# A Trek Through American and
# Texas Government

# A Trek Through American and Texas Government

*First Edition*

**Floyd Holder**
*Western Texas College*

cognella®
SAN DIEGO

Bassim Hamadeh, CEO and Publisher
Carrie Montoya, Manager, Revisions and Author Care
Kaela Martin, Project Editor
Alia Bales, Production Editor
Emely Villavicencio, Senior Graphic Designer
Alexa Lucido, Licensing Coordinator
Natalie Piccotti, Director of Marketing
Kassie Graves, Vice President of Editorial
Jamie Giganti, Director of Academic Publishing

cognella® | ACADEMIC PUBLISHING
3970 Sorrento Valley Blvd., Ste. 500, San Diego, CA 92121

To my fiancé, parents, siblings, friends, colleagues, and others I met along the way who helped me get to where I am today, thank you so much from the bottom of my heart. I love and enjoy each and every one of you.

# Contents

# Introduction

To the reader of this book, howdy. My name is Floyd William Holder IV. At present, I am an assistant professor of geography and government at Western Texas College in Snyder, Texas. In the fall of 2012, I found myself looking for my first teaching position after completing my Master of Arts in political science at Texas Tech University. I then landed at Texas A&M University at Kingsville as an instructor. During my time teaching there, and continually at my current institution, I have observed one key characteristic among students. Simply put, it was, and remains at times, very difficult to find ways to have students read and be prepared for class to further discuss the material.

In discovering ways to get students to read, I made some casual observations about my students' activities before class. One item that I noticed was the simple fact that many students, even in today's world of smartphones, watches, and other gadgets (and who knows what else is coming down the line), do still read, either on e-readers or actual wonderful-smelling paper books on occasion. Armed with the knowledge that students were actually still reading (just not what they needed to read for class), I further realized that what they were reading was all more or less in story format—maybe *novel* is the better term for it—in media like comic books, romance novels about werewolves and vampires, or even a kid who discovers that he's a wizard. In comparing what my students were reading to what I was assigning them to read for class, an obvious difference was observed. Much of what students are assigned to read in classes, from kindergarten to introductory college classes (English classes being the big exception), was really, at least in my opinion, nothing more than sentenced outlines. No continuity, flow, characters to fall for and hope the best comes their way, or process—something really tying it all together into a big picture that people can grab hold of and take with them as they enter the world. This is important, at least for the result of a government class, as government, in many more ways than even I care to admit, dramatically affects people more and more each day from a variety of angles. Offering an alternative to the status quo of textbooks is my inspiration for writing this book and the original. Hopefully, the interactive teaching style that my students enjoy experiencing in class comes through in this literature.

What follows in the 30 chapters of this book are the lessons that a fictional character named Champ Cove learned while visiting the various government agencies and affiliated organizations found here in the great state of Texas and the country at large. Major changes from the first iteration of this book, *A Trek Through Texas Government*, include the addition of chapters discussing government in general and the federal government, hence the name change. In addition, chapters have been organized into different sections in hopes of better developing story and substance of the topic at hand: government. Specifically, section I provides insight on the governing foundations of the nation, with chapters on American governing foundations, political geography, political culture, the impact of demographic shifts on government, our founding governing documents, federalism, and the history of politics in American and Texan experiences. Section II provides insight on the avenues available for the populace to get involved in government, with chapters on ways to influence the political process, elections from the perspective of voters and candidates, interest groups, and political parties. Section III provides insight on the various government agencies found in the country at the local, state, national, and international levels, alongside how they might interact with one another. The final section provides insight on the results of governing agencies, with chapters on domestic policy, foreign policy, civil liberties, government fiscal policy, and symbols used to represent themselves to the world. Lastly, a final chapter provides summary on what happened in the book. Each chapter is a read unto itself, so feel free to read them out of order on any topic that is of interest to you.

With that stated, I have one important memo. The stories that take place in this text are fictional. In no way did any of what is shown to occur *actually* occur, unless otherwise noted. However, the information presented here is real, much in the way that novels by Dan Brown are historical fiction/ novels. Enjoy the read.

Lastly, in writing this book, I conducted interviews, site visits, emails, and a multitude of other various forms of communication to gather information. THANK YOU VERY MUCH to each of you for your time and insight. In addition, to my editors and others at Cognella, Arek Arechiga, Alia Bales, Jamie Giganti, Kaela Martin, Carrie Montoya, David Rajec, and anybody else who helped along the way at Cognella, THANK YOU VERY MUCH for spending time and giving it your all to help get this amazing concept of a book written.

# Section I

## Governing Foundations

# Chapter 1

# American Governing Foundations

## Texas Higher Education Coordinating Board ACGMSLOs

*For Federal Government 2305: Upon successful completion of reading the book and taking the associated course, students will be able to do the following:*

1. **Explain the origin and development of constitutional democracy in the United States**
2. Demonstrate knowledge of the federal system
3. Describe separation of powers and checks and balances in both theory and practice.
4. Demonstrate knowledge of the legislative, executive, and judicial branches of the federal government
5. Evaluate the role of public opinion, interest groups, and political parties in the political system
6. Analyze the election process
7. Describe the rights and responsibilities of citizens
8. **Analyze issues and policies in US politics**

*For Texas Government 2306: Upon successful completion of reading the book and taking the associated course, students will be able to do the following:*

1. **Explain the origin and development of the Texas Constitution**
2. Describe state and local political systems and their relationship with the federal government
3. Describe separation of powers and checks and balances in both theory and practice in Texas
4. Demonstrate knowledge of the legislative, executive, and judicial branches of Texas government
5. Evaluate the role of public opinion, interest groups, and political parties in Texas
6. Analyze the state and local election process
7. Identify the rights and responsibilities of citizens
8. **Analyze issues, policies, and the political culture of Texas**

# The Hall of Presidents

I do not know how to begin to describe the events of today. I wholeheartedly believe that the main event of today, is the primary influence for what I want to do for the remainder of my life. In short, for the last week or so, my family and I have spent our time at the Walt Disney World® Resort in Orlando, Florida.[1] Seeing all the newest attractions surrounding Pandora—the World of Avatar at the Animal Kingdom—to the old haunts like *The Twilight*

FIGURE 1.1   Hall of Presidents Façade.

*Zone* Tower of Terror™ at Disney's Hollywood Studios® was fantastic (I hear the Tower of Terror may become a new *Guardians of the Galaxy* experience called Mission: Breakout[2]). One of the original attractions at the Magic Kingdom® stood out though among the rest, given my newfound look on life. Located in Liberty Square, just to the west of Cinderella's Castle, lies the Hall of Presidents[3] (figure 1.1).

We arrived at the park as a group a little after 11:00 a.m. During the day, we rode the classics like Space Mountain® and the Seven Dwarfs Mine Train, along with partaking in the newfound Monster's Inc. Laugh Floor Comedy Show among who knows how many other amazing attractions. Nearing 7:00 p.m., when leaving the Swiss Family Treehouse, we were hot, sweaty, and in need of a cold frosty beverage. We partook in libations at the nearby Tortuga Tavern. While there, my sister Charity commented, "The park is great, but the central Florida sun and humidity is starting to take its toll on me. I don't know what we are to do next, but if it involves staying out in the sun much longer, I am taking the monorail back to our resort with or without y'all to hit the pool."

The ultimatum took its toll on the mood of the group. Not wanting to see an end to the day as a group just yet, my dad chimed in, "I know where we can go. We can all learn a thing or two about the country where we live and love and keep our day going as a family."

---

1    https://disneyworld.disney.go.com

2    Joe Rohde, "Guardians of the Galaxy—Mission: BREAKOUT! Coming to Disney California Adventure Park Summer 2017," *Disney Parks Blog*, July 23, 2016, https://disneyparks.disney.go.com/blog/2016/07/guardians-of-the-galaxy-mission-breakout-coming-to-disney-california-adventure-park-summer-2017.

3    https://disneyworld.disney.go.com/attractions/magic-kingdom/hall-of-presidents

Deacon, Charity's husband, murmured aloud, "I know where you are taking us; let's go state representative."

A bit lost in my mind about what just happened, a short five minutes later, we found ourselves just outside the front façade of the Hall of Presidents showcase to partake in the 7:30 performance. The Hall of Presidents, which opened with the park itself in 1971, provides park-goers with an immersive experience into the mind and fortunes of the now 45 men who have held the highest office in the land. The main regular show focuses on the struggles faced by the presidents to perform their work alongside the obstacles faced by our country to find and continue with a national identity throughout our history to today. However, as part of an initiative to further drive interest into the history of our great nation, the shows for today paid special attention to introducing audiences to what government is, in addition to how our government differentiates itself from others around the world.

Once inside the building in the lobby, Charity gave a full address to the group: "Air-conditioning. Oh, thank you God for helping Willis Carrier invent this wonderful contraption."[4]

All chuckling to ourselves, we went off in different directions to explore the variety of items on display in the experiences lobby: Charity and Deacon found themselves going to the closest corner of the room to examine the various gowns worn by the first ladies; my mom and dad went to the heart of the room to stare in awe at the presidential seal that lies in the middle of the floor (figure 1.2). After reading a placard on the fencing surrounding it, I learned that it took an act of Congress to have it there, as the only other place in the world with the seal in this format is the White House itself.[5] I found myself taking a few steps toward the closest wall that happened to display a variety of artifacts from the presidents themselves.

FIGURE 1.2  Presidential Seal in Lobby of the Hall of Presidents.

My personal favorite was the pair of George W. Bush's cowboy boots with the presidential seal adorning them on the front. He was our 43rd president and the 46th governor of Texas.

---

4   https://www.carrier.com/carrier/en/worldwide/about/willis-carrier/
5   Jack Spence, "A History of the Hall of Presidents," AllEars.Net, July 7, 2009, http://allears.net/tp/mk/issue511.htm.

Just before 7:25, a Disney cast member[6] opened the doors at the far end of the lobby and allowed us into the seven hundred–seat theater for our showing. Once all were seated, the lights in the room dimmed, and the curtain went up to display a full gamut of truly lifelike animatronics representing each of our country's 45 presidents (figure 1.3). At that moment, from the speakers came the voice of actor Morgan Freeman asking, "George Washington?"

FIGURE 1.3    Panorama of all Presidential Animatronics.

A reply came from the animatronic of George Washington, "Present."

This process repeated itself until all 45 men were accounted for in attendance. After a short pause that built up the tension with each of the animatronics taking glances at one another, almost chiding one another to do something, the animatronic of the current office-holder, President Donald J. Trump, spoke: "Ladies and Gentlemen. What a great crowd here. Am I right?"

The room let out a mix of cheers, jeers, and applause. After another short pause, Trump continued, "As part of today's performance my fellow presidents and I are here to inform you of the entities that have been tasked by your duly elected leaders to provide you with the services, that, for a variety of reasons, cannot be reasonably provided to you on your regards or through some mechanism of the marketplace. Those entities are surmisable in one word: *government*. For those of you who don't know what that term *government* means, I was new here to this line of work myself, unlike many of my counterparts, when I took the position, so I had to look it up myself to make sure that I knew what I was getting into a little over a year ago. The government is simply the form or system of rule by which a state, community, etc., is governed.[7] In how this whole governing system works, a mixture of institutions, laws, and traditions work together to reinforce the legitimacy of the government so that it may hopefully help craft greater stability in the society it is governing."

---

6    This is what those who work for Disney are called.
7    http://www.dictionary.com/browse/government

## Institutions, Laws, and Traditions

From just behind President Trump, the animatronic of Abraham Lincoln interjected, "Donald, what do you mean by institutions, laws, and traditions?"

A bit put off, Trump continued, "Well now that you ask there Honest, let's start here by crafting an image. For our performance tonight, we shall use a chair, a great chair at that. That chair represents the whole of society, or the highly structured system of human organization for a large-scale community that normally furnishes protection, continuity, security, and a national identity for its members.[8] Getting back to what you requested of me Honest, there are laws that serve as the principles and regulations established in our community by some authority, like a city council at home, your state's legislature, or Congress up the Eastern Seaboard in Washington DC, and applicable to its people, whether in the form of legislation or of custom and policies recognized and enforced by judicial decision.[9] Those laws serve as the legs supporting said chair due to them being in place to support law and order. Without legs or laws, the chair and society simply can't stay up and together. Up next are institutions, which are any familiar, long-established person, thing, or practice;[10] a fixture so to speak such as us up here on the stage for our country, and traditions, long-established or inherited ways of thinking or acting,[11] such as a feeling that government should be kept small, which are used to reinforce the importance of having said laws. For the chair, this is the seat that you place your bottom when you use the chair and the seatback that helps you sit up in the chair."

It was then that James K. Polk spoke up. "Donald, it's great that we got the pieces and the overall form together, but what's holding everything together?"

Trump then orated, "Alright Napoleon, I've got just the right piece for you to consider. Holding everything together here is the active participation of people of the society in government, which includes holding government positions, volunteering your time to support institutions, or at a minimum going out to vote, just like my supporters, now constituents, did on November 8, 2016. The chair can only support us if we mend it from time to time by adding lubricant, seals, screws, and whatever else holds the pieces of the chair together."

## Power, Authority, and Legitimacy

Then, after Trump finished, the animatronic-playing former president Ronald Reagan chimed in, "Donald, do us all a favor and point out the various general types of government one said society could have."

---

8   http://www.dictionary.com/browse/society?s=t
9   http://www.dictionary.com/browse/law?s=t
10   http://www.dictionary.com/browse/institution?s=t
11   http://www.dictionary.com/browse/tradition?s=t

Settling into his presentation, Trump furthered, "Hold on there great communicator, or should I say Gipper; I think it may be best first to define some more terms. Lord knows how the press might go after me if I do not do everything in proper order more than they already are doing. Folks, those terms are *power*, *authority*, and *legitimacy*. When acting in a situation, not having all three will either prevent or, at a minimum, make it much, much harder to have your governing performance go off without a hitch, so to speak. First off, power is essentially the ability to accomplish something on your own or, at the very least, the capacity to get others to act in your stead.[12] Authority is a power or right delegated to a person,[13] whereas, legitimacy is the authority granted in a governing document to use a power.[14] Keep in mind that the last two terms are both grants of approval to act regarding some situation, with the difference being that authority is verbally communicated, and legitimacy, where the power to act is physically written down with which with associated seals and the like, is more believable for standing if an issue arises along the way when acting on the instruction."

The animatronic of Richard Nixon came into motion again and posited, "What kinda metaphor do you have for us to better understand those terms there, ehhh?"

Ready to pounce, Trump claimed, "Well folks, and you Nixon over there, I think you know me. I know myself well, so you should all know that when it comes to power, authority, and legitimacy, nothing serves to further our knowledge here more than the magical world known to us through the Harry Potter book series and movies. One of the greatest sets of laws that part of our society has ever implemented is the banishment of use of the three so-called unforgivable spells.[15] Those spells if performed are unforgivable; no redemption is possible due to the severity of their results, loss of free will, torture, and death on those they are cast. Such terrible spells, really curses, they are."

The animatronic belonging to Calvin Coolidge spoke up. "Get on with the metaphor good sir!"

Trump, looking flustered, continued, "Now, now, any witch or wizard has the power to cast said spell since, well, they are witches and wizards. It goes with the territory so to speak, unless, of course, their wands were taken away by the Magical Congress of the United States of America[16] or the Ministry of Magic in the United Kingdom.[17] The question is, does the

---

12    http://www.dictionary.com/browse/power?s=t

13    http://www.dictionary.com/browse/authority

14    http://www.encyclopedia.com/social-sciences-and-law/sociology-and-social-reform/sociology-general-terms-and-concepts/legitimacy

15    Spence, "A History of the Hall of Presidents."

16    J.K. Rowling, "The Magical Congress of the United States of America (MACUSA)," Pottermore, accessed March 19, 2019, https://www.pottermore.com/writing-by-jk-rowling/macusa.

17    Pottermore, "The Ministry of Magic," accessed March 19, 2019, https://www.pottermore.com/explore-the-story/the-ministry-of-magic.

witch or wizard in question have the authority and legitimacy to cast one of the Unforgivable Curses? The answer is, well, no. You see, in 1717, using the Ministry of Magic as a muse to discuss this concept, they made the use of said spells illegal under magical law. Accordingly, nobody has the legitimate right to use said spells since that time, as an official decree has been made to banish their use. However, during the first rise of Voldemort, Aurors, magical law enforcement, were given the verbal authority by the Minister of Magic to use them in hopes of getting information out of Voldemort's followers called Deatheaters, via the Imperious Curse that could be used to turn captured Deatheaters into unwilling spies, or the Cruciatus Curse, a torture spell like waterboarding done in our world, to get information out of them. Their use is still illegal under magical law, ours too by the way for that matter, but under the circumstances, the minister decided to look the other way in hopes of accomplishing a greater good, or at least in getting information. The use remained illegitimate due to the authority given to use the spells simply not being written down. Had the Minister of Magic made a public decree and posted it somewhere, like on the wall of Hogwarts, as was the case in the events of *Harry Potter and the Order of the Phoenix* for various magical decrees on education, it would have become legitimate. Very tricky stuff here this power, authority, and legitimacy. Thankfully, for me of course, and all my colleagues up here onstage, when in office we were the legitimate holders of the powers of the office due to the procedures as outlined in our Constitution for taking office, winning most of the votes in the Electoral College for most of us, being next in line for others, under the authority granted by voters in the prior applicable election having taken place."

## Some Types of Governments

From the corner of the room, the animatronic of President Dwight Eisenhower stood up at attention and commanded, "Commander in Chief, you are lollygagging around now. You shall complete your previous mission of talking about the general types of government right this moment. Dismissed!"

Visually taken aback but not knocked off his stump, Trump articulated, "Wow, that stern order there really brings me back to my days at the New York Military Academy in the Hudson Valley.[18] Okay, the main difference between each of the available governments for society is who has the power to act legitimately, or at least authoritatively (figure 1.4). The power may be vested in no one in particular, a single individual, or the masses in some voluminous concoction. For discussing this, we'll start with the smallest number of people in charge and then move onto those governments where many people are in

---

18    https://www.nyma.org

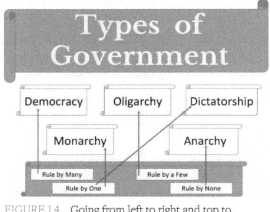

**Types of Government**

Democracy | Oligarchy | Dictatorship

Monarchy | Anarchy

Rule by Many | Rule by a Few

Rule by One | Rule by None

FIGURE 1.4 Going from left to right and top to bottom, the number of individuals in charge gradually decreases.

charge. First, and foremost, is where you have a system that has only one person overseeing the government. This form can either be a dictatorship or monarchy. The difference here is a dictator comes to power by taking force, usually via a coup d'état, a sudden and decisive action in politics, especially one resulting in a change of government illegally,[19] whereas a monarch gains their power through heredity due to the person before them either stepping down from the associated throne or passing away with the new guy taking over. Examples here would include Kim Jong-un of the People's Republic of Korea, commonly known as North Korea, and the Sultan of Brunei, respectively. Folks, should I keep going or what?"

People in the crowd were oohing and ahhing for him to do so. I think I even heard a chant here or there of "Make America Great Again." Offering some guidance, the animatronic for Rutherford B. Hayes chastised, "Donald, you know I don't like the concentration of power[20] for the same reasons various other presidents and I in the 1800s banned or highly restricted the use of alcohol and tobacco in the White House; they tend to ruin things. Move along with the less concentrated versions if you please."

After taking a moment to digest Hayes's remarks, Trump spoke, "Okay then, governments that have the power not fully concentrated with one individual, but not a lot, fall under the guise of being an oligarchy, a form of government in which all power is vested in a few persons or a dominant class or clique.[21] For an example of a 'true' oligarchy, see the rule of Kings Peter & Edmund and Queens Susan & Lucy as depicted in the movie and book, *The Chronicles of Narnia: The Lion, The Witch, and the Wardrobe*. In that case, the four brothers and sisters rule their world together as equals. What we more commonly see of this concept today is a solitary ruler with the condition that they must come from a certain group of society. This concept is where political scientists have gotten creative with the types of government. For

---

19    http://www.dictionary.com/browse/coup-d-etat

20    Christopher Klein, "A Brief History of Presidential Drinking," History.com, February 13, 2015, https://www.history.com/news/a-brief-history-of-presidential-drinking; Carl Anthony, "Nineteenth Century First Ladies & Liquor in the White House," *National First Ladies' Library Blog*, February 23, 2016, http://www.firstladies.org/blog/nineteenth-century-first-ladies-liquor-in-the-white-house.

21    http://www.dictionary.com/browse/oligarchy?s=t

example, you could reside in a theocracy where one must be a religious leader in some capacity to have the ability to take the highest position of rule just as how nearly every Pope in Roman Catholic history has first been a cardinal in the church.[22] Beyond that, you could have a gerontocracy where only older citizens may rule; think of societies in movies when somebody says 'we must consult the elders before we act,' an ethnocracy where only members of a certain ethnic group can be at the helm, as was the case in South Africa under apartheid and its white rule, matri- and patriarchies where only members of a particular sex can take power, women and men, respectively, corporatocracies where a business leader takes control of government and merges it with a business, and, most notably, single-party states where only members of a particular political party, such as the Communist Party in modern-day China and the former Soviet Union, could rule with other parties merely being banished, can govern."

Animatronic Lyndon Baines Johnson rose to suggest, "Get on with the ones that see power even less concentrated, rookie!"

Seemingly out of breath after President Johnson spoke intensely to him, Trump went on, "LBJ over there really can talk down one's throat. Can't he? Okay folks, on the complete opposite end of dictators and kingdoms you have anarchy where there is simply no government in place. A step up from there is an ochlocracy, where people have organized in the barest of all measures into traveling hordes of people who lay out justice, or whatever, as they see fit. For how to best visualize anarchy, I like to think about, all while hoping it never emerges here, the movie *The Purge*, because for 12 hours, one night a year, there are no laws, making murder, rape, and torture legal. For an ochlocracy, one should consider the film *The Dark Knight Rises* after Bane overthrows the Gotham government to clear the way for the prior movie villain Scarecrow to create a kangaroo court where the rich and powerful are taken in, tried, and sentenced to banishment or death by banishment. It's a court, but it's just thrown together on a whim to torture people due to the shocking lack of due process and the like providing a rule of law. Lastly, I don't think a truly anarchic society, one with no government whatsoever, is possible, as we as humans are prone to being part of a tribe so to speak, but to each his own. It is amazing how with nearly 200 different countries around the world you can end up with so few types of government."

At that moment the animatronic belonging to Harry S. Truman juxtaposed, "Could you summarize those groupings a bit for us, please?"

After some silent consideration, Trump spoke. "From what I just talked about, you have a system where one person is in charge, others where a group of people is in charge be it through heavily influencing the sole person in charge or making decisions as a small

---

22    Simon Rogers, "Every Pope Ever: The Full List." *Guardian*, February 13, 2013, https://www.theguardian.com/news/datablog/2013/feb/13/popes-full-list.

group, and those that, well, have the mob mentality so to speak. It's all about the concentration of power to rule. Hey there ahh ... Sage of Mount Vernon ... what should we talk about next?"

## What Is a Democracy?

At that moment the animatronic version of George Washington wound up and suggested, "Why good sir, since I was one of those founding fathers that got our country's democratic norms started, why don't you go a bit more into what exactly a democracy is there, Donald? It seems you, as they say, overlooked the concept when going from oligarchies to anarchy."

Trump contended, "Okay everyone, lend me your ear or whatever it is you need to keep up to date with the conversation. Democracy, for lack of a better term, is a massive step above an ochlocracy and anarchy due to the presence of very formalized government proceedings and is a step below oligarchies due to the ability of most members of society being able to join, or at least participate, in government. Regarding democracy, there are two types, direct and indirect. In the former, all those in society who are of age or any other prescribed minimums, such as being a landowner, would gather together as a group and make decisions about how their society will progress going forward, often voting together as a group in public. Due to the difficulties of getting large groups of people together to make decisions, this form of democracy is not a common practice today outside of town meetings in parts of New England[23] and two cantons of Switzerland, Appenzell Inner Rhodes and Glarus,[24] who continue the practice. Although, I must admit it would be quite fun to get on Fox News or C-SPAN and make an announcement along the lines of 'My fellow Americans, if you are of age and not a felon, do report to the National Mall in Washington DC, this Thursday night at seven so that we can vote on what to do about providing disaster aid to those impacted by the tornadoes in Oklahoma last week.' It would be a nightmare getting that many people together for that one item, am I right? Although, with the internet and phones, we could get a nifty voting system like what they had on *American Idol* a few years back and its reboot today; security concerns might get in the way, though.[25] Accordingly, that form only works well in

23   Amy Crawford, "What I Saw When I Participated in One of the Truest Forms of Democracy," Slate, May 22, 2013, http://www.slate.com/articles/news_and_politics/politics/2013/05/new_england_town_halls_these_experiments_in_direct_democracy_do_a_far_better.html.

24   Swissinfo.ch, "Landsgemeinde," February 15, 2007, https://www.swissinfo.ch/eng/landsgemeinde/245490.

25   Allison Piwowarski, "How Do You Vote on 'American Idol'? Here's How to Help Your Favorite Win, Romper, April 6, 2016, https://www.romper.com/p/how-do-you-vote-on-american-

areas with small populations. Now, what we have today is the latter form, better known as a republic. Under this system, due to having much larger populations and it being difficult to get that many people together, we elect representatives to go to Congress or your state legislature, in our country's case, and make decisions for the group. This is in the same ballpark as captains on a football team meeting on the 50-yard line for the coin toss to decide who will be defending which end zone and when their team will get the ball first. You don't need to send the whole team out there for that, so you send in your representatives."

## The Five Factors of a Stable Democracy

Suddenly, out of the blue, the animatronic version of Barack Obama intercalated, "Good work thus far my fair orange-headed replacement; care if I take over for a bit?"

Trump replied, "Why not? How about you drop some knowledge on what is needed to keep a stable democracy, republic in our case, running?"

Obama continued, "I think that might have been one of the smoothest transitions of power ever. During my time at Harvard Law School, I do believe that I took or taught a class or two on this subject. Per political scientist Larry Diamond, there are four key elements to ensuring our system survives. They are having a process for choosing and replacing the government through free and fair elections; the active participation of the people, as citizens, in politics and civic life; the protection of the human rights of all citizens; and finally, a rule of law in which the laws and procedures apply equally to all citizens.[26] I might add, though, that there should be in those free and fair elections notable differences between candidates so that voters have a meaningful choice to make and not just, for example, the lesser of two evils."

It was then that Trump interjected, "So do you believe that we have such an active system here today in our fair country?"

Obama continued, "Well Donald, let's take a closer look at the 2016 general election that brought you into office, shall we? You see, per Amendment 22, Section 1, 'No person shall be elected to the office of the President more than twice.' I was first elected in 2008 and again in 2012 and became term limited, preventing me from running for a third term in 2016, where Hillary ran under my party's banner instead. As part of finding my replacement, you and Hillary won a series of caucuses and primary elections to win your party's nominations after getting enough delegates. With your nominations in hand, you both competed for electoral college votes in the general election, of which you won by winning enough individual state contests

---

idol-heres-how-to-help-your-favorite-win-8444.

26    Hilla University for Humanistic Studies, "What Is Democracy?," lecture, January 21, 2004, https://web.stanford.edu/~ldiamond/iraq/WhaIsDemocracy012004.htm.

to win the required 270 electoral college votes, which are distributed to the states based on representation in Congress, even though you don't have any prior experience in government service. Along the way, anybody could have submitted their filing fees, or petition instead of the fees depending on state law, to run in the caucuses and primaries against you or later as an independent candidate in the general election. So, number one, yeah, we certainly do have free and fair elections. For item number two, 59.3 percent of the population eligible to vote did so, about 136,700,729 to be exact if I remember correctly.[27] I'd like to see a higher amount, say 80 percent or so, but nearly three-fifths is still most of the population, or at least those who could vote. Down-ballot may need some work as in those contests only around a quarter of the eligible population participated, but for our office, we are good to go."[28]

It was then, after a long pause in Obama's spiel, that I suddenly rose myself and shouted, "What about the other three conditions? Are we five for five or what?"

Obama, pivoting in my direction—I was on the front row to the left—furthered, "Well young man, I see that you are interested in politics. You should have faith that we are. As for factor three, the Voting Rights Act of 1965[29] and the Civil Rights Acts of 1957 and 1960[30] and their many updates since drastically altered the way in which American citizens vote by removing literacy tests and poll taxes, adding punishments for those attempting to block someone from registering, and outright prevention of discrimination in voting and related practices based on ethnicity and language. Regarding the fourth item, Section 5 of the Voting Rights Act of 1965 that establishes federal oversight of state registration practices, states are still primarily in charge of registering people to vote and conducting elections, but the federal overseers are known to be ardent administrators. Based on a formula derived in Section 4, states must obtain 'preclearance' before changes in their election laws may go into effect by submitting evidence that proposed alterations have no consequence of discriminating on the basis of race or minority language status."

I then knowingly interrupted, "Okay, I'll give you that we have four out of five then, but were Hillary and Trump all that different?"

After contemplating for a second, he said, "You really must be very interested in politics young man. Wow! For this information, on April 15th, 2016, and updated on September 23rd, Katie Zezima and Matthew Callahan of the *Washington Post* newspaper published a fascinating online interactive comparison of the candidates representing the four major political

---

27    United States Elections Project, "2016 November General Election Turnout Rates," last modified September 5, 2018, http://www.electproject.org/2016g.

28    Mike Maciag, "Voter Turnout Plummeting in Local Elections," *Governing*, October 2014, http://www.governing.com/topics/politics/gov-voter-turnout-municipal-elections.html.

29    79 Stat. 437.

30    71 Stat. 634; 74 Stat. 86.

parties, Democrat, Green, Libertarian, and Republican, in the 2016 general election.[31] Based on their work, major differences were found between Donald and Hillary on immigration, with Donald being for stricter controls than Hillary; on gun rights, with Hillary being for more stringent controls than Donald; on free trade, with Donald being for less and Hillary for more; on energy policy, with Hillary being for more green and Donald being open to all resources; on health care, with Donald being for less government intervention and Hillary for more; and on criminal justice, with Hillary being for less harsh punishments than Donald. While on education, campaign finance, Social Security, same-sex marriage, entitlements, the economy, the war on terror, and abortion, they were either quite similar or not enough data was available for an accurate comparison. Regarding Gary Johnson of the Libertarian Party and Jill Stein of the Green Party, Jill Stein was comparable to Hillary, while Gary Johnson was comparable to Donald, with both being more extreme in their respective beliefs to their most similar candidate. So, to summarize my point, yes, we certainly did have differences between candidates last year. Drop mic, boom. I'm out!"

## Theories on Leadership in the Government

After a brief pause, the animatronic belonging to Woodrow Wilson declared, "My oh my, my colleagues, as the only professor of political science in the theater I must admit that each of you who has spoken has done a splendid job at informing our patrons today on this wonderful topic. I want to work at bringing our discussion to an end by asking a question to the audience: Who is governing our country?"

A woman in the back of the theater chanted, "Trump is!"

A man in the middle of the theater opposite of where I was sitting then yelled, "No, Congress is!"

My brother-in-law Deacon noted, "That probably depends on who is asking and who is answering."

Nodding away at the responses, Wilson remarked, "I like that last answer there. With such a vast nation, it makes sense that nobody shares the belief that this or that group or that individual is truly in charge. From academia, my colleagues and I charge that three ruling theories to understanding government rule exist. On the one hand, you have majoritarianism, or the belief that those constituting a simple majority make the rules for all members of a group, nation, etc.[32] On another hand, you have the elite theory holding that a few select

---

31    Katie Zezima and Matthew Callahan, "Donald Trump vs. Hillary Clinton on the Issues," *Washington Post*, last modified September 23, 2016, https://www.washingtonpost.com/graphics/politics/political-issues.
32    http://www.dictionary.com/browse/majoritarianism?s=t

people dominate the government over society who only seek to further their interests by making decisions for the group.[33] On a final hand, you have pluralism or the distribution of power to multiple organized interest groups in society competing with one another to control as much or little of society as they see fit for their purposes."[34]

I then juxtaposed, "So what do we have here in the United States? From just a basic understanding of what you have said here, it could go either way."

After thinking for a moment, Wilson spoke. "Young man, your comments here are along the lines of what the man two seats down from you said before; it depends on who you are asking, which brings me to conclude that our country is truthfully a mixture of the three theories. Easier put, at the core, it is up to you and me to go out and vote in as many elections as we can, as whoever gets the most votes gets to run the government that they have been elected to serve, your simple majoritiarianism. Accordingly, we need to ensure that those blessed with power are working in our best interests as much as possible. The question then is, who is it that we are going out to vote on? Therefore, on the surface is where the other two theories come into play. For those who argue that it is elites in charge, consider the Bush family."

The animatronics of George H.W. and George W. Bush let out a big moan, which led Wilson to sigh loudly and then continue by stating, "Former president George W. Bush is the son of former president, former director of the Central Intelligence Agency, and former US congressman George H.W. Bush, who made his fortune in the oil and gas industry before public service. Beyond that, W's brother, Jeb, is also a former presidential candidate and governor of Florida. Their grandfather, Prescott Bush, was a US senator from Connecticut. For those advocating the pluralist model, look at how the presidency changes party often. Going back from President Trump, who is Republican, for now based on his history, you then have Obama, a Democrat; W. Bush, a Republican; Clinton, a Democrat; H.W. Bush and Reagan, Republicans; Carter, a Democrat; Ford and Nixon, Republicans; Kennedy and Johnson, Democrats; and so on and so forth. The individuals, outside of possibly Carter, are certainly elites, but the group from which they come fluctuates quite often. With that information in mind, you therefore have individuals giving their consent to elites who then go and rule in their stead along the lines of a shared political ideology, a mixture nonetheless of the three theories."

It was then that both former president Bushes spoke in unison: "Since you named us aloud there Woodrow, what do you mean by political ideology?"

---

33   Paul Johnson, "Elite (Elitist) Theory," *A Glossary of Political Economy Terms*, accessed March 19, 2019, http://www.auburn.edu/~johnspm/gloss/elite_theory.

34   Paul Johnson, "Pluralist Theory," *A Glossary of Political Economy Terms*, accessed March 19, 2019. http://www.auburn.edu/~johnspm/gloss/pluralist_theory.

After commiserating to himself for a moment, Wilson continued, "Well, first off, a political ideology is a set of doctrines or beliefs that are shared by the members of a social group that form the basis of a political system.[35] Regarding political ideologies in substance, four dominant ones exist, each of which differs based on the believed prescribed role of government in the process, along a left-right spectrum. At the far left is socialism and communism, which have government playing an active part in controlling primary economic drivers all the while promoting economic equality and community. Just to the left of the middle point on the spectrum is liberalism, which promotes an active role of government in the economy but falls short of taking over major sectors while promoting economic security, equal opportunity, and social liberty. After that, just right of the middle part of the spectrum is conservatism, which supports an active role of government in the economy to support capitalism while encouraging economic liberty, morality, and social order. Finally, at the far right of the spectrum is libertarianism, which advocates little to no regulation of economy by the government while promoting absolute economic and social liberty from government. From left to right you go from near total to a near nothing role of government in society. Ohh look at the time, class dismissed and thank you all for your attendance today at our special lecture presentation. For more information on that last topic, do some personal research on political culture!"

Being the presenter that he was, Trump even stood up and made a few bows and waves to the audience, which got a stable "Make America Great Again" chant or two going as the curtain went down before him. A crowd in the back even countered by also chanting "Stronger Together. Stronger Together."

Our group remained relatively quiet as we walked out of the theater. I could hear some grumbles here or there, though. My dad even said, when back out in the twilight, "I learned a thing or two in there about the different types of government that are available. I mean, theocracy, who knew?"

Deacon also mentioned, "I always thought that what we had was the only type of democratic society possible today. I know we get to vote on state constitutional amendments back in Texas,[36] but it's just not the same. It's good to see those towns in New England and I assume province-like areas in Switzerland keep the original form alive and well."

I didn't hear much after that. My head was spinning with all the terms, all the power plays, all the back and forth—all just for a presentation. No matter how I looked at it though, it is quite remarkable. Of any career or profession that I wanted to get into, the government is the one that deals with everything, since it makes rules for the marketplace and can even get rid of the market if it so desires, if certain individual actors begin to make up a significant portion of

---

35    http://www.thefreedictionary.com/Political+ideologies
36    Texas Constitution, article 17, section 1(a).

its membership. Then it hit me: This is where I wanted to spend my time and make my way in the world. I can always fall back on running the family business back home in Houston, but this is just such an essential aspect of society to get involved with understanding. Nothing could be more important. The proverbial door could be opened anywhere I wished if I selected the right path during or after my time in public service. The question is, where should I get myself involved in politics … err … government? I then pulled my dad aside as we were walking back to the monorail at the front of the park. "Dad, that show hit me. I want to learn more about what it is you do in government and then some. Could you help me do so in Austin this summer?"

He replied, "Of course son, but what about you working at the store before going off to college this fall? Are you even now still wanting to go off to college?"

I responded quickly, "I can work weekends and commute. Five days a week in Austin and two back at the store in Houston should do the trick! And yes, of course, I will, but now I know what to major and minor in, political science and business, respectively."

He shot back, "What about the work that goes on in Washington DC?"

I opined, "I have some planning to do, don't I?"

He nodded his head, and I knew that I had gotten on the track of learning about government. The question is, where exactly does that begin? I guess I'll figure something out on the plane ride home tomorrow.

**QUESTIONS TO CONSIDER** REGARDING AMERICAN GOVERNMENT:

1. The first main topic of the chapter discusses institutions, laws, and traditions regarding government and society. Please define each of these five terms. Then identify the city where you live and how your city relates to each of these five terms in detail.

2. The second main topic of the chapter discusses power, authority, and legitimacy. Please define each of these three terms and the scenario used to relate them to one another. Then identify a situation in your life that is similar and explain how so in detail.

3. The third main topic of the chapter discusses how you can decipher one type of government from another. Please identify what that differentiation is and where on the spectrum you would like to live in detail.

4. The fourth main topic of the chapter discusses the two types of democracies. Please identify the two types and explain what makes one different from the other. Lastly, indicate the one that you would like to live under and why in detail.

5. The fifth main topic of the chapter discusses the five factors that help ensure a stable democracy. Please identify what those factors are and whether you agree with the evidence presented here that indicates the United States does have a stable democracy and why in detail.

6. The final main topic of the chapter discusses theories on leadership in government. Please identify and define what each of those theories is and which one you believe to play the biggest role in your home and why in detail.

# Chapter 2

# Political Geography

# Leaving the Magic Kingdom®

I spent last night pondering what all it would take to fully grasp the decision I made yesterday to devote the work of my life to the world of government and politics. Thanks to the Hall of Presidents, I now have a solid grasp of what government is, the available types, and what exactly makes our republic here at home work so well. My dad has agreed to show me the ropes regarding the government as much as he can, but even I know there is more to the concept than what he can provide. A state representative and convenience store owner can only do so much, right? I did not know what the next step was, but I figured it was best to start on that when I had returned home. Little did I know that our flight home from Orlando, Florida, would prove fruitful in advancing my cause sooner than expected.

After leaving the Magic Kingdom just before nine o'clock in the evening, yesterday, we as a group took the monorail back to the Disney Contemporary Resort.[1] I went to my room and crashed along with most of our group. We left the resort the next morning on the nine o'clock run of the Disney Magical Express[2] to the airport. I thought it should be the Disney Magic Carpet Ride experience, but I'm not a Disney Imagineer, nor am I a cast member, so my opinion on the matter is null. At least the Magic Kingdom has the Magic Carpets of Aladdin[3] ride filling the apparent oversight in branding.

The venture to the Orlando International Airport[4] took roughly 40 minutes due to traffic along Interstate 4 and Florida State Highway 528. The express bus dropped us off at Terminal B on the south side of the main terminal building. We were checked in and through security in about 30 minutes. We proceeded to take the airport tram headed toward Airside 3 for our flight on United Airlines back home, nonstop to Houston. When there, I decided to obtain lunch at the Wendy's®[5] in the central rotunda as airline food has never really been that appealing to me and I didn't want to go hungry for the rest of the day. Everybody else just kind of moped around, while my mom and dad went to the lounge.

While waiting for our flight at Gate 36, I saw a redheaded man with rectangular glasses sitting on the bench across from me. He was examining a series of maps and reference pamphlets on southern United States heritage tourism. I felt the desire to ask him about his items, but he was nose deep in a map on streets in the United States named for Dr. Martin

---

1    https://disneyworld.disney.go.com/resorts/contemporary-resort
2    https://disneyworld.disney.go.com/guest-services/magical-express
3    https://disneyworld.disney.go.com/attractions/magic-kingdom/magic-carpets-of-aladdin
4    https://www.orlandoairports.net
5    https://www.wendys.com

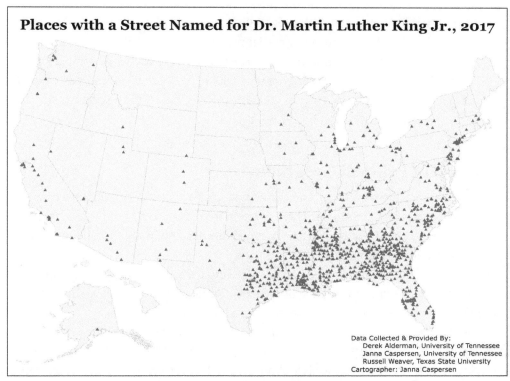

**Places with a Street Named for Dr. Martin Luther King Jr., 2017**

Data Collected & Provided By:
Derek Alderman, University of Tennessee
Janna Caspersen, University of Tennessee
Russell Weaver, Texas State University
Cartographer: Janna Caspersen

FIGURE 2.1   A majority of the streets are found throughout the Southern United States where Dr. Martin Luther King Jr. was from.

Luther King Jr.[6] (figure 2.1). There was a lot, primarily in the South, from what I could tell as the late-morning sun shone through the paper and highlighted the highlights he had made on the map. Just then, the gate agent announced, "United Airlines would like to begin pre-boarding flight 1788 with nonstop service to Houston from Gate 36."

I was in boarding group two, so I still had a few minutes before I needed to get up, and I was only about two-thirds of the way through my salad and fries. About ten minutes later, I was up and throwing my trash away when I heard the magical words, "United Airlines now requests all those in boarding group two to proceed to board the aircraft."

I ran back to my seat to get my things and head up to the jet bridge. The redheaded man was gone; I guessed at that point that he had already boarded. After waiting in the jet bridge for about ten additional minutes due to people putting tags on their gate-check bags—quite silly is the concept, really—I made the right turn to head down the aisle to my seat in row

---

6    Derek K. Alderman, "Martin Luther King Jr. Streets in the South: A New Landscape of Memory," accessed March 19, 2019, photo essay, pp. 88–104, http://web.utk.edu/~dalderma/mlkstreet/alderman_mlk_sc.pdf.

29 against the window in seat F. Luckily for me, the redheaded man was in E. My desire to ask him about the maps he was perusing earlier was now getting a bit overwhelming for my liking. I held back for now due to not wanting to be nosy. We did exchange some dubious "hi there's" and "pardon me's" as I entered my seat, though. Fifteen minutes later, we pushed back from the gate and taxied our way to Runway 36R for takeoff to the north before heading east after passing over Gainesville, Florida.

## The World of Political Geography

Just after hitting 10,000 feet, I heard on the PA system, "Ladies and gentlemen we have now climbed over 10,000 feet in altitude. Therefore, feel free to take out your large portable electronic devices and begin playing with them until our descent in about two hours into the George Bush Intercontinental Airport."[7]

The redheaded man began to take out his maps and to start perusing them again. At this point, I had to inquire, "Pardon me, sir, but what is all that material you have there? I've seen maps before, but yours at first glance seem to be a bit of a rarity."

Startled at the question, the redhead man stated, "Oh these, nothing much. I'm a geographer, and I study race relations, public memory, popular culture, and heritage tourism in the US South. One of my specialties is looking at how African Americans commemorate the past, and right now MLK memorials are all the rage and have been for quite a while now.[8] How's the view out the window, though?"

I looked out the window to make the most poignant reply and stated, "It's a bit swampy, and if we were about five months in the future, Florida[9] and Missouri[10] would be battling it out down there in Ben Hill Griffin Stadium[11]—in football of course, not with guns and canons. That would be bad."

Looking inquisitive, the man replied, "I agree with that final statement there. Oh, the world of political geography; it's just one big spatial problem."

I interjected, "What do you mean by political geography?"

---

7   https://www.fly2houston.com/iah/overview
8   Derek H. Alderman and Joshua Inwood, "Street Naming and the Politics of Belonging: Spatial Injustices in the Toponymic Commemoration of Martin Luther King, Jr.," In *The Political Life of Urban Streetscapes: Naming, Politics, and Place*, ed. Reuben Rose-Redwood, Derek Alderman, and Maoz Azaryahu (Abingdon, UK: Routledge, 2017), 259–73. Revised reprint of Social and Cultural Geography, 2013.
9   http://www.ufl.edu
10  http://missouri.edu
11  http://floridagators.com/facilities/?id=1

The man replied, "Well, using terms from the geographical glossaries published by Joe Naumann of the University of Missouri at St. Louis, geography is the study of how observable spatial patterns emerged.[12] Regarding politics and geography, it is the study of the organization and the spatial distribution of political phenomena. In other words, why cities, particularly capital cities, are where they are, why the borders are here and not there, or even why the Ottoman Empire failed, among other things in that corner of the map. You have an interest in this field, don't you? I can see it in your eyes and how they light up when I mention the world *political*."

I nodded in agreement with the statement and asked, "Would you mind continuing to talk about political geography? I made a life-changing decision yesterday, and I would like to know more, as your comments there relate to my newfound goal in life quite well."

The man furthered, "Politics, I assume is your chosen field then? And sure, why not, we don't have much else to do for a while but sit and enjoy the view out the window, as it allows us to take advantage of the bird's-eye view perspective that is the epitome of much in geography.[13] This is due to maps always being from above or else they'd be a bunch of pretty pictures not showing much useful information. I'm Dr. Derek Alderman, by the way, of the University of Tennessee at Knoxville and the current president of the American Association of Geographers,[14] or AAG for short. Political geography is not my specialty, but I did take a class or two on the subject during my time at the University of Georgia,[15] and my subject matter does go a bit into the topic here and there. Not to mention, as president of the association, I should know a thing or two about this and that in the major subfields of the field. What do you want to know first?"

## Country, Nation, and State

I sat back and murmured, "Why not some of the major terms? That should be a solid foundation to understand the government further. Oh, and ah, I'm Champ."

Dr. Alderman articulated, "Well Champ, nice to meet you. For this material, there are not too many general key terms to fathom, but the frequent misuse of the terms country, nation, and state is a good dialogue to consider. A *nation* is a group of people with a shared

---

12    University of Missouri–St. Louis, "Glossary Page," accessed March 19, 2019, http://www.umsl.edu/~naumannj/glossary page.html; All geographical and other definitions from here on come from the glossaries provided by Joe Naumann unless otherwise noted.

13    National Geographic, "From the Air: A Bird's Eye View of Spectacular Places," accessed March 19, 2019, https://www.nationalgeographiclodges.com/birds-eye-view.

14    http://www.aag.org

15    http://www.uga.edu

sense of cultural identity, typically based on language, religion, ethnicity, and historical associations of some kind, the Cherokee Nation,[16] for example. Meanwhile, a *state* is a sovereign country with a permanent resident population, land territory, organized system of government, international recognition, economic system, and circulation system of transportation and communications with control over said items by the government, our United States,[17] for example, whereas *country* is a colloquial crossover term for both, roughly meaning a political division of some kind. The difference in the first two, though, is simple, as the former refers to the citizenry with the latter referring to the government ruling an area with the citizens in it."

I opined, "I see a conflict of interest if the nations and states don't match up. So what about when you begin to get overlap between nations and states?"

Responding quickly, Dr. Alderman continued, "Well now, that is a subject complicated enough for further discussion. Regardless, nation-states are states that are overwhelmingly composed of people of one nation, Japan, for example, with its 98.5 percent of the population belonging to the Japanese ethnic group, according to the *CIA World Factbook*.[18] You then have binational or multinational states, where no one ethnicity has more than say 50 percent of the population, Brazil,[19] for example, with its population being roughly 48 percent white, 44 percent multi-racial, 8 percent black, and the remaining being Asian or Indigenous per their 2010 census.[20] You also have part nation-states, where you have a nation dominate over several, particularly contiguous, states. Look at how Arabs have a near monopoly of dominant ethnicities in southwestern Asia, more commonly known as the Middle East,[21] for example. And finally, you have stateless nations, which are where you have a nation without a state that the nation dominates in. A good example are Kurds, who occupy huge swaths of land covering northern parts of the states of Iran, Iraq, and Syria, in addition to southern and eastern portions of the state of Turkey[22] (figure 2.2), unlike their counterparts, the Tajiks or Uzbeks, who have their states, thanks to Tajikistan and Uzbekistan, respectively, in Central Asia. Granted, the Kurds are trying to change that by establishing their state with territory coming from places with large Kurdish

---

16   http://www.cherokee.org

17   https://www.usa.gov/about-the-us

18   https://www.cia.gov/library/publications/the-world-factbook/geos/ja.html

19   http://www.brazil.org.za

20   https://ww2.ibge.gov.br/home/estatistica/populacao/censo2010/caracteristicas_da_populacao/tabelas_pdf/tab3.pdf

21   *Mosaic*, "In Today's Middle East, Arabs Are No Longer Dominant," February 24, 2017, https://mosaic-magazine.com/picks/politics-current-affairs/2017/02/in-todays-middle-east-arabs-are-no-longer-dominant.

22   BBC News, "Who Are the Kurds?," October 31, 2017, http://www.bbc.com/news/world-middle-east-29702440.

populations, with mixed results.[23] This situation is a case where the placement of the border not controlling for an already present large minority population has led to a conflict, thanks to the presence of a separatist movement or organizations and activities within a country involving members of a group of people who want to establish their separate government or are trying to do so.[24] For an example of this concept closer to home, look at how Texas has flirted on and off with the idea of secession from the United States.[25] In a nutshell, though, it all comes down to demographics via the

FIGURE 2.2 The Kurdish Nation covers large swaths of land in multiple states, but not a majority in any one state.

ethnic breakdown of a state. The more dominant the dominant ethnicity is, the more likely it is to be considered a nation-state and vice versa to become a multinational state."

I inquired, "So what about a city-state? I hear that term a lot as well, regarding states in conversation."

Dr. Alderman concluded, "Simply put, city-states are states centered on a single important city with or without an immediate hinterland, which are regions or market areas composed of smaller towns and rural areas surrounding an urban center or core area. Singapore or the Holy See would be great examples, due to their small territories and lack of hinterland. If you'll excuse me for a moment, mother nature is calling, and I must answer her call."

23    Ellen R. Wald, "4 Key Points about the Kurdistan Independence Vote," *Forbes*, September 20, 2017, https://www.forbes.com/sites/ellenrwald/2017/09/19/4-key-points-about-the-kurdistan-independence-vote/#245b7b9f6ec9; https://thekurdishproject.org

24    https://www.collinsdictionary.com/us/dictionary/english/separatist

25    Amber Phillips, "Texas Secession Debate Starting to Get Kind of Real," *Fort Worth Star-Telegram*, April 19, 2016. http://www.star-telegram.com/news/politics-government/state-politics/article72788547.html.

## What Is a State?

With that statement, he tapped the woman sitting to his left on the aisle so that he could proceed to the bathroom. While he was gone, it appeared that the state, which seemed like another way of saying government, was core to understanding the world around us. When Dr. Alderman returned, I decided to ask for more information on how to realize what a state was. At that moment though, the flight attendant stopped by, and I took sparkling water with lime to sip while I waited. About ten minutes later, Dr. Alderman returned and stated, "Do you mind if I continue talking? I feel the need to discuss more on what a state is. The professor in me can't stop talking right now for some reason, as usual."

I replied, "You are reading my mind, good sir. Talk on."

After a brief pause, Dr. Alderman proposed, "For understanding a state, one must understand five pertinent different terms. First, an easy one is the size or the amount of physical territory occupied by a state. Of note, territory refers to the land and waters that belong to or are under the jurisdiction of a state, sovereignty, etc.[26] Per the *CIA World Factbook*, of the 254 different recognized countries—their term, not mine—the smallest is the Holy See, more commonly known as Vatican City, an enclave of Rome, Italy, at 0.44 square kilometers, while the largest is the Russian Federation at 17,098,242 square kilometers, or roughly 38,859,641 times larger than the Holy See (figure 2.3). Now keep in mind that size of the state is not everything, more the ability of those in government to manage the state's resources

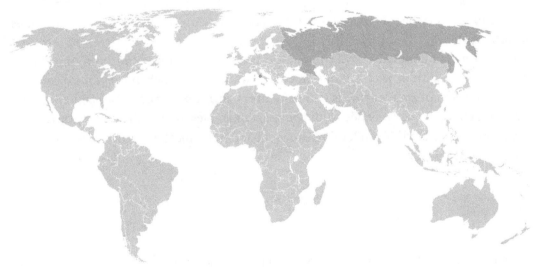

FIGURE 2.3   The Holy See is so small in comparison to Russia that an oversized green dot must be used to show where the state is.

---

26   http://www.dictionary.com/browse/territory

that makes the success of state, in my opinion. In short, getting more size gets you more resources to use, and that also gives you more influence at home and abroad. The problem is, the more territory you have, the more likely you are to have differences in your population, which leads to problems of its own, which could also lead to you becoming a failed state or a state whose political or economic system has become so weak that the government is no longer in control over the territory. Per the Fund for Peace's Fragile States Index, our current most failed states are South Sudan, Somalia, Central African Republic, Yemen, and Sudan.[27] Let's avoid that occurrence, shall we?"

I responded, "It's a plan, but if I understand you correctly, the larger size is paramount to a double-edged sword due to the larger size getting you more resources to proverbially mine and profit from while also letting the potential for internal conflict to arise due to a more diverse array of opinions on the matter due to the greater amount of people … er … nations?"

## State Shapes

Dr. Alderman held, "Well, let's talk about figures then. Consider houses. Each has its own shape, but you can group them into a few standard shapes like ranch or town or mansion. It's the same for the form or layout of a state. There are four main types of state shapes, and another that could occur concurrently with any of the main four. For this, remember the moniker OPIX-Target. The first shape of the main four is *compact*, which is a state that possesses a roughly circular, oval, or rectangular territory in which distance from the geometric center to any point on the boundary exhibits little to no variance. If you are trying to imagine this in your head, think of the capital form of the letter O, or the states of Poland (figure 2.4) or Iowa if looking at a world map. The second shape of the main four is *prorupt* or *protruded*, which is a state that features an elongated portion of territory extending from the main body of territory that is often compact in nature. If you are trying to imagine

FIGURE 2.4    This map of Poland represents a state with a compact shape.

_____

27    Fund for Peace, "Data for Peace," accessed March 19, 2019. http://fundforpeace.org/fsi/data.

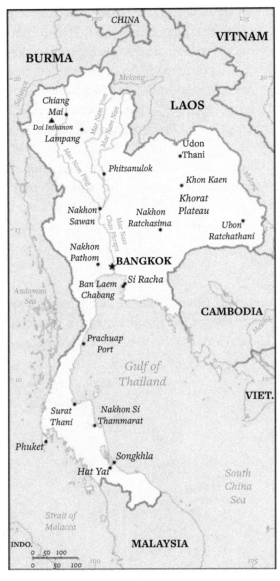

FIGURE 2.5  This map of Thailand represents a state with a prorupt shape.

this in your head, think of the capital form of the letter *P*, Thailand (figure 2.5) and Oklahoma if looking at a world map. The third shape of the main four is *elongated*, which is a state whose territory is much longer than its average width. If you are trying to imagine this in your head, think of the capital form of the letter *I*, due to the line that makes the letter going from top to bottom being very narrow with the extremes distant from one another, or the states of Chile (figure 2.6) and California if looking at a world map. The final shape of the main four is *fragmented*, which is a state that is composed of two or more noncontiguous segments. If you are trying to imagine this in your head, think of the capital form of the letter *X*, due to the two lines making the letter creating—in the negative spaces, of course—four definitively unconnected areas, or the states of the Philippines (figure 2.7) if looking at a world map. That fifth term is *perforated*, or a state that surrounds the territory of another state. If you are trying to imagine this in your head, think of the logo of the Target Corporation,[28] due to the largest circle surrounding the other two smaller circles, meaning that if you were trying to leave the center circles or state, you would have no choice but to go through the outer one to escape—the state of South Africa,[29]

which is perforated by Lesotho,[30] which is also an enclave (figure 2.8). There are no perforated states in the United States, though."

28  https://www.target.com
29  https://www.gov.za
30  https://www.gov.ls/

FIGURE 2.6  This map of Chile represents a state with an elongated shape.

FIGURE 2.7  This map of The Philippines represents a state with a fractured shape.

I remarked, "I had no idea that the different states were in such different and noteworthy shapes. However, would I be right in assuming that like one home layout over another, some are more attractive or efficient than others?"

Dr. Alderman reciprocated, "You could say that. For comparative purposes, let's use the term *suitability*, or the quality of having the properties that are right for a specific purpose,[31] governing a state in this case. A compact state is very suitable to govern, due

---

31  http://www.ldoceonline.com/dictionary/suitability

FIGURE 2.8   This map of South Africa and Lesotho represents a state with a perforation in it; South Africa is perforated by Lesotho.

to no two points in the state being exorbitantly far from one another, whereas a protruded state is only partially suitable to govern, due to a portion of the state being in an extension and exorbitantly far from those in the main area of territory. As for the last three, all are not suitable to govern, due to all areas being exorbitantly far from one another or not being able to quickly reach one another due to physical divides, such as wide waterways or other states, respectively, or some combination of the two. Granted, the real suitability of a state to be governed should be considered on a state-by-state basis, since high-functioning transportation or modern communications or a small size, in general, being present should help reduce the distance decay, or role of distance in making the decision for two places, parts of a state, to effectively interact with one another in governance."

## Enclaves and Exclaves

I interrupted to ask, "Where does the term *enclave* that you mentioned twice earlier fit into this?"

Dr. Alderman expressed, "Good transition there, but what about exclaves?"

I asked, "Exclave? What now?"

Dr. Alderman, while giggling to himself, continued, "Okay, an enclave is the entirety of a state or portion of a state that is surrounded by one other state. Examples are Lesotho, due it being surrounded by South Africa, and the Holy See, due to it being surrounded by Rome, Italy. An exclave is a portion of a state that is separated—or fragmented, to keep our terms in line—from the main territory of a state. For this, behold the state of Alaska[32] or the Kaliningrad Oblast,[33] the term for an administrative division corresponding to an

---

32   http://alaska.gov
33   https://gov39.ru

autonomous province in many Nordic countries[34] of the Russian Federation.[35] Alaska is separated from the mainland of the United States by Canada, while the Kaliningrad Oblast is separated from the main body politic of Russia by Belarus,[36] Latvia,[37] and Lithuania,[38] depending on the overland route you take. These two examples are not enclaves because they are not surrounded by another state. For an exclave that is also an enclave, look at the Dutch city of Baarle-Nassau, which surrounds parts of the Belgian city of Baarle-Hertog, which also surrounds parts of Baarle-Nassau as part of a second order or counter-enclave (figure 2.9). The border there has been laid out on the ground by fancy pavers, which places half of various structures in Belgium and the other in the Netherlands, among a wide variety of other comical circumstances that needed delineation due to centuries of conflict in taxation and control[39] (figure 2.10)."

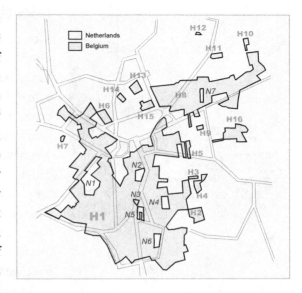

FIGURE 2.9  The main territory at the periphery is Dutch and completely surrounds the enclave belonging to Belgium which has further enclaves of the Netherlands within the original enclave of Belgium.

At that moment the flight attendant came by and asked for any additional food or drink orders. I stated, "Popcorn, please!"

The flight attendant replied, "Sorry sir, the popper is not operational today. Could I interest you in a bag of trail mix?"

I replied, "Sure, why not? That mix is just as good to graze on while listening."

Dr. Alderman inquired, "May I just have tonic water, please?"

The flight attendant, after preparing everything, remarked, "Here you go, loves. Enjoy!"

34    http://www.dictionary.com/browse/oblast
35    http://government.ru/en
36    http://www.belarus.by/en/government
37    http://www.mk.gov.lv/en
38    http://lrv.lt/en
39    Kaushik, "The Curious Case of Baarle-Nassau and Baarle-Hertog," Amusing Planet, accessed March 19, 2019, http://www.amusingplanet.com/2012/11/the-curious-case-of-baarle-nassau-and.html.

## Location

FIGURE 2.10 White pavers demarcate the border and land sovereign between Belgium and the Netherlands at Baarle-Nassau.

After taking a sip to drink and pondering a moment more to gather his thoughts about what to cover next, Dr. Alderman furthered, "Now, let's delineate that third term over there, location, or where exactly a state is relative to other states or geographic features. On one side of the proverbial coin, you have the absolute location, or where exactly a state is located on the planet. Using our plane, for example, if I were to turn on my iPhone[40] and turn on the FlightAware[41] app that I have, I could determine the exact location of our aircraft. Since this plane has Wi-Fi, let's take a gander at the map, shall we?"

A few minutes later, we could see not only the location of our flight if we were on the ground but also above it three-dimensionally. Not that it matters, but we were 29,500 feet above Pensacola, Florida, which is located at 30 degrees, 26 minutes, and 13 seconds north of the equator and 87 degrees, 12 minutes, and 33 seconds west of the prime meridian, the main two lines of the global latitude and longitude coordinate system used on earth to establish location. What came next from Dr. Alderman shed more light on our site, though. Pointedly, Dr. Alderman remarked, "For absolute location, we use coordinates of some kind. When the US government was releasing tracks of land 40 acres in size to settlers way back during, say, the Oklahoma land run of 1889,[42] they used the township and range system[43] to do so, which placed proverbial squares on the surface of the earth to be dealt out. Day to day, though, we use the geographic coordinate system, which uses the measures of latitude and longitude to locate points on the spherical surface of the earth. On the other side of the coin, you have relative location, or one's location based on one's distance and direction from another known location. For instance, as we saw before, we

---

40   https://www.apple.com/iphone
41   https://flightaware.com
42   Stan Hoig, "Land Run of 1889," *Encyclopedia of Oklahoma History and Culture*, accessed March 19, 2019, http://www.okhistory.org/publications/enc/entry.php?entry=la014.
43   "Township and Range," accessed March 19, 2019, http://www.jsu.edu/dept/geography/mhill/phygeogone/trprac.html.

are/were above Pensacola in the same way that the states south of the Saharan desert are in sub-Saharan Africa,[44] relatively speaking. Relative location uses very general terminology to describe the location, as opposed to the specifics of absolute location. And, of course, like shapes, some locations are better than others, thanks to the climate found there or items such as elevation or proximity to perpetual conflict."

## Core Areas

I posited, "That tallies up to three terms; two to go, if I am correct?"

Dr. Alderman offered, "Speaking of location, one important location in a state is its core area, or the main nucleus of activity within a state, its heart, so to speak. This area of the state is where the best transit options, major financial centers, a majority of the population, business headquarters, and, most importantly, the capital city or the municipality enjoying primary status in a country, state, province, or territory as its seat of government are. The core area here in the United States is the Northeast megalopolis (figure 2.11),[45] which includes our nation's capital in Washington DC, major business centers in New York City, and large

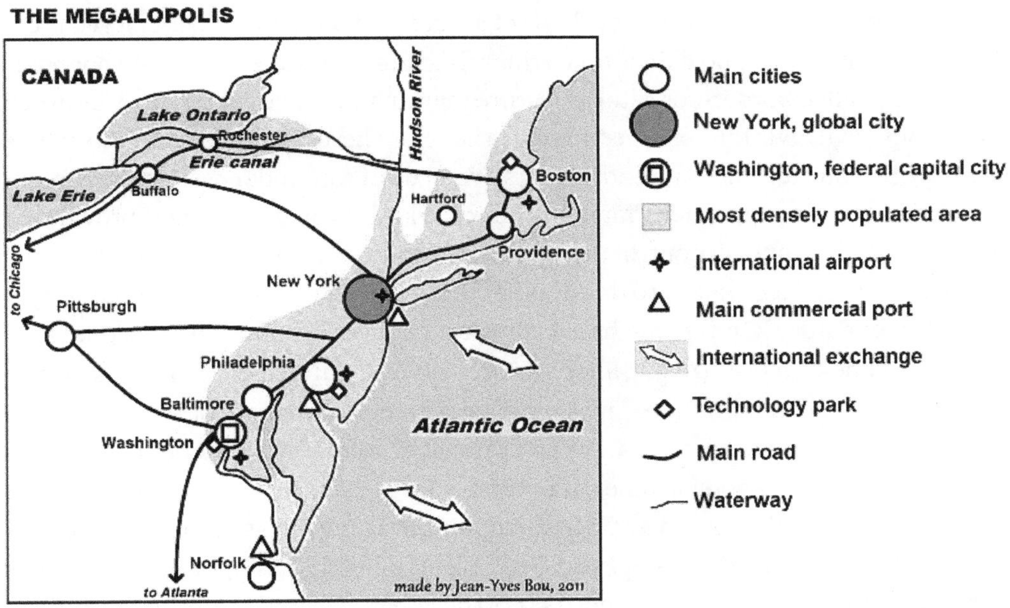

FIGURE 2.11   Basic Visual of the US Northeast Megalopolis.

---

44   http://www.newworldencyclopedia.org/entry/Sub-Saharan_Africa
45   http://www.america2050.org/northeast.html

populations, in general, along with the history of our nation thanks in large part to Baltimore, Maryland; Philadelphia, Pennsylvania; and Boston, Massachusetts, among others, stretching some 450 miles along the Atlantic Seaboard. Our nation's capital, as part of being a forward-thrust capital—or an introduced capital that is created by a state to spur economic development in relatively underdeveloped regions or to assert political control in a contested region—was moved repeatedly during the first decades of our country's existence before being permanently set up in Washington DC, in 1800, thanks to the Residence Act of 1790."[46]

## State Boundaries

I supplied, "The core area almost sounds like one's home, due to that being where one lives, eats, plans for, and, in some cases, works. A question, though: I've been looking out the window here and there; unlike the maps I saw growing up in school, there appears to be no blue, green, orange, red, and yellow states below with thick black lines neatly separating them. What gives?"

With a forlorn look on his face, Dr. Alderman said, "I'm going to assume that was a geography joke, an excellent geographical joke at that, but unlike maps, the world in person is not so neat and organized. The size or shape of a state would refer to those colored areas as you called them, but the bold lines now brings us to our final state term: state boundaries, commonly called borders, or a linear feature marking the edges of territory between states, regions, civil divisions, or other places. In general, these boundaries indicate where one state begins and another one ends. On its own side of a boundary, a state may regulate tax activities that occur there, make and enforce laws, provide currency, provide aid of various kinds, and overall control the society found there as much as it may have the power, authority, and legitimacy to do so. What makes up and goes into the boundary is a whole different story. On the one hand, you have geometric boundaries, or ones that are formed by one or more straight lines and arcs typically drawn on meridians or parallels. On the other hand, you have physiographic boundaries that are based on physical features such as mountains or rivers. For an example of both, if you look out the window now, due north of us by about 45 miles, if my app is up to date, you see the nearest point of the border between Louisiana and Mississippi (figure 2.12). That border includes the 31st parallel between the Mississippi and Pearl Rivers, the Mississippi River itself from the 33rd northern parallel down to the 31st northern parallel, and the Pearl River itself south of the 31st northern parallel down to the Gulf of Mexico: one border, three different boundaries utilizing both geometric and physiographic features."

---

46    Christopher Klein, "8 Forgotten Capitals of the United States," History.com, July 16, 2015, http://www.history.com/news/8-forgotten-capitals-of-the-united-states.

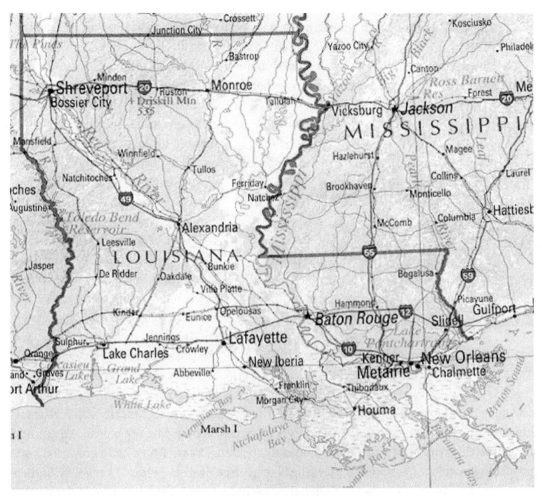

FIGURE 2.12    Map of the Border between Louisiana and Mississippi.

I inquired, "So what about when the border apparatus is being decided on?"

Dr. Alderman inquired, "What do you mean by the border apparatus?"

I replied, "I mean, so why is the border between the Baarle-Nassau and Baarle-Hertog not guarded while the one between North[47] and South[48] Korea is walled off, guarded, mined, and monitored entirely?"

After a minute of groveling to himself, Dr. Alderman continued, "I saw that you were talking to a group of people earlier. I assume that that was your family? May I ask why you aren't sitting with them?"

---

47    http://www.korea-dpr.com

48    http://www.korea.net/index.jsp

I responded, "I am not high enough on the family tree for first class, yet. One day though, I hope."

Dr. Alderman stated, "Think about who is up there in first class. Your better-to-do, your lifetime savers for that one big trip, among others. Those people aren't us. We're different. Because we are different, they get different seats, service, and, most notably, a fancy curtain separating us like a border does between two states. Back here nothing is separating us, not unless you count the annoying armrest of course, but that is a topic of discussion for another day. Regarding states, what gets placed on the border comes down to the relationship between the two states in question, economic differences between the two states, and the presence of violence in any one of the states. Let's use the border between North and South Korea as test subjects (figure 2.13). Relationship-wise, the two states are technically still at war following the end of the Korean War, as they only signed a cease-fire, not a peace treaty, and have little to no diplomatic ties.[49] Economically speaking, North Korea had a gross domestic product per capita of $1,700 in 2015, while South Korea's was at $37,700 in 2016.[50] Conflict-wise, per the Vision of Humanity's Global Peace Index—which is a measure of the level of safety and security in a society, the extent of the domestic and international conflict, and the degree of militarization[51]—South Korea is ranked as the 47th most peaceful nation—their term, not mine, once again—while North Korea is ranked as the 150th most peaceful. Due to those economic differences and the current state of affairs, the border is militarized, walled, guarded, mined, monitored, and God knows what else. In the case of Baarle-Hertog and Baarle-Nassau, Belgium and the Netherlands get along nice enough and overwhelmingly

FIGURE 2.13    North Korea as seen from the south and is the only portion of the Korean Demilitarized Zone where North and South Korean forces stand face to face.

49    Ji-Young Lee, "4 Things to Know about North and South Korea," *Conversation*, January 09, 2019, http://theconversation.com/4-things-to-know-about-north-and-south-korea-80583.
50    Central Intelligence Agency, "Country Comparison: GDP—per Capita (PPP)," *World Factbook*, accessed March 19, 2019, https://www.cia.gov/library/publications/the-world-factbook/rankorder/2004rank.html#af.
51    Vision of Humanity, "Global Peace Index 2018," accessed March 19, 2019. http://visionofhumanity.org/indexes/global-peace-index.

work together,[52] have similar strong economies with gross domestic product per capita of $45,000 and $51,000, respectively, and there is little to no major act of violence occurring, as Belgium and the Netherlands are both ranked the 19th most peaceful nations in the world. So they, once again, just put in pavers allowing you to walk back and forth whenever you want as part of the Schengen Agreement.[53] Other places like this include the quadri-point borders between the US states of Arizona, Colorado, New Mexico, and Utah, which features the Four Corners Monument, where they have just put lines on a cement foundation to demarcate the border and to allow for a nifty touristy photo with all members of the family in their own state[54] (figure 2.14). Let's go for a walk for what it's worth up here."

FIGURE 2.14    Four Corners Monument.

I thought to myself much more deeply about the curtain between coach and first class and what it represented and why it was placed there, to keep the two cabins, or states, apart, leaving only trusted agents, flight attendants, to be able to traverse the border until deplaning of the aircraft. About a minute later, Dr. Alderman and I found ourselves at the back of the plane, where the flight attendants work their magic to serve us drinks and snacks. There, Dr. Alderman spoke. "Okay Champ, we still have some more to go on borders. We saw the Louisiana-Mississippi border from our seats, but to truly understand waterway borders, we need to look out the other side of the plane. Look out the window of the A-B-C side of the plane for me and tell me what you see."

Once looking, I replied, "I see the rest of Louisiana for a few miles and then a whole lot of water—the Gulf of Mexico, if I am not mistaken."

Dr. Alderman replied, "Right you are Champ. The question is, out to sea, where does the United States end and Mexico begin? Is there a neutral area perhaps? The Rio Grande in

52    Government of the Netherlands, "Netherlands and Belgium Plan to Step Up Cooperation" press release, January 17, 2012, https://www.government.nl/latest/news/2012/01/17/netherlands-and-belgium-plan-to-step-up-cooperation.

53    https://ec.europa.eu/home-affairs/sites/homeaffairs/files/e-library/docs/schengen_brochure/schengen_brochure_dr3111126_en.pdf

54    http://navajonationparks.org/navajo-tribal-parks/four-corners-monument

Texas and various lines of latitude and longitude are used on the mainland, thanks to different treaties and agreements—the Treaty of Guadalupe Hidalgo following the end of the Mexican-American War,[55] for example. Unfortunately, water borders are not as clear-cut as land borders. If the distance between two states via a waterway is minimal, say a lake or river, the midpoint of the river controlling for islands and the like is used. In places like the Gulf of Mexico that we see out the window here, mandating what goes on requires consulting the United Nations Convention on the Law of the Sea.[56] Regarding inland waterways, those territories remain under full control regarding sovereignty, customs and immigration, and resources.

The first 12 miles out to sea are part of the territorial sea, where states still maintain full control regarding sovereignty, customs and immigration, and resources. This distance does vary by state, however. Following that is the contiguous zone, 12 to 24 miles out, where states have no sovereignty and minimal control over customs and immigration, but maintain full control over resources. From 24 to 200 miles out is the exclusive economic zone, where states have no sovereignty and no control over customs and immigration, but still maintain full control over resources. Granted, this may be extended up to 350 miles if the continental shelf is extensive enough, but no further. Beyond that is pure international water, where a state has no sovereignty, no control over customs and immigration, and no control over resources, and where it is essentially a free-for-all (figure 2.15). The border is where all the action is, I swear."

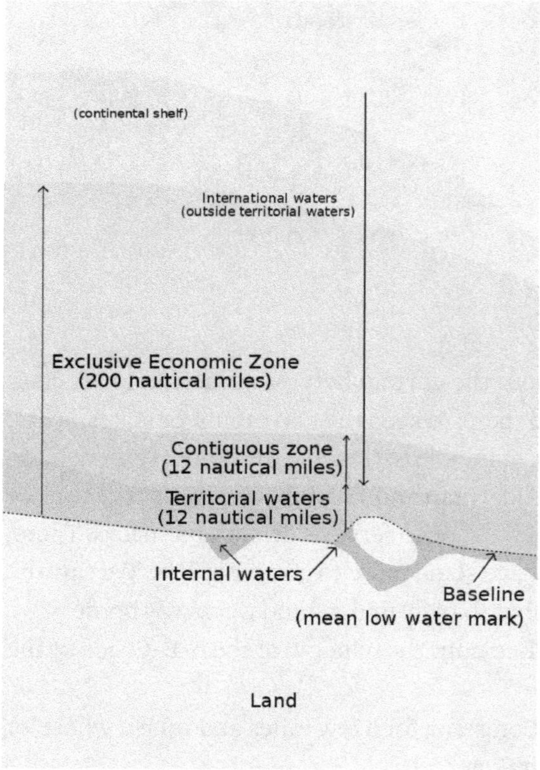

FIGURE 2.15  Map of Features, Limits, and Zones of Maritime Boundaries.

55   History.com Editors, "Treaty of Guadalupe Hidalgo," November 9, 2009, http://www.history.com/topics/treaty-of-guadalupe-hidalgo.

56   Division for Ocean Affairs and Law of the Sea, "United Nations Convention on the Law of the Sea of 10 December 1982: Overview and Full Text," last modified March 28, 2018, http://www.un.org/depts/los/convention_agreements/convention_overview_convention.htm.

I thought for a minute before asking, "What conflict may emerge from the placement of the border? It seems like if you don't control for this, conflict once again can emerge."

Dr. Alderman responded, "There are three classifications for borders that lead into the conflicts. First are antecedent borders, which are those that were determined before the intensive settlement of an area. An example would be the 49th parallel between the United States and Canada following the passage of the Oregon Treaty in 1846.[57] Following that are subsequent borders, which are those that are established during the process of intensive settlement. When establishing a subsequent boundary, they can be further classified as consequential or superimposed, where the prior controls for the present of any major nations and settlements, while the latter does no such thing and lets any potential conflicts emerge from doing so. For an example of the latter see the results of the Sykes–Picot Agreement that drew many of the borders in the Middle East that caused the Kurds to fall into their current predicament of being without a homeland.[58] A final classification is relict borders, or a boundary that no longer exists or is no longer enforced, although it may still appear on the cultural landscape. An example of the latter two border types is the Berlin Wall that was built as part of the Cold War separating East and West Berlin and that served as one of the official borders between East and West Germany; it was literally built overnight to keep people from escaping to the West and is now

FIGURE 2.16    Site of the former border between East and West Germany in Berlin after reunification at the Checkpoint Charlie Crossing.

derelict, due the reunification of Germany in 1990 following the collapse of the Soviet Union[59] (figure 2.16). Of note, the political and geographical areas near or beyond a boundary are called frontier zones."

57    History.com Editors, "U.S.-Canadian Border Established," last modified August 21, 2018, http://www.history.com/this-day-in-history/u-s-canadian-border-established.

58    Britannica, The Editors of Encyclopaedia. "Sykes-Picot Agreement." Encyclopædia Britannica. November 13, 2018. Accessed May 03, 2019. https://www.britannica.com/event/Sykes-Picot-Agreement.

59    History.com Editors, "Berlin Wall," December 15, 2009, http://www.history.com/topics/cold-war/berlin-wall.

I interjected, "But what about the conflicts?"

Dr. Alderman stated, "Calm down young man. Those conflicts are not in short supply. Besides, we already talked about the impact of large minority populations being present and the rise of separatist movements there. Remember, the Kurds, like Texans, remember the Alamo! Regardless, another conflict can emerge over the availability of corridor rights allowing entities from a landlocked state to pass through another state to get to the seas, as is the case off and on between Chile and Bolivia.[60] If using a ridgeline as a border, which also indicates where one drainage basin begins and ends, disputes can arise over determining where the ridgeline really is, as is the case with the Alps in Europe, where the watersheds for the Rhine, the Rhône, the Po, and the Danube Rivers, among others, all get their start or are heavily influenced by that area.[61] In other cases, when a river changes course, certain parts of a state can be cut off from the main section, as was the case of Carter Lake, Iowa, in the late 1800s that saw two different Supreme Court cases over the years determine the border as we know it today,[62] with the small town of Carter Lake, Iowa, being the only portion of Iowa west of the Missouri River, requiring one to traverse through Omaha, Nebraska, to get to the main portion of Iowa. Another issue is upstream obstructions like the Hoover Dam on the Colorado River running through the southwestern portion of the United States; the dam prevents river water from reaching Mexico and eventually the Gulf of California due to so much of the water being siphoned for drinking, irrigation, and recreation in the United States.[63] Another dispute arises from the fact that while borders can be drawn on the surface, resources underground do not follow the same divisions, as was the case between Kuwait and Iraq, which caused the first Gulf War to erupt over Iraq believing that Kuwait was taking oil reserves from the Iraqi side of the border.[64] A final dispute arises out of the claiming of land by foreign states. This situation is currently a major issue now in the South China Sea regarding the Spratly Islands, as China has claimed the islands as part of its exclusive economic zone, or at least built up large naval bases on them. The problem

60    Christopher Woody, "Chile and Bolivia Are Still Arguing over the Outcome of a War They Fought 131 Years Ago," *Business Insider*, October 4, 2015, http://www.businessinsider.com/chile-bolivia-sea-access-land-dispute-2015-10.

61    http://www.encyclopedia.com/places/germany-scandinavia-and-central-europe/central-european-physical-geography/alps

62    David Harding, "What's the Deal with Carter Lake (aka the Only Iowa City West of the Missouri River)?," Omaha.com, June 29, 2018, http://www.omaha.com/living/what-s-the-deal-with-carter-lake-aka-the-only/article_f16ae5e0-6a26-11e6-ab73-2b9ac4ed8a67.html.

63    Sarah Zielinski, "The Colorado River Runs Dry," *Smithsonian Magazine*, October 1, 2010, https://www.smithsonianmag.com/science-nature/the-colorado-river-runs-dry-61427169.

64    History.com Editors, "Persian Gulf War," September 13, 2017, http://www.history.com/topics/persian-gulf-war.

is, those islands are far closer to the Philippines and other states as part of their territorial sea and contiguous zones; a court case at the International Court of Justice ruled against China's efforts."[65]

I chimed in, "I had no idea that the borders have led to so much conflict. How does this all relate to keeping a state together, so to speak?"

It was then that a chime went throughout the cabin and the head purser at the front of the plane said over the PA, "Good afternoon. The captain has initiated our descent into the George Bush Intercontinental Airport. As we start our descent, please make sure your seat backs and tray tables are in their full, upright position. Make sure your seat belt is securely fastened and all carry-on luggage is stowed underneath the seat in front of you or the over-head bins. And, more importantly, if you two gentlemen in the rear vestibule could go back to your seats, that'd be great of you. Thank you."

## State Cohesion

After a moment, and embarrassed looks to each other, we went back to our seats. Once there, Dr. Alderman continued, "Champ, think of a state as your family; it might even be appropriate to use country here, if I am not mistaken. The same items that keep your family together are the same things that keep a state together. The critical term here to use is *state cohesion*, or the act of a state cohering, uniting, or sticking together. Not to rehash a term we used earlier, but the amount of cohesion found is a reliable measure of the suitability of a state to run, especially if there are multiple nations, climates, expansive territory, and the like. Those items affecting the suitability of a state on the one hand are centripetal forces that act to unite a state's peoples into a single nation based on religious, ethnolin-guistic, ideological, or other similarities, maybe more easily put as unifying forces, come to think of it. One important force here is nationalism, or a politico-territorial ideology based on collective feelings of belonging to a nation. For an example of this, look no fur-ther than President Trump's slogan, Make America Great Again, and platform of America First that is working to, and I quote, "lower taxes, repeal and replace Obamacare, end sti-fling regulations, protect our borders, keep jobs in our country, take care of our veterans, strengthen our military and law enforcement, and renegotiate bad trade deals, creating a government of, by and for the people."[66] It's practically nation building, or the process of fostering centripetal forces among diverse cultural groups inhabiting a state. Granted, a

---

65    Euan Graham, "The Hague Tribunal's South China Sea Ruling: Empty Provocation or Slow-Burning Influence?," Council of Councils, August 18, 2016. https://www.cfr.org/councilofcouncils/global_memos/p38227.
66    https://www.donaldjtrump.com/about

subnationalist group could work to undermine the state at large. Beyond ideology, there are institutions or social entities that work to build solidarity between people, like schools requiring everyone to stand for the national anthem,[67] religious entities that foster community through ministries like the Texas Baptist Men Disaster Relief,[68] and even the military, thanks to parades.[69] Also, strong communication and transportation links work well to unify states, such as the importance of Amtrak's Northeast Corridor services that connect the various cities of the Northeast megalopolis, in addition to the various forms of public transportation within each of the cities, without which that section of the country could not operate.[70] Lastly, the effective organization of a state's government is very beneficial as so much is dependent on it. Look back to the downfall of the Soviet Union and the many problems in the state-controlled distribution of resources beforehand.[71]

I interjected, "If those items are what builds a state up, what might be enough to tear one apart?"

Dr. Alderman continued, "Well, tearing apart a state is something better known as secession or the withdrawal of a people and their territory from a state to establish an independent state of their own. The forces at work here are centrifugal forces, or those items that act to divide a state's peoples into rival groups based on religious, ethnolinguistic, ideological, or other differences, maybe more easily put as destructive forces, come to think of it. One factor here is the globalization of the economy. No longer do we buy our TVs from the store down the street, made in the factory downtown; we drive up to the big-box store on the edge of town that brings in the set from a factory in Seoul or Taiwan.[72] Look at the impact of major corporations keeping money earned overseas to avoid paying taxes here at home, which leads to a decline in the suitability of a state to continue to govern said state.[73] States themselves, ironically enough, actually help that process along by entering into free trade agreements that create free trade areas in which two or more

---

67    Christine Hauser, "High Schools Threaten to Punish Students Who Kneel During Anthem," *New York Times*, September 29, 2017, https://www.nytimes.com/2017/09/29/us/high-school-anthem-protest.html.
68    https://tbmtx.org/
69    Michael Shear, "Trump Envisions a Parade Showing Off American Military Might," *New York Times*, September 18, 2017, https://www.nytimes.com/2017/09/18/us/politics/trump-4th-of-july-military-parade.html.
70    http://www.nec-commission.com
71    History.com Editors, "Soviet Union," September 01, 2017, http://www.history.com/topics/history-of-the-soviet-union.
72    Warren Fisk and Linda Qiu, "Donald Trump Says U.S. Doesn't Make TVs Anymore," Politifact, March 14, 2016, https://www.politifact.com/virginia/statements/2016/mar/14/donald-trump/donald-trump-says-us-doesnt-make-tvs-anymore.
73    Nilüfer Karacasulu Göksel, "Globalisation and the State," http://sam.gov.tr/wp-content/uploads/2012/02/1.-NiluferKaracasuluGoksel.pdf.

countries agree to eliminate tariffs and other barriers to trade between or among them so that goods flow freely across their mutual boundaries, such as the North American Free Trade Agreement, commonly known as NAFTA.[74] Also, don't be afraid to look at the impact of mass migration on the ability of a state to continue to operate. For example, as was written by Mandelbaum, during the mid-2010s Europe and the United States, both experienced massive influxes of new arrivals. The difference is that, that Europe has a minimal capacity to receive the migrants, much greater social and cultural gaps between the immigrants and the indigenous Europeans centered around religion in many cases, immigrants coming from sending states experiencing conditions that forced migration regardless of opportunities elsewhere, and the greater susceptibilities of the migrants to be more violent.[75] In northern Europe, one of the most severely impacted countries is Sweden, who has seen an uptick in terrorism since the start of the crisis.[76] Also, not help-ing are nongovernmental organizations, or NGOs, that organize individuals to perform a variety of service and humanitarian functions, bring citizen concerns to governments, advocate and monitor policies, and encourage political participation through the provi-sion of information often under the guise of the United Nations.[77] In short, the work of NGOs works best when they remain neutral in conflicts, put people and their needs first in delivering goods and services, and, most importantly, obtain community acceptance of their work to succeed most.[78] One major example of this is the influence of the Catholic Church, acting as an NGO, on the spread of HIV and AIDS, due to the church's advocation of no condom usage and church workers like nuns getting in the ways of the prophylactics being sent out in programs set up by the government or other NGOs.[79] Lastly, national-ism, when at the substate level, can actually serve to break up the state as a whole, as what may have happened in 1982 when Key West, Florida, protesting US policy of inland border checkpoints to prevent illegal immigration, staged a faux secession from the United States

74   https://ustr.gov/trade-agreements/free-trade-agreements/north-american-free-trade-agreement-nafta

75   Michael Mandelbaum, "The Impacts of Immigration: Europe vs. America." The American Interest. The American Interest LLC , June 14, 2018. https://www.the-american-interest.com/2018/06/13/the-impacts-of-immigration-europe-vs-america/.

76   True Publica, "Europe's Refugee Crisis Is Now Destroying Sweden," Global Research, July 3, 2017, https://www.globalresearch.ca/europes-refugee-crisis-is-now-destroying-sweden/5597450.

77   http://www.ngo.org/ngoinfo/define.html

78   Joseph Rostitano, "Https://Prezi.com/grzequjel9rt/Causes-Conflictngos/," June 4, 2019.

79   Kathryn Joyce, "The Catholic Church, Condoms, and HIV & AIDS in Africa," *Conscience Magazine* 33, no. 3 (2012), http://churchandstate.org.uk/2012/12/the-catholic-church-condoms-and-hiv-aids-in-africa.

FIGURE 2.17 Signage at the Key West International Airport leftover from when Key West, Florida, declared a tongue-in-cheek secession from the United States on April 23, 1982. Signage remains as part of a tourism marketing campaign.

and tongue in cheek formed the Conch Republic, named after the many seashells found there[80] (figure 2.17)."

At that point, the purser spoke over the PA system again. "Cabin crew, please take your seats for arrival."

Dr. Alderman spoke, "One final topic: Just like you and I when acting alone, states too can be weak. There is only so much to achieve by yourself. As the saying goes, you can get there quickly alone, but you can go further as a group. You and I can join up with our families. But what do states have?"

I replied, "A partridge in a pear tree?"

Dr. Alderman rebuked, "No, not that; keep it together now. No senioritis! States keep it together by evoking supranationalism, or ventures involving two or more states working toward common goals in cultural, economic, military, political, and other fields. Small-scale examples are defensive compacts like the North Atlantic Treaty Organization[81] to provide for the common defense of member states; economical compacts like the Economic Community of West African States[82] to create a common economic area for trade, customs, and currency in some cases; and energy compacts such as the Organization of the Petroleum Exporting Countries[83] to control the values of a resource, petroleum in this case. Meanwhile, large-scale examples include multifaceted arrangements like the United Nations[84] to provide consensus on a wide berth of issues for all states of the world, or the European Union,[85] which does the same for those states in Europe."

At that point, the wheels of the plane hit the ground, and the purser spoke over the PA system for the last time. "Ladies and gentlemen, welcome to Houston. Local time is 1:15 p.m., and the temperature is a muggy 95 degrees Fahrenheit. For your safety and comfort, please remain seated with your seat belt fastened until arrival at the gate. Feel free to use

80    M. Rebekah Otto, "The Conch Republic," Atlas Obscura, accessed March 19, 2019, https://www. atlasobscura.com/places/the-conch-republic-key-west-florida.

81    http://www.nato.int

82    http://www.ecowas.int/ecowas-law/treaties

83    http://www.opec.org/opec_web/en/about_us/23.htm

84    http://www.un.org/en/sections/about-un/overview

85    https://europa.eu/european-union/about-eu/eu-in-brief_en

your phones and small portable electronic devices. Please check around your seat for any personal belongings you may have brought on board with you and please use caution when opening the overhead bins, as heavy articles may have shifted around during the flight. On behalf of United Airlines and the entire crew, I'd like to thank you for joining us on this trip, and we are looking forward to seeing you on board again soon. Have a great afternoon!"

Dr. Alderman and I spent the 20 or so minutes it took to taxi to gate E-4 from runway 27 sipping the drinks that we kept from the cabin crew collecting them earlier. I thought a lot about what knowing the geographical aspects of government meant. Dr. Alderman heard me mutter a thing or two and brought up Friedrich Ratzel's organic state theory of state formation and development, which equated the state to a living organism that needed to expand through territorial growth or risk decay and death.[86] This need for more territory could be summed up as the concept of eating, as if I don't eat, I die. Even such small terms as *nation* and *state* were important to note, among other names often confused. Regardless, the government is important in and of itself, but where the government does its work may make all the difference; who knew?

A few minutes after we stopped at the gate, Dr. Alderman and I exchanged some goodbyes, only to find ourselves trudging up the aisle for his connection to Knoxville, Tennessee, and my reunification with my family. After passing through the jet bridge, I saw my family and moved toward them. Dr. Alderman shouted at me from a distance, "Be sure to get in touch later in your trek with a city, municipality, congressional district, gerrymander, reapportionment, and redistrict, as they are important territories and terms to visit on your trek through government, as the crossroads of politics and geography meet there.[87] Let me know if you want to be a volunteer on some of my work, and I hope to see you this fall!"

Charity and my dad both asked as I met them near the center of the concourse, "Who was that?"

I replied, "The first stop on my path to learning about government."

My dad replied, "You shouldn't talk to strangers, but I'm glad you learned something. Let's go home."

---

86    Geopolicraticus, "Geopolitics and Biopolitics," *Grand Strategy: The View from Oregon* (blog), February 2, 2012, https://geopolicraticus.wordpress.com/tag/organic-theory-of-the-state.

87    See the Congressional and Texas Legislative Chapters for this information.

**QUESTIONS TO CONSIDER** REGARDING AMERICAN GOVERNMENT:

1. The first main topic of the chapter discusses major terms regarding political geography. Please define what a nation and a state are, and then select a state from the world that you are interested in learning more about. Please use the *CIA World Factbook* to identify the nations of that state. Lastly, use that information to determine if your state is a nation-state, binational state, multinational state, or part of a much larger part nation-state.

2. The second main topic of the chapter discusses the five key terms to understand and visualize a state. Using the state you chose for question 1, please identify the size of your state, the shape of your state, the relative and exact location of your state, the geometric and physiographic boundaries of your state, and the core area of your state.

   a. It may be beneficial to find a blank map of your state online, print the map, and then write and draw on the map to answer this question.

3. The final main topic of the chapter discusses state cohesion. Please define *state cohesion* and then, using information from the *CIA World Factbook*, identify the centripetal and centrifugal forces found in the state you selected for questions 1 and 2. Lastly, using this information, indicate whether your state has the potential to remain intact long term and why in detail.

## FIGURE CREDITS

# Chapter 3

# Political Culture

# Institute of Texan Cultures

Thus far this week I learned a great deal about general options for how to construct a government and how to appropriately visualize nations and states. Today, as it would turn out, I focused on what exactly went into selecting one government structure over another for the state. Questions revolved around why one type is chosen over another and how issues emerge along the way that cause friction. Leading up to this situation, I came into the day knowing a few things left in my brain from my seventh-grade Texas history classes a few years ago. From those lectures, many of our state symbols derive from a vision of the state as one of self-determination, self-sufficiency, and hard work—a culture, you could say. On the other hand, the history of the state, at least regarding politics, centers on the goal of placing state government into a role that is limited in function and general ability to act on issues.

With that information in mind, I found myself in San Antonio, Texas, today at around 9:00 a.m., thanks to Charity setting up the first official stop on my trek. Over dinner last night when we got home from the airport, Charity asked sheepishly, "So, do you know what you are going to be up to next on your so-called trek that you are undertaking?"

I replied, "No, but it sounds as if you know what I should be doing next."

Overtly ready to respond, Charity spoke. "Well, as a matter of fact, I do have an idea. Are you willing to drive to San Antonio?"

I spoke again, "What exactly am I to do once there?"

Charity, while hurling a piece of paper into my hand, spoke, "This is the contact info for a colleague of mine named Dr. John Davis. He is the former full-time, and interim on occasion, director of the University of Texas at San Antonio's Institute of Texan Cultures.[1] This accomplishment is in addition to being the author of a social studies teacher's curriculum called *Texans One and All*[2] that he publishes with the institute. He would be a perfect individual to speak with and obtain information from about something called political culture. It fits, right, for what you are doing? Trust me!"

I responded, "I don't know if the stop fits, but the stop can only help, I guess. May I stop and get some authentic Mexican tacos and authentic German strudels for you on my way up to your house in Austin tomorrow after my visit in San Antonio?"

She replied, "I know Dr. Davis personally from the museum, as we consult back and forth with each other on a regular basis about our different exhibits, you see. Texas history coincides very intimately with Texas culture. Now finish your food before it gets too cold, and … what do you mean on the way up to my house?"

---

1  The information presented in this chapter was all gathered from an actual visit to the museum unless otherwise noted.

2  http://www.texancultures.com/texansresources/

I replied, "Most government in the state is found in Austin, and that's where you live. I figured I could stay with you for a while."

Charity remarked, "I talked myself right into that one, didn't I? Don't forget to call Dr. Davis after dinner to set everything up."

I replied, "Yes, yes you did, and thanks!"

With that stated, Charity and Deacon looked at each other sheepishly over what just happened, as they knew I might be staying for a while, messing up their groove. We finished eating, talked some more, and went about our evenings. Once the plates were cleared, I went out on the back patio to make the phone call. Seeing it was only seven o'clock or so in the evening, I figured it was still safe to call. After about three rings, Dr. Davis answered his phone. After a brief interlude on the phone, we agreed to meet in the main foyer of the institute at around nine o'clock in the morning near the big neon sign. Apparently, at the front of the museum, past the gift shop, of course, sits an 11-foot-tall, and God knows how vast, series of neon lights in the shape and perfect color orientation of a Texas flag. He advised that we were to examine the subject of political culture and how that influences the direction of politics on not just the state, but also the country at large.

I left my parent's house a little after six o'clock this morning to allow extra time for traffic and any other hiccups that might occur along the way. Getting out of the subdivision was a bit tricky, due to a busted water main on the main road, requiring a detour via a side street. I had to think for a minute for who to call to get it repaired but realized that I didn't know who to call and decided to let someone else make the call. I sent my dad a text at the store that would suffice, just in case. Once out of the subdivision, I turned southbound onto State Highway 6 for a 5 mile drive down to Interstate Highway 10. From there, I turned westbound onto Interstate Highway 10 for the remainder of the trip to San Antonio. The journey took about two and a quarter hours. Once on downtown San Antonio streets, I went through a drive-through and got some breakfast. The directions given to me by Dr. Davis were rather simple: "Go to downtown San Antonio and park at the Tower of the Americas—it's a big needle in the sky. You can't miss it. The institute is right across the parking lot and right across the interstate from the Alamodome.[3]"

With those directions in mind, I still found myself looking at my phone's GPS unit while traversing the streets with the easily visible spire always within sight. I pulled into the parking lot at 801 East Cesar E. Chavez Boulevard just after 8:45 and paid the ten-dollar parking fee. He was right: The institute shared a good deal of parking with the Tower of the Americas in something called HemisFair Park. Some of the signs advocating a significant redevelopment of the site seemed a bit excessive, though. The importance of this would be more evident later.

---

3   https://www.alamodome.com/

FIGURE 3.1 The Institute of Texan Cultures at HemisFair Park in San Antonio, Texas

Walking up to the building requires you to pass through a predominant structure designed to provide a formal entrance to the building and then go across a bridge, kind of like crossing a moat to enter a castle. In this case, it was the flags of the various large settlement groups that had settled in Texas over the centuries. The walk didn't feel like walking onto the field for a football game, but it made one feel connected to the rest of the world (figure 3.1). Once across the bridge, and through the front doors, I saw the massive neon flag Dr. Davis had referred to last night in the distance. The site was far more glorious to behold than I could ever have imagined. As I got closer, in shadow due to the brightness of the blaring neon, was Dr. Davis. It was easy to spot him, due to us being the only two there that early, outside of the museum docents.

On my way over to him, I was stopped by one of the docents to pay my eight-dollar admission fee. It seems like I should have gotten a free pass, but oh well. With that out of the way, I finally approached Dr. Davis and stated, "Dr. Davis. My name is Champ, and I am the one who you are scheduled to meet with today. How are you?"

He replied, "Well, thanks, I'm good, a bit Hemisfair to Midland from time to time. I hope your drive over from Houston was uneventful."

I said, "It was. Getting some nice authentic breakfast tacos made the drive worth the while all the more."

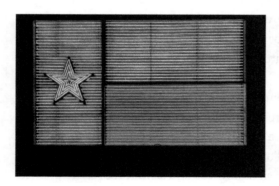

FIGURE 3.2 The Neon Texas Flag at the Institute of Texan Cultures

He continued, "Good. The tacos are one of the big things to enjoy around here. It was nice getting the call from you last night, and I am glad to play my part on your trek. Tell your sister, though, that I want access to a few new artifacts for my museum here that they have and she has prevented me from getting. Pass that on if you don't mind."

I said, "I will do my best, sir. So, where do we begin?"

Dr. Davis responded, "Oh I know, let's take the obligatory photo with your phone in front of the neon flag (figure 3.2)."

## Dependence on a Food Source

I winced in embarrassment at getting my photo taken in a big room like this. Thankfully, no one was there to watch, but it went well enough. Following this, Dr. Davis led me around the corner into the area of the museum that covers the American Indian in Texas. In getting started, he instructed, "Before we get into the nuts and bolts of what political culture is, let's go over these exhibits that divulge information on the native populations. Within them lies an important starter piece to the concept known as political culture."

Via my readings of the exhibit, I surmised the following:

Human settlements began in the area known today as Texas roughly 12,000 years ago, around 10,000 BCE. The first group was known as the Clovis people, named after the stone blades they used that were specialized for hunting colossal game, like mammoths. The Clovis were a hunter-gatherer society that was found near Clovis, New Mexico, just on the border with Texas, 90 miles northwest of Lubbock, Texas. Two thousand or so years later, the second group known to inhabit Texas rose, known as the Folsom people. They were named for the stone blades that were specialized for hunting large game, like buffalo, in their hunter-gatherer society and were found near Folsom, Texas, just outside of Amarillo. Folsom people are believed to be direct descendants of the Clovis people, only to be differentiated by their refined blade patterns and shapes for the relatively smaller game they hunted, showing an evolution in their hunting techniques. Following the Folsom people came the Archaic people, with their late, middle, and early stages, beginning roughly 8,000 years ago and lasting for around 6,000 years, with the most substantial stash of artifacts from these eras coming from throughout the Great Plains portion of the state. Archaic people are believed to be descendants of the Folsom and Clovis peoples due to an ever-more refined blade point that was now best suited for the small game, like deer, that they were forced to hunt due to the dying off of the buffalo and mammoths. Accordingly, the new people had to refocus their weaponry and lifestyle to match the game that was available. After this came the Neo-Indians, from around 0 BCE, who, due to advances in technology, were able to settle down and become farming societies. Finally, from about 500 years ago or so, Texas was inhabited by the Tonkawa, Pueblo, and Karankawa, who were hunter-gatherers, farmers, and fishers, respectively, due to living on the plains, desert, and coastal areas of the state, respectively. Lastly, it appeared that these final groups all perished or became less of themselves and were absorbed into other groups or the population at large following settlement by the Spanish and later immigrant groups to Texas.

Once I was done reading and making small talk along the way with Dr. Davis, he asked me, "What was the main item driving each of the native societies that have settled here in Texas over the millennia?"

I remarked, "It seems as if each society, at least as it is presented here, was dependent on their food source."

Dr. Davis went on, "Very good. Where the society went, where they stopped, what they did when they got there, et cetera, was dependent on their food source, which is more easily stated, or viewed, as their culture, or the way of life, especially the general customs and beliefs, of a group of people, at a time, at a place.[4] As we get closer to today, the availability of various food sources changed, so the various peoples altered their lifestyles to match via their available technology and prowess. The same arrowhead points needed to hunt the mammoth would not work for hunting buffalo, and so on and so forth, due to the need to be more accurate. The ability to farm and fish was and still is a game changer as they could settle down and better control their lifestyles. Overall, their food source was the main driving factor in society back then. So, now what do you think the main driving source in society today could be?"

I replied, "Well, based on the subject matter of my trek and other things I've learned thus far this week, I would say, government, or at least people's view of it?"

He furthered, "I would agree with that sentiment, among other things. As the availability of the buffalo changed, the American Indian populations had to adapt. Let's replace the buffalo as a driving factor with that of government. Today, as the government offers more services and becomes larger in general, it affects more people and dictates what it is the citizenry, you and I, can and cannot do more and more. Back then, every part of the buffalo was used—pelts for shelter and clothing, even the testicles were used. Ever tried a Rocky Mountain oyster?"

I could only make faint noises of dismay at hearing that and instructed, "Get to the point sir, please!"

Continuing, he went on, "Today, we are just as dependent on the government in a variety of ways just as the native populations were on their food source. For example, at the basic level, this includes identification in the form of a driver's license from the state or a passport from the federal government, all the way up to the fundamental infrastructure that

---

4    https://www.merriam-webster.com/dictionary/culture

we use to drive on and create commerce to gather more resources to provide for our own with. Who do you think provides for, builds, and maintains those roadways, the infrastructure fairy? Specifically, in fiscal year 2018, the federal government gave $41,420,520,075 to the states for their highways, Texas alone got $3,831,926,012 or roughly 9.25% of the money.[5] In short, the indigenous peoples used buffalo for food and clothing and shelter, and people do the same with government today—take advantage of all services that they offer: roads, public housing, food stamps, and other benefits."

I nodded in agreement.

Concluding, he said, "Accordingly, as the mammoth died off or the buffalo moved on, people had to decide to follow along or find a new food source and then adapt accordingly, without which they would die, due to not being able to get enough sustenance. Today, as the government moves in different directions for policy, people form an opinion as to whether that is a good decision for them and or the population at large. Look at what happened in 2016 with the election of President Trump: The citizens in most of the states, based on Electoral College votes, decided that a person with an America First principle for government was the right person for us to go forward with as our leader, as opposed to the more global view of Trump's opposition, Hillary Clinton, or his predecessor, former president Obama.[6] With that in mind, if enough people, as in a majority of the populace, get together, their opinions become permanent as their/the region's dominant political culture. The only difference is that people can tell the government what their views are and change the government to coincide with it, while the buffalo is, well, a wild animal and does whatever it wants regardless of your opinion."

We spent a few more minutes walking through the rest of the American Indian exhibit. I especially liked the clay housing used to display the pottery and intricate markings of the various cultures. Along the way, Dr. Davis advised that culture is something that is learned rather than genetically based, like your hair color, and that not learning your culture is dangerous to your survival. At one point he commented, "Had the tribes we discussed earlier not gotten to a better point when passing on how to catch their food, their continual existence as we've seen thus far today would not have been possible."

After looking at some of the more significant pottery found in the clay housing, I inquired, "So what might determine what we are taught?"

---

5    R.S. Kirk (n.d.), The Highway Funding Formula: History and Current Status. The Highway Funding Formula: History and Current Status. Washington, DC: Congressional Research Service.

6    Carol Morello, "Clinton, Trump Have Divergent Worldviews on Almost Everything," *Washington Post*, September 26, 2016, https://www.washingtonpost.com/politics/2016/live-updates/general-election/real-time-fact-checking-and-analysis-of-the-first-presidential-debate/clinton-trump-have-divergent-worldviews-on-almost-everything/?utm_term=.036a7896ef3c.

Dr. Davis replied, "Any number of items really, but probably more than anything your age, class in society, gender, and eventual profession. For example, in India prior to the 1950s, as part of their now heavily neutered cast system, an up-and-coming young maharaja or king would need knowledge of foreign policy and etiquette at state dinners, while a young girl of one of the lower castes would only need to, or probably just be allowed to, know how to clean the house, make a sari, and cook.[7] Also, what is learned here is passed down by one of two methods: imitation or being physically instructed on how to do something, such a hunting technique passed on from father to son. Speaking of which, the arrowhead itself, the ones we see here and in the prior exhibits, is an example of a culture trait or unit of learned behavior in society. Traits can be a physical item, a technique for how to use the item, a belief, or an attitude. When two or more traits are interrelated, they become culture complexes. Think of how having the best collection of something gives you greater amounts of influence in a situation—the big man on campus, so to speak. A group of complexes together becomes a culture system or a collection of interacting culture traits and complexes that are shared by a group. Add geography to the mix; you get a culture region, or a portion of the earth's surface occupied by people sharing recognizable and distinctive cultural characteristics. So, what group of people might come to mind here in the United States beyond the people we see here around us?"

I replied, "The Amish?"

Dr. Davis responded, "Right once again. I think the primary trait for them revolves around dressing.[8] For example, men wear dark-colored suits, straight-cut coats with no lapels, broad-fall trousers, suspenders, solid-colored shirts, black socks and shoes, and black or straw broad-brimmed hats. Shirts fasten with conventional buttons; suit coats and vests fasten with hooks and eyes. Meanwhile, women wear modest, solid-colored dresses, usually with long sleeves and a full skirt, a cape, and an apron. The clothing is fastened with straight pins or snaps. Bringing the clothing up to a complex is why it is done. Specifically, these are worn as the most obvious outward manifestation of their faith, purity, and social separation from the world. It demonstrates group allegiance and identity, as well as the willingness to yield to group standards. Add in the horse and buggy system. The no electricity thing and use of Pennsylvania Dutch, so on and so forth and you get your culture system all based on a literal interpretation of the Bible, as well as unwritten rules from the Amish Ordnung that

---

7    For general info on India see here: Kim Ann Zimmermann, "Indian Culture: Traditions and Customs of India," LiveScience, July 20, 2017, https://www.livescience.com/28634-indian-culture.html. For more specific info on the caste system today see here: What is India's caste system? (2019, June 19). Retrieved January 13, 2020, from https://www.bbc.com/news/world-asia-india-35650616.
8    "PA Amish Lifestyle: How the Community of Amish in PA Live Today." Discover Lancaster. Accessed April 28, 2020. https://www.discoverlancaster.com/amish/lifestyle/.

prescribes behavior, appearance, and other aspects of the Amish culture. Sealing the deal though is the agglomeration of their nation in and around Lancaster County, Pennsylvania, for your culture region. If you are looking for a more comical take on a more local example of these culture terms in our/a society, when you get home, look up a music video/song by Weird Al Yankovic's called "Amish Paradise"[9] that should help drive the point home."

Either way, after about 15 additional minutes here in the native population area of the museum, Dr. Davis signaled that we should head over to the Dome Show Theater and further our discussion. Once there, we grabbed a bench to sit on and watched the different panels light up with images of the main museum attraction, called the *Dome Show*.

## What Is Political Culture?

Once the 15-minute show was over, Dr. Davis stated, "Let's get to what political culture is. Per the *International Encyclopedia of the Social Sciences*, political culture is 'the set of attitudes, beliefs, and sentiments that give order and meaning to a political process and which provide the underlying assumptions and rules that govern behavior in the political system.'[10] In the study of political science, the field's founder is the late Dr. Daniel J. Elazar. In his 1966 seminal work, *American Federalism: A View from the States*, he defines *political culture* as 'the particular pattern of orientation of political action in which each political system is embedded.'[11] In other words, it is the foundation for what citizens living in a society and the governments regulating said organization are expected to do, respectively."

I butted in, "So what you are telling me is there is some invisible hand in society dictating the relationship between citizens and their government?"

Dr. Davis's rebuttal: "Yes. As remarked before, the food source in the early societies dictated a lot of their lifestyles. Now, the relationship between man and government has replaced said driving force in society in many ways, with today's added benefit of the free-market economy helping along the way."

I moved on, "So what cultures did Elazar theorize to be in society?"

## Political Culture at the National and Regional Levels

He continued, "Well. Elazar theorized about political culture at the national and regional levels. At the top, or national, level, we have two views to consider. One view is where

9   http://weirdal.com/videos
10   *International Encyclopedia of the Social Sciences*, 2nd ed. (New York: Macmillan Reference USA, 2008).
11   D. J. Elazar, *American Federalism: A View from the States* (New York: Crowell, 1966).

government serves as a political theater, featuring groups and interests bargaining with each other to achieve gains for themselves and others based on their own needs. On the other hand, you have people who view government as a commonwealth, allowing people to put aside their differences for the good of, and achievement of, common goals in the amelioration of society."

I intruded, "Why does this sound like the two main political parties today, from what I know of them? The Democrats advocate a larger government providing greater amounts of services, and the Republicans argue for a more limited government in scope and power."

He stated, "Because that is exactly what the two political parties represent today. It gets even more interesting when you look at what Elazar derived at the state and regional level (figure 3.3). He calls these subcultures. First is the 'individual subculture.' This culture is one where there is a marketplace of competitive individual interests who use the political system to better their causes, somewhat akin to the theater I mentioned earlier. Regarding government action on issues, none is taken unless a massive outcry from the public is made. Even then, the action taken is usually for electoral advantage and other gains of those in service. Rewards are based on patronage and party service, with a hint of corruption encouraged. Participation is left to the professional leaders, and average citizens are not encouraged to get involved. Looking at the two places where the government intervenes, economic and social affairs; the government would not take much action in either, so as to not rock the

FIGURE 3.3   Elazar's Culture Classification by State

boat of a hopefully churning society. Finally, if you were to look at a map, states in the mid-Atlantic region of the East Coast first adopted this culture and then brought it with them west as they settled along a similar latitude."

I remarked, "So this is the subculture that advocates a dog-eat-dog world: Everyone is seeking personal wealth, regardless of everything else, where you are left to fend for yourself and, as Jerry Butler puts it, 'only the strong survive'?"[12]

He concurred, "Yep. Luckily, for those of us who want some government intervention, but not too much, we have the 'traditional subculture.' This is the subculture where everything is set up to preserve the status quo and benefit the oligarchs of society who are leading it. Those oligarchs leading society could consist of the wealthy, landowners, business owners, or anyone who has a big hand in the game, like religious leaders in a theocracy. There is very little party competition, but the ruling party has competition from within, leading them to act to ensure they remain in power. Average citizen participation is discouraged, and low polling is the most common result of it. The direction of the state is left to the leaders of the ruling political party. Looking again at the two places where the government intervenes, the government would act in either social or economic affairs without prodding, but not in both to remain in power. Finally, if you were to look at a map again, states in the southern region of the East Coast first adopted this culture—look at the plantation culture of the Old South[13]—and then brought it with them in the same way that those who began the individual subculture did going west. More easily put, all the states from the old Confederacy would fall into this mainframe in some form or another."

In showing I understood, I surmised, "So this is the subculture that still advocates a dog-eat-dog world, but there is a general focus of those in control to act more in one area to keep their influence, an aristocracy so to speak, be it in economic or social realms, but probably not both. Also, here Jerry Butler would rename his song 'Only the People We Say Are Strong Survive.'"

He went on, "Once again, you are thinking in the right direction. Lastly, for those among us who want even more government intervention, we are left with the 'moral subculture.' This is the society where collective action through politics is called for, even if there is little public outcry for change in some form. Politics is focused on bettering society, even if it means holding back the stronger members to the benefit of everyone. Very little patronage or corruption is considered prudent, with items taking center stage on the merits of necessity, with higher levels of participation by society encouraged. Looking one last time at the two places where

---

12    https://www.youtube.com/watch?v=XPkd9ZQOtbI

13    USHistory.org, "Life in the Plantation South," accessed March 19, 2019, http://www.ushistory.org/us/5e.asp.

the government intervenes, the government would act in both social and economic affairs without prodding. Government is proactive, so to speak. Finally, if you were to look at that map again, states in New England first adopted this culture and then brought it with them once again in the same way that those who began the individual and traditional subcultures did."

I surmised, "So this is a subculture that does not advocate a dog-eat-dog world, as the focus of those in control is to act in a way that benefits the greatest number of people, regardless of mitigating circumstances in any possible measure. Also, here Jerry Butler would rename his song 'Only the Strong Survive, and That's Everybody'!"

## Political Culture at the Local Level

He furthered, "I think you have got the gist of everything as to what political culture is and the varieties that are found, at least at the state and national level. The better question is, what does the literature have to say about the local level? For that, it is wise to turn to Dr. Richard Florida's 2005 work, *Cities and the Creative Class*.[14] In this work, the study of political culture and how it exists is explored at the local level."

I mused, "So why was there a need for additional classification at a different level?"

Dr. Davis went on, "Simple enough. Political culture at the regional and national levels, as seen under Elazar, changes slowly. Of note, if you want to keep change at a minimum, you should isolate yourself and stabilize your circumstances. The slow change at the national and regional levels could take years, decades, maybe even a century for an entire region to switch cultures. Look at the South: The 2014 election saw every US Senate and gubernatorial office be held by the Republican Party for the first time in 150 years, since the height of Reconstruction, when it had been majorly Democrat.[15] What we have seen today is that urban centers are growing at massive rates while rural areas are remaining constant, population-wise, at best. This leads the urban areas to differ from the dominant subculture around them that is still, let's just say, running an outdated set of software. This growth causing the change is not people moving from the countryside to town, as the youth often do at the completion of their schooling, but by people moving in from distant places—be it Detroit to Dallas or Abu Dhabi to Austin—who bring with them their vices, virtues, and views regarding government that differ greatly from the region that they now inhabit. These differences bring to light an urban-rural divide that takes much greater precedence today than those argued by Elazar."[16]

14    Richard Florida, *Cities and the Creative Class* (New York: Routledge, 2005).

15    Molly Ball, "The Republican Wave Sweeps the Midterm Elections." *Atlantic*, November 25, 2014, https://www.theatlantic.com/politics/archive/2014/11/republicans-sweep-the-midterm-elections/382394.

16    Jose A. DelReal and Scott Clement, "New Poll of Rural Americans Shows Deep Cultural Divide with Urban Residents," *Washington Post*, June 17, 2017, https://www.washingtonpost.com/graphics/2017/

In considering what I just heard, I stated, "So I should think of a northern liberal moving to rural Texas or a conservative Arab family from Riyadh, Saudi Arabia, moving to liberal Austin. Just like water and oil, they don't mix well at first, but as enough people move there from their previous place of origin, they cause the urban area to differ from the dominant regional political culture surrounding them. This allows for the creation of this so-called new political culture as the communities adapt and adhere to the new order."

Dr. Davis expanded, "Precisely. Remember, allowing this to happen is the fact that we now live in a very mobile, postindustrial society that allows people to move to a destination, not out of chance, but out of precision, due to the knowledge of what is offered and expected of them there, especially as time wears on. Allowing people to move more freely is the fact that Americans are becoming wealthier and less tied to their original communities as the role and offerings of a traditional community have withered. Accordingly, with economic concerns gone by the wayside, people care more about social issues like same-sex marriage or women's access to services, such as abortion, as opposed to what are we going to eat tonight and how are we going to pay for it. Granted, the economy could always collapse in a heartbeat, and these issues move away from the foreground, but who knows when or if that is going to happen."

I chimed in, "So what now defines the places with these new local cultures?"

He replied, "Good question! The presence or lack of five different factors differentiates the four local political cultures. Factor one is innovativeness of the area, which is found in high-tech industries and creative centers. Second is diversity, which is common in high-tech industries and creative centers as well. The third is expected political involvement, commonplace in organizational-age communities and social capital communities. Fourth is the presence of a functional economy, which is prevalent in all but organizational-age communities. Finally, the fifth factor is the physical size of the city in question. High-tech industries and creative centers are quite similar. Both have an abundance of postindustrial, high-technology industry and service businesses."

I then asked, "What cities here in Texas best fit each of these communities?"

Dr. Davis then replied, "Easy, regarding high-technology industries and creative centers let's use Houston and Austin. Houston—indeed the greater Houston area, I should say best fits a high-tech industry—as it has a multitude of medical research occurring due to the presence of the Texas Medical Center,[17] the oil and gas industry,[18] shipping due to the ports

national/rural-america/?utm_term=.54e72d152b16.

17    http://www.tmc.edu/about-tmc/facts-and-figures

18    Roger M. Olien, "Oil and Gas Industry," Texas State Historical Association, last modified August 19, 2016, https://tshaonline.org/handbook/online/articles/doogz.

in nearby Baytown and Galveston,[19] while Austin, as an example of a creative center, has an abundance of high-tech firms like Dell Computers[20] driving their respective economies, with expected growth from those fields being channeled 'out' in Houston due to the inability of the different sectors to overlap (you don't want a hospital near a refinery), and 'up' in Austin due to the use of more traditional office buildings that are easier to overlap as various tech hubs mix easily. Regarding social capital and organizational-age communities, let's use the West Texas towns of Snyder and Ira as examples. Both are in Scurry County, with Snyder being the county seat and Ira being the bedroom community. Both are small farming and agricultural communities with an oilfield kicker in a rural area and with both not big enough to have a shape on a statewide map. What truly differentiates the two is that the social capital community is a functional city and municipality while the organizational-age community is more of a ghost town, with a school being the extent of services provided. Either way, in these areas, political involvement is expected, but the excellent economy is only found in the social capital communities. Here, who you know is still crucial, and there is little diversity."

## Factors That Develop Political Culture

With what makes the local political cultures vary explained, I asked, "So what are the factors that I should look for regarding determining the most likely culture that someone is from or influenced by the most?

Dr. Davis expressed, "It comes down to five things. They are race, due to the varying experiences people of different races have when interacting with government over time; religiosity, due to the various levels of it found around the nation and views toward intervention by different faiths in government, as evidenced by Jehovah's Witnesses not voting[21]; education, due to having more, leading to less dependency on government in most cases; family type, due to children often mimicking their parents' beliefs; and, most importantly, location, due to those in rural areas merely being less dependent on government; for example, many live off the power grid and water systems—both of which are typical functions of cities, better put as municipalities, not available in the middle of nowhere."

I asked him to further this by asking, "So what does not lead to developing a particular culture over another?"

He said, "Things like hair color, car being driven, and height. As the saying goes, blondes might have more fun, but they are all over the political spectrum. People's political culture

---

19    American Society of Civil Engineers, "Houston Ship Channel," accessed March 19, 2019, http://www. asce.org/project/houston-ship-channel.

20    http://www.dell.com/en-us

21    https://www.jw.org/en

drives their vehicle decision—not the other way around—and, finally, tall people and short people sit on both sides of the political aisle. Let's go for a walk."

## When Different Political Cultures Interact

Over the next hour, we viewed the remaining indoor exhibits of the museum. The rest of the museum, like the flags outside, displays the different ethnicities, nationalities, and religious groups who made the pilgrimage and decision to establish roots here in Texas. This included exotic places like Lebanon and China and people like the Wends, who are Germanic, alongside more well-known groups such as the Brits, mainland Europeans, Nordic people, and formerly enslaved people. However, one item bothered me about the seemingly happy coexistence of all these groups settling in one place together: It didn't seem legitimate. This was when the conversation became graphic.

Halfway through our walk, I inquired, "Don't these groups' differences get in the way of society going forward?"

Dr. Davis contended, "Well, yes, even people of the same group disagree from time to time. Why then would people of different groups not disagree on items? They would, of course. When social scientists look at these disagreements, we refer to these differences in society as something called a social cleavage, or the division of voters (or society in general) into groups based on the differing of opinions on a matter—political views, in this case."[22]

He continued, "Four common social cleavages have been identified in society at large. These include the center versus periphery as indicated earlier by the divisions between urbanites and rural citizens or coastal elites and those from the interior; owner versus worker and the divide between social or economic classes; land versus industry, representing the division between state and private control over industry; and finally the division of church and state over the acceptable influence of religious beliefs in government (figure 3.4). Other divides could be of gender or racial viewpoints.

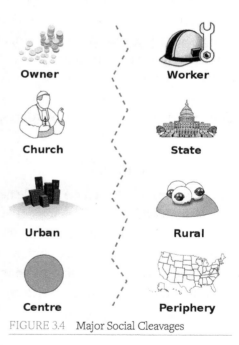

FIGURE 3.4   Major Social Cleavages

22   https://www.dictionary.com/browse/cleavage

Getting back to dealing with those differences, dealing with them is an action called 'cross-cutting' a social cleavage, or the simple act of finding an issue that all are concerned with, regardless of side, that people can come together and reach an agreement on.[23] For that better example, though, let me read you the script from one of my favorite movies, Marvel's *The Avengers.*"

After a short pause, Dr. Davis continued, "The line I want to tell you about is from the scene where up to that point in the film the Avengers are infighting with one another and causing a lot of distraction, preventing them from defeating Loki and his allies, to which Nick Fury says, 'These were in Phil Coulson's jacket. I guess he never did get you to sign them.' Keep in mind he says this while throwing blood-stained Captain America cards onto the table, and Steve Rogers picks one of them up. Nick Fury then further says, while walking toward Rogers, 'We're dead in the air up here. Our communications, the location of the Cube, Banner, Thor. . . . I got nothing for you. I lost my one good eye. Maybe I had that coming. . . . Yes. We were going to build an arsenal with the Tesseract. I never put all my chips on that number, though, because I was playing something even riskier.' Then after a long pause, Nick Fury looks at Iron Man and says, 'There was an idea, Stark knows this, called the Avengers Initiative. The idea was to bring together a group of remarkable people to see if they could become something more. To see if they could work together when we needed them to, to fight the battles that we never could.' Nick concludes his speech that rallies the group into action by saying, 'Phil Coulson died, still believing in that idea. In heroes.'[24] In this case, the need to save the world from an intergalactic invasion by Loki, and make sure Coulson did not die in vain, was enough for everyone involved to put aside their differences for the greater good. Overall, you need to find the issue that crosscuts differences in society and then progress can be found.

## Texas on the Brink

I could only think that I have a whole new perspective on life after that one. But I was still wondering aloud, "What does all of this say about Texas?"

In answering this question, Dr. Davis and I went to the rear of the museum on the first floor and out the door to an exhibition called the *Back 40*, which displayed an old one-room schoolhouse, a barn, a log cabin, a windmill, an adobe house, and a fort, reminiscent of how Texas may have looked to early settlers who had only fundamental infrastructure. Once out

---

23   https://www.youtube.com/watch?v=ORMlYi8F3UQ
24   IMDb, "The Avengers (2012): Quotes," accessed March 19, 2019, http://www.imdb.com/title/tt0848228/quotes?ref_=tt_ql_trv_4.

there, we sat on the grass under the windmill. In discussing how all of what I just learned related to Texas, Dr. Davis started with the question, "When you travel overseas, how do you reply when someone asks where you are from?"

I answered quickly, "Texan."

He responded, "Do you think people from Nebraska say Nebraskan? Not likely, I bet. It just doesn't sound right for some reason. They more than likely say American, along with most of the rest of the country."

I furthered, "What does that have to do with anything?"

He responded, "Everything. When you think of people from other states, it's kind of hard to get a basic idea of how the people from other parts of the country look. You may eventually think of mobsters from Jersey, farmers from Kansas, even surfer dudes from California. Texas, on the other hand—people could describe an imagined typical Texan in a heartbeat; Big Tex at the State Fair in Dallas says it all (figure 3.5). People think of Texans, and they think cowboys riding bucking broncos or people living off the land, being self-sufficient and capable of going when the going gets rough.

It's an oversimplification, but in many cases it still fits. Hell, people in business still wear cowboy boots to the office, and at the end of their senior year in high school, students ride tractors or horses to school for a day with encouragement from administrators.[25] This explains why Texas votes Republican, as Democrats often advocate greater roles of government, going against the grain of many places here in the state, Austin again being the exception, which is kind of funny, since the state capital is there."

FIGURE 3.5    Oversimplification of the Idolized Texas represented by Big Tex at the Texas Sate Fair in Dallas, Texas

I interrupted, "What facts exist that would prove this?"

He thought for a minute and went ahead, "Look at the log cabin over there. How developed a lifestyle would you say it is?"

I replied, "Primitive, at best."

He continued, "That would be a good term to use. Well, unfortunately, according to the Texas Legislative Study Group's report, *Texas on the Brink: How Texas Ranks among the 50*

25    Karla Blackstock, "In Rural Texas, High Schoolers Have 'Drive Your Tractor to School Day.'" Wide Open Country, February 26, 2019, http://www.wideopencountry.com/rural-texas-high-schoolers-drive-tractor-school-day.

*States,*[26] from 2013, that is how many Texans still live today, but with more modern materials, of course. Based on that report, the percentage of Texans living below the federal poverty level is the seventh highest in the nation, and Texas is the top producer of carbon dioxide emissions (the major presence of the oil and gas industry in the state explains that), has the fourth-highest teenage pregnancy rate, the 42nd-highest expenditures on education per student, and the second-highest public school enrollment. Does any of this sound like the results of a moralistic approach to government ?"

In shock, I shook my head to answer no.

He went on. "Health care, schooling, you name it. It all aligns with the state being very individualistic, although there are certainly tinges of traditionalistic culture in the East and South due to populations there stemming from more hierarchal societies. East Texas stems from the Old South, and South Texas stems from the ranchero culture (which was a quasi-feudal society) in Spanish Mexico, not to mention the dramatic conservatism of Mexico, thanks to the Catholic Church. Finally, as we mentioned before, Austin does have its shades of moralism due to its falling under the classification of being a creative center. Beyond that, it is all individualistic. Fight or flight, as the saying goes, to some other state or get to work here."

I replied, "So, we are a product of our political culture; we do not want more help from the government, so large portions of the society are worse off for it? How would you summarize everything we have gone over here today?"

Signaling with his hand, he motioned for us to go inside. On the way, Dr. Davis concluded, "Well, regardless of level and depending on which culture you live in, you can expect the size of government to differ dramatically, with the more moralistic places having larger governments per capita and more individualistic places having the opposite, with traditionalistic areas somewhere in between. More importantly, the expectations of the role to be played by citizens follow a similar line as the size of government for each of the cultures. Regardless, each culture reflects the political values and beliefs of people. It explains how people feel about their government and will determine the expectations of the government and the services provided. For change to occur, you need something massive to push an area over the borderline into the realm of a different dominant culture. I would reckon crosscutting one of the bigger cleavages should do the trick."

I mentioned, "Like immigration here in the state?"

---

26    Michael King, "Texas on the Brink UPDATED." Sixth Edition Ranks Texas Nationwide - News - The Austin Chronicle. April 15, 2013. Accessed May 03, 2019. https://www.austinchronicle.com/daily/news/2013-04-15/texas-on-the-brink/.

Dr. Davis replied, "Immigration will have an impact. What that impact will be is what we must wait for, especially as it relates to politics."

With that in mind, we had found our way back to the front of the museum and the large neon sign. It was just before noon, and I was getting hungry. I thanked Dr. Davis for his time and began walking toward the door. As I was on my way out, though, Dr. Davis interjected, "The Alamo is a short walk away through old HemisFair Park, along the Riverwalk, and an incline up the escalators inside the Rivercenter Mall. If you want to take a good look at what political culture in action is, go there."

I asked, "What do you mean by HemisFair Park?"

He looked on in amusement and spoke. "You don't know, do you? In 1968 San Antonio hosted the World's Fair and displayed the many cultures of the state to show Texas's connection to the rest of the world.[27] Texas is a very diverse place, you know. We just got to show off for a while. Why do you think the tower and museum are here? You are standing in history. Today there is a branch of the Universidad Nacional Autónoma de México[28] and several museums beyond this one. The building and the exhibits we saw today were crafted specifically for the events of that fair."

With that stated, I again thanked Dr. Davis for the information and made my way out the front door. Once over the bridge, through the flag-poles, and across the parking lot, I found myself at the foot of the massive Tower of the Americas (figure 3.6). Once there, I went to the base and found a map leading me to the Riverwalk. From there, it was a short ten-minute walk to the Alamo via the Rivercenter Mall.[29] After exiting the Bell Street entrance to the mall, I walked down the block, turned right onto Alamo Plaza, and came face to face with the historic relic in the distance (figure 3.7). It was at this moment that my seventh-grade Texas history class and the lessons I had learned today hit me: Texans at the Alamo fought for their independence from Mexico due to their belief in a limited government based close

FIGURE 3.6   Tower of the Americas in old HemisFair Park

27   http://www.worldsfair68.info
28   http://unamsa.edu
29   http://www.shoprivercenter.com

FIGURE 3.7   The Alamo

to home, not one that ruled from afar with a hammer. That is Political Culture 101, as the rebels were wanting to remove themselves from what is now known as a "moralistic society" to one that is more "individualistic" in nature. I saw the bullet holes that proved it.

**QUESTIONS TO CONSIDER** REGARDING POLITICAL CULTURE:

1. The first main topic of the chapter discusses the correlation between indigenous populations and their food source and how that relates to us with our experience with government today. Please indicate what that relationship is, what your gut reaction to that scenario is, and why in detail. Also, indicate something from your life that you can relate to this situation and indicate why in detail.

2. The second main topic of the chapter defines what political culture is. Please define what political culture is and identify a slogan from your life that helps you make decisions. Then relate that slogan to the definition of political culture in detail.

3. The third main topic of the chapter discusses political cultures at the national and regional levels. Please indicate what the regional cultures are and give a short explanation of each. Then, indicate where you live and what political culture best describes where you live. Then indicate whether you live in the proper place for you based on your view on life, and why, in detail.

4. The fourth main topic of the chapter discusses political cultures at the local level. Please indicate what the different local cultures are, what makes them different from one another, which one you would prefer to live in, whether that is where you live now, and why in detail.

5. The fifth main topic of the chapter indicates what factors develop your political culture. Please indicate what those factors are, which of those factors most impact your life, and how/why in relation to your political and personal beliefs, in detail.

6. The sixth main topic of the chapter discusses what happens when different political cultures interact with one another. Please identify and define this term and indicate what must be done to overcome the conflict. Lastly, identify a conflict from your life that you overcame, how you overcame that problem, and how that relates to question here at large.

7. The final main topic of the chapter provides insight into the Texas Legislative Study Group's report, *Texas on the Brink: How Texas Ranks among the 50 States*. Please rehash those finding and indicate how they relate to you in detail. Lastly, indicate if this set of circumstances should be changed, in detail.

## FIGURE CREDITS

# Chapter 4

# The Impacts of Demographics on Politics

# The Position of State Demographer

During my senior year of high school at Langham Creek[1] in unincorporated Houston, Texas, I took a sociology course as part of a dual-enrollment class with the local community college, Lone Star.[2] I remember one of the most groundbreaking lecture topics discussed in the class was how changes in the population could drastically impact the customs and norms in society. Therefore, I figured it was wise to learn about what exactly the population growth and makeup of Texas, and the country at large if possible, was during my trek around government this summer to offer some out-of-the norm insight. This nontraditional set of information seemed like an important step, as a growing—or even declining—population must impact politics in some form or fashion. In learning more about this, I scheduled an interview with the official Texas state demographer, Dr. Lloyd Potter of the University of Texas at San Antonio (UTSA), at the downtown campus.[3] Thanks, Dr. Davis, for the tip and the help to get this interview set up.

I left Charity's house at around 7:00 a.m. for the 9:00 a.m. appointment. It's only an hour and a half drive, but I wanted to leave time for the ubiquitous traffic jam along Interstate 35 that Charity advised would form en masse and delay my arrival. The trip down was very scenic and offered a wonderful glimpse of the German Hill country near New Braunfels, Texas, that I learned about yesterday at the Institute of Texan Cultures. About halfway, though, I realized that I should have probably just spent the night in San Antonio after being at the Institute of Texan Cultures in town there yesterday—oh well.

FIGURE 4.1   UTSA - Downtown Monterrey Building.

Nearing downtown San Antonio, Texas, I faced a small bit of rush-hour traffic but emerged unscathed, arriving at 8:45 a.m. outside the Monterrey Building (figure 4.1), at the corner of South Frio and Buena Vista Streets, the home of the Texas Demographic Center (TDC)[4,5]. Once parked, I called the TDC's main number as requested.

---

1   https://langhamcreek.cfisd.net/en
2   http://www.lonestar.edu
3   http://osd.texas.gov; https://www.utsa.edu
4   http://txsdc.utsa.edu/Index.aspx
5   Information in this chapter, unless otherwise noted, was obtained from an in-person interview with Dr. Potter in July 2014. Thank you, Dr. Potter, for your time and insight.

The receptionist then came down and delivered a parking pass to prevent my car from being ticketed or, more likely than not, towed away. Who knew college campuses were so strict about who can park there? She immediately went back inside, and I finished gathering my belongings. Once inside the building, I took the elevator up to the fourth floor and walked down a winding hallway to the main office of the TDC. The hum of computer hard drives from the various offices along the way was ubiquitous yet soothing. I assume it takes a lot of power to store and process all the data our population has to offer.

After entering the central office, I was wondering about where exactly to go once inside. After about ten seconds, the receptionist spoke up from out of sight because her desk was hidden from view at the doorway, slightly jarring me, and said, "Follow me this way. Dr. Potter is expecting you in his office."

I merely nodded my acknowledgment and followed her through the maze of office cubicles. When I finally entered the office, Dr. Potter left his desk at the far side of the room and joined me at his meeting table near the door. Following some good-natured introductions and stories about the day, we got down to business. At this point, I must admit that before I spoke with Dr. Davis about my idea to learn about demographics regarding my trek, I had no idea that the position of state demographer existed. A quick internet search once I got to Charity's last night showed that the job is possibly one of the most important in the state. Not knowing where to begin, the first question I asked was, "What exactly is a state demographer?"

Without hesitation, Dr. Potter said, "Well, how about a history lesson? Specifically, my position as state demographer was created by the Texas Legislature in 2001. This job creation occurred via the passage of Senate Bill 656 during the 77th regular session that met that year. The actual office was then passed around from one agency to another, finally ending up with UTSA back around 2010, when I was nominated to the position. The actual TDC was formed back in 1980, though.[6] At that time, I was serving as a professor and interim chair of the Demography Department here at UTSA[7]. Show and tell time—look at this."

At this point Dr. Potter handed me a copy of the actual legislation that created his current position; he had the copy framed on his wall. The only thing I could think was how cool it was to be able to trace your job to an actual piece of legislation and then be able to have a copy of the creation hang on your wall.

After a minute or so of obvious glaring at the document, on my behalf, Dr. Potter continued, "For me to specifically be named to the position, I needed to be appointed by the governor and be confirmed by the Texas Senate, have a 'graduate degree with specialization

6    http://txsdc.utsa.edu/AboutUs
7    http://copp.utsa.edu/demography/

in demography or a closely related field of study,' and have 'extensive experience in employing demographic and related socioeconomic data for use by legislative, public, and private entities,'[8] be a numbers whiz, so to speak, for this gig."

After reviewing the qualifications and the bit of history, he quickly showed me his doctor of philosophy in demography and sociology degree from the University of Texas at Austin also hanging on his wall, followed by a quick glance at his curriculum vitae showing extensive experience with the Centers for Disease Control and Prevention, alongside a stint at the Education Development Center in Newton, Massachusetts. I told him, "You seem more than qualified for the position! Me, on the other hand, not so much—better luck tomorrow in a few years, I guess. A query, though: What are the specific tasks of your position and agency?"

## Official Duties of the State Demographer

Dr. Potter recounted, "Let's look back the legislation that created my position. As the state demographer, I am tasked with six specific endeavors, five from Section 1 and one from Section 2 of SB 656.[9] Tasks one, four, and five from Section 1 are broad in scope. From there, I am charged with disseminating demographic and socioeconomic data to the public, providing information to the legislature relating to the effect of changes in demographics on the demand for state services and evaluating the type and quality of data to adequately monitor demographic population changes in the state and assess the effectiveness of delivery of state services. The other three, tasks two and three from Section 1, along with an unnumbered one from Section 2, are narrow in scope. For these, I am to provide annual population estimates for all cities and counties, along with biennial population projections for the state and all counties found within and serve as the state's official liaison to the US Census Bureau in Washington DC, in the Department of Commerce."[10]

I remarked, "Not to be repetitive, but being a numbers whiz doesn't seem to cut it. You also have to be well versed at leading an agency with solid communication skills, but what about the daily duties that must be done in fulfilling the constitutionally mandated roles you just pointed out?"

His response: "It depends."

I asked, confused, "How can it depend?"

---

8    Texas Senate Bill (TSB) 656, 77R, 2001.

9    SB 656, 77(R), 2001.

10   https://www.census.gov

He offered, "I am much more than the Texas state demographer. I am a public speaker, agency head, educator, enforcer, writer, and problem solver. With all the population changes that you learned about in your sociology class a few years ago that you told me about last night over the phone, I have become a trendy person to get in touch with here recently. Since taking office, I have been to several outreach groups like Rotary Clubs and have spoken at different library, real estate, and business industry events, along with a host of other important happenings—all to inform those groups about how the state population is changing so that they can then better suit their services to work more effectively with their ever-evolving clientele, citizens like you and me."

I interjected, "So, that's related to what the overall office and position are, but what exactly goes on here at the TDC?"

## Two Divisions of the Office of the State Demographer

Dr. Potter retorted, "Ah, you seek the heart of the matter here at work. This topic goes into what you just cut me off at speaking about earlier. Overall, there are two divisions to the agency, the first being the TDC, where we are right now, whose primary mission is to respond to requests for data and meetings (from both the public and those who are working directly with the agency on various projects) and to be the main data processing center, which explains the hum coming from behind the doors that you hopefully heard while walking to the office. The noise is very soothing when coming into work in the morning. One such example of this office usage was the move of the Toyota Motor Company's US headquarters when they were deciding to move from California to Plano, Texas, in 2014.[11] During that process, they visited my office here for estimates about the feasibility and business sense of making a move. In other cases, I often visit the clients as well when they request. Whether I go to them or they come to me here depends on the tasks needing to be commented on at that time."

To keep the conversation going, I suggested, "So what makes the other office stand out from the one we are located at right now?"

Dr. Potter replied, "The second division is located at the state capital in Austin, inside the Stephen F. Austin building on North Congress Avenue (figure 4.2) and is called the Legislative Liaison Office. Their primary task there is to be the go-to place for state lawmakers when they need data about the potential impacts of legislation on the state or in general that they are considering."

---

11    Tim Ciesco, "Toyota Celebrates Grand Opening of Plano Headquarters," NBC 5 Dallas-Fort Worth, July 26, 2017, https://www.nbcdfw.com/news/business/Toyota-to-Celebrate-Grand-Opening-of-New-Plano-Headquarters-Thursday-432862803.html.

FIGURE 4.2    Stephen F. Austin State Office Building.

It was here that I inquired, "Which office is busiest?"

His response: "It just depends on the season. When the legislature is in session, they do take up more of my time, but when they are out of session, other clients often take more precedence. Keep in mind, both divisions are designed for differing roles but provide essentially the same service: provision of and commentary on differing demographic data of the state. Also, beyond those two divisions, throughout the year I work with the various councils of governments, who serve as primary affiliates in providing much of the data that is processed here by the TDC. But then, there is always the teaching role of my position that takes up a fair share of my time. I teach one to two classes a semester here at UTSA, along with working with doctoral students on their dissertations. There is a lot of reading to do."

I interjected here, "I went to a Rotary meeting with my dad early last month. You could have been our guest, come to think of the matter."

He joked, "I, once again, have been to many of those. It's a great way to feed yourself, all while showing the importance of these changing times, the populace, and events on the state, as they have an impact on business."

## The Practice of Demography

It was here that he brought up a *Houston Chronicle* article entitled "Sharpstown Mall Getting a New Name—PlazAmericas."[12] This article conveyed how a declining shopping mall in southwestern Houston a few years back, most likely using data produced from his agency and his predecessors, revamped the mall's traditional setting into one of a Mexican/Spanish Zócalo, or central plaza. These actions were taken in hopes of transforming the mall to better fit its area's new predominantly Hispanic population and their shopping traditions to drive up business for the mall's tenants. I was just amazed at the real-world impact of his work. From what we could tell after reading the article, using the data to make those changes positively enhanced the future of the mall and the mall's tenants.

---

12    Nancy Sarnoff, "Sharpstown Mall Getting a New Name—PlazAmericas." *Houston Chronicle*, July 22, 2011, http://www.chron.com/business/real-estate/article/Sharpstown-mall-getting-a-new-name-1534020.php.

Afterward, Dr. Potter expanded, "For other daily items, like working with the data, I am responsible for ensuring the accuracy of the methods used to process the data, due to errors occurring on occasion. Therefore, I must lead the efforts to find the bugs causing havoc in the system when disaster strikes. Regarding the agency itself, I am responsible for making and getting approval for the budget, hiring and firing staff, and everything else that goes along with being the boss. The funniest part here, though, is dealing with those municipalities that are sometimes tardy in turning in their data and that, after a reasonable number of attempts by my staffers to get the data, I must act like Luca Brasi from *The Godfather* and get the data from them by any means necessary.[13] Not to mention, I do a lot of writing," he said, pointing to his bookshelf. "I have more than 40 pieces of published work in various formats. More importantly, all of this work must be done before I can even work to produce the data requested of me or mandated by law."

With that in mind, I could only imagine how crazy it would be if all of what he talked about as his daily duties required attention on the same day. While discussing his regular duties, I posited, "As you are a public official in more ways than one? What exactly are your roles in the governing process?"

Dr. Potter replied, "In short, I serve at the behest of the governor as he or she in that position is the one who gets to appoint me to the position. I do so by providing testimony with the mandated estimates and projections at various so-called legislative committee hearings."

With what the state demographer position entailed out of the way, I inquired, "Are you the only official state demographer in the country?"

Dr. Potter's response: "I'm one of a just a few, as most states use a conglomeration of different state agencies to compile the necessary data."

At this point, I asked, "It seems that we have covered what exactly goes on in your office to a large extent, and I have an idea of what demographics are from my classes in high school. However, I'm still not fully up to date on what demography is. What is that term, exactly?"

In response, Dr. Potter noted, "Demography is the study of population characteristics and trends, and there are two levels to practicing in the field. At the lowest level, demographers look at and report on basic demographic factors such as the race, gender, and age breakdown of various populations and what changes in those factors are over time—a positivist approach. Those working at higher levels inquire at what the impacts of changes in those basic factors are on society, most notably in that of the democratic process—a structural or humanist approach. In short, both levels monitor changes in the state demographics while the latter chooses to do something about the data."

---

13   http://godfather.wikia.com/wiki/Luca_Brasi

## Major Trends in State and National Demographics

At this point, it seemed as if the only real subject left to conquer was what the major trends in the state and country were. I, therefore, asked, "What changes are afoot, demographically speaking, for the state?"

After thinking for a minute, Dr. Potter stated, "Great question, but so that you can monitor major demographic trends yourself in the future after today, let's go to the state demographer's website, demographics.texas.gov."

Once the website was up and running and before Dr. Potter began talking again, I noticed a considerable number of updates from the center on its home page, links to when the agency was mentioned in the news, and additional links to its latest presentations. I could tell right from the start that it is an agency on top of its work. After a moment of silence, during which Dr. Potter could tell that I was taking in all to be seen on the website, he spoke. "Glad to see you are enjoying all my colleagues' and my work. Thank you. We'll get to the trends but hold on a little longer. There are three main tabs seen here for you to worry about when you leave here, okay?"

I stated, "Which three, sir? I see 11 to choose from."

Dr. Potter explained, "Ignore the four at the very top and focus on the next highest list of tabs for now. From that second highest list of tabs, let's look at 'Data.' This pathway is the quickest way to go after the various data sets we keep on file here at the TDC. For a glimpse at where we stand today regarding the state population, let's click on the subheading of 'Population Estimates' and look at the most recent estimated data from 2016 by opening the PDF file, which indicates that the state's total estimated population on July 1 was inclusive of 13,684,399 males and 13,998,197 females, with whites being at 11,498,484 total citizens, blacks at 3,218,511, other ethnic groups at 1,876,164, and Hispanics at 11,269,437.[14] Of note, if I remember correctly from the US Census Bureau website that I glanced over this morning, the national resident population on the same date was 323,071,342,[15] meaning that roughly 1 in 12 US residents at that time lived in Texas."

I interjected, "I'm a visual person; where can I get a picture language version of this information from, sir?"

---

14    http://demographics.texas.gov/Resources/TPEPP/Estimates/2016/2016_ASRE_Estimate_alldata.pdf
15    https://www.census.gov/data/tables/time-series/demo/popest/2010s-national-total.html; Annual Estimates of the Resident Population for the United States, Regions, States, and Puerto Rico: April 1, 2010, to July 1, 2018 (NST-EST2018-01).

Dr. Potter clicked on the tab labeled "Geography." From there, he further clicked on "Thematic Maps" and a whole slew of options came available to pick from. Dr. Potter stated, "There are thousands of maps to choose from on here, but you need to pick from the three pull-down options that you see here in order of 'Topic,' Sub-Topic,' and finally 'Map.' There is no specific map for the population data that we just looked up, but we can get something similar. Let's go with 'Population,' 'Total Population,' and finally, 'Total Population Size in Texas Counties, 2000' (figure 4.3). This data is a bit out of date, but nonetheless says a lot."

I interjected, "How so?"

Dr. Potter replied, "Simple—the counties in blue are those where over 500,000 people live and indicate where the big cities of the state are, like Austin, Dallas, El Paso, Fort Worth, Houston, San Antonio; and McAllen, Harlingen, and Edinburg are in the Rio Grande Valley, merging together as one ever so slowly. More importantly, the blue, orange, and pink counties, indicating the highest populated counties of the state, outside of the blue one for El Paso County, are all located in

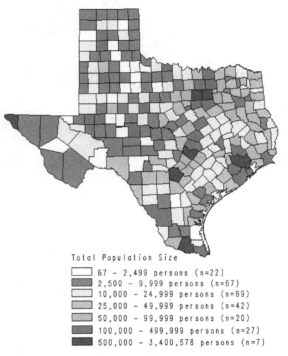

Total Population Size
- ☐ 67 – 2,499 persons (n=22)
- ■ 2,500 – 9,999 persons (n=67)
- ☐ 10,000 – 24,999 persons (n=69)
- ■ 25,000 – 49,999 persons (n=42)
- ■ 50,000 – 99,999 persons (n=20)
- ■ 100,000 – 499,999 persons (n=27)
- ■ 500,000 – 3,400,578 persons (n=7)

FIGURE 4.3  This map indicates that most of the population of Texas is not equally distributed throughout the state.

eastern Texas, while the white, red, yellow, and green counties, indicating the least populated counties in the state, are primarily concentrated in western Texas, indicating an unbalanced distribution of population. For how this compares to national trends, this is an opposing pattern, as since 1790, the mean center of the US population has gradually moved westward toward the middle of the country, now centered in Missouri. Here's a great map (figure 4.4)."

I muttered, "You are right sir, that map from the US Census Bureau indicates that the population center of the US had gone westward ever since our country's founding. Either way though, for us here at home that unbalanced population can't be good?"

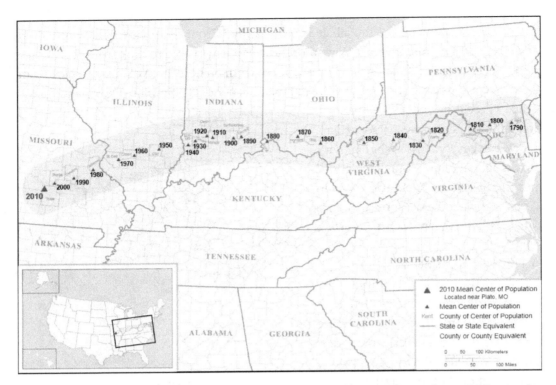

FIGURE 4.4   This map indicates that the center of the population of the United States has gradually moved westward thanks to Manifest Destiny and other factors.

Dr. Potter stated, "That depends on who is asking. For those out in West Texas, yes, it is; while for those back East, not so much, as there can be pressure applied by those growing East Texas communities to get a larger and larger portion of the proverbial government allocation pie. Regardless, it's not all bad, as all those people, regardless of location, help keep the economy going. Now, before we get into all those major trends, let's click on the 'Our Services' tab from the very top and then see how my staff and I can be of more service to you. If you wanted a specific presentation, we could tailor make one for you; we offer technical assistance, specialized analysis like the one we did for Toyota I told you about from before, and lastly, we put on regular workshops and training sessions to help those who will be using our services regularly avoid having to call on us for every tiny issue and data need. We are always here to help, but we also want you to be able to fend for yourself out there in the data realm."

I stated, "Thanks for the info on the website, but what major trends could I infer about the state if I went to every tab and looked at every piece of data available?"

In response to my question, Dr. Potter expressed, "There are four major trends now over the horizon.[16] First, the population of the state is continuing to experience a dramatic rise. Specifically, using the US Census's American Factfinder tool,[17] which uses the data provided by us here at the TDC, the state population from the 2010 census was 25,145,561; 25,640,909 in 2011; 26,060,796 in 2012; 26,448,193 in 2013; 26,954,436 in 2014; 27,454,880 in 2015; 27,904,862 in 2016; 28,304,596 in 2017; and finally, 28,683,724 in 2018—an increase of 3,538,163 citizens on July 1, based on projections and estimates from the 2010 census, in only eight years. This is an increase of roughly 14.1 percent since 2010. That is a large amount of growth in such a short time to cope with in the provision of services. The growth is about 1,039 people a day, with 524 of the 1,039 coming from natural increase (524 more births than deaths), and 515 of the 1,039 coming from net migration (515 more people moving into the state than out) due the stable, in relation to others, conditions of the state, and a booming economy.[18] Of note, using the same US Census Data we got before when we were discussing the 'Data' tab, the overall US population has been growing by leaps and bounds as well; on July 1, 2010, the resident population was 309,326,085 and was 327,167,434 on July 1, 2018, leading to an increase of roughly 5.8 percent since 2010, not quite the rate here in Texas but still quite the growth nonetheless."[19]

I was in awe at the growth and amazed to learn that the numbers are expected only to keep growing. I inquired, "Is all of this growth, and I'll call it a newfound wealth of population, spread evenly throughout the state?"

Dr. Potter rebutted, "No, and you should already know that from our conversation about the first map we looked at earlier."

I spoke, "That map is from 2000, and I thought maybe things have changed?"

Dr. Potter furthered, "Not in the slightest. Some things change, and some things don't. This is one trend that doesn't. That is trend number two if you're still counting. Despite the overall massive growth of the state, 73 of the 254 counties in the state, based on 2017 estimates against the 2010 census, saw their counties lose population, with Briscoe County seeing the biggest drop, percentage-wise, at 16.4 percent, going from 1,637 residents in 2010 to 1,368 on July 1, 2017; and the largest overall drop in total numbers belonging to Jefferson County at 4,722, going from 252,273 residents in 2010 to 247,551 on July 1, 2017. On the other hand, 179

---

16    These trends were first gathered in my initial interview with Dr. Potter in July of 2014 and confirmed to be still existent on January 14, 2019, via email conversations. Thanks for the update Dr. Potter and for all that you do for the state.

17    https://factfinder.census.gov/faces/nav/jsf/pages/index.xhtml

18    http://demographics.texas.gov/Presentations: Demographic Characteristics, Trends, and Transportation in Texas, slide 3.

19    https://www.census.gov/data/tables/time-series/demo/popest/2010s-national-total.html; Annual Estimates of the Resident Population for the United States, Regions, States, and Puerto Rico: April 1, 2010, to July 1, 2018 (NST-EST2018-01).

of the 254 counties in the state, based on 2017 estimates against the 2010 census, saw their counties gain population, with Hays County seeing the biggest increase, percentage-wise, at 30.8 percent, going from 157,107 residents in 2010 to 205,502 on July 1, 2017; and the largest overall increase in total numbers belonging to Harris County at 489,939 residents, going from 4,092,459 in 2010 to 4,582,398 on July 1, 2017[20]."

I sputtered, "I had no idea that I had spent so much of my time here lately driving through so much change."

Dr. Potter suggested, "Not only is all of this population change not even across all counties, it is not even across the state in general as, for trend number three, a majority of the growth is occurring in the so-called Southwest® Airlines Texas Triangle, named after the initial route map of the airline.[21] Essentially, the growth in Texas is primarily concentrated in the triangle of counties and their immediate surrounding ones, cornered by Harris for Houston, Bexar for San Antonio, and Dallas and Tarrant Counties for Dallas and Fort Worth, respectively (figure 4.5). Simply put, outside of the triangle, the only major growth is found in

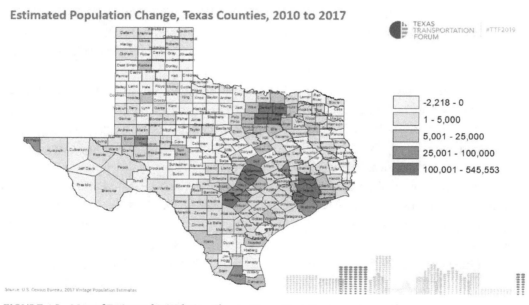

FIGURE 4.5   Map of Estimated Population Change, Texas Counties. 2010 to 2017.

20   https://demographics.texas.gov/Data/TPEPP/Projections/; To get these number, the num_chg_10_17 and pct_chg_10_17 columns were sorted in order from highest growth to highest decline.

21   Blusk, "Flashback Fridays: Closing the Texas Triangle and the Power of Three," *Southwest* (blog), January 20, 2012, https://www.southwestaircommunity.com/t5/Southwest-Stories/Flashback-Fridays-Closing-the-Texas-Triangle-and-the-Power-of/ba-p/39476.

urban areas like El Paso County for El Paso, Texas; Lubbock County for Lubbock, Texas; Ector and Midland Counties for Midland and Odessa, Texas; Nueces County for Corpus Christi, Texas; Webb County for Laredo, Texas; and Hidalgo for Edinburg and McAllen, Texas."[22]

I surmised aloud, "So being here in the triangle is like being in the safe zone, while being outside is akin to being in Pompei following the eruption of Mt. Vesuvius regarding growth in population?"

Dr. Potter furthered, "I wouldn't put it like that, but if it works for you, go for it. But let's move on to the fourth trend; the one that will most likely bring about the most significant change going forward in the state. Overall, all ethnic groups of the state are experiencing growth, but that growth is not equally distributed. Specifically, using July 1, 2017, estimates against July 1, 2011, estimates,[23] the "other" category for ethnic group (i.e., not black, white, or Hispanic) saw the highest percentage growth rate, as they started with 1,472,223 residents and grew by 403,941 residents to 1,876,164, a growth rate of 27.4 percent in population since July 1, 2011. Of note, the "other" group saw the second-highest overall growth in actual numbers. During the same time period, Hispanics saw the second-highest percentage growth rate, as they started with 9,813,362 residents and grew by 1,456,075 residents to 11,269,437, a growth rate of 14.8 percent in population since July 1, 2011. Of note, Hispanics saw the highest overall growth in actual numbers. During the same time period, blacks saw the third-highest percentage growth rate, as they started with 2,9,46,793 residents and grew by 271,718 residents to 3,218,511, a growth rate of 9.2 percent in population since July 1, 2011. Of note, blacks also saw the third-highest overall growth in actual numbers. Lastly, during the same time period, whites saw the lowest percentage growth rate, as they started with 11,442,303 residents and grew by 56,181 residents to 11,498,484, a borderline stagnant growth rate of 0.49 percent in population since July 1, 2011. Of note, whites also saw the lowest overall growth in actual numbers."

No matter how I processed those trends, it seemed as if society was going to be impacted in one way or another, better for some and worse for others. Therefore, I asked Dr. Potter, "Could you expand more on each of the trends than what you already have?"

After taking a few minutes to gather his thoughts, Dr. Potter uttered, "For the first trend, a growing population should lead to a healthy economy, which can be beneficial for everyone. For the second trend, some counties, or at least services in them, would need to be merged to reduce the cost of providing services, as the populations can no longer support

22    http://demographics.texas.gov/Presentations: Demographic Characteristics, Trends, and Transportation in Texas, slides 4–10.
23    http://txsdc.utsa.edu/Data/TPEPP/Estimates; divided the 2017 estimate population for each ethnic group by their 2011 estimate population and multiplied by 100 to calculate the percent growth rate.

the current number of service providers. More importantly, as people move away, the family farms are being sold off to major corporations, putting the means of food production into fewer and fewer hands who may not do as good a job at keeping the soil in a good productive condition, among other things. For the third, these overly populated areas may not be able to provide enough water and other basic needs of the citizens, ultimately overloading the system and causing it to deteriorate. However, the impacts of the last trend, I suspect, might be the longest lasting, especially regarding government."

I stated, "Dire as they may be, sir, go on."

For the fourth trend, Dr. Potter began by noting, "Growth in the Hispanic and other populations is not just increasing the overall population of the state but is also changing the overall look of the state. Certainly, as we've discussed earlier, half the growth is coming from natural growths, simply put as more births than deaths, but the other half is coming here from different places with their ways, languages, and customs. Do you think that those incoming will just shed their past overnight?"

I shot back immediately, "Some, yes, but probably not all."

Dr. Potter furthered, "That's probably the truth of it. Now, it's not to say that this change is bad in and of itself, but think about how the mass of different languages could impact communication, especially during a disaster. Also, odds are, many of the people coming here are coming to take advantage of our great economy; therefore, they may not be in the greatest of overall conditions when they get here. Therefore, they do not bring as many resources—used to represent a stable, producing, and growing economy—to the table as other parts of the population. Accordingly, if they do not bring as much to the table, there is less potential for aiding and abetting the labor force in its efforts to grow the state forward, leaving it short of high-skilled labor and possessing a glut of low-skilled laborers who may overload social programs designed for the poor, leading to generations of cyclical poverty. Overall, the economy today may be booming, but in the future, if current trends persist, we may be going full steam ahead into a wall of declining labor productivity due to the systems in place being overloaded by unequal and diverse growth in the population."

All I could say to this was, "Oh, the humanity of it all."

More importantly, I wondered aloud, "What could all of this mean for politics in the state?"

His response: "Massive realignment."

Furthering this response, Dr. Potter spelled out, "Most state political power is currently held by the Republican Party, which is more conservative, fiscally and socially, than the Democratic Party and the various third parties found in the state. By tradition, Hispanics and other ethnic minorities have typically voted in droves for the Democratic Party when they participate in the political process—which they do at a lower rate than that of the remaining population, at least here in Texas, where politics is dominated by whites due to a higher level of participation.[24] Therefore, if the current trends persist, political control of the state will no doubt undergo a massive change, placing the opposition in power (assuming minority voters increase their numbers at the polls and continue to vote for the Democratic Party as expected). I can only see a decline in power for the Republicans unless they broaden their appeal to this group. This shift, known as political realignment,[25] is felt to be unstoppable by many in the field."

At this point, I let out, "What terms are available to better and more thoroughly understand these trends?"

Dr. Potter responded, "The first would be majority-minority state. This term means that unlike other states—where white citizens are and have traditionally been the politically dominant race for an extended period—the total of all traditional racial minority groups (non-whites) are now the dominant state ethnic population. Texas falls into this category, alongside the fellow states and territories of California, Hawaii, New Mexico, Puerto Rico, and the nation's capital, Washington DC. Regarding why this has occurred, the non-white groups have higher birthrates, and Hispanics are the largest immigrant group today, driving up their numbers. Of note, at present, the mix of various non-white groups gives us this status, but in the next few years, Hispanics by themselves will be the dominant population in Texas. Now, the last two terms I want to inform you of here are known as push-and-pull factors, which are items in the starting location of potential migrants that give them cause to leave, as these are not favorable conditions to their futures, and items that are inaccessible to people in their current location but are readily available in a different, far-flung destination drawing them there, respectively. For many people, being poor in their homeland, and the promise of a better future being found in the new state and country at large, provides the necessary push and pull for people to make their legal and illegal treks to our state, not just from abroad but from other parts of the United States as well."

It was here that I inquired, "What events occur outside of just working with the data?"

Dr. Potter's eyes lit up here, and he offered, "Well, we have the annual Texas Demographic Conference.[26] At this event, I, or one of my staffers, gives a presentation about the current population trends in the state alongside other various presentations about certain subjects. The one earlier this year in Austin focused on the demographic impacts of and on infrastructure, the significant demographic trends, components of population change, and the road

---

24 Jolie McCullough and Alexa Ura, "Texas Voter Turnout Is Huge This Year. But Here's Who Doesn't Vote," *Texas Tribune*, November 3, 2016, https://www.texastribune.org/2016/11/03/texas-voter-turnout-huge-year-heres-who-doesnt-vot

25 https://www.encyclopedia.com/economics/encyclopedias-almanacs-transcripts-and-maps/political-realignment

26 http://txsdc.utsa.edu/AnnualConference/Current

to 2020, year of the decennial census. Beyond that, this annual event allows us to educate the users of our data on how to best use the data sets."

This seemed an informative and nice distraction to have from teaching and being stuck inside his office all day. It was then, just before noon, that the phone rang. When Dr. Potter picked up the phone, his tone became very professional. I overheard that he was being called into a meeting that afternoon in Austin. After that, he put down the phone and advised that our interview would have to end. Inquisitively, I asked, "Could I tag along to the meeting? I have to go back to Austin after this anyway."

His response: "Sure, why not? These meetings should be as public as possible."

## Meeting with Legislators

After writing down the address of the legislative liaison office in Austin, we both packed up our belongings and headed out of the office to get into our cars for the drive up to Austin. Before getting onto the freeway, I stopped at a burger place for lunch. An hour and a half later, I arrived outside the Stephen F. Austin State Office Building and was able to find parking next door at the coincidentally and conveniently located Bullock Museum. Once inside, I went up to the second floor and found the office near the doors of the elevator. When I entered the door, Dr. Lila Valencia, the legislative liaison office head, was waiting for me at the door.

After greetings were exchanged, she brought me into the conference room, where Dr. Potter was setting up the requested information. He instructed me to sit in a chair toward the back corner, as the legislators would fill up the remaining seven seats at the table. Following that, he told me that in a little over a week the state legislature was going to convene a special session—whatever that is—to draft a bill that would use funds from the state's rainy-day fund to finance various water-related projects around the state. More importantly, he advised that his role today was to inform the soon-to-arrive legislators what exactly the trends in population dispersion were going to be. This was to ensure that the parts of the states that would need the most water going forward would get more projects and related dollars to fund said plans.

Just after 2:00 p.m., all the legislators arrived, and the meeting began. Since they were in a hurry, the pleasantries were skipped. First, Dr. Potter gave his presentation, using much of the data we looked at earlier in the day to show that the state population is ever increasing on a variety of levels and ways. Then, the legislators asked questions about where the most growth was happening. Dr. Potter responded, noting that much of it was along the US-Mexico border and in the Texas Triangle. He also showed some fantastic population growth maps that I had not seen earlier in the day. After that, they inquired about what impact the increasing Hispanic population may have on water. He responded, noting that as this group has a higher birthrate and is increasing their numbers in the southern, arid areas of the state, they may best use as much desalinization water-production techniques as possible to avoid overusing the aquifers (underground water basins), alongside various types of water-reclamation methods. In concluding the meeting, some discussion was had over what the future look of the legislature may take, with no real insight other than simple realignment. Once the legislators had left, I said, "The meeting seemed rather simple."

Hearing this, Dr. Potter replied, "It typically is, although on some topics the legislators work to interpret my data to meet their desires. I avoid playing into their traps and stay as apolitical as possible, and it normally works well by plainly telling them what the data is indicating." After that, I thanked Dr. Potter for his time and wished him a safe drive back to San Antonio. While heading back to my car, I realized how diverse the state and country at large was becoming, alongside the benefits and challenges of how it was occurring. Can the state maintain its high growth rate? Will the country's westward expansion hold up? Will the newest immigrants assimilate quickly, or will they get left behind? Either way, I learned about the population trends of the state and country today. Overall, the state's population is growing, just not equally across locations and ethnically, which may lead to problems going forward. More importantly, control of the state may be changing, as a new dominant ethnicity is slowly becoming the majority. What happens next is anybody's guess, but no matter what, it'll be interesting to watch and experience, politically at least.

## FIGURE CREDITS

# Chapter 5

# Our Founding Documents

# Paper Is Still All Around

Charity woke me this morning at about 7:15. She was on her way out the door for work but still needed to ensure that I received a flyer she had gotten from the newspaper this morning. With her knowing that I was on a trek this summer to learn about the government, she had been keeping an eye out for any little thing that would be good for me to experience over the last week. I had no scheduled visits today, so this opportunity helped fill a nice

FIGURE 5.1   Texas State Library and Archives Building

hole in my schedule. The flyer read, "Come one, come all to the Lorenzo de Zavala Texas State Archives and Library Building[1] (figure 5.1) today for an immersive experience in the importance of our paperwork."

At first glance, this seemed to be one of the least exciting experiences in which an individual could find themselves partaking. After all, when was the last time I, or anyone else I knew, used a piece of paper for anything beyond cleaning up after themselves in the bathroom? The issue is, since it was the State Archives putting on the event, I knew that it would be wise for me to attend, as I imagined they had some important papers to read through. Luckily, the event didn't start until 11:00 a.m., so, after spending two days in San Antonio, I could get a bit more sleep before I made my first trek down to the Capitol Complex located in downtown Austin.

Just before 9:00 a.m., I finally got out of bed and went into the bathroom. After taking care of business, I was showered and ready to go just before 9:30 a.m. I skipped breakfast at home, seeking to get something quick on the road during my commute. After going through a drive-through, it hit me: Paper was a bit more critical than I thought. The bag, the food wrappers, and the receipt were all made from paper. Then I looked at the car a bit more and found scrap after scrap of paper, just sitting there with random jottings I had made last week. I looked around a bit more and realized that the sheathing for the straw was made of paper, and the flyer Charity had handed me was on paper. I realized that this experience in paper might be a bit more than I bargained for, not to mention that I needed to clean out my car. I even found myself wondering at this point, "Aren't we currently in this digitalization movement, and what happened to us all going paperless? Yeah, right!"

---

1   https://www.tsl.texas.gov/visit

Arriving downtown just before 10:30 a.m., I found myself pulling into the capitol visitor parking garage at 12th and San Jacinto. Luckily, the garage was not full, despite the preparations going on for the upcoming special session that my dad had told me about earlier in the week when I had updated him on what I had experienced thus far. About five minutes later, I had made the short walk across San Jacinto Street and continued around to the front side of the archives building, which faced the actual state capitol building's east side.

Walking through the grand portico gave me the feeling that I was about to step into something fundamental. Once through the set of doors between the statues of Sam Houston and Anson Jones, I found myself entering a large, two-story, open-air lobby. Behind me were small exhibits displaying artifacts related to letters written by some defenders of the Alamo. Excellent reads, after a glance, while above was the large, two-story mural entitled *Texas Moves Toward Statehood*. Seated behind the welcome desk was a young woman speaking to those who were checking in for the event or just visiting the library to look at various vital documents held there. Since I was there for the event, she instructed that I needed to go to the security desk located to her right and behind her.

When speaking with the officer on duty there, I was told that I was not allowed to bring anything with me into the room and that I was to leave all items in a free storage locker in a room to her left. With all my pockets emptied into a locker and a key strapped to my left wrist with Velcro so I could get my belongings back later, I took the adjacent elevator up to the second floor. When exiting the elevator door, I followed a series of signs leading myself and three other patrons to the left and the Darryl Tocker Learning Center. I found a seat toward the front of the large room. The funny thing was, though, several state troopers were posted throughout the room. It was then that the lights went dark.

Throughout the room, people slowly went silent. Then, in the front, a small podium began to glow ominously, with a mysterious unseen man speaking from behind it. "Welcome, everyone, to today's experience. Before a select few of the lights return to their normal glare, I would like to ask: How does everyone feel now with the lights so low?"

People began to shout, "It's a bit dark!"

Another person quietly spoke, "It's a bit difficult to see or do anything. If I move, I am liable to trip over something and break my neck."

The funniest thing I heard, though, was, "This must be how politicians work when they are making policy because they never seem to write anything well."

## Constitutions and Declarations of Independence

The mysterious man spoke again. "Folks, without what we will be discussing today, our lives as we know it now would operate much like you feel now—lost in the dark, to where if you make even the slightest of moves, it could lead to disaster. That disaster could be the on-a-whim decision-making of old King George III or General Antonio López de Santa Anna, deciding what to do in a situation that would lead to the absurdly high taxation of people over the tiniest of issues, like tea—not the Texas type more commonly known as oil, that is—the stuff you sip. Accordingly, today, we'll be discussing the various constitutions and declarations that govern our fair state and country."

With an immediate blinding capability, two spotlights came on at the front of the room. Those lights were showcasing two vault-like glass display cases that now stood on either side of the podium from where the speaker was talking. Inside those display cases seemed to be ancient documents that were handwritten with exquisite penmanship. Also, now slightly visible were the state troopers from before, but now with shotguns—ready to protect whatever essential items that were now visible—seated on either side of both display cases. Speaking again, the mysterious man from before (based on the similar-sounding voice) stated, "I am a professor of constitutional law at the prestigious University of Texas Law School.[2] Today, though, I do not claim to be the be-all and end-all expert on all things related to issues of law, but that is what I get paid to do my best at every day of the week—interpret the laws written for us to follow. What is visible before you today are items rarely

FIGURE 5.2   Texas Constitution of 1876

seen on full public display, unlike their national counterparts at the National Archives in Washington DC,[3] which are on view on a permanent basis when not stored at night in their bombproof storage containers. We tried to get them here for this, but those federal documents don't get out much. With that stated, to my right is the first page of text belonging to the Constitution of 1876 (figure 5.2) that currently dictates how the state of Texas shall operate its affairs with you, me, and those passing through the state. If you look at article 7, you might even read part of how the big school just north of here where I work was created. To my left is a lesser-discussed document in the state, but one that is probably just as important, or even more so. This document is our state's

2   https://law.utexas.edu
3   http://www.archives.gov

Declaration of Independence from Mexico (figure 5.3) that was written in 1836 following the disastrous events at the Alamo at Washington-on-the-Brazos. Another important document that aligns well here is our secession papers from the Union when Texas left to join the Confederacy in February 1861 (figure 5.4)."

After a short pause, the mysterious man continued, "In today's lecture, we will discuss many of the important fundamentals of each of these documents, not to mention a few good stories. Speaking of good stories, every academic's favorite TV show nowadays is probably CBS's *The Big Bang Theory*,[4] all thanks to their positioning of smart academic types, like myself, in the lead roles, not to mention a staff scientist ensuring that all the equations you see on-screen are the real McCoy.[5] The main characters of the show are

FIGURE 5.3    Texas Declaration of Idependence

Dr. Sheldon Lee Cooper, with his idiosyncratic and narcissistic behavior, alongside a prominent shortage of humility or empathy, and his roommate, Dr. Leonard Leakey Hofstadter, the straight man of the show, who is always having to face obstacles and deal with a constant lack of confidence in his actions. What I want to hear from the audience, though, is this: What is the item that—I guess I must now say 'formerly,' due to Sheldon moving out of the apartment—bound them together?"

A woman from the dark toward the rear of the room asserted, "The roommate agreement that Sheldon wrote—very deviously in his favor—most likely to torment his roommate, and the new room rental agreement that the two signed after Sheldon started renting his old room back as a place to work."[6]

The mysterious man went on, "Perfect; you too are up to date on your *Big Bang Theory* show lore. The thing to remember is, the roommate and room rental agreements and the various

4    http://www.cbs.com/shows/big_bang_theory
5    Neda Ulaby, "The Man Who Gets the Science Right on 'The Big Bang Theory,'" NPR, September 23, 2013, https://www.npr.org/sections/monkeysee/2013/09/23/224404260/the-man-who-gets-the-science-right-on-the-big-bang-theory.
6    https://the-big-bang-theory.com/episodeguide/episode/1114/The-Separation-Triangulation

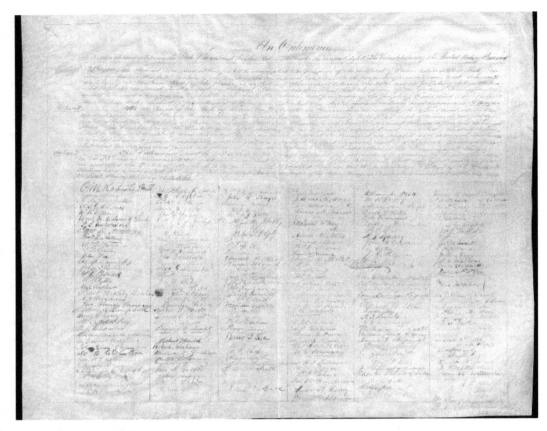

FIGURE 5.4    Texas Secession Paper's

constitutions we deal with are designed to dictate the proper procedures and who has the honor of dealing with them. Together, the agreements and constitutions are defined as 'the basic principles and laws of a nation, state, or social group that determine the powers and duties of the government and guarantee certain rights to the people in it.'[7] The difference is, the roommate and room rental agreements dictate how issues in the apartment, or at least in a section of the apartment, are handled, decisions are made, and how various day-to-day actions and issues will be progressed through when they arise, while our state's, the federal government's, and other states' versions establish governing institutions, assign those institutions powers, and place limits, either specifically or implicitly, on said powers that have been delegated in the entirety of the respective territory. It's all just a difference of what is specifically being created and regulated—actions in an apartment or an entire 'country-slash-state.' Regarding declarations of independence, 'an official, public, usually written statement of independence'[8] from

---

7    https://www.merriam-webster.com/dictionary/constitution
8    https://dictionary.cambridge.org/us/dictionary/english/declaration

something, the best example of the concept from the show being when they air the flashback of Leonard moving in with Sheldon; specifically, when they enter the room that will eventually become Leonard's, we see graffiti on the wall reading 'DIE SHELDON DIE' that was left by the former inhabitant, indicating that he will no longer live there under his dictatorship-like rule of tyranny that is more likely than not able to exist thanks to the roommate agreement."[9]

A guy in the back of the room remarked, "Hey buddy, why don't you turn the lights on for a change?"

The mysterious speaker remarked with a laugh, "Why would I do that? I couldn't make my next, and possibly a couple of following, points if I did. Also, the low light is good for keeping old documents written on parchment safe and sound from decay. This concept is important because if the documents dissolve, we technically are in a state of anarchy, and quite frankly, no one wants that. We have other copies, but without the originals, they are kind of for naught, just like with property and deeds. You need the original or it simply isn't yours, theoretically of course, as that is a whole other set of legal problems as the documents themselves are set of vested ideas we swear allegiance to."

## Interpreting Constitutions and Declarations of Independence

This led to an uproar of laughter, and the mysterious man continuing by remarking, "Back to the lights-out setting, though. We already established that having the lights on helps us see better. The lights being on or off is an excellent metaphor for one of the more prominent debates in the study of constitutions, specifically how one should interpret constitutions, with the word *interpretation* meaning 'a mental representation of the meaning or significance of something.'[10]"

A woman from in front of me then interjected, "Who's in what camp?"

The mysterious man then continued, "In one camp, you have those who argue that we should look at the document in a modern light, another way of saying with the lights on. Those people who camp here follow a legal philosophy based on the idea that the founding fathers could not have foreseen what the world would be like in the future and that the document that was produced must be interpreted in the face of any major or minor historical and societal changes seen today. Documents that would fall into this category would be known as living constitutions, also commonly referred to as 'loose documents' due to the way that the documents are written. An example of this comes from our very own US Constitution[11] (figure 5.5), which uses open-ended clauses to get its points across. Specifically, looking at

9    https://the-big-bang-theory.com/episodeguide/episode/322/The-Staircase-Implementation
10   https://www.vocabulary.com/dictionary/interpretation
11   https://www.archives.gov/founding-docs/constitution-transcript

FIGURE 5.5    United States Constitution–First Page

impeachment, or 'a charge of misconduct made against the holder of a public office,'[12] article I, section 2, clause 5 provides: The House of Representatives shall choose their Speaker and other Officers; and shall have the sole Power of Impeachment while article I, section 3, clause 6 provide: The Senate shall have the sole Power to try all Impeachments. Regarding how this clause makes the US Constitution a loose document, these clauses dictate that the House has the power to impeach government officials but gives to the Senate the power to try the case to remove the official in question with the only caveat being that two-thirds must be in agreement to convict and remove. Regarding how the trial is run, that is solely up to whomever oversees the Senate. Considering the movement in the House to impeach President Trump, current Senate Majority Leader Mitch McConnell is pushing for the use of the Impeachment proceedings rules used in the 1998 to 1999 that were crafted at that time while Speaker of the House Leader Nancy Pelosi decided to hold off for a period of time on sending the impeachment documents to the Senate to try and force Sen. McConnell for a rules change to allow additional witness testimony to occur in the Senate before voting to remove.[13] Followers here enact the spirit of the law in enforcement of the document."

A man then stated, "Wow, those founding fathers were dumb with a capital I. Why would you give someone a job and not properly tell them what to do? At best, you are going to have to go back and fix all the errors. I don't agree with that viewpoint, like probably many of the other people in this room. Am I right?"

An uproar of various forms of agreement rang around the hall. A little set back, the mysterious man spoke again, "Lucky for you, sir, there is a whole group of people minded like you who employ the opposing legal philosophy of judicial interpretation that severely limits or restricts the ability of later generations to view the document in their own light and time, as the document is viewed to mean exactly what it specifically says, lights off so to speak. Documents that would fall into this category would be known as 'dead constitutions,' also commonly referred to as 'strict documents' due to the absence of clauses like the one that I disclosed before from the US Constitution. An example of this is article 3, section 49a from our very own Texas Constitution of 1876, which reads, 'It shall be the duty of the Comptroller of Public Accounts in advance of each Regular Session of the Legislature to prepare and submit to the Governor and to the Legislature upon its convening a statement under oath showing fully the financial condition of the State Treasury at the close of the last fiscal period and an estimate of the probable receipts and disbursements for the then current fiscal year.

---

12    Impeachment: Definition of Impeachment by Lexico. (n.d.). Retrieved from https://www.lexico.com/en/definition/impeachment.

13    S. Hughes and N. Andrews, (2019, December 20). Pelosi to Delay Sending Impeachment Articles to Senate. Retrieved January 13, 2020, from https://www.wsj.com/articles/after-house-impeaches-trump-timing-of-next-steps-is-unclear-11576755097.

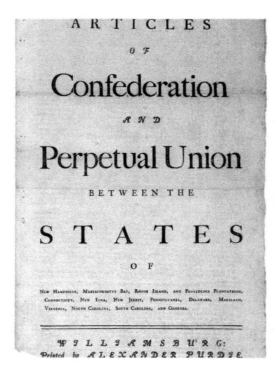

FIGURE 5.6   Articles of Confederation and Perpetual Union

There shall also be contained in said statement an itemized estimate of the anticipated revenue based on the laws then in effect that will be received by and for the State from all sources showing the fund accounts to be credited during the succeeding biennium and said statement shall contain such other information as may be required by law."[14] At no point in the US Constitution does the duty of an official have such strict restrictions or specificity placed on them. Other strict constitutions include the Articles of Confederation (figure 5.6), the Constitution of the Confederate States of America (figure 5.7), and, most notably, the roommate agreement, due to Sheldon saying it best— pardon the language, but here goes: 'You don't screw the roommate agreement, the roommate agreement screws you.'[15] There is no room for interpretation there considering current events, no matter how disastrous a situation is. Followers here enact the actual text of the law in enforcement as written with no alternation for the immediate circumstances present."

Then someone from the back remarked, "So can we shed some more light on the situation? Is there anything from that *Big Bang* show you mentioned earlier that we could discuss this matter of interpretation more through?"

Without delay, the mysterious man asked, "Someone who knows a lot about the show tell me, who are Sheldon and Amy?"

A girl, mockingly, said, "Amy and Sheldon sitting in the tree, k-i-s-s-i-n-g! First comes love. Then comes marriage. Then comes baby in the baby carriage.[16] The SHAMY!"

---

14   Constitution of 1876, article 3, section 49a.

15   https://the-big-bang-theory.com/episodeguide/episode/322/The-Staircase-Implementation

16   Dartmouth Folklore Archive, "The K-I-S-S-I-N-G Song," accessed March 19, 2019, https://journeys.dartmouth.edu/folklorearchive/the-k-i-s-s-i-n-g-song.

FIGURE 5.7    Constitution of the Confederate States of America.

The mysterious man went, "I couldn't put it any better myself. They are a couple, indeed. Sheldon even moved in with her after he moved out of the apartment with Leonard. Now, do they see eye to eye on a lot of things in their relationship?"

The girl replied, "NO!"

The man furthered, "Exactly, and just like between Leonard and Sheldon for the apartment, Sheldon and Amy adopted an agreement, better known as the relationship agreement, the general sense of wanting to be an intimate part of one another's lives', that was originally drawn up by Sheldon to handle what can and cannot occur in their relationship. They both eventually agreed to it, with some alterations being made. The problem is, they have a very different way of interpreting the now adopted document. Sheldon wants everything that goes on in the relationship spelled out, from when to hold hands, have coitus, and give a 72-hour advanced notice of when a trip is occurring, while Amy would just like the agreement to read that they can hold hands whenever she wants to, like a so-called normal couple, and not have so many items clearly spelled out. Overall, Amy is, for lack of a better term, okay with the agreement but longs and is not afraid from time to time go 'off script,' whereas for Sheldon that is just not acceptable."

At that point, a man yelled out, "Okay, thanks for the insight there, but what exactly people did argue over when writing the darn things?"

## Issues to Debate When Drafting a Constitution

It was then that the spotlight on our state constitution became a bit narrower, focusing on some random area, and the one on the Texas Declaration of Independence went dark. The mysterious speaker continued, "Excellent question. What I would like to do is respond by indicating that the goal of all constitutions is this: The writer simply seeks to match the government that is created with the needs of citizens who will live under the document by reflecting the interests and concerns of the people who write and go on to amend the documents in question. An example of this is the presence of plantation culture norms of allowing for slavery under our state constitutions of 1836, 1845, and 1861 that morphed into Jim Crow–like laws in 1866 and went away in the 1869 and 1876 versions. Not to mention that the 13th Amendment to the US Constitution forbid the practice of slavery outright after the US Civil War, except as a punishment for a crime.[17] Beyond that, four primary issues are debated in writing each type of document, beyond those that are specific to a given state's predicament. One item discussed is the degree of democracy, or the ability of people to participate in the political process, more naturally put as "we are deciding who is going to be responsible for making all the decisions in society." Are we going to have everybody in the state show up one weekend and have a big get-together to vote on every little issue directly? Or are we going to elect representatives to make most of those decisions for us? Will it be one guy named Chuck? This is a long-winded way of asking, how many democratic norms are going to be in place in society by allowing people to go vote? Beyond that, the issue of sovereignty is discussed, or the ability of a governing body to govern itself without any interference from outside sources or bodies below, above, or equal to them,[18] easier put, where power located in the state is. Is it with lower entities, like cities or counties of the state, or with higher entities such as the US Congress? Here in Texas, power is consolidated with the state, while under the federal government power is shared between it and the states, with norms to check each other's influence. A third important issue is the degree of political freedom or the ability of citizens to protest the actions of the government. Under the US and Texas Constitutions, people have the right to free speech, mostly unhindered, unless it presents a clear and present danger, for example.[19] Lastly, there is often debate over the ruling tribunal and how power is garnered. For example, will all power to lead be handed down to the next generation, like in a monarchy? Will we create a parliament like the one found in Great Britain, where the prime minister is the leader of the party in control of the House of

---

17    US Constitution, Amendment 13, section 2.

18    https://www.merriam-webster.com/dictionary/sovereignty

19    Andrew Costly, "A 'Clear and Present Danger,'" Constitutional Rights Foundation, accessed March 19, 2019, http://www.crf-usa.org/america-responds-to-terrorism/a-clear-and-present-danger.html; US Constitution, Amendment 1, section 1; Texas Constitution of 1876, article 1, section 8.

Commons (their version of a legislature), or will executive power be severed from that of the legislative assembly with a president, or governor in the case of a US state?"

I spoke up to ask, "So if you were to sum up what all those four things offer to the government beyond structure, what would you describe them as?"

The mysterious speaker concluded, "In a nutshell, I would say that they together as a whole offer legitimacy to rule for a respective government, that is, a willingness for the populace to be ruled over by that group over another potential group. As an example, look at snakes. Not all snakes are equally dangerous and scary. A garter snake is nothing to chagrin at, but you give a rattlesnake a lot more room to operate due to the additional fangs and rattler tail indicating that, 'Yes I'm a snake, and my bites can kill you,' not just annoy you from the pain as part of its defense system. Therefore, respect its authority. Without the documents, any government is just standing on a shaky foundation, like the mostly harmless garter snake, that could be overturned in a heartbeat via a coup d'état. For the government, its fangs and rattler come from the fact that we all got together and drafted these documents with one another and agreed on them together, at least enough to live with them for a short period depending on the document in question. The only problem here is how you keep the legitimacy of those being governed, by brute force or the governed following the law itself on their own regard. Also, this brings up another point, as when compared to many other countries, our state and our national constitutions typically garner a good deal of respect and are followed a majority of the time. Therefore, many other states, including many beyond those here in the United States, used our national version as a base model for when the individual states wrote their own, which typically go much more in depth since the US version is 7,762 words long, with the longest one being that of India, which is 146,385 words. Of note, Texas's is a mere 90,000 or so."[20]

After a brief pause in the events, a woman down the row from me asked, "So what can you tell us about the constitution we have today?"

## The Texas and US Declarations of Independence

After a moment, the mysterious man switched a few toggles on the podium and the light on the Constitution went dark, but the one on the Texas Declaration of Independence now relit. Following that, the mysterious man spoke aloud, "I would love to, but before we can

---

20   Chris Hooks, "Texplainer: Why Is the Texas Constitution So Dang Long?," *Texas Tribune*, August 25, 2011, https://www.texastribune.org/2011/08/25/texplainer-why-texas-constitution-so-long; https://www.laits.utexas.edu/txp_media/html/cons/0400.html; "Constitution Rankings," Comparative Constitutions Project, last modified April 8, 2016, http://comparativeconstitutionsproject.org/ccp-rankings.

continue traversing down that road, I'm afraid that we need to go back down it a slight and explore a side street. At this point, I would like to indicate that, traditionally, 'countries-slash-states' have been formed based on the combination of two characteristics. One is due to the limitations of geography, forcing people to live and work with one another in an isolated area without much outside influence. The other is the presence of a homogenous population, or group of people who share a common ethnicity or some other shared identity. When those two characteristics are present, one guy typically just went, 'I'm in charge now. Go away and serve me or off with your head.' Granted, there was probably a battle of some kind following such a statement, but it is relatively that simple. For example, look at Japan. The country was established several centuries ago via the rise of shoguns around the islands who took power out of nowhere over an isolated, homogeneous population that eventually consolidated into the constitutional monarchy we know today.[21] The idea of a piece of paper formally dictating how an entire country was going to be run was a new deal at the time, at least at a macro level beyond business contracts or other lesser types of agreements that may have been present."

At that point, a man from the front of the room interjected, "Didn't we have to sign some other document before we could write that there constitution?"

In response, the mysterious man furthered, "Yes, exactly. Thank you very much for bringing up where we now are. As we can all see here, lit up quite nicely is the Texas Declaration of Independence. This document was approved on March 2, 1836, by the general convention convened to declare our state's independence from Mexico at Washington-on-the-Brazos during the retreat of Texan forces following the fall of the Alamo.[22] The US version (figure 5.8) and the Texas version are quite similar in form. There is an opening introduction and preamble in both that was written to help others understand their decisions to leave and provide legitimacy for their movements. Following the preambles, there is a laundry list of specific reasons as to why American and Texan settlers had had enough of being a colony or state of their respective former domains known as the indictment and denunciation. For example, paragraph 12 of the US Declaration reads, 'He has erected a multitude of New Offices, and sent hither swarms of Officers to harass our people, and eat out their substance,' while paragraph 9 of the Texas version takes a similar tone and reads, 'It has dissolved by force, the state Congress of Coahuila and Texas, and obliged our representatives to fly for their lives from the seat of government; thus depriving us of the fundamental political right of

21  Prime Minister of Japan and His Cabinet, "Fundamental Structure of the Government of Japan," accessed March 19, 2019, http://japan.kantei.go.jp/constitution_and_government_of_japan/fundamental_e.html.
22  Texas State Library and Archives Commission, "Texas Declaration of Independence," Republic of Texas—Texas Revolution, accessed March 19, 2019, https://www.tsl.texas.gov/treasures/republic/declare-01.html.

FIGURE 5.8    Stone Printing from 1823 of the United State Declaration of Independence.

representation.' The only difference was that the American version directed its anger toward King George III of England and the Texas version geared its anger toward Mexico, led by General Antonio López de Santa Anna. Lastly, the final paragraph in both is a simple directive officially announcing their respective separations known as the conclusion. This is much in the way of Moses going down to Pharaoh to ask him to 'Let my people go, that they may serve me,' from Exodus, chapter 9, verse 1 of the Bible that led to the rain of frogs and the Jews fleeing Egypt and walking the desert for 40 years. The thing to remember is, the Jews, the Americans, and the Texans were all seeking to escape persecution, be it from or in their original homelands or a governing system that they no longer wished to be a part of."

## The Texas and US Constitutions

Another man spoke up. "Wasn't there something about unalienable rights in their somewhere?"

The mysterious man continued, "Why, yes, those rights to life, liberty, and the pursuit of freedom, which was a metaphor for land ownership—and being your own boss, might I add.[23] The more interesting thing, though, is what was later done to gain a foothold in achieving those certain unalienable rights. Remember, the US founding fathers sought to obtain a government that had a strict separation of powers, a weak executive, and power derived from the people, all within a single document. In achieving these ends, a document previously mentioned was the Articles of Confederation for the United States, written in November 1777 and formally ratified in March of 1781.[24] Under this document, the United States operated similarly to that of a firm league of friendship with one another, but never really getting close enough with one another to make it official as a single political unit, choosing to hold on to each of their own individual sovereignties and acting as much as possible as individual political states. In the case of the Articles of Confederation, issues revolved around war debts and states not wanting to give money toward paying them off, lack of a common currency, trade tariffs between states, lack of a national judiciary, unanimous approval in the Continental Congress being required to pass policy, no military call-up requirements, and the absence of a permanent executive, all of which led to the calling of the Constitutional Convention in 1787 that went on to write our current national constitution, the US Constitution."

One of the state troopers interrupted the mysterious man by tapping him on the back with his shotgun and stating, "So then what happened with that whole new document drafting?"

The mysterious man continued, after a small chuckle, by mentioning, "Funny thing to note about that convention is that they were originally convened to make changes to the Articles of Confederation but ended up writing a whole new document.[25] That convention

---

23    Center for Civic Education, "Terms to Know," accessed March 19, 2019, http://www.civiced.org/resources/curriculum/911-and-the-constitution/terms-to-know.

24    Library of Congress, "Articles of Confederation: Primary Documents in American History," accessed March 19, 2019, https://www.loc.gov/rr/program/bib/ourdocs/articles.html.

25    Ibid.

met from May 25 to September 17 in 1787 in Philadelphia, Pennsylvania. Rhode Island was a no-show, New Hampshire left early, and the group debated over plans from New Jersey and Virginia, which was settled with a compromise from Connecticut.[26] The New Jersey plan's source of lawmaking power was derived from the states having an equal number of votes in a unicameral legislature, a plural executive, and a judiciary having no power over the states, but with the government having the authority to compel states to follow national policy. Opposingly, the Virginia plan's source of legislative power was derived from the people, based on popular representation in a bicameral legislature with an executive branch of undetermined size, a judiciary with justices having life tenure and being able to veto legislation in a council of revision—all with the states being able to override federal law. Finding a median point in the debate was the Connecticut Compromise, which sought to have power in one legislative body coming from the people (with population-apportioned membership) and power in the other lawmaking body coming from the states (with equal representation in a bicameral legislature), both serving equitably with a single executive who could be removed by the legislature, with judges having life tenure and an ambiguous authority to review policies and pass judgment on them all under the guise of national supremacy, with ratification conventions in each state allowing for the states and people to have a say in the process."

A woman toward the back spoke up to ask, "Could you summarize that in a few short sentences?"

The man concluded that part of his spiel by stating, "After 9 of the 13 states ratified the document, the compromise established the republic that we have to this day, barred tariffs between states, and included a system of checks and balances between the states and the federal government (and within the federal government itself—better known together as federalism), a single currency, and a postal system, among many other things, but most importantly, it established a sentiment to compromise later on over various issues. The issue is, though, the Constitution left many things up to the states, like slavery (beyond banning further importation of them after 20 years) and establishing the right to vote, not to mention the blatant lack of clauses dealing with basic civil liberties. Overall, though, the first article of the US Constitution created and crafted the legislature, the second did the same for the executive branch, and the third did the same for the judiciary. Also, the fourth article established rules for interstate relations, the fifth made rules for amending the document, the sixth established the supremacy of the federal government, and the seventh made rules for ratifying the document."[27]

---

26   History.com Editors, "Constitution," October 27, 2009, http://www.history.com/topics/constitution.

27   National Archives, "The Constitution of the United States: A Transcription," accessed March 19, 2019, https://www.archives.gov/founding-docs/constitution-transcript.

I spoke up again. "Wasn't there a big debate over ratification, which is why it was not approved for another two years after being written?"

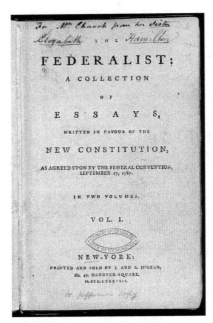

FIGURE 5.9   Title Page of Publius: Volume 1

The mysterious man toggled a few more switches, which ended up dimming the light on the Texas Declaration of Independence and turning on the one on the Constitution of 1876, and said, "That debate was between two groups, better known as the Federalists (supporters of the new constitution), and Anti-Federalists (those opposed to the new document).[28] Beyond simple support over the new document, the sides varied over their views toward the amount of power granted to the states, the necessity of a bill of rights for citizens, the necessity to alter or renege on the Articles of Confederation, and the size of the country regarding its ability to protect people's rights. Finally, swaying approval of the new constitution came in the form of the Federalist Papers (figure 5.9), 85 articles published in the magazines *Independent Journal* and *New York Packet*, which were written by a consortium of Alexander Hamilton, James Madison, and John Jay (under the pseudonym of 'Publius'), calling for the ratification of the US Constitution.[29] Many of the papers are still cited today in court cases and are direct evidence of what our founding fathers sought to achieve all along during this troubled era in our nation's history. With the votes swayed in their favor, thanks to the use of the Federalist Papers, the Constitution went on to be ratified, with the Bill of Rights immediately passed as tender rendered to sway the Anti-Federalists into adoption, and 17 additional amendments to follow since."

Another man asked, "I'm a newly arrived immigrant who is not yet fully naturalized. Could you further explain my rights in general as a person found here?"

The mysterious man continued, "Sure, why not? The Bill of Rights, also known as the first ten amendments to the US Constitution that were passed to placate the pessimistic Anti-Federalists, comes down to two basic aspects: the rights of citizens and the accused. Amendment 1, which protects your right to free speech, assembly, petition, and the ability

---

28   Gordon Lloyd, "Federalist-Antifederalist Debates," Teaching American History, accessed March 19, 2019. http://teachingamericanhistory.org/fed-antifed.

29   https://www.gutenberg.org/files/1404/1404-h/1404-h.htm

to practice your own religion; Amendment 2, which protects your right to bear arms; Amendment 3, which prevents you from being forced to quarter soldiers in your home against your will; Amendment 7, which guarantees you the right to jury trials in civil proceedings; and Amendments 9 and 10, which guarantee you additional rights not enumerated in the Constitution—these all represent additional rights granted to individual citizens. The remaining all deal with those rights belonging to the accused. For example, Amendment 4 protects you from illegal search and seizure; Amendment 5 protects you from double jeopardy—not the ones on the game show, though—and self-incrimination while guaranteeing you due process, a grand jury hearing, and retribution for any eminent domain proceedings; Amendment 6 guarantees you a speedy and public trial by an impartial jury, requires you to be formally charged with crimes, allows you the ability to compel and confront witnesses, and the right to counsel; and Amendment 8 bars any cruel and unusual punishment after any court proceedings. In addition, the 11th, 12th, 16th, 20th, 22nd, 25th, and 27th Amendments all either expand or contract the ability of the federal government to operate, which leaves the remaining amendments to expand the amount of democracy allowed in the country via the expansion of voting rights or the guaranteeing of citizenship, alongside the 18th and 21st Amendments prohibiting and then repealing the prohibition on alcohol sales. Of note, while on amendments, to alter the US Constitution per article 5 'whenever two thirds of both Houses shall deem it necessary, shall propose Amendments to this Constitution, or, on the Application of the Legislatures of two thirds of the several States, shall call a Convention for proposing Amendments, which, in either Case, shall be valid to all Intents and Purposes, as part of this Constitution, when ratified by the Legislatures of three fourths of the several States, or by Conventions in three fourths thereof, as the one or the other Mode of Ratification may be proposed by the Congress.'[30] The Constitution was so important, because of many of these rights and regulations, that Washington, in his farewell address, went so far as to call for citizens to protect the document against all enemies and to resist political pressure to change it.[31] I would talk more about these items, but that would take a whole day in and of itself."

A puzzled-sounding girl a few rows behind me asked, "So what about our state constitution? Is it or is it not a big deal?"

The mysterious man posited, "That would depend on how you define what a big deal is. Is it the length or impact it had? Let's go with length. The US Constitution, once again, is roughly 7,800 words in length, while Texas's is over 90,000 words in length. Also, while the US version has been amended 27 times, the current Texas version has had 677 proposals go

---

30    US Constitution, article 5.
31    http://avalon.law.yale.edu/18th_century/washing.asp

before the citizenry, with 498 being approved and 179 rejected as of November 2017.[32] This sheds more light on the dead-versus-living debate, as the Texas version has been amended so much it's dead, with the US version being alive due to such a low number of amendments, indicating that we can look at it in modern light without having to change the document to decide on an issue, whereas with ours, we can't. Besides, the national government is on its second edition, while our state is on its seventh, for that matter."

After that, a woman yelled out, "Feel free to keep us physically in the dark, but get on with our state constitutions already."

Then, with much haste, the mysterious man sternly continued, "Yes, of course! Our original constitution was the Constitution of Coahuila y Tejas.[33] This document was our state's governing document from 1827 to 1836. It established us as a full-fledged Mexican state that later went on to break down over General Santa Anna trying to centralize all power in Mexico City and limiting trade with the United States, alongside meddling from the Catholic Church. This was our time growing up under the rule of our parents. Following that, our second constitution was the Republic of Texas Constitution[34] that was in effect from 1836 to 1845. That document established us as a full-fledged independent state. It included a strict separation of church and state (thanks to the prior meddling of the Catholic Church), required legislative approval for the freeing of slaves, and denied citizenship for current slaves and their descendants in response to the efforts of Mexico to free them in the past. This was in addition to Spanish traditions of homestead exemptions and community property laws in marriage, alongside some English common law implementation. This document broke down due to Texas achieving US statehood and represents a young adult moving out on their own for the first time who then decides to get into their first adult relationship. Our third constitution was the Constitution of 1845,[35] which was in effect from that year to 1861 and established us as a full-fledged US state. Beyond that, this version was fairly like the prior one and had requirements such as biennial legislative sessions and two-thirds legislative approvals for corporations. It set a debt limit of no more than $100,000 and established the permanent school fund, with later amendments establishing a plural executive. This document broke down over our decision to join the Confederacy over issues of northern economic tyranny and slavery and represented our first time in an adult relationship only

32    https://tlc.texas.gov/docs/amendments/Constamend1876.pdf

33    S. S. McKay, "Constitution of Coahuila and Texas," Texas State Historical Association, June 12, 2010, https://tshaonline.org/handbook/online/articles/ngc01.

34    Joe E. Ericson, "Constitution of the republic of Texas," Texas State Historical Association, June 12, 2010, https://tshaonline.org/handbook/online/articles/mhc01.

35    S. S. McKay, "Constitution of 1845," Texas State Historical Association, June 12, 2010, https://tshaonline.org/handbook/online/articles/mhc03.

to have the relationship go belly up when things got tough. This series of events led to our fourth constitution, better known as the Confederate State Constitution.[36] This document established us as a full-fledged state of the Confederacy, banned the freeing of slaves, and increased the debt ceiling. This version broke down due to us losing the Civil War and was in effect from 1861 to 1865 and more or less represents us having a rebound relationship after getting out of our first adult relationship. This led to our fifth state constitution, known as the Constitution of 1866.[37] Our fifth constitution lasted for three years and represented our first attempt at rejoining the Union. Its goal was to satisfy the Union enough to permit us back into the Union under the mild form of Reconstruction pushed by Andrew Johnson and sought to do this by nullifying secession, abolishing slavery, and renouncing Confederate war debt. The issue is, the US Reconstruction Acts of 1867,[38] led by the Radical Republicans who took over the US Congress in 1866, required the new southern state constitutions to be approved of by Congress. Our first attempt was not enough under the new federal legislature and is akin to going back to our ex and wanting to go to counseling in hopes of getting back together. This led to the creation of the Constitution of 1869.[39] Now, folks, this is where the proverbial poo hit the fan."

While the mysterious man was taking a breath and having drink of water, a man in the back row asked, "What happened? Did the document go all over the place like when I had Montezuma's revenge when I visited Mexico over spring break last year?"[40]

With a drink of water now down his throat, the mysterious man furthered, "Obviously, this constitution made its way around the state; it was in effect from 1869 to 1876. The 1868 convention[41] called to draft the new document, and the ratification election afterward, saw many whites either boycotting the convention in protest or not being allowed to participate due to their service for the South during the Civil War. The leader of the convention was Edmund J. Davis, who later went on to become the first governor of Texas under the new system. The constitution's writers here drafted a document that centralized power in the hands of the governor, who had a four-year executive term and the ability to appoint all major state officials. This was on top of the new annual legislative session, which centralized

36    Walter L. Buenger, "Constitution of 1861," Texas State Historical Association, June 12, 2010, https://tshaonline.org/handbook/online/articles/mhc04.

37    S. S. McKay, "Constitution of 1866," Texas State Historical Association, June 12, 2010, https://tshaonline.org/handbook/online/articles/mhc05.

38    Texas State Library and Archives Commission, "The Reconstruction Acts: 1867," last modified August 25, 2011, https://www.tsl.texas.gov/ref/abouttx/secession/reconstruction.html.

39    https://tshaonline.org/handbook/online/articles/mhc06

40    https://www.urbandictionary.com/define.php?term=Montezuma%27s%20revenge

41    Buenger, "Constitution of 1861."

public schools and weakened the local governments. The actions under Davis as governor are viewed in retrospect as the instrument for an era that most Texans view as the most corrupt and abusive in state history."

A man in the back interjected, "Why was that? Our gang works well with strong central control."

After thinking for a moment, the mysterious man offered, "Davis gave large public gifts to supporters, increased taxes to fund ambitious and wasteful public programs, and increased public debt. Have you ever wondered why many people here in the state are so anti-liberal rhetoric? This was all on top of using the state police forces to terrorize the population, arrest political opponents, and intimidate newspaper editors who wrote articles in poor taste, instead of enforcing public safety, as many rural parts of the state often fell victim to American Indian and outlaw attacks. This was all on top of personally regulating the voter registration system of the state. All of this might be good for control, but it is so unethical and detrimental to the public good that it could not stand for long. Overall, this is our young adult from before and their significant other going to couples counseling to realize that they want to be together but are still in need of drastic changes."

A young-sounding man at the front questioned, "So how did we move away from that tyranny?"

After another quick pause, the mysterious man continued, "In the election of 1874, many formerly disenfranchised parts of the population, former Confederate troops, and officials got the right to vote back and showed up in full force to elect Democrat Richard Coke as governor. The issue is, Governor Davis used the placement of a semicolon in the constitution and a group of handpicked Texas Supreme Court justices to invalidate the results. Come time for the new government to take place in the original capital building, Davis holed up in his office with state police protection, who also barred access to the newly elected legislators so that they could not take office. In response, armed legislators, singing 'The Eyes of Texas Are upon You,' stormed the capitol and used ladders to get up to the second floor to convene the session and swear in the new governor. As you all can probably tell at this point, this era of governance permanently etched into the minds of Texans a healthy fear of centralized government on top of what was already there from our time as a Mexican state. This set the tone of the next constitution: Deny power at all costs. Some historical revisionists argue that Davis was not personally corrupt and that Reconstruction brought many progressive reforms, like school systems, which are still beneficial to us today. Either way, people at the time were tired of the hassle and were ready for a new direction."

I spoke up. "So what does our current constitution consist of?"

The mysterious man continued, "The Constitutional Convention of 1875 drafted the Constitution of 1876,[42] so named for when it went into effect, which you once again see here in part next to me. This new document cut the salaries of state officials, placed strict limits on income and property taxes, restricted state borrowing, stripped the governor of most power (including a shift from a four-year to a two-year term), and required that all justices and the attorney general be individually elected, establishing a formal plural executive. Not to mention, the legislature returned to a biennial legislative session and the creation of a bicameral supreme court. The writers here responded to the abuse of power by denying the offices their power. Specifically, they drafted the second-longest constitution in the country, behind Alabama. Article 1 proclaimed a bill of rights, which included section 18 banning prison for debt, section 23 protecting your right to bear arms, and my favorite one—thanks to an amendment in 2009—unfettered access to all public beaches. Beyond that, article 2 creates the different branches of government and a system of checks and balances between them. Articles 3 to 5 define the legislative, executive, and judicial branches of the government, while the remainder covers specific topics not seen anywhere near the federal version. This includes voting laws in article 6, education in article 7, and what to do about taxes and revenue in article 8. Article 9 created counties, article 11 created municipalities (easier put as cities), article 12 covers how to create private corporations, article 14 created the Texas General Land Office, article 15 covers impeachment, article 16 covers items that weren't big enough for their own section nor a good fit for others, and finally, article 17 covers how to amend the document . . ."

It was then that a woman interrupted. "I was a math teacher, and I believe you left out articles 10 and 13."

Very kindly, the mysterious man replied, "That is because the state legislature and our fair citizens followed the state constitutional amendment process of two-thirds of both houses voting to send amendments to the voters, of which, afterward, a simple majority of voters went on to approve of them and removed article 13, which covered Spanish and Mexican land grants, in its entirety. Beyond that, in 1969 large portions of articles 10, 12, and 14 were also removed. And finally, the state, in 1971, saw voters approve of a referendum to hold a convention to draft a new constitution for the state that occurred in 1974. After months of work, the convention fell three votes shy of sending the new document to be approved of by the voters.[43] Overall, this is our couple finishing couples counseling and reentering their relationship with a new outlook forever."

42   https://tshaonline.org/handbook/online/articles/mhc07
43   Mary Lucia Barras and Houston Daniel, "Constitutional Convention of 1974," Texas State Historical Association, June 12, 2010, https://tshaonline.org/handbook/online/articles/mjc07.

## An Educational Game

It was then that the mysterious man toggled a few of his switches, turning up many of the lights in the room but leaving him in the dark as much as possible. With the lighting settled, the mysterious man spoke: "Everyone, if you could please reach for the small balloon of flour taped to the underside of your chairs. . . . Now that you all have your balloons, we shall play a game. The rules are oyez, oyez, oyez, I call this country into order."

After that, the mysterious man said nothing. I and others in the audience just sat there staring at each other with a flour-filled balloon in our hands. A few moments later, some people in the back began throwing the balloons between them, and others just started tearing into theirs. The mysterious man stopped and questioned us in the audience: "How did you feel without direction?"

The elderly woman from before spoke. "I was confused."

Another man yelled, "You left us out to dry in a pasture, buddy. We didn't know what to do, and people just started improvising, doing all sorts of different things. The back of the room is now literally covered in flour from floor to ceiling."

The mysterious man further questioned, "So what would you have wanted me to say additionally earlier after I did my oyez's?"

The man in the back expressed, "Rules would have been nice, or even some specific directives."

The mysterious man offered, "Okay everyone, or at least those of you who still have unbroken balloons, please pass them up and down your rows."

Following that, for about a minute, we all orderly passed the balloons. It was then that the mysterious man yelled out, "Why are the bald people touching the balloons? This game is only for the haired to endeavor. You baldies need to give all your balloons to the haired in the audience at once."

It was then that I became a wealthy man, having about ten balloons handed to me. The issue is, though, I was getting some of those looks that you only get when you have pissed someone off. Thankfully, the mysterious man asked, "So, for those who just lost everything, how do you feel?"

A bald man down the row from me said, "Discriminated against."

The man went on. "Wait-a-minute all you bald complainers, I thought you all wanted rules to follow."

The bald woman from before then iterated, "Yes, but what's the problem?"

The mysterious man then furthered, "You failed to provide the document's writer, myself in this case, rules to follow when crafting said rules. Regardless, let's remedy the problem by all continuing to pass the balloons. Everybody can participate again now, but you must only transfer the balloons with your feet."

With that statement out in the open, people began to take off their shoes and haphazardly pass the balloons. The room started to smell, and people were dropping balloons all over the place, causing even more of a mess. More importantly, people started to act frustrated because, even though everyone was now allowed to participate, it was still difficult to do so due to the new, stringent requirements, particularly amongst the people in the room without legs. Then the mysterious man questioned again, "Originally, y'all were confused. Then many of you were offended. Now, how do you feel with all the fancy rules?"

A man way in the back shouted, "Exhausted. The rules are now too strict for us to work and pass the balloons under efficiently."

Several other people groaned in agreement. The mysterious man concluded his speech: "Unfortunately, everyone, no ideal constitution exists. There is no one-size-fits-all for every state. No document is perfect forever. No document can be good without people following the rules set before them. Constitutions can be too strict or too loose in interpretation. The activity we just participated in is a modified version of the paperclip game.[44] This game is designed for teaching people about the value of a good constitution. A good constitution is one that is fair to all concerned and is designed to help regulate society but not go so far as stopping everything from occurring in said society. Our current constitution here in the state did not do the best at preparing state leaders for what would come, as evidenced once again by 500 or so amendments, but how could they? I think, though, if you were to ask me whether our current constitution is good, I would say it is like Schrödinger's cat (figure 5.10),[45] often discussed on *The Big Bang Theory*, which can be dead or alive until we check the box that it has been placed into; we know not how the document drafted itself will perform until we implement it and see what happens and make the decision to make additional changes or leave good enough alone. Although, due to the low number of amendments in our national version, they might have done a better job. I can't tell you what will happen tomorrow, and there is no way they could have seen the automobile, much less the internet, coming down the line.

FIGURE 5.10  Visual of Schrödinger's Cat Concept

44    https://teachingcivics.org/lesson/paperclip-game-and-the-value-of-rules
45    Elise Andrew, "Schrödinger's Cat: Explained," IFLScience, March 20, 2018, http://www.iflscience.com/physics/schrödinger's-cat-explained.

What is known, though, is they acted out of paranoia from the memory of Santa Anna and the recent reconstructive behavior of Governor Davis, like how our national founding fathers decided to reject the authority of King George III. It is now that I leave you for today. Goodbye."

It was then that all the lights in the room went dark, only to all turn back on again a minute or so later. The man was gone, but the documents were still there, with the officers asking people to form lines so that they could come and view the documents up close if they so wished. I took my time and considered each one with awe and confliction. I thought, "Who knew so much conversation and debate could come from paper, albeit essential paper! Either way, it is what's written on these papers that governs so much of what goes on in our governed societies."

On my way home all I could think was, "What would happen if we did rewrite our constitution? Would it be better to stick with the original, or could we ruin what we have worked so hard to prosper under? I guess I need to get active and vote when the next amendment election occurs so that I can be part of or block what our legislature puts before us. Either way, constitutions are vital pieces of paper dictating that our fair state is run based on the feelings of those who wrote and those who went on to amend those documents."

**QUESTIONS TO CONSIDER** REGARDING OUR FOUNDING DOCUMENTS:

1. The first main topic of the chapter discusses the fact that paper is still all around us. Please indicate how you feel about this predicament and either confirm or deny this situation in your life.

2. The second main topic of the chapter defines what constitutions and declarations of independence are. Please define each of those terms, provide an example of both from your life, and explain why they are good examples, in detail.

3. The third main topic of the chapter discusses how one may interpret constitutions and declarations of independence. Please identify and gather information on the different ways to interpret. Lastly, please identify how you would prefer to interpret a document and indicate why, in detail.

4. The fourth main topic of the chapter discusses the critical items to debate when drafting a constitution. Please identify what those items are, the item that you feel is most important to debate, and why, in detail, to offer the most political legitimacy.

5. The fifth main topic of the chapter identifies the different sections of the Texas and US Declarations of Independence. Please identify the various segments of a declaration of independence, what you feel is missing, and why, in detail.

6. The sixth main topic of the chapter discusses current Texas and US Constitutions. Please identify the constitution that you feel to be drafted best and indicate why, in detail, based on the readings.

7. The final main topic of the chapter introduces a game to help further the discussion on drafting constitutions. Please identify a way that you would want to be taught this concept and compare it to the game mentioned in detail.

## FIGURE CREDITS

# Chapter 6

# State and Federal Relations

# The Concept of Sovereignty

I had a great weekend looking back at all I had learned from the week before. I think political geography might be my favorite, but I can't discount seeing the state constitution. Overall, I'd been having fun and was looking forward to more adventures. The problem is, I still didn't know where to venture off to next. However, before I went to bed last night, Charity gave me the number of a young woman who was interning at the Bullock Museum this summer under her guidance. Charity described her eloquently as a "delightful young woman with sense and sensibility."

More importantly, she also argued that I could learn a thing or two from her about an important topic on my trek this summer and that I should ask as many questions as possible about her major at university.

Underlying her mantra, Charity was worried that I was not having enough fun this summer—socially, of course—and wanted to make sure that I was following through with my educational goals as well. Accordingly, I called and spoke with the young woman over the phone before I went to bed. We agreed to meet for lunch at the 1886 Café & Bakery, in the Driskill Hotel[1] (figure 6.1) in downtown Austin the next day at noon. With that all said and done, I went to bed pondering what we would be spending our time talking about concerning her major.

This morning, though, I crawled out of bed and took care of my morning procedures a little after 9:00 a.m. I watched the news, read the newspaper, and finished writing up my journal entries from last week. Before I left, though, I did a little recon work on where we were meeting for lunch, as she had suggested the place. The Driskill Hotel is the oldest hotel in the Austin metropolitan area. It was built

FIGURE 6.1    Driskill Hotel Front Exterior.

in 1886 by cattle baron Jesse Driskill, who was looking to diversify his assets following the making of his fortune selling beef to feed Confederate soldiers during the Civil War. Since then, the building has been the location of many gubernatorial inauguration balls since

---

1    http://www.driskillhotel.com.

1887, along with the actual inauguration of Governor Sul Ross.[2] In addition, the building was where former president Lyndon B. Johnson heard the announcement of his wins in the 1948 US Senate, 1960 vice presidential, and 1964 presidential elections, each of which was followed by him making a speech from the Governor Jim Hogg Room's balcony to cheering crowds below, not to mention meeting his wife there on a date in 1934.[3] Not wanting to be late, I left the house at about 11:15 a.m. for the short drive to downtown Austin.

Just before 11:45 a.m., I pulled up in front of the hotel at the corner of Sixth and Brazos Streets. Located at the Sixth Street entrance was a valet parking service that I took advantage of due to the lack of clear alternative parking options available in the area. Once inside via the Sixth Street entrance, I was amazed by the Romanesque-style architecture of the building that melded perfectly with the western ambiance of the decor, from the paintings to the frescos and even the floor, as I walked around the lobby. The large portrait of Mr. Driskill on the wall above the staircase made me chuckle to myself, "This place is almost bigger and better than Texas itself."

Located to the left of the Sixth Street entrance is the 1886 Café & Bakery, where we were supposed to meet. I told her that I was going to be wearing a light blue button-down dress shirt and a pair of plain khakis, and she had advised me that she would be wearing a grey pencil skirt with a red blouse. When I walked in, I did not see her from the reception desk, so I went ahead and requested a table. Luckily, the lunch crowd had not yet arrived, so I was able to get one of the beautiful booths by the big picture windows facing Sixth Street. The early model Ford van permanently on display in front of the hotel was right outside the window—a very cool sight to behold. Then, just after 12:05 p.m., an attractive brunette approached the table and spoke. "Hi, Champ, I presume? I'm Leia Chester."

I rose from my bench and stated, "Hi Leia, I'm Champ. It's nice to meet you in person. Phone calls never seem to do introductions justice."

Leia motioned for us to take our sides of the booth. We made small talk about what our hobbies were and exciting items that we had experienced over the summer thus far. She had some novel tales about eclectic visitors to the museum, and I brought up some of the more notable sites that Dr. Aldermen and I had seen when looking out the windows of the plane the week before. Our waitress arrived and asked, "Could I get the two of you something to drink?"

I replied, "I'll have a glass of iced tea, please."

Leia requested, "Lemonade would make a nice treat on a hot summer day like this, if possible?"

---

2   Ibid.
3   Ibid.

Our waitress said, "I'll be right back with the drinks and to get your food orders."

In hoping to break the silence, I said, "Charity advised me that I should ask you about your major. What are you studying?"

Leia, after a moment's pause, went on. "Well, that is a great question. I just finished graduate school at UT here in Austin. I majored in political science.[4] This fall, I am beginning my first year of law school. However, one of my favorite subtopics to research is something called federalism, which is a fancy term for the relationship currently found between the different levels of government we have here in the country and the distribution of power between them."[5]

I replied, "Aren't you a little young to be finishing grad school?"

Leia declared, "For most people, yes, but I graduated from high school when I was 13 and finished my undergrad when I was 15. Then I took the last three years to complete my master's and doctorate. I'm the female version of Dr. Sheldon Lee Cooper."

Stunned, I posited, "That's . . . impressive and I completely get the comparison, but back to your favorite subject, though. What exactly does the relationship between the different levels of government consist of?"

Leia remarked, "Let me introduce a term to you called sovereignty. Sovereignty is the full right and power of a governing body, be it vested in one man, like a king, or an entire legislative assembly—all depending on the governing scheme, of course—to govern itself without any interference from outside bodies of government, be it below, equal to, or above them.[6]

I interjected, "So sovereignty is another way of saying independence, the freedom from control, influence, support, aid, or the like, from other entities,[7] right?"

## Power Structures for Government

Before Leia could answer, our server returned, and we placed our orders. Leia continued, "Exactly, but federalism is just one of the three main governing system classifications available for those relationships between central and regional authorities (figure 6.2). Of those three governing classifications, their main difference is based on the degree of centralization present in their constitutional foundations for power or authority. For example, the most common classification is called a unitary governing system, where all constitutional authority rests with a national government or some other central authority. In these states, regional or local governments are subordinate to the central government and primarily serve the

---

4   https://liberalarts.utexas.edu/government
5   https://www.merriam-webster.com/dictionary/federalism
6   https://en.oxforddictionaries.com/definition/sovereignty
7   http://www.dictionary.com/browse/independence

| Form of Government: | Many Small Separate States | International Organization | Confederalism | Federalism | | Devolution | Decentralisation | One Large Unitary State |
|---|---|---|---|---|---|---|---|---|
| Political System: | Many Small Separate States | International Organization | Confederation of States | Federal Union of States | Federal State | Devolved Government within a Unity State | Decentralisation within a Unitary State | One Large Unitary State |

*Increasing separation* &larr; &rarr; *Increasing integration*

FIGURE 6.2   States falling on the left side of the spectrum are more decentralized than those on the right that are more centralized.

function of being administrative agents for the policies passed by the central government. Also, those local and regional councils do have some limited leeway in policy implementation as required, but due to their being created by the central authority, they do run the risk of being shut down should they stray too far from the herd. States that employ this system are typically smaller in land area due to a greater number of similarities among the populace than states found in the other classifications that are much bigger (figure 6.3). Some examples are democratic states such as the United Kingdom of Great Britain and Northern Ireland, and Japan, or more authoritative examples like the Kingdom of Saudi Arabia or the Democratic People's Republic of Korea . . . er . . . North Korea."

In ensuring that I understood the concept, I contended, "So in this case, all of the power would be highly centralized with the national government, and the local governments are found to be dependent on them for all of their legitimacy to act?"

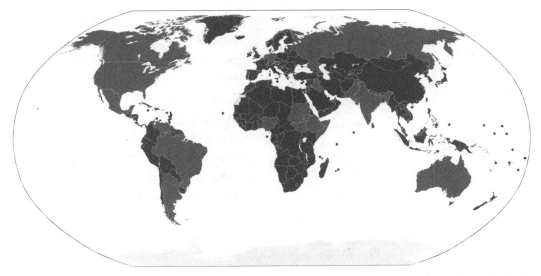

FIGURE 6.3   The larger the state the more federal while the smaller the more unitary. Also notice the lack of confederal states.

Leia expressed, "That would be correct. Keep in mind now; this is the relationship within each of the 50 individual states and their local government counterparts that are currently within our country as a whole. On the opposite, and much less common, end of the spectrum for this concept is confederal governments, where member states or regional governments have all the authority, with any central government over them being dependent on said member states for any power that they might have. This was the governing system initially set up in our country under the Articles of Confederation, namely due to article 2 of the document stating, 'Each state retains its sovereignty, freedom, and independence, and every power, jurisdiction, and right, which is not by this Confederation expressly delegated to the United States, in Congress assembled,'[8] with the keywords being 'expressly delegated.' This model was found to be unworkable because the member states retained too much sovereignty over their realms, which made it difficult for commerce and other items to function properly, as each of the states had developed separate economies that did not mesh well with one another within the country. This option was also the form of government set up for the Confederacy during the Civil War under the Confederate States Constitution (figure 6.4), which was in response to a rise of centralizing authority by the Union government before the war, most notably with slavery. A more modern example of this government system would be the European Union, which consists of 27 separate states that have the full freedom to govern themselves without much interference by their European Parliament outside of their adoption of a common currency, erased border controls

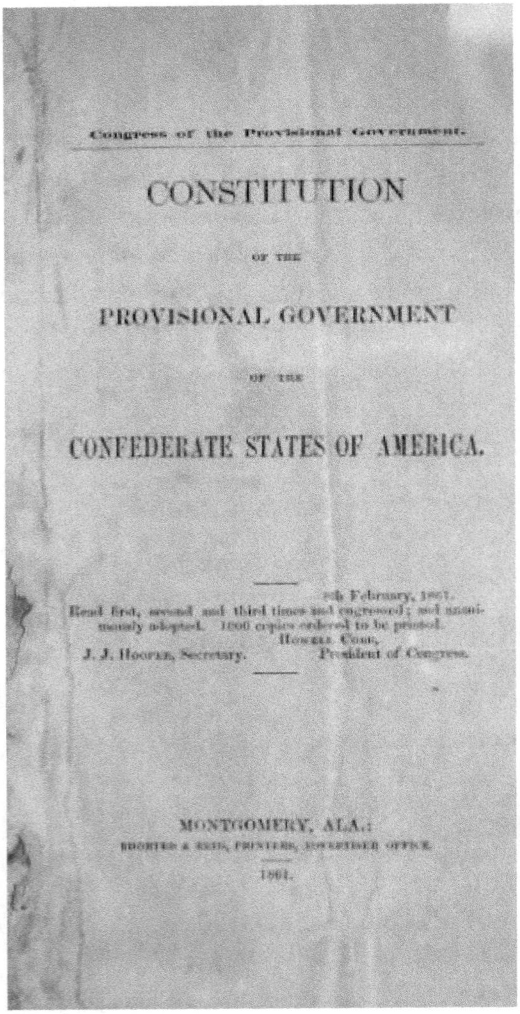
Congress of the Provisional Government.

CONSTITUTION

OF THE

PROVISIONAL GOVERNMENT

OF THE

CONFEDERATE STATES OF AMERICA.

MONTGOMERY, ALA.:

1861.

FIGURE 6.4 Constitution of the Provisional Government of the Confederate States of America.

8 Articles of Confederation, article 2.

between them, and other authority over various aspects in society, with a multitude of exceptions for each.[9] It used to be 28, but the United Kingdom decided to leave.[10] Their governing documents make it a bit harder to decipher what is in effect. Beyond those examples, there is no other country or system of countries that uses that organizational scheme."

In ensuring that I understood the expanded concept, I further contended, "So in this case, all the power would be highly decentralized, with the local governments requiring the national government to be dependent on them for their legitimacy to act?"

Leia concluded, "Once again, Champ, you have the concept down thus far. As I mentioned before, the final governing system classification is called a federal system, which is a system of government where government power is, for lack of a better term, equally divided and shared at the same time between a national or central government and the member state or regional governments, even with additional levels of government in some cases. This option is the governing relationship system that we have here in the United States between the 50 states and the federal government that they as a group created. We adopted it here in response to the inefficiencies found in the Articles of Confederation and not wanting to go back to a unitary system found when we were under Great Britain with King George III. Typically, larger countries like Brazil, Russia, and Australia adopt this system. This situation is due to there being such great differences in the various states found within the country, requiring the various regions to have greater levels of sovereignty or autonomy than what is allowed under a unitary system, but not as much as they would have under a confederal system. This scenario is kind of similar in formation to the confederal system, but instead, the central government is granted much more authority and can operate independently, within reason."

## Types of Power

In ensuring that I understood the entire concept, I further contended, "So under the unitary government, all power is centralized with the national government. Under a confederal government, all the power is decentralized with the member states that all essentially run their own countries but go to a national government for a few select issues, while here, in a federal system, the power is not fully decentralized, nor is it fully centralized. Overall, the states are fully in charge of certain things while the federal government is fully in charge of

9   http://europa.eu/about-eu/facts-figures/index_en.htm
10   Alex Hunt and Brian Wheeler, "Brexit: All You Need to Know about the UK Leaving the EU," *BBC News*, January 31, 2019, http://www.bbc.com/news/uk-politics-32810887.

others, all while acting independently of one another. So, what exactly is our federal system made up of, then?"

Before Leia could answer, our food arrived. It all smelled delicious and was quite tasty. After a few bites, Leia continued: "Well, our federal system is all about power sharing. We started with a big pile of available powers and then divided it up according to what was indeed a local matter—say, how education needs in Texas are dramatically different than those in, say, Connecticut—and what needed attention at a nationwide level. Let's use national defense as an example, since at the time we needed to protect ourselves as a group from a vengeance-minded Great Britain following the loss of their American colonies, us, in the American Revolution. Now in this power-sharing system, three types of power exist. Those going to the federal government are called delegated powers, as dictated by the US Constitution. In delegating those powers, they are obtained by one of three methods. First are expressed powers that are clearly written in the Constitution, mostly under article 1, section 8. This list includes, in no particular order, and I quote: 'to coin Money, regulate the Value thereof,'[11] 'To establish Post Offices and post Roads,'[12] 'To raise and support Armies . . . . To provide and maintain a Navy,'[13] 'To regulate Commerce with foreign Nations, and among the several States, and with the Indian Tribes,'[14] and 'To declare War,'[15] or in some cases by denying the power to the states, and thus giving it by default to the federal government, and I quote again from article 1, section 10: 'No State shall enter into any Treaty, Alliance, or Confederation.'"[16]

I interjected, "So these are expressed because they blatantly grant power to perform a clearly identified and defined task in the document?"

Leia continued, "Exactly. They are different from the second class of delegated powers, which are called implied powers, and are assumed to exist to allow the federal government to operate their expressed powers more fluidly. These powers hail from article 1, section 8, and come in the form of a clause that reads, 'To make all Laws which shall be necessary and proper for carrying into Execution the foregoing Powers, and all other Powers vested by this Constitution in the Government of the United States, or in any Department or Officer thereof.'[17] This clause is formally called the necessary and proper clause,' which in many

---

11  US Constitution, article 1, section 8.
12  Ibid.
13  Ibid.
14  Ibid.
15  Ibid.
16  US Constitution, article 1, section 10.
17  US Constitution, article 1, section 8.

ways grants the federal government a blank check to make rulings on unspecified manners so long as it can relate the power to one of the expressed powers we discussed previously."

I opined, "Wasn't there a US Supreme Court case about this issue?"

Leia continued, "Yes, there was. That was the decision rendered in *McCulloch v. Maryland* when the state of Maryland wanted to prevent the federal government from setting up its bank.[18] The federal government argued that, based on their ability to collect taxes, this required them to set up a system for holding those raised funds, in this case, the Bank of the United States.[19] Accordingly, the United States won, thanks to Chief Justice John Marshall interpreting the Constitution as viewed by the federal government and granted them considerably more power.[20] The difference here is that, while these powers are explicitly given, they are not clearly defined to indicate what said power entails. Just so long as they relate to one of the expressed powers, as determined by the decision in *McCulloch v. Maryland*, they are legit. In this case, the real question is, though, what additional powers are necessary and proper to perform a task? If you attended the event last Friday at the archives building, you probably had an excellent introduction to that conflict of interest."

I interjected again, "I did attend. Regardless, then these powers are implied because a grant of power is clearly expressed without clearly identifying what that power entails?"

Leia concluded, "That's basically about it. The last power grant comes in the form of inherent powers, better put as delegated powers that come with an office or position. Using the presidency as an example, per article 2, section 2, 'The President shall be Commander in Chief of the Army and Navy of the United States, and the Militia of the several States when called into the actual Service of the United States.'[21] This wording clearly delegates to the president the ability to command our military without telling him how he can or needs to do this. With the first passing of the document, the only real limitation on this inherent grant was the requirement from article 1, section 8 that gave Congress the power to declare war. Once stated, though, there was no real limit on what the president could do unless some restriction was granted. No other practical power limitations were found for this expressed power until the War Powers Resolution of 1973, which further allowed the president to send our armed forces abroad in the instance of 'a national emergency created by attack on the United States, its territories or possessions, or its armed forces.'[22] In this further regulation, the president is required to notify Congress within 48 hours of committing armed forces to

---

18   McCulloch v. Maryland, 17 U.S. 316 (1819).
19   Ibid.
20   Ibid.
21   US Constitution, article 2, section 2.
22   87 Stat, 555 or Public Law 93-148; http://www.gpo.gov/fdsys/pkg/STATUTE-87/pdf/STATUTE-87-Pg555.pdf.

military action and forbids armed forces from remaining in combat for more than 60 days, alongside a further 30-day withdrawal period, without an authorization of the use of military force or a declaration of war by Congress. This law further defined the ability of the president to make war but still doesn't set more of what the limits of actual action by troops are."

I stated, "So these inherent powers are like implied powers in that they grant an unspecified amount of power but are specified to a specific position. So, what is the next overall grouping of powers?"

Leia expressed, "This group of powers consists of those belonging to the states. These powers are better known as reserved powers and are primarily deemed to be heralded from the Tenth Amendment of the US Constitution, which reads, 'The powers not delegated to the United States by the Constitution, nor prohibited by it to the States, are reserved to the States respectively, or to the people.'[23] This power grant, once again, more or less writes a blank check of power to the states, allowing them to act as they wish on anything not mentioned in the Constitution, nor explicitly denied to them. That so-called blank check can consist of powers over education, to conducting elections, to providing for public health and safety, and even establishing the local government. This power is in addition to the explicitly enumerated power of ratifying US constitutional amendments from article 5."[24]

To clarify what Leia stated, I commented, "So these reserved powers are like the implied delegated powers in that they clearly grant a power but are not specific to what those powers are for the states. Are there any controversies coming from this grant of power?"

Leia commented, "Well, we are essentially here on a lunch date. If things go well, I might agree to a second date with you. If things continue to go well, we might even become an item. After that comes marriage and even a baby in a baby carriage. The question is, though, what would we need to have to go get married?"

I slowly responded, "A ... uhh ... marriage license that is issued by the state, of course."

Leia posited, "What is a marriage license, essentially?"

I even more slowly responded, "That ... uhh ... would be ... I guess a ... a contract between two people that is issued by the state."

Leia continued, "Another item not mentioned in the Constitution is marriage. Accordingly, the states then have the right to define under what circumstances people may get married, per the Tenth Amendment. In doing so legally, per their state constitutional rights a few years ago, 36 states and the District of Columbia have legalized gay marriage, leaving 14 states that

---

23   US Constitution, 10th Amendment.
24   US Constitution, article 5.

have banned the practice in some form or fashion.[25] Complicating matters, there is the Ninth Amendment, which reads, 'The enumeration in the Constitution, of certain rights, shall not be construed to deny or disparage others retained by the people,'[26] that guarantees additional rights to people who were not included in the Constitution. In this case, people most likely under the amendment have the right to get married. Further complicating matters is the full faith and credit clause from article 4, section 1, which reads, 'Full Faith and Credit shall be given in each State to the public Acts, Records, and judicial Proceedings of every other State.'[27] This requires any contract formed in one state be honored elsewhere as is."

I interjected, "That sounds simple enough."

Leia continued, "In shedding additional light on this matter, there is the US Supreme Court case of *Obergefell v. Hodges et al.*, which sought to determine the constitutionality of same-sex marriage and which has all of the trappings of constitutional decision-making as, no matter how they decide,[28] there is some aspect of the Constitution that will get trampled on: the states and their ability to regulate, people and their unmentioned rights, or the guarantee of contracts being recognized everywhere, all of which is being argued under the due process clause of the 14th Amendment, section 1, which reads, 'Nor shall any State deprive any person of life, liberty, or property, without due process of law; nor deny to any person within its jurisdiction the equal protection of the laws.'[29] Put together, you have evidence that the US Constitution is a living document that can be viewed in light of the times and quite the problem in how to best to interpret just this one case. Fortunately, depending on how you look at the situation, the US Supreme Court ruled in the matter for the right of same-sex marriages to occur nationwide."[30]

I interjected, "So the states have the right to regulate marriage, all people have been granted the right to get married in multiple implied places, and any license issued by one state must be recognized elsewhere. However, some states have banned gay marriage while others have begun to allow the practice. You are right, that is quite the conundrum in handling these contracts, as no matter how a court would rule on this, some part of the Constitution gets

---

25    Haeyoun Park, "Gay Marriage State by State: From a Few States to the Whole Nation," *New York Times*, March 31, 2015, https://www.nytimes.com/interactive/2015/03/04/us/gay-marriage-state-by-state.html.

26    US Constitution, Ninth Amendment.

27    US Constitution, article 4, section 1.

28    US Supreme Court. *PDF*. Washington, DC, June 26, 2015. https://www.supremecourt.gov/opinions/14pdf/14-556_3204.pdf

29    US Constitution, 14th Amendment, section 1.

30    In rectifying this puzzle, on June 16, 2015, in *Obergefell v. Hodges et al.*, the US Supreme Court decided on the matter siding with the appellees, allowing for same-sex marriage to occur going forward in the entirety of the Union.

construed with someone or some governing institution losing a right somehow. On a more solidified note, what is that last grouping of powers you mentioned earlier?"

Leia continued, "Well, the controversy continues, just not as much as before. In this case, the controversy revolves around how exactly the last set of powers are granted not just to the federal but also to the state governments, alongside who has more standing regarding how laws go into effect, as it is not as obvious as before. This last group of power is known as concurrent power. Examples of these powers include the ability to borrow money, levy taxes, make and enforce laws, establish courts, and even charter banks. None of these items are barred from being performed by the states, so, according to the Tenth Amendment once again, they can perform them at will. For the federal government to have these powers, they must be expressed, or construed to be implied or inherent to a position by them, in the Constitution. For example, looking at the power of the courts, article 3 reads, 'The judicial Power of the United States, shall be vested in one Supreme Court, and in such inferior Courts as the Congress may from time to time ordain and establish,'[31] alongside article 1, section 8, stating, 'To constitute Tribunals inferior to the Supreme Court,'[32] which gave the power to establish lower courts to Congress. There is nothing stating that they are concurrent; there has to be no banishment of the power from the states, and there must be an explicit delegation or implication of them at the same time to the federal government."

I inquired, "What other controversies are there with this?"

Leia speculated, "Additional controversy occurs when laws and/or decisions in court are being made that may at times conflict with one another. When this happens, the supremacy clause from article 6, which reads, 'This Constitution, and the Laws of the United States which shall be made in Pursuance thereof; and all Treaties made, or which shall be made, under the Authority of the United States, shall be the supreme Law of the Land,'[33] goes into effect. This clause acts much like the popular baseball rule where the tie goes to the runner. In this case, the state is the baseman catching the ball, and the federal government is the runner; the federal law stands, not the state law. The only exception is that whatever the federal government is regulating, state versions may stand if the law governs more strictly, for lack of a better term, than the minimums established by the federal form of the law. California auto-emission limits are an excellent example of this, as many cars sold elsewhere

---

31   US Constitution, article 3, section 1.
32   US Constitution, article 1, section 8.
33   US Constitution, article 6.

cannot be sold there due to not meeting their emission standards, which are much stricter than the national average."[34]

I articulated, "So this last category of powers is held by both the states and the federal government. What differs is how they get them and who's right when similar legislation is produced. Any thoughts on how we arrived at our current federal system?"

## Eras of Federalism

Before Leia could answer, our waitress arrived and took away our plates. Before she left, though, Leia asked, "Could we have a slice of the three-chocolate layer cake, à la mode for good measure, and a slice of the strawberry-vanilla marble cake, please?"

I joked, "You must be looking for a nice sugar high to get you through the afternoon!"

Leia replied, "Well, to some extent, yes. More importantly, though, the slices will provide a nice visual to answer your latest question."

I articulated, "How so?"

Leia held, "Overall, there have been two distinct eras of federalism, and one that requires people to take out a grudge. The first took place from the founding of the country under the US Constitution to the early 1930s. As contended by Edward Corwin in his 1950 work, 'The Passing of Dual Federalism,' during this era there was an understanding that federal and state governments were both highly sovereign in their domains-slash-spheres of influence while being equal in importance to one another.[35] The national government primarily functioned using only its enumerated or delegated powers and had few opportunities to promote policy.[36] The relationship was one of tension after strict interpretations of the Tenth Amendment served to clearly demarcate a line between the responsibilities of the federal and state governments. One of the few examples of the federal government during this time making an impact on domestic national issues was the passing of the Reconstruction Amendments that banned slavery, had the due process clause applied to the states and enforcement of their laws, and prohibited discrimination based on skin color or former status of servitude on voting.[37] Going forward requires understanding how to accurately interpret the Tenth Amendment as to where that line between federal and state powers stands. A question: How does the Tenth Amendment define powers that are 'delegated to the United States by the Constitution'?"[38]

---

34   PBS NOW, "Air Wars," April 15, 2005, http://www.pbs.org/now/science/caautoemissions2.html.
35   Edward S. Corwin, "The Passing of Dual Federalism," *Virginia Law Review* 36, no. 1 (1950): 1–24.
36   Ibid.
37   US Constitution, 13th, 14th, and 15th Amendments.
38   US Constitution, Tenth Amendment.

I remarked, "It doesn't specify which powers are delegated to the federal government. It just says 'delegated,' which could also include the implied or inherited ones, leaving them quite possibly free to regulate almost anything they please."

Leia continued, "That is the issue that guides the federalism eras going forward. Where does the line exist? Is the Tenth Amendment a clear line in the sand, or is it more of a broken rope allowing for spillage one way or another in favor of the federal government? Whether or not adding the term *exactly* to the amendment would make a difference was a big item of debate during the amendment's drafting. Representative Thomas Tucker of South Carolina tried to squeeze the word in, only to be rebuffed by James Madison and Roger Sherman.[39] The Supreme Court, in *United States v. Sprague*, held that 'The Tenth Amendment was intended to confirm the understanding of the people at the time the Constitution was adopted, that the powers not granted to the United States were reserved to the States or to the people. It added nothing to the instrument as originally ratified.'"[40]

Our waitress at this point brought our desserts to the table. At my first attempt to get a bite, I was slapped away from getting a piece, as Leia wanted to continue speaking. She submitted, "The three-chocolate layer cake we see here represents the era of federalism that we have just discussed. The upper white chocolate layer is the federal government's power; then there is the layer of icing separating it from the dark and milk chocolate layers beneath it representing the state and local governments, respectively, which are also separate from one another. Fans of strictly interpreting the Tenth Amendment of the Constitution vastly prefer this era. For the one or two eras since, depending on how you look at it, we must examine the marble cake. If you look closely, no clear, distinct layers exist. The white, dark, and milk chocolate forming the tiers of the layer cake are physically replaced here with the strawberry and vanilla that are now all mixed after fighting for turf in the oven when being baked, with no strict limit as to what each is responsible for governing. In our case, those powers are no longer clearly separate from one another. The official term for this changeover is the newfound era of cooperative federalism. More importantly, people who prefer the loose interpretation of a constitution or marble cake view of federalism prefer this and the final era."

I interposed, "So what caused the layers to mix?"

Leia went on, "No one event, but rather the realization that certain items required multiple levels of government to work together in hopes of resolving issues. More importantly, as Edward Corwin (from the piece I told you about earlier) puts it, 'The National Government and the states are mutually complementary parts of a *single* government mechanism all of whose powers are intended to realize the current purposes of government according to their

---

39    *Annals of Congress*, August 18, 1789.
40    U.S. v. Sprague, 282 U.S. 716 (1931).

applicability in hand.[41] Such 'current purposes' include actions revolving around the Great Depression, World Wars I and II, civil rights discrepancies, the Cold War, and advances in technology that all required greater coordination of responsibility to deal with in bettering the country properly."

I interjected, "So what exactly happened during this cooperative era to make this all possible?"

Leia continued, "Well, for that, we need to look back to the year 1913 and the passage of the 16th Amendment, which allowed for the federal government to collect a tax on incomes. Throughout the history of the country, the federal government has always given money to the states for various programs through the issuance of grants-in-aid, which is monies coming from central government for a specific project to help its progress that is run by a government at a lower level. What changed with the 16th Amendment was the amount of money the federal government had available to give away-slash-return to the states, as that is where the funds originally came from via taxation of the citizenry. Looking at the numbers, in 1910, three years before the 16th Amendment, the federal government's revenues were roughly $800 million, based on ad valorem taxes, fees, and other business interests.[42] Later on, in 1920, seven years after the 16th Amendment went into effect, the federal government revenues were roughly $7.3 billion, a ninefold increase in revenues, based on the new income tax and the prior ad valorem taxes, fees, and other business interests being in effect.[43] Fifty-four percent of the $7.3 billion came from the new income tax, totaling nearly $4 billion in and of itself, a more than fourfold increase in the entirety of federal government revenues from just a decade prior. Simply put, as the old saying goes . . . talk walks and . . ."

We stated together, ". . . money talks."

I inquired, "But how did the money talking, talk?"

Leia continued, "That is how grants-in-aid work. It is up to the states to begin and operate the programs. Then the federal government, using those newfound income tax dollars, helps to prop up the program by offering additional matching financing. Those grants can come in the form of categorical grants, where the federal aid is to be used for strict purposes, under steep restrictions, and is to be matched by the receiving entity. Or the grants can be in the form of block grants that can be used for general purposes and with fewer restrictions, while still being required to be matched in most cases, which brings up concerns of devolving power back to the states, but that's a different matter altogether."

I juxtaposed, "What is a specific program of this era to signify this program?"

---

41    Edward S. Corwin, "The Passing of Dual Federalism," *Virginia Law Review* 36, no. 1 (1950): p. 19.

42    http://www.usgovernmentrevenue.com/year_revenue_1910USmt_16msin#usgs302

43    http://www.usgovernmentrevenue.com/year_revenue_1920USmt_16msin#usgs302

Leia concluded, "Using a specific program—that's easy, silly! One of the significant events that caused the transition over to the cooperative era, as I previously mentioned, was the Great Depression. Economies of the states and their local governments faced economic disparity for themselves and their citizens in ways never seen beforehand. As part of President Franklin Roosevelt's New Deal program, the Social Security Act was enacted on August 14, 1935.[44] This program was intended to provide those of old age, survivors of the dead, and the disabled with a steady income.[45] Later on, as part of Lyndon B. Johnson's Great Society program, he and his administration, under the aid of Congress, created the Medicare system in the United States after the passage of the Medicare Amendment to Title 18 of the Social Security Act.[46] Under this amendment, each of the states is required to operate and pay for half of their programs, with the remaining funding being matched via those grants-in-aid, which are funded by an additional Medicare tax on your income allowed under the 16th Amendment. In operating the program, each state establishes its eligibility standards, benefits package, payment rates, and program administration under broad federal guidelines. As a result, 56—inclusive of national territories and Washington, DC—different Medicare programs are in existence today. Initially, and until today, those federal funds are categorical grants and must be spent on Medicare programs. Overall, the federal government provides matching cash, and the states offer the service (i.e., cooperating on concerns of the day) to this day."

I posited, "You said earlier that there was something that could be construed as a third era of federalism. Why the hesitance to call it a third official era for what occurs today?"

After a short pause and a couple of bites of cake, Leia contended, "Do you know what addiction is?"

I remarked, "Somewhat, yeah. In biology class, we learned that it's a primary, chronic disease of brain reward, motivation, memory, and related circuitry regarding inappropriate or unsustainable behavior.[47] People do things they shouldn't be doing, but can't stop, essentially."

Leia continued, "The money from the federal government can be quite enticing to act on and eventually functions like a drug that gets people—governments, in this case—addicted to it. The third era is marked by the emergence of a feeling in people—the state governments in this case—that their addiction or reliance on these programs, the funding at least, has gone too far and they need to make a change and stop doing whatever it is that they are doing. In this case, the states are alcoholics deciding that they need to put down the bottle

---

44    http://www.legisworks.org/congress/74/publaw-271.pdf; Pub. L. 74-271.
45    Ibid.
46    http://www.legisworks.org/GPO/STATUTE-79-Pg286.pdf; Pub. L. 89-97.
47    https://www.asam.org/resources/definition-of-addiction

and stop drinking—better put, possibly, as taking money from the federal government—so that they can do better in their domain and focus on what they truly need. The problem is, that is easier said than done, as those programs funded by the federal dollars are deeply woven into the lives of people. Just ask any recovering alcoholic how hard it can be to quit without the intervention of someone else on their behalf."

I suggested, "This situation sounds like a line from *The Incredibles* movie, where Mr. Incredible goes, 'It got smart enough to wonder why it had to take orders,'[48] when referring to the Omnidroids created by Syndrome he has been hired to defeat. That's where we are today, I guess: The federal government, the Omnidroid in this metaphor, is wondering why it must take orders from the people who created it, the states. The federal government does what it wants to, despite the differing needs of the different states, particularly on issues that the federal government has had no purview on before due to its growth into a behemoth far bigger than the founders had intended. This sounds like a lot of what my dad talks about when he returns home from the legislature."

After a pause, I further inquired, "So what is this era called?"

Leia noted, "Well, this is the so-called era of coercive federalism, in which the feds are now directing the states on policies the states must implement. This era has its foundations in the 1970s, when a report issued by the US Advisory Commission on Intergovernmental Relations found that most of the federal preemption laws were the invalidation of a US state law that conflicts with federal law.[49] This is different from the cooperative era because programs here are often tied to other unrelated programs, as opposed to a straight-up matching funding for service-provision agreement requirements. One of the most notable examples of this is the passage of the National Minimum Drinking Age Act of 1984. This policy did not set the drinking age at 21. It merely stated, 'The [Transportation] Secretary shall withhold 10 percent of the amount required to be apportioned to any State [highway funding dollars] . . . on the first day of each fiscal year after the second fiscal year beginning after September 30, 1985, in which the purchase or public possession in such State of any alcoholic beverage by a person who is less than twenty-one years of age is lawful.'[50] In this case, the federal government is requiring the states to shift policy in one area before they can act in another, probably more important, space, against their wishes. This is important, as, say, a state like Louisiana and its annual Mardi Gras festival, which would like to sell alcohol to those 18 years of age to make the extra revenue, but now they can't

---

48    Brad Bird, "'The Incredibles,'" Internet Movie Script Database, 2004, http://www.imsdb.com/scripts/Incredibles,-The.html.

49    Advisory Commission on Intergovernmental Relations, "Federal Preemption of State and Local Authority" (draft report, Washington, DC , 1989).

50    23 U.S.C. § 158. National minimum drinking age.

unless enough of those in their late teen years can plunder enough alcohol to make up the difference for the highway dollars lost from the federal government, of which, using the state of Louisiana's Fiscal Year 2015 highway funding dollars, as part of the Highway and Transportation Funding Act of 2014, totaling $677,413,014, would have cost the state $67.7 million.[51] Of which, getting more specific, using the Louisiana state excise tax of $12.50 per 31-gallon barrel of beer or the $.80 excise tax per liter of liquor, they would have needed to sell an additional 541,931 barrels of beer or 8,467,663 liters of liquor to make up the difference.[52] I don't think they could make up the difference in revenues if they tried. Therefore, the age there has been 21 since 1995.[53] The issue of raising it there got so contentious that several court battles were fought under the guise of age discrimination to prevent the state from raising the drinking age from 18.[54] Overall, the situation is the federal government punishing states for not adopting policies that they are not in favor of while possibly having no real jurisdiction over the additional issue."

I inquired, "So why is this so bad?"

Leia argued, "Whether or not it is bad may be a personal opinion. Some states and their citizens don't mind so much being marched around, as they are more in favor of government intervention—central, in this case."

I interjected, "Like those living in moralistic political cultures?"

Leia continued, "That would be correct. In the bigger picture, though, this debate brings us back to the Tenth Amendment. Specifically, this debate again brings up the question of where that line in the sand exists between state and federal powers in our federal system? John Kinkaid, a federalism scholar, writes on the matter, 'Liberals, lacking revenue for major new programs, and conservatives, lacking public support for major programs in equity programs, [saw the federal government switch] from fiscal to regulatory programs.'[55] Dislike of this era is often due to the feeling that states' rights have been trampled and taken away from them, like how some alcoholics feel after sobering up a bit and realizing that they just bought a new set of hardbound encyclopedias for a cool three grand—which is not good, as they lost control, even though the purchase might be beneficial in the long run to them. The complaint here is that they may be unfunded mandates that require policies to be enacted

---

51  https://www.fhwa.dot.gov/legsregs/directives/notices/n4510788/n4510788_t1.cfm; .1* 677,413,014 (The apportioned total.)

52  http://www.rev.state.la.us/ExciseTaxes/AlcoholicBeverageTax

53  Associated Press, "Louisiana Court Upholds Drinking Age of 21," *New York Times*, July 3, 1996, http://www.nytimes.com/1996/07/03/us/louisiana-court-upholds-drinking-age-of-21.html.

54  Ibid.

55  John Kinkaid, "From Cooperative to Coercive Federalism," *Annals of the American Academy of Political and Social Science* 509 (1990): 139–52.

without the provision of necessary funding to do so. The states have no control over whether to continue offering the program, even if they don't need it, as other unrelated programs elsewhere are affected. This matter over power control has gone so far that former Texas governor Rick Perry tossed around the idea that secession from the Union may be an option, without actually calling for it.[56] More recently, as attorney general and again later as governor of the state, Greg Abbott has gone forward and sued the federal government on issues ranging from immigration to nuclear power regulation.[57] This is all over the issue of who is responsible for what, how they are supposed to do it, and more importantly, who is going to pay for it. It's a complicated issue that brings to light the old saying, don't bite . . ."

We said together, ". . . the hand that feeds you!"

Leia continued, "In this case, the hand that feeds Texas, at least as one of the bigger sources of revenue, is the federal government itself, as they provided, in the fiscal year 2018 of the state from September to December, $13,369,149,000 or 37.1 percent of state income."[58]

I posited, "That's a lot of money. So, what system are the states advocating that is better?"

Leia speculated, "You have let me do a lot of the talking today. More importantly, you have been a gentleman and paid me your full attention. Even more so, you have shown that you understood a fairly complex topic."

I interjected, "You are welcome. But what has that got to do with anything?"

Leia held, "Well, when you are trying to court a woman, what do you do?"

I answered, "I work to show what I have to offer—like having a job or some other meaningful future. Other items, like a place to live, a car, and even a cool social life would likely help my cause."

Leia continued, "So what do all of those represent?"

I continued, "It's like a lifestyle playlist of all the things I have on offer."

Leia surmised, "Close enough. Better put, though, you and I are like the 50 states. We are our independent bodies, or states in this case, and our parents are like the federal government. Only we can indeed make decisions for ourselves, and typically we get mad when someone else tries making them for us, just like many of the states during the last two eras

---

56    Robert Farley, "What Perry Really Said About Secession," FactCheck.org, August 23, 2011, http://www.factcheck.org/2011/08/what-perry-really-said-about-secession.

57    Sue Owen, "Greg Abbott Says He Has Sued Obama Administration 25 Times," Politifact Texas, May 10, 2013, http://www.politifact.com/texas/statements/2013/may/10/greg-abbott/greg-abbott-says-he-has-sued-obama-administration-; Enrique Rangel, "Abbott: Texas Likely to Sue Feds on Obama's Immigration Order," *Lubbock Avalanche-Journal*, November 24, 2014, http://lubbockonline.com/texas/2014-11-24/abbott-texas-likely-sue-feds-obamas-immigration-order#.VZMCv_lVhBc.

58    https://comptroller.texas.gov/transparency/revenue/watch. Download the most recent All Funds File. Total all federal revenues in the period and then divide into all funds to get numbers cited.

of federalism. As a woman, I am faced with multiple suitors who are like the other states trying to sell me on why I should listen and buy into their—as you put it—'lifestyle playlists.' If I just blindly go out and buy into one of the suitors and don't investigate what's really going on in their lives, I am likely to get into a relationship that I simply don't want or something that, while cool, I have no use for and will only take up valuable space in my life. This is a social comparison to what was coined by US Supreme Court justice Louis Brandeis in his dissenting opinion from the case of *New State Ice Co. v. Liebmann*. In his opinion, Justice Brandeis argued that 'state[s] may, if its citizens choose, serve as a laboratory; and try novel social and economic experiments without risk to the rest of the country.'[59] Overall, this notion shows how, amid the federal framework, a system exists where state and local governments act as autonomous social 'laboratories,' where laws and policies are created and tested at the state level of the democratic system—in a demeanor very much related, in theory at least, to the scientific method—before other states adopt a similar policy. Therefore, it is just up to the states' personal preferences in what they want to do, listen up or go their own way."

I interjected, "Kind of like the same-sex marriage topic we discussed earlier?"

Leia continued, "Exactly, but I have an even more controversial topic to discuss this further. Same-sex marriage is simple: They can either get married, get a civil union, or none of the above. Any effects are secondary to the simple act of marriage. Marijuana use is a far bigger tug-of-war to hassle over, as the effects are not secondary; they are direct. Marijuana can be outright legal or outright banned, and there is a far bigger middle ground to figure out. Can we allow for medicinal? If we go with recreational, how much can we allow to be legal? Can people grow their own, or do they have to go to a dispensary? When people do get it, how much are we going to tax it, or how can we make sure it is all safe? What is the blood-pot-content limit going to be before someone is driving while stoned? There are so many questions to figure out. So does this sound like a good thing for a one-size-fits-all solution from the federal government?"

I replied, "Absolutely not! That is a lot to figure out."

Leia concluded, "That's why too much federal influence is regarded in some states as a bad thing. The states we're discussing are so different. Alaska is sparsely populated, at around 1.3 people per square mile, with a total of 663,268 square miles. All the while, New Jersey is a fraction of the size of Alaska, with over 1,200 people per square mile, with a total of 8,722 square miles. Would the regulation of pot use have anywhere near the same needs? Not in the slightest. Currently, Alaska, California, Colorado, Maine, Massachusetts, Nevada, Oregon, Vermont, Washington State, and Washington, DC, have legalized marijuana under state

---

59    New State Ice Co. v. Liebmann, 285 U.S. 262 (1932).

law.[60] Twenty-three states have allowed for decriminalization, which is transferring punishment from a felony to something akin to a speeding ticket, or some medicinal use, leaving 18 states with no legal marijuana of any kind; and those numbers seem to be changing daily.[61] More importantly, those states that have some form of legalization all have different rules for when use or possession becomes illegal. This whole situation is a call for a return of the states and the federal government back to their proper roles under the dual era of federalism, where everyone knew what they were supposed to do and did it, alongside staying out of other levels of government's business."

## Policy Diffusion

I asked, "So what dictates when a potential policy will diffuse to one state or another?"

Leia surmised, "That depends on the amalgamation of two sets of conditions the state is facing. First, as I am sure you already know from when you visited the Institute of Texan Cultures down in San Antonio, as argued by Daniel Elazar in his perennial book, *American Federalism: A View from the States*, states will have differing cultural preferences toward government intervention behavior.[62] Accordingly, states will be more or less apt to adopt policy than others. Focusing this condition on diffusion of policy, one set of scholars, led by Jack L. Walker in his seminal research, entitled "The Diffusion of Innovation Among the States," argues that policies are most likely to diffuse based on geographic proximity and regional emulation from larger to smaller states, or the federal government for that matter, that took earlier risks and determined the sustainability and applicability of a policy.[63] Opposingly, there are those scholars, such as Virginia Gray in her work entitled "Innovation in the States: A Diffusion Study," that argues in-state conditions, like resources available and the actual need for a similar policy, better explain when policies will further diffuse among states, as opposed to the mere fact that a more affluent or larger state nearby adopted the policy.[64] Overall, it's merely a waiting game for when a favorable set of conditions emerges, not to mention where that line in the sand is viewed to be drawn by the Tenth Amendment."

60    Jeremy Berke and Skye Gould, "This Map Shows Every US State Where Pot Is Legal," *Business Insider*, January 4, 2019, http://www.businessinsider.com/legal-marijuana-states-2018-1.

61    Ibid.

62    Daniel Elazar, *American Federalism: A View from the States*. (New York: Crowell, 1966).

63    Jack L. Walker, "The Diffusion of Innovation among the States," *American Political Science Review* 63, no. 3 (1969): 880–903.

64    Virginia Gray, "Innovation in the States: A Diffusion Study," *American Political Science Review* 67, no. 4 (1973): 1174–85.

I could only remark, "In applying the discussion we just had, what are my chances of you adopting my playlist?"

She replied, "Hmmm . . . I don't know. Since I am in a more resourceful state, I guess I could take a risk on you going forward, but like any good conservative state, I will have to think about it more before I say yes."

With that stated, we both rose from the table and went to the cashier to pay for lunch. I, wanting to enhance my chances for a second date, immediately paid for everything. Before going our separate ways, we hugged and wished each other a good day. It was nearly 1:30 p.m. when I began to get into my car. Then it hit me. Activities between, within, and above with the federal governments are a lot like regular relationships, be they romantic, parental, friendly, employer-employee, or with man's best friend. Each relationship develops its dynamics, all of which depend on how the different parties view their roles, how those characters mesh with others, and how they entered those roles and relationships. Depending on all that, the connection can be very beneficial or quite toxic. It just relies on the ability of those involved to be willing to work together and be in the right state of mind to make it all happen for the bettering of those societies.

**QUESTIONS TO CONSIDER** REGARDING STATE AND FEDERAL RELATIONS:

1. The first main topic of the chapter discusses the concept of sovereignty. Please define that term, relate the concept to some event in your life, and explain why sovereignty relates to the situation, in detail.

2. The second main topic of the chapter discusses the different power structures available for a system of government. Please identify and explain how each of the structures work, select the option that relates most to your life, and explain why, in detail.

3. The third main topic of the chapter discusses the different groups available to wield power in our country's federal system of government. Please identify each group of power and give an example from each, identify the power group that you would like to have most, and explain why, in detail.

4. The fourth main topic of the chapter discusses the different eras of federalism. Please identify and provide insight into the era that most relates to your life and explain why, in detail.

5. The final main topic of the chapter discusses policy diffusion. Please define the term, explain why people and governments of certain states prefer that over a more centralized approach, and explain why you like or dislike this decentralized approach, in detail.

## FIGURE CREDITS

# Chapter 7

# Parallel Political Histories

**Texas Higher Education Coordinating Board ACGMSLOs**

*For Federal Government 2305: Upon successful completion of reading the book and taking the associated course, students will be able to do the following:*

1. **Explain the origin and development of constitutional democracy in the United States**
2. Demonstrate knowledge of the federal system
3. Describe separation of powers and checks and balances in both theory and practic
4. **Demonstrate knowledge of the legislative, executive, and judicial branches of the federal government**
5. Evaluate the role of public opinion, interest groups, and political parties in the political system
6. Analyze the election process
7. Describe the rights and responsibilities of citizens
8. **Analyze issues and policies in US politics**

*For Texas Government 2306: Upon successful completion of reading the book and taking the associated course, students will be able to do the following:*

1. **Explain the origin and development of the Texas Constitution**
2. **Describe state and local political systems and their relationship with the federal government**
3. Describe separation of powers and checks and balances in both theory and practice in Texas
4. **Demonstrate knowledge of the legislative, executive, and judicial branches of Texas government**
5. Evaluate the role of public opinion, interest groups, and political parties in Texas
6. Analyze the state and local election process
7. Identify the rights and responsibilities of citizens
8. **Analyze issues, policies, and the political culture of Texas**

# Why Texas Is Texas

History is defined as "a chronological record of significant events (such as those affecting a nation or governing institution) often including an explanation of their causes."[1] For people, life is one long series of decisions that can be traced to discover why someone is afraid of something, enjoys an item or pastime, or merely performs a task out of habit. Accordingly, the past has a way of dictating, or at least influencing the future.

The question is, how does this relate to today? Well, today was about learning why Texas today is—politically, at least—Texas. What were the significant events that led us to be one of the most influential states in the nation today? Who played a role along the way that got us here? What factors influenced those decision makers to act the way they did? Was it all divine intervention? Was it just pure happenstance? Or was it in the cards all along, as people who are too different from one another only go in different directions? Is it right for us going forward? My goal for the day resonated off these questions. That goal was to learn about the political history of Texas. However, little did I know that much of what I learned reflected a near-mirror image in many ways to the history of our country at large.

FIGURE 7.1  Bullock Museum.

Luckily, staying in Austin has its perks for learning about state history regarding politics. The first break of the day came from the fact that Austin is the state's capital; everybody who knows somebody, or something, is already there, waiting to share their insight on government. Second, my sister, Charity, works at the state history museum, the Bullock Museum[2] (figure 7.1). Accordingly, I was to go into work with her this morning, so she could give me a full hands-on tour of the exhibitions and adequately educate me on what the 411 is on the history of the state, at least as it relates to state politics. I could only hope that the information gathered would be able to expand on, or at least streamline, what I had learned five years ago in my Texas history class—a rite of passage for any youth growing up in Texas in their seventh-grade social studies class. What I learned in the required 12th-grade American government class would also pay big dividends in due order.

---

1   https://www.merriam-webster.com/dictionary/history
2   https://www.thestoryoftexas.com

On the way to the museum from Charity's home in Lost Pines, Charity, being the tour guide at heart that she is, treated us to a chorus of famous Texas songs. She had compiled them on her iPhone the night before to help get me into the mood for today's history lesson. The list of songs included "Texas, Our Texas," which is the state song,[3] "Yellow Rose of Texas," "Deep in the Heart of Texas," "The Aggie War Hymn," "The Eyes of Texas," and more regional favorites like "Cotton-Eyed Joe," "Luckenbach, Texas," "She'll Be Comin' 'Round the Mountain," and even one by an actual former governor of the state (W. Lee "Pappy" O'Daniel), "Beautiful, Beautiful Texas." After listening to those songs, I was ready to go and expand my knowledge about the state, as they helped get me in the mind-set of the state's history. After a 23-minute car ride, due to traffic, we arrived at the museum just before 8:50 a.m. Once out of the car, in the parking lot across Congress Avenue from the museum, we walked across the street and into the front plaza of the museum. The day then marked its moment in time as our path met a critical juncture.

Charity remarked, "Little brother, as tradition dictates, to properly experience the museum and cap off the prep work I got started with in the car, you need to walk through the five-hole of the giant Lone Star that sits out in front of the museum that we now stand before."

This request seemed a little odd, but I only remarked, "Okay."

Doing it really didn't seem to have that much of an impact at first, but when I came out the other side and looked up, it felt as if I was back playing high school football and entering the stadium to a raucous crowd minus the crowd due to the grandiosity of the museum building standing before me. We then "hit the field" by walking through the front door of the museum after finishing the walk across the plaza.

However, when we were inside, Charity's boss came running up to her, ranting frantically, "I was about to call you, but I saw you through the window coming in, so I just ran over. Thank God! Your project at the zoo was damaged last night from the thunderstorms that hit the area. The Austin Zoo needs you to go over and work on helping to get everything all figured out, so they can get the complex back up and be running fully. Some of the live animals are on an unplanned walkabout."

I then got my marching orders from Charity, which were, "You stay here and go on a tour of self-discovery. This museum is cool like that. Information on the history as it relates to Texas politics starts on the second floor to the right of the stairs, not the one here in the rotunda, but the one behind the paid admission area entrance. Here's 30 bucks for admission, and maybe a movie or two. Use your student ID for a discount, and the rest is for lunch. I will retrieve you at the end of the day, or hopefully sooner."

---

3    Added by Acts 2001, 77th Leg., ch. 1420, Sec. 7.001, eff. Sept. 1, 2001.

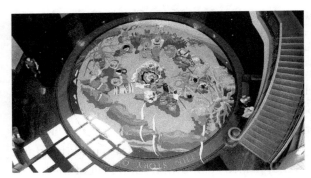

With that said, Charity ran back out the door to her car across the street and headed over to the zoo for some damage control while her boss went back to whatever he was doing beforehand, leaving me to stand there twiddling my thumbs. Looking for where to begin, abandoned to the wolves it seemed, I glanced around and noticed that the floor of the rotunda had an inscription set into the marble floor: "THE STATE OF TEXAS, BORN AROUND THE CAMPFIRES OF OUR PAST" (figure 7.2). Apparently, the floor of the building's rotunda is a giant granite mural of a campfire from the Wild West, with the different peoples of the state gathering' round. I then thought to myself, "'Ring of Fire'[4]— what an excellent place to get started. Thanks, Johnny, for the poignant reminder of what politics in the state has been through on more than one occasion, as I would learn later. This act seemed a lot like the team huddle before kickoff. How funny!"

## Early Texas History

I then walked over to the back left corner of the room to buy my ticket. The problem was, it was not quite 9:00 a.m., so I needed to wait about five minutes for the ticket counter to open. Once the box office was open, I decided to walk around the exhibitions no matter what, but I had to choose between seeing *Texas: The Big Picture* on the most massive IMAX theater in the state or watching the *Star of Destiny* in the Texas Spirit Theater, Austin's only 4D theater, last I checked. I asked which one had more information on the history of the state. The ticket taker, Stephanie Stephens, replied, "They both do, but regarding a longer timeline, it is *Star of Destiny* by a mile. All the big shots are in it, from Sam Houston to George W. If you come back later, though, we have IMAX versions of all the Hollywood films as well."[5]

With my student ID discount, my total came to $14 for everything. I proceeded farther back to the left and entered the main exhibition hall. My only thought was, "This place has about everything you would need to know about Texas on display, nice and neatly."

---

4   https://www.youtube.com/watch?v=It7107ELQvY
5   https://www.thestoryoftexas.com/visit/buy-tickets

The docent at the entrance advised everyone to make our way around the first floor as we pleased and to explore the remaining stories clockwise for the best experience possible.[6] This routing was due to much of the space being under reconfiguration for the new exhibit, *Becoming Texas*, that will "explore the people and events that shaped Texas long before its famous boundaries or name appeared on maps."[7] After walking around the first floor, Charity's telling me about how the primary politics of the state started on the second floor made more sense, due to the first floor only covering early native life of the state that I had gathered up pertinent information on a few days earlier at the Institute of Texan Cultures up to the French and Spanish ambitions of the area that ended in the early 1800s. The most notable exhibition on display here, though, is the Royal French Ship, *LaBelle*.[8] Apparently, this massive sailing ship sunk in Matagorda Bay, Texas, in 1686 during the French custodianship of the state from 1684 to 1689. The vessel was raised from the murky shallows in the 1990s, only to face an ownership crisis between Texas and France that was settled by having France become the owner but placing the vessel on permanent loan to the museum to help avoid further destruction from a transatlantic voyage back home. Essentially, what information was available is pertinent, as it covered the people who initially settled the land here in the state. However, in the grand scheme of things, after exploring the second floor, Texas politics, as it relates to today, got its start on that floor, as promised by Charity. Inspiringly, my Texas history textbook from way back in seventh grade came to life once I had begun.

From this point forward, the museum functions as a timeline. However, instead of just looking at pictures and lines on the wall, you walk through it. All the rooms either displayed actual relics from what was (or physical recreations of the places where the people who made the history back then had experienced the events) to get us on the path to where we are today; some of them even had a right combination of the two. Using the advice from the docent again, I turned right at the top of the stairs and found myself in the rooms entitled "Building the Lone Star Identity" and "A Separate Identity," taking up a quarter of the floor. At this point, in deciding how best to recount my day and the events that I discovered here, it seemed best to take notes on the individual circumstances and then go back and summarize each of the different eras and associated factoids to make a short story of some kind. The story from when the state was under Mexican rule went a lot like a bad divorce making headlines on *Maury*.[9]

---

6    An actual tour of the Bullock Museum was performed to gather the information for this and all following sections that take place there unless otherwise noted.

7    https://www.thestoryoftexas.com/visit/exhibits/first-floor-galleries

8    Texas Highways, "Landing of *La Belle*," December 2014, https://texashighways.com/culture/history/landing-of-la-belle-exhibit-la-salle.

9    http://www.mauryshow.com

Mexico gained its independence from Spain after years of fighting that was brought about due to political tensions under the Bourbon Reforms, discrepancies in the leadership of Spain, and general liberalization of views toward being under the Spanish Crown by settlers. Once free of Spain in September of 1821, the new state faced two weighty issues. The first dealt with the fact that much of the new country, a territory that stretched from the Yucatán Peninsula to today's Pacific Northwest in the United States, was in shambles, economically and physically, from over a decade of revolution and poor economic times. The second was how to cope best with the ever-expanding territory of the United States, with its recent purchase of the Louisiana Territory from France in 1803 that literally doubled the size of that state, not to mention the likely probability, under the guise of manifest destiny, that the United States would eventually want to expand further west soon, where, coincidentally, Mexico had just acquired vast territory.

In handling its two difficult issues, Mexico decided to act preemptively by trying to kill two birds with one stone. Mexico decided it was best to create a buffer zone with the ever-expansive United States by inviting Europeans and Americans to settle Texas, or Tejas at the time. It was hoped that the new settlers would bring their wealth and spirit to ignite an era of economic revitalization to the area by developing it. The most notable group of settlers to the area came under the auspices of Moses Austin in 1821 (and later his son, Stephen F. Austin, following Moses's death in June 1821), which saw 300 families settle into an area south of where the city of Austin sits today, extending to the gulf coast.

The issue is, while many of the early settlers who came followed the rules of swearing allegiance to the Mexican government, learning the Spanish language, and converting to Roman Catholicism, most settlers, due to being so distant from the capital of Mexico and closer to the United States, were able to stay Americans at heart and in action, following their own prior traditions in an autonomous state of existence. For three years, this was a light issue until the state of Coahuila y Tejas was formed, with its capital being in the city of Saltillo, and eventually in Monclova, in 1833. While closer than La Ciudad de Mexico, Saltillo and Monclova were still too far away from the settlers in Tejas for comfort and to have any real impact on integrating them into Mexican culture. Many felt that Tejas deserved to be its own state. Feeling left out of the process, settlement leaders Sam Houston and Erasmus Seguín each eventually went to La Ciudad de Mexico to request that Tejas be formed into its own Mexican state, only to find themselves thrown into jail for extended periods.

Along the way to eventual independence from Mexico in 1836, Mexican leaders, culminating with the actions of General Antonio López de Santa Anna, made a series of decisions on issues that would doom them to disgrace in the eyes of Tejas settlers, setting the stage for an eventual revolution. First came the decision and lengthy fight to ban the practice of slavery. This item was an issue, as many settlers to Tejas had brought slaves with them to help develop the land, especially within the expanding cotton industry. In 1823 the national government decided to end the slave trade and grant freedom to children of slaves at the age of 14, but not to ban slave ownership outright. Later, in 1827 Coahuila y Tejas's legislature outlawed the importation of new slaves, freed the children of slaves at birth, and required that any new slaves brought into Tejas be released within six months. Finally, in 1829 slavery was officially outlawed in Mexico, causing the desire to revolt within Tejas to percolate among the settlers; however, Tejas was temporarily exempted from the rule. In 1830 Tejas was ordered to comply fully with the mandate, leading many colonists to convert slaves to indentured servants on 99-year-term contracts. In attempting to abolish slavery, the Mexican government interfered with the heart of the economy in Tejas, to the dismay of settlers.

Second, the whole existence of Tejas as it stood under Mexican rule was due to the opening of the territory to immigrants by authorities in hopes of invigorating the area. That policy began to change on April 6, 1830, when the Mexican government implemented a series of laws intensively restricting immigration from the United States and eventually abolishing further immigration in 1833. Most importantly, the laws canceled all unfilled "empresario" contracts and called for the enforcement of customs duties on all goods imported from the United States. These actions angered Tejans, leading a group of armed settlers to dispose of the commander of the military outpost in Anahuac in June 1832 while a second group concurrently overthrew the outpost at Velasco. These actions were taken in part to protest the centralist policies of Mexican president Anastasio Bustamante. It is important to note that by 1835, roughly 80 percent of Tejas residents were either from the United States or born of those immigrants. This divide in population created an identity crisis for the region that, like 25 years later in the United States and the Civil War, would eventually lead to war—or revolution, depending on how you looked at it. Once again, the actions of Mexico caused tension with residents of Tejas by attempting to restrict links with their homelands, which hit home at a social level, as for many those homelands were still closer than the capital of Coahuila y Tejas, not to mention La Ciudad de Mexico.

Up to this point, the Mexican government had attacked the main livelihood of Tejans, alongside cutting off many of the connections of citizens to their homelands after letting them initially live in an autonomous state. The final straw that broke the camel's back of Mexican authority in Tejas was the revocation of the 1824 Federal Constitution and the reorganization of Mexican states into military departments/districts in October of 1835 by new leader General Antonio López de Santa Anna. This action attacked settlers on a legal level by removing many protections that they had enjoyed. Overall, the actions of Mexico were unforgivable in the eyes of Tejans—actions that would no doubt, as seen later, lead to war, based on the contents of these rooms.

## Founding of Texas Mirrors That of the United States

From what I could tell after walking through the first quarter of the museum's second floor, the seeds of distrust in central government, especially in those governments that are far away, had been sowed into the soils of Texan mentality. In the bigger picture, the actions of the Mexican national government essentially put Texas residents in the position of being backed into a corner, leaving them no other choice but to fight for their livelihoods. It was not until I had reached the threshold of the access to the next room that I needed to stop and ponder. At this moment, lectures from my senior government class now flooded my memory. The events of the previous rooms were a near mirror image to what our country at large had experienced leading up to the American Revolution with Great Britain and King George III. I could only summarize everything that came flowing back into my head yet again as another episode of *Maury* with all the mudslinging occurring.

Comparatively, those venturing into the new world came to start new lives just like those who went to Texas. Some came to escape religious persecution, as was the case with the Pilgrims,[10] while others sought to better their futures economically, as was the case with those heading to Jamestown,[11] later the Massachusetts and Virginia Colonies, respectively. The difference here is that

---

10    History.com Editors, "The Pilgrims," December 2, 2009, http://www.history.com/topics/pilgrims.
11    History.com Editors, "Jamestown Colony," March 8, 2010, http://www.history.com/topics/jamestown.

those heading to Texas, officially at least, came legally, while those settling the New World just showed up uninvited by the native population. Beyond that, these and other colonies that emerged up until the mid-1750s operated under governments like that at home in England. Each colony had a royal governor who served as a surrogate for the king in the colony assigned. In addition, each colony had a governor's council that served a role like that of the House of Lords, with membership limited to the most elite men in the colonies' society; the council ultimately functioned as a supreme court alongside a general assembly that served a role like that of the House of Commons, with membership falling to those elected by the populace to help a lawmaking agenda and govern their colonies. For the most part, due to diverse histories of their colonies and economies, not much action warranted greater collaboration by the 13 colonies in existence beyond trading.

A greater desire to work together came because of the French and Indian War between Great Britain and France. This war was fought over further territorial expansion in the New World. Following this conflict won by the British, like Mexico and its war of independence with Spain, Great Britain now had a new massive territory that stretched from the Arctic Ocean to the Gulf of Mexico and westward to the Mississippi River that was very expensive to run, along with sizable war debts. The drive to begin working together came because of the government of Britain's response. Just as Mexico had started to place more significant restrictions on the Tejans, so too did Great Britain, with theirs leading to disastrous results regarding their control over the colonies in the long run.

Specifically, Great Britain passed a series of acts that sought to get the help of the colonists in paying for the territory that they now occupied. First came the Proclamation of 1763 that prevented the colonists from developing the land west of the Appalachian Mountains. Second came the Sugar Act of 1764 that increased duties on sugar; new import duties on textiles, coffee, wines, and other goods; and doubled the tariff on foreign goods shipped from England to the colonies. Following this came the Stamp Act of 1765 that required a tax to be paid on nearly all paper documents produced or purchased in the colonies. The year 1765 also saw the Quartering Act come into existence, requiring colonists to house British soldiers in their homes. Parliament also passed the American Colonies Act in 1766 that asserted Parliament's legal right to adopt binding laws over the colonists in America alongside repealing the Stamp Act entirely and watered down the Sugar Act. Then came the Townsend Acts of

1767 that imposed further duties on items brought to the colonies and created a Board of Customs Commissions to enforce the various acts and collect monies owed. The colonies then had to deal with the Tea Act of 1773 that lowered import tariffs on imported tea to make it more competitive against colonial-produced teas, which led to the Boston Tea Party forming. Lastly came the 1774 Intolerable/Coercive Acts that sought to punish the now rebellious colonies by requiring them to quarter British soldiers, again, closed the port of Boston, and reshaped colonial governments administratively. Overall, colonists of the New World did not take kindly to having the core fundamentals (economically, legally, and socially) of their lives massively redrafted to suit the needs of their distant leaders, just as what happened with Tejas and Mexico years later.

## The Road to the Texas Revolution

With the political beginnings of Texas and America now established in my head to be similarly centered around the development of a massive distrust in distant governments, I then fully entered the next room, entitled "The Road to Revolution." The situation presented in the room made it apparent that the Tejans had chosen to fight. That fight was the Texas Revolution. Even before entering, though, I could also already sense the comparison to America's early plight oozing to the surface just at the sight of what was to come.

Events in the Texas Revolution experienced three periods of ebb and flow. Control after the first ebb came to the Tejans after victories at Gonzalez, Goliad, and Bexar. Activities at the Battle of Gonzalez centered on a cannon that Mexican authorities had given to settlers in 1831 for protection from the Comanche nation. The issue is, with the multitudes of revolt from outlying Mexican states, the military decided to retrieve the cannon, as those in revolt should do worse without firepower. In late September 1835, troops from the garrison at Bexar (now San Antonio) arrived to retrieve the cannon, only to face days of settlers doing everything from blocking access to the town to outright fighting them in the streets. This battle, known as the Battle of Gonzalez, is most notable for being the first skirmish in the Texas Revolutionary War and for the flying of the world-famous "Come and Take It" battle flag that showed a cannon, the preceding words, and a star, all in black, placed on a field of white.

Building off the victory at Gonzalez, settlers near Goliad then attacked the garrison at Mission La Bahia, facing little to no opposition from the under-staffed and unprepared Mexican troops based there. While not strategic, this battle influenced the later actions of Mexican general Cos, who had been sent to San Antonio de Bexar right after Gonzalez to reinforce the garrison there and protect the city, which was next in the line of sight for Texans to take. For the next two months, Cos and the Tejan army, led by Stephen F. Austin, were in a stalemate, until December 4, when Texas leader Ben Milam spoke his famous words: "Who will go with Ben Milam into San Antonio?" The words rallied the troops. Four days later, after a vicious door-to-door, street-to-street siege that saw Milam killed halfway through (serving to inspire his troops to continue), Cos signaled for a truce that saw him exchange the town and supplies in return for the pardon of his forces and safe passage to the Rio Grande. Most notably, the Tejans took the Alamo from this conflict. Overall, the first ebb of the Texas Revolution saw Texans win three strategic and symbolic battles that saw Mexican troops, in their entirety, be removed from the territory for a time. The issue is, what goes around seems to come back around and haunt you.

Actions in the second ebb consist of the response of General Santa Anna and his Mexican forces. Most notable from this reaction was the retaking of the Alamo by Santa Anna that ended on March 6, 1836, as part of the notorious Battle of the Alamo. Lasting for ten days, Tejan troops remaining at the Alamo, led by Jim Bowie and William Travis, held back two initial attempts by Mexico to retake the mission, but their defenses failed in the third attempt, which saw the demise of nearly all combatants on the Tejan side. This battle was one prong of a two-prong approach by Mexican forces to retake the territory.

On the coastal front, General Urrea led troops. Near Goliad and Coleto Creek, Urrea and his troops came across James Fannin and a regiment of around 300 soldiers who were leisurely retreating from the fort at Goliad on the orders of Sam Houston. Deciding to fight, the 300 or so Tejans lasted for two days, only to surrender. Instead of being released as expected, on March 27, 1836, all soldiers captured (along with 40 or so from other, smaller battles that occurred in the area around that time and who were all being held as pirates) were marched out onto a nearby road, surrounded by two columns of Mexican soldiers, and executed in what would later be called the Massacre at Goliad. The importance of these two events is that they went on to serve as the impetus and rally cry

FIGURE 7.3  On March 2nd, 1836, the Texas Declaration of Independence from Mexico was signed here in this building.

for Tejan soldiers in the final ebb of the Texas Revolution.

Of note, during this stretch of the war, the signing of the Texas Declaration of Independence on March 2, 1836, at Washington-on-the-Brazos occurred (figure 7.3).

In the final ebb, Texans, at the Battle of San Jacinto, finally won their independence. Following the actions at Goliad and the Alamo, Santa Anna and his forces continued their march toward the retreating Texas forces, which were moving eastward toward Houston as part of the "runaway scrape." After the two crushing military exercises, Sam Houston and other Texan forces reorganized at Gonzalez, moving the Texan capital to Harrisburg (and eventually Galveston), and finally settling Houston's forces at Lynch's Ferry weeks later. Santa Anna, in full pursuit, arrived at the area on April 19, 1836, to rest his troops and then attack on the 22nd. Deciding not to wait for Santa Anna to make his move, on the afternoon of the 21st, Houston launched a surprise attack on the "siesta"-ing Mexican soldiers (who were without sentries or lookouts on the camp for an unknown reason) in the Battle of San Jacinto. After attacking at 4:30 p.m., the battle was over in 20 minutes, thanks to the ridgeline and trees used to camouflage the approaching Texans working far better than expected, giving the Texans total victory. A month later, on May 14, 1836, Santa Anna signed the Treaty of Velasco (after initially escaping during the battle, only to be recaptured when one of his own soldiers ousted him after telling Texan soldiers that Santa Anna dressed in infantry robes to hide from them), ending the revolution and establishing the Texas-Mexico border as the length of the Rio Grande.

## The Ebbs of the American Revolution

Based on what I saw in the second quarter of the second floor, Texans had fought for and eventually won their independence from a distant power they despised. The impetus to fight came from the actions taken by their now former government to restrict their ability to function as seen best fit. In battle, Santa Anna and his forces sought to retain control of what they had helped establish, only to find themselves being kicked out by soldiers who they more than likely outnumbered but who were far more apt at fighting a war than initially thought. As I was approaching the threshold to the area of the museum explaining the aftermath of the conflict in starting the new Texan nation, I found myself looking out over the balcony to the first floor considering how the events of this room related to what American colonists had gone through following their own conflict. The comparison still held firm.

Regarding actions by the colonial governments, as part of a first response, specifically to the Stamp Act, a Stamp Act Congress met in 1765 in New York City. That Congress issued a Declaration of Rights and Grievances that reiterated the colonist's allegiance to the Crown while also emphasizing their right not to be taxed without their consent, resting on the fact that they had no specific representation in Parliament.

As part of a second response to the continual actions put forth by the Crown, primarily the Intolerable Acts, the First Continental Congress met in September 1774 with 56 representatives from all colonies other than Georgia. This Congress, via the Declaration of Colonial Rights, enacted a boycott of British goods that was enforced via the Continental Association, published a list of grievances such as no taxation without representation, and petitioned King

George III for change regarding their injuries. Also, plans were laid out for a second Continental Congress to meet the following year. Unofficially, plans were also laid out to build a stockpile of arms in Concord, Massachusetts. In response to the eventual buildup of the arsenal, the governor general of Massachusetts sent British troops to capture the arms and destroy them. This led to the Battle of Lexington and Concord, the first battle in the American Revolution, when colonists at both sites fought back, earning a victory for themselves.

Officially leading America through the Revolutionary War and into independence was the Second Continental Congress. This congress met from May 1775 to March 1781. Beyond declaring independence from Britain in July 1776 at Independence Hall

FIGURE 7.4  On July 4th, 1776, the 13 Colonies Declaration of Independence from Great Britain was signed in Independence Hall, this building..

in Philadelphia, Pennsylvania (figure 7.4), this legislature took on the role of being the de facto national government of the newfound United States; it raised armies, directed war strategy, appointed diplomats, and made formal treaties to help establish the newfound country.

Militarily, the American Revo-lutionary War saw its own series of ebbs and flows in control. In the first ebb that lasted from 1775 to 1776, following the creation of the Continental army by the Second Continental Congress, General George Washington, and his forces, scored a moral victory in the Battle of Bunker Hill in Boston. Following that battle, through fall and winter, Washington and his troops continually worked to keep the British held up in Boston. Following a later conflict at Fort Ticonderoga in New York that saw the American regimes capture a large cache of weapons, the British led by General Howe were forced to evacuate from Boston to Canada in March 1776; they spent the next several months there regrouping to plan an invasion of New York. In the summer of 1776, Howe and over 34,000 troops returned and met with Washington and his troops on Long Island and forced them to evacuate across the Delaware River into modern-day Pennsylvania. This ebb ended with the Americans led by Washington making their famed trek back across the Delaware River, making a surprise attack on Trenton followed by one at Princeton, both victories for the Americans. Hostilities ended here, with Washington making his winter quarters at Morristown and the British in New York.

The second ebb of the American Revolution saw the British make a series of strategic moves in fall 1777. Specifically, a two-pronged approach aimed to divide the colonies into north and south physically was implemented. In this method, British general Burgoyne first moved his troops south from Canada with an aim to meet up with Howe on the Hudson. En route, at Fort Ticonderoga, Burgoyne and his troops retook the fort. Meanwhile, Howe then decided uni-laterally to move his troops south to take on Washington in the Chesapeake Bay area; Howe went on to take victories at Brandywine Creek on September 11 and the overtaking of Philadelphia on September 25. Washington made a successful blow against the British by striking at Germantown in October, followed by setting up Winter Quarters near Valley Forge. However, left to their defenses, Burgoyne encountered American general Gates in the First and Second Battles of Saratoga, where he and his troops were forced to surrender on October 17. This ebb ended with these last two battles serving as a turning point in the war, due to the American victories officially bringing the French into the war on the side of the Americans, bringing with them aid, expertise, and training beneficial in the final two ebbs.

As part of the third ebb of the American Revolutionary War, a stalemate emerged in the northern states and battles raged in the southern states. During June 1778, Sir Henry Clinton, the new British supreme commander, successfully evacuated British troops from Philadelphia to New York. En route, though, Washington's army met them at Monmouth, New Jersey, and fought in a battle that ended in a stalemate. All the while, a joint American-French attack on Newport, Rhode Island, held by the British, failed. Meanwhile, early 1779 to mid-1780 saw Georgia and South Carolina fall to the British under the helm of Lord Cornwallis. August saw a victory for the British at Camden, South Carolina, while October saw a victory for the Americans at King's Mountain under General Horatio Gates. This ebb ended with a win at Cowpens, South Carolina, in January 1781 for the American effort by newly enshrined American general Nathanial Greene, who replaced Gates.

Action in the final ebb of the American Revolution saw total victory for the Americans. Continuing from his success at Cowpens, by the fall of 1781, Greene and his forces saw the retreat of Cornwallis and the British troops to Yorktown, Virginia. In the Battle of Yorktown, supported by a fleet of 36 French ships offshore, the Americans on land forced the surrender of Cornwallis and his forces on October 19, 1781. While the end of the war is often noted as being the Battle of Yorktown, the British still held sturdy bases at Charleston, South Carolina, and the main army was still found to occupy New York City. The year 1782 saw no significant battles, but by late that year British forces entirely withdrew from the South, and preliminary negotiations of the Treaty of Paris occurred in November. Almost a year later, in September 1783, Great Britain formally recognized the independence of the United States and ended the eight-year-long war, followed by the last remaining British forces in the United States leaving New York on November 25, 1783, on Evacuation Day.

## From Republic to State

Based on what I had recollected at this point, not only had the events that led to seeds of distrust in distant government been nearly identical, so too were the efforts needed to fully gain independence, fight in war, and eventually sign a peace treaty. Granted, the Texans were more efficient at driving out the Mexicans in a little over a year, while it took eight for the Americans to do so with the British. I supposed that Mexico being a lot closer to Texas than Britain was to America helped, not to mention the warmer climate being more suitable for continual conflict. Looking ahead to the next room, "The Republic of Texas," I could tell that the future of Texas, politically, faced some teething issues. Here too, did I get tinglings of relatability to their early American counterparts along the way.

Once free of Mexican rule, the politics of the state centered on the future direction of the new republic. On one side were nationalist supporters, led by Mirabeau Lamar, who advocated for a Texan empire that spread from the Gulf of Mexico to the Pacific Ocean and the expulsion of Native Americans and other people they considered "less desirable" in the process. On the other side were annexation supporters, led by Sam Houston, who advocated peaceful relations with native populations.

On the issue of annexation into the union, despite having just fought for independence, overwhelming public support existed for the procedure.[12] Holding up approval from the United States were two dissociated issues. First was the desire of the United States to avoid war with Mexico, which had vowed to go to war with the United States if Texas were ever to become a state. In the second case, slavery became an obstacle to overcome, as the balance found at the time in the United States (between free and slave states) would be altered in favor of slave states had annexation occurred outright immediately.

Beyond annexation concerns, other more nuanced issues that played significant roles in Texas politics during this era—such as being recognized by other nations to make the new Republic of Texas official, how to deal with the borderland with Mexico, a worthless currency, Spanish and Mexican land grants, and where to place the capital—were dealt with. These issues were all eventually settled with the annexation of Texas into the US in December 1845, after a joint resolution by the US Congress went into effect.

According to the timeline in this room, Texas faced issues that any other state, now and then, would go through when forming a new entity. Furthermore, based on a glance at the room, issues faced here seemed to compare to that of the song "Should I Stay or Should I Go?" by the Clash.

Following the annexation in 1845, Mexico, as promised, immediately ended diplomatic relations with, and declared war on, the US by starting the

---

12    D. Malone and B. Rauch, *Empire for Liberty: The Genesis and Growth of the United States of America* (New York: Appleton-Century-Crofts, 1960), 590.

Mexican-American War. This war ended in 1848 with the signing of the Treaty of Guadalupe Hidalgo. This treaty forced Mexico to give up the territories of Alta California and New Mexico to the United States in exchange for $15 million, assume $3.25 million of debt owed to US citizens, and most importantly, officially rescind their claims to Texas. In this treaty, both sides finally recognized the Rio Grande as the official border. Altogether, this added nearly as much land to the Union as the Louisiana Purchase had almost 45 years before, in 1803.

Despite the conflict with Mexico, four oddities in some form or another came out of the annexation. First, Texas was admitted as a slave state, which would later impact our actions regarding the Civil War. Second, the United States did not accept land for the repayment of debts associated with the annexation and prior sovereignty. Therefore, the areas currently in New Mexico, Colorado, Wyoming, and Kansas that were initially part of Texas were sold off and the proceeds given to the United States in exchange. Meanwhile, the portion going to Oklahoma was later surrendered as part of the Missouri Compromise in 1850. The remaining public lands allowed for the land grant institutions of the University of Texas and Texas A&M University to be formed, alongside the creation of the permanent school fund that today receives countless sums of money from oil and gas leases on the land and goes toward lower education in the state. Third, while not noted officially anywhere, yet still held highly in popular lore, Texas may have been given the right to leave without a fight if it did not enjoy being a state, which also impacted our actions regarding sides during the Civil War. Finally, and still in existence today, Texas, due to its size, has the right to divide into four additional states, for a total of five, if the state ever so wishes to take that action.

## More Similarities between Texas and the United States

Once I had left room on Texas as a republic up to joining the Union, I had a solid feeling about more comparisons between Texas being independent and the founding of the country. At this point, the further apparent comparisons became even more evident. Those teething issues are ever so familiar to me.

As stated prior, the Second Continental Congress had been selected for the leadership of the country beginning in 1775. Beyond war efforts, they also focused on the items of need to run the country. To handle such affairs, the Congress drafted the Articles of Confederation that formed a so-called League of Friendship between the states that let each remain sovereign to rule over its own citizens while providing a bare minimum of power to the Congress for other affairs. The document was approved of and implemented by the Congress in 1777 but was only fully ratified in 1781. Powers beyond waging war consisted of a single vote for each state in the unicameral Congress, the power to coin but not print money, sign international agreements and treaties, provide postal service, and deal with Native American affairs. Almost at the start, the document proved unworkable due to 9 of 13 states needing to approve of legislation, no separate executive or judiciary, no regulatory ability over interstate or foreign trade, no tax levying and collection abilities, no power to raise an army, and the unanimous consent requirement for changes to the articles.

Following the war, an economic downturn emerged that was exacerbated by the loss of trade with Great Britain and the West Indies. The year 1785 saw the meeting of a committee to discuss issues with trade with other nations that ended with no action being taken, due to the nine-state requirement. Other committees were called that also saw no action being taken on a federal court system and the implementation of a solicitation system to collect taxes and other resources from the states. At this point in the new country's history, the lack of a war for the Congress to rally cooperative efforts behind also hampered efforts by the new states to work together now that their safety was more secure. Change only came following a September convention in Annapolis, Maryland, on the issue of interstate commerce that had delegates from just five states attend. There, the product of a committee led by Alexander Hamilton called for a convention to meet the following year in Philadelphia, Pennsylvania, to discuss all needed efforts to make the articles "adequate to the exigencies of the Union." It was at this convention that the actual future of the country, as a whole, lay. Beyond the governing problems, the country at this time saw a rebellion in Massachusetts led by farmer Daniel Shays and his compatriots in agriculture to protest the foreclosure of properties due to the failure to pay taxes. This rebellion instilled in leaders the perils of a limited and passive government, due to their inabilities to swiftly deal with the uprising's economic underpinnings. Under these dire conditions, in February 1787 Congress gave its blessing for the Constitutional Convention to occur later in the year.

The convention that became known as the Constitutional Convention of 1787 convened on May 25, 1787, and lasted for four months. Fifty-five delegates from 12 states attended, sans Rhode Island. General George Washington was selected to lead the convention. Attendees united on four fronts: (1) the need for more action on trade with other nations, (2) the unfortunate consequences of dealing with the potential for conflict like Shays's Rebellion to occur elsewhere, (3) the inability of the current government to provide protection from native people due to encroachment on their lands, and (4) the need for more central action on ending the economic depression. The division occurred, just as it did with Texas, along what to do with the direction of the country.

One side of those at the convention, led by Virginia and its plan, was primarily the largely populated states. This group proposed a system of three branches of government inclusive of a legislature with two houses, with membership proportionate to state populations, having one group elected by the people of each state and the other by that state's legislature. The legislature would have the power to make laws when the states were incapable of doing so or to keep the harmony of the states. The Congress would also be able to select an executive and judiciary. The executive and members of the judiciary would serve on a Council of Revision that would be able to veto legislative actions.

Opposing the Virginia Plan were minimally populated states led by New Jersey and its plan. This second path called for a unicameral legislature with equal representation of the states that had the power to levy taxes, regulate interstate trade, and assert federal law as the law of the land. Also, the legislature would still be able to select the executive and judiciary. Regardless of these differences, both plans sought a limited executive. Deadlocked over the direction of the country, a smaller committee of members was implemented to reach some compromise in July 1787.

The committee produced the Connecticut Compromise, which was submitted by that state's delegate, Roger Sherman. This compromise called for a bicameral legislature with equal representation in the upper house, known today as the Senate, and proportional representation based on population in the lower house, known today as the House of Representatives. Further stipulations called for all revenue bills to start in the House, two-thirds approval for appointee and treaty approval by the Senate, and the power in general for Congress to regulate interstate and foreign commerce. The executive would be slightly plural due to the people directly electing the president and vice president via the Electoral College; the president would then have the power to negotiate treaties, serve as commander in chief of the armed forces, and veto legislation of the legislature—a system of checks and balances and a clear separation of power, to put it frankly. On the issue of population, representation, and distribution of tax revenues, slaves were to be counted as three-fifths of a person to ensure that those states were not overly represented and compensated.

This compromise went on to be approved of by a vote of five-to-four, with the smaller states of Connecticut, Delaware, Maryland, New Jersey, and North Carolina supporting and the larger states of Georgia, Pennsylvania, South Carolina, and Virginia going against, with the New York and New Hampshire delegations being absent and the delegates from Massachusetts unable to vote one way or the other. Final draft submission to the states came on September 17, 1787, with all 12 of the delegations present voting in favor.

While the delegations at the Constitutional Convention divided between small and large states, the real divide came between individual citizens who became known as Federalists, those in favor of the new constitution, and Anti-Federalists, those against the new constitution. This divide was based on fears of the ability of a strong central government to abuse their power and the preference for more states' rights. Anti-Federalists were primarily farmers and rural citizens in general, while Federalists were from urban areas and came from the business class and felt that a stronger central government was needed to help regulate the economy.

Most notably, helping to sway Anti-Federalists to the cause were the Federalist Papers, published under the pseudonym "Publius" by Alexander Hamilton, James Madison, and John Jay, that argued for the ratification of the Constitution. Opposing these arguments were letters written under the name "Brutus" that explained that the new system of government and its taxes simply replaced one tyrant with another, alongside being most critical of the lack of a Bill of Rights to protect citizens from government. With promises, most notably by James Madison, for the new legislature's first order of business to be the creation of a Bill of Rights, ratification came on June 21, 1788, with the approval of New Hampshire to the cause. Beyond the papers and promises of a Bill of Rights, Federalists used winter ratifying conventions to ensure that rural citizens were less likely to participate, the requirement for needing only 9 of 13 states to ratify the document, and a ban on reporting the day-to-day events of the special conventions be implemented as part of the ratification process. On July 2, 1788, the Congress of the Confederation, still operating under the Articles of Confederation, appointed a committee to prepare for the new government. The new government went into effect on March 4, 1789, with the start of the new Congress, followed by Washington being inaugurated to office as president on April 30, 1789.

Lastly, the United States faced off with the British years later in the War of 1812. This war was not so much about Great Britain seeking to retake its former colonies, as was the case of Mexico in the Mexican-American War. The conflict was fought over British restriction of US trade with its neighbors, notably France, the Royal Navy's impressment of American seamen and the enlistment into their forces, and desires by the United States to further expand its territory in the direction of Canada. This conflict ended on December 24, 1814, with the signing of the Treaty of Ghent in something of a stalemate.

## Nation Building

Based on what I had just recollected, the United States, like Texas, had experienced its own set of teething issues regarding its conception, both of which centered on the eventual direction of the new nations once established, with clear proponents for each available option: for the United States, a series of fiefdoms or a unified front, and for Texas, being just another one of the states or its own republic. Both even had to fight a war with their previous master, twice, to reach those points in their establishments. It was at this point I wondered aloud, "What does all of this mean? What does this all add up to?"

Not expecting an answer, I got one. A female voice spoke, "Separatism and nation-building, you dummy."

I spun around to find Leia, the woman who I had a delightful lunch with yesterday, staring at me with that look only a woman can give showing support and disappointment all at the same time. I replied, "Define your terms, young lady."

Not waiting, Leia replied, "Separatism is defined as 'the advocacy or practice of separation of a certain group of people from a larger body based on ethnicity, religion, or gender,'[13] or in this case, over economic and geographical differences. Nation building, on the other hand, is 'government policies that are designed to create a strong sense of national identity.'"[14]

I requested, "Go on."

Leia furthered, "As I am sure that you are aware after walking through the exhibits, certain actions were taken by Mexico that enraged the Texan settlers, just like what happened between the American colonists and Great Britain on the remarkably similar fronts of

---

13  https://en.oxforddictionaries.com/definition/separatism
14  https://www.collinsdictionary.com/us/dictionary/english/nation-building

economics, socialization, and legalities. In response, not all at once mind you, the colonists in their respective areas decided to leave based on those actions, your separatism. Following that, with their respective declarations of independence signed, nation building began with the respective revolutionary wars needing to be fought. Those actions then precipitated the decision for what the future of each was to be—being a US state, for the Texans, and having a strong central government, for the Americans, your nation building."

What Leia had said perfectly capped off everything that I had recollected and read. I could only ask, "What happened next?"

Leia motioned that we move on to the next room. We had some small talk along the way about how she had seen me walking around for a while and then stop to ponder and then do it all over again. Walking, stopping, and then staring had made me seem strange and in need of assistance, so she decided to come over and help after letting me suffer for a time. Upon entering the next rooms, "Secession and the Civil War" and "There Is Work to Be Done," I saw that the museum's timeline of history for Texas turned to the first era of statehood, which came with its own remarkable set of drama. Texas history right before, during, and immediately after the Civil War is rehashed to show that, like divorce, secession, yet again, does not go smoothly. More importantly, the history of the state and the rest of the nation from this point forward seemed to be in alignment with, or at least run alongside, one another, as they were the same. In the next two rooms I learned, with Leia showing me:

> During the initial period of US statehood, politics in Texas once again centered on Sam Houston, who was for staying in the United States, while the opposition was for secession and possibly joining the Confederacy as time wore on (or at a minimum going back to being a republic). Tense relations with native population and the potential loss of federal troop protection were significant concerns if secession occurred. Consensus on reasons for the start of the Civil War revolved around the practice of slavery and its influence on other issues such as states' rights and the ability to bring slaves when traveling to the North; sectionalism in the differing economies of the various states; northern merchants and southern agriculture dependent on slavery; and whether slavery would be allowed in future territories. Since Texas was a slave state, any action taken by the United States to outlaw or further restrict slavery was viewed as a threat to the state and its economy. More importantly, driving home the issue throughout the 1850s and culminating with the inauguration of Abraham Lincoln in 1861 was the rise of the Republican Party on the sole

basis of limiting slavery to its current areas and eventually ending the practice. Texas was not in favor of this during this period, just as it wasn't during Mexican statehood.

Therefore, Texas officially left the Union to join the Confederacy on February 1, 1861. Ten other states did as well, starting with South Carolina on December 20, 1860, and ending with Tennessee on June 8, 1861. During the war, very few battles took place in the state, as Texas was located far away from the main battlegrounds in Maryland (Antietam), Mississippi (Vicksburg), Pennsylvania (Gettysburg), Tennessee (Shiloh), and Virginia (Bull Run, Spotsylvania, and Antietam). In helping with the war effort, Texas supplied much of the cotton used by Confederate forces. The few battles that took place in the state were mostly concentrated to skirmishes associated with the Union blockade of southern ports. Texas, along with the rest of the Confederacy, went on to lose the war after the surrender of Confederate troops in April 1865 at Appomattox.

With the conclusion of the war, general chaos was flush throughout the state and much of the South due to a mass of freed slaves, thanks to the Emancipation Proclamation and little to no distinguishable, established government on the ground providing order. Union troops began to arrive in June 1865 to provide much-needed law and order. The first order of business under federal troop occupation saw voters go on to pass the Constitution of 1866 that changed Confederacy to the United States in the Constitution of 1861 of the state of Texas and outlawed slavery in a minimal attempt to merely satisfy the US government with a show of a change of heart. Also, despite being required by Congress to approve of the 13th and 14th Amendments, lawmakers ignored them and voted in the "black codes," severely repudiating the rights of former slaves.

The issue is, President Johnson was also impeached, but not convicted, and the more moderate Republicans were overtaken by the Radical Republicans, who were hell-bent on punishing the South for the war, in the 1866 midterm elections. Once in office, with full veto-override capability, the Radical Republicans went on to pass the Reconstruction Acts (on March 23, 1867), which required southern states to write brand-new constitutions and approve of the 13th, 14th, and 15th Amendments, alongside severely limiting the voting rights of former Confederate soldiers and governing officials in order to officially rejoin the Union. In response, Texas went on to ratify and approve the amendments and the Constitution of 1869 in July of that year, which led to issues of its own, with the other Confederate states being readmitted to the Union at the same time following the adoption of their own Reconstruction-mandated constitutions. Federal occupation of the state did not end until July 1869, for Texas at least, when the voters approved the Constitution of 1869. Reconstruction, as a whole, for the South did not end until 1877 with the Compromise of 1877 that led southerners to accept Republican Rutherford B. Hayes as president in exchange for the last of federal troops occupying the South to leave.

During this era of politics, Texas left, fought against, and rejoined the Union, along with several of the other states in the South. This was separatism at its finest, once again. Accordingly, like any separation, issues were worked on when separated, and there were some hurdles crossed when officially reconciling, as was evident in the nation-building process during Reconstruction experienced by all the states in the South. Overall, no matter how I tried to separate the two political histories, the continuous parallels were ever so evident.

The time was nearing noon, and I was feeling famished. Feeling confident, I asked, "Are you up for that second date yet?"

Blushing, Leia rebutted, "How about dinner and a movie?"

I replied, "How about lunch and a movie right now?

Leia stopped me and said, all while walking away, "I have to get back to work, silly. Meet me here at 6:00 p.m. when I get off work, and we can see *Solo: A Star Wars Story*. See you then! In the meantime, though, be sure to finish the museum or I'll get you in trouble with you-know-who."

## Reshaping Identity

Figuring it was best to continue to follow my marching order, I kept on into the final main room of the floor entitled "Reshaping Identity." Once the issues regarding Reconstruction were dealt with, new ones arose with the document that the US Congress required the state to procure. Overall, Texas was not entirely done with its own individual reconciliation.

Looking at the events from this era, it is wise to look back at what occurred before the events of the American and Texas Revolutions. Mexican forces, under the leadership of Santa Anna, had centralized power in Mexico City and used military districts to enforce power that eventually caused the citizens of Tejas to revolt, with King Gorge III doing the same to the colonies with strikingly similar results. Events that occurred under the seven-year run of the Constitution of 1869 in Texas were amazingly similar. Leading the charge during this era was a former Union brigadier general known as Edmund J. Davis. Before the war, Davis had aligned with anti-secessionist forces, even attempting to join the secession convention to stop the separation from occurring. When secession and war happened, he fled to Union-held New Orleans and eventually Washington, DC, where he received a commission in the Union army. During the war, Davis spent much of his time on the Rio Grande frontier working to subdue the southern slave and cotton trade. After the war, he was a member of the 1866 Constitutional Convention and president of the 1869 Constitutional Convention.

Davis, a Radical Republican, is most remembered, though, for his time in the governorship from 1869 to 1874. His time in office, and most events in state affairs from 1869 to 1876, later became known as the most oppressive era in the history of Texas government. Brought along to the office with him were his views, which were in line with the Radical Republican mantra of punishing the South and increasing civil liberties for former slaves and their supporters. Making good use of his expanded appointment powers, he posted many of his close allies to powerful state offices to extend the reach of radical politics.

While in office, Davis succeeded in the implementation of a state police force and reorganizing a militia, the reorganization of the public school system, and higher welfare spending, among many more initiatives. The issue was, much of the revenue for the state came by way of a property tax. The most significant property in the state, up to 1865 at least, was slaves. Without that tax base and no other new primary source of revenue coming into play, budget deficits were faced, with a later increase in taxes being implemented to cover the shortfall. All the measures implemented—and how to pay for them—faced strong opposition from both sides of the political aisle. Despite their differences, both sides were also united in their general opposition to the creation of a strong central government. It became so sorry that in 1873, after former Confederate soldiers and governing officials were refranchised, Davis was voted out of office by a two-to-one margin. Only adding to the hysteria of the era, Davis, in January 1874, refused to vacate his office and used state troops to block access to the statehouse for the newly elected Democratic legislature. Not giving up, the newly elected legislature used tall ladders to get to the second floor of the building, where the legislative floor was, so that they could inaugurate the new administration and officially remove Davis from office.

With Davis removed, a constitutional convention was called in August 1875, and it took place from September 6 until November 24 of that year. The document produced by that convention was voted on by the public on February 15, 1876, passing by a 2.5-to-1 margin. Convention production centered on the provision of a document that would severely limit any future government from functioning smoothly. Most notably, the document created a decentralized state government. In the legislature, a bicameral legislature was created, with an uppe and lower body. For the executive, a true plural form was created that saw many of the most important officials (like the lieutenant governor or attorney general) required to be directly selected by the voting public in statewide elections. Most interestingly, though, were changes to the judiciary and the creation of two courts of last resort, one for civil and another for criminal cases. With the goal of making power as decentralized as possible in mind, additional restrictions were also put into place, such as the requirement for a balanced budget and a plethora of restrictions on how new officials could act while in office. Essentially, using emotions and experiences from the past decades of conflict over control, Texans learned from their past how a strong central government could severely limit their freedoms and did everything possible to ensure that the oppression would never happen again.

The events depicted on the second floor of the museum saw Texas go through many relationships (and stages of them). It seems as if, up to this point, Texas was a part of one country, became its own, joined another, left it, and then got together all over again. Likewise, America left Britain and started its own country, only to deal with a brief separation of half the country. The last quarter of the floor discussed some minor events from the next 60 or so years that got us to the 1936 centennial of the state. Other than images projected onto the wall, this area did not bring much to the table regarding the political history of the state.

After going up the stairs to the third floor, I discovered events that influenced Texas into the 20th century. Texans had found the land useful for their wishes. Most notable of this occurrence is the development of ranchlands throughout, with more well-known ones like the King Ranch in South Texas and the XIT Ranch in the Plains Panhandle, which are, or were, respectively, more significant in size than the US state of Rhode Island. Other than ranching, agriculture was very much prevalent, with rice paddies being developed on the gulf coast, cotton farming in the West, produce in the far South, and timber production in the East, along with a variety of other crops throughout the remainder. Finally, what came from below the ground seemed to have had the most significant impact—"Texas Tea," more commonly known as oil. This product became so prevalent that much of the state economy until the 1980s was based on this commodity, which really brought the state into its own. The only issue is, the exhibits on this floor, while I felt they were of Smithsonian quality, really did not add much to the political history of Texas or the United States in this context. What was left of the floor was reserved for special events and exhibitions that were currently closed off. The last bit of earlier advice from Charity—to go to the LBJ Museum for modern politics—made more sense as I walked around this area. In short, the politics of the state of Texas over time mirror those that were experienced by the country at large, to the point that those histories even became the same at the end.

---

**QUESTIONS TO CONSIDER** REGARDING PARALLEL POLITICAL ACCOUNTS:

1. The first main topic of the chapter displays how the founding of Texas relates to that of the United States as a whole. Please make a timeline of general events that occurred for Texas and the United States and indicate in detail if said political histories indeed are parallel in your opinion; offer information to support your position.

2. The second main topic of the chapter displays, once again, how the founding of Texas relates to that of the United States as a whole. Now, with your initial timeline made, please make a timeline of major events in your life and indicate if the way we establish ourselves in life is relatable to how our state and country were founded and offer information to support your position, in detail.

---

## FIGURE CREDITS

# Section II

## Getting Involved in Government

# Chapter 8

# Getting Involved in Government

# Getting Politically Active

When I woke this morning, I spent a few minutes contemplating where I'd been and what I'd learned thus far on my trek. The Hall of Presidents lesson on what government is, the plane flight back from Florida and geography lesson on what a state comprises, cultural and demographical influences on politics, the relationship between the states and the federal government, and the history of the state of Texas compared to the United States together provided an excellent foundation on which to place further information. Everything I'd seen thus far could be categorized as governing foundations. Not knowing where to turn next, I grabbed my cell phone and made a call. My Uncle Tommy picked up his phone begrudgingly and yelled, "What?"

A bit taken aback due to the demeanor, I replied, "Hi Tommy, it's Champ. Could I follow you around work today?"

He replied, "What and why? Does this relate to that trek of yours your father told me about last week when I was in Houston?"

I replied, "Yes, sir. You are the participation guru last I checked, so I thought I'd give you a call."

Tommy furthered, "Fine, be at my office at 9:00 a.m. and don't ever call me at this hour ever again. Bye and say 'hi' to Charity for me."

The phone clicked off, and I decided to get my day started even though it was only 6:00 a.m. Once in the shower, I thought about Tommy. He runs an Austin-based political rally consulting firm group called Capital Activists. Mostly, he runs different political events and rallies around town for politicians and other various groups. At this point I figured we could hopefully discuss the multiple ways that one could get active in politics beyond joining a political party or getting a job with government somehow. Looking back, I now know that there are a lot more ways to get politically active than what I thought possible when I made that first phone call.

Once out of the shower I did a bit of light reading to pass the time before I left the house at 8:15 a.m. Just before 8:45 a.m., I found myself going northbound on Interstate Highway 35 after State Highway 71 merges into it. After leaving the interstate at Exit 234B, I turned west on to East Sixth Street. Six blocks later, I turned south onto Brazos Street, where two blocks later I turned right into the guest parking area of the Frost Bank Tower[1] garage (figure 8.1). After parking, I went into the lobby of the building on the first floor. From there, I took an elevator up to Tommy's office on the 29th floor of the building. Once out of the elevator, I found Tommy waiting for me in a chair in the lobby, reading a magazine. He remarked at that moment, while standing, "Champ, welcome! How was the rest of your morning?"

---

1   http://frostbanktoweraustin.com

I replied, "Thank you. The drive in went well, but I didn't get any more sleep. How is your morning going?"

Tommy responded, "Quite well, even though you woke me so early. Beyond that, I don't have any major events planned for this week, so I get to do a bit of housekeeping around the office, and, more importantly, show you the participatory political ropes. Lucky for you and your father, giving you a tour is all I can do, seeing as how your dad's actions down Congress Avenue in the state legislature give my staff preparing demonstrations so much to do when they are in session. Regardless, let's go sit down in my conference room over here for a little while to get some of the essential information on the table and in your brain."

About a minute later we were seated around a sizable oak table ready to get going. I asked, "So, what should I know first?"

FIGURE 8.1 Frost Bank Tower in downtown Austin, Texas.

## What Is Participation?

At that moment Tommy took out his iPhone, opened the iTunes App Store, and downloaded a song. With his media player, he started the song. The song's first lines went, "Get up, stand up, stand up for your rights! . . . Get up, stand up, stand up for your rights! . . . Get up, stand up, stand up for your rights! . . . Get up, stand up, don't give up the fight!"

I interjected, with the song still playing in the background, "Why are we listening to a Bob Marley song?"

Tommy replied, after pausing the music, "Well Champ, "Get Up, Stand Up" by Bob Marley and the Wailers[2] is the epitome of getting involved in politics. The song is calling you into action to stand up for your rights no matter what the obstacles. This is what you are doing when getting politically active. Sometimes you are getting active for the rights of others, like when an antiabortionist is protesting outside of an abortion clinic regarding the unborn, such as David Gittrich.[3] Sometimes you are doing so for everyone at large, like Concepción Picciotto, who held a vigil outside of the White House in Washington, DC, to

2   https://www.youtube.com/watch?v=F69PBQ4ZyNw
3   Jonathan Shorman, "David Gittrich, Prominent Kansas Anti-abortion Activist, Dies," *Wichita (KS) Eagle*, October 18, 2017, http://www.kansas.com/news/politics-government/article179474031.html.

encourage our leaders to rid ourselves of nuclear weapons.[4] But for the most part, you are motivated by aspects of your own experience, like Edith Windsor, who fought for her entire life to legally marry her same-sex partner, Thea Spyer.[5] Each, of course, had varied results from their actions. With that stated, participation, in general, is, 'the fact of taking part, as in some action or attempt, in an activity.'[6] Meanwhile, political participation is 'any action that supports or opposes state structures, authorities, and/or decisions regarding the allocation of public goods, among others.'"[7]

I inquired, "So what does participating in the political process do for me? I mean, I shouldn't do something unless I get something out of it, right?"

Tommy, after humming and hawing for a few seconds, continued, "Good point; you shouldn't do something unless you get something out of it, be it a tangible item or that tingly feeling in your heart you get after a good deed. Specifically, though, political participation does quite a lot, but it comes down to a few positive aspects, like fostering stability and order in society by reinforcing the legitimacy of political authority. This offering is in addition to providing a sounding board for public policy debates, deliberations, and discussion by officials due to the voice of the people being heard, not to mention doing so helps you understand the working of and make improvements to transparency of the government. And, most importantly, doing so can directly impact the direction of the country at large. Alternatively, though, doing so may erode society as we know it to be. Think of the work done by British citizens during the Brexit proceedings[8]. The citizens of the United Kingdom voted to leave. Initial reports do show that the British people may rue the day that they decided to leave[9]."

## Levels of Participation

I responded, "Tommy, wait a sec, the people of a country voted to leave a union. Why was this decision not made by the government itself. Does this mean that once you enter politics, you can climb to higher ranks or something?"

---

4  http://prop1.org/conchita
5  http://ediewindsor.com
6  http://www.dictionary.com/browse/participation
7  There are thousands of different definitions for this, this one makes the most sense to me.
8  Kimberly Amadeo, "Brexit Consequences for the U.K., the EU, and the United States." The Balance. .Dash, December 26, 2019. https://www.thebalance.com/brexit-consequences-4062999.
9  Ibid.

Tommy spoke, "Actually, yeah, you can. In his 1985 work, *Political Participation*,[10] Lester Milbrath provides us with three categories, depending on how you choose to get involved politically. Those categories are spectator activities, transitional activities, and gladiatorial activities. Think of these categories as akin to the different divisions of baseball under the helm of the Little League Baseball organization, from Tee Ball to Little League to Senior League Baseball, all the way up to the major leagues.[11] Let's start at the bottom; this is where, more likely than not, most people fall into, those spectator activities. In short, those that fall here go out and vote, encourage others to vote in some form or specific way, have discussions over issues, expose themselves to the issues and stances to take on them, and/or wear a button of some kind to show their support. Your Tee Ball players, so to speak; not professional in any aspect, but still participating as much as they possibly can with their limited abilities and resources. The other two categories above spectators are home to smaller portions of society where, as President Trump puts it, people are either entering or actively involved with 'the swamp,' due to this being where all the political mudslinging goes on. In short, those going with the transitional activities attend political party events, actively support a political party financially, give up their time to volunteer for the party, or provide other resources and, at least, make it a point to contact those who hold party offices to influence them. They are taking an interest by being more than just a voyeur, but they only feel comfortable testing the waters while staying in the shallow end of the pool. Your Senior Leaguers, so to speak, they are well versed in the goings on of baseball but are still not professional. Finally, those in gladiatorial activities either join the political party hierarchy by being the chair of a level of the party or run for office under the party banner, hold fund-raisers for the party, or even actively campaign on behalf of the party, your Major Leaguers, so to speak, due to them getting paid to play the game full time in some capacity for a team or, dare I say, party. Those protesters from before, like the Gittrich fellow, would fall under the transitional banner as they are doing more than voting but not actually joining the government, which would make them a gladiator."

I took a minute here to digest the baseball comparison. Then I suggested, "Everybody plays Tee Ball or Pee Wee football, but very few people go on to play professionally or in one of the other higher classifications, due to any number of items getting in the way, like injuries, fewer teams being available, and the like. In the same way, a lot of people go out and vote, but there are only so many elected offices and party positions to hold, with fewer being available in say Washington, DC, than here in Austin? Also, could we discuss the election process next?"

---

10   Lester Milbrath, *Political Participation* (Chicago: Rand McNally, 1985).
11   https://www.littleleague.org/who-we-are/

## Voting and Elections

Tommy replied, "Champ, you are spot on in that mind-set there. However, for a full explanation of how we vote here in Texas, keep an eye out for the Texas secretary of state's big annual summer voter registration later this week that you should attend, I think, as that specific topic is a discussion for another day, entirely. But, for sanity sake, remember that voting is a 'formal expression of opinion or choice, either positive or negative, made by an individual or body of individuals,'[12] while an election is 'the selection of a person or persons for office by voting.'[13] In a nutshell, voting is informal and could be on almost anything, whereas an election is formal and is only used when hiring people for a job by voting. The prior could be something as simple as what toppings to have on your family's pizza or simply where to go out to eat for dinner, while the latter is picking someone to decide where your tax dollars are spent for an extended period. However, in both cases, you are still casting a vote, or the expression of your choice, for or against someone or something.[14] It's the most common way for you to have your say, for lack of a better term."

## Active and Passive Participation

Tommy then furthered after a pause, "In the same work we talked about before by Lester Milbrath,[15] the various political participation methods themselves could be categorized as active, an activity involving physical effort and action,[16] and passive, an activity not involving visible reaction or active participation,[17] due to differences in time needed, energy allotted, and means available when partaking in the activity. You can go back and sort all the activities into one or the other, but depending on how you chronicle the activity, you could go one way or the other on some. Therefore, going forward, when we discuss or experience each activity today, I am just going to give you the definition, or the formal statement of the meaning or significance of a word, phrase, idiom, etc.,[18] of the activity in question in addition to what the activity does and the goal of participating in that activity, alongside any other relevant information. The question is, where to begin. There are so many options and so many possibilities, but what are we doing right now?"

---

12    https://www.dictionary.com/browse/voting
13    https://www.dictionary.com/browse/election
14    There are literally hundreds of different definitions for these terms, these makes the most sense to me for the purposes here.
15    Milbrath, *Political Participation*.
16    http://www.dictionary.com/browse/active
17    http://www.dictionary.com/browse/passive?s=t
18    http://www.dictionary.com/browse/definition

I replied, "Having a discussion (figure 8.2)?"

Tommy continued, "Very good. Voting is important due to you having a formal say in the political decision at hand, but discussing the issues beforehand by having, say, an important issue–themed discussion is just as important due to the knowledge gained by doing so. Nothing is better than a fully informed voter to work with on a project. Partaking in a discussion helps you and others develop your opinions. This ideal is important, as you should not support something unless you can effectively support it. People love nothing more than shooting you down when you fly unprepared for the task at hand. Regardless, discussions can occur in the form of debates, or regulated

FIGURE 8.2    "Discussing the War in a Paris Café" – a scene from the brief interim between the Battle of Sedan and Siege of Paris during the Franco-Prussian War.

discussion of a proposition between two matched sides or candidates that people observe,[19] or having a town hall meeting, which is an event at which a public official or political candidate addresses an audience by answering questions posed by individual members.[20] Funny thing though, at these events that I help put on by making room and catering reservations as part of my work for the company, more commonly than not, people just demand answers from governing officials or those running for office about issues that they are concerned with or are being affected by. See the protests at Republican official's town hall meetings by those who may lose their health care if Republican legislators ever succeed at dismantling the Patient Protection and Affordable Care Act, where they just showed up and started shouting the legislators down, forcing them to stop the event cold turkey, as an example.[21] Another form of discussion here is people appearing on a TV talk show to discuss an issue, provide commentary, or even just deliver a statement. My favorite, though, is getting together with a group of buddies at a coffee shop or a bar, just sitting around a table hashing out our differences or coming to terms on a matter one way or the other. I guarantee you that if you

19    http://www.dictionary.com/browse/debate?s=t
20    https://www.merriam-webster.com/dictionary/town%20hall
21    Lauren C. Williams, "Angry Protesters Are Swarming Republican Town Hall Meetings over Trump's Agenda," ThinkProgress, February 18, 2017, https://thinkprogress.org/protestors-fight-trump-gop-at-town-halls-9afa11922ed5.

go to a McDonald's®[22] on any given day at around seven or so in the morning, you will find a bunch of elderly gentlemen just shooting the proverbial breeze with one another on anything and everything."

I had no idea up to that point that just discussing the day's events was so important. While pondering, Tommy poked at me with a five-dollar bill and stated, "Go get a snack from the convenience store in the lobby and a copy of the newspaper for me. You are probably famished, and I need to take care of some things. On the way, though, go to a website called Reddit[23] to see how people your age today share information by posting to message boards to reach consensus on issues. It's kind of like when you go and post on Facebook® and Twitter to get your points across to society at large via posting on your wall or feeds alongside posting on those of others or some initiatives, page,[24] but more discursive."

## Ways to Communicate with Public Officials

About ten minutes later, I found myself walking back into the conference room with a cold Dr. Pepper®[25] and that day's edition of the *Austin American-Statesman*.[26] Couldn't help thinking that Tommy was right—the Reddit® website did indeed have a plethora of useful information to be had from various postings on literally everything. I pulled out a chair and sat down. Tommy took a second to gather his thoughts, then stated, "Champ, open up the front section and tell me what you see on any random page."

I followed the command by opening the paper. To my surprise, I found a series of ads and spoke, "What's the point?"

Tommy rebutted, "Well the ads are how the papers make money beyond subscriptions to be able to continue to fund the paper, but what do you see beyond the ads?"

While blushing and chuckling to myself, I replied, "Yeah, but there is lots and lots of text, some photos, and a random cartoon here or there in the paper, but what does all this add up to?"

Tommy continued, "Okay, Champ. The main item that you will see in any newspaper is the stories of the day written by the writers of the newspaper on sports, big events, and the minutia of the time, called articles. Beyond that are special sections investigating more long-term stories,[27] most notably that of Spotlight with the *Boston Globe* and its series of pieces on the

---

22  https://www.mcdonalds.com/us/en-us.html
23  https://www.reddit.com
24  https://www.facebook.com/help/333140160100643/; https://support.twitter.com/articles/15367
25  https://www.drpepper.com/en
26  http://www.statesman.com
27  http://www.statesman.com/news

Catholic priest abuse scandal over the last decades.[28] Therefore, on the one hand, newspapers (figure 8.3) serve to inform you of the major happenings of the day. However, if you look at the second or third page of the front section of any newspaper, or under the tab of the associated newspaper's web page,[29] you will see a series of items called editorials, or an article in a newspaper or other periodical or on a website, presenting the opinion of the publisher, writer, or editor.[30] These editorials could come in the form of

FIGURE 8.3   Protesters used newspapers to keep up to date on events occurring around them during the protesting.

letters to the editor, general essays on a subject by a reader, or, my favorite, after comparing the three, editorial cartoons—more commonly referred to as political cartoons. These cartoons use symbolism, captions and labels, analogies, irony, and exaggeration to comedically get their points across as to why something that is occurring in politics is good or bad for us going forward. Each of these three methods is used by citizens to go out and voice their opinion without actually having to leave their homes or find an audience to speak with, yet be able to get a fairly large promotion and readership of their stance on an issue."

I interjected, "So this is the La-Z-Boy®[31] method then?"

Tommy nodded his head in agreement with discouragement, but then posed a poignant question: "So, what is something that people of your generation have probably never done before that mine may constantly have?"

I replied by stating, "Write an actual check?"

Tommy rebutted, "Close, because for this next one you have to write something. Keep guessing though!"

I listed off, "Use a landline telephone or watch cable television or mail an actual letter via the US Postal Service."[32]

---

28   https://apps.bostonglobe.com/spotlight/tips; Editors, "The Story behind the 'Spotlight' Movie," *Boston Globe*, accessed March 20, 2019, http://www.bostonglobe.com/arts/movies/spotlight-movie.

29   http://www.statesman.com/opinion

30   http://www.dictionary.com/browse/editorial?s=t

31   https://www.la-z-boy.com

32   https://www.usps.com

FIGURE 8.4   At the Second Annual Bay Area Human Rights Conference on February 28, 2009, students from the Amador Valley Human Rights Club write letters to their senators to urge them to support taking action to end the Darfur genocide.

Tommy continued, "Not a bad list there of how the times are changing, but let's focus on the last one you listed off. Writing your elected officials a letter, or a written or printed communication addressed to a person or organization,[33] is still very important (figure 8.4). This method formally communicates your opinion to the official. This choice is a good method for effectiveness at communicating your opinion, as despite being much, much slower to get to the official the letter is addressed to, once the letter is there, it's there. It can't be deleted at the click of a mouse, put in a junk folder and forgotten about, or ignored, as the letter takes up physical space on a desk somewhere, meaning it must be dealt with if the official wants to keep the image that they are on top of things by keeping a clean office. Now, to bring us up into the 21st century regarding communicating with your representative, many representatives have a way for you to go to their websites and leave a message for them."[34]

## Service Clubs

I thought for a second that there are a lot of ways to communicate with our public officials—I kind of wonder, though, what they do with all that data. I made a mental note to ask about that the next time I speak with one of those officials. After a brief pause, Tommy noted, "Even though it's only 11 o'clock now, we can go ahead and head somewhere for some lunch and get started looking at the activities that would require you to get more physically active. Let's go."

Once downstairs, we found Tommy's car just outside the main entrance of the tower in his reserved parking spot on the street. Once we were going, Tommy spoke: "We are now on our way to the weekly meeting of my Rotary Club.[35] We are officially known as the Rotary

---

33   http://www.dictionary.com/browse/letter?s=t
34   https://www.whitehouse.gov/contact
35   https://www.rotary.org/en/about-rotary

Club of Austin-Southwest.[36] We meet on Tuesdays for lunch around noon at the Red Lobster®
on South Lamar.[37] We'll be there in a few minutes."

In getting to the restaurant, we immediately turned south on to Congress Avenue for about half a mile before turning west onto Baton Springs Boulevard. After three-quarters of a mile, we turned south onto South Lamar Boulevard. Two and a half miles later, we turned left into the parking lot. After parking, we walked up to the door, and the hostess, Melody, let us in and stated, "Welcome back, Tommy! Here for Rotary again?"

Tommy replied, "You betcha, Melody! Is our sergeant at arms in his position yet?"

Melody replied, while wagging her finger scoldingly, "You'll have to see for yourself."

After walking down the hall to the left of the hostess stand for a few feet and taking the turn, I saw a person who I would learn is the president of the club at the door of the restaurant's group meeting room, greeting people. Seeing Tommy, he said, "Tommy, welcome to the meeting today. Sue is sick, so I am doing the hosting duties today for her. Who is the guest you have with you here?"

FIGURE 8.5 The Rotary Club Charity Shop.

Tommy replied, "Well Bob, this is my nephew Champ. He is learning a few things about the government this summer. So, I brought him with me today so that you could inform him of the value of a political participation method called service clubs (figure 8.5)."

While shaking Tommy's hand, Bob replied, "Tommy, you go get your button and then watch the door for me. In the meantime, I will fill Champ in on the pertinent information."

Once Tommy had gone into the room to get his badge, Bob advised, "Now Champ, service or social clubs are organizations with the main function of social contact."

I asked, "So how does all of this work? I mean, what's the purpose of these clubs as it relates to politics, I guess? Do we eat for the cure or something?"

Bob replied, "Well, in general, we do first have a meal for about 20 minutes, followed by club announcements and, seeing as how many of us are leaders of the community in various fashions, we each mention events that are going on that may be of interest to our fellows

36  http://www.rotaryaustin-southwest.org
37  https://www.redlobster.com

that you may not hear about otherwise, or those that may need volunteers so that they may go help out in some way that we know of based on our jobs and the like. As an example, the mayor of Sunset Valley is a member, and he always keeps us up to date on the big events coming up in our part of the greater Austin area. This is important, as often those events will impact you in some way regardless of your interest in them. Oh, lastly, beyond hearing speakers and eating a meal together, we go out and provide volunteer support to various charity groups or nonprofits around the city as a group. Our big fund-raiser is the Rotary Club of Austin-Southwest Charity Golf Tournament each April,[38] and we have smaller initiatives that occur throughout the year, like our Dictionary Project, coat drive, and—my favorite—the Easter Egg Hunt at our YMCA down the street."[39]

Tommy, who had returned to us, interjected, "Champ, let's go sit at the back table and get eating. We'll be starting shortly, and I want to speak on two last things while we're here. Thanks, Bob!"

Bob replied, "Anytime, Tommy!"

Once we were seated, Tommy continued, "There is a fine line we cannot cross at these meetings. Simply put, discussing politics is officially non licet conversation. Guests can be political figures who discuss the programs being put on by their associated agencies and how their group's actions may be affecting us in some form or fashion; the speaker just can't give a stump speech for funding or electoral support."

After taking a few bites of my shrimp alfredo pasta, I asked, "So, what is the other thing?"

Tommy noted, "Beyond what Bob told you about earlier, a lot of us here, myself included, attend meetings to get something called social capital, or the interpersonal relationships, institutions, and other social assets of a society or group that can be used to gain an advantage in various avenues.[40] Essentially, we hope to accomplish goals, political in your case, through built relationships. Bob did a great job a few minutes ago on that by telling you about the club and what goes on here. Developing friendships as a kid helps you get a better social life, have more opportunities, and simply get out more. The same thing occurs here, but instead of help in getting that cute guy or gal's number so you can ask them out, you are hoping to get them to donate to your event, be able to meet someone important to help put on your event, or even advance your career in some way. Easier put, we just work to get some numbers to call in case of an emergency. Make some friends now, you hear me?"

I nodded in agreement as Bob rang the bell and began the meeting.

---

38  http://www.rotaryaustin-southwest.org/page/2017-golf-sponsors
39  http://www.rotaryaustin-southwest.org/sitepage/service-projects
40  http://www.dictionary.com/browse/social-capital

## Political Apparel

After the meal and presentation, at around 1:00 p.m., Tommy decided that it would be prudent of us to attend a meeting of the Austin City Council. After we were in the car, we left the parking lot and proceeded north on Lamar Boulevard. Just after crossing Bluebonnet Lane, on Congress Avenue, we almost hit a jaywalker. We only missed him thanks to being able to turn into the parking lot of an old auto-repair shop. After collecting himself, Tommy, still breathing heavily, advised, "Okay Champ, we have the chance here for a participation option that I was going to tell you about later, but now it is awkwardly prudent to do so. Look back at the guy back there who we almost hit. You can still see him running in and out of traffic behind us in the rearview mirror—crazy. Take a long look at him; specifically, at his apparel. He is wearing a shirt, hat, and button combo that indicates to others his political views, which is the point of putting on those clothes. Political apparel is any piece of clothing with a political statement on it. Beyond the shirt, hat, and buttons you see right now, you can also wear socks, watches, bibs, rings, hoodies, ribbons, and, tattoos, among many other options that are out there to support the cause. Accordingly, Champ, even you can make a statement by simply getting dressed in the morning. Oh, here's a shirt for you to have as a souvenir that I got laying around in here."

I could only balk at Tommy when I read the shirt; it had "Trump 2020: Keep America Great!" emblazoned on the front. I said, "Come on, man. I can't support anyone yet. I haven't even spoken to someone with one of the political parties yet, other than my dad. Let's go to the city council meeting already. Besides, get me one of his hats (figure 8.6). You know I'm a hat man, right? You all right, though, after that near fender bender?"

Tommy, I think, nodded his A-OK status but said, "It never hurts to get started campaigning early. The early bird does get the worm."

FIGURE 8.6    Close-up of then candidate-Trump in a Make America Great Again hat.

## Political Advertisements

Going forward, to avoid any future near misses, I decided that I might help keep an additional set of eyes on traffic and told Tommy as much. Tommy, though, took the initiative to introduce an additional form of political participation that is commonly seen on roadways. Tommy iterated, as we were waiting at the Barton Springs Road light, "I am all right, thanks for checking in back there. But since you are looking out the window so fervently over there now, keep an eye out for the various advertisements, or paid notices that tell people about a product or service,[41] that you may see out on the road. For political purposes, these advertisements hope to get you to support a candidate or even vote against an initiative. There are three types of political advertisements that you can see—the only difference being their size. The smallest are found on the rear of cars and are called bumper stickers; these are 3¾

FIGURE 8.7   Candidates' posters on display in front of a polling station in Ward 1, Manchester, New Hampshire, Feb. 9, 2016. (Photo: K. Gypson / VOA).

inches tall by 11½ inches wide. The mid-sized one is yard signs, which are commonly 18 inches tall by 24 inches wide (figure 8.7). The largest, though, are billboards, which are 14 feet tall and 48 feet wide. The nice thing is, though, they all have the same purpose: to get the candidate's or group's initiative message out to the people. The key to making them work the best is the requirement for a short and sweet message. This is due to you only having a second or so to look at them while on the highway. They may be distracting to most, but what better thing to do in bumper-to-bumper traffic than be educated about relevant civil matters of the day? Well, also I guess, the price tag will be dramatically different for each, and you could get the sign in any size you want. Those three from before are just the most common."

FIGURE 8.8   Anti-Obama Bumper Stickers.

While we were pulling through the intersection, I read aloud a rather impressive set of bumper stickers (figure 8.8) that read, in order, "TIME FOR ANOTHER TEA PARTY," followed by "I'LL KEEP MY MONEY, YOU KEEP THE CHANGE," and ending with, "WHERE'S THE BIRTH CERTIFICATE?" There was also a taped Bernie Sanders slogan in the rear window of the car that read "FEEL THE BERN!" (figure 8.9).

Tommy chimed, "Those stickers are in response to the 'He Won Again' button the guy who we almost hit

---

41   https://dictionary.cambridge.org/us/dictionary/english/advertisement

earlier was wearing, as not everyone agrees with the current president's policy plans for the country. Oh, well."

I thought aloud, "These advertisements can be very entertaining, can't they, and not to mention, they are everywhere. Back in my subdivision in Houston, Copperfield, there aren't any signs allowed, and I don't remember seeing any of them en masse, I believe, due to deed restrictions."[42]

Tommy noted, "Deed restrictions are great for keeping out derelict properties. We'll be at city hall in about two minutes. Keep your guard up now, ya hear!"

FIGURE 8.9   "Feel the Bern" Slogan of Bernie Sanders for President 2016.

## Public Service in Action

After crossing the Colorado River, on Lamar Street, we made the U-turn that takes traffic down to West Cesar Chavez Street. We then turned left for five blocks. We then turned north onto Lavaca Street and parked at the public garage on the first block to the right. After leaving the garage, we walked across Lavaca Street to arrive at Austin City Hall, located at 301 West Second Street, at about 1:45 p.m. We then made our way to the city council chambers on the second floor. Once standing in the aisle on the right side of the very crowded hall, Tommy advised, "For us, this meeting is all about seeing the political participation method of public service in action. People who provide public services are known colloquially as public servants, or people who hold government positions by election or appointment.[43] People in these positions include people you know of, from firefighters, even the volunteer ones, to school board members, mayors, police officers, the person who helped you get your driver's license, and, my most feared, jury members in court. Don't forget about members of the armed forces. Older citizens, I find, are most often found serving in these positions, as they have more time and do not need to be paid in many cases for their efforts, making them perfect candidates to volunteer here. Let's see what is going on here at the meeting."

During the meeting, some exciting events occurred that were relevant to my trek. After some opening remarks, a group seated toward the front rose and shouted in unison, repeatedly, "S-O-S, save our springs, now!"

---

42   http://www.copperfield.org/documents.php
43   http://www.dictionary.com/browse/public-servant

I interjected, "What are they shouting? The city council can't be polluting the water by talking, can they?"

Tommy explained, "I had a few things planned for later, on this topic, but here goes. Those people shouting are putting into motion one of the four ways to practice the art of civil disobedience, or the refusal to obey governmental demands or commands, especially as a nonviolent and usually collective means of forcing concessions from the government.[44] The goal here is to disagree with the government and let them know. Acts of civil disobedience vary in three different ways. This includes the presence or lack of violence, vocality levels, and what exactly it is that you are doing in the process. This group here is protesting, which is an expression or declaration of objection, disapproval, or dissent, often in opposition to something a person is powerless to prevent or avoid.[45] Protesting is known to be nonviolent and has people get together in a group to show strong disapproval of something by chanting and walking in circles with large signs. It can be kind of annoying to the people they are yelling at, like the council members there, but it is effective at getting their point across. One of the more famous protests is the Professional Air Traffic Controllers Organization that saw more than 12,000 members of the union walk off the job in 1981 only to be fired two days later by President Ronald Reagan for not going back to work[46]".

I interjected, "Is it just me, or does this seem like there is the potential for something more to come of this than just chanting?"

Tommy replied, "Yeah it does, but give me a minute, I think the group is now going to give a more concise statement."

After a few minutes the protestors finally sat down, and a woman from the Save Our Springs Alliance[47] spoke during the "statements from the public" section of the agenda: "Nothing can be more important than to protect our water supplies and their high quality here in Austin. We use it to clean ourselves, nourish our thirst, and entertain ourselves by swimming in the nearby Barton Springs Pool[48] to cool off during the hot summer season. The population is ever growing, and we must do something about it now.[49] Last year the population growth was over 5.1 percent, alone, in the Austin Metropolitan area. I now hold

---

44    https://www.merriam-webster.com/dictionary/civil%20disobedience

45    http://www.dictionary.com/browse/protest

46    Kathleen Schalch, "1981 Strike Leaves Legacy for American Workers," NPR, August 3, 2006, http://www.npr.org/templates/story/story.php?storyId=5604656.

47    https://www.sosalliance.org

48    https://austintexas.gov/department/barton-springs-pool

49    John Egan, "Austin's Booming Population Growth Blows past the Rest of Texas," CultureMap Austin, March 23, 2017, http://austin.culturemap.com/news/city-life/03-22-17-austin-population-growth-census-report.

in my hand a petition[50] in hopes of appealing to our authorities in charge of our supplies and bringing the water to our homes for some action—water usage, in this case. We are making this appeal before the council to get city policy more aligned with the highest of water conservation strategies and cleanliness standards available, even more so than those of the Environmental Protection Agency[51] and our state's own Texas Commission on Environmental Quality.[52] Overall, we would like to have further reduced pumping from the Edwards Aquifer so that our springs will flow for the ages!"

Tommy interjected, "Stepping away from civil disobedience for a moment, the woman who spoke brought up a petition (figure 8.10), which is but one form of political participation called legal action. Legal actions are judicial proceedings brought by one party against another.[53] That petition could be used to get a measure on the ballot to require the city to use stricter water standards for the area going forward. More directly, though, you could just sue the city by filing a lawsuit, which is a legal proceeding between two parties in the courts, instituted by one party to compel another to do something, regardless of whether the action is based on law or equity.[54] Regardless, you are seeking to force a response by the opposite party to your concerns."

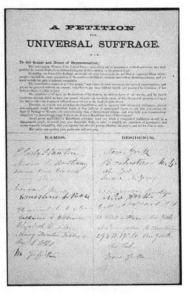

FIGURE 8.10    Petition of E. Cady Stanton, Susan B. Anthony, Lucy Stone, and others asking for an amendment of the Constitution that shall prohibit the several States from disenfranchising any of their citizens on the ground of sex.

It was at that point the protesters from before began their chant again. Tommy whispered in my ear, "Let's hope this doesn't turn into a riot, as rioting is a noisy, violent public disorder caused by a group or crowd of persons, as by a crowd protesting another group, in the streets.[55] Compared to protesting, there is an increase in the vocality of the group and the actual use of violence. Think of the supporters you see here with pitchforks, instead of signs, that are being thrown. I DON'T LIKE IT! STUFF GETS DESTROYED! One of the most notorious riots in American history occurred in 1992 following the not guilty verdict of four police

50    http://www.dictionary.com/browse/petition?s=t
51    https://www.epa.gov/standards-water-body-health
52    https://www.tceq.texas.gov/waterquality/standards/WQ_standards_intro.html
53    https://www.merriam-webster.com/dictionary/legal%20action
54    https://legal-dictionary.thefreedictionary.com/lawsuit
55    http://www.dictionary.com/browse/riot

FIGURE 8.11   Images from the 1992 L.A. Riots.

officers who were on trial for the beating of Rodney King during a traffic stop.[56] The events lasted for nearly six days, officially killing 63 people, and caused billions in property damage (figure 8.11), which led to citywide curfews and the US Marines[57] being called in to restore order."

I was in utter disbelief at the extent of the incidents and asked, "Is there a safer form of civil disobedience, or do you just have to get up and in people's faces to make some changes happen?"

Tommy motioned that we should go and mentioned, "That's our next two stops, and we'll be outdoors to liven up and get us some fresh air."

## Nonviolent Protest

Once we were back in Tommy's car, we exited the garage back onto Lavaca Street. We then went north for 17 blocks, followed by one block west on Martin Luther King Boulevard, then turned north on Guadalupe street for four more blocks. We then turned left on to 22nd Street and parked on the left in the lot just after Nueces Street. We then walked east toward the University of Texas at Austin campus. After we walked across Guadalupe Street and a block farther north, Tommy said, "Look to the east here. This is the university's West Mall. It serves as the university's official Free Speech Zone. These zones are places on university campuses around the country where many of the actions that we have seen earlier today can all take place. These zones are important, as protests held in a classroom would prevent the class from occurring, so people wanting to reach students must reserve space to talk here. These spaces are also quite controversial, as they are believed to be a violation of several First Amendment rights due to their speech and assembly being somewhat restricted to a sole place on campus. Now look over there in the distance."

Tommy and I stood and observed something that he explained was called a peace vigil. It was nothing more than a group of people just standing around in silence with lit candles in their hands. The group also had signs on the ground that read "S-O-S, Save Our Springs," so I figured that they were in coordination with the protest that we had just observed going

---

56   Los Angeles Times Staff, "The L.A. Riots: 25 Years Later," *Los Angeles Times*, April 26, 2017, http://timelines.latimes.com/los-angeles-riots.

57   http://www.marines.mil

on over at City Hall. I concluded to myself here by mumbling, "A peace vigil is the silent, nonviolent form of civil disobedience due to everyone just sitting around letting your displays to do the talking. More importantly, the action is obviously at the opposite end of the activist scale from rioting."

When we were walking away, Tommy notified me that "the longest-running vigil in the American context ended just three years ago back in 2015. A woman by the name of Concepción Piccotto and her group called Peace House, that I casually mentioned earlier today, spent 35 years of her life, yes 35, in Lafayette Park, just across Pennsylvania Avenue from the White House in DC (figure 8.12), advocating for the nuclear disarmament of the US arsenal."[58]

FIGURE 8.12    White House Peace Vigil.

When we were back in the car, Tommy said, "Let's go get a shake."

I spent the next 15 minutes in afternoon traffic, pondering what Tommy was up to in his preparations. There had been a small, silent chuckle at the end of his last statement, so I was suspicious. After going ten blocks or so, I think, farther north on Guadalupe Street, we turned into the parking lot of a small diner. TV crews were everywhere, and people were standing around looking through the windows of the diner. We joined in and observed the events. Tommy indicated, "Champ, look here. Those people there, my clients, all dressed in the blue tie-dye outfits are performing a sit-in, which is another form of civil disobedience that sees a person or group enter a place and refuse to leave until certain demands have been agreed to.[59] It is the same as the peace vigil that we just left, but their actions do the talking to get the point across, rather than their visual displays."

I interrupted, "Why are they doing it, though?"

Tommy replied, "It is part of the water protests that we saw a while ago at city hall. The Save Our Springs group hired me to help coordinate their activities so that they could get

58    Bill Chappell, "Longtime White House Protester Dies, after Vigil That Started in 1981," NPR, January 26, 2016, http://www.npr.org/sections/thetwo-way/2016/01/26/464420101/longtime-white-house-protester-dies-after-vigil-that-started-in-1981.

59    https://dictionary.cambridge.org/us/dictionary/english/sit-in

their point across and not worry about the logistics of getting to and fro. For their sit-in here, they are arguing that restaurants giving away free water is bad for the aquifer, which is any geological formation containing water. They don't want the restaurant to give away free water, as they believe that if you charge people for water, they will use less of the liquid. Either way, if the restaurant makes the water not free, they will leave. My group over there in the black vans brought them and will take them away when they feel that they have made their point. No more than three hours left, though, as that is all that they paid me for my group's services. Let's go back to my office. I got some ice cream there that will do the trick for some energy, seeing as how the place is not in service for the time being. For an example of this concept in action, in the big bigger picture, though, think of the work done by activists during the Woolworth lunch counter sit-ins where they refused to leave until they were served after not being done so due to the color of their skin.[60]"

Another example of a protest in this neck of the woods that doesn't really fit into any of the categories seen here, think of the work done by Rosa Parks when she refused to give up her seat to a white man to protest the segregationist policies of the bus company; four days later the Montgomery, Alabama, bus boycott began"[61].

I asked, "Wait, are you helping put on the peace vigil, and the protest, as well?"

Tommy replied, "Yep, that's part of the job. Sometimes I am helping build the stage and getting speakers; other times my employees just bring people to the event, so the group can just worry about making their point. It's a dirty job, but somebody's got to do it."

On the way back to the Frost Bank Tower, I spent some time pondering the benefits of this career choice, as putting on events would be quite fun. Once again in his reserved spot, Tommy said, "On second thought, I have some work to do. We'll pick this up another day, as there is one other form of political participation you need to learn about, and that is something called lobbying, but that is an activity that requires a day in and of itself, like voting in elections. See you later and keep an eye out for cops.

I began to get out of Tommy's car. Just as I was standing up, I stuck my head back in the car and went, "Hold up, who pays for all of this?"

Tommy replied, looking exhausted, "You do, of course. Maybe not you directly for every little thing, but people like you do who support the cause, the candidate, the program, etc. You and others make so-called political contributions, a voluntary gift (as of money or service or ideas) made to some worthwhile cause, politician, political campaign, or a political

---

60  "Sitting for Justice: Woolworth's Lunch Counter." Woolworth's Lunch Counter - Separate Is Not Equal. Smithsonian National Museum of American History Behring Center. Accessed January 13, 2020. https://americanhistory.si.edu/brown/history/6-legacy/freedom-struggle-2.html.

61  History.com Editors, "Montgomery Bus Boycott," February 3, 2010, http://www.history.com/topics/black-history/montgomery-bus-boycott.

party to show direct support of an endeavor of theirs.[62] The Save Our Springs group took donations and used it to pay for my services. In other cases, your tax dollars pay for your congressman or congresswoman to read your letters, or at least an office staffer to do so. In others, your subscription to the newspaper keeps the publisher afloat to print your letters. It all comes back to your wallet. If you don't want something to happen, you must kill it by draining it of resources, that is, not giving it money or attention. Have a good night and say hi to Charity for me."

## Ways to Get Politically Active

It took me about an hour in late afternoon traffic to reach Charity's house in the Lost Pines neighborhood just outside of the city. When I walked in the door, Charity, who was off for the afternoon, came up and gave me a big hug. We then walked up the stairs to the guest bedroom. Just before the door, Charity asked, "So what did you explore today?"

I replied, "Today was a very politically active day. Tommy and I traveled around Austin and learned about the different forms of political participation. The forms of political participation range from items that can be done without leaving the house to forms that take place right in the heart of government in Texas. It appears I need to pick a team to support and get out there to support them for the best politically active experience. Protecting water supplies might also be a good place to get started. What did you do?"

Charity replied, "Not a lot, I went in to work this morning and finished up a few exhibits at the museum. I then came home early and cooked dinner. Work and travel always make me hungry. Let me know if you need anything, and have a good night. Do you know what you are doing tomorrow?"

I replied by stating, "Nope, I'll just wake up and see what happens."

Charity then went downstairs to finish something else she was working on. I thought to go and eat some dinner, but as soon as I put my things down, the text app on my phone buzzed. Picking it up, I read, "Little bro, follow this link, night!"

I clicked the link, my phone's web browser opened, and I came across a CNN article that brought to light 25 ways to get politically active no matter your political affiliation.[63] When reading, a few other options stood out from what I had seen before. This list included what I would refer to as odds and ends. One of the simpler ones, viewing government in action, Tommy and I had been doing when we sat in on the city council meeting. Another

---

62   https://www.vocabulary.com/dictionary/political%20contribution

63   A. J. Willingham, "25 Ways to Be Politically Active (whether You Lean Left or Right)," CNN, January 23, 2017, http://www.cnn.com/2016/11/15/politics/ways-to-be-more-politically-active-trnd/index.html.

interesting one was to plant a victory garden so that we could be self-sufficient and not drain resources away from the troops, or wean ourselves off oil by growing olives to use the olive oil to power our cars. My favorites required attendance at either a summer camp or the theater. The Young America's Foundation holds retreats to learn about the benefits of conservatism at the ranch owned by President Reagan in California.[64] Or the next time that I head to New York City, I should take in the musical *Hamilton* due to the show being a bastion of political theater, the term denoting "theatre productions used for political purposes, usually as part of a campaign or movement, sometimes as part of the work of a political party."[65] I guess they all help somehow in the bigger picture to make change. I'm going to go change and sleep.

---

64  http://www.yaf.org/events/?filter_category=reagan-ranch-events&filter_site=
65  http://www.hamiltonbroadway.com; http://www.dramaonlinelibrary.com/genres/political-theatre-iid-2514

**QUESTIONS TO CONSIDER** REGARDING OPTIONS FOR POLITICAL PARTICIPATION:

1. The first main topic of the chapter discusses who you can be an advocate for when getting politically active. Please identify those groups, the ones you feel you should be active for when participating, and why, in detail.

2. The second main topic of the chapter defines political participation and what participating does for you. Please write down that definition, explain what participating does for you, and indicate whether you have ever been politically active. Explain why or why not in detail.

3. The third main topic of the chapter discusses the different levels at which you may participate politically. Please identify what those levels are and consist of you doing, the level that you would like to join, and changes needed in your life to achieve that level, in detail.

4. The fourth main topic of the chapter discusses voting and elections. Please define those terms, provide examples of both from your life, and explain in detail why they are good examples of both.

5. The fifth main topic of the chapter discusses active and passive participation. Please identify what the difference is and explain in detail why one would be better than the other to participate in to get your point across when participating politically.

6. The final main topic of the chapter goes into detail on the various ways that an individual could get politically active. Please select your favorite option, define that option, indicate what the option does for you, and state the goal when taking that action, alongside what issue you would choose to act on using that method.

# Chapter 9

# Elections and the Candidates

# Who Is Needed to Run a Campaign?

I remember watching the returns from the 2016 general election for president of the United States. Throughout the night, multiple people from the campaign made speeches onstage. Reporters were set up to cover the twists and turns of the night as they emerged. Speakers onstage then went on to speak directly to the reporters, and so on and so forth, on how they played a role in the candidate getting to that point in the campaign, I assume to ensure their 15 minutes of fame were achieved. Until today, I had not put much effort into realizing how each of those people onstage related to one another, or even if they did, throughout the process of going through a campaign for public office, nor how much of an actual campaign the events leading up to that night were in total.

Yesterday, my Uncle Tommy had begun the process of informing me on the ways to get involved in politics while going to his Rotary Club meeting, visiting Austin City Hall, and other politically related locations around the city of Austin. With him being the political consultant that he is, I knew that there had to be more to the process that he could share than what could fit in one day. Surprise, surprise, while on my way home from my tour, he sent me a text to meet him again at his office the next day. His message stated, "Get ready for a behind-the-scenes tour of a real, live election campaign." Accordingly, for today, the goal was to introduce me to the process one would need to take to run for and, hopefully, win a public office—a step in the political process, which is the bulk of his other day job, beyond lobbying, running campaigns.

Unlike last time, I arrived a bit earlier at Tommy's office, close to 8:30 a.m. He was waiting for me this time in his conference room, reading some materials about the changing demographics of Texas. Once I sat down, we started the basic jibber-jabber about how I was taking in the various methods to participate that I learned about the prior day. He was especially interested in the fact that my favorite way to do so was rioting, due to the rarity of people liking that method. To begin our discussion on the heart of today's matter, I got around to asking, "So what is a campaign?"

Tommy replied, "Well, Champ, a campaign is 'a connected series of operations designed to bring about a particular result,'[1] which, in the case of today's proceedings, is getting a person elected to political office."

I remarked, "If I wanted to run for office and start my campaign, where might a good place to start be?"

In response, Tommy indicated, "Well, Champ, the first step for any individual seeking to run for office is simply deciding to run. In any case, there are friends and family in the background urging someone to do so and sometimes telling them not to do so, not to mention

---

1   https://www.merriam-webster.com/dictionary/campaign

people jilted from other avenues providing their pressures to do so. For a local city council or school board position, the decision to do so might simply come down to the person who will be running saying, 'I'll do it!' This decision is done over a couple of beers at the from time to time, sometimes even over a bar bet, I might add. I'm thinking of your dad and his job down the road from us here now. From there, the rest is history. For higher offices, like the presidency, the decision to run is more of a group effort. For an example of what I mean by that, answer me this: Who is Nick Fury?"

I responded, "The leader of the Avengers?"

Tommy responded, "What did he set out to do with the main heroes of the Marvel Universe?"[2]

I replied, "He gathered them together to fight crime and the like in that universe?"

Tommy furthered, "Exactly, for these bigger positions you have to be like Nick Fury and build your own Avengers! For now, let's call them your exploratory committee, or 'an organization established to help determine whether a potential candidate should run for an elected office.[3] More importantly, once the campaign begins, they become campaign staffers. Finally, at some point, they may advise the candidate to throw in the towel and drop out of the race due to poor performances at campaign events, poor polling numbers, or even health concerns that may arise. On larger campaigns, there are roughly eight, at least in my opinion, major individuals whose opinions you must consider before the potential candidate makes a decision, granted, depending on circumstances various personnel roles can be expanded or further delegated to keep costs in order. For example, in the pole position is me, the campaign manager. I am the person who oversees the personnel in charge of the various major aspects of a campaign for a candidate so that they may concentrate on getting their message out to the public, attending events, and swaying their hopeful future constituents' votes in their favor. Regarding the exploratory stage of the campaign, I would be the one gathering the various opinions of the other individuals to help the future candidate make the decision to run. Overall, you could say that I am the chief executive officer, or CEO, of the campaign."

I asked, "As CEO, who is the first person you might speak with about joining your campaign, or should I say the company, or at least get their advice to consider?"

Tommy articulated, "After getting myself situated, I like to bring in a press secretary. This person serves as the 'doorman' or 'bouncer' of the operation. Necessarily, this person is the individual for those seeking specific information about the campaign or candidate regarding items like their official stance on an issue, the time and place of a major campaign event, significant changes in the campaign structure, or even when the candidate will be

---

2    http://marvel.com/characters
3    https://www.definitions.net/definition/exploratory%20committee

taking a day off to gather themselves as needed. Mostly, they deal with people who monitor the progress of the campaign full time, like a reporter for the news, who would then go on to file daily stories and news briefings on the happenings of the campaign. Overall, this person is the first line of defense for a candidate regarding the public and begins their role when the candidate makes their decision to run."

Right then, the Facebook app on my smartphone pinged. Embarrassed, I turned it off, looked up, and saw Tommy grinning slyly. Thankfully, Tommy just said, "Speaking of technology getting in the way, after the press secretary, I then bring in staffer number two, my tech guy, better known as a media consultant. This individual's role boils down to being the 'e-doorman' of the campaign, so to speak. The press secretary deals with those individuals who have full-time jobs working for CNN,[4] Fox News,[5] or the *New York Times*.[6] Now, thanks to the rise of social media like Twitter,[7] Facebook,[8] Pinterest,[9] etc. over the last decade, more than just those reporters who deal with the press secretary have ways to reach out to the campaign for information, who also in many cases want to voice their opinion to the campaign directly. Therefore, you need somebody to deal with those new avenues of information being spread and received. For example, now, instead of issuing a press release, in some cases I tell this person to post that the candidate will be speaking at this or that location on social media and the public is welcome to attend."

"In some cases, those reporters are happy to go with those tweets. Also, this person can post photos of what occurred at events, share information about what the candidate did that day, or answer basic questions about the campaign. Also, this person may be responsible for managing the candidate's website, which covers a lot of the information that people would be after to learn. In other cases this person may even be sent to events ahead of time and ensure that any technology needed at the venue is there and working. During the exploratory phase, this person would be the actual one compiling various information, while I would process it to build a big picture about whether the campaign has a real chance at success."

After a pause, I inquired, "Who deals with all those people tweeting about wanting to get involved? I know you deal with the major players as a campaign manager, but what about all the potential volunteers?"

Tommy remarked, "That would fall to the staff director. This individual is akin to that of a sheepherder or hand on the ranch. For the most part, they get started with their duties

---

4   https://www.cnn.com
5   https://www.foxnews.com
6   https://www.nytimes.com
7   https://twitter.com/?lang=en
8   https://www.facebook.com
9   https://www.pinterest.com

after I, as the campaign manager, get started with the campaign. With the word out, thanks to the media consultant and press secretary, people call or tweet or what not in wanting to volunteer. The person in the staff director role then gives the volunteers the opportunity to do so. This could be asking for help hanging up flyers around town. If you look in the corner behind you, I have boxes of campaign materials—signs, in this case—which are ready to be distributed to and then around by those who show up and help. At events, when a candidate is speaking, this person helps get people into the right place for the best image to be distributed among media outlets later by the press secretary or the media consultant. For some larger campaigns with official headquarters, they also get people to man the post and sell merchandise, collect donations, answer the phone; you name it. There are thousands of items that a campaign needs help with, and volunteers through the staff director play a pivotal role in getting items completed for the campaign. Having a lot of volunteers is like a well-lubed engine; they both just run smoothly with them in place and a good driver behind the wheel. They don't have much to do with the exploratory phase, but if they were to indicate that a lot of people wanted to help with the campaign, that is information alone that might be worthwhile to consider in deciding to run."

I interjected, "Speaking of good communication, do many of your candidates write their speeches?"

Tommy replied, "That, honestly, depends entirely on the candidate. Some are English majors from college and don't need help writing a speech, while others are farmers strolling in from the pasture and have no clue how to organize their beliefs and thoughts or even why they are running for office. If a speechwriter was needed, they could write the entirety of or help a candidate draft a speech for the candidate to use at an event. They may also issue excellent talking points to the candidate for use in interviews. More importantly, this person's duties could range from just one of the duties a regular aide has, or it could be a full-time position, all of which depends on the need for help and the position being sought mixed in with the intricacies of the candidate or campaign. Either way, just like action movies with big explosions, they, like a candidate with a good speechwriter, are always better with the memorable lines provided by a good writer. This person would be the scribe of the campaign."

After a brief pause, I inquired, "After speaking with the state demographer last week, the situation appears that it is beneficial to keep up to date with the numbers. Who do you have for that?"

Tommy yelled, "Mona, come in here!"

A few minutes later, a young woman with a pencil behind her ear entered the room and asked, "What do you need, boss?"

Tommy continued, "Mona, would you mind informing my nephew, Champ, over here on your role in the firm?"

Mona replied, "Certainly, sir!"

After sitting down, she furthered, "Champ, I am Tommy's pollster and researcher. For the first position, I partake in the activity of polling. Polling is 'a sampling or collection of opinions on a subject, taken from either a selected or a random group of persons . . . for analysis.'[10] Data from these polls can be used to better plan out the campaign, along with just deciding to run in the first place. This data includes learning about which groups of individuals have a poor view of the candidate, what about the candidate is poorly viewed by the public, and simply just getting a gauge of what the district in question is feeling now that is important to consider. With that data, campaigns can shift their focus, add a platform plank, which is 'stated principles or objectives comprising the political platform of a party or individual campaigning in an election.'[11] or decide to avoid the subject altogether. On the other hand, I also gather information as a researcher. Polling deals with getting the mood of the people. Researching deals with obtaining the facts of an issue. Nothing can bring down a candidate more than looking incompetent on stage. Take former Texas governor Rick Perry, who ran for president in 2012 under the Republican banner. He couldn't name three federal government departments that he wanted to shutter when in office, and the moderator roasted him for not being able to do so live on stage. He even checked his notes and still couldn't muster up a good answer. This error led to him having to drop out of the race a short while later.[12] Some good research, with a little help from a speechwriter in Perry's case, could have gone a long way toward the success of his campaign by ensuring that he had a list of agencies that could be placed on the chopping block with background substance as to why they should be there, such as being unconstitutional in the case of the US Department of Education. Granted, a better candidate probably should need my services at a minimum for things beyond fact-checking purposes. I would view myself as the investigator of the campaign and voice of the people during the exploratory phase of the operation. Questions?"

I could only reply, "No, but it seems as if the right candidate might not need that much help and all the help they could get all at the same time when running for office."

---

10    http://www.dictionary.com/browse/polling

11    http://www.dictionary.com/browse/plank?s=t

12    Amy Gardner and Philip Rucker, "Rick Perry Stumbles Badly in Republican Presidential Debate," *Washington Post*, November 10, 2011, https://www.washingtonpost.com/politics/republican-presidential-candidates-focus-on-economy/2011/11/09/gIQA5Lsp6M_story.html?utm_term=.09412c200fed; CNBC and Associated Press, "Rick Perry's Energy Department 'Oops' Moment," *New York Times*, December 13, 2016, https://www.nytimes.com/video/us/politics/100000004820721/rick-perrys-energy-department-oops-moment.html.

Tommy and Mona both nodded in agreement. Tommy articulated, "Thanks for your help, Mona. Keep me posted on those polls for our candidate on the Southside."

Mona left, stating, "On it, sir!"

Tommy stated, "You are right about having the right candidate. Don't get me wrong, I can work with anyone, especially if they pay promptly for my services, but a good person with lots to sell regarding their clear vision for what they want to be done while in office, few or no skeletons in their closest, and an overall good personality is essential for success. Of note, the candidate is essentially the main event or headliner of a show or concert and could be construed as a product of all our work done behind the scenes for them. Without them, there isn't a campaign to speak of."

At this point, close to 11:00 a.m., Tommy's cell phone rang. After speaking for a few minutes, Tommy said, "I have one of my candidates on the phone who's running for a vacant Austin ISD school board post. He's a paying client and, unfortunately for you, requires my attention first and foremost. Let me make a few phone calls for you real quick, though, okay?"

## Financing a Campaign

Ten minutes later, I found myself being sent on my way to the local office of US Representative Sandra Ridge. Nearing 11:30 a.m., I arrived at her office on the west side of town, near Lake Travis. Once inside, Sandra herself was in a meeting. Therefore, to get the most bang for my buck, I was ushered to the office of one of Representative Ridge's assistants, Cindy. Once I was at the door, I knocked and was allowed in. The woman began by stating, "Well, Champ, welcome to the office of the final essential person one would need to run for office successfully. That last role has me in the position of being a financial advisor. I'm the one who keeps track of the money flowing into and out of a campaign's coffers. As the financial advisor, I know who sent in donations and how much they sent. I also keep track of what money is being spent on what, as I am required to do so by law. With the pollster, we can determine if we should continue to campaign in a method that is being used or switch to some other method that we can more afford. Now, a candidate does not technically need to raise money, but it helps if the person does. Signs aren't inexpensive. For funding, a variety of sources are available. This is the point where we transition to step number two in the process of campaigning for a public office: fund-raising, or 'a campaign to raise money for some cause,'[13] the campaign in this case. Fund-raising options include the candidates themselves, individual citizens making donations, interest groups and political action committees' contributions, various taxpayers' funds that many candidates may have access to but avoid for image

---

13 http://www.thefreedictionary.com/fund-raising+campaign

concerns (especially conservative ones), and the respective candidate's political party. For the actual campaign, I am the 'treasurer' of the operation, but while in the exploratory phase I would advise if the potential is there for the potential candidate in question to be able to afford to campaign . . . er . . . run for office. All the other people that you have heard about up to here don't exactly work for free. They might even expect a cushy position in your office if you win the election. Therefore, we have to look at some numbers to ensure that running for office makes 'cents.'"

While Cindy was gathering up some data to run with on her computer, I asked, "How big can these numbers get?"

Her response: "Big. For what occurs in Texas elections, you should head to the Texas Ethics Commission's website.[14] They have guides on what candidates can and cannot do and what they must do to do keep their campaigns legal.[15] However, since you wanted to see just how big these numbers can get in a campaign for public office, we need to turn to the Federal Election Commission's website[16] and the campaign reports from the 2016 presidential election between Donald Trump, Hillary Clinton, Gary Johnson, and Dr. Jill Stein, specifically, the Campaign Finance Disclosure Portal[17] for access to all the hard numbers. Keep in mind, all the numbers that we are about to discuss come from this website unless I say so, okay, and are up to date as of February 22, 2018."[18]

I nodded in acknowledgment. Cindy continued, "First, regarding how much money they received, these dollars are better known as contributions or 'a payment exacted for a special purpose';[19] funding of the candidate's campaign in this case. For the 2016 presidential election cycle, 'the applicable period in which [a series of] elections occur,'[20] individual donations of all kinds (typically sorted as large and small) gave $399,670,200 to Hillary, $132,232,785 to Donald, $9,980,093 to Dr. Stein, and $11,143,927 to Gary. Regarding their own money, Hillary put up $1,450,335, Dr. Stein contributed $40,000, Gary put up none, but Donald Trump put forth a whopping $66,141,714. Political action committees donated $1,785,191 to Hillary, $144,764 to Trump, Dr. Stein took none, and Gary took a paltry $5,000. Only Dr. Stein took public money totaling $456,035 out of the Presidential Election Campaign

---

14   https://www.ethics.state.tx.us
15   https://www.ethics.state.tx.us/main/guides.htm
16   https://classic.fec.gov/index.shtml
17   https://classic.fec.gov/pindex.shtml; https://classic.fec.gov/disclosurep/pnational.do
18   This was the date the author accessed them.
19   https://www.thefreedictionary.com/Contributions
20   Austin Graham, "What's an Election Cycle? Depends Where You Are," *National Conference of State Legislatures Blog*, June 26, 2014, http://www.ncsl.org/blog/2014/06/26/whats-an-election-cycle-depends-where-you-are.aspx.

Fund.[21] Finally, the Democratic Party donated $20,039, Republicans donated $9,303, the Libertarians donated $239, and the Greens failed to support their respective candidate's campaigns monetarily. Overall, the Clinton campaign took in $402,925,765, the Trump campaign took in $198,528,566, the Stein campaign took in $11,050,026, and the Johnson campaign took in $11,149,166 in total, respectively."

At this point, I was perplexed by all the numbers. Cindy continued, "Let's now look at the expenditures or 'payments [made] . . . for goods or services, or a charge against available funds in settlement of an obligation,'[22] like buying television and radio ads, billboards, polling services, campaign signs or ads, transportation to and from events, the events themselves in certain cases, and of course, Tommy, along with all of the other people running the campaign. Regarding Hillary and her campaign, they spent $579,241,676 of their own money alongside their party spending $812,980,633 on them, for a total of $1,392,222,309. Trump's campaign spent $341,296,207 while the Republican Party spent $646,655,733 on them for a grand total of $987,951,940. The website didn't have expenditures for the individual Green and Libertarian Parties, but their candidates' campaigns spent $11,050,026 and $11,625,727, respectively."

I interjected, "This can't get any worse, can it?"

Going along with what I said, Cindy responded, "I would say more informative than worse, but using the number of total popular votes won by each candidate, 65,853,652 for Hillary, 62,985,134 for Donald, 1,457,226 for Dr. Stein, and 4,489,235 for Gary,[23] Hillary and the Democrats spent $21.14 per vote and still lost to Donald and the Republicans, who spent $15.69 per vote. Meanwhile, for posterity, Dr. Stein and the Greens spent $7.58 per vote, and Gary and the Libertarians spent $2.59 per vote, using the information that is available. Overall, I'd say it's not how much it is you spend, it's how you spend it."

At this point, I needed to put some controls on the proceedings, lest I go insane. I asked, "So what regulates all of this?"

Cindy explained, "On where the money comes and goes, physically, we must consider the great and oh-so-powerful Title 15 of the Texas Election Code that regulates political funds and campaigns in Texas, at least, all nonfederal offices, that require an election to fill.[24] For federal positions, you must consider the regulations put forth by the Federal

---

21   Marylyn W. Thompson, "How Is Jill Stein Paying for Ads, Parties, and Pricey Office Space?," *Boston Globe*, September 21, 2016, https://www.bostonglobe.com/news/politics/2016/09/20/how-jill-stein-paying-for-ads-parties-and-pricey-office-space/ATNDEtfj7GDK5GoJMAzHHK/story.html.

22   http://www.businessdictionary.com/definition/expenditure.html

23   David Leip, "2016 Presidential General Election Results," Dave Leip's Atlas of U.S. Elections, accessed March 20, 2019, https://uselectionatlas.org/RESULTS/national.php.

24   https://www.ethics.state.tx.us/statutes/title15.html

Election Campaign, Presidential Election Campaign Fund, and the Presidential Primary Matching Payment Account Acts.[25] Regardless, in general, from Title 15, per sections 252.001 and 253.031, each candidate must appoint a campaign treasurer, which can be themselves, before any donation can be accepted. Per section 253.001, you may only contribute in your name. Per section 253.033, all donations over a $100 may not be made in cash. Per sections 253.094 and 253.099, corporations or labor organizations may not make any contributions, at least not directly, to a campaign other than a get-out-the-vote initiative. And what I find to be most important, per section 253.102, businesses or labor groups are specifically barred from any coercive behavior, like bribery, that may influence the election in any way, among a wide array of other important measures. Oh, all of this must be reported to the respective agency, the aforementioned Federal Election Commission or Texas Ethics Commission. Beyond that, we can, should, and need to gather funds continuously, lest we fall behind and become unable to keep up with our opposition. Any questions?"

I could only respond, "How far would the hundred bucks in my pocket take me?"

She replied, "Not far; luckily that is all the distance you need to go now, which is next door into the break room where Sandra is waiting for you."


## Campaigning

A few moments later, I found myself face to face with Representative Ridge who thankfully had a sandwich waiting for me for lunch. After I went inside, we sat down together and made some small talk. After a while, I inquired, "I know now who is involved and how much this show costs to put on, a small fortune in some cases, but what comes next?"

In getting started, Representative Ridge stated, "For my role as the candidate, or 'a person who seeks or is nominated for an office, prize, or honor,[26]' it's all about getting my message out. Doing so requires that I campaign, or embark on 'an operation or series of operations energetically pursued to accomplish a purpose,[27]' to get elected to the office, in this case. Now, depending on what kind of office I am pursuing, I must select one of two options as the core of my plan of action. Now, when I ran for school board a decade or so ago, a local position in the grand scheme of things, I implemented a campaign strategy involving a lot of 'boots on the ground,' so to speak, to get my message out, which involves mostly pursuing activities that get myself out among the people due to being so physically close to the voters in districts that are physically small. The problem here is, it means that I must physically get out there and do

---

25    https://classic.fec.gov/law/feca/feca.shtml
26    https://www.thefreedictionary.com/candidate
27    http://www.thefreedictionary.com/campaigning

things with other people, which, around this time of year, can be tiring because of the heat or be less than secure, depending on the area in question. On the other foot, if the race is for a national or statewide position, like being the congresswoman I am today, my campaign strategy will place more media and technological means of getting my message out at the heart of our plan. This is required due to the race taking place in a much more significant geographic area, mixed in with the fact that I need to reach a more meaningful and more diverse set of people in far-flung places that I can't get to in person as easily. Now, this strategy doesn't exclude any activities that bring me to face-to-face events, but they are done less often and more strategically. The problem here is, as I am sure you just learned, creating ads and then airing them in any format is costly. Regardless, going from the first strategy to the other requires switching from carpet bombing to strategic bombing in the mission, so to speak."

I interjected, "So what exact activities are included when you are out campaigning among the people?"

Representative Ridge continued, "There are actions that I have to do personally and ones that others can do more effectively on my behalf. One option that is fun is called stumping, 'a place or an occasion used for political or campaign oratory,[28] better known as publicly speaking about the issues and taking a stance on them in front of a crowd (figure 9.1). I no longer must stand on an actual tree stump, which is what political candidates back in the day were required to do in many cases to get above the crowds and where the term got its

FIGURE 9.1   Republican presidential candidate Donald Trump speaks at a rally where he was endorsed by former Alaska Gov. Sarah Palin at Iowa State University in Ames, Iowa, on Tuesday, Jan. 19, 2016.

start. My favorite example of this, though, is old-timey politicians who stood on the back of trains speaking to crowds as they passed through a town. Other times, I get to appear on local television stations or live on the radio. I've done that several times."

I asked, "So what do you do when not stumping?"

Representative Ridge furthered, "I recently made a new slogan with my speechwriter that goes, 'Sandra Ridge holds the Conservative Line for America.' This helps my supporters and me in promoting my cause by giving them a chant that people can easily grab hold

---

28   https://www.thefreedictionary.com/stumping

FIGURE 9.2  Hillary Clinton Supporters holding a sign with her campaign slogan "Stronger Together" on it.

FIGURE 9.3  President Barack Obama kisses a baby on the tarmac following his arrival at Denver International Airport in Denver, Colo., Nov. 1, 2012. (Official White House Photo by Pete Souza).

of and spread. 'Remember the Alamo,' ring a bell for why this is so important? For whatever reason, based on what happened in the 2016 presidential election, 'Make America Great Again' just sounded more impactful than 'Stronger Together' (figure 9.2) or not having a noticeable one at that for Dr. Stein and Gary. Other times, I walk door to door to get close to my constituents. I have answered phone calls at call centers during the final push before Election Day to drive up the vote once or twice. You would be surprised to know how important it is to call someone personally. Lastly, I would say that I have mastered the art of using social media to my advantage."

I inquired, "Didn't you kiss a baby once?"

Blushing, Representative Ridge admitted, "I have and will continue to do so (figure 9.3). Babies just let the personal side of you out when it happens. Also, doing so makes you seem more reachable to the average person, which helps if someone is on the fence about supporting. The line 'you could have a beer with him' from the Broadway smash hit *Hamilton* song entitled 'Election of 1800'[29] provides a lot of evidence for doing the little things like kissing a baby, as Burr built a lot of support by just going out and speaking with people and going with the flows of what occurs when doing so."

At this point, after hearing about all these different activities, I had one question: "Why take all of these different actions?"

29   Lin Manuel-Miranda, "The Election of 1800: Original Broadway Cast of Hamilton," Genius, accessed March 20, 2019. https://genius.com/Lin-manuel-miranda-the-election-of-1800-lyrics.

Representative Ridge quickly remarked: "Doing so makes us, me, look as good as possible, not to mention, as I have said repeatedly, get my message out! I mean, if I don't get my message out, no one knows about me, and that is never a good thing. More importantly, I leave myself open to criticism for not saying anything or having a vision. Even more so, when campaigning, depending on what point in the race the campaign is in, I must focus on what I am saying. For example, before the field of potential candidates for my party is set, it's best I stick to talking wonderfully about myself. Once the field is set and the process for getting the nominations begins, when caucuses and primaries are going on, I must also talk badly about my fellow party competition to show, as I said before, I'm the best conservative of the bunch. Lastly, once I secure the nomination, during the general election season, I switch to talking badly about the other party's candidates to show, as I said before, that I am the best candidate, but now overall."

## Debates

At this point, Ron, Representative Ridge's office manager here in Austin, entered the room. Representative Ridge instructed, "Ron, join us. You are just in time for our conversation."

Looking a bit disappointed that his lunch might be longer than expected, Ron joined us. Representative Ridge stated, "Ron, during my last campaign, what event were you responsible for putting together?"

Ron replied, "The debates?"

Representative Ridge nodded her confirmation, followed by Ron continuing, "Well, if I have overheard your conversations well enough from across the hall, this would be step four, and we'll call it seven as well for timekeeping purposes due to both being the same thing, but with a different set of contestants. Regardless, debates are 'a formal contest of argumentation in which two [or more] opposing teams defend and attack a given proposition.'[30] In general, political debates differ in the first case by who gets asked questions. As part of step four, formally known as intraparty debates (figure 9.4), the various candidates vying for the nomination of a specific party are found onstage. Here, the

FIGURE 9.4   Former Hewlett-Packard CEO Carly Fiorina, former Arkansas Governor Mike Huckabee, and former Virginia Governor Jim Gilmore at the Republican Party debate in Iowa in 2016 at the Iowa Events Center in Des Moines, Iowa.

---

30   https://www.thefreedictionary.com/debate

FIGURE 9.5 Green Party (USA) national convention, Chicago, 12 July 2008, after Cynthia McKinney wins nomination.

candidate is working to show that they represent the party better than the other contenders. As part of step seven, formally known as interparty debates (figure 9.5), the various candidates representing the different parties vying for the office in question, after being nominated by their parties for the role, are found onstage. Here, they are working to show that they are the best overall person for the office, not so much the best conservative, in our case here, in the field."

I inquired, "What are the differences beyond who is getting asked questions?"

Ron furthered, "No matter what, there is always a moderator, 'the person who oversees the discussion and makes sure that the debate is conducted in a fair and organized way.'[31] This brings us to who is asking the questions. Questions could be posed by the moderators themselves, a person from the audience, a question submitted through various methods read by the moderator or emcee, or even by a video played in front of everyone. This is important, as a person from the audience, compared to a professional moderator, can ask questions with vastly different qualities and types, leading them to play a huge role in the success of the debate for a candidate, going forward, to live with, on the campaign trail. A third difference is the format of questions being asked. When you see a debate on TV, Sandra sometimes gets to stand behind a podium; other times, it's a town hall format where Sandra and her opposition get to walk around while answering; and finally, there are ones where the candidates are sitting across from one another at a table. A nervous fidget or leg shaking can be hidden by a table a lot more easily than a podium, which helps make Sandra look better. Had it not been for the televised debate format between Nixon and Kennedy that was used in 1960, Nixon would have been elected then, not in 1968, to the office, due to him appearing under the weather up against the calm collective visual put forth by Kennedy, whereas those on the radio felt that Nixon had won.[32] Beyond that, the focus of a debate may switch from subject to subject or focus on one issue. For example, one contest, assuming it was for the presidency, might concentrate

31    https://www.collinsdictionary.com/dictionary/english/moderator

32    History.com Editors, "The Kennedy-Nixon Debates," September 21, 2010, http://www.history.com/topics/us-presidents/kennedy-nixon-debates.

questions on foreign policy, another on domestic policy all mixed in with questions on the personal characteristics of the candidates themselves from time to time. Finally, if there is more than one debate, as there was in 2016 for the presidency, the events are spread out across the country to give as much access as possible to different groups, with the first occurring at Hofstra University in New York,[33] the second at Washington University in St. Louis, Missouri,[34] and the final one at the University of Nevada, Las Vegas.[35] Also, the vice presidential candidates have a debate of their own at some point in the process."

## Getting Nominated

Representative Ridge stated, "Ron, thank you very much for the valuable insight. Feel free to go finish your lunch in peace."

Ron remarked, "I'm good. I got started in this, and I seek to finish this campaign of knowledge. Now, with all the work that you have put forth as a candidate fund-raising, speaking your mind, and facing your competition head to head, it's time to get some hard results in step number five, obtaining your party's nomination. There are two options used by the major parties: a caucus, or 'a closed meeting of a group of persons belonging to the same political party ... to select candidates or to decide on policy,'[36] or a primary election, in which 'an election by the voters of a [district], belonging to a particular party, . . . meet and nominate the candidates of their party to stand at an approaching . . . general election.'[37] For all offices in Texas and most other states, all you need to get is 50 percent plus one or more of the vote in a primary election. At the state level, California is the big exception, due to the use of a so-called jungle primary, in which all potential candidates, regardless of party, are thrust together in a primary, with the top two vote getters being the only two candidates to advance to the general election ballot later on,[38] whereas due to the presidency being elected by the whole of the country, a candidate need not get the most number of votes, but the most number of delegates. The number of delegates to win each party's nomination is set by the parties themselves and divided up to each of the states. For example, in 2016 Hillary needed to win a majority of the 4,766 delegates up for grabs, while Donald needed to win a majority of the available 2,474 for Republican candidates, to which they received,

---

33   https://www.hofstra.edu
34   https://wustl.edu
35   https://www.unlv.edu
36   https://www.merriam-webster.com/dictionary/caucus
37   https://thelawdictionary.org/primary-election
38   http://www.sos.ca.gov/elections/primary-elections-california

2,811 and 1,542, respectively.[39] Complicating this process is the presence of what are known as unpledged delegates for the Republican Party and 'superdelegates' for the Democrats. These are individual votes held by essential party officials, elected officials, and whoever is deemed worthy by the parties to have one use to vote for their parties' nominee for president and are not bound to how their state's delegation voted, which has the same worth as one delegate vote earned by a candidate from a state primary win. A majority of these primaries and caucuses occur in January to June in even-numbered years, with the most prominent day being Super Tuesday, when the highest number of states hold their contests with the most number of delegates being on the line for the presidential nomination. Finally, for the presidential election, depending on how you do in the primaries, your campaign staff would advise you on whether to stay in the race. How are you feeling so far on this?"

I replied, "As good as I can be. There is just so much to consider and go through when running for political office."

Ron, now cheerful, yelled, "Cindy, get in here, it's time to party."

## Party Conventions

A minute or so later, Cindy entered the room and filled the final seat at the table. Representative Ridge remarked, "Champ, even though I earned enough votes in my primary earlier this year, it's not quite over, yet. The results must be formally counted as part of step six, the party conventions, 'a meeting of delegates of a political party at "various" levels to select candidates for office and to decide party policy[40]. These events are run by the political parties themselves. Now, to harken back to step five, parties in the state that did not get 20 percent or more of the vote for any statewide office in the last general election do not have primaries and do all the work of selecting their nominees by a vote of delegates at the convention. Beyond formally selecting the party's nominee, the party platforms are formally selected, important party officials and candidates make speeches, protesters make their scenes, a wide variety of socials are undertaken, and future party events are planned out. Finally, the convention ends with a major speech by the candidate for the principal office on the ticket—in this case, a speech by the candidate for governor at the state level and president at the national level. It's a massive show, like an infomercial on TV, but it is a weeklong affair. Also, if at the national conventions, the presidential

39    Wilson Andrews, Kitty Bennett, and Alicia Paralapiano, "2016 Delegate Count and Primary Results," *New York Times*, April 14, 2015, https://www.nytimes.com/interactive/2016/us/elections/primary-calendar-and-results.html.

40    https://www.britannica.com/topic/political-convention

nominees would announce their selection of a running mate for vice president. Overall, all those involved there are rallying party support and morale for the upcoming final push for the win, kind of like how we are all here getting you up to speed on what goes on during these campaigns here."

I inquired, "So what is the next step?"

Cindy chimed in, "Remember those numbers that we talked about earlier, Champ?"

I replied, "Yes?"

Cindy continued, "Think about who won the election."

I replied, again, "President Trump, but he didn't have the most votes. Hillary did, so what gives?"

## Winning an Election

Cindy furthered, "That is step number eight, winning the office. First off, the presidency is special. Due to wanting to keep impact as equitable as possible between the states when selecting our nation's leader, our founding fathers decided to give one vote for the presidency to each state for each of their representatives in Congress. This system is formally known as the Electoral College.[41] Using Texas as an example, we currently have a total of 38 electors in the Electoral College, due to us having two senators and 36 representatives. Each state has at least three—including the District of Columbia, thanks to the addition of the 23rd Amendment to the US Constitution.[42] The minimum is three, due to always having two senators and at least one representative. In 2020 a new census will be undertaken, and, based on the results, Texas and other states will then gain or lose additional House seats as part of the reapportionment process and, along with that, official votes for president. At present, the magic number to win the presidency is 270 Electoral College votes, a true majority of the 538 available. A candidate earns them by winning the various contests held in the 50 states, plus Washington DC. On election night in 2016, Trump won 30 of the 51 contests, getting 306 votes against 232 for Hillary from her 21 contests (figure 9.6). The real drama came over the next several weeks, when the official voting of the electors commenced, which saw several electors cast their votes against the wishes of their electorate. Despite not being on the actual ballot in many cases, General Colin Powell won three and Faith Spotted Eagle won one in Washington State, despite Hillary winning that state; former US representative Ron Paul and Ohio governor John Kasich each got one in Texas; and Bernie Sanders received one in Hawaii as part of a series of

---

41   https://www.archives.gov/federal-register/electoral-college/about.html

42   U.S. Constitution, Amendment 23.

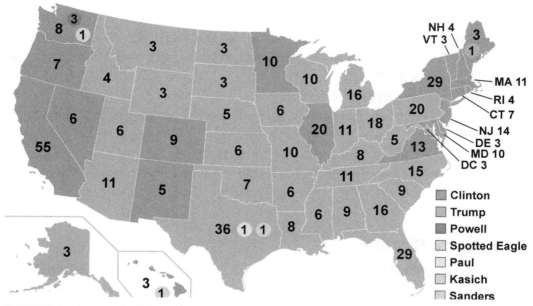

NH 4
VT 3

3
1

MA 11
RI 4
CT 7
NJ 14
DE 3
MD 10
DC 3

8
3
1

3

3

10

7

4

3

10

10

29

6

3

5

6

16

20

55

6

9

20

11

18

5

13

11

5

15

8

9

11

11

7

6

9

6

9

16

3

36  1  1

8

6

29

3
1

■ Clinton
□ Trump
■ Powell
□ Spotted Eagle
□ Paul
□ Kasich
□ Sanders

FIGURE 9.6   This map displays the split of electors for Maine who divide their votes in the college by congressional district and the validated faithless electors in Hawaii, Texas, and Washington states.

protest votes formally called faithless electors. Certain states also have laws against state electors going against the wishes of their state's electorates.[43] Despite protesting the win by Trump, their faithless actions gave Trump an even bigger margin of victory had the results been the same from election night.[44] People reacted so violently to Trump winning the presidency that at electoral vote casting and counting people openly protested in legislative halls around the country.[45] With that in mind, if no candidate gets the needed 270 votes in early January when the votes are tallied on the floor of the House, each of the state delegations in the body is then granted one vote to select the president between the top three earners in a contingent election. The same goes for the vice president in the Senate, but only from the top two vote getters. In both cases, votes are taken until someone gets a true majority. This last occurred in the election of 1824. This process is undertaken to prevent one state, like California today, from having too much say in the direction of the

43   http://www.fairvote.org/faithless_electors

44   https://www.270towin.com/maps/2016-actual-electoral-map; Kiersten Schmidt and Wilson Andrews, "A Historic Number of Electors Defected, and Most Were Supposed to Vote for Clinton," *New York Times*, December 19, 2016, https://www.nytimes.com/interactive/2016/12/19/us/elections/electoral-college-results.html.

45   https://www.youtube.com/watch?v=_lmcQobJU-g

country due to its large population. Of note, Maine and Nebraska divide their Electoral College votes proportionally based on the popular vote of the state."

I chimed in, "So what about offices other than the presidency?"

Cindy continued, "Every other office, so long as they are elected, only need get the largest number of votes on election night to secure the office. For example, in the 2006 Texas governor's race, incumbent Rick Perry, '(referring to the present time) a person who has a particular office or position,'[46] only received 39 percent of the vote, garnering 1,716,803 votes, with the Democratic candidate, Chris Bell, getting 29.8 percent of the vote, due to getting 1,310,353 selections. Causing this situation to occur was the presence of two strong independent candidates, the then state comptroller Carole Keeton Strayhorn and musician Kinky Friedman, getting 797,577 or 18.1 percent and 546,869 or 12.4 percent of the vote, respectively.[47] Rick Perry won here with a plurality, a situation in which the number of 'votes cast for a candidate in a contest of more than two candidates . . . is greater than the number cast for any other candidate, but not more than half the total votes cast.'"[48]

## Final Steps

At this moment Tommy entered the room and pulled up another chair to the table. Tommy stated, "Based on what I just heard, it's time for step nine, postelection events, which, oddly enough, initially calls for another party! Specifically, on election night, political parties and the candidates host a watch party to view the returns as a group. Once the final tallies have been posted, the losing candidate typically calls the winning candidate to concede the race, each of whom then tends to go on and make a speech to their supporters, an acceptance one for the winner and concession version for the loser. Hillary Clinton held her election night watch party at the Javits Center (figure 9.7), where had she won she would

FIGURE 9.7   Jacob K. Javits Convention Center.

46   https://dictionary.cambridge.org/us/dictionary/english/incumbent
47   David Leip, "2006 Gubernatorial General Election Results—Texas," Dave Leip's Atlas of U.S. Elections, accessed March 20, 2019, https://uselectionatlas.org/RESULTS/state.php?f=0&fips=48&off=5&year=2006.
48   https://www.merriam-webster.com/dictionary/plurality

have 'broken' the real glass ceiling that makes up the structure of the building, and Donald Trump held his at the Midtown Hilton, about 1.2 miles apart from one another on Manhattan in New York City, New York. From there, the winner proceeds to build their administration by hiring officials, laying out policy,[49] speaking with future colleagues, meeting with other presidents from around the world,[50] and, as a first known to me, president-elect Trump even went on a victory tour.[51] The year 2016 also saw recounts occur, due to such tight margins seen in individual states; these were called for and led by Green Party candidate Jill Stein, most likely on behalf of Hillary Clinton,[52] and by George W. Bush and Al Gore following the 2000 election, with both leading to calls for a pure direct election of president afterward.[53] Lastly, per tradition, the incoming president visits the White House to get a tour and valuable insight on how to handle the future position they are to take. Much of the same occurs at the state level as well, just not with as much fanfare."[54]

I surmised, "So all is not said and done on election night; a lot must occur before the person takes office. What happens next?"

Cindy spoke, "I finally get to take office. Step number ten. This is formally called Inauguration Day. Per the 20th Amendment of the US Constitution, the beginning and end of the terms of the president and vice president were moved from March 4 to January 20, and of members of Congress from March 4 to January 3. The biggest event of the day is the taking of the oath of office by the incoming official, which for president occurs exactly at noon on that day.[55] Beforehand, there are a wide variety of events. Of note, the inauguration of the next governor of Texas is on the third Tuesday of January, and the new state legislature begins at noon on the second Tuesday in January of each odd-numbered year.[56] President Trump hosted the Make America Great Again Welcome Celebration, which saw a

---

49   https://www.greatagain.gov

50   https://twitter.com/realdonaldtrump/status/80484871159988224o?lang=en

51   Matthew Nussbaum, "Trump Team Planning 'Victory Tour' of States He Won," Politico, November 17, 2016, https://www.politico.com/blogs/donald-trump-administration/2016/11/donald-trump-victory-tour-of-states-won-231576.

52   Collin Brennan, "Remember the Recounts? Here's Where They Stand in These 5 States," *USA Today*, December 7, 2016, https://www.usatoday.com/story/news/nation-now/2016/12/06/election-2016-recount-where-5-states-stand/95052042.

53   Jonathan Chait, "The Rigged 2000 Florida Recount and the Path to Donald Trump," *New York Magazine*, October 19, 2016, http://nymag.com/daily/intelligencer/2016/10/the-rigged-2000-florida-recount-and-the-path-to-trump.html.

54   Billy Hallowell, "Texas' Governor-Elect Reveals the Message That Rick Perry Left for Him Inside This Coveted Bible," Blaze, December 13, 2018, https://www.theblaze.com/news/2015/01/19/texas-governor-elect-reveals-the-message-that-rick-perry-left-for-him-inside-this-coveted-bible.

55   https://washington.org/DC-guide-to/presidential-inauguration-washington-dc

56   Texas Government Code 301.001.

wide variety of musical performances the night before the inauguration.[57] Following that, on the actual day, there is an interfaith prayer service at the National Cathedral, all of which is followed by another prayer, the national anthem being sung, and various speeches and songs being sung.[58] Once the swearing-in is performed (figure 9.8), the new president, or governor in the case of Texas, makes a speech, a luncheon is held inside the old chamber of the House in the Capitol, the outgoing president is sent off into the sunset, and everyone finishes the night by having a gala in honor of the new president."

FIGURE 9.8    President Donald Trump being sworn in on January 20, 2017 at the U.S. Capitol building in Washington DC. Melania Trump wears a sky-blue cashmere Ralph Lauren ensemble. He holds his left hand on two versions of the Bible, one childhood Bible given to him by his mother, along with Abraham Lincoln's Bible. Photo by Jonathan Adams (2017-01-20).

At this point, I asked, "What's left?"

Representative Ridge and her colleagues all said in unison as they left the room, "We gotta get to work! Have a nice rest of your day."

I replied, "Is there anything I can help with?"

Representative Ridge stated, "Normally, we would need some help with this or that, but we don't have all that much going on until the fall. We are in that lull between primaries and the general election when we restock our war chests and other supplies. Check back then, okay?"

Rejected and following them out of the room, I said, "Thanks for your time, and I will."

While walking back to my car, my head was spinning. It seemed as if the whole process was just a person interviewing for a job, except it was a very public process. Still, though, it looked as if it all needed to be gone through, with the multitude of different items along the way, due to what is on the line, managing the public's affairs. Either way, along with the campaign trail, a candidate needs help from a diverse group of people who are all charged with helping them get the message out about the issues. Representative Ridge shouted as I was about to exit the main door, "Don't forget your bumper sticker!"

---

57    Bri Watkins, "Trump Makes Appearance at MAGA Welcome Celebration," *University Star* (San Marcos, TX), January 19, 2017, https://star.txstate.edu/2017/01/19/trump-makes-appearance-at-maga-welcome-celebration.

58    Stephen Collinson, "Trump Becomes 45th President of the United States," CNN, January 21, 2017, https://www.cnn.com/2017/01/20/politics/donald-trump-inauguration-highlights/index.html.

**QUESTIONS TO CONSIDER** REGARDING RUNNING FOR ELECTED OFFICE:

1. The first main topic of the chapter discusses the various people needed to run a successful campaign. Please identify those individuals, name the one you feel is most important to the process, and indicate why, in detail.

2. The second main topic of the chapter discusses financing a campaign. Please identify the different fund-raising resources available for getting funds, the one that you would like to use the most, and why, in detail.

3. The third main topic of the chapter discusses candidates campaigning. Please identify an office that you would like to have, describe the type of campaign that you would need to run for that office, and outline the different physical activities that you would need to do to campaign using that method successfully, in detail.

4. The fourth main topic of the chapter discusses debates. Please define debates, describe the ideal debate format for you to go into, and indicate why, in detail.

5. The fifth main topic of the chapter discusses the candidate obtaining the party's nomination. Please identify your state, the procedure that your candidate must take to secure a party's nomination there, and whether you like that process, and why, in detail.

6. The sixth main topic of the chapter discusses party conventions. Please indicate what party conventions are and whether you think they are an excellent endeavor to proceed through in a campaign, and why, in detail.

7. The seventh main topic of the chapter discusses how candidates win their elections. Please indicate what the path to victory is for candidates in your state and compare that to how a candidate wins in Texas or the US presidency, in detail.

8. The final main topic of the chapter discusses the last two steps of a campaign. Please identify those steps and compare them to how you plan on acting at graduation from your current educational institution.

## FIGURE CREDITS

# Chapter 10

# Elections and the Voters

# Minimum Qualifications

When I woke up this morning, I did not have any government-related activity planned. Seeing as how it was summer, this did not worry me much, even though I had this whole mission to learn more about government before me that was nowhere near complete. There is always attendance at the Barton Springs Pool[1] to consider to pass the time. This week had begun with learning about what provides the government with a foundation to govern and transitioned into how one may get involved with a government, based on what I had experienced over the two prior days with my uncle Tommy, various political participation methods, and the art of running for office.

Accordingly, at around 9:00 a.m., I finally rolled out of bed, crawled on the floor to the stairs, and made my best impression of an armadillo moving down the stairs. Once downstairs, I decided that it would be better for me to walk the rest of the way to the kitchen like a reasonable person, lest I look a total sloth to Charity and Deacon. Lucky for me, they had both already left the house, and I was all alone. Accordingly, I got a bag of potato chips, a Coke, and for good measure, a can of Cheez Whiz, the quintessential 18-year-old's breakfast of champions. After that, I ran to the couch in the main room and prepped for a lounge day in front of the television.

After an hour of some comedy show, during a rerun of *Family Feud* from when Richard Dawson was the host,[2] a rather exciting commercial presented itself to viewers. The primary person in the ad was a gentleman by the name of Rolando B. Pablos, and he introduced himself as the Texas secretary of state. The announcement began with Secretary Pablos declaring, "Hello to all my fellow Texans viewing this program, especially those of you living in Austin. I am Texas secretary of state Rolando Pablos. I am here today to ask you five simple questions."

At that point, I could only imagine what this could relate to on my trek. The most interesting of my thoughts was, "What program is he trying to pawn off on the public from the government now?"

Interestingly, though, the secretary's questions proved to be quite relevant, as I instantly learned of a significant event that I should attend, as it would advance my lofty quest. I tuned back in to hear Secretary Pablos stating, "Are you at least 17 years and 10 months of age and will be 18 years of age by the next Election Day, on November sixth of this year? Are you a fellow citizen of the United States like me? Are you currently a Texas resident? Have you not been declared by 'a court exercising probate jurisdiction to be either mentally incapacitated or partially mentally incapacitated without the right to vote'? And finally, are you not a convicted felon, or, if you are, are you at least two years beyond the end of your incarceration,

---

1   https://austintexas.gov/department/barton-springs-pool
2   https://www.familyfeud.com

parole, and probation? If you were able to answer yes to all these questions, I am proud to declare that you—yes, you, my friend—are eligible to register to vote, and later on to go vote here in the great state of Texas.[3] Today, from noon to three this afternoon, I will be located on the campus of UT in the West Mall area—their free-speech zone. If you qualify to register, I look forward to seeing you there later today to get you registered, thanks to help from the registrar of voters in Travis County, County Clerk Dana DeBeauvoir.[4] Time is of the essence. I'll be voting in our next election, which is only 140 or so days away, and I know you want to be there, too. So, come on down and get yourself registered to vote, today!"

Afterward, the next commercial moved on to some ad by a personal injury attorney, so I tuned out and began tabulating with my fingers and speaking aloud: "Eighteen? Just about a month out. US citizen? Yep. Texas resident? Uh-huh. No criminal record? Yes! I also have not been declared mentally incompetent. I think I about qualify to vote. You know, I should go register."

Since it was only 10:00 a.m., I had a bit of time before I needed to get ready to go. I finished watching *Family Feud* and switched over to another station and watched a rerun of *Jeopardy!*—that Ken guy was smart.[5] Just after 11:30 a.m., I was ready to go and hopped into the car for the drive, yet again, to downtown. Once downtown, I did not want to walk too far, so that I could avoid the summer heat that was creeping up earlier and earlier in the day. I found some parking in a car park at 22nd and Nueces Streets, roughly four blocks due west of the campus's West Mall, just before 12:30 p.m.

After I paid the attendant, I began the short walk. Along the way, though, I could hear a man's voice being projected into the distance above the roar of engines going down the street. About a block away, in front of the University Baptist Church, at the corner of 22nd and Guadalupe Streets,[6] the stage, located over the mall's now derelict fountain, where the man's voice was coming from, came into view. When I first heard the voice, I thought it belonged to Secretary Pablos, but now I had visual confirmation. Luckily, I caught him at an essential part of his speech: "You all again so much for being here today! Registering to vote is one of the most critical parts of our democratic process. Without you registering, you cannot cast your ballot to voice your opinion on the direction of not only our great state but also the local and federal governments. For those of you who are declared to be ineligible today, remember that you can go to voteTexas.gov and print out an application to mail in for free, get a registration form at the post office for free, or ask to be registered for free

---

3   https://www.votetexas.gov/register-to-vote/index.html
4   http://traviscountyclerk.org/eclerk/Content.do?code=Elections
5   https://www.jeopardy.com
6   http://ubcaustin.org

when you go renew your driver's license when your disqualifications have been cleared up to register.[7] Keep in mind, once you are registered, you need not update your registration unless you move, as a new card is mailed out automatically every election cycle that cannot be forwarded to keep the records up to date, as when the card gets returned you are scrubbed from the list of those registered in the county at that address. Lastly, keep in mind, the act of voting is an informal affair, as it is the decision to declare or pronounce by general consent on an issue, while elections are far more formal and important, due to them being 'the act or process of choosing someone for a public office by voting.'[8] The prior is akin to selecting what your family will have for dinner, while the latter refers to the long-standing procedure we have in place to decide who will be the next leader of the state. With that stated, thank you all for being here, again, and I will be over near the blue tent with the state seal on it, there on the north side of the mall, for any of your questions. Good day and God bless Texas!"

## Preparing to Vote

Once across Guadalupe Street, I decided to go and try to speak with the secretary first and foremost. Luckily, most of the people who were standing to view the speech had dispersed or gone to register. Accordingly, there were just a few people waiting to have their one-on-one with Secretary Pablos. When I stood fourth in line, the woman who was currently speaking with the secretary asked, "Why are we having this registration drive now, when the next Election Day is, what, four-plus months away?"

Secretary Pablos remarked, "Well, young lady, yes, Election Day is a 140 or so days away, but you must be registered to vote no later than 30 days before the election so that your local election clerk or voter registrar can obtain the official registration lists to ensure that only qualified voters actually vote on Election Day.[9] You don't want people from elsewhere making decisions for our great state, now do you?"

The same woman interjected, "Well . . . no, I guess not. Regardless, though, if I do register to vote today, what do I need to do next?"

Secretary Pablos responded, "Simple. A few days before the election, download a sample ballot to determine who the candidates are in elections that you are eligible to vote in so that you can decide how you would like to vote. For those of us here in Travis County, we can turn to our local chapter of the League of Women Voters for their voter guide[10]

---

7    https://www.votetexas.gov/register-to-vote/where-to-get-an-application-2.html
8    https://www.collinsdictionary.com/us/dictionary/english/election
9    http://www.votetexas.gov/register-to-vote/you-must-register-by.
10   http://lwvaustin.org/voter-guide

(figure 10.1), or we can go to the county clerk for a nonexplained version of the ballot.[11] This information will help you know what is being voted on. Then, on Election Day later this year, just show up and cast your ballot, but remember: To meet the photo identification requirement, you will need to bring either a driver's license, an election identification certificate, an identification card from the Texas Department of Public Safety, a military ID card, a US passport, your concealed-carry permit, or your US citizenship certificate containing your photo.[12] This action will help ensure that you have everything you need to be able to vote. Without one of those, you will simply be sent away; although, if, for whatever reason, you forget your ID and your name doesn't appear on the roster, you can cast a provisional ballot to have a say, if everything gets sorted out, paperwork-wise, later."[13]

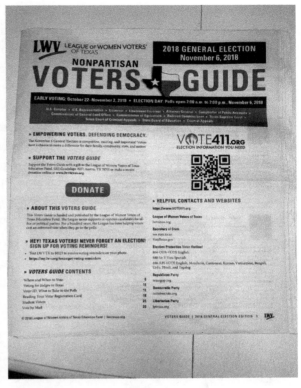

FIGURE 10.1   League of Women Voters Guide for the 2018 General Election in Texas.

The woman stood, thanked Secretary Pablos, and began to walk away. The funny thing was, though, Secretary Pablos added on, "You might also consider doing some research beforehand regarding how you will be voting."

The woman replied while turning around, "What do you mean do some research beforehand? Isn't it just like tapping buttons on my smartphone?"

Secretary Pablos furthered, "It depends. For example, if, for whatever reason, you know that you will be unable to go vote on the main Election Day, 'a day legally established for the election of public officials,'[14] the first Tuesday after the first Monday in November, early

---

11   http://www.traviscountyclerk.org/eclerk/Content.do?code=E.3

12   https://www.votetexas.gov/register-to-vote/need-id.html

13   http://www.votetexas.gov/your-rights

14   https://www.merriam-webster.com/dictionary/Election%20Day

voting is available for everyone 17 to 4 days (excluding weekends, typically) before the general election.[15] Also, voting by mail may be possible if you are over 65, in jail but not convicted of a felony, serving in the military, or sick with a major health condition like cancer.[16] However, if you do choose to vote on the actual Election Day, there are multiple precincts open on Election Day to accept voters and keep the lines short or at least convenient, as they will be located all over town.[17] You must ensure that you go to the correct one or you may be turned away, but in early voting, the locations are much more centralized."

The woman interjected, "What might I physically be facing when I get to the polling station?"

Secretary Pablos continued, "You might be able to get ahold of a ballot that is in some genuinely foreign language to you. This requirement is due to the state's ever-diversifying population. Accordingly, per section 203 of the Voting Rights Act of 1975 that amended the Voting Rights Act of 1965, alternative language ballots must be provided where the number of United States citizens of voting age is a single language group within the jurisdiction is more than 10,000, or is more than five percent of all voting age citizens, or, if on an Indian reservation, exceeds five percent of all reservation residents; and the illiteracy rate of the group is higher than the national illiteracy rate.[18] For example, Vietnamese was just added to the list of available ballots in certain parts of Houston in Harris County a few years ago.[19] Now, beyond the language of the ballot, the actual voting device you come across may be a Scantron-like paper ballot or an electronic version.[20] Regardless of the type, each of the ballots in Texas will be in the office-block format, with each office listed followed by the available candidates to select (figure 10.2). Other states use a party-column format, where each office is listed on its row and, if the party has nominated a candidate for the

FIGURE 10.2 The ballot shows the option to vote straight party or go race-by-race in filling out the ballot.

15    https://www.votetexas.gov/faq/early-voting.html
16    http://www.votetexas.gov/faq, under the question titled: "Can anybody vote early by mail (also referred to as 'absentee voting')?"
17    https://www.votetexas.gov/mobile/voting/wwwww/where.htm
18    United States Department of Justice, "About Language Minority Voting Rights," accessed March 20, 2019, http://www.justice.gov/crt/about-language-minority-voting-rights.
19    http://amarillo.com/stories/2002/08/01/new_harriscounty.shtml#.VkjfJnarTIU
20    https://www.sos.state.tx.us/elections/laws/votingsystems.shtml

office, their candidate is contained in the column reserved for that party. Therefore, if someone wanted to vote for all members of the same party, they could go down the row, checking, clicking, or punching chads to their heart's content, depending on the voting apparatus the precinct is using. Of note, specific formats of ballots do make a difference regarding the ease of voting, to the detriment of some and benefit of others.[21] Beyond that, I guess you could say that voting here in Texas is quite easy, so be sure to register before you leave here today. Just remember, long gone are the days when the state required some combination of a poll tax or a literacy test and that voters be nonmilitary, male, over 21, ready to perform jury duty service, and have resided in the state for one year.[22] Those requirements were designed to prevent, so viewed at the time, 'less desirable' parts of the population from voting. Thanks for the questions and stopping by."

## Who Is Most Likely to Vote?

With the original woman now gone, the twosome of female students in front of me standing in line together then sat down. The taller of the two girls asked, "We were wondering, who is most likely to vote?"

Secretary Pablos said, "Would you like to know the specifics or the basics?"

In unison, the girls replied, "Just the basics, please! At least for now."

Secretary Pablos continued, "Well, about five years ago, Jan Leighley and Jonathan Nagler published their book, *Who Votes Now? Demographics, Issues, Inequality, and Turnout in the United States*,[23] which sought to update the original compendium of knowledge looking at this subject, which was entitled *Who Votes?*, published by Raymond Wolfinger and Steven Rosenstone[24] in 1980. From the original piece by Wolfinger and Rosenstone, demographic factors such as increased wealth, being male, lighter skin-toned, more educated, and older, alongside having more considerable interest in politics and having a political party that you are more in favor of, made you more likely to vote.[25] Today, though, interest in politics and a political party alongside increased wealth, education, and age still make one more likely to vote, but based on evidence provided by Leighley and Nagler, women are now more likely to

---

21    Lena Groeger, "Forms Matter: How the Design of Forms Can Decide an Election, Affect Racial Profiling & Shape Identity," Source, November 1, 2017, https://source.opennews.org/articles/forms-matter.

22    United States v. Texas, 384 U.S. 155; Carrington v. Rash, 380 U.S. 89; U.S. Constitution, 19th Amendment; U.S. Constitution, 26th Amendment; and Beare v. Smith, 321 F. Supp. 1100, respectively.

23    J. E. Leighley and J. Nagler, *Who Votes Now? Demographics, Issues, Inequality, and Turnout in the United States* (Princeton, NJ: Princeton University Press, 2013).

24    R. E. Wolfinger and S. Rosenstone, *Who Votes?* (New Haven, CT: Yale University Press, 1980).

25    Ibid.

vote than men. Economic conservatives are as well, along with churchgoers. Differing voting rates based on race or ethnicity have disappeared.[26] Therefore, let's do an experiment and look at the man standing second in line right now. Sir, what is your name?"

I shook after being jolted from my sturdy listening ear and said, "Me? Ughh . . . I'm Champ."

Secretary Pablos invited me over to sit on the couch with them. Once I was seated, he continued, "Champ, welcome. I want to make a few assumptions to prove a point, all right?"

I remarked, "Sure, go ahead."

Secretary Pablos asserted, "Champ, you look a fair bit younger than me. You don't wear the fanciest of clothing, so you are probably not the most affluent. You're a dude. I don't see a college ring. You don't have a cross or some other religious item around your neck, so that tells me that you may not be the biggest of churchgoers, and I'll bet that you are conservative fiscally. Not looking at the political factors, I would say that you only meet one of the six factors to make you more likely to vote. Now tell me, did you vote in the election last year?"

I could only say, "Close enough, sir, on sizing me up, and you are right, I didn't vote, but that was only because I was not yet 18 last November. One month to go for me, yippee!"

Secretary Pablos stated, "I hate that 5 percent that just can't be explained when using econometrics[27] like this. However, just to let you know, so long as you meet the other qualifications, and seeing as how you will turn 18 before the next election, you can go ahead and register to vote now, as you are at least 17 years and 10 months of age at the time of registration,[28] which will be today, I hope."

As I was sitting there, a question popped into my head. I asked, "Why should I vote, sir?"

Secretary Pablos thought for a minute. "Son, I am reminded of a saying that is often attributed to Pericles, which goes, 'Just because you do not take an interest in politics doesn't mean politics won't take an interest in you!' Government is one of those multiheaded beasts, much like a Hydra, that just won't go away; whether you want it to or not, it comes at you from multiple angles and levels, all at the same time. Even if you fight it, the only thing you can do is control it; you can't kill it, that would be anarchy, and the only way to control it is to vote in an election that goes a long way toward determining the direction it—and you, because you are along for the ride—will go. More importantly, think about the Bush family here in Texas; a majority of those found in that family meet all the demographic factors that make one more likely to vote, even the political ones. This, more likely than not, gives them more to lose from the results of the election. If someone was elected with plans to redistribute the wealth, they would run the risk of having a lot of their wealth stripped away from

---

26    Leighley and Nagler, *Who Votes Now?*

27    https://www.investopedia.com/terms/e/econometrics.asp

28    http://www.votetexas.gov/register-to-vote

them and redistributed. Any vote on their behalf to support an opposing candidate of the one that I just mentioned would be a great investment of their time. Now let's get to specifics regarding these young women's original question."

Before he could continue, the shorter of the two young women I was now sitting between said, "You answered our question well enough, sir, and we need to get to class. Thank you, and have a good day."

## VAP and VEP

After they were gone, I remarked, "Feel free to continue your answer, sir!"

Secretary Pablos furthered, "Champ, there are three terms that I would like to introduce to you now. First and foremost is the term *voting-age population*, also known as the VAP, which is the number of persons in the territory that you are evaluating who are old enough to vote, which is 18 years of age or older here in Texas. Its cousin is the term *voting-eligible population*, or VEP for short, which is the number of persons in the territory under question who meet all the voter registration requirements, such as being 18, a state resident and US citizen, mentally competent, and a nonfelon.[29] The VAP is a bit of an imperfect measurement, as it may account for people living in an area who are not citizens and exclude residents who live abroad or are away at school but are 18 years of age. The final term is called *voter turnout*, which is the percentage of the VAP or VEP who voted in an election.[30] Due to VEP being more accurate, let's use the VEP, and our good friends at the United States Elections Project at George Mason University,[31] who are notable for keeping track of this particular set of data, to look at the turnout figures in Texas and what that means."

Secretary Pablos took out his smartphone and brought up the website of the group that he had just referenced. He went on to state, "As we just discussed, specific groups of people are simply more likely to vote than others, so it is logical to conclude that not everyone will show up and do so. The question is, how many will and how many won't? If we look at the last few election cycles going back to, say, the 2000 election, for Texas, these are the VEP turnout rates (and keep in mind that these are for the highest office on the ballot): 49.9 percent turned out to vote in 2000, 34.2 percent in 2002, 53.7 percent turned out in 2004, 30.9

---

29    United States Elections Project, "Why Should I Care If Turnout Rates Are Calculated as Percentage of VAP or VEP?," accessed March 20, 2019, http://www.electproject.org/home/voter-turnout/faq/vap-v-vap.

30    https://www.youtube.com/watch?v=_rz5I899h1c

31    Michael P. McDonald, "Voter Turnout Data." United States Elections Project. Accessed May 04, 2019. http://www.electproject.org/home/voter-turnout/voter-turnout-data.; https://docs.google.com/spreadsheets/d/1or-N33CpOZYQ1UfZooh8yGPSyzoDb-xjmZOXg3VJi-Q/edit#gid=1670431880; all data discussed here came from this spreadsheet.

percent in 2006, 54.1 percent in 2008, 32.1 percent in 2010, 49.6 percent in 2012, 28.3 percent in 2014, and 51.6 in 2016.[32] The average state, inclusive of the District of Columbia, had a turnout of 59.2 percent in 2000, 42.3 percent in 2002, 62.1 percent in 2004, 43.1 percent in 2006, 63.2 percent in 2008, 43.3 percent in 2010, 59.9 percent in 2012, 39.3 percent in 2014, and 60.8 percent in 2016. From those turnout rates, two apparent trends and a significant concern emerge."

I interjected, "Does one of those trends have something to do with when the president is elected?"

Secretary Pablos continued, "Yes, precisely. People, for whatever reason, just become more engrossed in politics when the presidency is on the line in the election. The president was on the ballot in 2000, 2004, 2008, 2012, and again in 2016. Compare the voter turnout rates of those years to elections that occurred in between, called the midterm elections because they happen at the halfway point of the president's current term;[33] the turnout is lower by about 20 percentage points to around 40 percent of the population. The most significant drop-off occurred in the '06 election cycle, when the turnout rate fell by 22.8 percentage points, a borderline 50 percent drop-off from the previous election.[34] Overall, half the state VEP votes every four years, and then about half of them don't vote again two years later."

I interjected, "What's wrong with that drop-off, though, if the voters only care about national politics, which, if I'm not mistaken, is pretty important, right?"

Secretary Pablos shrugged and muttered, "Simply put, elections for the governor, the other members of the state executive branch, half the state senators, all of our national and state representatives in the House, and many of the local government positions are held during that midterm election cycle. The concern is that those figures mean that only one in four state citizens who are eligible to vote when the direction of state politics is up for grabs makes their mark on the process. So, as Jeremy Bird, the leader of Battleground Texas, put it on *The Colbert Report* on February 26, 2013, 'You are getting a government that is for half the people and by half the people.[35] A quarter of the people, though, in reality, making his statement even worse than it sounds. Therefore, if only a small percentage of the people who did not vote, did vote, we would have a drastically different-looking state—state government, that is. How people physically look is a whole different story!"

We laughed a little at that one-liner. Then I asked, "What's the other trend?"

---

32    Michael P. McDonald, "Voter Turnout Data." United States Elections Project. Accessed May 04, 2019. http://www.electproject.org/home/voter-turnout/voter-turnout-data.

33    https://definitions.uslegal.com/m/midterm-election

34    Ibid.

35    *The Colbert Report*. Comedy Central. April 26, 2013.

Secretary Pablos concluded, "That would be how we compare to the average state when it comes to turnout. Using those VEP numbers from before, our turnout in 2000 was 9.3 percentage points less than the average state, 8.1 percentage points less in 2002, 8.3 percentage points less in 2004, 12.2 percentage points less in 2006, 9.1 percentage points less in 2008, 11.2 percent points less in 2010, 10.3 percentage points less in 2012, 11 percentage points less in 2014, and 9.2 percentage points less in 2016. Not only does Texas follow the trend in dropping off during midterm elections, but we also drop off far more than other states, as our turnout is roughly 80 percent of other states, percentage-wise, in any given election."

I asked, "Would you mind if I listened in on some of the other questions that people have, to keep the line going?"

Secretary Pablos said, "Sure, but go sit at the far end of the couch so that the next groups of people can get up close and personal."

I moved to the far end and said thanks. Once I scooted over and was seated, an older woman came in under the tent and introduced herself. She inquired, "Why are those rates that you were just talking about so low?"

Secretary Pablos iterated, "Well, ma'am, if you heard what I said earlier, many positions are on the ballot, making it quite long. Accordingly, if things take too long—especially now with our smartphones making us wired for high-speed operations permanently—that can be off-putting, keeping people from voting, all despite the straight-ticket option for people, where a voter can check one box and vote for everyone listed under that party name and then leave after about a quarter of a second—granted, the state legislature is doing away with that option following the 2018 general election.[36] Also, our more traditional and individual political culture is not the most inclusive at supporting political involvement. Finally, many people think of Texas as the home of the Big Rich, limousines as far as the eye can see, and servants with servants. The issue is, looking at poverty-rate data from the US Department of Agriculture, Texas isn't.[37] The average county in Texas has 17.5 percent of its population living in poverty. Only 14 counties out of 254 have a rate of less than 10 percent.[38] Eighty-five counties have rates of more than 20 percent.[39] The national average is only 14.5 percent.[40] Our population, on many fronts, has the odds stacked against it and is not likely to vote because of it."

---

36    National Conference of State Legislatures, "Straight Ticket Voting States," December 3, 2018, http://www.ncsl.org/research/elections-and-campaigns/straight-ticket-voting.aspx.

37    http://www.ers.usda.gov/Data/povertyrates/#Pa6c5e4a868154209a331befacce91b64_2_382iT4

38    Ibid.

39    Ibid.

40    https://www.census.gov/data-tools/demo/saipe/saipe.html?s_appName=saipe&map_yearSelector=2017&map_geoSelector=aa_s

# Keeping Elections Secure

The woman rose to her feet and thanked the secretary for his time. After that, a man walked in and asked, "How does the state ensure that the voting process is secure?"

FIGURE 10.3   Sign indicating the beginning of a no electioneering zone to ensure a neutral polling station.

Secretary Pablos, with a big grin on his face, replied, "Good sir, we have a five-step process for that here in the state based on the state election code.[41] First off, before you even enter the polling station, there is a 100-foot neutral zone (figure 10.3) between where people can campaign and where the actual booths are located, to keep undue influence out. Also, each polling station has observers from both parties to keep the peace as much as possible. When voting, as I already discussed, you must present an ID, and, more importantly, we have been using the Australian balloting system since 1913, which has you voting in private on a uniform ballot that has no identifying characteristics. Finally, if the spread between the top two candidates is less than 10 percent, the loser can request a recount.[42] We do our best to avoid the whole election fiasco in 2000 that occurred in Florida, which helped Jon Stewart coin the term 'Indecision 2000.'"[43]

The man looked up and said, "Good to know, Secretary, that we are keeping the process private and secure for selecting our governing officials in the state. Thanks for your time. I'm going to register. I just wanted to check proper protocols were in place beforehand."

# Texas Elections

After that, a football player who was in full uniform and a bit odorous from morning two-a-days walked in. "Sir, this evening I have a government class exam on Texas elections. Could you give me the 4-1-1 on what exactly the process is? I want to pass."

---

41   http://www.statutes.legis.state.tx.us/?link=EL

42   http://www.sos.state.tx.us/elections/laws/recounts.shtml

43   Peabody, "The Daily Show with Jon Stewart: Indecision 2000," accessed March 20, 2019, http://www.peabodyawards.com/award-profile/the-daily-show-with-jon-stewart-indecision-2000.

Secretary Pablos handed the player a pad of paper with a pen and proceeded to continue showing the mastery of his field by responding, "Son, look here. You are on the football team. Let's use that and the process of running an entire play to get the message across to you."

The football player articulated, "So what's step number one, sir?"

Secretary Pablos continued, "Okay, in running a football—American, not European—play, there are three steps. First, before each play, you and the rest of the offense circle the wagons in a huddle and have a big discussion on what play to run next (figure 10.4). In that huddle, Coach puts in his call, y'all discuss it, and if someone has a better idea, you go with that option, which sometimes *is* the option. Regarding the election process, there are also three steps. Step number one is called the primary election, 'a preliminary election in which voters nominate party candidates for office,'[44] where each of the parties, represented by the offense and defense in the football metaphor I am working here, decide who will represent them in the next step—their play call, if you will. Selecting a play in football is just like the parties selecting their candidates in a primary election; a bunch of options are presented, and we try to pick the best option available for our side. Of note, other states use a party caucus to do their play call-

FIGURE 10.4   Players go into a huddle to prepare for the play, like how voters vote in the primary to select the best candidate for their party.

ing, which involves 'a meeting of the local members of a political party especially to select delegates to a convention or register preferences for candidates running for office.'[45] They still vote in the caucus, it's just very public and all at once."

The football player interjected, "What special items should I know about the primary process?"

Secretary Pablos furthered, "Specifically, a political party in Texas must have a primary if their party received at least 20 percent of the last vote for the governorship.[46] To get on the primary ballot, you must pay a filing fee or present a nominating petition in place of the

44    https://www.thefreedictionary.com/primary+election

45    https://www.thefreedictionary.com/Party+caucus

46    CBS News, "Your Guide to the Wild and Crazy Texas Primaries," February 28, 2018, https://www.cbsnews.com/news/your-guide-to-the-wild-and-crazy-texas-primaries.

filing fee, along with an application with the local party that you are seeking the nomination. Those filing fees, though, range from $3,750 for any position on the Texas Supreme Court of Court of Criminal Appeals all the way down to $300 for the State Board of Education, with the other positions all requiring a fee somewhere in between.[47] Keep in mind; the state reimburses the parties for the costs of holding the primary elections, minus the filing fees collected. Also, the parties run the elections. Also, you must get 50 percent of the vote plus one vote to win the nomination. This election occurs typically on the Tuesday after the first Monday in March of years ending with even numbers. If there is no winner the first time through, the top two vote getters face off in a runoff election to obtain the nomination. Finally, and probably most importantly, we here in Texas use something called the open-closed primary system. A full open primary system is open to everyone, while a closed system is only open to members of said party. Here in Texas, each of the primaries is open to everyone, but on a primary day, you can only vote in one primary that you get to choose. Therefore, the primary is open and closed all at the same time. This process was selected to prevent something called crossover voting, which is when a voter who is registered as a member of one political party but who votes in the primary of another party.[48] These actions, when done, are taken to help ensure that the worst candidate available of the opposing party is selected to run against the favored candidate of their preferred party. If there is a runoff, you can only vote if it was in the original primary that you voted in. A very treacherous process is this primary election mess."

The football player, very taken in by the conversation, spoke up. "It sounds like you are saying that step number one is all about planning for what is to come next by putting your best foot forward and nominating the right play call or candidate to run for your team, respectively."

Secretary Pablos continued, "Exactly, son. Now, step two for football is when you run the play that you called back in the huddle against the play called by the defense, hoping that your call is better than the one called by the other team (figure 10.5). Step two for the election process is called the general election, 'a regularly scheduled local, state, or national election in which voters elect officeholders,'[49] where each of the political parties—the offense and defense from the football metaphor—put their candidates selected from the first step into the race, and whichever party chose the candidate that is most favorable to the electorate should win—or score points, if looking at all of this from the football play vantage point, that is."

47   https://www.sos.state.tx.us/elections/candidates/guide/2016/demorrep2016.shtml
48   "Crossover Voter - Dictionary Definition." Vocabulary.com. Accessed January 13, 2020. https://www.vocabulary.com/dictionary/crossover voter.
49   http://www.dictionary.com/browse/general-election

The football player asked, "So what special about the general election should I know?"

Secretary Pablos, after thinking for a few seconds, remarked, "Well, to win here a candidate does not need to get 50 percent plus one of the votes, just the most, which is called winning the plurality.[50] Government officials and other volunteers run these elections. This election takes place on the Tuesday after the first Monday in November every year, at least here in Texas. Finally, for candidates to get on the ballot, parties who win at least 5 percent of a statewide office are automatically on the next ballot."

FIGURE 10.5  Players run their offensive and defensive plays to try and earn points for their team while preventing the other team for doing so just as voters go to the poll to get their preferred candidate or party elected to office.

The football player inquired, "But what about everyone else?"

Secretary Pablos continued, "Other parties, per Title 9 of the state election code,[51] must file a petition with a variable percentage of the last gubernatorial vote, depending on the office level, which, if I am not mistaken, is 1 percent for statewide offices, 3 percent of the district for multicounty districts, and 5 percent for all other districts. Lastly, if a candidate wanted to get onto the ballot without a party—here, they're called write-in candidates—they must declare their candidacy with me 70 days before the election, with the filing fee or a substitutive number of signatures. After that, the name of the person is posted in each of the relevant polling places' voting booths. I think that answers your last question. What question do you have specifically, sir?"

The football player remarked, "So here it seems like this step is all about selecting a candidate to fill an office, just like selecting the right play means you scored a touchdown. But how is there a third step if you score, or win office on the plurality, in step two?"

Secretary Pablos, getting the smile of Rafiki on his face (from the *Lion King*, when he hits Simba on the head), then went, "My boy, what is it that everyone hates that the referees do during the play?"

The football player went, "Ohhhh . . . call a penalty?"

---

50   https://definitions.uslegal.com/p/plurality-voting-system
51   http://www.statutes.legis.state.tx.us/?link=EL

FIGURE 10.6  Referees after a play review the call on the field for accuracy in the same way that voters have special elections to ensure that they are represented in the state legislature.

Secretary Pablos continued, "Right on, but let's mix in a play review here as well for good measure, as both ensure what happened on the field occurred (figure 10.6). In this case that third step in the election process is called a special election, which would occur right after the general election if we did not use the plurality mode. In Texas, though, we use special elections for when a vacancy occurs in a position that has pure lawmaking authority, which is how it is in the legislature for example. The governor fills all other vacancies until the next general election. In addition, the general election for constitutional amendments in odd years that I was discussing earlier on the stage is another use of special elections here in the state, as this election is only called for if the legislature actually creates any amendments to be approved of by the citizens. The special items you need to know about this election are that they are nonpartisan, so anyone at any point can be a candidate for the open position,[52] and a winner needs to get a simple majority to win, or the two top vote getters get to participate in another runoff election. Overall, we are ensuring that everyone has representation and that the call on the field was correct."

At that point, the football player looked down at his watch and said, "Oh, I'm late for the second half of two-a-days. Gotta go, but just to summarize: The primary election is for the parties to select their candidates, the general election is about the people selecting who will hold the office, and the special election is where we fill an early vacancy?"

Secretary Pablos concluded, "Once again, young man, you got it spot-on. Have a good practice and do well on your exam tonight!"

Before the next person sat down, a string of thoughts ran through my head: "Why is everyone asking this guy, of all things, about elections? What right does he have? Why is he the expert? Where did he get the knowledge from?"

I interjected as the next person was anxiously waiting, "Why are you the one answering all these questions and putting this event on?"

Secretary Pablos iterated, "It's my job, per article 4, section 3, of the state constitution, and I quote: 'The returns of every election for said executive officers, until otherwise provided

52    https://definitions.uslegal.com/n/nonpartisan-election

by law, shall be made out, sealed up, and transmitted by the returning officers prescribed by law, to the seat of government, directed to the secretary of state.'[53] In other words, I am the chief election officer for the state. Secretary of the state is my name, and elections are my game. Also, per article 4, section 19, I am responsible for keeping the state seal safe of all things.[54] Lastly, other than verifying the results from across the state, well before Election Day, I am responsible for constructing the state portion of the ballot. For the local elections, the county clerk or designated election official does that. In some cases the process requires that people draw numbers out of a hat."

Secretary Pablos noted, as the next person in line sat down, "How are you doing, sir? Welcome. Sorry for the delay, but this young man over here has quite a good list of questions."

The old man now seated stated, "I know. I heard him outside for a bit, and I want to know about that too, so keep talking, Secretary."

Secretary Pablos asked, "What questions do you have sir?

The old man thought for a few seconds and asked, "Who wins?"

Secretary Pablos acknowledged, "Locally, or further down the office hierarchy of the ballot in the state, it's like a boulder rolling down a mountainside: It's anyone's guess as to what's going to happen, but whoever is most representative of the area has the highest probability of being elected. Statewide, though, more likely trends do exist. Remember, section 1 of article 4 of the state constitution creates five officials who are elected statewide. I get appointed by the governor to serve at his behest, so long as I get confirmed by the state senate. We should also include the land commissioner—created by article 14, section 2, who also gets elected via statewide ballot—in this for good measure. Of the 20 people who have served in those positions since 1995, there have only been two women: Carole Keeton Strayhorn as comptroller from 1999 to 2007, and Susan Combs, who succeeded her from 2007 to earlier this year. Of note, before being comptroller, Combs was the commissioner of agriculture during the same years that Strayhorn was comptroller.

"Regarding Hispanics, during that same time, Dan Morales—who was attorney general from 1991 to 1999—is the only one, although if you go halfsies, current land commissioner George P. Bush's mother is Hispanic. So that's 4 out of 20—or 20 percent of our state leaders over the last 20 years who have been something other than white and male. More importantly, the last group of Democrats to hold any statewide office ended following the 1998 general election when John Sharp, the comptroller of public accounts, Bob Bullock, the lieutenant governor, Daniel Morales, the attorney general, and Garry Mauro, the General Land Office commissioner, were all voted out of office; another 4 out of 20,

---

53  Texas Constitution of 1876, article 4, section 3.
54  Texas Constitution of 1876, article 4, section 19.

so 20 percent, again. The good ol' Republican boys' club might be in effect here. Champ, remember the quote I used earlier from *The Colbert Report*? There is more truth to that than you can imagine, as, if I recall correctly our latest report from the state demographer, Hispanics are on the rise in the state."

The older man and I looked at each other in amazement over what we had just heard. Then an aide to the secretary poked his head into the tent and mentioned, "Sir, it is time that we departed, as you are late for your next event today with the governor."

Secretary Pablos rose and stated, "Boys, it is time for me to run, and thanks for your time and ears. Duty calls. Don't forget to register before y'all go."

We rose, shook the secretary's hand, and followed by leaving the tent. We both immediately made our way over to the booths on the other side of the mall to register. My companion was a veteran, so the event organizers had a unique enclosure for him and his fellows. I, however, had to wait in the regular line. While I was waiting, I pondered everything that I had learned that day. I met the five qualifications that I needed to reach to be able to register. I also learned about who is most likely to vote, who is most likely to win, how we keep the process secure, and what the steps are for the populous to put someone into office. The question is, though: Who could I turn to for help in getting elected to an office?

**QUESTIONS TO CONSIDER** REGARDING VOTERS IN AN ELECTION:

1. The first main topic of the chapter discusses the minimum qualifications needed to be met before registering to vote. Please identify what those minimum qualifications are, name the ones you fit, and indicate clearly whether you qualify to register.

2. The second main topic of the chapter discusses what a voter needs to do to prepare to go vote. Please identify what different things voters need to do before they go vote, state the one you view as least important to perform beforehand, and indicate why, in detail.

3. The third main topic of the chapter discusses those who are more likely to go vote. Please identify what those factors are that make someone more likely to go vote, state the ones you meet, and indicate clearly whether you are likely to go vote.

4. The fourth main topic of the chapter discusses the terms *VAP* and *VEP*. Please define what those terms are, the one that you would like to use if writing an article on voter turnout for partisan purposes, and why you chose that option, in detail.

5. The fifth main topic of the chapter discusses the protections used by Texas to keep elections secure. Please identify what those protections are, name the one you feel to be the most important, and indicate why, in detail.

6. The final main topic of the chapter discusses the different elections held in Texas. Please indicate what elections you as a voter participate in and why, your process for choosing an elected leader, and what that process relates to in your life, in detail.

## FIGURE CREDITS

# Chapter 11

# Special Governmental Interests

# What Is a Lobbyist?

Last week I had the opportunity to drive around town with my uncle Tommy, a political activist in the Austin area. When with him, I was exposed to numerous ways that I could participate in the political process. If I remember correctly from that day, you can put a bumper sticker on your car or wear a T-shirt with whatever you want on it and be able to consider yourself active in the political process, amid a variety of other methods, like going out and voting in an election. The issue is, though, many of those activities seemed to be, for lack of a better term, informal methods of getting your point across, and mostly unregulated. What I learned today covered the most important way a person can directly influence government beyond merely voting or getting a job in government. Overall, I learned about the special interests of the state, better known as interest groups, and their lackeys called lobbyists. Compared to what I learned with Uncle Tommy earlier on, I could see why this involvement method demanded a full day unto itself.

My day began just after 7:00 a.m. when I awoke from bed. I went on to shower, get dressed, and have some breakfast. The only thing is, before 8:00 a.m., there was a knock at the door. Charity and her husband, Deacon, had already gone for the day due to early meetings, so it was up to me to answer the knock at the door. To my surprise, at the entrance were two Texas state troopers.[1] I opened the door and stated, "Good morning. How can I help you?"

The shorter of the two officers spoke. "Yes. Good morning, sir. My name is Trooper Tim Turner, and this is Trooper Shane Spinster. We have a bench warrant issued by the chair of the Texas Ethics Commission[2] for one Champ Cove."

Shocked, I replied, "Uhhh . . . that's me, but what in the world does the Texas Ethics Commission have for me to respond to?"

Trooper Spinster responded, "That's a good question, son, but we are not privileged to that information. We are just here to collect you."

Before going to their vehicle, I changed clothes from the pajama shorts that I had been wearing, then shut down the house for the day. I sensed at this point I was in trouble, but not trouble, trouble. As I was being taken to their car, though, all I could think about was what in the world was going on. I knew I had been all around town getting information about government found here in the state, but other than what Tommy and I had done earlier in the week, attending those various political demonstrations, none of what I had done seemed to be all that controversial. Maybe it was just that spur-of-the-moment decision to pick up the sign for the woman who dropped hers, or perhaps I said something wrong to the secretary of state. Once in the car, though, I just sat there as we made the half-hour or so

---

1   http://www.dps.texas.gov/tle/index.htm
2   https://ethics.state.tx.us

drive into downtown. Toward 9:00 a.m., the vehicle we were in pulled into the spot reserved for police vehicles located in front of the Sam Houston State Office Building (figure 11.1) on 14th Street.

I was escorted up the front steps. Once in the building, we went through security and into a block of elevators that took us down into the basement. I inquired, "Shouldn't we be going up, not down?"

FIGURE 11.1   Sam Houston State Office Building.

Trooper Spinster stated, "Yes, and no. The Texas Ethics Commission offices are upstairs, on the tenth floor to be exact, but the commission and its members do not meet there. Their meetings are in the Capitol Extension committee rooms. Today, they are on Extension Floor 1, Room 14."

Once out of the elevator, we turned left and made the short walk through the underground tunnel to the Capitol Extension. That tunnel took us through the E1.900 hall of the extension. Once in the Central Galley, we crossed the short bridge and turned right toward the room entrance. Once in front of the chamber, we turned left and entered through the left door of the room. I was seated toward the back of the hall. The meeting had already started and, noticeably, one of the chairs in the commissioner seating area was empty. Trooper Turner handed me a meeting agenda so that I could figure out what exactly was going on. Upon reading through the document, I found that I was listed under agenda item 14, which read, "Discussion and possible action regarding the investigation into governments found in the state of Texas being led by one Champ Cove."

I could only think, "Wow, what have I gotten myself into now? I knew it could be awkward to ask and get answers to questions and all, but don't I have some basic civil liberty or right to learn about my government or something? I guess maybe my dad may have violated some ethical norm along the way when he spoke with me or called in a favor. He is a state legislator, after all, but he's not even here."

An hour and a half later, nearing 11:30 a.m., my presence at the front of the room was requested when the commission chair stated, "If I am not mistaken, we are now on agenda item 14. I now request that one Champ Winston Cove be seated at the front table. While he approaches, this item asks us to obtain information about what exactly the called witness is doing when going to the various governmental offices found in the state."

After a short pause, the commission chair articulated, "Once seated, you may begin by making a statement, Champ."

Once seated, I posited, "Good morning. Thanks for hearing from me, I guess? I am not sure what exactly I have done to require an investigation into what I am doing this summer. Specifically, though, this summer I am on a trek to learn as much about the government as I possibly can. I seek to follow my father into politics in some form or fashion, but I have no clue as to what I should do or where exactly I should go. Accordingly, the only thing that I figured that I should do is show up at places, make appointments at others, or simply get involved with something that I could learn from here. For that, I would like to apologize for any potential waste of time or public resources I may have incurred. That is all."

The commission chair proclaimed, "Young man, do you think that you are actually in trouble? Heavens, no. If anything, we are here to advise you on how to avoid getting into trouble when going around to wherever it is that you are headed. You see, there is nothing wrong with going around asking people for information and working to get them to make decisions in your favor in government. *Do see the First Amendment to the US Constitution for that right.* The issue is, many people today have gone forward and made a full-time job of influencing government in their favor. Like many other professional jobs here in the state, the position therefore requires regulation. Simply put, when visiting each of the offices you have been to thus far, or in the future for that matter, you are somewhat playing the role of someone most commonly referred to as a lobbyist. Before I define that term, though, please take note of the booklet located there in front of you; it is essential. That ten-page packet is chapter 34 of the Texas Ethics Commission Rules, entitled 'Regulation of Lobbyists.'[3] Please turn to page 1 and look at section 34.1, entitled 'Definitions,' subheading 3. Specifically, a lobbyist, when performing his or her job, is someone who has '*direct communication* with and works toward preparing for direct communication with a member of the legislative or executive branch to influence legislation or administrative action.' When looking for a more general example of a lobbyist, be sure to think of Tom Hagen and Luca Brasi from the *Godfather* movies.[4] When Godfather Vito Corleone needed opinions swayed, he sent them in to get his point across, either with basic conversation from Tom or brute force from Luca. All of this occurred under the Corleone family name, their clientele group."

I interjected, "What do you mean by 'direct communication'?"

---

3    https://www.ethics.state.tx.us/legal/ch34.pdf
4    Roger Ebert, review of *The Godfather*, March 16, 1997, https://www.rogerebert.com/reviews/great-movie-the-godfather-1972.

The commission chair responded, "Well, there is another packet there in front of you. That packet is entitled 'Lobbying in Texas: A Guide to the Texas Law.'[5] Under the heading of 'Direct Communication' on page 1, that concept is defined as 'contact in person or by telephone, telegraph, or letter.'"

I remarked, "I do believe that I have made some direct communication, but I can't definitively say that I was trying to influence any decisions. More to the point, I just went through and learned about what the different governing officials were doing. I mean, when with the state demographer, I just learned about what he did beyond teaching at UTSA, such as reporting on data regarding population figures, but at no point in time did I tell him how to spend money on acquiring population figures. I could see how, with my dad being a state legislator and all, that that could be a small conflict of interest, but nothing more serious than that."

The commission chair furthered, "Good point, young man, but the better question is whether you need to actually register as a lobbyist. That will determine your guilt or innocence here."

## Registering as a Lobbyist

Another commissioner three people to the left of the chair interjected, "I will take the lead in deciding that. Now Champ, I am Commissioner Dell Lenovo, one of the four appointees of the governor himself to this commission. In determining whether you need to register as a lobbyist, there are two separate thresholds that, if crossed, would require you to register. First and foremost, there is an expenditure threshold. Specifically, you would have to register if, per pages 3 and 4 of the first packet we gave you, the lobby guide, you 'expend more than $500 in a calendar quarter for certain purposes,' not inclusive of certain expenditures reimbursed by a state officer or employee, a gift to a state agency, their own personal expenditures for getting there, and any taxes or tips paid in the process of communicating directly with one or more members of the legislative or executive branch to influence legislation or administrative action. Over the first two weeks of your—as you put it—'trek,' how much have you spent to influence the policy decisions of those you spoke with?"

I speculated, "I would say that since I only spent money on myself in getting to different places and nothing on the officials, my answer would be none."

Commissioner Lenovo declared, "Okay then, since you have not spent more than $500 on lobbying expenses in your two weeks thus far, you have not passed that threshold. On the other hand, though, there is the compensation and reimbursement threshold. This threshold comes into play when, per pages 2 and 3 of the first packet we gave you, you receive or

---

5    https://www.ethics.state.tx.us/guides/lobby_guide.pdf.

are 'entitled to receive under an agreement under which the person is retained or employed, more than $1,000 in a calendar quarter as compensation or reimbursement to lobby,' not inclusive of any reimbursed office or personal expenses from one or more other persons used to communicate directly with a member of the legislative or executive branch to influence legislation or administrative action. How much have you been reimbursed for the last two weeks of your trek from your parents, your uncle, and your sister for lobbying expenditures?"

I speculated again, "I would say that since I am paying for most things that I am doing from my savings, outside of when my sister Charity gave me some money for lunch and entrance fees, that would also be none. Going forward, I will be sure not to take any more money, to avoid any issues or conflicts of interest."

Chair Lenovo concluded, "Well then, since you have not been reimbursed for any expenses used to wine and dine a governing official, nor are you collecting a paycheck, you do not meet this threshold. Accordingly, you need not register as a lobbyist and have committed no fouls. Also, keep in mind, there are several exemptions to many of these thresholds. These are listed on pages 6 and 7 of the *Guide to Lobbying* packet. Specifically, you are exempt from the compensation and reimbursement threshold if you spent no more than 40 hours of your time in a calendar quarter lobbying. This situation is commonly referred to as incidental lobbying. Also, certain activities—like if the persuasion attempt is recorded in public records kept in connection with a legislative hearing, requesting information about the interpretation of a law, or if you are responding to a request for information from a board or commission, such as ours, that is responsible for regulating the lobbying industry found here in the state—are exempt. Also, public officials acting in their official duties, news media outlets collecting information for the dissemination of news, or if you are compensating or reimbursing someone for lobbying, are all exempt as well if that, for lack of a better term, is the entirety of their lobbying activities."

Another chair seated next to Chair Lenovo proposed, "Now Champ, I am Commissioner Spot Light, one of the two appointees of the House Speaker. Let's assume that you did meet the qualifications to register as a lobbyist. Per the *Guide to Lobbying* packet you received earlier, on pages 8 through 12, beyond paying the annual lobbying fee of $750 and registering within five days of your meeting one of the thresholds, you must also state the subject matter (better known as the policy area or areas that you will be seeking to persuade people over), how much you were paid and/or how much you were compensated or reimbursed to lobby, who is paying or reimbursing you to lobby, and who your assistants are, to make sure that you don't have anyone working for you on the inside. Once registered, you must periodically report your activities. Keep in mind that if you expend less than a grand annually, you may file your Lobby Activity Report annually. Expend even a cent more, and you are required to report monthly. When you report your activity, each report must detail who you were lobbying for, how much you spent, and, most importantly, who that money was spent on."

I interjected, "You don't have to report on what exactly it was that you and the official talked about?"

Commissioner Light concluded, "Well, no. Thanks to the efforts of, oddly enough, lobbyists seeking to keep lobbying regulation at a minimum, this is all that we require. I'm looking at the page on my laptop now from the National Conference of State Legislatures,[6] one of the most formidable resources monitoring these requirements, and there is certainly a variance in registering requirements. These variances include how the states define lobbying, who is required to report, and what exactly is reported, among more minor nuances. For example, for those seeking to lobby in Washington DC, to the federal government, based on the Lobbying Disclosure Act of 1995,[7] you must only register if your organization spends more than $20,000 a year or, as an individual, you spend more than $5,000 a year, alongside spending 20 percent or more of your time, on lobbying. Also, you can be exempt if you are part of a grassroots lobbying effort or a tax-exempt organization like a religious group. More importantly, semiannual reports only disclose the general nature of the lobbying effort, the specific bills, and bill numbers, the costs of their work, and the branches they have spoken to, not the individual names. Beyond that, further legislation came in 2007 via the Honest Leadership and Open Government Act[8], which reinforced House and Senate ethics rules, increased the delay between leaving the legislature and working for a lobbying firm, and increased reporting requirements for expenditures to quarterly reporting, which is also now done electronically. We at least require the names of who you spoke with, so we are indeed stricter than the federal government on specific items, not by much, but still in line with them on other reporting requirements. With other states, it just depends on their beliefs about reporting standards."

The chair spoke up again. "Champ, in case you didn't get my name from before, I am Jeffrey Ocean, one of the two appointees put forward by the lieutenant governor. Beyond those registration and reporting criteria, per the *Guide to Lobbying in Texas* packet, other prohibitions and restrictions do apply. For example, per pages 13 to 17, you cannot blatantly bribe an official, nor may you give them cash or material gifts or buy lodging for a ceremonial or pleasure trip. You can only pay for food or beverages if you are present, you cannot offer contingency fees, and most importantly, you are barred from the legislative floors unless specially invited. Lastly, per page 17 of the *Guide to Lobbying* packet, breaking the rules on bribery or contingency

6    http://www.ncsl.org/research/ethics/50-state-chart-lobbyist-report-requirements.aspx
7    http://lobbyingdisclosure.house.gov/lda.html
8    https://www.congress.gov/bill/110th-congress/house-bill/2316

fees is a felony, while everything else is a misdemeanor, like paying for lodging of a pleasure trip that in no way could be construed as part of one's job. Overall, though, what we have discussed here with you are the basics of lobbying regulations of the state. Keep in mind that those rules only apply when seeking to deal with the executive and legislative branches; any lobbying toward the judicial branch and local government is exempt from regulation.[9] Beyond the rules, though, we are not in the best of positions to discuss this subject further. For how to lobby, if you look to the back of the room, one of our favorite influential customers and fellow member of this commission is here to speak with you. You are dismissed."

When I turned to look at the back of the room, Tommy, my uncle, was sitting there waiting for me with a big grin on his face. After a second or so, he waved me over. Once there, he patted me on the back and stated, "Son, that was quite the grilling you took there. Let's get some lunch over at the Capitol Grill and take a stroll around downtown to see some applicable sights on today's subject. . . . Thanks, guys, for playing along up there!!"

## Types of Interest Groups

With full stomachs now in tow and getting near 1:00 p.m., Tommy and I walked our way out of the state capitol building, via the elevators that go through the original building to the first floor, and then exited through the western entryway. Along the way, Tommy declared, "You now got the idea behind the regulation of my work. For the rest of the day, we are going to cover what there is to know about lobbying beyond the simple act of regulating the industry. For starters, people may act alone in attempting to influence government, but as we all know, life is a bit of a numbers game. The greater the numbers you have, the better off you'll be in influencing government. Accordingly, people then get together and form influential organizations. When people get together in these like-minded organizations to influence government, they are called interest groups, also referred to as pressure groups, 'an interest group organized to influence public and especially government policy but not to elect candidates to office.'[10] These interest groups are half the players in something called the 'political game,' which is a fancy way of describing the process of determining who gets what from where and how they end up needing to spend their gained resources."

As we were walking down West 12th Street, but still on the capitol grounds, I asked, "Why do those pressure groups then feel the need to take action?"

Uncle Tommy furthered, as we hit Lavaca Street, "Look at the situation like this. Texas has a vast economy and enough government spending for a lifetime every year, in my opinion.

---

9    https://www.ethics.state.tx.us/guides/lobby_guide.pdf, page 2.

10    https://www.merriam-webster.com/dictionary/pressure%20group

Many of the groups that go out and lobby are therefore seeking their slice of that pie, because they all, for the most part, depend on government outlays to do their work, or in other cases, their beliefs empower them not to want any government spending on an item. For example, teacher organizations work to compel greater spending on public education, and a road construction firm would see to it that that the state build and maintain more roads, while a religious organization (like the Southern Baptist Convention[11] and their missions) would seek to impair any further government spending on abortions or even seek to have the practice outright banned here in the state due to their beliefs."

I asked, "So how can we go back and organize all of these pressure groups?"

Tommy furthered, "Speaking of the devil in timing, if you look south, you can see the local headquarters of the American Federation of Labor and Congress of Industrial Organization (AFL-CIO). This group is a good example of the first type of interest groups, economic-minded, as they seek to obtain financial benefits of some kind for their members. The AFL-CIO[12] would go after better workman's compensation, stricter workplace safety laws, and even higher minimum wages. Beyond labor unions, agriculture groups, business organizations, and professional occupational advocates would also fit this category, with groups such as the Texas Farm Bureau,[13] the Texas Chambers of Commerce,[14] and the Texas Association of Realtors[15] representing them, respectively. Let's keep walking west to get to the next category."

Halfway between Lavaca and Guadalupe Streets on 12th, Tommy had the two of us look to the north. He continued, "In front of us is the office of the Texas State Teachers Association,[16] which is part of the National Education Association (figure 11.2). This group represents the category of mixed interest groups. This naming is because this group represents not only the eco-

FIGURE 11.2    Texas State Teacher's Association Building.

---

11    http://www.sbc.net
12    http://www.texasaflcio.org
13    http://texasfarmbureau.org
14    http://www.tcce.org
15    https://www.texasrealestate.com
16    http://tsta.org

nomic interests of members but also social injustice causes. For example, on the one hand, they seek to get better pay and teaching conditions for the teachers they represent, while on the other, they seek to expand education program offerings found here in the state for students. Other than educational groups, groups that focus on race relations and gender issues would also fit this category, with groups such as the National Association for the Advancement of Colored People,[17] the League of United Latin American Citizens,[18] and Planned Parenthood of Greater Texas[19] representing them, respectively. Let's go a bit further west."

FIGURE 11.3    Texas Chapter of the Sierra Club Building.

A block and a half later, we turned to the north onto San Antonio Street and stopped two buildings farther down. Tommy continued, "In this small structure here is the headquarters of the Lone Star Chapter of the Sierra Club (figure 11.3).[20] They represent the final category of interest groups, noneconomic organizations. These organizations seek to lobby the government for increasing standards in society without positively or negatively affecting members' finances— easier put as social injustice causes. These groups could range from increased civil liberties to merely seeking increased government efforts to clean the environment more and get us fresher air. The Sierra Club would advocate for policies that ensure the protection of the environment and your right to a fresh breath of air, for example. Other environmental groups, patriotic groups, personal liberty seekers, public interests, and religious rights advocates would be classified under this category, with organizations such as the American Legion,[21] the Texas State Rifle Association,[22] Texans for Public Justice,[23] and the Christian Coalition of America and their Texas chapters[24] representing them, respectively. While we

17    http://www.txnaacp.org
18    https://lulac.org
19    https://www.plannedparenthood.org/planned-parenthood-greater-texas
20    http://texas2.sierraclub.org
21    http://www.legion.org
22    https://www.tsra.com
23    http://www.tpj.org
24    http://www.cc.org

are standing here, other than interest groups, who else might you want to speak with to learn about additional opportunities to join the government?"

## Comparing Interest Groups and Political Parties

I remarked, "Seeing as how we are talking about getting politically involved, all that I can think of to be left is political parties."

Tommy, with no immediate reply to my response, instructed us to go east back down 12th Street toward the capitol building. When we were standing once again in front of the Texas State Teachers Association building, Tommy had us look south. He furthered, "Well, Champ, you are spot-on to your reply earlier. We are now looking at the Republican Party of Texas headquarters. In many ways, political parties, such as the Republican Party, and interest groups are very similar. For example, both groups seek to influence the government and have a lasting impact on society regarding various issues. In how the groups and political parties go about doing so is where the difference lies. Political parties are the other half of the competitors in the 'political game' I mentioned earlier. One of the items that you should ask party leaders about is their party platforms. Question: How many pieces do you think those chairs have a plank on?"

I surmised, "From what we've discussed so far today, I suspect that each of their party's platforms is going to be several pages long and cover nearly every issue imaginable with a statement about every subject in some form or another, taking different stances on the matter at hand."

Tommy contended, "Well, interest groups don't do that. Typically, they have a very narrow opinion or view on one specific subject. Let's say that they are single-issue focused. Environmental interest groups like the Sierra Club a while back on our walk only care about one thing: protecting the environment; nothing more, nothing less. Now, it could be argued that their protect-at-all-costs view is not the majority opinion of society, so this does bring up fear over their minority view being taken over by the unorganized masses, but it's hard to argue against clean air in most cases. Another question: Who is the local Sierra Club candidate for the lieutenant governor's office in the last election?"

I replied, "I do not remember there being one—granted, I did not get to vote, so I may have missed that."

Tommy said, "Either way, that's right; the second difference is that these organizations do not put candidates up for election on ballots. Now, that doesn't mean that there isn't a Sierra Club candidate on the ballot; it just means that these groups have thrown their support behind someone from a political party who agrees with their viewpoint. Last question: Which candidates would the Sierra Club probably support?"

I speculated, "Based on what I've heard on the news over time, I would say Democrats, as they typically hold similar views."

Tommy concluded, "That is only half correct, as these groups will play along with anyone who will agree with or listen to them, no matter their political affiliation. That's the third and final difference; they get to play both sides. They do what Jeff Saturday did during the 2013 NFL Pro Bowl. He was the main ball snapper for the NFC squad, but since this was going to be his last game, he decided to cross over for one play and have his final career snap go to his former Indianapolis Colts teammate of 13 years, quarterback Peyton Manning of the AFC, who was playing for the Denver Broncos at the time.[25] Now let's take a geographical look at our situation. What are we surrounded by?"

I replied, "Well, based on the short walk we just went on, influence central, as one major political party and several interest groups are headquartered right here."

Tommy contended, "Why can all those entities exist?"

I remarked, "State and federal law?"

Tommy replied, "Close enough. Remember, last week you had the critical document experience at the state archives. You should have learned that, from our state and federal constitutions, we are technically guaranteed the right to form these groups. Explicitly, the First Amendment of the US Constitution states, 'Congress shall make no law . . . [restricting] . . . the right of the people to peaceably assemble, and to petition the government for redress of grievances,'[26] while article 1, section 27 of the Texas State version reads 'The citizens shall have the right . . . to . . . apply those invested with the powers of government for redress of grievances or other purposes by petition, address, or remonstrance.'[27] Overall, both documents allow citizens to go forth and complain to governing officials. Keep in mind that there are almost no limits on what you can form a group about. When I was in college, there was this professor who had diabetes. He was an avid volunteer with the Juvenile Diabetes Research Foundation[28] to help garner support for a cure to that dreadful disease. More importantly, why do you think that there are so many groups?"

I opined, "I read an article online last month that talked about a set of girls from Overton, Texas, who had their lemonade stand shut down for not having a peddler's license, not to mention a health permit[29]—all despite that activity serving as a national pastime for chil-

25    Jon Benne, "One Last Snap," SBNation.com, January 28, 2013, https://www.sbnation.com/nfl/2013/1/27/3922910/pro-bowl-2013-jeff-saturday.

26    U.S. Constitution, Amendment 1.

27    Texas Constitution of 1876, article 1, section 23.

28    https://www.jdrf.org

29    Deena Zaru, "Texas Cops Shut Down Kids' 'Illegal' Lemonade Stand," CNN, June 12, 2015, https://www.cnn.com/2015/06/11/politics/lemonade-stand-shut-down-texas/index.html.

dren growing up. So, I would say that it sounds like because the government is practically everywhere."

Tommy interjected, "Very good. The ever-increasing size of government is having a greater and greater influence on items in society. I once knew a guy who worked for a timber company out West. On their millions of acres of property, they have roads throughout. To keep water flowing from plot to plot, they have culverts going under their roads. The Environmental Protection Agency then wanted to require water-quality monitors to be installed on either side of the conduit to ensure that the water was the same quality on both sides, despite the fact the water had no outside influence along the way from, say, a sewage treatment plant or something. I didn't get the backstory, but he was irate over the seemingly excessive regulation. It got so bad, though, that he went out and joined an interest group of his own free will. It's like backing an animal into a corner; people, like the animal, get so nervous about their livelihood they feel that they are left with only one option: Fight back for their right to operate."[30]

I suggested, "Who and why would someone join an interest group?"

Before he answered, he motioned that we make our way back to the capitol building so that we could get out of the sun. About ten minutes later, we found ourselves sitting down on a bench in the first-floor hallway. Tommy continued, "The members of an interest group are probably not the average members of society. The burger flipper at the restaurant here in the capitol may be unionized, but he probably won't be anywhere near something other than a picket line protesting or paying his dues. The owner of the restaurant and other professional types of individuals, like CEOs and doctors, are much more likely to join. Also, members will typically be well educated and affluent. Regarding why they join, though, it could be a simple desire to influence government and the decisions it makes, the work requirements for continued employment at a company, or the networking opportunities offered for people if major downsizing occurs in the industry, and they find themselves outside looking in, in need of someplace to end up."

## What to Know When Lobbying

I asked, "So what do you do as part of your position when going around lobbying?"

Tommy articulated, "Champ, lobbying and interest group activities can be done either directly or indirectly. Directly is when we are acting openly, frankly, or candidly about getting our point across. This option includes going and visiting with legislators or other officials in their offices, filing a lawsuit in court, being elected or appointed to a governing

---

30    See author or source material.

board like I am to the Texas Ethics Commission, and what I specialize best in, organizing public demonstrations. Indirectly occurs when we are acting without making direct contact in some form or fashion with those governing officials. Actions here include something called electioneering, which is working toward the successful election of a candidate, political party, or ballot issue by making signs and buttons to display; this is in addition to going out and educating the public at events on an issue, alongside attending social events with politicians where we can make donations but not ask for anything specific, as that would be bribery. Let's go down the hall. Time for you to jump into the deep end of the pool."

On the way, I could only take deep breaths to keep from nervously shaking. I asked, "So what is it that you want me to do?"

FIGURE 11.4    Texas Secretary of State's Office.

Once on the east side of the capitol building, we found ourselves stopped in front of Room 1E.8, the central office for the Texas secretary of state (figure 11.4). Tommy replied, "The Texas secretary of state is one of the most important executive branch offices found here in the state. I want you to set up an appointment to speak with the officeholder tomorrow. This office is an important stop on your trek. Now go."

I was all of a sudden thankful that the state troopers from before had allowed me to change into formal clothes. I proceeded to open the door. Seated at a desk was a nice young woman answering the phones. She inquired, "How may I help you, sir?"

I replied, "I would like to set up a meeting with the secretary of state sometime tomorrow."

She replied, "Who are you, and what is the subject of said meeting?"

I remarked, "My name is Champ Cove, and I would like to learn about the position."

She stated, "So you know nothing about what goes on here and expect the secretary to drop everything to tell you anything you want to know? I can pass a note along. Write your contact information on this sheet of paper, but don't expect anything. Have a great day, sir."

After putting my information on the sheet of paper, I turned and walked out the door. Once I was outside, Tommy had a smirk on his face again, knowing that I had just walked into a bear trap, and said, "You just walked in there blindly. You didn't even ask for topic ideas. You just went for it. A for gall, F for lunacy. Let's go sit on this bench over here."

Once we were seated, Tommy continued, "When lobbying, you have one overall basic goal: Influence government to a means you see fit. More importantly, that goal varies, depending on who it is you are speaking to. I don't think that you have gotten here yet this summer, but everything involved in government deals with some portion of the lawmaking process. The legislature oversees drafting laws, so your goal there would be to help shape the policy being created. The executive branch oversees approving and then enforcing laws. Accordingly, your goal here is to curb the implementation of the newly minted laws to a more desirable standing. Lastly, if you didn't get the bill drafted or implemented the way you wanted, you must lobby the judiciary—which determines the constitutionality of policies—where your goal is like that of a wall: Block policy from going forward and becoming an established law due to the law not being to your liking. The big item we all use to decide when to act is the Texas and Federal Registers,[31] where agencies and the legislature publishes all laws and agency decisions for public dissemination and response."

I interjected, "When going in to lobby, what specific information do pressure groups need to bring along with them?"

Tommy continued: "In achieving all those goals, interest groups draw in elite officials—call them the industry all-star team—to go in and lobby on their behalf, alongside trained hires like me. Let's use the development of a football team to get this point across. First off, each player must know his capabilities—a lobbyist's views, in this case. Is he tall and lean, making him better for a quarterback, running back, or even a wide receiver, or is he a wide load, which might make him perfect for being a lineman? Knowing this allows you to go out for the best position. No sense in going for defensive lineman if you can't keep back the 400-pound opposing lineman who will be in front of you. For lobbying, being sure about your position on an issue will help you be more confident in asking for terms to be found in the following policy. Secondly, the team must know their program inside and out—the lobbying organization in this case. Coach needs to draw up the best plays possible; is the team short of receivers, leaving them to focus on running the ball, or vice versa, forcing them to go for the air attack? For lobbying, the more you know your organization, the better you can organize people to get your point across. Third, the team must know who their next opponent is—an opposing lobbying organization in this case. In prepping for their next game, the coach and the players watch tapes of the other team so that they know how best to defeat them via the exploitation of their weaknesses. As the saying goes, 'Keep your friends close but your enemies closer,' so your enemies can't get away from you. For lobbying organizations, it's the same concept."

---

31   http://www.sos.state.tx.us/texreg/index.shtml; https://www.federalregister.gov

I interrupted, "If I am not mistaken, those three items all relate to knowing your team/lobbying group, but what about actually getting your point across?"

Tommy concluded, "Also, the team has to know what their mission is, beyond just winning. Lobbyists, in this case, must understand their issue. At the beginning of the season, everyone has their eyes on the prize of winning the championship. As the season progresses, though, some teams face the harsh reality of still wanting to win, not just winning for the sake of winning, but preventing a better team from advancing past you. For lobbying, this is knowing your issue. The issue is, if you go out spewing information about how your view is essential and evidence to the contrary emerges, you lose all your political clout. I mean, you are there to provide info; be sure it's accurate and legit. Lastly, the team must know what the rules are, alongside who will be enforcing them—the official a lobbyist will be speaking with at the time. Case in point: In the US House of Representatives, American Samoa, Guam, the Northern Mariana Islands, Puerto Rico, Washington DC, and the Virgin Islands each get their representatives. The thing is, those members don't get a vote beyond any committees they are assigned to. Therefore, it would behoove you to avoid spending your time there and not waste any resources on them once a bill leaves a committee that they serve, as they have no more direct influence. There is an excellent *Colbert Report* video that you should check out sometime.[32] For football, this is like needing to avoid tossing a forward lateral."

I commented, "So if I know all of that important information, I should be able to get my point across without much hassle. All of that is assuming a single decision-making process, but what should the official keep in mind when deciding to listen or not?"

Tommy asked, "What's another term for food or the other things you use on a day-to-day basis?"

I replied, "I guess the term I would use is resources?"

Tommy expressed, "Exactly. Resources, 'a source of supply or support'[33] are the most prominent thing an official can depend on from a lobbyist. During opinion-making sessions, a lobbyist could pull out an information packet to help a legislator decide what to do. Also, if the decision has already been made, the group could pledge volunteers to help get the program off the ground at events or only spread the word. Finally, if the office is elected, a lobbyist could provide a public endorsement of some kind or even go so far as donating to their campaigns, which aren't cheap to manage—which you know already."

---

32   Comedy Central, "The Colbert Report," accessed March 20, 2019, http://thecolbertreport.cc.com/videos/6quypd/better-know-a-district---district-of-columbia---eleanor-holmes-norton.

33   https://www.merriam-webster.com/dictionary/resource

## Controls on Interest Groups

I mentioned, "That seems to be a very lucrative trading scheme. I change my mind on something, and I get all those 'resources' to come my way. So, what regulates the trade-offs?"

Tommy contended, "Let's look around at our present situation. You already know about one: the regulations—easier put as laws—which regulate their transactions. The more laws there are, the less power lobbyists have to influence. Another one, though, is, look at all the people around us. Many of the people who work here got their jobs by being elected. The more people vote, the less power lobbyists have, because all the governing officials know that if they make a dumb decision, their position is toast. The more votes cast, the less power lobbyists have to influence. Another control revolves around the offices we saw earlier today; there is more than one lobbying group on many issues. If your group is the new kid on the block, don't expect to have much of a sway on issues. This may be because you would have fewer so-called resources to dole out. More experienced groups have more power to influence. From our earlier conversations, who should you try to learn about tomorrow?"

I replied, "Political parties?"

Tommy continued, "That would be correct. Here in Texas, right now, the Republicans are the dominant political party as they hold all the offices. Therefore, they don't have to spend as much time listening to Democrats to reach a consensus on matters, giving them more time to deal with lobbyists, giving the lobbyists more power to influence. Lastly, there are two structural controls that come into play. On the one hand, we have a short legislative session, giving a reduced—in comparison to other legislatures—amount of time for legislators to deliberate on issues. This situation gives interest groups more power to influence, as they can shorten the time needed to flesh out the important points of an issue by providing more of those resources, which fits in nicely with the short sessions. On the other hand, much of the power here in the state is spread out thin, making it easier for lobbyists to speak with officials, as the officials have more freedom to make up their minds and not fit in with the governor's wishes, giving the lobbyists more freedom."

I remarked, "So several items give power to lobbyist persuasions. It just depends on the greater or lesser presence of them."

Tommy said, "Lobbyists are very powerful in what they do; it all just depends on the playing field that they can play on. Let's go walk down the back side of the complex, and I will fill you in on the last thing you should know about interest groups."

After walking back through the rotunda and out the exit doors, we stopped and looked down on the rear driveway. Tommy continued: "Now, Champ, with everything we do in life, there will be positives and negatives. One major negative impact that you touched on earlier is the fact that, beyond reporting who people like me have spoken to, everything we specifically talk about is kept private, which is shady. This leads to the second negative: If we don't have to report what exactly it is that we say, we can say almost anything and get away with it. I've heard stories of representatives being threatened with manufacturing plant closures by corporations in their districts if they voted favorably on certain pieces of legislation. Lastly, these kinds of groups, once again, have very narrow interests, so if they get their way on something, nothing else really matters, one way or the other."

I interjected, "So what's the upside to all of this fuss?"

Tommy concluded, "As we talked about before, lobbyists and interest groups bring a lot of resources to the table. Those resources, particularly the information, provide three major positives. First, access to that information (assuming the information is accurate, of course) is a gold mine, as it is traditionally off-limits to non-industry eyes. Secondly, that information is a big cost saving to taxpayers, as the different government research bodies do not have to go out and produce duplicative information. Lastly, remember all the participation events that we went to earlier this week? Pressure groups represent the final positive; while lobbying events are typically closed to the public, there are still large education functions within these groups. Now, if I'm not mistaken, that's really about all that there is to know, unless you want to get into the nitty-nitty-gritty of it all. Anything else that you can think to ask about?"

I got an idea and asked, "Tommy, how much do you care about me?"

Tommy replied, "A lot."

I continued, "You would do anything to help me, right?"

Tommy, getting an inquisitive look on his face, went on: "I would not, but what are you after?"

I concluded, "Since I know that you care about me and would do anything for me, would you make sure that I get home safely by giving me a ride?"

Tommy grunted and went, "Oh, that's good—you knew what your issue was, who it was you were lobbying to, and everything else, like the fact that you don't have a car here with you. You learned well, kid. I knew setting up that pickup this morning was going to come back to haunt me. All right, let's go. You talked me into it."

Based on that last conversation, it appears as if I may have found my calling in this political game. Beyond that, though, I could see why this participation method, lobbying, needed a whole day. If you want to go through and get your view to make a difference, you must go in and speak to people, not just stand on the corner waving a sign, although that might not hurt in the short run. More importantly, because the lobbyists and the interest groups they represent work full time, they have the same amount of regulation as any other primary profession found here in the state. Lastly, this aspect of the political game is all about being very persuasive, to your benefit.

**QUESTIONS TO CONSIDER** REGARDING SPECIAL GOVERNMENTAL INTERESTS:

1. The first main topic of the chapter defines lobbyists. Please define that term, identify an example of that term in your life, and explain why they are an excellent example, in detail.

2. The second main topic of the chapter discusses the thresholds to meet before you must register as a lobbyist. Please identify the thresholds that you need to meet, the ones you meet, and indicate if you need to register as a lobbyist. If yes, please identify the information that you need to report as it relates to your situation.

3. The third main topic of the chapter discusses the different types of interest groups. Please identify the different types of interest groups, what they seek to accomplish, the type that you are most drawn to, and why, in detail.

4. The fourth main topic of the chapter compares interest groups to political parties. Please identify what differences there are, the one that indicates to you that the two are truly different from one another, and why, in detail.

5. The fifth main topic of the chapter identifies the things you need to know when lobbying. Please identify what those need-to-know items are, the one you feel is most important to know, and why, in detail.

6. The final main topic of the chapter discusses different controls on interest groups. Please identify what those controls are, the one that you would least fear as a lobbyist, and indicate why, in detail.

FIGURE CREDIT

# Chapter 12

# Political Parties

# What Are Political Parties?

Growing up with my dad being an active member of the Republican Party in the state as a Texas state representative, I was exposed to more political parties than the average kid. The issue is, being a kid, mainly until the beginning of this summer, I never really appreciated all the intricate nuances that went along with so-called party politics, the infighting between members of a party or different political parties, hence the reason that I am on this fun little trek this summer in the first place. In rectifying that nonappreciation of the insight that had been made available to me, I figured it would be wise to spend the day, as part of my trek, speaking with various leaders of the different political parties operating here in the state, to learn more about them. The question was, how do I do such a thing?

**TEXAS ★ DEMOCRATS**

FIGURE 12.1    Texas Democratic Party Logo.

FIGURE 12.2    Republican Party Logo.

In deciding who I should speak with, I decided to do an internet search for political parties in Texas. As always, the internet never failed to surprise me with the vaunted amount of material. The two main parties that I had been exposed to in my senior government class last fall, Democrats (figure 12.1)[1] and Republicans (figure 12.2),[2] had fully functional websites that were easy to find contact information on; even their national contingent's versions were easily accessible. Beyond those two parties, links to a smattering of other lesser-known, even a few very fringe, parties came to light, some with versions just for Texas, just for national, and some for both, including the Communist Party,[3] Constitution Party,[4] Green Party,[5] Guns and Dope Party,[6] Independence Party,[7] Libertarian Party (figure 12.3),[8] Objectivity Party, Reform Party,[9] Socialist Party,[10] U.S. Marijuana Party,[11] Vermont Progressive

---

1    https://www.txdemocrats.org; https://www.democrats.org
2    https://www.texasgop.org; https://www.gop.com
3    http://www.cpusa.org; https://www.cp-texas.org
4    https://www.constitutionparty.com; https://www.constitutionparty.com/tag/constitution-party-of-texas
5    http://www.txgreens.org; http://www.gp.org
6    http://www.gunsanddopeparty.net
7    http://www.theuniversalfoundation.com/tipotx.html; http://aipca.org
8    http://www.lptexas.org; https://www.lp.org
9    http://reformparty.org; http://reformpartytx.org
10    Socialistpartyoftx.org; https://www.socialistpartyusa.net
11    http://usmjparty.org

Party,[12] and the Working Families Party,[13] among many others.[14] After reviewing the links, just after 9:00 a.m. and a quick phone call to my dad to get any other options that I may have missed that were worthwhile, I called the office numbers of the chairpersons of the Democratic, Libertarian, and Republican Parties of Texas to arrange a meeting. The other political parties either didn't have an office in the Austin area or didn't appear to have much of a permanent contact link for the turnaround time that I required.

FIGURE 12.3   Texas Libertarian Party Logo.

In deciding how best to foster a constructive conversation with the representatives of the different parties, I decided that it was best that I implement two pieces of knowledge I had gained over the years. First, after several joint Thanksgiving dinners with my father's more conservative family and my mother's more liberal family, I learned that it becomes hard to start an argument—or stay angry, for that matter—with someone you disagree with on issues when you have a full stomach. Second, I learned that the Swiss had avoided being involved in two world wars and countless other conflicts by becoming a neutral territory. Accordingly, picking a place to go where no one had an advantage seemed wise. Sadly, in obtaining neutral territory with food, Switzerland, unlike Mexico, doesn't have a consulate in the Austin area to use for a meet-and-greet. Therefore, I decided to go with one of the 800-pound gorillas in the room that would ensure strict order, despite their, albeit minor, meddling in the 2016 presidential elections.[15] Without hesitation, I called in the Russians via the Russian House Restaurant (figure 12.4),[16] located at 307 East Fifth Street in downtown Austin.

FIGURE 12.4   Russian House Restaurant.

12   http://www.progressiveparty.org

13   http://www.workingfamilies.org

14   https://en.wikipedia.org/wiki/List_of_political_parties_in_the_United_States

15   *New York Times*, "Russian Hacking and Influence in the U.S. Election," accessed March 20, 2019, https://www.nytimes.com/news-event/russian-election-hacking.

16   http://russianhouseofaustin.com

Coincidentally, the restaurant was located centrally to each of the three party's central headquarters.

When making the phone calls to arrange everything, I had to leave messages with Democratic chair Gilberto Hinojosa,[17] Libertarian Party chair John Wilford,[18] and Republican Party chair James Dickey.[19] Accordingly, I had to let the spirits determine if the chairpersons would attend. I told each of the chairpersons in their message that I would arrive early for the scheduled meeting time of 11:30 a.m. to get a table and that I would be wearing my Texas-flag, cotton button-down shirt in a quiet corner of the restaurant, to avoid any mishaps from people seeing the three of them together.

Since it was only 9:30 a.m. and I had some time to use wisely before I needed to depart, I decided to do some preemptive research on what exactly each party was supporting. In doing this, I downloaded the most up-to-date version of each party's platform,[20] which is the "party's formal statement of its basic principles, objectives, and positions on major issues"[21] (figure 12.5). In fostering conversation later, I decided that I would pick four issues that would hopefully help clear the water regarding what differentiates the parties beyond what I hear about on late-night TV or the news. This move would later prove to be a wise decision. Accordingly, with platforms in hand, flag shirt on, and a mind-set in place needed to corral the most significant political players in the state, I left Charity's house just after 10:30 a.m. I went into town on Highway 360, north on MOPAC, and exited at Sixth Street for the drive across downtown to the restaurant.

Since I didn't know how long I was going to be there, I parked in a long-term garage two blocks west of the restaurant, at the corner of Fifth and Brazos. After the quick walk to the restaurant, I entered the

FIGURE 12.5   Electoral Program of 1912 for the Progressive Party.

17   https://www.txdemocrats.org/our-party/leaders/officers

18   http://www.lptexas.org/state-leadership

19   https://www.texasgop.org/leadership-directory/party-officers/

20   https://3npv5loo75n4f1mrxbxvz8hv-wpengine.netdna-ssl.com/wp-content/uploads/2016/05/PERM-PLATFORM-as-Amended-by-Gen-Body-5.13.16.pdf; https://www.txdemocrats.org/our-party/texas-democratic-party-platform; http://www.lptexas.org/platform

21   https://definitions.uslegal.com/p/party-platform

establishment to begin my preparations just after 11:00 a.m. At the front of the restaurant was a stuffed bear, standing on its back legs next to a wall of former Soviet military garb that you could wear as you mingled in the establishment. After the entrance is a traditional bar and lounge-type area, but in the back, through a door which appears to have come straight off someone's house in Moscow, you enter the dining area, which I could tell with one glance provided the atmosphere I sought. The aura of the room was set from the moment one enters, due to a multitude of Russian nesting dolls, mismatched silverware, table linens, and family portraits everywhere that really made it feel as if you were back in Moscow during the Cold War, with the KGB ready to jump out at you at any time to quell any attempts against the state.

In the time before the chairpersons arrived, and after I was seated by a woman with a thick Russian accent, I reviewed my notes and put in an order for a round of water and a dish called meat delicacy, which consisted of a platter with three different varieties of fish, their famous Hungarian salami, beef tongue, and various smoked meats.

Roughly ten minutes later, with the waters already on the table, Chair Wilford arrived, along with the delightful-looking appetizer in tow behind him. I immediately rose from my seat and shook his hand. Once seated, Chair Wilford also thanked me for including him in my roundtable, as what he called "third parties," or "a political party formed as a dissenting or independent group from members of one or both of the two prevailing major parties,"[22] do not typically get invited to such events. As evidence, he brought up the fact that, outside of the 1992 presidential debate, third parties are not normally invited to participate, at least in modern times.[23] It was then that I heard a loud utterance behind: "You there, in the flag shirt. Are you Champ?"

I once again stood up to find two gentlemen now approaching the table in a hurry. I replied, "Yes, sir. Who might you be?"

Immediately, the same gentleman who had spoken before responded, "My name is James Dickey, chair of the state Republican Party, and this is my counterpart from the Democratic Party, Gilberto Hinojosa."

I ushered the chairpersons to find a seat at the table with Chair Wilford, who had also stood to shake their hands. Apparently, from what I could hear of their conversations, a meeting between these three gentlemen, or at least those in their position, was a rare experience. This piece of information made sense, as every other year their parties are locked in competitive electoral campaigns in which they seek to destroy each other, or their chances of winning various offices, at least. Once they were seated and eating the appetizer, Chair Hinojosa spoke up.

---

22    http://www.dictionary.com/browse/third-party

23    Pete Tucker, "How Third Parties Are Kept Out of Presidential Debates," Huffington Post, August 3, 2017, https://www.huffingtonpost.com/pete-tucker/what-the-hell-how-third-p_b_11277474.html;

"You are a very lucky man to have this opportunity to speak with us. We don't typically like to play nice with each other, but I guess in this special situation we can make an exception. Also, had your father not contacted James over there, who called me about all this, we would have thrown your message in the trash. You have no idea how many people are always working to speak with us. We are all very important here in the state, even John over there. Once again, be sure to appreciate the access you now have. Good appetizer choice, by the way."

I remarked, "Thanks, Dad, and thank you, each of you, for your time. I want to follow my father into government somehow, and I am spending my summer learning about the various aspects it entails. On that trek, y'all are an important waypoint, as it appears that so much is initiated by y'all, or your candidates, at least, in government."

Chair Wilford chimed in, "So what exactly is it that you want to know?"

I responded, "Quite frankly, everything each of you can offer on the subject, but if you want to come to a consensus on questions for me to focus on, feel free. Let's get started with defining what political parties are, I guess."

Chair Hinojosa noted, "That's simple, political parties are 'an organization of people who share the same views about the way power should be used in a country or society (through government, policy-making, etc.),'[24] in other words, your teammates in the struggle for control over the government. What next?"

I replied, "A history of political parties, if that's all right."

Before the chairpersons could respond, the waitress came over and took our main entrée orders. We ended up splitting orders of Russian pelmeni, pork schnitzel, and a few shashliks of lamb and chicken. Once through ordering, Chair Dickey spoke up. "For political party history, you cannot look at one party by itself. You must look at how the parties relate to one another at that point in time. This set of circumstances is in the same way that you cannot look at one team in a sports league by itself; they are part of a league where they are competing for something more by selecting a different strategy over a possibly more traditional one, and they could achieve a higher level of success. Let's use the 2002 Oakland A's and their use of a new team-building tool, called sabermetrics, that used modern sophisticated statistical analysis that concluded that teams should emphasize a player's on-base percentage and slugging percentage in determining their potential offensive success, rather than the simple, traditional measures of stolen bases, RBIs, and batting average that had been used over the prior century. In both cases, without competition, it is just one team—or party, in this case—playing by itself. Therefore, doing so is silly and lacks that particular sense of excitement.[25] Overall, competition is what makes up the history of political parties, and

24   https://www.collinsdictionary.com/us/dictionary/english/political-party
25   Michael Lewis, *Moneyball: The Art of Winning an Unfair Game* (New York: Norton, 2003).

that history can best be viewed via the string of party systems that have been in existence in our country over time."

I asked, "'Party system' what? Please go a bit more in-depth. My government teacher didn't exactly mention that term in high school very comprehensively."

Chair Dickey continued, "Well, 'party system' is a phrase used by those scholars studying politics to refer an era in time when a relatively durable system of political parties and voter alignments, electoral rules, and policy priorities in a democratic political system's electoral process is in effect. Each party system provides evidence of how the dominant political party controlled the government, mobilized a voting bloc, and obtained financial resources, all in hopes of retaining office by working toward selecting the right candidates. A one-party system has one dominant political party, a two-party system has two, and a multiparty system has at least three, sometimes even more, dominant political parties vying for control and having control of the government. To indicate when one system ends and another begins, it is wise to focus on a critical election that alters significant portions of the now-defunct system into a newer one."

## How Political Parties Form

I spoke up. "Let's go back a step here. So parties and their politics operate in a series of systems, but how do they emerge to take part in a particular system?"

Chair Hinojosa remarked, "James, I'll take this particular question. You see, political parties can form by one of two methods. In the first case, let's assume that we have a legislative body that has recently formed. Let's also assume that in that legislative body, there are no present official divisions—political parties, for example. Then one day, an important enough issue emerges that divides the body permanently, causing it to develop into parties."

I interjected, "That issue, you could say, is a cleavage, right? More importantly, though, it's one that the body members could not crosscut."

Chair Hinojosa continued, "Very good. You've already learned about political culture, haven't you? On the other hand, though, political parties may form, external from a legislative body, over an issue that the parties in power are neglecting to a great enough extent to where, eventually, they gain enough momentum in wanting to deal with said issue and use that momentum to gain a prominent role in the legislative body. In some cases, a new party could completely replace one of the current parties in power."

I interjected, again, "So, regardless of circumstances, political parties form over an issue that emerges, and, depending on where and when the issue emerges, they fall into one of the two formation methods that you mentioned."

Chair Hinojosa continued, "For an example of internal political party formation, see our first party system.[26] The system was in place from the founding of our country, under our current system, in 1790 to 1824. During this time, Congress had no parties to speak of in their sessions. The main issue during this era was the passage of the 1794 Jay Treaty with Britain that angered southerners, with their desire to align more with France.[27] What later emerged from this disagreement on one side in Congress was the Federalist Party, based in the North, which sought to employ the financial system of Treasury Secretary Hamilton, which emphasized federal assumption of state debts, a tariff to pay off those debts, a national bank to facilitate financing, and encouragement of banking and manufacturing industry—a strong central government, in a nutshell. Opposition came from the Democratic-Republicans, or Jeffersonians, who held power in the South and mid-Atlantic sections of the country and opposed strong executive powers, any permanently standing military force, or any federal financial program, and who emphasized a strict reading of the Constitution. These would be the holdovers from the anti-Federalist contention left over from the agreements put in place to ratify the US Constitution. Also, the constituencies of both were limited and weakly organized, stressing strong coordination by elites in society to accomplish legislation. Overall, there were no parties in Congress at the founding of our fair country. However, when a big enough issue emerged, finances and foreign alliance in this case, the members quickly picked sides and created our first party system."

I inquired, "So what caused the system to break down?"

Chair Hinojosa continued, "Simple, the Federalist Party self-destructed. This self-destruction occurred due to internal disputes over policy, the inability to organize public support, opposition to the War of 1812 with Great Britain, and the Democratic-Republican Party co-opting, meaning 'to take or assume for one's use'[28] many of the ideals of the Federalist Party. During this time, Federalists quickly dissolved into a few strongholds and then nothing afterward, being seen as too elitist by society. Emerging from this era to form the parties that would partake in the second party system were the two main factions of the Democratic-Republican Party that saw the Jacksonian faction evolve into the Democratic Party that continues to today, and the Henry Clay faction, which became the Whig Party, from 1828 to 1852. Those Democrats were supported by small farmers, frontier citizens, foreign-born people, and Catholics, while the Whigs were supported by middle- to upper-class citizens, native-born people and Brits,

---

26   For a good quick summary of information of the history of party systems in the United States, see http://www.u.arizona.edu/~norrande/pol231/hist-06-bw.pdf.

27   Office of the Historian, "John Jay's Treaty, 1794–95," U.S. Department of State, accessed March 20, 2019, https://history.state.gov/milestones/1784-1800/jay-treaty.

28   https://www.thefreedictionary.com/co-opt

and evangelical Protestants. Democrats favored limited government and a hard money policy, while Whigs favored economic development and societal reform in general."

Chair Wilford forwarded the conversation by stating, "For more background on this, during the second party system, which formed in the aftermath of the hotly contested presidential election of 1824, Andrew Jackson won the popular vote but not a majority of electoral votes. In deciding who would become president, the House of Representatives was left to make that decision and ended up selecting John Quincy Adams as the next president. This set of circumstances left Jackson supporters so upset that they organized the previously mentioned Democratic Party to stand against the administration of Adams. Four years later, with the first major use of the grassroots party-development scheme—which is building support from the ground up, essentially—Democrats successfully got Jackson to replace Adams in 1828. Reeling from their loss in 1828, those opposed to Jackson's policy ended up forming what turned out to be a temporary political party, the previously mentioned Whig Party. This party system differed from the first by the legitimization of parties, patronage systems, mass-based party support, and the use of party conventions for presidential candidate nomination. Specifically, the Republican Party that came to power with Lincoln in 1861, when they formed externally with a focus on ending slavery and replaced the faltering Whigs."

I posited, "You said that the Republicans ended up replacing the Whig Party—the same Republican Party that we have today?"

Chair Dickey replied, "Yes, the same Republican—and Democratic, for that matter— Parties that we have today. The big item that you will notice going forward is that these parties just have constantly varying issues that they support and backing constituencies. Regardless, the third-party system—which ran from 1856 to 1894—saw Democrats, with support from a coalition of southern current or former slave owners at the beginning and support later on from the working class and immigrants, facing Republicans supported by business owners primarily found in the North and West and former Free Soil and Know-Nothing Party members—ended due to Reconstruction efforts in the South. Following that era, the fourth political system was in effect from 1896 to 1932 and saw the rise of real legitimate third parties, like Kurt's Libertarian Party, as well as the Prohibitionist, Populist, and Socialist Parties, more commonly referred to as protest parties. This system saw these protest parties going against strong former slave owners supporting the Democrats, and northern business owners supporting the Republicans, and ended due to economic collapse following the stock market crash of 1921. After that era came the fifth party system, which was in effect from 1932 to 1960, with the same business owners supporting the Republicans and a group called the New Deal Coalition—a group of unions, intellectuals, professionals, southern farmers, Jews, Catholics, and African Americans who were dominant during this time—supporting the Democrats. The Democrats' dominance here faced its eventual demise due to their coalitions' diverse factions no longer being able to work with one another, and those remaining conservative Democrats eventually had enough of the policies pushed forward by the more liberal aspects of the party mentioned earlier."

## Nolan Chart

Our waitress appeared at the table with another round of waters for the group and, most importantly, the main entrées for our meal. Once the platters were divided, we had about five or so minutes of silent chewing and glee over the delicious food. Then I posited to the group, "So that is the history of political parties, at least regarding the US experience. Better question: How can we look at the political parties today?"

Between bites, the three chairpersons exchanged murmurs and quick thoughts to the point where Chair Hinojosa answered for the group, "There is one more system era to discuss, but that would be best to end our discussion on, as that really gets to the heart of what happened regarding Texas. A question though: Have you heard of the Nolan Chart (figure 12.6)?"

I answered with an immediate "No, not really. What does that portray?"

Chair Hinojosa continued, "Well, it has to do with one's political orientation. People assume that they and others are either on the right or the left or somewhere in between. Let me show it to you."

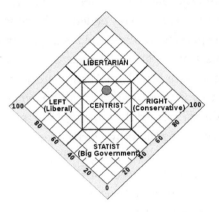

FIGURE 12.6  Nolan Chart of Political Ideology.

After a few minutes on his phone, Chair Hinojosa concluded, "For a while, Down's traditional left-right political spectrum was enough to explain people and their politics.[29] People with more populist views were on the left, and those with more laissez-faire views were on the right, but now, with other issues emerging, like social normative ones beyond just economic issues that have dominated politics until the latter half of the 20th century, it is easier to explain modern politics on a more planar basis. This here is the chart. It is nothing more than a simple x-y coordinate plane, besides being tilted to the left to have a zero-zero point found at the bottom, as opposed to its normal spot at the bottom left. On the bottom right axis is the view of an individual toward economic freedoms, and on the bottom left axis is the individual's view toward personal freedoms; the further up to the left or to the right you go, the more individual values each of those items.

---

29    A. Downs, *An Economic Theory of Democracy* (New York: Harper, 1957).

Stretching from the total economic freedom point to the total personal freedom point on a diagonal is the simple linear Down's political spectrum I mentioned before, but the new visual system seen here now allows for the emergence of not just the economic but also the social views. The top of the spectrum is for those who value high levels of both economic and personal freedoms, like Kurt's Libertarian Party, and the bottom is for those who value low levels of economic and personal freedoms—your Communist or Socialist Parties, for example. Left wingers or liberals, like myself and my party who take up the far left corner, are those who value high amounts of personal freedoms but are willing to give some economic freedoms for the collective good, while the right is for conservatives, like James and his party currently, who value high economic freedoms but are more willing to part ways with personal freedoms."

Chair Wilford spoke up and showed me a web page on his smartphone. "One of the most popular versions of this chart is found on the website of a group called Advocates for Self-Government, who are seeking to plant the seeds of liberty, via the process of a quiz they crafted.[30] This quiz is commonly referred to as the world's smallest political quiz, as it provides you with five statements on personal issues and five additional statements on economic issues that you must indicate whether you agree with, disagree with, or maybe support. Depending on how you answer, you fall into one of the categories by having a dot placed on the chart you just saw. Let's find out where you stand."

I remarked, "I'll consider that my homework for today, but can we take a look at who falls into each of the corners beyond what you said earlier?"

Chair Dickey remarked, "Relax, we still have dessert for that. Let's finish off our entrées with a discussion on the basics of what political parties are and how they operate."


## Functions of Political Parties

With everyone in agreement, Chair Wilford spoke up again after a few minutes of eating. "When enough people, for lack of a better phrase, gather at the various points along the political plane we just discussed, such as a corner stronghold, they have shared political interests, a single or several issues that they care about. With those shared interests, as was the case of Republicans and slavery, among other issues, those groupings can get together and form a political party if they seek to hold public office and affect change in society. If the grouping does not seek to obtain political office, they will fall under the category of being an interest group, but that's not a topic for this discussion."

---

30   http://www.theadvocates.org/quiz/quiz.php

I interjected, "I learned about those special interest groups yesterday. Horrifying stuff there. A lot of cloak and dagger, so to speak, seeing how they communicate their ideas to your representatives in office."

Chair Wilford continued, "Once formed, the new party then works together to gain political office through popular elections and focus all their activities on supporting that goal by recruiting new, like-minded members who are electable. This need is important, as our parties primarily function to provide a sensible link between people and the government."

At that moment, Chair Hinojosa spoke up. "Speaking of functions in the big picture, there are four basic aspects that all political parties work to achieve. Beyond nominating people and getting them elected, there is an education function that is accomplished by simplifying the issues for voters.[31] For example, if you want the option of having abortions be available to you, vote for us, etc. Also, parties have a mobilization function that is accomplished by having voter registration drives alongside actually driving people to the polls, hosting forums for candidates to meet with voters or discuss an issue, all in hopes of increasing turnout[32]— in their favor, of course. Finally, an operational function comes into play once the party's representatives get into office, which is patterned by running the office as they, the party and members, see fit."[33]

## Characteristics of American Political Parties

Chair Dickey moved onto another critical aspect by remarking, "Beyond functions and goals, American political parties share three basic characteristics. In the first case, as we talked about before, the United States, for much of its history, has had a two-party system: all Democrats and Republicans since the 1850s. Keeping this two-party system alive has been a smattering of circumstance. On the one hand, third parties, like that of the Libertarian Party chaired by our colleague John over here, are often much smaller than the mainstream political parties. Accordingly, when their promoted issues rise to a large enough scale, Gilberto's and my party take sides on the issue and absorb their members accordingly, for the most part. The

---

31    https://www.texasgop.org/about; https://www.txdemocrats.org/our-party

32    Christine Birkne, "After 26 Years, Rock the Vote Is Still Driving Young People to the Polls," *Adweek*, July 31, 2016, http://www.adweek.com/brand-marketing/after-26-years-rock-vote-still-driving-young-people-polls-172593; Ryan Grim, "Alyssa Milano Wants to Drive You to the Polls in Georgia," Huffington Post, March 27, 2017, https://www.huffingtonpost.com/entry/alyssa-milano-wants-to-drive-you-to-the-polls-in-georgia_us_58d97c2be4b018c4606a48b8; Beth Walton, "Groups Offer Voters Transportation to the Polls," *Citizen Times* (Asheville, NC), November 2, 2016, https://www.citizen-times.com/story/news/local/2016/11/02/groups-offer-transportation-polls/93159160.

33    Peter Baker, "For Trump, a Year of Reinventing the Presidency," *New York Times*, December 31, 2017, https://www.nytimes.com/2017/12/31/us/politics/trump-reinventing-presidency.html.

Libertarian Party will probably not face this issue, as they take a stand on multiple issues and are not focused on a single item—like most third parties are—that, once handled, takes the wind out from beneath their wings, and they fade into oblivion. If anything, though, the Libertarians stand the best odds to replace one of us going forward. Also, not helping the third-party cause here is the use of single-member districts, which, due to people not wanting to vote for a losing cause, help reinforce the driving force of the main parties. Also, third parties can be viewed as extreme, which goes against the mostly middle-of-the-road voting population that we have, at least for the time being. Not to mention, people can be very repetitive, giving them a lot of historical inertia to vote for one party, election cycle after election cycle, and requiring a massive jolt to get them to vote for another party. Have you heard about the tidelands controversy?"

I immediately chimed in, "Yes, sir. It began the split-up of the Democratic Party here in the state back in the 1950s."

Chair Wilford interjected, "Texas was a strong one-party system from 1876 to 1978, with all power being held by the Democrats. This situation was due to, as previously mentioned, larger parties adopting the platforms of smaller third parties in this case. For Texas, this was the Populist Party and their planks being adopted by the Democratic Party. Also keeping that strong one-party system alive was the adoption of party primaries that allowed for elections within the Democratic Party between the various factions.[34] That kept more conservative members in line with the Democrats for a while longer. Finally, the Great Depression of the 1930s gave a lot of clout to Democrats, as that party was throwing money at people, and that can be difficult to draw people away from heading toward. Thankfully, as mentioned by Chair Dickey, the tidelands controversy then came along and began to pry things apart and create a two-party system for a while, until we reached our current de facto one-party system, dominated by the Republicans."

Wanting to move on from one sore subject to another, Chair Hinojosa iterated, "Well, on a less tainted note, American political parties are also traditionally very nonpragmatic. This situation means that politicians and the parties they represent get elected more based on their ideology and their image, as opposed to some expected series of results when in office. For evidence of this on the campaign trail, take a look at President Obama's Hope poster or the campaign effort—built on Wendy Davis's shoes after she filibustered the Republicans' attempt back in 2013 at outright banning abortion here in the state—called "Stand with Wendy." These slogans don't exactly say a lot about what the candidate will do exactly in office, but they help reinforce the image that the person will help you in some aspect that

---

34    O. Douglass Weeks, "Election Laws," Texas State Historical Association (TSHA), last modified July 25, 2016, https://tshaonline.org/handbook/online/articles/wde01.

you want them to, all while remaining a bit wishy-washy on the details. More interestingly, if you look at the cold, hard numbers, the tendency still exists when the parties take office. For example, look at President Trump and the promises he made during his campaign for office in 2016 before he was elected on the campaign trail. Specifically, as accounted for by Politifact and their Trump-O-Meter, run by the *Tampa Bay Times* newspaper,[35] when looking at Trump's scorecard of promises made on the campaign trail, as of 1/23/19, if the Wi-Fi in here will keep up, 17 have been kept, 11 have been compromised on, 18 have been broken, 28 have had efforts stalled, and 28 are in work in some form or fashion. Better put, ask yourself: If you only fulfilled 16.7 percent of an order that you were tasked with accomplishing, would you keep getting your customers' business? Not likely, I bet, not to mention compromised on 10.8 percent and outright broke a further 17.6 percent. For historical perspective, look at the numbers for Obama's two completed terms and his top 25 promises made on the campaign trail; he was only able to keep 9, he compromised on 8, and the remaining 8 were broken in the various lawmaking processes needed to accomplish them.[36] Only in politics and baseball could this happen. This characteristic is an issue because it's like the blind leading the blind; we think we are going in the right direction, but nobody has confirmed if that's where we want to be going until now. Granted, with the parties at extremes, and tight electoral margins in the legislature, this is realistically par for the course, though."

Chair Wilford spoke up, "Seeing as how you mainstream parties talked yourself a bit into a hole there, I will attempt to bring us out of it to save face by widening it, at least. That last American political party characteristic is the basic position that, while much of the action taken by the parties, especially our national contingents, gives the idea that we are all the same, we are all independent entities at different levels that function separately from one another. In other words, parties are decentralized. There is not one great spirit floating around telling us all what to do and how to do it in a party. The precinct, county, state, and national versions are all different organisms of the greater whole. It's like the Russian nesting doll here on the wall: Each of them fits nicely into another, but they are each their own piece of art, just as a party encompasses slightly varied goals, opinions, and member types. That doesn't mean that the different levels don't work together, but they are fundamentally different."

I asked a question of the group: "So how do the different levels work together?"

Chair Dickey answered, "It's fair to say that national parties have access to a lot more resources than most of the precinct or county contingents and even some of the states,

---

35   Politifact, "Trump-O-Meter: Tracking Trump's Campaign Promises," accessed March 20, 2019, https://www.politifact.com/truth-o-meter/promises/trumpometer.

36   Politifact, "Promises about PolitiFact's Top Promises on The Obameter," accessed March 20, 2019, http://www.politifact.com/truth-o-meter/promises/obameter/subjects/politifacts-top-promises.

while at the same time those local contingents have a lot easier access to actual citizens due to already being in the communities. Therefore, in making an exchange, the national contingent of the party helps by providing polling services, research information, money for television, radio ads and direct mailers, and, of course, the almighty dollar when needed, so long as the local contingents continue to get people involved with the party by sending them to higher conventions and voting in their favor come election time. My personal favorite service though is when the national bigwigs are brought in to help state and local candidates get elected. Trump might be from New York, but he can wear a cowboy hat with style, like when he came to help with Hurricane Harvey recovery efforts and to campaign for Ted Cruz in the Senate here recently."

## Political Party Platforms

Chair Hinojosa interjected, "On a different note, though, even with this exchange of services, the lower levels are still able to toot their horns on particular items from time to time. For example, we had the States' Rights Democratic Party (more affectionately known as the Dixiecrats), which was a short-lived segregationist political party in southern states during the 1948 elections (figure 12.7). That party originated as a breakaway faction of the Democrats and was dead set on ensuring that what they saw as the southern, somewhat racist, way of life was protected from an oppressive federal government. In preserving their way of life, their supporters gained control of the state Democratic Parties—in part, or entirely, in several southern states—leaving those at the national level to be cut off at the knees in keeping Republican Dewey out of, and Truman still in, the White House. The national Democrats still won, but their efforts were definitively undermined by the varied versions of the party at the local level that were opposed to the national party goals, to some success in the general election."[37]

While getting out a copy of each party's platform and the list of issues that I had made earlier in the day, I chimed in, "So American political parties are characterized by being nonpragmatic, decentralized, and operative in a two-party system, for now at least. What do the current political parties represent, though?

Chair Hinojosa spoke up by saying, "I'll get started by talking about liberals. Liberals tend to vote Democratic (my party) and believe that it is imperative for the government to regulate the economy in support of greater social equality and avoid concentration of wealth that threatens equal access to control over government, destroys economic competition, and weakens economic freedom. Liberals support welfare programs, wage laws, unions,

---

37    United States History, "Dixiecrats," accessed March 20, 2019, http://www.u-s-history.com/pages/h1751.html.

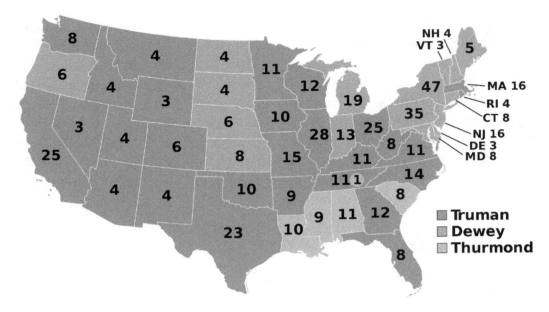

FIGURE 12.7   The Dixiecrats carried Louisiana, Mississippi, Alabama, and South Carolina, and received one additional electoral vote in Tennessee (colored in orange). States in blue voted for Democrats Harry S. Truman and Alben W. Barkley; those in red voted for Republicans Thomas E. Dewey and Earl Warren.

insurance mandates, educational programs, and progressive taxes. This circumstance is in addition to having a desire to protect civil liberties and rights, alongside being suspicious of conservative efforts to legislate morality. Our main membership groups are, per our website,[38] African Americans, Asian Americans, Americans with disabilities, environmentalists, Hispanics and Latinos, LGBTQ Americans, women, and finally, students and young Americans with outreach groups for rural Texans and veterans."

I commented, "That is a very diversified group of individuals."

He replied, "Yes, they are. This group of individuals, on occasion, does produce its problems, as each group can have some very diverse opinions. For example, our position calling for more paths to citizenship might be beneficial for our Hispanic contingent, but more Hispanic immigration might draw ire from the African American contingent, as this would increase competition for jobs held by them at the lower levels of the economy. More importantly, our work to ensure greater rights and protections for the LGBTQ community or women might not be of concern for anybody else in the party, so the issue stays on the fringe. It's tough to determine what exactly that is that would make everyone happy; it's a lot of white noise, so to speak."

---

38   https://www.txdemocrats.org/our-party/our-people

I had one more question for Chair Hinojosa: "Where in the state do Democrats, then, have a majority of control?"

Chair Hinojosa replied, "Using a map of 2016 US presidential election returns for Texas provided by the *Washington Post* that I have a photo of here,[39] for Democrats that would be along the US-Mexico border, where Hispanics dominate the population, and in urban areas like Houston and Austin, where your more philosophical liberals tend to congregate. It's not a lot of territories, but that is where most in the state live, so it has its advantages. Therefore, we must be optimistic toward our ideals and efforts to achieve them in government. All other areas of the state, primarily your rural areas, are dominated by the Republican Party. It's a lot of territories, but just not where most people now live in the state. Unfortunately, though, many of those rural voters are more likely to vote, so we are at a disadvantage. Libertarians are not quite making enough of an impact on state politics to dominate an area—one day, though. I suspect it will be the suburbs and exurbs of the counties immediately surrounding the major cities in the United States (figure 12.8)."

FIGURE 12.8   The darker the red the greater the margin of victory for President Trump and the greater the blue the greater the margin of victory for Hillary Clinton. The blue counties in the sea of red counties and the blue counties along the Rio Grande River Border with Mexico indicate the Democratic Party.

Not wanting to be left behind, Chair Dickey continued the conversation by going, "Looks like it's time for the conservative opinion to be heard. Conservatives tend to vote Republican (my party) and believe that individuals should be left alone to compete in a free-market economic system, unfettered by government control, with what controls are in place being minimal. Controls that do get put in place should support business development, fund highways and other infrastructure, and include tax incentives for investment. These items will encourage economic development via the trickle-down process of wealth distribution. We favor the status quo, proper moral values, and harsher punishments for criminals, and we oppose efforts to redistribute wealth directly. Our disciples typically include big businesses

39   *Washington Post*, "Who's Winning Texas: Live Election Results," last modified November 9, 2016, https://www.washingtonpost.com/2016-election-results/texas/?utm_term=.4953142e845b.

and their owners, rich people in general, social traditionalists, the religious right, libertarians, fiscal conservatives, and the military. We also tend to be skeptical of the influence and role played by the government and work to reduce its impact."

Breaking up this line of conversation was the waitress, who took our plates. We all looked at the menu for what desserts would be excellent. We ended up ordering Kiev cake, ptichye moloko, and mini cheesecakes. Now, with the orders all taken, Chair Dickey continued, "From those groups, fiscal and social conservatives typically tend to be the dominant factions. Unlike the dominant Democratic factions that create a muddled message, our dominant factions tend to create a solid platform to run on that most everyone agrees with in lockstep. The issue is, due to that platform being so strong, it tends to isolate people away from the party. Simply put, it can be difficult to get LGBTQ people to join the party, even if they are the most avid of fiscal hawks, if you want to take away their right to get married. Picking one party over another then requires making difficult decisions."

Bringing up the rear was Chair Wilford, who remarked, "Seeing as I am the only third-party representative here, I guess that I will explain not just my party, but everyone else's, as best as possible. Looking back at the Democrats and Republicans with the diamond form of the Nolan Chart, they are each on the left and right, respectively. Libertarians would again fall at the top, due to having a high value of respect, not just for personal freedoms, as is the case with Democrats, but also for economic freedoms that are most prized by Republicans. For lack of a better term, though, third parties fall into the middle, with either a focus on full government control—as is the case with the Communist or Green Parties as an extreme of the Democratic Party—or little to no government control—with my party, the Libertarians, as an extreme of the Republican Party. I see that you have a copy of our platforms there with you. Let's do some comparing and contrasting."

I stated, "Could we do this comparing and contrasting over these issues I have listed here?"

The chairpersons all replied in unison, "Sure, that will work. What's on your list?"

I replied, "That would include health care, immigration, same-sex marriage, and government taxation."

Chair Wilford spoke up. "That's a good mix of issues, mostly social, but they do cover a good deal of economics as well."

I responded, "When I read the different platforms this morning, the Libertarian was nice, short, sweet, and to the point, while the Democratic and Republican ones were lengthy and somewhat overly complex.[40] One pattern that did emerge, though, was that a lot of things revolved around granting access to items."

---

40   The GOP, Democratic, and Libertarian Parties' platforms can be found in footnote 20. All items below discussing the party platforms were found in those links.

In unison, the three chairpersons responded, "What makes you say that?"

I continued, "For example, in regard to same-sex marriage, under the heading of 'LGBTQ Rights,' from the Democratic platform, it states, 'denounce efforts to not comply with the U.S Supreme Court decisions which guaranteed marriage equality to all couples,' which is a basic call for ensuring continual access to marriage rights by same-sex couples, which is fairly in line with item article 2, section 1, subsection e of the Libertarian platform, which reads, 'The Libertarian Party of Texas . . . believes that marriage is a matter of private contract, and should not be defined or licensed by the government. We believe that the government should not treat individuals differently based on their marital status.' The only difference is the Libertarians want marriage to be free from government regulation one way or another, while Democrats still want some amount of funneling through the government to ensure the sanctity of the process, whereas in total opposition, the Republican platform, under principles 79 and 80, states, 'We support the definition of marriage as a God-ordained, legal and moral commitment only between one natural man and one natural woman,' and calls for the overturning of the decision in *Obergefell v. Hodges* under the belief that it 'has no basis in the Constitution and should be reversed, returning jurisdiction over the definition of marriage to the states.' No matter how I sliced it, Republicans want to restrict access to marriage to heterosexual couples, while Libertarians and Democrats want to have near-unlimited access to it by everyone, no matter the circumstance."

Once again in unison, the three chairpersons responded, "That makes sense. What other evidence is there that you have?"

I further added on to make my point by stating, "Regarding health care, under the heading of 'Healthcare,' from the Democratic platform, 'Texas Democrats continue to believe healthcare is a fundamental human right for all Texans and not a privilege reserved for those able to afford it,' which is a basic call for socialized, government-run health care, while the Republican platform, on page 18, under principle 111, reads, 'Health care decisions, including routine preventative care such as immunizations, should be between a patient and health care professional and should be protected from government intrusion,' which, once again, reads very similarly to article II, section 2, subsection a of the Libertarian platform, which reads, 'Government should neither provide, control, nor require health care. We do not believe that people have a right to be provided with health care at other peoples' expense.' Overall, Democrats want to promote access to health care via government intervention, while Libertarians and Republicans want to have little to no government intervention in the provision of healthcare. No matter how I sliced it, it's the same pattern, except Libertarians now align more with Republicans on this issue."

I added on, "Regarding immigration, under the heading of 'Immigration,' from the Democratic platform, it states we 'support comprehensive immigration reform, including an attainable path to citizenship,' which is a basic call for illegal immigrant amnesty and more open borders, while the Republican platform, under principle 259, states, 'Any form of amnesty with regard to immigration policy should not be granted, including the granting of legal status to persons in the country illegally,' the exact opposite stance. Lastly, article 3, section 1, of the Libertarian platform reads, 'The Libertarian Party of Texas . . . seeks to encourage immigration of students, workers, and business owners willing to invest in Texas.' This one seems to call for more open borders in a way without getting into specifics, placing the party somewhere in the middle due to the requirement to invest. Overall, Democrats want more access to the state for immigrants, while Libertarians and Republicans want to have some restrictions applied. No matter how I sliced it, it's the same pattern of accessibility, except Libertarians align more with Republicans on this issue."

Once again in unison, the three chairpersons responded, "You are making your point, but let's take a look at that last comparison you have there son, just to make sure your point holds up."

I completed my point here by stating, "For the last issue, I chose taxation by government. The Democratic Party platform, under the heading of 'Principles Of The Texas Democratic Parties,' reads, '[T]he burden of taxes should be fairly distributed,' which is fairly self-explanatory. Meanwhile the Libertarian Party Platform reads, 'Taxation should be used only for services that cannot be provided by free market solutions,' and aligns well with principle 175 of the Republican platform, which reads, 'We believe the most equitable system of taxation is one based on consumption and wish to see reforms towards that end at all levels of government,' alongside article 1, section 1, subsection b, General Taxation, from the Libertarian Party Platform that reads, 'All taxes should be for a specific purpose, and have specific sunset dates. This will allow every legislative session to be held accountable for establishing excessive taxation and prevent perpetual funding of governmental growth.' In this case, Republicans and Libertarians want to tax, but just for specified reasons, while the Democrats are for more taxation in general, as it grants citizens access to more services. As I've said before, it all comes down to access; Dems want to grant more in some areas and less in others, with the Republicans displaying similar goals, and the Libertarians not caring what it is you do as long as you leave government out of it all."

Chair Wilford posited, "That last statement says a lot more than just how much access parties wish to grant when in office. It also indicates that third parties often fall in between the other parties on various issues, as they/we agree with one party on certain issues and then agree with other parties on other issues."

While hearing that position, it made a lot of sense. We have the dominant parties that have their views, but what about those who are okay with same-sex marriage but also want a fiscally solvent government that has a limited role in society, or vice versa? Third parties are the way to go in that instance. Who knew?

## Party Structure

At this point, our waitress finally brought out our desserts. After my big compare-and-contrast session, I needed a sugar rush to get me over the finish line. Chair Hinojosa spoke up: "From what we all talked about today—good conversation, guys—the last thing we need to advise you on is how the structures of political parties are organized. Simply put, at the bottom rung is something called a party primary. This is an election held in Texas during March of years ending in even numbers. On the ballot are people seeking the nomination of their party to run under that party's banner in the general election later in the year, along with a simple way of voting on platform planks of the party, at least at the lower level. Beyond that, though, this is the only way to officially join the party, as voting allows you to access half of the upper-rung, temporary party mechanisms, better known as conventions. Conventions are held at the precinct level on the day of the primary and at the county, state, and national levels later in the election cycle, in order. Of note, the national convention is only held if the presidency is on the ballot in the general election. Conventions are just party planning, as they help create permanent party structure, approve of party platforms, and select delegates to attend those higher conventions. The other half of the upper rung is the permanent party structure. This structure is based in party headquarters and headed by us chairpersons that you see here at the table and by executive committees that operate with the main goal of organizing events and party fundraisers, as well as keeping continuity between current and future campaigns. We were elected to our positions by the electorate at the various conventions. Simply put, the permanent party structure is all about party conducting."

With dessert now finished, I was looking for a way to end our discussion on a high note. I asked the group, "What I should know going forward?"

Now Chair Wilford spoke up again by stating, "Going back to the old conversation we had at the beginning of our meal, we left out one important term. This is called realignment, or the simple act of people switching from one political party to another. An extension of this term is called dealignment, which sees people no longer identify with one party and begin to vote for multiple parties in a single election, in a process called split-ticket voting. Looking at the modern political history of the state following the tidelands controversy, President Johnson bringing the Democratic Party further left on the political spectrum, and not to mention the Sharpstown scandal shedding a poor light on the party; many conservatives of the state had had enough of the Democratic Party. Accordingly, those citizens quickly realigned with the Republican Party, which better represented their conservative values. This was aided and abetted via the rise of a strong national icon when Ronald Reagan came to power in the 1980s as president, a large number of conservatives moving to the state—all thanks to our booming economy increasing the wealth of many individuals—and a majority of Hispanics, who typically vote Democratic, not voting, and culminated with James's party taking complete control of politics since 2002. Also, of note here: After Reconstruction, every southern state went Democratic from top to bottom for the better part of the next hundred years. In the 1970s those states began the process of becoming Republican, with the process of complete realignment—or inversion, depending how you see it—in the South finally ending in 2014, when every southern governorship, US Senate seat, and state legislative body became controlled by the Republican Party for the first time in over a century and a half."[41]

I asked, "So what could change that to a great extent?"

Chair Hinojosa closed our conversation. "The Democratic Party once again has its strongholds in cities and along the border, both of which are predominantly populated by nonwhites who also tend to vote less, yet outnumber the majority of voters who are white. If we as a party can get those urbanites voting, increase immigration to the state by like-minded voters to ourselves, and have the Republicans isolate enough of the population, we have a fighting chance to begin the process of taking over some small shred of politics here in the state and hopefully parts of the South, at that tipping point. This would end the current, sixth, party system."

On that note, I once again thanked each of the party chairpersons for their time and walked them to the door. On my way back to the table, I settled the tab with our waitress but told her that I would like to sit for a bit longer. While sitting, I brought up the world's smallest political quiz that I learned about earlier and answered the questions. I ended up falling right on the line between being a Libertarian and a conservative, like how my dad is. I learned a lot today about what political parties are and how they form. Political parties are more than just the smiley faces I see on television, as there is a whole mass of machinery going on behind the candidates who represent them, helping people learn about, get involved with, and further support the party going forward. This information is essential, as, based on the history of political parties, they are living, breathing organisms that change and sometimes die as time progresses, only to be replaced by something else. Going forward, I will have to choose. Luckily, I still have more time to determine precisely what I will do.

---

41   Nate Cohn, "Demise of the Southern Democrat Is Now Nearly Complete," *New York Times*, December 21, 2017, http://www.nytimes.com/2014/12/05/upshot/demise-of-the-southern-democrat-is-now-nearly-compete.html?abt=0002&abg=1.

**QUESTIONS TO CONSIDER** REGARDING POLITICAL PARTIES:

1. The first main topic of the chapter defines political parties. Please define what they are, provide an example of who from your life fits the bill, and indicate why this is so.

2. The second main topic of the chapter discusses how political parties form. Please identify what those two methods are, identify how and when your group of friends formed, indicate which of the two methods relates most to your group of friends' formation method, and explain why, in detail.

3. The third main topic of the chapter discusses the functions of a political party. Please identify what those four functions are, the one that relates to how your group of friends interacts with others at school, and why, in detail.

4. The fourth main topic of the chapter discusses the three characteristics of American political parties. Please identify what those three items are, the ones that relate to your group of friends, and why, in detail.

5. The fifth main topic of the chapter introduces political party platforms. Please identify what party platforms are (you may need to go back to the first few pages for this), the main differences between the party platforms discussed in the book, the platform that relates most to your group of friends, and why, in detail.

6. The final main topic of the chapter discusses party structure. Please identify what the two structures are, the one that your group of friends is most similar to in reality, and why, in detail.

## FIGURE CREDITS

Fig. 12.1: Copyright © by Txdemocrats (CC BY-SA 3.0) at https://commons.wikimedia.org/wiki/File:TexasDemocraticParty_Logo_2019.png.

Fig. 12.2: Source: https://commons.wikimedia.org/wiki/File%3ARepublicanlogo.svg.

Fig. 12.3: Source: https://en.wikipedia.org/wiki/File:Libertarian_Party_of_Texas_logo.png.

Fig. 12.5: Source: https://commons.wikimedia.org/wiki/File:PamphletFrontPageProgressivePartyPlatform1912.jpg.

Fig. 12.6: Copyright © by William Saturn (CC BY-SA 3.0) at https://commons.wikimedia.org/wiki/File%3A60-60_score.jpg.

Fig. 12.7: Source: https://commons.wikimedia.org/wiki/File:ElectoralCollege1948.svg.

Fig. 12.8: Copyright © by Ali Zifran (CC BY-SA 4.0) at https://commons.wikimedia.org/wiki/File:Texas_Presidential_Election_Results_2016.svg.

# Section III

## Government Office Spaces

# Chapter 13

# Special Governing Districts

# Services Provided by Governing Districts

After the events of today, I feel as if another change in course has been brought on my trek. The first seven days of my trek covered topics akin to establishing the foundation of the house we call government in the United States. The last five days seemed similar to building the house due to my trek teaching me how I could get involved in government. What began today brought on me the actual offices that governing officials hold. This third phase seemed to be akin to deciding how each room of the house will be used. In addition, compared to some of my previous day's adventures, the pace of today was somewhat ratcheted down. At this point in the summer, I was getting tired from all the travel: back-to-back drives to San Antonio, more trips to downtown than I can count, and even a road trip back home to Houston last weekend, all of which brought me more information to digest than a 30-foot anaconda could in a lifetime. For one day at least, the long drives were over, and the information was few and far between, but notable nonetheless. Today I was grateful to have reached a point that I was able to walk to my next place of discovery. Overall, I was able to get an inside look at a local government agency that was truly special.

Close to 9:00 a.m., after sleeping in until 8:00 a.m. (a pleasant surprise in and of itself), I walked the half mile from Charity's house on Bay Hill Drive in the Lost Creek subdivision (figure 13.1) to the headquarters of the Lost Creek Limited District[1] at 1305 Quaker Ridge Drive (figure 13.2). Also in the building were the offices of the Lost Creek Neighborhood Association,[2] the homeowners association of the subdivision. I could also tell that I was in the right spot due to the building

FIGURE 13.1   Lost Creek Subdivision Entrance Sign

FIGURE 13.2   Lost Creek Subdivision Clubhouse

---

1   http://lostcreekld.org/default.aspx
2   https://www.lcna.com

having the zoning-standard look of the community but having enough parking spaces for a convention out front. Waiting for me by the front door was General Manager Jim Emmons.

After so much travel during the summer, I was a professional at meeting new people. I broke the ice by stating, "Mr. Emmons, nice to meet you! I'm Champ. Thanks again for meeting with me today."

Jim replied, "You are welcome and glad to do it. Your sister is on the board that approves my budget, so I am glad to make time for her and the board. At a meeting a few years ago, the board added giving field trips to my job list. You are number one, so let's see how this goes."

After walking through the office and waving at the secretary, we found ourselves in the community room also used for small meetings. Not knowing where to begin, I inquired, "What exactly puts the 'limited' in the limited district?"

In response, Jim offered, "Well, we are limited concerning the number of services we can offer. In the bigger picture, the limited district is one example of something in Texas called a special district, which are set up around the state to provide a single solitary service to a set geographic region."

I interjected, "Similar, in a sense, to one of those single-serve cereal bowls I ate breakfast out of in kindergarten?"

He replied, "Exactly. Those breakfasts offer one serving of food for one person in the same sense that we can only offer one service, used to be a lot more, to those found here in the community. Also, these districts are not just for utility services like water/sewage, natural gas, telephones, or electricity. These special districts are used for anything ranging from ports to pipes, public transport, and most notably, school districts."

I asked, "So what exactly do you provide for the community?"

Jim replied, "Overall, we here at the Lost Creek Limited District are focused on being a resident-run entity that funds and oversees maintenance of the community areas of Lost Creek. These include the entrance monument facade and landscaping, parks, and trails within the neighborhood.[3] Lastly, we enforce the various deed restrictions on properties found within the community on items like color schemes and roofing materials.[4]

I asked, "So how was it that you became the freestanding government entity that you are today?"

It was here that Jim put on his lecture cap and iterated, "That is a story that has some actual noteworthy history to it. Overall, the Lost Creek Limited District is the only standing entity left over from the subdivision's founding in July 1972. At that time, there was

---

3  http://lostcreekld.org/default.aspx?section=about_us
4  http://lostcreekld.org/default.aspx?section=deed_restrictions

an agreement between the property developers and the Texas Water Commission,[5] which later required approval from the state legislature, to create a municipal utility district, more commonly referred to as a MUD. Until recently, we were also responsible for handling all the fresh and wastewater services and negotiating trash services for the community here in Lost Creek. Over time, this developer's tool evolved into an official local governing entity for those residing within it, which gives us the full ability to levy annual taxes, charge periodically for services, provide various recreational facilities, condemn noncongruent properties, enforce restrictive deed covenants, and make any legitimate regulations to accomplish our purposes."[6]

## How Special Governing Districts Are Run

I inquired, "It seems as if the limited nature of your name makes sense due to the minimal amount of functions you provide, but for now, how is the limited district organized and run?"

Jim advised, "We have our layperson board of directors, as they all do. Ours is the one I mentioned earlier that your sister is on. The board consists of five directors who are residents of the community. Each person is elected to the board and serves a four-year term.[7] Two or three people are up for election every two years, which provides continuity in case all those up for reelection are ousted. As part of their duties, they decide on tax rates, changes to the deed requirements, and anything under the purview of the limited district. Most notably, though, the board tells me what to do."

I asked, "What do you mean, 'tells you what to do'?"

Jim continued, "As you already know, I am the general manager of the district. I oversee the day-to-day activities that occur within what we have under our purview. Today this includes enforcing those significant deed restrictions, ensuring that the park trails get maintained, and seeing to it that the front community façade is well-maintained. In the past, when we were the MUD, that list of duties also included negotiating service contracts with outside operators for our trash pickup, maintaining the pipes that move water and waste about the service area, and any other related water infrastructure. Once I decide on a service change, the measure goes before the board for public debate and eventual approval by the board of directors, hopefully. The most notable topics to discuss at the meetings are tax rates for the payments of bonds and other services we offer. We are our little corner on the pyramid of government that houses local entities."

---

5   https://www.lcna.com/info.php?pnum=15a68f661e0d16
6   Ibid.
7   http://lostcreekld.org/default.aspx?section=about_us/directors

I asked, "Do you do everything as your entity, or do y'all team up with other governments?"

In response, Jim went on. "For what we do today, we may hire a landscaper for a significant project, but not nearly as much as we used to. For example, when we also provided water services, we entered into service agreements with the various other local governments in the area. Specifically, we formally purchased our water from the city of Austin through a service agreement we had with them.[8] With the deal in place, the water was taken from Ladybird Lake (better known as the Colorado River), piped to the Ullrich water treatment facility for purification, and finally, pumped to the subdivision-slash-district for use.[9] Once in the district, the water was either stored in two large tanks (located behind my office) for emergencies when power in the area is lost, or immediately sent out into the system for use by residents—or to one of 130 fire hydrants for use by firefighters if a residence goes up in smoke.[10] Once used and treated in our on-site facility, the cleaned wastewater was shipped over to the Lost Creek Country Club for use as the exclusive water instrument for the golf course, helping them save money on watering and ensuring that the water is reused as much as possible to preserve and protect the environment."

I interjected, "Was?"

## Issues Faced by Special Governing Districts

Then the discussion took a negative turn when Jim replied, "Was—remember we are now a limited district, though we used to be a much more full-service MUD. This drawdown brings us to the issues regarding special districts. Overall, three main issues are commonly associated with running special district governing entities. In the first place, very few people know about us and what we do, beyond paying a bill for when they rent out space in the community park and a line item on their annual tax bills distributed for us by the county. Also, since few people know about us, there is naturally low participation in our monthly meetings and elections for board positions. At last month's meeting, there was nobody in attendance out of a few thousand residents. Finally, there is an issue with economies of scale. Even though we only provide one service, we still must have various other supporting departments that provide background assistance to the implementation of the main offering—again, community maintenance, in our case. To compensate for this, we outsourced much of this—bill paying, in our case—to reduce our costs, among other things. At a certain point, though,

---

8    http://www.austintexas.gov/edims/document.cfm?id=227010
9    Ibid.
10   Ibid.

with this final issue, the best way to deal with it is to end the district and have our services absorbed into the various departments of the city of Austin."

I interjected, "Wait a minute. Charity was telling me about the recent annexation of your former, I guess, MUD by the city of Austin."

Jim advised, "The changeover occurred a few years ago, in December 2014. This was done to decrease the costs to consumers, our residents, due to the economies of scale offered by the city of Austin, as the city will add another set of customers to their roster and get rid of the middlemen in the service of water provision—us, the MUD. They took over the pipes, the treatment plant, etc. Ever since, the district has continued in a limited capacity to provide maintenance of the various parks and entryway to the community."

Then one of the funniest things of the summer occurred. Jim simply stated, "Come to think of it, that's it. That's all we do. No fire protection, no road maintenance, no police patrols, no social services, nothing else, service provision–wise for us. If it's not park provision, deed restrictions, or affecting the front signage, we typically don't care much about it, outside of letting the city of Austin know about a major leak somewhere in the pipes so that they can come and fix the issue. Most of those problems are now theirs. Let's go for a tour."

I could only reply, "That limited service provision makes you very special."

Nodding in agreement, Jim furthered our adventure with a short walk out of the building to the two large storage tanks (figure 13.3) we had discussed earlier in his office. Jim advised that the two tanks have a combined storage capacity of 2.5 million gallons, which would provide the community, assuming nobody else is connected to the pipes alongside, full usage, with enough water for about four days during a power outage. Between the two storage tanks was a special pressure tank that is used to ensure that enough pressure exists in the system to get water out over the 15 miles of pipes formally handled by the district.[11]

FIGURE 13.3    Lost Creek Subdivision Water Tanks

Next, we drove about 2 miles to the end of Turtle Point Drive to see the wastewater treatment facility. Once we were there, I saw that the labyrinth of pipe runs and tanks were enough

---

11    Ibid.

to make a Rube Goldberg–device fan very excited. Surprisingly, though, the smell was nowhere near repugnant; this explains why two families have homes right next door, although the vast swarm of trees separating the three places probably helped. While walking around, Jim noted that the facility can treat up to 520,000 gallons of water a day, but that that much capacity has never been needed in a day. That factoid shed a little light on why the city of Austin wanted access to the facility and agreed to take over the former MUD's central service as Jim further advised that prior to the takeover Austin only had two major wastewater treatment facilities and this one facility added 34 percent more capacity to the system.[12, 13]

Finally, we got back in his truck and drove the 2 or so miles to the end of Caribou Trail to see the two large reservoirs that are still used to provide water (after it has been cleaned) to the golf course. On the golf course, someone with a five wood on the eighth hole could easily hit the closest reservoir; talk about a hole-in-one.

Nearing 11:00 a.m., Jim looked over and said, "Once again, that's about it regarding my special district. We don't have much. We used to have all this water infrastructure to manage, but now all we have is the front sign, deed restrictions, and the nature trails to work on."

In response, I replied, "Jim, thanks again for the tour and your time. Could I get a ride back over to Bay Hill Drive? Your old pickup is nice to ride in."

On the way there, I thought about what little I had been through today. Simply put, there was not a lot to the district in its present form. Before, as the MUD, they handled buying the water, maintaining the pipes, cleaning the used water, cleaning the trail, fixing the sign, and submitting the budget. Now it's just mowing the grass, enforcing deed restrictions, and repairing damage to the sign. Compared to what little else I knew about local government, the other groups were capable of handling so much more; Jim said as much. I could only wonder at how many of these tiny, single-service providers existed in the state. There must be a lot more going on behind the scenes at the local level of government than I realized.

---

12    Ibid.

13    "Wastewater Treatment Plants." WASTEWATER TREATMENT PLANTS. City of Austin. Accessed January 14, 2020. http://www.austintexas.gov/department/wastewater-treatment-plants.

**QUESTIONS TO CONSIDER** REGARDING SPECIAL GOVERNING DISTRICTS:

1.  The first main topic of the chapter discusses the number of services provided by special governing districts. Please indicate how many services that is, who from your life is comparable, and why, in detail.

2.  The second main topic of the chapter discusses how special governing districts are run. Please indicate what that structure is, what that structure is comparable to in your life, and why, in detail.

3.  The final main topic of the chapter discusses issued faced by special governing districts. Please identify what those issues are, the one most similar to issues in your life, and why, in detail.

# Chapter 14

# Municipalities of Texas

# The Difference between Cities and Municipalities

Over the years, I have written postcards back to my family while I was away from home. Many of them enjoy receiving the cards; some even have a good laugh at my expense because they think it's silly. It is a bit old-fashioned, yes, but I would much rather fill up my grandmother's mailbox than her inbox, assuming she had one of those, of course. Each trip, I bring a list of mailing addresses, which includes the person's name, street address, city, state, and zip code. One particular item from that list that I have never really much thought to was the city on the address of the envelope. What exactly is meant by that term *city*? Is it a legal jurisdiction of some kind, or is it just another word in the dictionary? Today's mission was, therefore, to learn the story behind the word *city* and the men and women who provide services in those jurisdictions. This day would continue my march through local governments.

FIGURE 14.1  Austin City Hall with Frost Bank Tower in background.

Thanks to Charity's work at the zoo, she had gotten to know Austin's city manager, Spencer Cronk. Thanks to that relationship, Charity had made a call on my behalf to schedule a day when I could shadow Manager Cronk in his duties.

Close to 8:00 a.m., I arrived at Austin City Hall (figure 14.1) and went up to the second floor to the city manager's office. Spencer was speaking with the young woman behind the front desk. After I walked in, the two of them looked up to greet me and said in unison, "Good morning, sir. How can we help you?"

I replied, "Hi there. I am Champ Cove. My sister Charity arranged for me to meet with the city manager today."

Spencer, straightening himself up, reached out to shake my hand and said, "Welcome to Austin, Champ. Let's go back to my office. We have a lot for you to learn about today and such a short time to do so."

Once back in his office, we were seated. He continued, "For the next hour or so, we are going to talk about whatever it is we can. At ten o'clock, I have an important meeting for us to attend. After that, you will get some lunch, and then I am going to send you to the wolves at our various agencies. So, what would you want to learn about first?"

It took me a few seconds to think of something, but then it hit me. I proceeded to ask, "What exactly is the city?"

Thinking for a few seconds himself, Spencer replied, "What you and most people do when thinking of Austin is to call it a city. The issue is, a city is nothing more than 'a human settlement, the mass of people living in the area.'[1] What we, as the misnamed city of Austin, are is a municipality, or 'the administrative division having corporate status to self-govern a specified jurisdiction—the governing body over the settlement.'[2] Both work when referring to us, but, per article 11 the state constitution, we are officially known as municipal corporations.[3] What next?"

Building on what Spencer said in his last statement, I asked, "As the governing jurisdiction that you say you are, what is it that you can and cannot do?"

Spencer continued, "That would depend on how it was that we were created."

I interjected, "Not all cities are created equally?"

## Types of Municipalities in Texas

Spencer continued, "You bet, under the rules of the Constitution of 1876, article 11, that is how the pie is sliced. Specifically, section 4 of article 11 provides for the creation of general law municipalities. For a municipality to form in this mode, it must have fewer than 5,000 citizens.[4] Duty-wise, these cities are limited to providing only essential services such as police and firefighters, alongside basic utilities and roads. General law municipalities have minimal opportunity to pass more stringent policy on other matters."

I interjected, "So what is the other group of municipalities about?"

Spencer continued, "Once the population in their governing territory gains more than 5,000 citizens, via the process of a ballot referendum or the granting of a new charter by the legislature, those municipalities may assume home-rule control of their charters and amend them as seen fit, but no 'oftener than every two years.'[5] In differentiating the two in a general sense, if you have never heard of the city and it only appears as a dot on a road map, it is most likely going to be a general law city; if it begins to have a shape to its form on a map and you have heard of it, the city is most likely home rule, at least in Texas. The latter organization method came after a constitutional amendment election in 1909 and was further strengthened by an additional amendment in 1911, which lowered the threshold for cities to obtain this higher rank.[6] Amarillo, in 1911, was the first city to do so."

---

1   https://www.merriam-webster.com/dictionary/city
2   https://www.macmillandictionary.com/us/dictionary/american/municipality
3   Texas Constitution of 1876, article 11, heading.
4   Texas Constitution of 1876, article 11, section 4.
5   Texas Constitution of 1876, article 11, section 5.
6   Texas Senate Joint Resolution 6, 31R (1909), and Texas House Joint Resolution 10, 32R (1911), respectively. Texas Constitution, article 11, section 5.

During a pause in his speech, I asked, "So how can the municipalities further amend their charters?"

Spencer argued, "That depends on who is leading the charge. At times, the municipality puts a referendum on a ballot to let citizens have a say on a matter when, due to some political matter, they are unable to act further without citizen guidance. It's a cop-out of one's duty, but it is paramount to let citizens have a say. On the other hand, when it is citizens leading the charge for change, the ballot measure is something called an initiative. Typically, this is done when a group of citizens feel so strongly about an issue that they cannot wait for the municipality to do something about it, so they decide to put the action on an issue on the ballot themselves.[7] The only real restriction is that their additional regulations cannot violate the state or federal constitutions. A special type of initiative, though, is something called a recall election, where an individual, or group of citizens for that matter, thinks that a governing official is doing such a horrible job that the person needs to be removed before the next regularly scheduled election. I believe that this is how the state of California elected the 'Governator' to power in 2003."[8]

I spoke up: "Who?"

Spencer, looking annoyed that I was not more up to date on my political knowledge, replied, "Arnold Schwarzenegger, the guy who played the Terminator in all those old movies. Drop 'term' and add 'govern,' and you get the coolest nickname of all time. What else you got for me to answer?"

## Dillon's Rule

I asked, "You brought up the fact that the legislature must create your organization. Can you further explain that?"

Spencer furthered, "In 1868, in the US Supreme Court case of *Clinton v. Cedar Rapids and the Missouri River Railroad*, the relationship between Texas and our municipalities, really all local governments for that matter, was cemented in legal reasoning.[9] This case introduced Dillon's rule—named after Justice Dillon, who wrote the opinion—to provide direction on what services a city could offer." In quoting the case, Spencer stated, "'Municipal corporations owe their origin to, and derive their powers and rights wholly from the state legislature. It breathes into them the breath of life, without which they cannot exist. As it creates, so may

---

7   For more info on the differences between referendums and initiatives see this link: http://www.ncid.us/initiative_referendum

8   Andrew Glass, "Schwarzenegger Elected Governor, Oct. 7, 2003," Politico, October 7, 2009, http://www.politico.com/story/2009/10/schwarzenegger-elected-governor-oct-7-2003-027970.

9   Clinton v. Cedar Rapids and the Missouri River Railroad, 24 Iowa 455 (1868).

it destroy. If it may destroy, it may abridge and control."[10] The state is like our master: They can, and did, bring us into the world many years ago and may tell us how to run our municipal governments, but most importantly they can extinguish our existence if we fall out of line with their mantra. This situation is a standard biological commensalistic relationship: The state can survive on its own, but we are entirely dependent on them for what we are and can do. This relationship is real for all local governments in the state, as this is what the state, via the Texas State Board of Education, did with North Forest ISD in 2013—they shut the school district down due to poor test scores and general operating issues.[11] Overall, they can shut us down and start all over again with something new or shift the responsibilities to another already present similar agency—as the Texas State Board of Education let Houston ISD[12] takeover over the district in the North Forest ISD matter."[13]

I inquired, "What is the story behind the founding of Austin?"

Spencer immediately replied, "Officially, Austin was founded as the city of Waterloo in March 1839 to serve as the capital of the newly founded Republic of Texas. Waterloo was renamed Austin later that year, to pay tribute to Stephen F. Austin. We were then incorporated on December 27 of that year as our municipality under the rules of the Constitution of 1836."[14]

Going full circle, I asked, "What else differentiates the general law and home-rule municipalities?"

Spencer advised, "Other than population size, of course, and the additional ability to govern with those direct-democratic initiatives in home-rule municipalities, it all comes down to the size of their theoretical waistline. Let me get something for you."

After digging through his bag for a minute, he handed me a sheet of paper with a drawing on it. Spencer stated, "Champ, this is a map I made this morning just for you from our website. Anyone can go to it and make their own (figure 14.2).[15] This map focuses in on the south side of our municipality and Travis County, with parts of neighboring Caldwell and Hays Counties, and with Buda, Kyle, and Mustang Ridge municipalities' jurisdictions mapped out as well where relevant. The areas that are tan all belong to the municipality of Austin. I put our city council districts (with identifying numbers for each district) on there as well to make the area stand out a bit more. The furthest extent of those lines is called our city limit; we have full regulatory control over those living within that line. What I want you to focus

10    Ibid.
11    ABC13 Archive, "Texas Education Agency Rules to Close North Forest ISD and Merge into Houston ISD," ABC13 Houston, accessed March 20, 2019, http://abc13.com/archive/9047790.
12    https://www.houstonisd.org
13    Ibid 11.
14    http://www.austinlibrary.com/ahc/faq1.htm
15    http://www.austintexas.gov/GIS/JurisdictionsWebMap

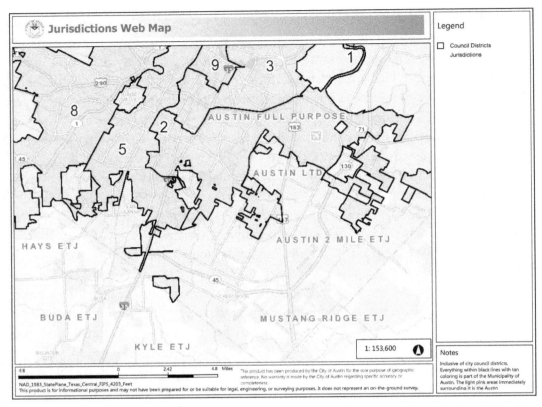

FIGURE 14.2 South Side of Austin Map with City Limits, City Council Districts, and Extra-Territory Jurisdiction.

on, though, is the pinkish area that immediately surrounds the lined areas with the terms 'AUSTIN 2 MILE ETJ' and 'AUSTIN LTD' on them. These are areas that the city of Austin does not have full control over. LTD stands for limited control, where we, as the municipality, are in the process of annexing—which is the forcible acquisition of territory, claimed or unclaimed, by a group[16]—these areas, which means that we are working to place them under our full regulatory control. ETJ, on the other hand, is shorthand for extra-territorial jurisdiction, a control buffer that surrounds the city and which we have insufficient control over. This area can extend a half mile to a full 5 miles beyond the city limit, depending on the current size of the city. Ours is 2 miles, but due to having more than 100,000 people, it should be 5 miles.[17] The influence of other nearby municipalities gets in the way of us having further control. We, as cities, like these ETJ and LTD areas, because it prevents us from being

16    http://www.dictionary.com/browse/annexation
17    http://www.bhlaw.net/8%20MUNICIPAL%20REGULATION%20ETJ%20-%20COG%20Basics%20of%20Planning%20and%20Zoning%20-%20April%202005%20Edition.pdf

boxed in by so-called bedroom communities. We here in Austin are, unfortunately, boxed in to the south by Buda, to the north by Cedar Park and Round Rock, Lakeway to the west, and Manor to the east."

I interjected, "Wait a minute. What is the issue here?"

Spencer continued, "Well, that waistline I referred to earlier is a nice metaphor for their city limit-slash-ETJ. When the area within the limit grows and begins to expand beyond it, the city wants to go forward and expand its waistline via the process of annexation. This arrangement is typically done to help control development within the current ETJ area and expand the city's tax base to keep its coffers full."

I interrupted, "I bet people tend to have an issue with that annexation, as it may mean additional taxes and higher fees for various services."

Nodding his head, Spencer furthered, "Yep. So, to control annexation, home-rule and general law cities have to play by different rules, all of which were founded under the Municipal Annexation Act of 1963, which later became section 43 of the Texas Municipal Code. In either case, the property to be annexed must be in their ETJ. Looking at the Texas Local Government Code, chapter 43, subchapter B, general law cities, for the most part, must receive a petition of some kind from landowners or voters before proceeding with any annexation of property,[18] while home rule cities have much more freedom to do so without consent, depending on the wording of their charters.[19] Once annexed, if done unilaterally by the municipality, utility services, if offered by the city, must be extended to the newly annexed area within three years' time. If not, some annexed areas have the right to secede, all once again depending on the wording of their charters. Of note, I believe, Senate Bill 89 in 1999 was the last major alteration to municipal annexation here. Specifically, that bill drastically rewrote annexation rules in the state and required a plan in most cases to be set up before any annexation proceeds. Speaking of proceedings, let's get going to that meeting."

After a bit of a stretch, once standing, Spencer and I proceeded out of his office, through a cubicle farm, and out into the main hallways. We found our way over to the city council chambers (figure 14.3). This was the same chamber where I had

FIGURE 14.3 Austin City Hall Council Chambers.

---

18    Texas Local Government Code, section 43.
19    Ibid.

been with my uncle last week to visualize the public service form of political participation. Little did I know, my education about cities . . . er . . . municipalities—I still can't get the terminology straight—was just about to hit center stage, or should I say the podium.

## Managing a Municipality

It became apparent when we walked into the chambers that I was not the only one there learning about municipal government, as the room was filled with summer-school kids from the Austin Independent School District. Spencer, at this point, ushered me over to the podium, where I was told, "You are going to be emcee of the first part of the meeting. Ask this question for me: 'How is a municipality managed?'"

Right at ten o'clock, the city council and mayor entered the chamber. The gavel was hammered by the person in the middle, who looked a bit more important than the rest and called the meeting to order. After the obligatory pledge and prayer, the person at the center said, "Welcome, everyone, to today's special meeting of the Austin City Council. My name is Steve Adler. I am the mayor of Austin. Seated in his traditional seat to the side is our city manager, Spencer Cronk. Also with us today is a nice young man at the podium who I believe has a question for us to discuss today. Go ahead, young man."

I took a deep breath and said, "Good morning, council. Thank you for letting me speak here today. I was here a little while back, and things seem to be a lot calmer today. I guess my question is, how is a city, or should I say municipality, managed?"

Everyone on the council let out a bit of a giggle at the correction. Then Mayor Adler said, "Funny you should ask that. Depending on how you look at it, there are three or four different methods. For a good listing of these, you should see the National League of Cities about this for further information that we might miss giving you today.[20] As you can probably guess by my introduction, we here in Austin use a technique called the council-manager system. This system sees power separated between either lay or professional city councils that work to make and set policy for the city—acting as the legislature of the city. On the other hand, the city manager—Spencer, in this case—is a professionally trained individual who in many cases has a master's degree in public administration and a bachelor of science in urban and regional planning to provide him with expertise on the matter. His duties are to implement the policies set forth by the council while advising us on the potential impact of what we are doing, or want to implement. Like us here on the council, his powers are granted and

---

20    National League of Cities, "Forms of Municipal Government," accessed March 20, 2019, https://www.nlc.org/forms-of-municipal-government. Information on each of the different types of municipalities discussed in this chapter was pulled from this website.

restricted by the city charter. For what it's worth, he physically runs the city, just the same as the president runs the country. This process is done by him hiring and firing individuals, submitting a budget, and simply being an advisor to us on the council. For you kids out there in the audience, Spencer is like your teacher running your classroom, and your school board is like us, the council telling your teacher what they need to teach."

The kids and I were eating this stuff up at this point. I jokingly said over the microphone at this point, "Let me guess: In the next system, you'd have all the power, Mayor Adler?"

Mayor Adler replied, "Why, yes, I would. That would be one of the two forms of the mayor-council system: strong. Under the strong form, the mayor is not only in charge of deciding policy, with the approval of the council, of course, but also is actually fully in charge of running the city, in the same way that Spencer is here in Austin. On the other hand, the weak mayor functions like another city council member does, but with a fancier nameplate. Together, the mayor and council set policy and instruct city officials on how their policies should be implemented. Our neighbor down US Highway 290, Houston, uses the strong-mayor format."

Wanting to stir up even more pizazz, as the students were really on edge after that last discussion, I stated, "I don't like the idea behind having a strong mayor, or a mayor, for that matter. What system do you have up your sleeves for me now to ponder?"

With the look of a tiger ready to pounce, Mayor Adler continued, "Well, if you must know, there is the commission form of municipal government. Here, citizens elect commissioners to serve in a small legislative body. Those commissioners are responsible for one specific aspect of running the government. One is in charge of firefighters, one is in charge of police, and so on down the list. One commissioner is delegated to lead each of the commission meetings, earning the title of mayor along with their original elected position. All of these people, after deciding on the direction of policy together, then go forth and manage their executive departments individually. People do tend to like this system, due to it giving credence to experienced officials of their field. However, young man, I got some more systems up my sleeve. Care to try me?"

At this point, all the students were up in arms with the biggest chorus of "Oohhhhhhhhhhh" that I had ever heard.

Not wanting to disappoint, I said, "What if I just wanted to get rid of all of you and give all the power to the people? Come on, guys and girls, who's with me? Yeah!"

After a few seconds of teachers shushing the crowd, Mayor Adler remarked, "Well, for those of you who want something slightly more than anarchy, but not a true leadership group, there is something called the town meeting system, where everyone who is eligible, depending on their system, gets together as a group to decide basic policy and then goes on to nominate someone to see those policies put through to fruition."

It was then that one of the quietly sitting council members, Joe Jacobson, who I later learned is a local government professor at UT Austin, spoke up: "Mayor Adler, thank you for that energetic lecture on how municipalities are specifically run. I would like to point out that the main difference between each of these systems is the person who has the day-to-day control over the city—the manager in the first, the mayor/council in the second, the individual commissioners over their individual departments in the third, and finally, society as a whole in the latter. The first is most common, the second is the second-most common, and so on, down the line."

I inquired, "So which one is best?"

Councilman Jacobson furthered, "Picking one form or another is like picking your poison; each system has its downside, but some are certainly better than others. We here in Austin switched from the strong-mayor form in 1924[21] to the council-manager system because we wanted to avoid the likelihood of the mayor going mad with power, although the current council-manager system has its downside, in that the person who is in charge of the city is not selected by the electorate, but by the council. If the wrong sort of people got elected to the council, the city manager could be forced to implement policies he or she disagreed with and were bad for the city overall, regardless of opinion. More importantly, the weak-mayor form leaves voters perplexed as to whom they should hold responsible, because when problems emerge there is no clear person to blame for what occurred, as the council acts as a group. For the commission, fractured responsibility is a major concern, as everybody knows what their position is responsible for managing. Get a citywide issue, though, no one takes full responsibility, and getting an overall solution is nearly impossible. Lastly, for town meetings, the danger is groupthink, where, due to a feeling of the necessity for a solution, the group decides to go with an option that is irrational, unnecessary, or dysfunctional, leading to disaster, all because no one has any experience at running an actual municipality to guide them appropriately."

I asked, "So how can I get a job working with y'all on the council?"

Another council member by the name of Arnold Hey mentioned, "Great question. Municipal elections in Texas, keep in mind, are all nonpartisan. No one serves as a Republican or Democrat or whatever. Getting an actual seat requires you to run for either a single-member district, like that of our state and federal legislature, or an at-large seat, which is where you run in a citywide election, like that of a US senator who runs statewide. At-large systems come in two methods: Pure is the first, where, for example, five people are running for three open seats on the council. The top three vote getters all win a seat. In the second,

---

21   http://www.austintexas.gov/department/city-manager/about

people are still running in an at-large election, but the candidates have to select a specified place or seat on the council."

After hearing all of this, the schoolkids and I were in awe at what the options were for how a city could be managed and led. I stated, "I think that I have learned enough for one meeting. I'm going to get some lunch. Thank you for your time and answers."

After I sat down, Mayor Adler proceeded to call a recess for people to leave or use the restroom. Spencer came over to me with a sheet of paper in his hands. He stated, "This is a list of different city departments that you may go to visit after lunch. Go get some food, and then go as you see fit. All the city department heads know that they might get a visitor. Have a great day, and pleasure meeting with you."

I replied, "Thank you so much again!"

## Departments of the Municipality of Austin

With five hours before the city closed for the day, I picked four places that I wanted to visit and learn about the specific services they provide. I then walked out of city hall to get some lunch and brainstorm what I would ask when I arrived at each of the places. During lunch, I came up with the following questions:

What does this office do for the public?
When would I need to visit?
What role does this office play in the running of government?

Since I was inside all morning, I decided that it would be good to go to departments that would get me outdoors. Once back in my car at the garage across from city hall at 301 West Second Street, I found myself going west on Cesar Chavez Boulevard. I then went on the loop that put me southbound on Lamar Boulevard. During the loop, I could see what appeared to be the former Mexican consulate and thought, "What role do they play here in the United States?"

Once on the south side of Lady Bird Lake, I took an immediate right onto Riverside Drive that ended in the parking lot of the Austin Parks and Recreation Department. Once parked, I made my way inside, going through the xeriscape garden out front.

After speaking with the secretary, I was sent to the back office of the department head, Kimberly McNeeley. With some small talk out of the way, in response to the first question, she replied, "Our department owns, operates, or maintains 300 parks, 13 off-leash dog parks, 147 playgrounds, 227 miles of trails, 40 pools, 11 museums, 35 baseball diamonds, 24 historic

FIGURE 14.4  The Zilker Park Entrance Portal, Austin, Texas, United States. The Art Deco sign was built by the Civil Works Administration in the early 1930s.

buildings, 5 historic cemeteries, and so much more,[22] most of which is free, or has a small fee, to use. The main facility includes the famous Zilker Metropolitan Park, home to Barton Springs Pool and the Austin City Limits Music Festival, which, if you look out the window behind me, is available for all to see[23] (figure 14.4). Regarding your second question, citizens would need to visit the main office, where we are now, when wanting to reserve a space for an event, complain about a particular service not being up to snuff, or simply get information about the numerous facilities we operate. My favorite is the botanical garden in Zilker Park. For that last question, though, we provide a service to the citizens of the municipality, really the whole region, by providing recreational services that all have equal access to use and enjoy. Is that it?"

I replied, "For here, yes. Thanks for your time."

On my way out, she tossed me a pin to remind me of my time there and stated, "Enjoy the great outdoors. It is our greatest treasure!"

Once back in my car, I went east on Riverside Drive for two long blocks, past the Palmer Events Center[24] and the Long Center for the Performing Arts,[25] which are the primary large concert venues for the area outside of the Austin City Limits[26] venue in downtown and the Circuit of the Americas Pavilion[27] on 290 toward Bastrop. I then turned right onto South First Street. A block later, I arrived at the city annex, located at 505 Barton Springs Road (figure 14.5). While there, I would visit two additional city departments.

Once inside, I first made my way to the Planning and Zoning Department. Inside their office, I went up to the receptionist and advised that I was there to speak with director Gregory Guernsey.

22   Austin Parks and Recreation Department, "Austin Parks and Recreation Department FY17 Annual Report," Issuu, January 7, 2018, pp. 6–7, https://issuu.com/atxparksmarketing/docs/annual_report_fy17.

23   http://www.austintexas.gov/department/zilker-metropolitan-park

24   https://www.palmereventscenter.com

25   http://thelongcenter.org

26   http://austincitylimits.com

27   http://www.circuitoftheamericas.com

Unfortunately, she replied, "I'm sorry, young man. He is not available. But if you are the boy being sent around to visit different people, he authorized me to speak to you on his behalf. What is your first question?"

I replied, "What does this office do for the general public?"

For the first question, she replied by reading straight from the department's website and stated that their mission is to "provide planning, preservation and design services to make Austin the most livable city in the country. What's next?"[28]

FIGURE 14.5  City of Austin One Texas Center.

I replied, "When would I need to visit?"

She replied, "Dearie, a person would need to visit us to obtain a building permit, schedule a site inspection, ensure compliance with drainage plans, select appropriate foliage, or request a deviation from the overall city zoning plan to ensure that their future property is compliant with building regulations put forth by the city if found within the limits. Give me one more good question, and then I've got to get back to the phones."

I hurriedly responded, "What role does this office play in the running of government?"

For the last question, she indicated, "We provide a service to the city, in that we ensure buildings are safe for people to use."

Following the quick experience, I thanked her for her time. She too gave me a pin to remember my time here. I became a bit suspicious at this point but decided to make sure that I did not lose the pins. After the Planning and Zoning Department, I visited the Public Works Department[29] down the hall, expecting to learn about water. Boy, was I wrong. When I entered, Director Cilpub, a tall Danish man, approached and asked, "Are you the boy who is touring city departments today?"

I responded with a definitive "Yes, sir!"

He handed me a hard hat and said, "Let's go."

After we got into his truck, we headed east on Barton Springs Road, which led us right onto the Congress Avenue Bridge (figure 14.6). Instead of going all the way across, we stopped about a third of the way across the bridge, right behind a work crew going about their business.

Once out of the car, I asked, "So what are we doing here?

28    http://www.austintexas.gov/department/planning-and-zoning/about
29    http://www.austintexas.gov/department/public-works

FIGURE 14.6 Ann W. Richards Congress Avenue Bridge is home to the world's largest urban bat colony, which is composed of Mexican Free-tailed Bats. The bats reside beneath the road deck in gaps between the concrete component structures. They are migratory, spending their summers in Austin and the winters in Mexico. According to Bat Conservation International [1], between 750,000 and 1.5 million bats reside underneath the bridge each summer. Since Austin's human population is about 750,000, there are more bats than people in Austin during the summer.

He replied, "Bridge maintenance. We do not want ours collapsing like the one in Minneapolis did a few years ago on Interstate 35 a thousand or so miles north of here."[30]

As we continued to walk past the lot of the repair work going on and toward some scaffolding, I asked the first question. He replied—and being the top director that he is, he spoke from memory—with the department's vision statement from their website: "This department designs, manages, and inspects major capital improvement projects; promotes bicycle, pedestrian, safe routes to school, and urban trail projects; and maintains the city's network of trails, roadways, and bridges once the structures are built."[31]

That helped bring clarity as to why we were on the bridge and not scuba diving through a pipe somewhere.

Once at the midpoint of the bridge, we walked onto some scaffolding that took us over the side and under the bridge. Director Cilpub explained, "We are replacing the expansion joints with newer ones that help provide structure, as part of the regular maintenance of the road surface and bridge to ensure that it does not collapse."

While looking at a gap between two sections, I asked, "The main reason for a citizen to visit your office is to get a pothole fixed, correct?"

Director Cilpub replied, "Typical citizens, yes, but developers would need to visit to ensure that local roads were capable of handling traffic for their developments and the like."

This response sounded like a reasonable statement, due to a large number of skyscrapers going up around the city. On our way back up the scaffolding after an hour or so, I heard some chirping. I stopped and looked at a section of the bridge that was not being disturbed. All I could see were thousands of bats sleeping. I quietly moved, not wanting to be hit in the face by all the bats in the world if they got spooked and flew in my direction. I then remembered

---

30    MSNBC.com staff, "9 Thought Dead as Minneapolis Bridge Collapses," NBCNews.com, August 2, 2007, http://www.nbcnews.com/id/20079534/ns/us_news-life/t/thought-dead-minneapolis-bridge-collapses.
31    http://www.austintexas.gov/department/public-works

that, during the summer, millions of Mexican free-tailed bats, the state flying mammal, make their home in the bridge.[32]

Once back in the truck, I asked the third question. Director Cilpub's response: "I play the role of construction manager by providing reliable transit facilities for citizens to use, via servicing of the facilities. For questions about using the facilities, speak with transportation[33] or Capital Metro."[34]

In the parking lot, Director Cilpub dropped me back off next to my car and handed me a pin. Now I knew that I would hear about these things later. I asked him to sign my form, too, just to be safe.

Once in my car, I proceeded east on Riverside Drive and south on Interstate 35. After a few miles, I took the eastbound ramp for State Highway 71. After passing State Highway 183 just before 4:00 p.m., I exited at Spirit of Texas Drive. Going south on the road, I found myself parking in the short-term parking lot. Once inside the Austin-Bergstrom International Airport Terminal (figure 14.7), I went to the upstairs offices and found myself in the Aviation Department[35] director's office.

FIGURE 14.7 Aerial View of Austin-Bergstrom International Airport.

Of all the people I had been speaking with today, Director Nitsua Tropria seemed to be the most straightforward. In response to the first question, he replied, "We ensure that the airport is ready to accept commercial and general aviation airplane traffic for the capital region by meeting Federal Aviation Regulation 141, part 139—the certification for the safe operation of an airport."[36]

I joked, "It seems as if everyone has to get certified for everything."

Director Tropria replied, "Well, yes. Without certification, you would or could have someone who could barely drive a car deciding to open their backyard up for landing planes, and it would be perfectly disastrous. The planes we get here are as long as some small skyscrapers are tall and go over 500 miles an hour. Regulation is essential for the safe operation of aircraft.

---

32    Bat Conservation International, "Congress Avenue Bridge," accessed March 20, 2019, http://www.batcon.org/index.php/our-work/regions/usa-canada/protect-mega-populations/cab-intro.

33    http://www.austintexas.gov/department/transportation

34    https://www.capmetro.org

35    http://www.austintexas.gov/resident/aviation; http://www.austintexas.gov/airport

36    https://www.faa.gov/airports/airport_safety/part139_cert

The regulation is what has helped keep the United States free of major accidents since 2009, outside of the poor woman who died after getting sucked out of the plane last year when the window burst due to the engine containment system failing when the engine exploded."[37]

To keep things going, I posited, "I bet most people come to complain about noise levels of the airport or to advise about some issue with the airport facilities."

Director Tropria replied, "Oh, yes. Planes are big and noisy, not as noisy as they used to be, but people still love to complain."

Regarding the third question, Director Tropria responded, "We do not play any role in running the government; instead, we provide a service, like many of the departments in the municipality, by operating an entity that, outside of Branson, Missouri, few private entities operate.[38] Would you like to end your day on an adrenaline rush?"

I could only reply, "Sure."

I was handed a yellow vest and told to follow him down to the basement. After the elevator ride down and through a doorway, we were on the same cement surface as the multitude of planes. Waiting for us was a white Ford Expedition with a huge flashing light display on its roof. In the car, I was told, "We are now going to proceed to the runway for an inspection."

This facility being an airport, Director Tropria began speaking a weird code into his radio: "Austin ground, OPS One at the terminal. Request permission to proceed to approach of Runway One-Seven-Right via taxiways Romeo and Charlie."

Ground responded, "OPS one, proceed as requested."

Director Tropria: "Roger, Ground. OPS One proceeding as requested."

On the way to the runway, we passed the new midfield concourse being constructed. Once there, Director Tropria contacted the tower: "Austin Tower, OPS One at approach One-Seven-Right on Charlie. Request permission to proceed onto One-Seven-Right for inspection."

Tower responded, "OPS One, proceed as requested. Advise when clear."

After that, I do not remember much, as we had to get on and off quickly due to the daily evening British Airways flight wanting to land.[39] Who knew a city provides so many diverse services or has so much control over what people could do with their properties? More importantly, I am amazed that municipalities can be organized and run in a variety of different

37    Vince Lattanzio, Alicia Victoria Lozano, Denise Nakano, and Brian X. McCrone, "Woman Killed, 7 Hurt in Mid-Air Exploding Engine Incident," NBC 10 Philadelphia, April 23, 2018. https://www.nbcphiladelphia. com/news/local/Airplane-Makes-Emergency-Landing-at-Philadelphia-International-Airport-480008613. html; Dan Reed, "In a Dangerous World, U.S. Commercial Aviation Is on a Remarkable Safety Streak," *Forbes*, January 3, 2017, https://www.forbes.com/sites/danielreed/2016/12/28/in-the-last-7-years-you-were-more-likely-to-be-run-over-by-a-car-than-to-die-in-an-airline-crash/#743e1d8428a2.

38    http://www.gcr1.com/5010web/airport.cfm?Site=BBG

39    https://www.britishairways.com/en-ca/destinations/austin/flights-to-austin

ways that best suit their local desires and needs. Municipalities seem much more capable of service provision than their special district counterparts.

When I got home, Charity asked, "Let me see your pins. I want to report to Spencer that you did what you were told." I showed them to her and went to bed to get some rest after a busy day learning about the municipalities that manage the cities.

---

**QUESTIONS TO CONSIDER** REGARDING MUNICIPALITIES:

1. The first main topic of the chapter discusses the difference between cities and municipalities. Please identify what that difference is, a situation from your life that is similar, and indicate how, in detail.

2. The second main topic of the chapter discusses the different types of municipalities in Texas. Please indicate what the two types are, the one that you would like to live under most, and why, in detail.

3. The third main topic of the chapter discusses Dillon's rule. Please define what Dillon's rule is, describe something similar from your life, and explain why it fits the bill, in detail.

4. The fourth main topic of the chapter provides insight on the different ways to manage a municipality. Please indicate what the different ways are, the one you would least like to live under, and why, in detail.

5. The final main topic of the chapter provides insight on select agencies of the municipality of Austin. Please select the one you were intrigued by the most, go to its website to learn more about it, and write down what you learned, in detail.

---

# Chapter 15

# County Government in Texas

## Counties as Arms of the State

Earlier in the week, the Lost Pines Limited District, serving as a medium to learn about special districts, taught me that they oversaw one specialized task. The city of Austin yesterday seemed like a special district on steroids, as they could do several jobs at one time as they saw fit. In both cases it seemed as if the responsibilities were for items that I needed on a regular basis. In what I learned about today when spending time with the Travis County authorities, the services they offer seem to be required a lot less regularly, but are still very important when needed. Therefore, today was all about the basics—basic government services, that is.

Just after 8:00 a.m., I left Charity's house for the quick half-hour drive to the Travis County Courthouse (figure 15.1). Just after 8:30 a.m., I found the courthouse, located two blocks southwest of the state capitol building on Guadalupe Street. After parking my car in the garage, catty-corner to the courthouse and across the street from Wooldridge Square Park, I crossed the street and made my way up the short path to the front entrance. Once inside, I made my way up the stairs to the second floor and found myself entering the offices of County Judge Sarah Eckhardt.[1] Once inside the door, I noticed Eckhardt was speaking with her secretary about some missing form she needed for a meeting later in the day. Eckhardt then looked up and said, "You must be Mr. Cove. Come on

FIGURE 15.1 Travis County Courthouse.

into my office. I've been looking forward to this since speaking with your father a few days ago."

Once in her office, Eckhardt stated, "Welcome to the Travis County Courthouse. I hope finding your way here was easy enough. It's not like city hall here, where people have to go regularly."

I replied, "Well, yes, it was. I've made the drive in from Lost Pines so many times now that the road signs for downtown Austin are etched into the back of my mind. The trick is, look for the signs you haven't been needing on previous trips. By the way, the coffee smells great, too."

Eckhardt replied, "I can get you a cup if you want."

---

1    https://www.traviscountytx.gov/commissioners-court/county-judge

I replied, "No thanks. I just had a cup in the car. If I heard correctly, you have a meeting soon, so I'll just get started with some questions if you don't mind. What exactly is a county?"

Eckhardt remarked, "Sounds like a plan. Just remember, you will be at that meeting, too. To your question though, article 9 (via sections 1 and 2) of our current state constitution regulates the creation and duties of counties like us here in Travis,[2] beyond what other responsibilities are assigned to us by the legislature.[3] In the broadest of general definitions, a county provides general-purpose government, alongside serving as an administrative arm of the state, bringing state policy down to the community level. We function to help all citizens of the county, but due to cities having precedence within their limits, our presence is reduced there, unless a segment of a county or state road is running through the city limits. Then we are responsible for that road's maintenance. The funny thing is, though, besides primarily operating in the rural parts of a county, most services we offer are in cities, or at least based in the largest city in the county, called the county seat, and based in the county courthouse like the one we are in right now. Overall, there are 254 counties found in the great state of Texas. Of note, counties are very similar throughout the country, the only difference being that in Louisiana they are known as parishes."

I asked, "What do you mean by general purpose?"

Eckhardt replied, "Your father said that you were with the city yesterday. The city does provide a good amount of exceptional services, like regulating land use. We here in the county, unless it is truly public land that we own, don't get into any of that. The only duties specifically given to us are from section 1a of article 9 of the state constitution, which grants us the power to regulate beach access by motor vehicles if we are on the coast.[4] Section 12 gives us the authority to create airport authorities in our territory.[5] Section 14 allows us and I quote 'a Manual Labor Poor House and Farm, for taking care of, managing, employing and supplying the wants of its indigent and poor inhabitants.[6]' One of our most important tasks is the creation of countywide hospital districts.[7] We don't get to do a lot of our own choosing beyond what I've discussed; everything else is to service the needs of the state. Other general-purpose tasks include, from the Local Government Code's chapters 85 and 86, rural law enforcement by the sheriff and constable."

I remarked, "Tell me more about servicing the state. That sounds very burdensome."

---

2    https://www.traviscountytx.gov
3    Constitution of 1876, article 9, sections 1 and 2.
4    Constitution of 1876, article 9, section 1a.
5    Constitution of 1876, article 9, section 12.
6    Constitution of 1876, article 9, section 14.
7    Constitution of 1876, article 9, section 4.

She replied, "I would, but my fellow officers of the county will do a better job at that later today."

Hitting a wall, I requested, "What service do you provide for the county?"

In response, Eckhardt advised, "I am the lead administrative official of the county for as many four-year terms as I can get elected to serve.[8] I could be thought of as the 'mayor' or 'president' of the county. Contrary to the title, though, I have very few, if any, judicial duties. Smaller counties have the county judge lead the county constitutional court, but in bigger ones, like Travis or Harris, I tend to stick to the administrative functions due to them demanding so much of my time. Also, I can perform weddings, supervise elections, prepare the county budget, conduct hearings for alcohol permits, and even tell people that they can go to a mental asylum. Most importantly, my primary function is to lead the commissioner's court, the legislative body of our county, in decision-making and what services the county will provide going forward."[9]

After that, I asked, "What are the structural and organizational differences between various counties in Texas?"

She responded fervently, "County management does not vary from county to county. Each county is run with the same set of positions and a basic set of rules. We are like general law municipalities, to be honest; we, once again, don't have a lot of say in what it is we can or cannot do. Many of us wish that we could be like home rule cities. For example, whether there are the roughly 134 inhabitants in the 677 square miles of Loving County or just north of 4.65 million or so residents in Harris County, covering 1,778 square miles, the county government is the same from top to bottom. Although, in smaller counties, many of the similar positions, like those for finance, are combined, due to them being redundant or small enough not to require a separate person to handle each one, alongside being easily condensable. As the counties grow, the special positions emerge in some form or fashion."

Getting close to 9:45 a.m., Eckhardt stated, "It is time for us to go to that meeting I was telling you about earlier. You have some more questions to ask."

At this point, I stated, "This feels a lot like what happened yesterday, and what are those questions?"

Eckhardt replied, "You'll figure it out!"

---

8   http://www.county.org/texas-county-government/texas-county-officials/Pages/County-Judge.aspx
9   Texas Local Government Code, section 81.005; http://codes.lp.findlaw.com/txstatutes/LG/3/B/81/A/81.005.

## County Positions

We then headed down the hall to the commissioner's court. Once in the county commissioner's court chambers, I found a meeting agenda sheet. Right at the top, just like yesterday, I was the first agenda item on the list. Right at 10:00 a.m., Eckhardt banged the gavel, calling the meeting to order, and led the court in the pledges and a prayer. Following a quick round of comments from the public, I was invited to the podium to speak. Not being given a script like yesterday, I went with, "Commissioners, thank you for letting me come and ask questions of you today. I would like to know: How do the commissioners of the court get their positions?"

Commissioner Nightly Dayson spoke up and advised, "Each of us commissioners represents one-quarter of the county's population in something referred to as a precinct, like that of a state or US legislative district, but in the county. Also, we serve four-year terms like that of the judge, but the terms are staggered to provide continuity for the court's business. Think of county commissioners as the 'representatives' of a county, but with additional nonlegislative duties. Our charter provides additional information on this matter."

Building on the response, I asked, "What are those 'nonlegislative' duties?"

From the court, Commissioner Francine Firestorm, Precinct 2, then offered, "Our main duty is to oversee the county roads or whatever other county facilities are in our precincts that have no specified elected or nonelected official to oversee them, like the sheriff and the jailhouse. The Texas Association of Counties[10] refers to this as 'hands-on service delivery.'"[11] Beyond that, the county government is very much like that of the state government, in that power is fragmented. Each of the positions that you are going to speak with this afternoon is individually elected by the public. For example, the only real power that we as the commission have here is influencing the direction of the county via our budgeting authority. The only other duties of our court are to set the tax rate for the year and pass ordinances for an insufficient number of items, like what Judge Eckhardt told you about in her office earlier, if what she just whispered in my ear is correct. Beyond that, that is about it. We do get to go to other counties to negotiate a service contract with them, though, which is essential to cut costs for everyone."

Then, out of the blue, Commissioner Travillian of Precinct 1 announced, "This set of circumstances leads to two issues for the county. In the first case, the fractured responsibility of power in the county leads to no concise direction. Specifically, the judicial and law enforcement positions can arrest a bunch of people, but since the sheriff does not control the

---

10    https://www.county.org/Pages/default.aspx

11    http://www.county.org/texas-county-government/texas-county-officials/Pages/County-Commissioner. aspx

budget, he or she could be faced with overcrowding in the jail. In the second case, people do not like voting in our elections due to 11 different positions being on the ballot, not including any actual 'judgy' judges, the list of which can be quite a lot in larger counties like Harris, where there are 40 county-level judges.[12] People are unable to keep up with the different positions to make sensible decisions, although the ability of people to vote straight Republican or Democrat and be in and out in ten seconds does help."

I concluded, "If I am not mistaken, that is about it for general purpose. Thank you for your time, commissioners."

I sat down and watched the rest of the short special session. The court was discussing the purchase of some land for the county from the state's General Land Office for the county to add additional territory to Zilker Park and put in a small wind farm for power generation. After a while, I was handed a document by the judge's secretary, outlining my schedule for the rest of the afternoon.

Unlike yesterday with the city of Austin, where I had a choice of places to see, I was being sent everywhere today. Instead of listening to the events that were occurring in the meeting, I took out my smartphone and looked for where everything was. Most everything seemed very close by, so it looked like it was going to be another fun scavenger hunt today. What I learned at each of the places is how many of them are there to be administrative arms of the state.

What helped bring home the idea of being the administrative arm of the state was my first stop with the county clerk. After the meeting at noon, I took the brown-bag lunch and pad of paper I had with me and went upstairs to the county clerk's office for my lunch appointment. Waiting for me in the lobby of her office was County Clerk Dana DeBeauvoir.[13] When I walked in, she invited me to her office and told me to have a seat. Once I was seated, she asked, "What did you think of that meeting? There was not a lot to it, right?"

I replied, "Yeah, just me asking some questions and then debating over purchasing some land, a straightforward process, if I am not mistaken. Could you clarify something for me? What does everyone mean by 'administrative arm of the state'?"

DeBeauvoir articulated, "An arm of the state refers to an agency created by the state to operate as an instrument of it. In general, courts decide on whether it is an arm if it runs with little to no substantial autonomy from state regulatory functions.[14] This job includes funding or rulemaking for the agency."

---

12   http://www.ccl.hctx.net; http://www.jp.hctx.net; see the bottom of the sites.
13   http://www.traviscountyclerk.org/eclerk/Content.do?code=Home
14   http://definitions.uslegal.com/a/arm-of-the-state

I posited, "How does that relate to your duties, beyond taking notes of what goes on in the commissioner's court meetings,[15] of course?"

DeBeauvoir replied, "During election season, unless the commissioners give my authority away to an elections commission, I administer the election in the county.[16] If the parties wish, I may also administrate their primaries as well.[17] About your question, as you may have learned, the secretary of state is the chief election official of the state. Seeing as how their office cannot be everywhere on Election Day, the other county clerks and I do that job for them and run the election, outside of constructing the statewide portion of the ballot. Also, the state is required to keep track of people and other operations in the state. Accordingly, I also keep records of all misdemeanor court proceedings, births, deaths, marriages, cattle brands, hospital liens, deeds, deeds of trust, liens, and Certificates of Release or Discharge from Active Duty, known as a DD 214.[18] I would also take on the duties of the district clerk,[19] who handles the records of the state district courts, if our population is less than 8,000 people, but that boat sailed a long time ago for us.[20] All of this is to help the state keep up their records. I mean, why set up another state agency when the county could do it for them?"

I asked, "So what role would you say that you play in the running of government?"

DeBeauvoir replied, "I would be considered the record keeper of the government. Wanna see 'em?"

Confused, I took out my smartphone and remarked, "What's the web address?"

Laughing, she replied, "Wrong computer, and room, for that matter. Follow me."

We walked down the hall and entered a room labeled Records Room. When walking through the door, I realized that it was not a regular door, but rather the face to a huge walk-in safe. What I saw when inside made me blurt out loud, "Are we in the library or what?"

DeBeauvoir continued, "Close enough, on most occasions. When I say we keep all records, I do mean all records, dating back to the founding of the state—or should I say county for us here in Travis—depending on the record. What you see here in these books and map casings are the records of every plot, property purchase, birth—you name it—from around 1840 to the early 1970s, when the state switched over to computerized records. Those people sitting at the desks most likely have the job of landman, and they are trained to go through old records to determine the proper ownership of air, ground, mineral, and other rights of everything in the county. Those books weigh in at around 35 or so pounds and cover somewhere around

15    http://www.traviscountyclerk.org/eclerk/Content.do?code=Commissioners
16    http://www.traviscountyclerk.org/eclerk/Content.do?code=Elections
17    Ibid.
18    http://www.traviscountyclerk.org/eclerk/Content.do?code=Recording
19    https://www.traviscountytx.gov/district-clerk
20    Ibid.

40 years of records apiece, depending on the amount of activity going on in the county at the time. They are not typed; they are all handwritten. This map over here dates from when plots of land in the city of Austin were first sold. We are a library of records. This room is my file cabinet, it just has a lot more records and is the size of an entire house, which I turn to if someone needs something important to make their case. The women behind the counter outside this room are there to help you retrieve your records and file for licenses like marriage."

During her talk, I just stood there taking it all in. I could only think how bad it would be if this room caught fire. People could lose everything with the right legal challenge if that happened, I bet. All I could say was, "Thanks for your time and energy. The answers were short, but the view is impressive. Also, how do I get to the County Tax Office from here?

DeBeauvoir replied, "You need to go to the Airport Boulevard Annex at 5501 Airport Boulevard."

With an address in hand, I went downstairs, out the door, and across the street to the garage to get into my car. Once in the car and back on the road, I went east on 11th Street to I-35 North. I left the interstate at exit 237A and then went north on Airport Boulevard. A mile later, the annex was on the right (figure 15.2). I parked my car and went inside. The office was conveniently located just inside the east entry. Once I was in the office, three well-dressed officials were waiting. County Treasurer Dolores Carter spoke: "Young man, are you Champ?"

FIGURE 15.2 Travis County Annex Building.

I replied, "Yes, ma'am."

"Welcome to the County Tax Office. We three are to see that you understand the fiscal processes that exist in the county."

Tax Assessor-Collector Bruce Elfant[21] said, "Don't mind her rhymes. She does not get to deal with a lot of people, just money all day. We have a conference room set up for us. Let's go."

A few minutes later in the conference room, Auditor Nicki Riley[22] advised, "Champ, if you were looking to get a term that describes each of our positions, we all serve as the accountants of the county. We all have a different spot in the dealing-with-money process, though."

Then a man barged in through the door and asked, "Am I too late?"

---

21   https://tax-office.traviscountytx.gov
22   https://www.traviscountytx.gov/county-auditor

Elfant stated, "No, not all. We are in the perfect spot for you. Tell them what your office does, Cad."

The man said, "Champ, before my colleagues can do their jobs, I must first do mine. My name is Cad Prayser. I am the chief appraiser for the Travis County Central Appraisal District.[23] Our duties in the district are to determine the value of property in the county.[24] We are not affiliated with the county, other than the fact that we operate in the same jurisdiction with a similar sounding name. After I get done . . ."

Elfant interrupted, "I get to do my job. Based on the assessed value of the properties, I then get to calculate or assess the taxes owed by the property owner.[25] Also, depending on where you are in the state, some places have combined tax districts, where we at the county collect taxes not only for the county but also for any other public agency that is levying a tax in the county. All of this occurs after I advise the commissioner's court about what tax rate is needed to fund the services that they as the commissioner's court wish to provide. Of note: The maximum county tax is 80 cents per $100 valuation of property. The collector part comes from the fact that I also collect the payments made by citizens paying their tax bills. As an example of this that shows the breadth of my office work, I also register and license all motor vehicles owned by county residents for the Texas Department of Transportation, their annual tax bill for their vehicles. That is also one of those 'arm of the state' functions you may have heard about earlier. We in my office are like the billing and collecting agency of a credit card company, but for the county-slash-state."

I stated, "So the appraiser first sets how much the properties are worth. Then the assessor-collector says how much is owed by the property."

In unison, they both replied, "You got it."

Treasurer Carter said, "Now that the county has told people they owe money, someone has to collect said requested cash and do something with it. Specifically, I am the chief custodian of all county funds collected, where I, as the county treasurer, am in charge of receiving all funds and ensuring that the funds are placed into the proper account.[26] Then, once the commissioners or other county officials decide to spend money, it is up to me to ensure that the items requested are paid for in full.[27] I am essentially the 'bank' of the county."

Auditor Riley interjected, "Speaking of spending money, we all know that people try to cheat the system or take advantage of it by spending on things that are less than appropriate.

---

23    https://www.traviscad.org/organization
24    Ibid.
25    http://www.county.org/texas-county-government/texas-county-officials/Pages/Tax-Assessor-Collector.aspx
26    http://www.county.org/texas-county-government/texas-county-officials/Pages/County-Treasurer.aspx
27    Ibid.

When the commissioners spend, they must first make a budget. When implementing that budget, it is my job to ensure that what the commissioners spend was budgeted for and, more importantly, is legal.[28] I'm the real accountant of the bunch, thank you very much."

I stated, "So once again, the appraiser sets how much the properties are worth, and the assessor-collector says how much is owed. Then the treasurer actually handles all the money coming in and going out, with the auditor making sure it all adds up?"

In unison, they all replied, "You got it."

I asked, "So where is the district attorney located?"

Riley remarked, "That is located back downtown, at 509 West 11th Street."

I thanked them all for their time. Once back in the car, after I entered the address into my GPS, I realized that my last stop was right next door to the county courthouse, where I was earlier. After the drive back, I parked my car, a couple of spaces away from where it was previously, just before 3:00 p.m. After walking across the street and around the building to 11th Street, I entered the justice center through a hefty amount of security. The room where I was told to go earlier on my list took me to a conference room up on the eighth floor.

Waiting for me in the room were two officers in uniform and two people in suits. The more senior looking of the two officers rose and spoke. "Champ, welcome to the Blackwell-Thurman County Justice Center. From the emails that have been sent around, you've heard about the record-keeping and taxation functions of the county. We here deal with those who have violated the laws of the state. I am County Sheriff Sally Hernandez. I am the chief law enforcement officer of the county.[29] My deputies and I perform criminal investigations, write traffic citations, provide security for the building we are in, and operate the county jail.[30] Our service jurisdiction is primarily outside the city limits, with some exceptions. This person here is my colleague."

The officer said, "Precinct 1 County Constable Danny Thomas. We in my office have what I would like to call variable responsibilities. What the community needs, we help with achieving, depending on the county in question.[31] In some counties, it is real law enforcement. In others, we are the principal court process officers, serving court summons, providing bailiffs, and executing orders. In some counties, we are no longer even in existence, with our duties being taken over by the sheriff and her band of merry men."

I asked, "So y'all see to it that the laws are enforced, but what about you two?"

28   http://www.county.org/texas-county-government/texas-county-officials/Pages/County-Auditor.aspx
29   http://www.county.org/texas-county-government/texas-county-officials/Pages/Sheriff.aspx
30   Ibid.
31   http://www.county.org/texas-county-government/texas-county-officials/Pages/Constable.aspx

It was then that the other woman in the room spoke up. "I am Margaret Moore, the district attorney. This person here is my colleague, David Escamilla, the county attorney. Once the sheriff and the constable arrest and house the accused, our offices prosecute the accused of any charges levied against them.[32] The difference is that I am responsible, along with my assistants, for felony cases, and David is responsible for misdemeanors. In some cases, like smaller counties, our jobs are combined, but . . ."

Escamilla offered, "I have one additional function. Essentially, I advise the county commissioners and other elected officials, but I do not represent them when someone accuses them of wrongdoing in court proceedings.[33] They bring in outside counsel for those matters. Essentially, we are the 'legal aides' or 'lawyers' of the county."

I posited, "So all of you are two sides of the same coin. Half of you enforce the law and half ensure that justice is served."

In unison, they all went, "You got it."

Sheriff Hernandez asked, "Wanna go on a ride-along and learn more about how the law is enforced?

I replied, "No, thank you, but how do I get to the office of Precinct 1 Commissioner Jeff Travillian?"[34]

Constable Thomas replied, "Go down to the second floor and take the sky bridge across to the county courthouse, and it will be down the hall to the left."

Once I was back in the main courthouse, Travillian was waiting for me at his office door. After shaking hands, he said, "Let's take a walk around the floor."

After a few minutes, he continued, "I hope that you have enjoyed your day thus far. What we are to discuss now is an issue for not just us here at the county, but also those in the special districts and municipalities. You already know about the issues of lengthy ballots and a strong state getting in the way. What I want you to comment on is term consolidation. What does that term mean to you?"

After thinking for a second or two, I remarked, "The combination of different things, local government agencies in this case, I assume."

Travillian furthered, "If you were combining agencies, what would you do?"

I thought some more and stated, "Get rid of excess positions?"

Travillian continued, "Why?"

I immediately replied, "Save money for the public, of course."

Travillian offered, "But what if you could not do that?"

---

32   https://www.traviscountytx.gov/county-attorney
33   Ibid.
34   https://www.traviscountytx.gov/commissioners-court/precinct-one

I replied, "Then excess government would continue to be in existence and be a detriment to the public good."

Travillian posited, "I bring this up because different types of local government agencies may not do this in the state. Municipalities with one another may do so under the guise of Title 2, subtitle E, and chapter 6 of the Local Government Code, with an election of those involved.[35] There is, however, no provision for us to do so. A new county cannot be formed unless it is at least 700 square miles and that territory must come from an already created county as the state has been fully divvied up.[36] I bring this up to show the drastic differences in county populations and the . . ."

I interjected, "You mean the roughly 134 inhabitants in the 677 square miles of Loving County and just north of 4.65 million or so residents in Harris County, covering 1,778 square miles?"

Travillian continued, "Loving County is not much of an issue, as there is no incorporated city, just a postal-named place called Mentone. The issue is in Harris County, where the municipality of Houston, which occupies 627 of those square miles, is found. The city of Houston and Harris County occupy almost the same territory, not to mention all the smaller enclave cities located there as well. Getting rid of the county or city and school governments would be very beneficial through reduction of duplicated services like road repair. This would be one of the most beneficial things that could occur in the reformation of local government. The only thing that the cities and counties can do is a contract with each other for services, leading to a patchwork of agreements maintaining public facilities."

I asked, "So what can you do?"

Travillian concluded, "Keep governing and making those agreements. It's five o'clock, time for us to go for the day. Have a great rest of the week."

We shook hands, and I stated, "Thanks for the lecture."

One the way home, all I could think about was how counties are much more cookie cutter than municipalities and special districts. Special districts could be for anything, and cities can do almost anything they want. However, I felt that as cities grow within their jurisdictions, counties face the ever-dreadful option of losing jobs due to duplication. The future is mixed, so to speak, for counties, but their services are essential and focus on the business of the state.

---

35   Texas Local Government Code, Title 2, Subtitle E, Chapter 6.
36   Constitution of 1876, article 9, section 3.

**QUESTIONS TO CONSIDER** REGARDING COUNTY GOVERNMENTS:

1.  The first main topic of the chapter discusses how counties serve as arms of the state. Please define that term, provide an example from your life where you serve as the arm to someone in their business, and explain how, in detail.

2.  The final main topic of the chapter discusses each of the county positions. Please select the position that interests you the most, provide insight on what that person does, identify what that position is similar to in the real world, who from your experience fits the bill of being that person, and why, in detail.

# Chapter 16

# Councils of Governments

## COGs in Texas

Wednesday through Friday of last week, I visited the offices belonging to the lowest (special districts) and midlevel (cities and counties) rungs of the local government hierarchy in Texas. Today I was going to focus on the highest rung: regional planning commissions, more commonly known as councils of governments (COGs). This experience helped tie each of the lower levels together and cap off my experience with local government. In doing this, I spent the better part of the day with the executive director of the Capitol Area Council of Government[1] (CAPCOG) to learn about the services they provide. After experiencing the day, I got the feeling here that "sharing is caring."

I left Charity's house at 8:30 a.m. for my shadowing start time of 9:00 a.m. I knew how to get to their offices at 6800 Burleson Road in southeast Austin, near Austin-Bergstrom

FIGURE 16.1 Front Entrance to the Capital Area Council of Government Offices.

International Airport, due to seeing the building on Thursday of last week when on my way to a tour of Austin's airport. It was an easy drive on TX-360 and US-290 that took all of 20 minutes. Once I arrived, I parked outside of Building 310 and headed to their offices on the first floor (figure 16.1). After checking in with the receptionist, I waited in the lobby for the director to retrieve me.

Just after 9:00 a.m., Director Betty Voights appeared at the door separating their offices from the public spaces and called me back to her office. After walking

through another small cubicle farm, we arrived at her office in the northeast corner of the area. Her office was small and compact, but I could tell that she worked with a variety of people on a variety of endeavors and made good use of it due to the placards and mementos on the wall. Once seated, we exchanged pleasantries and watched out the window as a plane or two took off. In figuring out where to begin looking at COGs, I asked, "What is the extent of COGs in Texas?"

In response, Voights stated, "There are 24 different COGs in the state[2] (figure 16.2). More importantly, each of the COGs consists of 3 to 26 counties grouped geographically,

1    http://www.capcog.org
2    Texas Association of Regional Councils, "Regions," accessed March 20, 2019, https://www.txregionalcouncil.org/display.php?page=regions_map.php.

FIGURE 16.2 Map of Texas Council of Governments Regions.

depending on the size of the local metropolitan area, and are named for whatever region the COG represents. One of the more obviously named ones is the Alamo Area COG, for counties surrounding San Antonio, along with the various Rio Grande COGs that have counties in groups at various points on the river. One of the funnier ones is Ark-Tex Council of Government, so named due to it having a county from neighboring Arkansas included."

I replied, "I just hope those COGs covered any jurisdictional and state sovereignty issues!"

After hearing that, she perked right up and said, "You bet those COGs are covered for that. There is an entire section of Chapter 391 of the state's Local Government Code that allows for this to occur. It's important to have this ability, as the state is growing right up to its borderlands. Oh, and for your information, chapter 391 of the state government code is the portion of state law regulating regional councils."[3]

---

3    Texas Association of Regional Councils, "Regions."

I asked with a small laugh, "So can the COGs down in the Rio Grande Valley join with entities in Mexico?"

She replied, "Better double down on that first bet; you could make a fortune because COGs can. Just remember, though, that our COG cannot, as we have no border with a neighboring state, nor with a state of Mexico unless you include the Mexican consulate down the road from here, but that is neither here nor there."

## What Is a COG Region?

Based on what Voights had just said, it seems that the COGs are grouped based on simple geography. With that in mind, I inquired, "So what factors are used to determine where one COG ends and another begins, other than simple county borders? More easily put, what officially is a COG region?"

In response, Voights brought out an actual copy of chapter 391 to define what a region was. She read aloud from section.002 (3): "Officially, a region is 'a geographic area consisting of a county or two or more adjoining counties that have, in any combination: common problems of transportation, water supply, drainage, or land use, similar, common, or interrelated forms of urban development or concentration, or special problems of agriculture, forestry, conservation, or other matters.'"[4]

I interjected, "So beyond where the county borders are, the actual borders selected are those where the influence of one major area ends and another begins to take precedence. Where does the influence of Austin end and the other big cities nearby begin?"

She brought out a map and stated, "Look at this map here (figure 16.3). Our council has ten counties within its jurisdiction, which includes those of Bastrop, Blanco, Burnet, Caldwell, Fayette, Hays, Lee, Llano, Travis, and Williamson, with a slightly more than '90 member governments and organizations, including cities, counties, school and appraisal districts, utilities, chambers of commerce and more,' making up the actual roster of CAPCOG members.[5] Now getting at the extent of our influence, Interstate 35 runs due north and south within our jurisdiction, with Highway 290 more or less due east and west. Going south, along 35, when you leave Hays County, the influence of San Antonio in Bexar County, the home of the Alamo Area COG,[6] begins to take over, so the border between Hays and Comal Counties was used. To the north on 35, when you leave Williamson County, the influence of Belton in

---

4  Ibid.
5  http://www.capcog.org/regional-directory; http://www.capcog.org/about-capcog
6  http://www.aacog.com

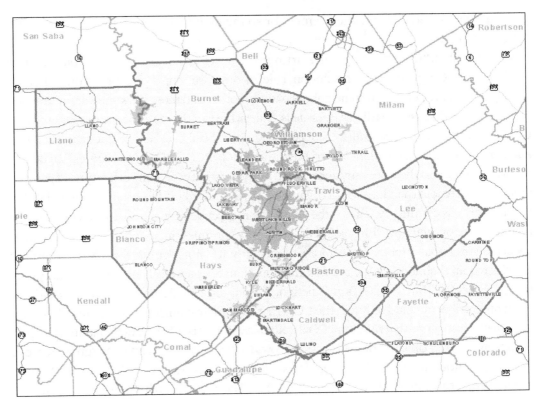

FIGURE 16.3 Detailed Map of the Capital Area Council of Governments.

Bell County, the home of the Central Texas COG,[7] begins to take over, so the border between Williamson and Bell Counties was used. To the west on Highway 290, when you leave Llano County, the influence of San Angelo in Tom Green County, the home of the Concho Valley COG,[8] begins to take over, so the border between Llano, Mason, and San Saba Counties was used. Finally, to the east on Highway 290, when you leave Lee County alongside to the east or when you leave Fayette County, the influence of Houston in Harris County, the home of the Houston-Galveston Area Council,[9] and a lesser extent the Brazos Valley COG,[10] begins to take over, so the border between Lee, Fayette, Burleson, Austin, and Colorado was used."[11]

7   http://www.ctcog.org

8   http://www.cvcog.org

9   http://www.h-gac.com

10   http://www.bvcog.org

11   http://txregionalcouncil.org/regional-councils; see here for a comprehensive list and map of all COGs in Texas.

I interjected, "So how did these ninety or so member agencies go about joining your regional council?"

Voights stated, "It's quite simple. In starting a COG, any grouping of cities or counties may establish a COG by ordinance, resolution, rule, or order (among a plethora of other items), so long as they are geographical neighbors of one another and meet the state's definition of a region that we discussed earlier. The issue is, the entirety of the state is now relegated to one COG or another; this is due to all 24 COGs of Texas have been in existence since the late 1960s and early 1970s with a creation date of June 1970 for CAPCOG. Thus, no entities can decide to form a COG, and the rules only apply when a city or county (or some other type of government) wishes to join their local COG organization. Accordingly, if a local government decided to join—or, less commonly, leave—the COG, the respective agency can do so with a simple majority vote of their governing council, the county commissioner's court or city council or special district board, for example. More importantly, it is not required for local government entities to join their local COG, as there are more than the previously mentioned ninety governing agencies within our COG's jurisdiction. The only other real rule, therefore, is that a local government agency could only join the COG that their main county was zoned into, based on state planning regions that mimic all COG boundaries. Ours is officially State Planning Region 12. Granted, if over time the city of Houston grows to the point that its influence grows more in the area, counties in our COG may begin to switch over to the Houston-Galveston COG with the approval of a variance by the governor of Texas. The borders can be quite fluid in reality."[12]

## How Are COGs Managed?

Nearing 10:15 a.m. with a lull in the conversation I decided to ask, "How is the COG run?"

Voights replied, "Each member group is, once again, required to have a ruling tribunal of some kind, akin to a commissioner courts for counties, and some form of council set up for cities. More importantly, like them, and any good governing agency for that matter, the COG, too, must have one. The difference is, due to us being more of a confederation of entities than a unified entity in the way that counties or cities or special districts are, our leadership is a bit more complex as we have more than one legislative assembly. Regardless, though, the COG operates as an official political subunit in Texas."

I nodded that I understood and motioned for her to continue. She furthered, "Overall, like the state government or the national government, we have a system of checks and balances via the separation of powers. Legislatively, the direction of the COG is provided by the executive committee, the general assembly, and the various regular committees—a

---

12    Texas Association of Regional Councils, "Regions."

three-pronged approach, if you will. The primary legislative group is called the executive committee.[13] This committee is a 29-member board whose primary duty is to meet monthly and provide direction to COG staffers on program implementation, budgets, contracts, and general policies and procedures for managing the agency.[14] Membership on this committee consists of city and county elected officials, along with three nonvoting state legislators who are all nominated and have their districts in the region.[15] Lastly, this group meets monthly to perform their duties and functions similarly to that of the Texas House and Senate."

I interjected, "What about the other two?"

Voights remarked, "The other two entities are somewhat subordinate to the executive committee and serve the role of advising them on their decision-making in some form or fashion. On the one hand, you have the CAPCOG General Assembly.[16] This group is responsible for approving the CAPCOG annual budget and amendments to the CAPCOG bylaws made by the executive committee, alongside appointing and approving of members to serve on the CAPCOG Executive Committee. Membership here is held in proportion to the population of the cities and counties of the COG. Therefore, the bigger counties and cities found within the region, primarily those of Travis and Williamson Counties, have a greater share of the seats, as most of the region's population is found there. On the other hand, there are a variety of committees that formulate plans on special topics for the general assembly and executive committee, like aging, solid waste, criminal justice, geography, homeland security, law enforcement, clean air, economic development, transportation, and emergency management.[17] Overall, these committees and the assembly act a lot like the legislative process you could experience down the highway at the state capitol building."

I inquired, "So what exactly is it that you do here?"

With a delay, she replied, "I am akin to the executive branch of the state and federal governments as I oversee the COG's day-to-day operations as the executive director. I am like that of a governor, president, or city manager. In determining what those daily duties are, I rely on standard business practices and the guidance of the committees. And before you ask, we don't have a judicial branch, as any fraud and the like committed would be investigated by the local police departments and court systems, but we would certainly have a committee to evaluate what happened internally."

I asked, "How does financing of the COG work?"

---

13    http://www.capcog.org/about-capcog/executive-committee
14    Austin: Capital Area Council of Governments, September 9, 2015, p. 8, sec. 5.8.
15    Austin: Capital Area Council of Governments, September 9, 2015, p. 6, sec. 5.2.
16    http://www.capcog.org/about-capcog/general-assembly
17    http://www.capcog.org/committees

Voights informed me, "In performing our duties, the COG is unable to tax citizens who live in our jurisdiction and must rely solely on member distributions and grants applied for, despite being an official government entity. Also, once the money is collected and budget made, we must submit reports to state auditors or face being shut down. Overall, we live and die by our ability to raise funds and by contributions from members entities."

Nearing 11:00 a.m., I suggested that we look at the purpose and goals of COGs in governance.

In response, she said, "COGs fill some pretty important roles, but for today, I'm not the best person to go over these with you."

I suggested, "Field trip time?"

She replied, "Yep, but only down the hall. Therefore, get some fresh air, maybe lunch, and stretch your legs. Then, come back to my office in about 30 minutes. I need to check some emails and make a few calls."

During the 30 minutes, I went down the main building's hallway and got a light snack from the vending machine. The funny thing was, while I was sitting on a bench near the door in the lobby at around 11:15 a.m., I saw three very important-looking vehicles arrive in the parking lot. On vehicle number one, the marking read "CPPD." "TDEM" was on vehicle number two, and "TCEQ" appeared on the third one. I got that feeling again that these were for me, as the occupants of each of the vehicles came inside and went into the CAPCOG offices in short order.

After the 30 minutes were over, I went back inside and found Voights waiting for me at the main door. She said, "Follow me. I have set up a special meeting for you."

I replied, "Let me guess: a cop, a fireman, and a state bureaucrat all walked into a bar?"

She said, "Close. Just the Monterey Meeting Room, nothing as fancy as a bar."

## Service Categories of COGs

I just laughed and followed her down the hall. After entering the room, she introduced me to Cedar Park police chief Sean Mannix,[18] Texas Department of Public Safety Division of Emergency Management public affairs organizer Jahns Jacobson,[19] and Texas Commission on Environmental Quality agency director Jam Marmalade.[20] After the pleasantries were exchanged and we all sat down, Voights indicated, "The offerings of the COG are designed to encourage local governments to join forces in the provision of services to ensure the highest quality of provision, at the lowest cost to taxpayers as possible, all while getting the biggest

---

18    http://www.cedarparktexas.gov/departments/police-department
19    https://www.dps.texas.gov/dem
20    https://www.tceq.texas.gov/

bang for the buck. In doing this, on whatever the COG has been charged with resolving at the regional level, the COG creates a plan for member units to follow."

I interjected, "If everyone in the region is not a member, how does this work?"

Voights furthered, "Well, the plans the COG produces can be adopted in whole or in part, or they can simply be ignored by member agencies, leaving a patchwork coverage of solutions that often obtain the rank of recommendations. This situation is only made worse when including local agencies that are not part of the COG. Overall, all our services fall into one of three categories. Chief Mannix, take the helm in discussing category one."

Mannix explained, "In essence, the programs in the first category are designed to achieve a better economy of scale by performing them at a regional level. As an example of this category, let's look at the Law Enforcement Academy (operated by the COG for local law enforcement agencies), which provides initial training for new officers and continuing education for veterans, using local agencies' headquarters for operational sites.[21] This provision is an essential function due to there being several police agencies in the COG that are quite small, with maybe only five to ten officers and a secretary or two, making it unreasonable for them to have pure training officials or facilities, as it would take away too many resources from their patrols."

I thought to myself that this seemed especially prudent, as he went on to mention that it is quite expensive and time consuming to train a new police officer. I said, "So, on the other hand, large cities like Austin, due to being so much bigger and needing many officers, can have their academies, as the greater need makes it a more fiscally sound case for them to do so. Accordingly, having a single entity for this necessary function in the region cuts down on duplicative costs and allows for officers to form working relationships that may benefit responses to more significant crises in the future."

Mannix concluded, "Therefore, it makes no sense to have 100 or so different law enforcement trainers and facilities in the area, so member agencies got together at the regional level via the COG and made one big training center for everyone to use."

Jacobson spoke up, saying, "Chief, you brought up disasters, financial ones at least. May I take over, then?"

Mannix said, "Sure. I have to get back for a class that is being held at my station this afternoon, anyway."

As Mannix walked out the door, Alexandra thanked him for taking time out of his busy day. Then Jacobson started in on a fascinating spiel about a disaster scenario: "Hurricanes in Texas are a fact of life. Every year, every other, or once a decade some portion of the Texas coast is going to be ravaged by one of these storms. These storms will cause massive

---

21    http://www.capcog.org/divisions/regional-law-enforcement-academy/in-service-training

destruction along a large swath of coastline. The closer to where the eye hits the coast, the greater the destruction."

I asked, "So what exact role does the COG play in this scenario?"

Jacobson spoke, "That is the second function of a COG, perform services that achieve a higher level of efficiency and effectiveness by doing it at the regional level, and disaster relief is a perfect example of this. Specifically, for example, the Coastal Bend COG[22] has created a wonderful disaster relief plan[23] that sees all member agencies agreeing to share resources, such as school gyms as shelters, city utility workers being sent in for repairs from areas that aren't affected by the storm, and police units working with the highway patrol to create contraflow highways to speed up predisaster evacuations and continue law enforcement throughout the emergency. Also, if the governor requests federal disaster aid, my group would help coordinate where to provide aid to state forces, especially if the disaster struck an entire region. Overall, the groups working together are more effective at getting aid to people in need and can, therefore, use their resources more efficiently than if they worked alone."

Marmalade spoke up, saying, "Speaking of disaster relief, Champ, have you ever smelled the air during a disaster, much less during a regular day? There can be some filthy air out there."

Jacobson looked a bit perturbed at the intrusion, but he could probably not say anything, as he had interrupted Mannix earlier. I replied, "No, but I agree that at times the air can be somewhat heavy and humid, leaving a very muggy feeling in the atmosphere."

Marmalade asked, "Where does the air for one city end and begin?"

I replied, "It doesn't end and begin, it's everywhere all mixed and if one area has bad air it sort of tapers off the further away from the source."

Marmalade nodded in agreement with my response and then indicated, "The third role of COGs is to handle issues that cannot be done at the city or county level, like improving air quality, as the air is quite literally everywhere. Therefore, the COG develops a plan, like disaster relief, to help member agencies reduce their air pollutants and save money by using more fuel-efficient items. My specific agency, the Texas Commission on Environmental Quality, is required to aid and abet the COGs in drafting and implementing these plans when requested."

I mentioned, "I spoke with the state demographer earlier this summer. We went to a meeting up here in Austin where he was advising some legislators on demographic shifts of the state. Was he doing the same thing in that case?"

Marmalade replied, "That's exactly what he was doing! We all, the state, must help the local governments."

---

22   http://cbcog98.org
23   http://cbcog98.org/em

## Like a Jedi High Council

I asked a fascinating question to everyone left in the room: "Do the COGs then function like the Jedi High Council from Star Wars?"[24]

As everybody took this question in, I noticed some very odd-looking expressions hitting their faces. I figured that I better provide some clarity. I started off by stating, "The Jedi High Council is like a COG, in that it takes the greatest minds, Jedi minds that is, of the galaxy who have mastered the force in the Jedi Order—or cities, in this case—and puts them together to solve issues facing the whole of the Republic."

I continued, "In the movies, this great issue was most commonly that of the Sith Lords, who have mastered the dark side of the force, and terrorize the galaxy. They are essentially a hurricane or poor air quality in Texas. In facing a threat, the Jedi were brought together, like the COG committees and assemblies are to work together to fight the concerns common to them all, the dark side and hurricanes, respectively."

I think that the group that I was speaking to understood this analogy, but I didn't let the issue float out there for too long. I quickly thanked them all for their time and information to end the day without argument from the group.

Voights thanked me for stopping by the COG to learn about their services, but before I left, she did leave me with one last bit of information. She stated, "COGs do provide many of the same services, but in many cases, COGs are very much tailored to the different needs of the area, as the state of Texas is diverse in a variety of different measures, from ethnicity to climate, right down to the most popular mode of transit."

I shook everyone's hand and left the office at around 2:00 p.m. for an early afternoon snack. While on the way to Franklin's Barbecue, I felt amazed at how the state of Texas has a whole government entity designed to let other entities on the same level of government, local, share resources. It made sense, as it makes no sense for smaller agencies to have their police academies (due to the costs and time consumed in running them), neighbors should help neighbors (as disasters are not typically limited to only a specific area), and the fact that some things impact everybody equally. Anyway, sharing is caring, especially with the pocketbook and this government entirely.

---

24    Wookieepedia, s.v. "Jedi High Council," accessed March 20, 2019, https://starwars.fandom.com/wiki/Jedi_High_Council.

**QUESTIONS TO CONSIDER** REGARDING COUNCILS OF GOVERNMENTS:

1. The first main topic of the chapter discusses how the state has been divided geographically into COGs. Please look at figure 16.1 and determine which COG your hometown and your school is in, determine if those are good groupings, and indicate why, in detail, based on personal experience.

2. The first main topic of the chapter defines what COGs and regions are. Please define what COGs and regions are, indicate whether this definition is a good approach at divvying up the state, in your opinion, and why, in detail.

3. The third main topic of the chapter discusses how COGs are managed. Please identify what the different management entities are, which you think is the most critical part, which one needs the most improvement, and why, in detail.

4. The fourth main topic of the chapter discusses the three service categories of COG provisions. Please identify what those service categories are, the one that you will most likely need in life going forward, and why, in detail.

5. The final main topic of the chapter discusses an analogy on how to understand what COGs are. Please rewrite that analogy in your own words, using something that you are familiar with from your own life.

FIGURE CREDITS

Fig. 16.2: Source: https://comptroller.texas.gov/transparency/reports/expenditures-by-county/2012/cogs/cogmap.php.

Fig. 16.3: Source: http://data.capcog.org/Information_Clearinghouse/download-interface/roadsdownload.html.

# Chapter 17

# Texas Legislative Structure and Process

# Contexts of the Capitol Complex

Today began the portion of my trek experiencing the state level of government in Texas, specifically, the legislative branch, "the branch of government having the power to make laws."[1] I spent today at the state capitol building in downtown Austin. I had been looking forward to this day since Uncle Tommy took me here last week and nearly killed me of embarrassment when giving me the quick training version of how to properly lobby the government. With that information in mind, the primary goal of this morning was to gain information on the structure and the setting of the state's legislative branch, while the afternoon focused on how laws and other state business are crafted and given approval by the required entities. Overall, so much goes on here that it takes a whole day to experience it all, just like driving from Orange to El Paso in Texas, and vice versa.

FIGURE 17.1  The Texas State Capitol Building

Since Charity works at the nearby Bullock Museum and I was going to be staying at the same spot all day, we carpooled to downtown together instead of driving separately as usual. After she dropped me off at Congress Avenue and 11th Street just after 8:00 a.m., I made the long walk down the picturesque pedestrian path, called the Great Walk (figure 17.1), to the front of the building. Suddenly, just before I got to the main entry doors, my dad, Chuck, a state representative from Houston, snuck up from behind and scared the living daylights out of me. After I scolded him for doing that, we had a robust embrace, and he told me that he was going to be preaching to me about what goes on here—not the house speaker, Joe Straus, as originally planned, due to the speaker needing to prepare for the special session that would begin later in the next day.

Instead of going inside as I had initially planned, we started walking back south along the walkway I had just progressed along. After the last bit of small talk, my dad stated, "Son, what we are to discuss now, and the whole morning, has to do with a term known as *context*, or 'the set of circumstances or facts that surround a particular event or situation.'[2] While I am sure that you know by now the main item we partake in here as legislators is to make

---

1   http://www.dictionary.com/browse/legislative-branch
2   http://www.dictionary.com/browse/context?s=t

the laws of the land, in Texas at least, but so much more occurs here. You see, in the first case, the capitol grounds overall serve as a memorial to those who died defending the state or represented something that dealt with the state's heritage. In total, there are 19 different monuments and a plethora of historical markers on the grounds. On either side of here as we walk back toward Congress Avenue on the Great Walk are two large fountains and memorials to the defenders of the Alamo (figure 17.2), Terry's Texas Rangers, volunteer firemen, and Confederate soldiers."

I had to take a deep breath after that morbid piece of information to keep my wits about me while my Dad handed me a map of the capitol grounds to keep track of where we were going (figure 17.3). Following that, getting close to 11th Street, we turned east and walked past the Tejanos Memorial on one of the multitudes of manicured, tree-covered walkways

FIGURE 17.2    Defenders of the Alamo Memorial

found on the capitol grounds surrounding the main building. In the distance, we saw the Texas Capitol Visitors Center[3] and the Texas Insurance Building and walked toward them. Then, about halfway between the visitor's center and insurance building, my dad stopped our progression and told me to turn around and look back at the capitol building to take in the beauty of the building that was best this time of day from afar in the early morning light. The next bit of information he offered said a lot about the state and how we view ourselves.

Without hesitation, looking right at me, he said, "Son, the Texas state capitol building before you was designed in 1881, began construction in 1882, and was opened in 1888. It is constructed in a beautiful Italian Renaissance Revival form, reaching 308 feet in to the sky, opened with electricity, and was purposely designed to be 19 feet taller than the US Capitol Building to show how great the state, and formerly the Republic, of Texas really is, as everything here is bigger and better, just like the mosquitoes. Most importantly, topping the

---

3    https://tspb.texas.gov/prop/tcvc/cvc/cvc.html

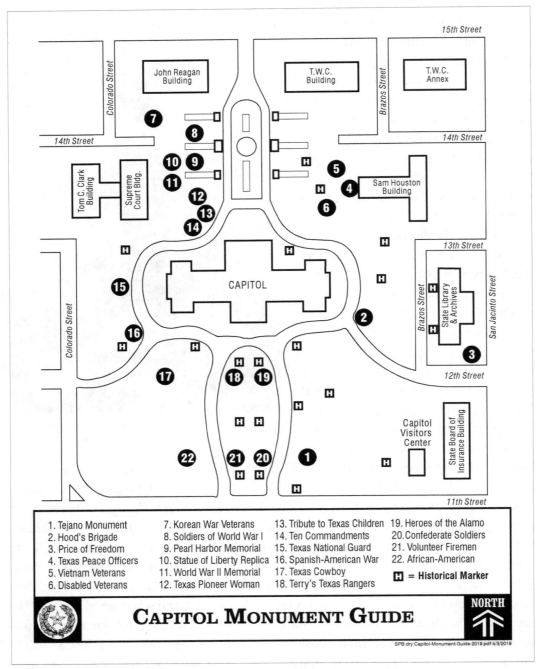

FIGURE 17.3 Capital Complex Monuments Guide

structure is the Goddess of Liberty, holding the five-point Texas star representing all that is fair and just in the state."[4]

The only thing that I could think to reply to that information that made sense was, "How beautiful the Marble Falls Sunset Red granite is on the building."

Continuing our walk to the north, we came across the Hood's Brigade Memorial. Then we reached the Lorenzo de Zavala State Archives and Library Building. My dad wanted to go inside, but I told him no, as I had already been there and seen the current state constitution, but to impress him, I ended by stating, "This building serves the same function as the nearby LBJ Presidential Library[5] and the National Archives Building[6] in Washington DC, as all three house important artifacts and documents of their respective primary occupiers."

Impressed, my dad continued walking around the capitol with me. Still heading north, we passed the Sam Houston State Office Building, whose primary tenant is the Texas State Preservation Board, which oversees the maintenance of the Capitol Complex. In the distance, we could see the Texas Workforce Commission buildings. Between us and those buildings were the Peace Officer and Disabled Veterans monuments.

Just as we were reaching the Texas Workforce Commission's main building's south entrance, my dad again stopped our progress and asked, "Each of the office buildings you see surrounding us at our present location represents the second context of the complex, office space, as this is where the work of the government is performed for the citizens. Now, though, let's turn around; what do you see around us while we stand here beyond the buildings?"

My response was, "Hedgerows and very short greenhouses?"

This guess proved to be only half correct, as my dad went on to assert, "Hidden behind what are actual hedgerows are skylights (figures 17.4 and 17.5) that provide light to the underground Capitol Extension Project,[7] which was completed in 1993. This extension," he went on after a pause,

FIGURE 17.4    Texas Capitol Skylights–Aboveground

---

4    Texas State Preservation Board, "Capitol History," accessed March 20, 2019, http://www.tspb.state.tx.us/prop/tc/tc-history/history/index.html.

5    http://www.lbjlibrary.org

6    https://www.archives.gov/dc

7    Texas State Preservation Board, "Capitol Restoration and Expansion," accessed March 20, 2019, http://www.tspb.state.tx.us/prop/tc/tc-history/restoration/index.html.

FIGURE 17.5    Texas Capitol Skylights–Underground

FIGURE 17.6    Texas Capitol Extension Reverse Rtounda

"houses additional office space for nearly all of the state legislators and added 667,000 square feet of space to the building, nearly tripling the floor space, all without blocking the region's legally mandated 30 unhindered views of the capitol, which recently has been under attack due to growth here in Austin."[8]

Now walking southwest, we went between the most northern pair of the eastern set of skylights and could look down at the two floors visible from above, right into people's offices. We proceeded to cross the northbound track of North Congress Avenue on the capitol grounds and past a central set of skylights. Before continuing to cross the southbound drive of North Congress Avenue, my dad and I looked down into the inverted rotunda that finishes the Capitol Extension's mirroring of the original structure (figure 17.6). This was the coolest part of the day, thus far in my opinion, as people were there just milling around in what looked to be a reverse of the main building's dome.

In deciding to get out of the summer heat and humidity that was on the rise in what seemed awfully early in the day, we walked over to the Texas Supreme Court building, on the west side of the Capitol Complex, which houses the two courts of last resort found in the state and served as context three of the day, judicial proceedings. On the way, we walked through another set of skylights, past the statutes dedicated to Pearl Harbor veterans, the Statue of Liberty

---

8    Preservation Austin. Background on the Capitol View Corridors Issue.

replica, monuments to World War II veterans, Texas pioneer women, a tribute to Texas children, and the granddaddy of them all, the Ten Commandments statue. Here, my dad chimed in and stated, "This is the most controversial structure on the grounds, due to a very perceivable violation of the separation of church and state requirement as mandated by the First Amendment to the US Constitution, as the Texas attorney general actually went to the US Supreme Court and won the state's right to keep the statue on the ground, against the wishes of the American Civil Liberties Union."

I could only think that it was a bad omen that we had to have the monument when the commandments are simple to follow in the first place, but that is Texas politics for you. Finally, my dad also noted here that the main building's legislative chambers served as a part-time church in a prior time, due to them being the most significant rooms in the city, giving local ministers a break in the number of services they were necessitated to provide each Sunday. I also seemed to remember a public elementary school near where I lived being used on Sundays by churches at this point. Either way, I think context four is religion, as so much of it in various capacities occurs here.

Once inside the supreme court building, I told my dad that we should focus on the legislative branch side of things, as I was hoping to spend a whole day learning about the judiciary here later in the summer. Then, to my surprise, he took us down into the basement of the building and led us to a guarded tunnel entrance. After flashing his congressional identification, we were let through. Three minutes later, we found ourselves walking past some of the offices that we had seen earlier from above and entered the first floor of the airy Central Gallery of the Capitol Extension, beautifully lighted from above by the sun. These passageways served as context five, underground connections, as all the buildings surrounding the capitol building—the Sam Houston State Office Building, for example—are connected to the capitol itself via these walkways (figure 17.7). I got a bit of a lousy flashback at this point to last Friday when the state troopers dragged me before the Texas Ethics Commission through one of these hallowed halls.

While walking along the gallery, we saw the Capitol Grill restaurant, the gift shop (context six, shopping opportunities), and the eight committee chambers that lined the corridor. At the center of the gallery is the open-air, inverted rotunda that anybody can walk into and explore. In the

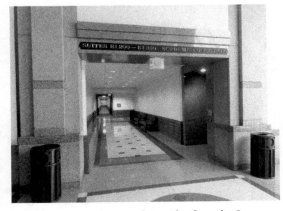

FIGURE 17.7   Underground Corridor from the Supreme Court Building to the Capitol Extension

dome, the group of people milling about that I saw a few minutes earlier was now officially protesting. I got that sinking feeling again that I was going to be involved in this activity eventually in some form or fashion.

After seeing the extension rotunda from inside, getting close to 8:30 a.m., we made the long walk to the main building of the capitol and went up the stairs to the capitol's basement floor, informally known as "the Crypt." In the middle of the circular stairwell, though, on the ground, as my dad pointed out, was the backside of the state seal, which had the Alamo and various state symbols, on display. Once in the basement, we could see some of the original generators that powered the building back in the day, a local children's art display, support structures, pictorials of past legislative sessions, and other various state agency office space.

Once in the basement rotunda, we made a U-turn to the left and went up one of the grand staircases found in the main building. At the top, we took a few short turns in a tight passageway and found ourselves at the bottom of the grand, four-story central building rotunda. This room housed portraits of every single governor in order of their terms in office, with the newest on the bottom floor and the more historical leaders on the top level, and a few Republic of Texas presidents in there with them. Whenever there is a new governor, all the portraits slide over one place and/or move up a floor to make room. Atop the rotunda, on the underside, was a massive bronze star with the letters T-E-X-A-S emblazoned around it in the negative space between the points. However, the most exciting area at this point was the south lobby entrance that houses artwork displaying the surrender of Santa Anna (following the Battle of San Jacinto) and Davy Crockett, alongside marble statues of prominent figures like Stephen F. Austin (figure 17.8) and Sam Houston in full regalia. It was also worthwhile to notice here the abundance of 6-inch bronze door hinges that state "State Capitol" on them, door handles that display the lone star, and surrounding handcrafted door frames on each doorway (figure 17.9). Along with the height of the building, in hindsight, I do believe that context seven is that size

FIGURE 17.8   Statue of Stephen F. Austin in the Southern Entrance to the Texas State Capitol Building

matters in Texas. Before heading farther upstairs, we walked down the east corridor to the entry there and the Agriculture Museum. We poked our heads in but didn't stay long. I had a feeling here, though, that I would be back later.

Wanting to rest his feet, my dad said, "Let's go to my office."

I responded, "What about the west corridor?"

His response, "More executive offices not relevant to today. Nothing special."

After going up the east stairwell, we took a left and went out to see the rotunda floor from above. This vantage proved pertinent, as on the rotunda floor is the front side of the state seal, which majestically displays smaller seals of the six national flags that have flown over the state (France, Spain, Mexico, Texas, the Confederacy, and the United States) (figure 17.10). One thing my dad pointed out here was some ever-so-slight wear and tear on the floor from casket holders placed during funerals that take place here when vital state officials lie in state postmortem. I hated how it distracted from the fantastic seal emblazoned on the floor. Oh, well.

My dad's office was in Room 2S2, one of the most prominent rooms in the building, as it was right outside of the house chamber floor. He was able to get it thanks to his seniority in the house after nine consecutive terms there. Inside were rooms for each of the legislators who shared the office and desks for the pooled staffers they used who were stationed here and not back in their districts. Decorations included items from the local

FIGURE 17.9   Texas State Capitol Door Hinge

FIGURE 17.10   Reverse of the Texas State Seal in the Capital Extension

FIGURE 17.11    Texas House Chamber

schools and famous places that can be found back home. I liked my old Langham Creek Lobo football helmet on the shelf the most. After the dime office tour, we started with the nickel lawmaking tour to preview where I was going to be spending a lot of my time this afternoon and see more about what was going on in the capitol.

To get started, we toured the Legislative Reference Library, located in the north wing of the second floor, where legislators wanting to get some quick info about a bill they are writing or about to vote on can go to get help with how they should progress. Factoring in the state archives, museums, artwork, and the like, I do believe that context eight here is that the complex is a great place to learn something. Leaving the library, we headed back toward my dad's office but went straight into the house chamber (figure 17.11).

## Requirements for Serving in the Texas Legislature

Sitting in the historical chairs located along the walls, I began to ask my dad about the layout of the room, but my dad went straight into advising me what it takes to be eligible to run for office here officially. Mainly, as he put it, "For the house, a person need only be a US citizen, a registered voter, a resident for one year in their district, 21 years of age, and live at least the last two years in the state before running. For the senate, the first three qualifications are the same, but you must now be 26 years of age and live for the prior five years in the state."

I interjected, "Is that it? Those qualifications seem so minimal."

Then and there, the conversation moved on in hushed tones as my dad advised, "Unofficially son, it helps to meet four additional qualifications. First, it helps to be of the dominant race in your district, as that is how citizens in the state are typically drawn/grouped in their districts. Second, it also helps to be an attorney, as attorneys are typically political science undergrads, and a large amount of their time in law school goes far in-depth on the various aspects of lawmaking, such as constitutional law classes, giving them special training. Third, having access to large amounts of capital is also very beneficial, as it costs a lot to run for office."

I, again, interjected, "You don't have to tell me that twice, as when I spoke with Stormy Ridge a week or so ago those numbers were divulged thoroughly to me."

My dad continued, "Finally, it also helps to be a Republican, or at least a conservative Democrat, in Texas, as most citizens are prone to vote more conservatively than elsewhere, at least for the time being, which you should have the inside track on, as you learned about the future of Texas from the state demographer a while back, right?"

I replied, "Yes sir, but how many people serve in this chamber?"

## Facts about the Legislature

My dad furthered, "There are 150 members in the house and 31 members in the senate, who serve two- and four-year terms, respectively, albeit staggered in the senate, with the caveat that all seats in that body go up for election after being redrawn following the decennial census. On top of that, there are no term limits in either house. More importantly, each member solely represents their own equally populated districts and earns $7,200 a year with a per diem of about $150 a day for expenses when in session, giving a total salary of $35,400 every two years, not including special sessions, for the privilege of doing so."

I did the math in my head and realized that I made more in a year running the counter at one of the family gas stations and corner stores back home, not including the expense pay than each legislator gets in two years. Reading my mind, my dad contended, "This keeps any illicit desires of members to make more laws than necessary at a minimum, as we have to support our families otherwise with our day jobs. This information explains why I never sold any of our stores and remain an avid business owner first and foremost, not a legislator since I became a member here 18 years ago. Now turn around."

I remarked, "At this group picture set?"

My dad replied, "The one and only. At the start of each session, each member gets their photo taken to make a log of who was serving at that time. One exists for each of the prior 85 regular sessions. The one on the left is from the fifth back in 1885 (figure 17.12), and the one dead ahead of us is the prior one. What are some of the differences you see?"

I replied, "From what I can see, the body used to be entirely male and predominately white. Today, though, there is a large contingent of Hispanics and blacks and women, albeit nowhere near most of the membership. I would gander that this is far more representative of the state than it used to be, but why the change?"

My dad suggested, "Each changeover has its history behind it. For example, until the 1960s women were not expected to participate in politics, as they were expected to focus on fulfilling domestic duties such as child rearing and cooking. But as views toward women's participation outside the home in various ways have altered, their numbers are slowly but surely increasing. For ethnicity, the changeover is the result of laws now in place, like the Voting and Civil Rights Acts, alongside a growth in population numbers making their

FIGURE 17.12   Collection of House Member Headshots from the 1885 Texas House

participation more probable. Growth-slash-diversification in other categories, such as age, education, and religion, is occurring for various attributable reasons, mostly centering on the diversification of society itself. These trends are seen nationwide, even if one in two state representatives are still 'a white, male, Protestant baby boomer, with a graduate degree and a business background.'[9] Look here at the portrait from the 82nd Texas House."

---

9    Karl Kurtz, "Who We Elect: The Demographics of State Legislatures," National Conference of State Legislatures, December 1, 2015, http://www.ncsl.org/research/about-state-legislatures/who-we-elect.aspx.

Before we left the room to view the senate chambers, my dad mentioned that, beyond lawmaking, the room is the scene of the biennial governor's State of the State address and the occasional bickering between representatives, which can be moved into the speaker's apartment located behind the desk to keep things from reaching a boiling point in the chamber and get away from the cameras. Mixed in with the protesters outside in the reverse rotunda, I do believe that context ten is that visions are made and fought for here on both sides of the aisle. Then the tour got special. Flashing his congressional ID to the docent giving a tour, we crossed the fabric barriers blocking visitors from using the original desks and chairs from the 1880s and went up to the speaker's chair, where the leader of the house sits. Once there, we saw the remnants of the Battle of San Jacinto battle flag on display in a case behind the desk. Here, a tidal wave of history swept over me and hit home, not to mention a couple of "oohs" and "ahs" at the fact that we got to see more than the average tour. It pays to know people, I guess.

On the way over to the senate chamber, we made a pit stop in the Governor's Reception Room, which is open to the public. Located in that room was a desk where any citizen could walk in to request an appointment with the governor. I signed my name on the list with the sturdy Texas Ranger stationed there and learned that this is where the current governor keeps his office. I assumed that context 11 is that this is a great place to relax and have a good time following a legislative success of some kind.

After viewing the courting chairs, various pieces of art, and the state troopers on the post in the room for a while longer, we left and made our way over to the senate chamber floor (figure 17.13). Once there, we walked right in and went to the center of the room. At that point, my dad pulled me in and had me look at the desks of the room, followed by him turning me around to have me to look at the galleries of seats surrounding the room up on the third floor. He stated, "Those seats are reserved for the citizens of the state. At any time, especially when the legislature is in session, any citizen can view our proceedings in action. More importantly, those seats cannot be reserved or held for anyone, under any circumstances, and are therefore available on

FIGURE 17.13   Texas Senate Chamber

a purely first-come, first-served basis. And if you haven't been keeping track, this is the final context, viewing government in action. Unlike in many other countries and states of the world, in places like Texas and the other modern democratic realms of the world, you can view so much of the process of government, and not just in lawmaking. Think about it, even down to the courts themselves, you can walk right in and watch and even ask questions on occasion. Now, look at the ceilings, the light you see there is actual light shining through skylights, and more importantly, the large chandeliers are in the same shape and lettering as the bottom of the main rotunda. The Lone Star State motto is clear in this building's design. Lastly, if you now look behind the desk of the lieutenant governor, the leader of the senate, you can see one more bit of history, one of 15 placed throughout the room—a historical portrait of the city of Austin's namesake, Stephen F. Austin, by an unknown artist. Let's go over here."

## Sessions of the Legislature

We went to the southern wall of the room and found a set of seats to discuss the business of the state legislature further and to rest our now tired again feet. When seated, my dad explained the different sessions that can be convened in the chamber. He began by stating, "Primarily, the legislature meets in a biennial 140-day regular session, which begins on the second Tuesday in January of odd-ending years following a general election in the state with the last day for new legislation to be introduced on day 60 of the session and only legislation received from the opposing house to be considered from the 125th day onward, with no lawmaking allowed on the final day.[10] Typically, these sessions end in late May, with any legislation passed going into effect 90 days later, on or about September 1, the start of the state's fiscal year. Here in this session, topics can cover anything a legislator wants to pass a bill about. Secondarily, the legislature may meet in special sessions, which can only be called by the governor. When called, these sessions can only last a maximum of 30 days and can only discuss what the governor wants us to talk about. If the governor does not get his way, he can call as many as he wants until he gets his way."

I commented, "This seems brutal for the opposition of a bill, as they can't get a break."

My dad furthered, "Some of the more exciting topics in recent years for special sessions have been abortion rights[11] and redistricting controversies,[12] leading many to believe these sessions to be a waste of time and money, as they are topics that do not do much in the way

10    Sharon Carter and Hugh L. Brady, "Rules of the House of Representatives of the State of Texas," 2019, https://house.texas.gov/_media/pdf/hrrules.pdf; Senate of Texas, "Senate Rules," January 11, 2017, https://senate.texas.gov/_assets/pdf/SenateRules85.pdf.

11    Matt Smith and Joe Sutton, "Perry Renews Texas Abortion Battle with Special Session," CNN, June 28, 2013, http://www.cnn.com/2013/06/26/politics/texas-abortion-bill/index.html.

12    Legislative Reference Library of Texas, "Congressional Redistricting 2001–2003," January 16, 2004, http://www.lrl.state.tx.us/legis/redistricting/redistrict.cfm.

of progressing the real business of the state. Regardless, in both types of sessions, there is often inadequate evaluation of bills and only special interest bills being discussed, with everyone running around like chickens with their heads cut off due to the general chaos of the short sessions. Here, look at this video on my phone. This first is a YouTube video of a 2007 KEYE Austin news report showing potentially illegal voting going on in the body, called 'ghost-voting,' along with the environment that exists in the chamber."[13]

I felt it was an excellent video, showing the body violating its own voting rules with comments from the rep who pushed through the law requiring citizens to use IDs when voting in elections. The second was a highlight, but probably more of a gag reel, of the actions seen on the floor during the 2011 general session.[14] I could only give myself a facepalm at the sight of these videos and how unprofessional it all seemed.

## Key Terminology

My dad's comment on the matter went, "We're busy all over the place for those 140 days, and we gotta do what we gotta do to get the job done, and along the way, some crazy stuff happens. Regardless, what we will discuss for the remainder of the morning will be some key terminology for you to understand better what will be occurring this afternoon. To get started, notice how you and I are always talking about the House and Senate found in the Texas Legislature; there is a formal term for that. That is *bicameral*, or 'a governmental body with two houses or chambers."[15] All legislation before us must first be approved by both houses before being sent to the governor for final approval and eventual implementation."

I chimed in, "That process seems a bit excessive to go through, but how common is that format?"

My dad replied, "Believe it or not, that legislative format is quite common in the United States. The only exception is the Nebraskan unicameral legislature that only has one legislative assembly, which is further distinguished by the fact that they also forbid political parties from the legislature.[16] Speaking of differences between different state legislatures, not all operate at the same aptitude. Simply put, some are more professional legislatures than others, meaning that some have better accumulations 'of all the qualities that relate to trained and skilled people.'"[17]

---

13    http://www.youtube.com/watch?v=SrBLxAt63Ks

14    Justin Dehn and Thanh Tan, "The 82nd Lege Session: The Highlights Reel," *Texas Tribune*, June 2, 2011, http://www.texastribune.org/2011/06/02/the-82nd-lege-session-the-highlights-reel.

15    http://www.dictionary.com/browse/bicameral-legislature

16    https://nebraskalegislature.gov/about/about.php

17    https://dictionary.cambridge.org/us/dictionary/english/professionalism

I responded, "So what does a more professional legislature have that a less professional one does not?"

My dad stated, "The California legislature is highly professional due to their assembly's year-round sessions, high salaries, and full staffs, among other things, while New Mexico's is entirely nonprofessional due to its short sessions, low staff levels, and lack of salaries for legislators. Ours here in Texas is known as a hybrid since our legislators do get paid, albeit not that well, have short and infrequent sessions, and have proper staffing only during the sessions.[18] Regarding the long-term effects on the legislature, a less-than-fully professional body leads to a less-than-apt group of members, due to high turnover and a higher-than-typically tolerable level of influence from lobbyists. Let's go stretch our legs out a bit more."

FIGURE 17.14   Old Texas Supreme Court Room

After leaving the Senate floor, we went up the first set of stairs and found ourselves on the third floor. When there, we proceeded to the north wing and found ourselves standing between the entry doors of the old Texas Supreme Court and the former Court of Criminal Appeals courtrooms, where those courts met before 1959. Once inside the old supreme court chambers (figure 17.14), my dad mentioned that, during the last bit of renovation, the State Preservation Board was able to find old carpet and drapes that allowed them to refurbish the room to historical conditions—simply an amazing feat, I felt. It was then that my dad stated, "Son, here is where I want to introduce you to two important terms regarding the actual makeup of the legislative bodies that we have just walked through. But first, a question: What are your thoughts on pie?"

I said with a grin, "Pie is delicious, but what does that have to do with anything?"

My dad retorted, "Everything. The first term here I want to introduce you to here is reapportionment, best defined as 'redistribution of representation in a legislative body . . . according to changes in the census figures as required by the Constitution.' The only legislative body in the United States that faces reapportionment in the amount of representation is the US Congress, where all 50 states send representatives, as every ten years following

---

18   National Conference of State Legislatures, "Full- and Part-Time Legislatures," June 14, 2017, http://www.ncsl.org/research/about-state-legislatures/full-and-part-time-legislatures.aspx.

the decennial census some states get more representatives and other states lose representatives. Our numbers there all depend on how much population our state gains or loses and ultimately has at the end of a decade. We typically gain membership as of late. With that in mind, that brings us to our second term here to discuss, *redistricting*, 'the actual process of drawing the boundaries of the legislative districts. Causing both terms to play out is the requirement that all districts must have approximately the same amount of people in them, as required by law following that census.[19][20]"

At this point I wondered, "Dad, tell me now, you've got this image in my head of a pie. Would the pie being cut into slices be like that of reapportionment and the individual states doing what they will with their 'slices' of Congress be akin to redistricting?"

My dad replied, "Well, yes. I would agree with that. The main thing to remember in that scenario is that the more representatives a state would get in say, the US Congress, the larger the slice of pie that state would get. Speaking of slicing up the pieces of pie, that can be done in a variety of ways."

I replied, "Explain."

My dad furthered, "In short there are three ways to eat a pie, or redistrict legislative districts in our case. The first method is pairing. This situation is where two current members of the body are forced to compete for a single seat after their residences have been drawn into the same new district. Second is homogeneity, which is where all citizens of the district are similar regarding political ideology and have been drawn together because of that, leading to little competition in winning the district for whoever falls in line with the dominant ideology of the area. Finally, the last method is heterogeneity, where there is a solid mix of various political ideologies among the citizens living there due to the way the district has been drawn, leading to a great deal of competition in winning the district."

I asked, "Why would one choose one method over another?"

He replied, "That would depend on your goal. For example, for homogeneity, the simple goal is to keep the currently dominant party in power, as they would also do the redistricting. Since 2002 my party, the Republicans, have taken all efforts possible, including calling extra sessions of the legislature into order, to make sure the state was as Republican as possible. This situation most notably occurred during the 2003 redistricting controversy, which saw the state legislature redraw US congressional boundaries without an official decennial census happening[21] (figure 17.15). During the controversy, Democrats left the state to pre-

---

19    Texas Legislative Council, "Texas Redistricting," accessed March 20, 2019, http://www.tlc.state.tx.us/redist/process/summary.html.

20    Ibid.

21    Texas Legislative Council, "Texas Redistricting 2000s Chronology," accessed March 20, 2019, http://www.tlc.state.tx.us/redist/history/chron_2000s.html.

## 2002 Election Results

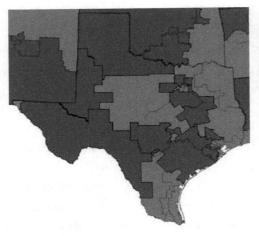

## 2004 Election Results

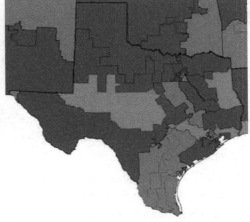

FIGURE 17.15   Texas Congressional Redistricting–2002 and 2004

vent the legislative quorum from meeting and acting on the matter, and when that wouldn't work, they all came back and sued in court, to no avail. We merely served to put as many Democratic citizens into as few districts as possible. Check out this video."

He brought out his smartphone again and brought up a good *Daily Show with Jon Stewart* video that gave highlights of the controversy.[22] The fact that they went to a Holiday Inn was funny as all get-out, but I felt they had a good reason to leave in the first place. After the video, my dad continued, "When we use the pairing method, for example, it is instrumental in getting less desirable members of the legislature out of the legislature when it is time for them to go after, say, a scandal, or at a minimum, disagreeing too much with the chamber leader. It is simply the parties fighting over control of the state, with the power of the magic marker and hired guns like Kimball Brace to wield them."

I asked, "Who's Kimball Brace?"

Once again, my dad got out his smartphone and brought up another *Daily Show* clip, where Brace (the interviewee of the video) is featured, showing how states get districts to be very homogenous.[23] Brace's job was to draw congressional districts into shapes that put groups—based on similar demographics and political affiliation, as my dad said before— into as few districts as possible.

22   *The Daily Show with Jon Stewart.* Comedy Central. May 13, 2003. http://www.thedailyshow.com/ watch/tue-may-13-2003/austin-powerless.

23   *The Daily Show with Jon Stewart.* Comedy Central. December 10, 2013. http://www.thedailyshow. com/watch/tue-december-10-2013/american-horrible-story---gerrymandering.

At this point, he handed me two stapled sheets of paper from his coat pocket. The sheet on top was a map of the 2019–2020 Texas House districts (figure 17.16). The second was a map of the 2019–2020 Texas Senate districts (figure 17.17). He stated, "Take a look at these maps for a bit. We need to bring this construct down to the local level."

After a minute or two of evaluation, my dad asked, "Well, son, what are some of the patterns that you notice about the maps you are holding there?"

I replied, "For the districts out in the western part of the state on both maps, they appear to be large, somewhat squared areas. However, for those in or around the urban areas, the districts seemed to be shapes of all sizes and contorted beyond belief."

My dad replied, "These districts in the urban areas have been something called gerrymandered, as they are far from the squares you use in west Texas and are drawn to be very obtuse, to get as much of a less desirable population or the opposing party into one district as possible. Here in recent times, Democrats are most often gerrymandered in Texas redistricting efforts. Look at this map here of the current Texas 35th Congressional District " (figure 17.18).

After shuffling the maps around in my hand, my dad continued, "This district covers citizens living in Bexar, Comal, Guadalupe, Hays, and Travis Counties. This long, thin district was designed, back in 2011, to marry as many liberals in Austin, San Antonio, and parts in between, to get more conservative districts out of the state and as many liberals into as few districts as possible. This situation is bad news for the Democrats, as they must now match different factions of their party that do not always get along with one another: Hispanics from San Antonio and mainstream liberals from Austin. Overall, we did our job and protected our Republican majority at all costs, both sides do it[24]—up until 2013, with the overturning of Section V of the Voting Rights Act. Due to the extensive practice of gerrymandering, many states are now required to gain further approval from the US Department of Justice for their legislative redistricting."[25]

Since it was getting close to 10:30 a.m., my dad decided that was enough information for now and that he needed to go to his office and work for a while. He instructed me to be back at his office in one hour sharp. We hugged, and I left.

---

24    "How to Rig Elections, the Legal Way." The Week. The Week Publications Inc., May 22, 2016. https://theweek.com/articles/625095/how-rig-elections-legal-way.

25    Adam Liptak, "Supreme Court Invalidates Key Part of Voting Rights Act," *New York Times*, June 25, 2013, http://www.nytimes.com/2013/06/26/us/supreme-court-ruling.html?_r=0.

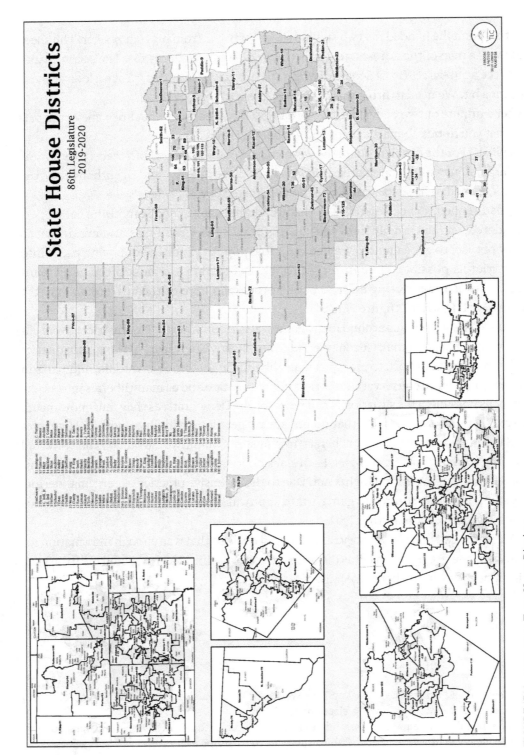

FIGURE 17.16  2019–2020 Texas House Districts

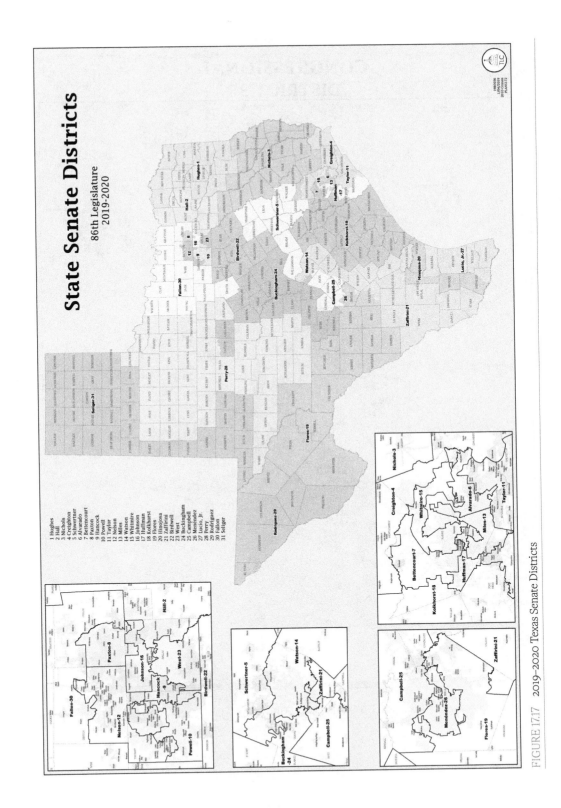

FIGURE 17.17  2019–2020 Texas Senate Districts

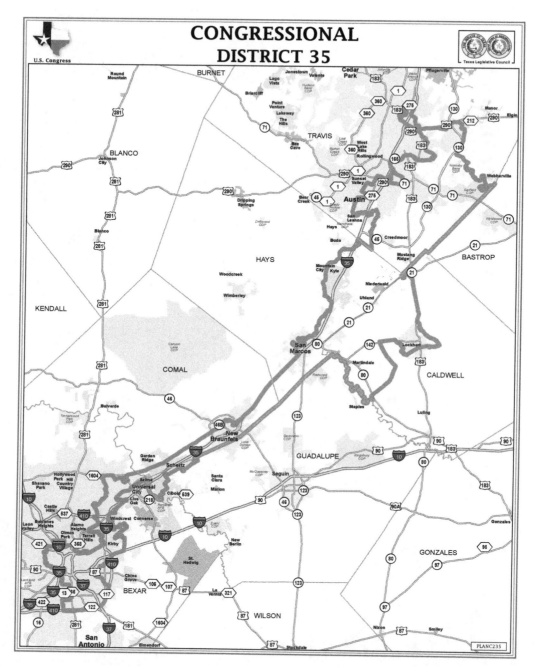

FIGURE 17.18　2019–2020 Texas 35th US Congressional District

## Presiding Officers

In the meantime, I took a hike down Congress Avenue to Lady Bird Lake and back, getting a hot dog from a street vendor along the way. While doing so, I concluded that the Capitol Complex serves as more than just a place for the state to develop policy; it serves as a memorial, a symbol, and the brain, body, and soul of the state, as this is where the direction of all the action of governance stems from. More importantly, in setting the structure of the legislature, much work is done behind the scenes to allow them to work in as favorable conditions as possible. I could only think, "I can't wait to find out what's going to unfold this afternoon under those very favorable conditions, but will it work?"

Just a hair before 11:30 a.m., after going through security at the north entrance of the capitol, I made my way up the eastern grand staircase to the second floor and arrived at my dad's office door. Then the fireworks started.

After his aide showed me to his door, I went in and found two prominent-looking men sitting across from him, discussing the day's agenda. The gentlemen turned out to be Lieutenant Governor Dan Patrick and House Speaker (at the time) Joe Straus. Once they were introduced and the requisite formalities were performed, the men informed me together that they are the presiding officers, or "[those] who preside[] over a forum or debate,"[26] over lawmaking in the different houses of the state legislature—the senate and house, respectively. I asked them to tell me about how they obtained their jobs.

About getting their jobs, Patrick first explained, "Joe and I had to follow two very different paths. Simply put, I had to win two statewide elections, the Republican Primary and the subsequent general election. Once fully elected to the position, my term lasts a total of four years, with no limit on the number of times I may run for office. More importantly, as a holder of this position, I am a hybrid official, as I am officially elected to the executive branch, but I primarily serve in the legislative branch, where I earn a similar annual pay during my term. More interestingly, currently, I am in the same party as the governor. It is entirely possible, though, that the lieutenant governor could be a member of an opposition party, unlike the vice president, who runs as a team with the president and is also a hybrid official, except that position is tied to the US Senate."

Straus then took over. "I had to win three elections to get my leadership position. The first was the primary election in the spring prior that gave me the opportunity to run for my seat in the legislature on the Republican Party ticket, just like the lieutenant governor, except it was my small district, not statewide. The second was the general election last fall to represent my district against other parties, and the third occurred on the first day of the last general session. In the third election, which took place on the house floor, I was elected

---

26    https://www.thefreedictionary.com/presiding+officer

by my peers in the house to lead them through the policy-making process of the term. For my term, I serve in the position for a two-year stint, and by tradition, rarely does anybody in my position serve more than one term. Although, I am on my fourth and final, last I checked, due to my impending retirement from the legislature. This position is typically filled by a moderate of the ruling party to provide a bridge to reaching agreements in the lawmaking process, which is organized nonpartisan, better known as not along party lines."

I remarked, "As presiding officers, what powers pertain to your positions?

Straus began by saying, "Our positions are like that of a sports league commissioner who oversees organizing what events will occur during the season, or session, in the case of the legislature. At the basic level, we assign which committees hear which bills, who serves on which committees, and who will be the chairperson, or leader, of the various committees.[27] In assigning membership, we work as best as possible to match people's competencies—or day jobs and/or the main industry in their district—with their committee assignments to get the best people available to review the proper bills. For example, a doctor or someone who represents the Houston Medical Center would serve on a health care committee, so on and so forth."

I interrupted the conversation here by asking, "Could you explain what committees are?"

Straus responded by saying, "Not now. I'll guarantee, though, that you'll get into the basics of them later today when the Texas house and senate are in session."

I replied, "Okay, I think, but is that it for your powers, or is there more to the story?"

## Texas Legislative Process

Straus's knowledge of the position and the role as commissioner really came into light when he stated, "I am also in charge of controlling the pace of discussion on the floor and, when conflict arises, I, or one of the appointed senators placed in charge of the chair for a time, must interpret the rules on how the conflict will be resolved."

I looked at my dad and asked, "So what exactly is it that you do here?"

He responded, "The only thing I can do is vote; the presiding officers have all the other power. If I want to get stuff done, I must get real intimate with them and work a little magic. Even then, it usually doesn't work, but once in a blue moon, and only then, it does, if I'm fortunate."

Despondent about this knowledge, I replied, "It seems as if you presiding officers are in charge here, but what can I do to influence your decisions if I absolutely must?"

---

27    Texas House of Representatives, "Speaker of the House: Powers and Duties," accessed March 20, 2019, http://www.house.state.tx.us/members/speaker/#powers.

Speaker Straus responded, "In the first place, my attitude will play a huge role. This control boils down to how helpful I choose to be when dealing with legislators trying to muscle a bill through that I, and other important people, do not fully agree with. For example, when dealing with the opposition, it would be wise to help a bill through that I am not totally in favor of, nor totally against, if it means getting help later with a bill that is going to be close to passing and that the ruling party is truly in favor of, but the opposition is skittish about. Second, when the opposition gets their act together as a group effort, they can get in the way. For example, enough of the Democrats in 2003 left the state to block our efforts to convene the special session to redistrict the state."

I interjected, "Hey, Dad, isn't that what you told me earlier today?"

My dad replied with a nod, and Straus continued: "Since the membership overturns frequently, the extensive legislative experience is lacking. Overall, there are only a few handfuls of members who have been in office longer than two or three terms, giving them inside knowledge and an advantage in working the system, better than the average member of the chamber. Since the senior members know how to work the system better, they can use that knowledge to overrule Lieutenant Governor Patrick or me on many important issues, if so desired."

Up next, Patrick interjected, "The next group of controls revolves around the antics of the governor. Our current governor can veto, or kill, the bills we produce in different ways. We'll let Governor Abbott fill you in on the specifics of that later, although we really do hate it when he says stuff like, in general, 'If that bill reaches my desk I'm not going to pass it, so don't waste your time on it,' as it stops the process of passing a controversial bill cold before it even begins to be discussed."

This act seemed to be a brilliant policy maneuver and a bit Trumpian.

After that, Patrick mentioned, "Our state constitution is very strict. Thus, the legislature must follow a multitude of microcosmic rules to get a bill passed. One such example is the fact that each proposal must be read allowed on the floor three times, which typically takes place over three days, before it can be officially voted on, which takes time and purposely slows down the process and potentially wastes a whole lot of effort that could be used to consider additional legislation.[28] Also, the political climate of the time can play a crucial role in a bill's passage, as a massive spending bill amid an economic downturn, or a lot of the legislature being caught up in a scandal, can hold an agenda up as the atmosphere becomes toxic. Lastly, Speaker Straus and I have been here a while and have done so much to get here. Along the way, we had to check our ambitions for this or that. This power check revolves around the fact that if we continue to seek higher office and also push through too much controversial legislation, we could be seen as too partisan and unfit for holding higher office."

---

28    http://www.house.state.tx.us/about-us/bill

It was getting close to 12:30 p.m.; the presiding officers and my dad all looked down at their watches and said, "It's time."

Then Lieutenant Governor Patrick and Speaker Straus got up and left the room. Following this, my dad looked at me and said, "Let's go pass some legislation, yeah!"

The funny thing is, my dad did this all while lugging out a 20-page-long typewritten bill from his briefcase to show me. He stated, "Son, this is a bill that is going to authorize the state to spend some of its surplus from the last regular session on water projects around the state. Since I've been here for many years, I know what I am doing, but if I was new, I could call on the services of the Texas Legislative Council[29] and get help with the bill drafting and any other research that I may need. Also, since it is a spending bill, the Legislative Budget Board [30]and state comptroller gets to have a say in the matter before I am authorized to produce it on the floor of the House to ensure that we have the money to progress forward."

It felt good to know that the new members of the legislature were not sent in with a 20-dollar bill pinned to their suits and wished the best of luck for the remainder of the term. He also indicated that there is the Sunset Advisory Commission,[31] which advises the state budget writers about which agencies have gone beyond their necessity and should be defunded—the easiest way to shut down parts of the government. Following this, my dad stated, "In getting a new law passed in Texas, each bill must go through 21 steps to become law—22 if the governor disapproves of the bill. For today's bill, the first nine will occur in the House, due to the constitution requiring it to start there as it is a spending bill, the next nine in the Senate, and then it hops around to different places for the last three or four steps. Let's go down to the House floor for our proceedings of the day. On the way, though, feel free to follow along on the nice diagram of how all this works, made by the *Texas Co-op Power* magazine" (figure 17.19).

With that information in tow, we left the room and proceeded out of the office and into the house chamber and its floor for the proceedings. Once we were in the hall, the various members were milling about, waiting for the speaker to read the governor's proclamation and call the special session into order. My dad told me to go over to the same chairs we sat in earlier in the day so that I could watch the proceedings. Once I was in my seat, things quickly went into full swing, and, after looking at the complex diagram, I knew that I was in for a busy afternoon. Per the house rules,[32] the proclamation was read, the pledge was said,

---

29   http://www.tlc.state.tx.us
30   http://www.lbb.state.tx.us
31   https://www.sunset.texas.gov
32   Ibid 10.

the

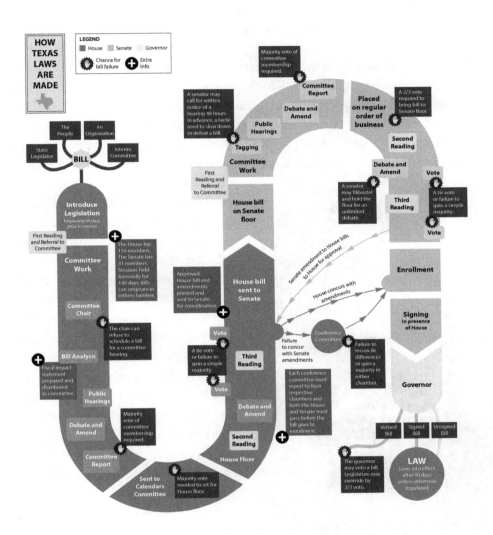

**HOW TEXAS LAWS ARE MADE**

LEGEND
- House
- Senate
- Governor
- Chance for bill failure
- Extra Info

**The People** / **An Organization** / **State Legislator** / **Interim Committee** → **BILL**

**Introduce Legislation**
beginning 60 days prior to session

First Reading and Referral to Committee

**Committee Work**

The House has 150 members. The Senate has 31 members. Sessions held biennially for 140 days. Bills can originate in either chamber.

**Committee Chair**

The chair can refuse to schedule a bill for a committee hearing.

**Bill Analysis**

Fiscal impact statement prepared and distributed to committee.

**Public Hearings**

**Debate and Amend**

Majority vote of committee membership required.

**Committee Report**

**Sent to Calendars Committee**

Majority vote needed to set for House floor.

**House Floor**

**Second Reading**

**Debate and Amend**

**Third Reading**

A tie vote or failure to gain a simple majority.

**Vote**

**Vote**

Approved House bill and amendments printed and sent to Senate for consideration.

**House bill sent to Senate**

Senate amendment to House bills to House for approval

House concurs with amendments

Failure to concur with Senate amendments

**Conference Committee**

Each conference committee must report to their respective chambers and both the House and Senate must pass before the bill goes to enrollment.

Failure to reconcile differences or gain a majority in either chamber.

**House bill on Senate floor**

First Reading and Referral to Committee

**Committee Work**

**Tagging**

A senator may call for written notice of a hearing 48 hours in advance, a tactic used to slow down or defeat a bill.

**Public Hearings**

**Debate and Amend**

**Committee Report**

Majority vote of committee membership required.

**Placed on regular order of business**

A 2/3 vote required to bring bill to Senate floor.

**Second Reading**

**Debate and Amend**

A senator may filibuster and hold the floor for an unlimited debate.

**Third Reading**

**Vote**

A tie vote or failure to gain a simple majority.

**Vote**

**Enrollment**

**Signing**
In presence of House

**Governor**

Vetoed Bill / Signed Bill / Unsigned Bill

The governor may veto a bill. Legislature may override by 2/3 vote.

**LAW**
Goes into effect after 90 days unless otherwise stipulated.

FIGURE 17.19   Adapted from: Diagram of the Texas Lawmaking Process

prayer was prayed, the podiums were turned on during the roll call, and the session was then called into order.

My dad left his seat and moved to one of the podiums at the center of the room where, if a house member wishes to speak—to introduce a bill, in this case—they must move to be recognized by the speaker. After arriving at the podium, Speaker Straus called on my dad to introduce the bill that he had been discussing earlier in the day with the lieutenant governor and the speaker.

While there, my dad completed the first step in the process of passing a bill in the state legislature. In short, he introduced the bill to the floor and then had an intern give the document to the clerk of the house for processing, numbering, and reading—the second step.

For the life of me, I cannot remember the exact text of the bill, but mostly they were belatedly following the directive of a 2013 state constitutional amendment that authorized the state to spend $2 billion of the state's rainy-day fund on water-related projects for the state.[33] Some of the projects included desalinization plants along the gulf coast, a piping system to bring water to the arid west of the state from more fluid regions, and a multitude of other seemingly more and more important endeavors. After the bill was read aloud, the speaker completed the third step by assigning the bill to be heard in the next half hour by the Natural Resources Committee and recessed activity on the floor, as there was no other authorized business to be discussed until the committee returned with its report later.

With everybody leaving their desks and seats, my dad came over and told me to follow him down to the Capitol Extension to the committee rooms. It took about 15 minutes to get there after wading through the crowd, using the restroom, going down the stairs, etc. (figure 17.20). It felt like a

FIGURE 17.20   Set of Stairs Leading to Upper Floors of the Texas Capitol Building

33   Elizabeth Koh, "Ballot Order Set for Nine Proposed Constitutional Amendments," *Texas Tribune*, August 5, 2013, http://www.texastribune.org/2013/08/05/nine-constitutional-amendments-appear-nov-ballot.

big maze, once again. The conference room was E1.010 (figure 17.21), right next to the restaurant on the west side of the Central Gallery.

When inside, we sat down on the left side, as the center seating was already filled. Before the proceeding began, my dad told me what a legislative committee is precisely. He stated that they are "a body of members appointed by the presiding officer (or another authority specified by the chamber) to consider and make recommendations concerning disposition of bills, resolutions and other related matters"[34] and that their primary responsibility is to review policy for the legislature.

FIGURE 17.21    Texas Capital Building Extension Conference Room E1.010

He went on to argue that the committee could take one of three options on the bill—the fourth step in the process of lawmaking in Texas. First, the committee could ignore it, better known as pigeonholing. This result seemed unlikely, as they were all only here to discuss the one bill. Second, they could alter the bill to reduce the amount spent, get rid of projects they felt were unnecessary, or amend the wording for a variety of reasons and then pass or fail it. Finally, the committee could flat out approve or disapprove of the bill immediately. Straight approval seemed most likely, as the speaker and lieutenant governor had already given their blessings, not to mention the fact that the committee was held purely by Republicans who were all in favor of the bill.

The chair called the meeting into order at 1:00 p.m. and surprised everyone by inviting me to the front for questioning about the bill—a power that they have to ensure full and proper review of the bill.

My dad patted me on the back and said, "You wanted to learn about the government this summer. This endeavor is what you wanted. Welcome to the big leagues, Slugger. Have fun!"

I gulped and faced the music.

The music thankfully only consisted of Chair Susan Lockerby telling me about what the standing committee process was. Initially, she asked me to view the action of the legislature

---

34    National Conference of State Legislatures, "Glossary of Legislative Terms," accessed March 20, 2019, http://www.ncsl.org/research/about-state-legislatures/glossary-of-legislative-terms.aspx.

as that of a football game. In this case, the bill was the ball, the parties were the teams fighting over it, and the house floor served as the playing field. This and other committees served as the on-field referees, with the speaker serving as the league's head official in charge of assigning officials to work each of the games—or merely review potential future policy, in their case. This result made sense, as I would learn later that the game took all afternoon, and along the way, the bill was sent to various committees for review, just like throughout a football game when multiple penalties are called. She went on by stating that their committee was permanent and had lawmaking authority, with the primary goal being to consider legislation for the main body floor by reviewing it.

It was then that Representative Memo Ochoa (R-Corpus Christi) chimed in and mentioned that there was something called subcommittees, where three or four members of the first committee would break off into their little group and review the legislation for the whole of the committee. This seemed like the head on-field referee at a football game going to the small sideline tent to watch replays when one of the head coaches challenges the ruling on the field.

Taking back over control of the hearing, Lockerby said that more than 10,000 pieces of legislation[35] are submitted to be considered during each of the general sessions, and there was no way that each bill could be considered by the entire house. Therefore, a multitude of standing committees are created to review the different pieces of legislation for the main floor, ensuring that only the best bills made their way back to the floor for final consideration.

Once finished, Lockerby dismissed me from the chair. Then she and the other members further discussed the bill, made about six changes to some of the wordings, and cut a project that they felt unimportant (better known as marking the bill) to keep the state from building near the Padre Island National Seashore. This seemed all good. Close to 1:15 p.m., the committee voted and approved the bill, eight to one. The lone "nay" came from Ochoa, whose district holds the project that was cut. With the voting done, the chair sent an edited version of the bill, called a report, with a congressional intern to the house clerk so that it could be added to one of the house calendars—the fifth step—and let the speaker know of their progress. This is important, as calendars, not bills, are scheduled time on the floor, and if time runs out on the floor for that calendar, the bill dies.

After that, my dad collected me, and we walked back up the various stairwells to the house chamber for floor discussion of the bill—the seventh step. On the way, my dad explained that before the legislature could further discuss the bill, it had to be reread—the sixth step—and

---

35    Bobby Blanchard, "On First Day Allowed for Filing, Legislators Submit More than 350 Bills," *Texas Tribune*, November 11, 2014, http://www.texastribune.org/2014/11/10/first-day-pre-filing-draws-more-300-bills.

that only then could the seventh step take place. More importantly, he indicated that three main rules had to be followed beyond the standard Robert's rules of order for parliamentary procedure.[36] The first was that each person speaking on a bill was limited to what commonly amounted to about ten minutes each. Second, trial votes could be had. And finally, it only takes a simple majority of those present on the house floor to approve of the legislation—if enough are present for a quorum, that is.

After I returned to my seat, Straus called the house back into session at 1:30 p.m. and had the clerk read the updated version of the bill. Once the bill was read, the floor was opened for discussion of the bill, which lasted for all of about ten minutes, thanks to Ochoa trying to get the cut project back on the bill via an amendment. He made a dull, pointless speech that fell on deaf ears, leading to a roll-call vote that failed to get enough votes to get the item back on the bill. With no changes or further discussion desired by other members, the eighth step commenced, with the clerk reading the bill once again to make sure that everybody involved knew exactly what was in the bill. As expected, during the ninth step—officially voting on the bill—it passed, 148 to one, with the speaker abstaining by tradition and the guy who had his project cut trying to make a point by voting "nay." Following this, the house recessed at 1:45 p.m. until the bill came back to the house.

Immediately after that, Senator John Jacob Jingle Heimer Schmitt from New Braunfels came over to my dad and told him that he would be the one to sponsor the legislation in the senate—the tenth step—and get the bill heard there, a fancy way of saying introducing the bill, but in the other legislative assembly. With the senate scheduled to be called to order at 2:00 p.m., I told my dad that I would grab a snack for us at the extension's restaurant and meet him at the third-floor senate gallery to watch the events that would happen there.

With food now in hand, I was making my way back up to the third-floor gallery just after 2:00 p.m., thinking that mall walkers in search of a challenge could up their training if they switched to here. However, since I had entered the restaurant, the central gallery and the main rotunda had become full of protestors who were against a portion of the bill that would fund the construction of a dam on the Sabine River that would flood parts of the East Texas wetlands. With so many protestors in the way, I just grabbed a corner of the central gallery and ate, all while hoping that my dad would not starve to death.

Near 2:15 p.m., I saw a divide open in the protestors, with Texas Rangers at the helm and the senate members who were trying to get the senate Natural Resources Committee meeting from their chamber in tow. I did not see my dad, but I followed the group into room E1.012 anyway to get away from the protestors. Once seated, I asked one of the staffers who came down with the senators what happened up in the senate chambers.

---

36  http://robertsrules.com

A staff member responded, "Senator Schmitt sponsored the bill and got the needed two-thirds approval of the body to hear the bill in the senate. Then the bill was read as finally approved by the house. Following that, Lieutenant Governor Patrick assigned the sponsored bill to the senate Natural Resources Committee and then recessed the session until the committee reported back. And here we are just for that."

I said thanks and noted that steps 11 and 12 were now accomplished. Then the chair called the committee meeting—the 13th step in the state lawmaking process—into order close to 2:30 p.m. to discuss the bill. It was a bit hard to hear, as the protesters were outside the room chanting away against the legislation. I guesstimated that since the bill by this point had already been marked up considerably, and no one there really had any desire to make any further changes, they would proceed to vote on the bill for good measure. However, just like this morning, I was called forward to testify.

I gulped and faced the music again.

Thankfully, Chair Hill Ary kept her comments focused as she introduced two other committees in the legislature that would not usually convene during a special session. She talked about interim and joint committees. She began by explaining that, since the general sessions were only 140 days, this left roughly 590 days between sessions, with everybody just twiddling their thumbs. Therefore, to make those 140 days the most productive, legislators get together in interim committees to draft legislation, make further changes, and prepare final drafts so that, on day one of the 140 days, multiple pieces of legislation can be submitted right away for consideration and not have too much opposition or barriers to passage, as everybody has already unofficially approved it. This made sense, as doing your homework in advance allows you to also get it out of the way early on and even get extra credit for it in one way or another. This seemed a lot like offseason workouts or training camps by players in the NFL[37] or spring training in Major League Baseball®.[38] The joint committee, on the other hand, had members serving from both houses, with the primary direction to advise the executive and other state officials on how they should act on matters. This seemed a lot like player associations for competitors in major sporting leagues who bring in players from the different teams to work on common causes affecting everyone playing in the league. When finishing her talk, she concluded by stating, "Your dad is going to be waiting for you in the gallery of the senate, and he still wants his snack."

Embarrassed, I stepped down after being dismissed and went back to my chair. The meeting concluded at 2:45 p.m. after the members voted 6 to 0 on the bill before them without

---

37    https://www.nfl.com
38    https://www.mlb.com

any changes being made, to approve it. Once again, the bill was handed to an intern, who took it the clerk of the senate and got it placed on the sole senate calendar—the 14th step in the process. In leaving the room, the Texas Rangers posted at the building cleared a path in the crowd of protestors for the members to use in getting back. Feeling wise, I tagged onto the rear of the procession with my dad's snack in hand and made my way up to the senate gallery, with the floor to come back into session at 3:00 p.m.

As instructed, my dad was waiting there for me in the back row of the viewing gallery with a seat being kept warm for me by a protestor, which he proceeded to move from after my dad put on his world-famous puppy-dog eyes. While waiting for the senate to be called back into order, my dad explained some of the rules here. He said that there are no trial votes, that it still takes a simple majority of those present to approve of most bills, and that I probably already knew about the two-thirds approval to hear the bill on the floor. The thing that stood out is that there is no limit on the amount of time that a legislator can spend talking about a bill on the floor—better known as a filibuster. The only rules for filibusters are that those on them have three strikes and that if they talk about something other than the bill, lean against a support, or eat or drink something, they then lose a strike and, in some cases, lose all of them at once, ending their speech. He noted here that Wendy Davis, the 2014 gubernatorial candidate for the Democratic Party, was known to be an avid filibusterer, made famous by her 2013 abortion bill filibuster, that saw her, and her pink shoes, make a 12-hour successful blockage of a bill, during a special session, that would basically have shut down abortion activity in the state.[39] That worked until the governor just called another session to get the bill passed. Dad also stated that, at the federal level, senators could speak about whatever they want, bringing up the famous reading of Dr. Seuss's *Green Eggs and Ham* by Senator Ted Cruz in 2013.[40] With that in mind, at 3:00 p.m., Lieutenant Governor Patrick called the senate back into order.

After the session was restarted, the 15th step occurred when the bill was read by the senate clerk. During the floor debate, the 16th step, a few speeches by various senators were given about the greatness of the bill and how we were saving the state from going dry like the situation Californians were dealing with. The big difference here is that senators may speak at their desks. I chuckled a few times at the grandiosity of the speeches during this floor debate that lasted until 3:30, when the discussion was closed.

---

39    Manny Fernandez, "Filibuster in Texas Senate Tries to Halt Abortion Bill," *New York Times*, June 26, 2013, http://www.nytimes.com/2013/06/26/us/politics/senate-democrats-in-texas-try-blocking-abortion-bill-with-filibuster.html.

40    Michael McAuliff, "Watch: Ted Cruz Reads 'Green Eggs and Ham' on the Senate Floor," Huffington Post, September 25, 2013, http://www.huffingtonpost.com/2013/09/24/ted-cruz-green-eggs-and-ham_n_3985336.html.

One amendment passed that required that at least 50 percent of the projects be bid out to Texan firms to keep the money as close to home as possible. Following this, the clerk read the bill—the 17th step.

After that, the chamber voted—the 18th step—30 to 1 to approve the bill, with the lone senator from Corpus Christi voting "nay," in solidarity with the house rep who did the same earlier. Then the lieutenant governor recessed the session until the conference committee—the 19th step—could meet at 4:00 p.m. Before we left the chamber, my dad indicated that, since the house and senate passed different versions of the bill, the different versions of the bill had to be reconciled. If the two houses hadn't passed different versions, the conference committee could have been skipped.

To get to the conference committee room (E1.004) in the extension's auditorium, we had to once again wade through the crowd of people. We made it through, thanks to the Texas Rangers' escort. It took about 15 minutes to reach the room. Along the way, the only thing that I could think about was that the only real hurdle in getting legislation passed here is the size of the building, with its copious number of stairs that people must climb and avoid falling on in getting to the next step. Sheesh. Also, my dad enlightened me here about the powers the committee had, beyond the actual reconciling. This committee, as my dad put it, "unless so directed to, could not alter, amend, or omit text that is not in disagreement from their houses' final report on the bill, nor may the committee add text on any matter that is not in disagreement or that is not included in either version of the bill in question." Simple enough, I thought.

After arriving in the auditorium, my dad and I found some seats toward the front, thanks to some badge flashing to the guards at the door. It was getting close to 4:00 p.m. The five senate members, of whom two must be from the senate standing committee that initially approved of the legislation, and five house members in a similar capacity convened onstage to reconcile. Once assembled, it took about 30 minutes for them to bicker on the wording of the amendment made by the senate in defining what a contract was and how they determined what a Texas firm is. This seemed prudent.

In speaking to the crowd, the committee chair, but I swear she was looking right at me, announced that once they approved of a final version, it would go back to each of the chambers to be reapproved of—the 20th step. They proceeded to vote, thankfully without calling me up for questioning, and approved the reconciled version nine to one. The one "nay" voted in sympathy for Representative Ochoa, whose project was cut earlier in the house committee. Once the vote was completed, the bill was sent back, and the committee was closed at 4:25 p.m. It was at this point that my dad said I could skip this last vote process in each of the houses, as it was kind of quick, and that he wanted me to see the signing ceremony with the governor more than a revote, which was a simple majority vote. He directed me to the Governor's Reception Room (figure 17.22) once back in the second-floor rotunda balcony, while he went back into the chamber to vote.

Near 5:00 p.m., the doors to the reception room I was now sitting in swung open, with a man who I assumed to be Governor Greg Abbott leading the way in his wheelchair, with various members of the legislature in tow. In the middle of the room, a small table had been set up with fancy pens placed on it ready to be used to give the governor's John Hancock a whirl on the final wording of the legislation—the

FIGURE 17.22    Texas Governor's Reception Room in the State Capital Building

21st step. After everybody got behind him to watch him sign, my dad included, the governor looked up and said, "There is a special young man who is here today learning about how to pass laws in the state of Texas. Could you please stand up and come forward? I want to make sure that you know exactly what my powers are in this situation, as your father requested."

I gulped again and walked forward with flashes from the cameras whirling about and sat down in a spot on the floor where the governor requested. The governor went on for about ten minutes, discussing what his powers were. In summary, he could approve of the bill or veto the entire legislation right then and there. Unfortunately, he could not ignore the bill, as the bill would go into effect, with or without his approval, after 10 days (if the legislature was still in session) or 20 days if out of session. Besides, if he liked the bill but hated certain portions, he could use his line-item veto powers to get rid of those pieces he disliked, although he admitted that he could only cut items related to the state budget and spending. He concluded by remarking, "I like the bill, so I am going to sign it in its entirety, but if I did veto it, each house of the legislature could override the veto with a two-thirds majority vote, and, since each house nearly unanimously passed, I better sign it to avoid a 22nd, if needed, step, you could say."

To great applause, the bill was signed. Following this, people left the room, and in the distance, I could hear the lieutenant governor and speaker simultaneously close their legislative chambers sessions in the background. I met up with my dad and said, "That was exhausting."

He nodded in agreement and remarked, "Try doing that for 140 days repeatedly."

I decided not to ask any more questions but did wonder aloud if there was anything else that I should learn while there regarding the legislative process.

Looking at me, he asked, "Wanna go climb to the top of the dome?"

I said, "Sure, why not? It's only more stairs to climb and hurdles to get in the way of me crashing in Charity's car for a nap, just like what the bills here have to deal with to become law."

After that, we made our way up the stairs to the fourth floor. Unfortunately, the area was under construction due to a leak from a recent rainstorm, and we could not progress. With that last hurdle insurmountable, we just looked out the windows and watched the sunset for a few minutes before I said, "I'm hungry, and I ought to get outta here."

My dad gave me a hug, told me how brave I was for facing the music, and wished me on my way. I left for the long hike back to Charity's car at the Bullock Museum after getting a burger from the capitol's restaurant on my way out the door. Overall, I spent today learning about how state legislation is structured and proceeds through a process that is designed to weed out the bills that do not pass muster via a multitude of inspections, readings, hearings, and debates. It is incredible how anything gets passed at all due to the lengthy process that must be navigated through.

---

**QUESTIONS TO CONSIDER** REGARDING THE TEXAS LEGISLATURE:

1. The first main topic of the chapter discusses the various contexts of the Capitol Complex. Please define the word *context*, indicate a context that is special to your existence, and explain how that context influences your life decisions, in detail.

2. The second main topic of the chapter discusses the minimum requirements to serve in the state legislature. Please identify what those minimum requirements are, the ones you meet, and whether you may serve in the state legislature.

3. The third main topic of the chapter discusses the size of each legislative body, the terms and limits of representatives, and their pay. Please identify what the information here is, the one piece of information that worries you most as a citizen, and why, in detail.

4. The fourth main topic of the chapter discusses the sessions available in Texas by lawmakers to make legislation. Please identify those sessions and explain what each session consists of, the one that would worry you most as a representative, and why, in detail.

5. The fifth main topic of the chapter discusses key terms relevant to the legislature. Please define each of those four terms, the one that would relate to you and your life the most, and why, in detail.

6. The sixth main topic of the chapter discusses presiding officers. Please explain what presiding officers are, who they are in the Texas Legislature, what powers they have, what controls exist over them, your opinion on their necessity in the legislative process, and why, in detail.

7. The final main topic of the chapter discusses the process the Texas legislature goes through to pass legislation. Please identify in detail what that process is and explain what from your life is similar in length and how it relates, in detail.

## FIGURE CREDITS

Fig. 17.1: Copyright © by LoneStarMike (CC BY-SA 3.0) at https://commons.wikimedia.org/wiki/File:TexasStateCapitol-Nov2007. JPG.

Fig. 17.2: Copyright © by John Cummings (CC BY-SA 3.0) at https://commons.wikimedia.org/wiki/File%3ATexas_State_Capitol%2C_Austin_26.JPG.

Fig. 17.3: Source: https://tspb.texas.gov/plan/maps/doc/capitol_complex_maps/capitol_monument_guide.pdf.

Fig. 17.4: Copyright © by Larry D. Moore (CC BY-SA 3.0) at https://commons.wikimedia.org/wiki/File%3ATexas_capitol_skylights. jpg.

Fig. 17.6: Copyright © by Another Believer (CC BY-SA 4.0) at https://commons.wikimedia.org/wiki/File:Austin,_Texas_(2018)_-_113. jpg.

Fig. 17.12: Copyright © by John Cummings (CC BY-SA 3.0) at https://commons.wikimedia.org/wiki/File:Texas_State_Capitol,_Austin_11.JPG.

Fig. 17.15: Copyright © by Alfredsp39 (CC BY-SA 3.0) at https://commons.wikimedia.org/wiki/File:Texas_redistricting_-_2002_and_2004.png.

Fig. 17.16: Source: https://tlc.texas.gov/redist/pdf/house/map.pdf.

Fig. 17.17: Source: https://tlc.texas.gov/redist/pdf/senate/map.pdf.

Fig. 17.18: Source: https://fyi.capitol.texas.gov/fyiwebdocs/PDF/congress/dist35/m1.pdf.

Fig. 17.19: Source: http://www.texascooppower.com/texas-stories/life-arts/the-legislature-and-you.

Fig. 17.20: Copyright © by John Cummmings (CC BY-SA 3.0) at https://commons.wikimedia.org/wiki/File:Texas_State_Capitol,_Austin_16.JPG.

# Chapter 18

# The Texas Governor

# The Governor's Mansion

I had planned on sleeping in today and then doing some touristy sightseeing and seeing some nongovernmental entities for once. However, little did I know that signing my name on a list yesterday in the Governor's Reception Room at the state capitol building would wreck those plans like a fire-ant hill beneath a picnic blanket in Zilker Park. That list, the Governor's Appointment Request Log,[1] was an item that any person could make their mark in and request an appointment to meet with the governor in some capacity or another. After getting home yesterday, I went online and discovered that it typically takes months to set up an appointment, much less have it occur, after signing that list. The thing is, when your dad is a vital state lawmaker, one little phone call can get you bumped to the front of the line and parts unknown in between. What happened? Exactly that.

Accordingly, at 6:00 a.m., my cell phone rang, with the nice Texas Ranger I had met the previous day in the reception room waking me from my summer slumber.

Her message was very brief, more of an order: "Please meet the governor at the Governor's Mansion, located at 1010 Colorado Street across from the capitol building, at 7:45 this morning. When you arrive, go to the back entrance of the complex on Lavaca Street, where the gate guard will inspect you and your vehicle, followed by showing you where to park. Also, bring some items with you for an overnight stay. It's going to be a long day for you. Most importantly, be wearing a suit when you arrive."

I replied, "Yes, ma'am." Then I thought, "How cool; I may get to sleep in the big house of Texas government!"

Accordingly, I was invited to be a guest of the governor for the next 24 hours as he went about his business, which turned out to be the significant business of the state, alongside some downright hilarious antics. After showering and getting dressed, I left Charity's house at 7:00 a.m. and made the quick trip downtown. Luckily, the morning traffic had not yet amassed.

When I arrived into downtown Austin at about 7:20 a.m., I quickly found the mansion and went to the back entrance, met with the guard, passed my inspection, and parked my car where told to in the lot. I got the items for the night out of the trunk and readied for the day ahead. When walking out of the lot, I went around the north side of the mansion to the sidewalk that led up to the front door. This path was my only big mistake of the day, as three uniformed state troopers immediately stopped me from heading directly to the front door, all while giving me a very thorough frisking. The troopers then searched my belongings, confirmed my identity against their list of approved visitors, and concluded everything by making a quick call inside. I missed the back entrance and tripped an alarm.

---

1   https://gov.texas.gov/organization/detail/scheduling-and-advance

Ten minutes later, nearing 7:45 a.m., Governor Greg Abbott met me on the porch, where I was being held, with the grace of a man who is on top of his game. Once nearby, he extended his hand and shook mine with an excellent, firm grip. He motioned for me to leave my items with the troopers so that they could take them to the vehicles we would be traveling in later in the morning.

After that, he said, "Champ, it is nice to make a more personal acquaintance with you after our very public Q-and-A session yesterday."

I replied, "Me too. I'm excited about what's in store for the next few days?"

He went on, "What exactly are you doing this summer? What your dad said on the phone seemed like a tall tale not even a real Texas cowboy could spit out over a campfire and be believable."

I explained, "Since I want to follow my dad into politics in one form or another, I need to get in the trenches beforehand and learn what government is. Therefore, I'm spending my summer visiting with different governing agencies and entities found here in the state."

He smiled. "Well, you have come to the right place. This residence is the home of the highest office in the land. Well, for Texas, at least. Let's go for a quick tour, as we need to hit the road for an event that starts at 10:15 this morning, and for this one you can't be late."

At the news of this, I could only look on with faith in God-knows-what, as I still had no idea what exactly it was that we were going to be doing today, or even tomorrow morning, for that matter. Still on the porch, he asked me to walk back down the front steps onto the walk and look up at the flagpole. When standing at the base of the pole, Abbott said, "Now Champ, alongside Old Glory and the state flag waving in the wind, a rare third one flies with them. This third one, unofficially in use since around 1964 by Governor Connelly, as no exec-utive order or legislation has made the flag official, is the state governor's flag, which consists of the state arms, a lone star encircled by live oak and olive branches laid on a light blue circle, which is further laid on a dark blue field with one lone white star in each corner (figure 18.1). This is one of 16 known official and unofficial governor flags in use in the United States. The state legislature in 2007 and 2009 have attempted to make the flag official, but the bills died in committee. Lastly, the Texas

FIGURE 18.1 The Texas Legislature failed to adopt this flag.

FIGURE 18.2 The Texas Legislature failed to adopt this flag for the governor.

Flag Code[2] gives me the right to call for flags, including these, to be flown at half-mast to commemorate an occurrence. Let's keep walking down to the front gate."

I could only think aloud, "I want a personal flag, too. Oh well!"

Once at the gate, Abbott continued, "Let's turn around and gander at the edifice perfectly lit up now by the sun shining on it through the trees. This glorious building is the Texas Governor's Mansion (figure 18.2). This white Greek-revival structure adorned by six 29-foot columns on the facade was completed in 1856 and has housed the first family of Texas ever since, outside of when it was being renovated here and there. The most notable occurrence of this was from 2007 to 2012, due to an initial renovation that had to be extended near its completion due to a yet-to-be-brought-to-justice individual throwing a Molotov cocktail at the building, burning the front facade and much of the interior to a crisp in the middle of the night. Thankfully, most of the treasures we'll see within were not inside at the time of the fire."

We both sighed in unison at the stupidity of people sometimes.

I asked, "Does the mansion look like another essential executive household in the country, like the White House in DC, to you, or is it just me?

He responded, "Yes, it does, and this is the only thing in Texas that the state did not make bigger and better, as at the time the state was on a strict budget that we have kept ever since."

Moving on from there, we went inside the mansion for a quick gander around the building. When entering, any visitor goes directly into the tremendous two-story front corridor, which houses an incredible, grand, U-shaped staircase at the rear[3] (figure 18.3). On the walls are new paintings depicting essential events in state history, like what I had seen over the previous day in the state capitol. We first decided to see the upstairs, but the governor

2    "Government Code Chapter 3100: State Flag," accessed March 20, 2019, http://www.statutes.legis.state.tx.us/Docs/GV/htm/GV.3100.htm.

3    Texas State Preservation Board, "The Texas Governor's Mansion," accessed March 20, 2019, http://www.tspb.texas.gov/prop/tgm/tgm/mansion.html; This link provides all source material for information on the mansion.

remembered his wife was still getting ready and changed course.

Abbott said, "Let's stick to the first floor. Upstairs is the private residence where I live with my wife, who is not ready to receive people, alongside the Pease Bedroom (figure 18.4), which serves the same function as the Lincoln Bedroom at the White House: historical value and guest quarters. While we are here, though, check out the scars on the banister from the tacks put in by Governor Hogg over 100 years ago to keep his kids from sliding down the darn thing."

We went off to the left and ventured into the small parlor, where a guest could wait on the governor if the governor was behind schedule. On the wall was a portrait of former Governor Sam Houston so that, as Abbott surmised, "he can keep an eye on things to make sure that we are not messing up what he got started so well many years ago."

After that, we went into the large neighboring parlor, which is only accessible through the small parlor (figure 18.5). This room housed some mementos from the family of Governor Sam Houston and is primarily used for more formal entertaining. Abbott said, "My favorite item in the room, though, is the Hepplewhite grandfather clock, which dates back to the 1790s and still works."

Once back in the front entry hall, we crossed straight ahead into the library (figure 18.6). After a moment in which we stared in awe, Abbott mentioned, "I like

FIGURE 18.3 The Front Entry Hall, with original staircase, in the Texas Governor's Mansion in Austin, the capital of Texas.

FIGURE 18.4 The Pease Bedroom on the second floor of the Texas Governor's Mansion in Austin, the capital of Texas.

FIGURE 18.5 The Large Parlor in the northwest corner of the 1856 section of the Texas Governor's Mansion in Austin, the capital of Texas.

FIGURE 18.6 The Library in the southeast corner of the original portion of the Texas Governor's Mansion in Austin, the capital of Texas.

the particular history that has occurred in this room regarding Texas lore. As legend tells it, during secession in 1861, then-governor Sam Houston read, and then tossed, a letter from President Lincoln into the fireplace, which stands to the right of the doorway when entering—a letter that was offering him a commission as a general in the Union Army, along with 50,000 troops to help keep the peace, in return for keeping Texas in the Union.[4] Depending on how you evaluate the situation, that decision, if true, may have changed the direction of our fair state."

The story sent a chill up my spine. I responded, "That's the truth, after what I learned about a few weeks ago at the Bullock Museum. What else is important in this room?"

Abbott replied, "Besides the tale, three significant items stand in the room. The first is a portrait of Stephen F. Austin that hangs over the fireplace, followed by his desk, and, finally, a chandelier from 1856, which is the only light fixture that has hung in its original place since the mansion's opening. This is where informal entertaining takes place at the mansion."

Following this, we moved into the blue-walled state dining room (figure 18.7) that housed

FIGURE 18.7 The State Dining Room, looking towards the west wall of the Texas Governor's Mansion in Austin, the capital of Texas.

the oldest piece of furniture, a sideboard, and the only non-American-made piece of furniture in the mansion, the table itself. This room was refreshing to see, but Abbott rushed me through another wall into the conservatory, which had to be the most historical room in the building.

Abbott started by getting the basics out of the way by noting that this is where he and his family primarily eat meals, but beyond that, history buffs could have their lunch and dinner here as well to their heart's content and never be satisfied.

---

4    Howard C. Westwood, "President Lincoln's Overture to Sam Houston," *Southwestern Historical Quarterly* 88, no. 2 (October 1984): 125–44. doi:10.1093/anb/9780198606697.article.0400528

Explicitly, he stated, "This room houses half of the Governor's Memento Collection (figure 18.8), which began in the 1960s when First Lady Gene Daniels, a direct descendant of Governor Sam Houston, started gathering mementos that symbolize each of the past governors' time in office. This later led to the tradition—started by her husband and followed by every governor since—of leaving a piece to the collection upon leaving office. The piece I find most interesting is the sword of former governor Edmund J. Davis."

FIGURE 18.8 The Conservatory, part of the 1914 addition on the west side of the Texas Governor's Mansion in Austin, the capital of Texas.

At around 8:35 a.m., we were interrupted by a state trooper, who indicated that it was time for our departure from the mansion. Following this, we headed out the back door past the kitchen and to the porte cochere, where a small motorcade was waiting to whisk us away. Once we were in the vehicle and headed down Congress Avenue, I asked, "Where are we going, and what are we doing once there?"

He responded, "You'll find out eventually. I hope you like to fly, though."

I said, "Yeah, but I do like to know the final destination, as I'll need to buy a ticket."

He hushed me up by handing me an envelope and saying, "I told your dad about this adventure yesterday, and he got you a ticket. Here you go. He wanted to surprise you as much as possible."

I flipped it open to see a United Airlines boarding pass for Flight 3569 to Newark, New Jersey. I said, "He certainly did, and then some, but wait one cotton-picking moment. What is the Texas governor doing in New Jersey? Gambling enough to save the Jersey casinos? Wouldn't Louisiana be a lot easier to travel to?"

He replied, "Actually, the borough of Manhattan in New York City is our final destination, to be more specific, but as there is no airport there, we have to fly into Jersey and then cross the Hudson River to get there. For what we are doing when there, you'll have to wait until we arrive. And if you don't have any other questions, sit back, relax, and enjoy the thrill of getting to avoid a lot of annoying stoplights."

I had a lot more questions to ask, but I decided that they could wait, as we had the better part of the day left to chit-chat. Just before 9:15 a.m., we arrived in front of the Barbara Jordan Terminal at Austin-Bergstrom International Airport. The state troopers in the motorcade had already cleared a path to the front door and on into security, which, thankfully, was only a short walk away. Interestingly enough, even the governor still has to go through security when flying commercial. I giggled at the sight of Abbott going through the motions of being in security at the airport. Once through, we were whisked away on one of those fancy golf carts to Gate 21 for our flight. I must admit, though, it was cool having people look at you like, "Who is that kid with the governor?"

When we were at the gate, the plane had already been unloaded from its prior flight, and we could preboard the aircraft to help keep the peace in the waiting area, as, I was later told, many Austinites disagree politically with Abbott, who is a conservative, as they are predominately liberal politically. The lesson learned with Dr. Davis about local political culture came back to me full force. We boarded, and then the politician/showman came out as Abbott stood at the door with the flight attendant to help greet passengers. I figured he did this to help keep the few autograph seekers at bay during the flight itself. "Very smart," I later thought. Overall, he looked like a rhinestone cowboy up there under the boarding lights.

Once boarding had finished, Abbott sat down next to me in the front row of coach. The plane then taxied to the runway and took off without a hitch for an on-time departure. About ten minutes into the flight, his aide tapped him on the shoulder and gave him a folder with things for him to work on while we flew. From what I saw, it was standard office fare, like what his opinion on a matter was or signing his approval on committee work, etc. Funny thing though, 34 minutes after that, the same aide took the folder away from him and said, "Sorry, sir, I need the folder and its contents back. We're now over Arkansas."

I looked on in puzzlement and said, "You can't work on stuff over Arkansas? Aren't you just sitting here with a tabletop in front of you begging to be used?"

He stared back, responding, "Per state law, section 16 of article 4 of the state constitution to be specific, whenever the governor leaves the state, the lieutenant governor becomes the head honcho, and I get to play the role of Cinderella when the clock strikes midnight.[5] Everything goes away until I get back. Funny thing though, I can still call myself governor."

I asked, "Why?"

He replied, "Remember, under the current state constitution, people wanted to have a weak executive whose primary focus was on Texas, not some far-flung place or office. Therefore, what better way to ensure this than to castrate their power if the officeholder ever chose to leave the state, if only until they returned?"

In response, I plotted out, "So when former Texas governor and US president George W. Bush was running for president in 2000, running around the country, he held the title but none of the powers of the office during much of that time?"

He nodded yes and said, "Remember, though: Once the legislature is not in session, which it had been in for over 15 months at that time, there are not a lot of opportunities, outside of

---

5    Texas Constitution of 1876. article 4, section 16.

a major crisis, to use any of it. Speaking of powers of the office, you probably want to learn more about what the office of governor is, right?"

I replied, "Yes," but then I persuaded him to keep it simple in getting started, and to begin with the necessary qualifications, then to get on with the big stuff.

## Minimum Qualifications to Serve as Governor

Abbott's response was candid. Primarily, it came down to four vital minimum qualifications, and I quote: "Be 30 years of age, a US citizen, registered to vote in the state, and have spent at least the last five years as a resident of the state before the election."[6]

"Simple enough," I thought, but wondered aloud, "That seems too easy to be true, as many people would meet that but do not run for office."

He went on to say, "Unofficially, it helps to be male—although that may change in time, thanks to more women in politics at the state level—and middle-aged . . . roughly 40 to 60, and be a businessperson or attorney to give voters that feeling that you are competent to run the state, either from knowing how to run a business or being very well versed in state law. Politically, be moderate to conservative, which is essentially saying be a Republican. Religion-wise, be a white Anglo-Saxon Protestant, aka a white Christian. Finally, most importantly, though, have access to a whole lot of cash, as it takes a lot of it to get elected. Free bumper stickers, buttons, and T-shirts are expensive, not to mention the TV spots."

That response cleared up a lot of confusion about the simplicity of the formal qualifications. He went on and talked a bit about the perks, which included the mansion and office in the capitol that I saw late yesterday on top of formal offices in the Texas Insurance Building. These turned out to be in addition to a $150,000-a-year salary that is just about on par with the rest of the states, which range from $70,000 a year up to $174,000.[7] "Not bad for a public official," I thought. Speaking of perks, the flight attendant just happened to stop by and ask, "Drinks, gentlemen?"

I ordered a soft drink, and Abbott ordered tonic water and ice. I asked him to comment on how he got his job and how long he could be governor.

He retorted, "Well, if I like the job, which I certainly do, I can have it for as long as I want, as I face no limits on the number of terms I may serve, just like the legislators you met yesterday. The only hurdle to that feat is that I must first get elected during a presidential midterm election, just like the other members of the executive branch, and again every four

6    Ibid, section 1.
7    Vicki A. Benge, "State Governor's Salary & Benefits," Chron.com, April 4, 2017, http://work.chron.com/state-governors-salary-benefits-1734.html.

years[8] after that until I resign, get voted out, get impeached, or God forbid, start my dirt nap. Thankfully, though, I don't need more than 50 percent of the vote to win reelection. I only need the most votes, not a majority, better known as a plurality for the smart people like you, to win my general election. Got to get a true majority in the primary, though, now that I think about the process. This allows me to face a bad term or a lot of stiff competition and avoid a long runoff process. For example, when Rick Perry was reelected governor in 2006 for the second time, he received 39.09 percent of the vote, while his nearest opponent, a Democrat named Chris Bell, got 29.79 percent,[9] and still won without getting a true majority of the votes in the general election."

I inquired, "What if you have a bad term and people want you out sooner rather than later, or, God forbid, if disaster strikes?"

Perturbed, he responded, "Just like the president, I can face removal through the impeachment and conviction process. The first part, impeachment, is like having criminal charges filed against you in a court of law. You are not guilty or innocent; you are just charged with criminal mischief while in office by the Texas House, which your father is in, by them casting a majority vote in favor of filing charges. After that, I would face a trial, with the chief justice of the Texas Supreme Court serving as the main judge, the Texas House prosecuting the matter, and the Texas Senate serving as jurors and courtroom. If convicted, which has not happened since Jim Ferguson was kicked out of office in 1917,[10] I would be removed from office and barred from public office for life, and the lieutenant governor would become the official governor of the state. Now if disaster strikes, the line of succession goes from me to the lieutenant governor, to the president pro tempore of the senate, to the speaker of the house, to the attorney general, and then, funny enough, to the chief judges of the courts of appeals, in court number order.[11] That last one is important, as very rarely are justices placed into the succession line of an executive position, but this is Texas, so everything's just a bit different, or better if you choose to view it like that."

---

8    Texas Secretary of State, Qualifications for Office," accessed March 20, 2019, https://www.sos.state.tx.us/elections/candidates/guide/qualifications2018.shtml.

9    David Leip, "2006 Gubernatorial General Election Results—Texas," Dave Leip's Atlas of U.S. Elections, accessed March 20, 2019, http://uselectionatlas.org/RESULTS/state.php?f=0&fips=48&off=5&year=2006.

10   Ralph W. Steen, "Ferguson, James Edward," Texas State Historical Association, last modified February 24, 2016, https://tshaonline.org/handbook/online/articles/ffe05.

11   Texas Politics Project, "Who's Next? Order of Gubernatorial and Presidential Succession," accessed March 20, 2019, http://texaspolitics.utexas.edu/archive/html/exec/features/0304_01.html.

## Legislative Powers of the Governor

After hearing that, I was ready to eat, so when the same friendly flight attendant came back by with the snack boxes available for purchase, I ordered a snack box, which amounted to a nice-sized meal. Following this, I encouraged Abbott to speak about his duties while in office.

He responded by indicating that the powers he holds—when he gets back to Texas, of course—fall into one of two categories: legislative, or lawmaking, and executive, or officiating powers, which can be further divided into duties as head of state and head of government.[12] He first went into the legislative powers, most of which I remembered him speaking about the day before. In no short order, he went on, he could just sign a bill into law, better known as approving of legislation, veto the entire bill (just not ignore the bill, known as a pocket veto), or use the line-item veto (which is killing parts of a bill related to budgeting), alongside calling for a special session to get something he wanted to be discussed further now instead of waiting for the next regular session.

Beyond what was sanctioned by law, Abbott indicated that he could impact the direction of a potential future state law that was interesting. First, he went on about how he could kill a bill by threatening to veto it. I remembered here that the legislature only meets 140 days every two years, so if he didn't really like a bill, he could just threaten to veto the darn thing, and no one will spend any time on it, as the legislature has so little time to spend on something that would be dead on arrival. He brought up here the story of how Rick Perry (his predecessor from late 2000 to early 2015) threatened to veto a bill that funded the Public Accountability Office, located in the Travis County District Attorney's office, which has the additional responsibility of prosecuting public crimes. The issue is, the now former district attorney Rosemary Lehmberg was arrested for drunk driving and refused to resign, despite the apparent conflict of interest because she pled guilty and was sentenced to 45 days in jail.[13] When the bill funding the office reached former governor Perry's desk, he killed it, just like he promised. This led to the politically charged indictment of coercion of a public official—a felony—charges that were eventually dismissed.

After that, he went on about his ability to bargain for what he wants in a bill. This seemed straightforward until he went into five key factors that impacted his ability. First was his level of commitment to a measure. If he wanted it, he could go all in, or, if not, he could mention something and leave it to be added or not at the will of another. The

---

12   Office of the Texas Governor, "Duties, Requirements & Powers," accessed March 20, 2019, https://gov.texas.gov/governor-abbott/duties.

13   Sarah Rumpf, "Political Payback: Rick Perry Indicted in Power Struggle with Democrat-Controlled DA Office," *Breitbart*, August 15, 2014. http://www.breitbart.com/texas/2014/08/15/political-payback-rick-perry-indictment.

second was his timing. Endorsing a bill too early or too late won't help the bill advance, but speaking out at the right times could provide the right kick to get the bill passed on up to his office. The third was the amount of opposition or support derived by the legislature. Essentially, if he liked the bill but the legislature didn't, there would be nothing that he could do, and vice versa. The fourth was what the cards foretold in the future if he supported something he was on the fence about now. In other words, he could gain some valuable future benefits on a bill that he might like to be approved in the future if he passed a bill now that he doesn't like—a tit-for-tat situation. Last up was the bill writer. Even though I learned yesterday that there is an enormous amount of turnover in the legislature, some do stick around for decades. For example, Abbott brought up the tenure of State Senator John Whitmire from Houston, who served in the Texas House from 1973 to 1982 and has served in the Senate from 1983 to the present, giving him a great deal of authority and respect for pushing through legislation from experience.[14] I was impressed after all of this. He also mentioned that if he does his bargaining before the session, he can save a lot of time and push bills through more quickly if everybody already agrees about what is to be in the darn thing.

His last two legislative powers seemed a bit odd but very worthwhile nonetheless. The first one boiled down to him calling a fact-finding commission into order. These commissions can call witnesses, make recommendations on options for going forward, and merely do research on an item that the governor feels needs attention. This power made sense, as it is prudent to get all of the applicable data on a matter before making an important policy decision. On the other hand, though, I could see how these groups could be sent on a wild goose chase to make people think that they are doing something when in reality they are not. This seemed very similar to his ability to call special sessions of the state legislature into order, which is what happened late yesterday when I was there. Regardless, he did bring up the 9/11[15] and Warren[16] Commissions Reports (figure 18.9) as good examples of how important these groups can be in making a change.

His last power here, I felt, was like a sports coach bringing in his ringer in a game. This one was public speaking. When he was discussing this, all I could think about was him standing in front of the door during boarding and greeting people. He had a knack for it; what could I say? The most critical example he discussed of this power was his State of the

14    Texas Senate, "Senator Whitmire's Constituent Questionnaire," accessed March 20, 2019, http://www.senate.texas.gov/member.php?d=15.

15    National Archives and Records Administration, "9/11 Commission Records," accessed March 20, 2019, http://www.archives.gov/research/9-11.

16    National Archives and Records Administration, "Warren Commission Report: Table of Contents," accessed March 20, 2019, http://www.archives.gov/research/jfk/warren-commission-report.

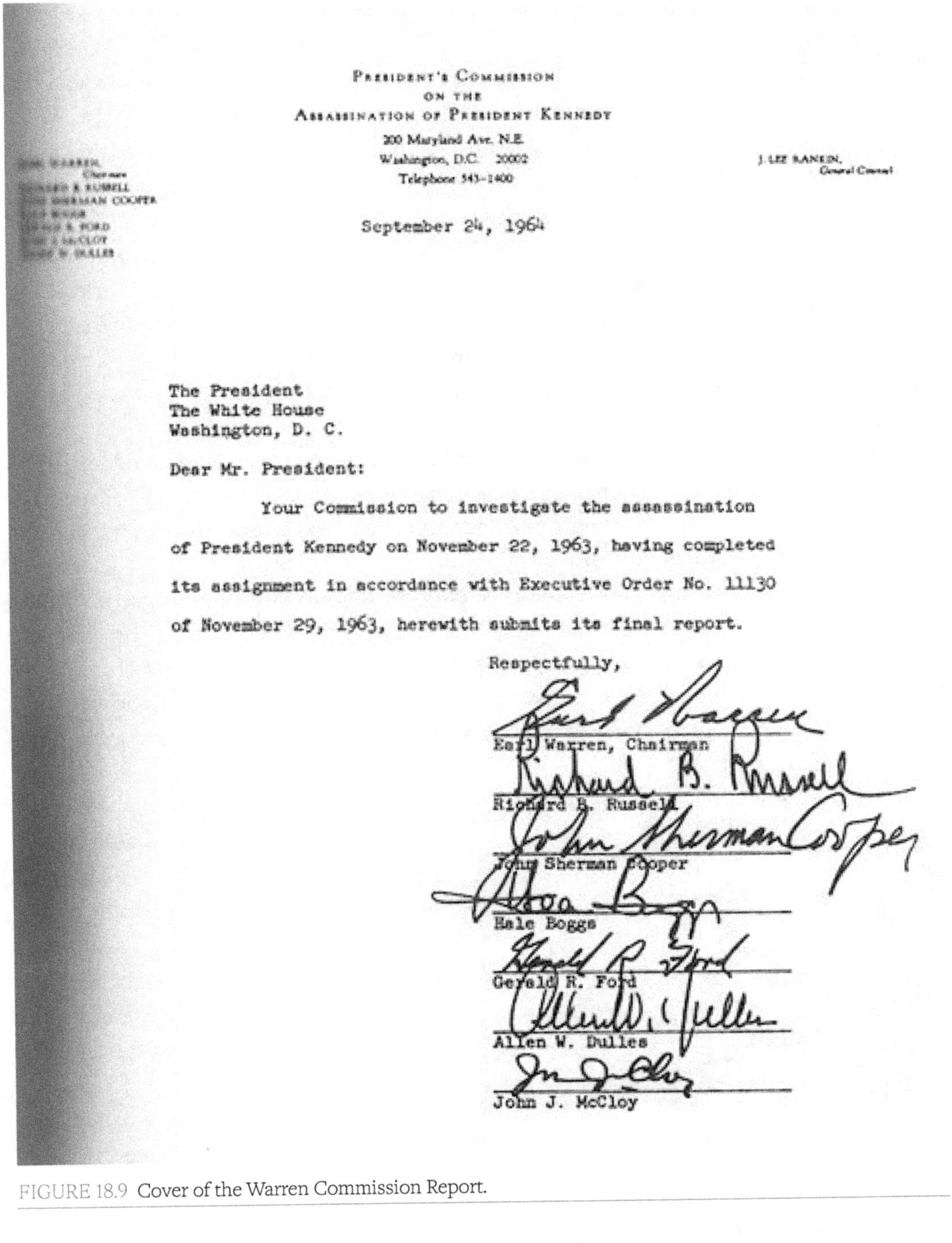

President's Commission
on the
Assassination of President Kennedy
200 Maryland Ave. N.E.
Washington, D.C. 20002
Telephone 543-1400

J. Lee Rankin,
General Counsel

September 24, 1964

The President
The White House
Washington, D. C.

Dear Mr. President:

Your Commission to investigate the assassination of President Kennedy on November 22, 1963, having completed its assignment in accordance with Executive Order No. 11130 of November 29, 1963, herewith submits its final report.

Respectfully,

Earl Warren, Chairman

Richard B. Russell

John Sherman Cooper

Hale Boggs

Gerald R. Ford

Allen W. Dulles

John J. McCloy

FIGURE 18.9 Cover of the Warren Commission Report.

State address at the opening of the biennial legislative session, where he could proselytize about what direction he wanted the state to go toward during the session and his term.[17] He made a funny comment here: "It's a lot like the president's State of the Union address, the difference being that people here tend to like and agree with me more on my policy, as we all typically share something of the same view on how things should go a majority of the time."

That one big speech sounded important enough, but then I inquired, "Can you make other speeches about something at any point in time?"

He nodded yes and nodded off for a nap. Talk about timing—he's a talker, and now he wants to sleep. Then, amazingly enough, it was nearing our arrival time in Newark, as the flight attendants started coming by to collect trash and other things to ready the cabin for arrival. After that, we touched down at Newark Liberty International Airport right on time, at 3:02 p.m. EDT. I was amazed at how our conversation had eaten up so much of the flight time.

As we were VIP, we could deplane first, even before the first class. We arrived into Gate C98 and were met by another fancy golf cart that whisked us away, outside of security and to a waiting shuttle for our venture into Manhattan. The strange thing was, instead of going into the city, we ended up at another terminal, called Signature FBO, just before 3:20 p.m. More interestingly, we avoided the building and drove straight up to a waiting helicopter on the tarmac. When out of the shuttle, we went straight onto the chopper. Minutes later, with our hand luggage in the storage bin, we took off for a breathtaking ten-minute ride to the VIP heliport at West 30th Street and 12th Avenue, on the west side of Manhattan (figure 18.10). On the way, I asked, "Why are we taking a helicopter when we already had a shuttle?"

FIGURE 18.10 Helicopter Landing at the E. 34th St. Heliport in New York City.

The aide who earlier gave and took back Abbott's work chimed in. "The traffic in New York and Jersey is so horrible and unpredictable that we fly coach to save money on the flight that got us here, but flying like that saves us enough money to charter a helicopter and help us avoid the nightmare traffic. Also, Abbott over there likes to fly."

"Not bad," I thought. Once back on the ground at the West 30th Street heliport,

---

17  Office of the Texas Governor, "Governor Abbott Delivers State of the State Address," January 31, 2017, https://gov.texas.gov/news/post/governor_abbott_delivers_state_of_the_state_address.

we clamored into another waiting bus that took us 22 blocks to the to the north, where we went east on 52nd Street for one block and immediately arrived at our destination just before 3:45 p.m. Once again, Abbott was at a place where he could perform under the lights.

Our destination was the filming location of *The Daily Show with Trevor Noah*[18] (figure 18.11). Now, I must admit that I was shocked that we flew all this way to be on TV, but who cares? I get to watch one of my favorite shows, live, even with the new host.

FIGURE 18.11  The Daily Show with Trevor Noah Studio.

## Executive Powers of the Governor

On the way to the studio, Abbott pulled me over to offer some more advice. "What comes now will be prime examples of my executorial powers. For now, though, what we are doing here in New York City are my duties as head of state, the highest-ranking position in a sovereign state that is vested with powers to act as the chief public representative of that state, a small portion of my executorial powers."

After him saying that, we hung out a bit into the green room to wait for taping to begin just after 4:00 p.m. While waiting, I pondered what a head of state was, but then I remembered my senior government class, and it hit me: He's like the queen—Queen Elizabeth of England, that is—just a lot younger and the opposite gender. This became even more relevant when I remembered that he had no real governing powers as governor when out of state, just like she doesn't, albeit not on a permanent basis. Mainly, over the next hour, he went on national television and acted out the first two of the three main roles as head of state.

The first became self-evident when he returned from the restroom. In a nutshell, Abbott looked as if he was the epitome of a hyperbolic Texan, as he had changed his clothing into a bluebonnet tartan button-down shirt adorned with a bolo tie, cowboy boots and hat, blue jeans, a big silver belt buckle from a famous Texan artisan who made it mainly just for him a few years back, and a Texas blue topaz ring. I chimed in, "What are you wearing, sir?"

He replied, "I am serving as a state symbol to the extreme as nearly everything that I am wearing are official symbols of the great state of Texas."

---

18   http://www.cc.com/shows/the-daily-show-with-trevor-noah

A few minutes later, he was brought out onstage to a roar of applause as he glistened under the lights. I was positioned just off to the side of the cameras, in the audience. Trevor Noah started the conversation with quite a bit of banter over Abbott's outfit and said, "I feel like I am talking to a museum, as opposed to just visiting one, as I like to do."

Abbott responded, "If I am going to keep the tradition of Texas governors appearing on *The Daily Show* alive, I need to dress for the occasion to give it my spin. Not to mention, I have now promoted many a state business, as everything I am wearing was manufactured in the state. This is a second important part of my head-of-state duties, promote the cow patties out of the state. My favorite was promoting Blue Bell Ice Cream when that delicacy came back into production back in 2015."[19]

This banter went on, leading to uproarious laughter from the audience time and time again. The more interesting part was when Noah, the liberal of the conversation, and Abbott, the strident conservative, got into it over whose state had a better business environment.

I enjoyed the conversation had between the two. I remembered why I like politics: People arguing over things that matter, like protecting freedoms, keeping government solvent, and the like. After about 30 minutes of discussion, nearing 5:00 p.m., the interview ended to great applause, and we left the studio for our next stop.

Once back in the car, Abbott and I talked about the interview. We both agreed he did a good job discussing the virtues of limited government while balancing it with the needs of society that needs the government to enforce them. It then hit me: "It's Tuesday, and we're in New York. What else does he have up his sleeve?"

Since I said this out loud, Abbott heard it, and a grin grew on his face. His blabbering followed the grin. "Do you like a good dinner party? Because we are going to the most gubernatorial one of them all, the National Governors Association[20] 2018 Annual Gala."

I thought out loud, "So this is why I needed to wear the suit."

Abbott said, "You got it. Driver, let's boot scoot on over to the Javits Convention Center" (figure 18.12).[21]

The journey took all of five minutes, going south on 11th Avenue for 16 blocks right up to the front entrance. Once out of the cars, we went through the main door and into the Crystal Palace main lobby for the building that I remembered from Hillary Clinton's 2016 election night party that didn't go off as planned. In the enclosure we got our passes for the event and then went directly into the 3B exhibition hall for the evening's events. Along the way,

---

19  Office of the Texas Governor, "Governor Abbott Celebrates Return of Blue Bell at Texas Capitol," August 31, 2015, https://gov.texas.gov/news/post/governor_abbott_celebrates_return_of_blue_bell_at_texas_capitol.

20  http://www.nga.org/cms/home.html.

21  https://www.javitscenter.com/

we spoke with the media (where Abbott shined, of course), glad-handed the other governors, and talked a little bit of shop. I was also introduced to many other prominent officials, and I made a lot of great contacts for future stops on my trek going forward, I hoped.

Just before 6:00 p.m., dinner bells rang, and people went to their seats. We were seated just to the left of center in the middle of the room. Braised duck was then served. Following this, 20 minutes later, Governor Andrew Cuomo of New York approached the podium. Once there, he proceeded to give the opening remarks of the gala. He called the meeting into order, recognized essential dignitaries, and went through the basics of the evening's events and conferences over the next few hours. Abbott and others were congratulated on their recent election success. For once, Abbott was quiet for the occasion, although, 20 minutes through the speech, he leaned toward me to explain the last of the three duties as head of state. Per him, "As a head of state, I am required to attend ceremonial events that are representative of an institution, the governorship, but have very little authority or influence in matters. They are for the matter of show as signing paperwork is not all that exciting. If I were staying the whole week for some of the other events, I would attend meetings and gain some knowledge about items that are influencing many of our states in the country, but I already read about most of the issues in my daily briefings. Closer to home, I would meet the Boy Scouts or Girl Scouts[22] visiting the capitol, march in a parade, pose on a magazine cover, attend a college's graduation, fire a gun, meet the president when he comes to visit the state, as President Trump did in 2017 following Hurricane Harvey (figure 18.13), things like that. In other words, I am representing the office without doing anything for the position other than put on a smiling

FIGURE 18.13  Governor Abbott with President Donald Trump during Hurricane Harvey Recovery Efforts.

---

22    http://www.scouting.org; http://www.girlscouts.org

face for the people. Also, I have the voice of the people during a disaster in requesting federal assistance."

Once the New York governor's speech was over, all governors in attendance were called up to the stage for a photo op of them together. The stage was a bit small, but the governors all got in well enough, as a shot was later displayed on the screen. This seemed to make sense, as much of what went on that evening was a lot of pomp and circumstance. Once done, the main floor was opened for dancing and reveling. I could only comment to Abbott, "You governors know how to have fun."

He replied, "With as much stress as we face, it is nice to get down and have some fun."

Getting close to 9:00 p.m., our group left the convention center the same way we had entered the building. Once on the road, we headed for the same heliport we had arrived at earlier for our flight to Newark Airport. From the convention center, we could have walked, but the cars were quicker for getting back to the chopper. The drive took us six blocks south on 11th Avenue and then one block west on 30th Street. The helicopter ride took just over 12 minutes, once in flight, to get us back to Newark Airport and the Signature terminal. The car was waiting for us on the tarmac and quickly took us right back to Terminal C for our flight home upon arrival.

Once inside the terminal, we cleared security and were once again whisked away by a cart to our departure gate, C97. When we were there, we were once again allowed to preboard, but instead of glad-handing at the door, Abbott decided to take his seat, as he did not want to delay people from getting some shut-eye and getting home quickly. Once boarding was done, United Flight 322 pushed back from the gate and left a few minutes late, just before 11:15 p.m.

Just before we nodded off, I whispered, "Governor Abbott thanks for letting me shadow you today."

He replied, "It ain't over yet, son. And besides, I have a whole lot more official duties to tend to tomorrow to tell you about when we get back. From here on out, these are my duties as head of government, the highest official in the executive branch of a sovereign state who often presides over a cabinet that leads executive departments."[23]

Three and a half hours later, we arrived at the Austin-Bergstrom International Airport without much of a fuss, outside of some turbulence during landing due to some storms about to roll through. Once at the gate, we deplaned to a waiting cart that ushered us to the terminal roadway and our waiting vehicles. Twenty-five minutes later, close to 2:00 a.m., we arrived at the mansion. We went into the now-obvious back entrance and to the living quarters. I found my bags in the Pease Bedroom, changed clothes, and went to bed. I also heard Abbott waking his wife to a less than enthusiastic "Oh, good morning. 'Night."

---

23   http://www.yourdictionary.com/head-of-government

At 6:00 a.m. the next day, I awoke to the smell of maple sausages filling the mansion. I went into the bathroom, used the facilities, showered, and got dressed. Fifteen minutes later, I went downstairs to the conservatory for breakfast. No breakfast had yet been placed on the table, but as soon as I walked in, Abbott came in from the kitchen across the hall with the sausage and some pancakes. After eating three of both, I was ready for the day. Since Abbott needed some prep time before we left at 7:30 a.m., I was sent to wait in—you guessed it—the small parlor room at the front of the mansion.

Just before 7:15 a.m., Abbott and his wife appeared, ready for the day. From their conversation, I could tell that she was off to work at her charity organization, Texanthropy,[24] a group that seeks to promote volunteerism and service to others in the state. We exchanged some pleasantries as she walked out the door. With her on her way, Abbott approached me and said, "Ready to learn all that's left to know about the governor?"

All I could say was, "You bet!"

With that out of the way, we went out the back porte cochere and into the vehicles for the short trip across the street to the capitol building. We entered on the north side of the capitol from 15th Street and drove down North Congress Avenue right up to the back entrance of the building. Once out of the cars, we went through the large doors into the elevators just past the north lobby and up to the second floor. We exited the elevators and walked around the rotunda floor viewing gallery past a lot of the previous governors' portraits and into the governor's office via the reception room.

When we were in the room, Abbott sat at his desk and told me to sit in the chair across the desk from him. Once situated, Abbott spoke, "Let's get you educated in what head-of-government powers I have remaining. I'll get started with budgeting. Per state law, I am the chief budgeting officer of the state. Through my Budgets and Policy Division,[25] I am responsible for preparing the state's biennial budget and distributing it to the legislature for further changes and approval before coming back to my office for any final tweaks using my line-item veto and final approval. Then, once the legislative session is out of session, The Legislative Budget Board and I are responsible for seeing the budget through and responding to any major events occurring in the state that may impact the budget, like a hurricane, per section 130 of the State Government Code."

I replied, "So that's budgeting; what about law enforcement?"

Abbott furthered, "That might depend on what you mean by law enforcement. On the one hand, when disaster strikes, I am responsible for declaring martial law[26] to help ensure

---

24    https://gov.texas.gov/first-lady/texanthropy
25    https://gov.texas.gov/organization/bpp
26    Texas State Library and Archives Commission, "Proclamation of Martial Law in East Texas, August 16, 1931," last modified March 30, 2011, https://www.tsl.texas.gov/governors/personality/sterling-oil-2.html.

law and order is maintained along with deploying the state guard to help, like when I did earlier this year to help secure our southern border with Mexico.[27] I would say, though, the most controversial power here—wait a minute, I'll let you read it for yourself."

Abbott took a piece of paper out of his Pendaflex. It read, "Execution Postponement."

I asked, "What does this mean? "

Abbott furthered, "My only true day-day-to-day law enforcement power is the ability to freely delay the execution of condemned criminals for no more than 30 days at a time; outside of that, I can only grant pardons in line with or less than the recommendation of the Board of Pardons and Paroles,[28] and the Public Safety Commission and local law enforcement are in charge of policing the state,[29] unlike the president, who has unlimited authority to commute sentences in these situations. Today's condemned is Clifton Williams out of Smith County, who was convicted of murder stemming from a 2005 home invasion that left a 93-year-old woman dead.[30] I do not often grant postponement outside of extreme circumstances. After you leave, I will call the warden in Huntsville with my decision."

Wanting to move on from the awkward situation, I asked, "What comes next?"

## A Plural Executive

Sounding glad for my conversational switch, Abbott mentioned, "I have some various official duties that include requesting federal aid dollars to help recover from a disaster, as I did last fall following the hurricane that hit the state,[31] serving on various committees like the Legislative Budget Board that I mentioned earlier, and merely coordinating multiple activities of the state. Now, before you go, there is one last power I should discuss that will lead you to your next stop on your trek for today. Unlike the president of the United States, who gets to appoint all federal judges and significant executive branch officials, I cannot do that. This is due to those positions—such as the attorney general, railroad commissioners, and

---

27    Elizabeth Mclaughlin, "Texas Governor Pledges 1,000 National Guard Troops to US-Mexico Border," ABC News, April 10, 2018, http://abcnews.go.com/US/texas-governor-pledges-1000-national-guard-troops-us/story?id=54349075.

28    Texas Board of Pardons and Paroles Executive Clemency Page, "Clemency," last modified January 2, 2019, http://www.tdcj.state.tx.us/bpp/exec_clem/exec_clem.html.

29    https://www.dps.texas.gov/public_safety_commission/index.htm

30    Texas Department of Criminal Justice, "Offender Information: Williams, Clifton," Death Row Information, accessed March 20, 2019, https://www.tdcj.state.tx.us/death_row/dr_info/williamsclifton.html.

31    Office of the Texas Governor, "Governor Abbott Requests Federal Funding for Flood and Water Infrastructure Projects," September 9, 2017, https://gov.texas.gov/news/post/governor-abbott-requests-federal-funding-for-flood-and-water-infrastructure.

lieutenant governor—getting elected independently. Now, I do get to make some appointments,[32] but those nominations are for minor positions, like the Texas Racing Commission, that—regarding the overall spectrum of running the government—play a minimal role. Even then, those appointments are not all made when I am elected; I sometimes must wait for their terms to expire two or four years into my term; they are left over from the prior administration. No clean slate protocol for me."

I responded, "This one sounds most interesting. Why did you save it until the end?"

He asked, "What's the definition of *plural*?"

I responded, "Yeah, it's . . . when there is more than one in a situation."

He replied, "Good. Close enough. Now, what do you think when I say the term *plural executive*?"

I answered, "More than one governor?"

He nodded his head in concurrence and spoke: "Well, Champ, we here in Texas have one true governor—that's me—but the executive branch is plural in that the power of the executive is spread across several individually elected offices that may act independently of my wishes, to be as aligned as possible with the view of citizens or some other calling. That's where you go to next. Go down to the grill in the extension, get a snack, and then meet the lieutenant governor in the main rotunda. Anything else before you go?"

I could only reply, "Nope, thanks for the good show!"

Abbott concluded, "Here's a good metaphor for you, using one of my favorite movie trilogies, the Austin Powers film saga, and two of its main characters, Dr. Evil and Mini-Me. Dr. Evil, at the beginning of the second film, gets a clone. The problem is, the clone is a miniature version of himself. People think that the clone has just as much power as Dr. Evil, but he is just another mindless drone of the leader who must comply or face the leader's wrath. They might look alike, but they are vastly different. Or, more easily put, the president and I may both wear suits and rule a land territory, and though my territory is a part of the president's, we do not rule equally. I am weak, and the president is strong."

After leaving Abbott's office and on the way down to the grill, I could only wince at the look on his face when Abbott told me about his situation in the executive branch in Texas. I remembered our conversation from yesterday, when he said to me that when out of the state he loses what authority he has, and I realized that, even though he's back home, there is not that much power to wield, outside of his veto when the legislature is in session. Beyond that, I could only think that being governor sounded fun, but the overall duties as head of government seemed a little dull in the grand scheme of things; still, they are essential items to consider, like being the head of state. Overall, I felt that a governor is the real leader of

---

32    https://gov.texas.gov/organization/appointments

the state but is often shackled by rules that are designed to weaken him or her. After what I learned with Dr. Davis a while back, it made sense, but I wondered how this could impact the future of the state if the governor cannot lead effectively.

---

**QUESTIONS TO CONSIDER** REGARDING THE GOVERNOR OF TEXAS:

1. The first main topic of the chapter discusses the Governor's Mansion. Please identify one thing you learned about the Governor's Mansion, state how that object relates to your life, and explain why, in detail.
2. The second main topic of the chapter discusses the minimum qualifications necessary to serve as governor. Please identify what those minimum qualifications are, state the qualifications you meet, and explain whether you may run for governor.
3. The third main topic of the chapter discusses the extent of options that the governor has to act with on behalf of the state. Please indicate what that limit is, describe a similar odd rule from your life, and explain how the two compare, in detail.
4. The fourth main topic of the chapter discusses the legislative powers of the governor. Please identify what those powers are, the one most like how you make changes in your life, and why, in detail.
5. The fifth main topic of the chapter discusses the executive powers of the governor. Please identify the two types of executive powers, give examples of those powers, identify the set you feel is more powerful, and explain why, in detail.
6. The final main topic of the chapter discusses the concept of a plural executive. Please define what is meant by a plural executive, state how that concept relates to your life, and explain how it relates, in detail.

---

## FIGURE CREDITS

Fig. 18.6: Source: https://commons.wikimedia.org/wiki/File:The_Library_in_the_southeast_corner_of_the_original_portion_of_the_Texas_Governor%27s_Mansion_in_Austin,_the_capital_of_Texas_LCCN2014632018.tif.

Fig. 18.7: Source: https://commons.wikimedia.org/wiki/File:The_State_Dining_Room,_looking_towards_the_west_wall_of_the_Texas_Governor%27s_Mansion_in_Austin,_the_capital_of_Texas_LCCN2014632019.tif.

Fig. 18.8: Source: https://commons.wikimedia.org/wiki/File:The_Conservatory,_part_of_the_1914_addition_on_the_west_side_of_the_Texas_Governor%27s_Mansion_in_Austin,_the_capital_of_Texas_LCCN2014632028.tif.

Fig. 18.9: Source: https://commons.wikimedia.org/wiki/File:Warren_commission_cover.jpg.

Fig. 18.10: Copyright © by Beyond My Ken (CC BY-SA 4.0) at https://commons.wikimedia.org/wiki/File:Helicopter_landing_E_34th_St_heliport_NYC.jpg.

Fig. 18.11: Copyright © by Tdorante10 (CC BY-SA 4.0) at https://commons.wikimedia.org/wiki/File:52nd_St_11th_Av_td_(2019-01-03)_04_-_The_Daily_Show_Studio_(733_11th_Avenue).jpg.

Fig. 18.12: Copyright © by Javitscenter (CC BY-SA 4.0) at https://commons.wikimedia.org/wiki/File:Mainphoto_javitscenter.png.

Fig. 18.13: Source: https://commons.wikimedia.org/wiki/File:Hurricane_Harvey_Response_(36806293711).jpg.

# Chapter 19

# The Executive Branch Beyond the Governor

## Texas Higher Education Coordinating Board ACGMSLOs

*For Federal Government 2305: Upon successful completion of reading the book and taking the associated course, students will be able to do the following:*

1. Explain the origin and development of constitutional democracy in the United States
2. **Demonstrate knowledge of the federal system**
3. **Describe separation of powers and checks and balances in both theory and practice**
4. **Demonstrate knowledge of the legislative, executive, and judicial branches of the federal government**
5. Evaluate the role of public opinion, interest groups, and political parties in the political system
6. Analyze the election process
7. **Describe the rights and responsibilities of citizens**
8. **Analyze issues and policies in US politics**

*For Texas Government 2306: Upon successful completion of reading the book and taking the associated course, students will be able to do the following:*

1. Explain the origin and development of the Texas Constitution
2. **Describe state and local political systems and their relationship with the federal government**
3. **Describe separation of powers and checks and balances in both theory and practice in Texas**
4. **Demonstrate knowledge of the legislative, executive, and judicial branches of Texas government**
5. Evaluate the role of public opinion, interest groups, and political parties in Texas
6. Analyze the state and local election process
7. **Identify the rights and responsibilities of citizens**
8. **Analyze issues, policies, and the political culture of Texas**

# Bureaucracy and Bureaucrats

Continuing from where I left off yesterday, early this morning I was in the middle of transitioning from the guidance on government from the governor to that of the lieutenant governor, who was to advise me of what occurs in the executive branch of government beyond that which is under the direct control of the governor. From what I remember about that sector of the government, one of the most common things I hear other people complain about during the day is how the government is so often stupid, inefficient, and only capable of messing up everything that was working fine for everyone in the first place. Therefore, the goal for today was to learn about the people who were supposedly responsible for all that proposed inefficient activity, at least those who primarily function at the state level. Just before 9:00 a.m., with a morning snack in hand, I found myself entering the main floor of the capitol rotunda and looking at the portraits of past governors (figure 19.1), the massive seals on the floor, and the robust star on the underside of the rotunda's dome again. A short while later, Lieutenant Governor Dan Patrick tapped me on the shoulder from behind, and in a smooth voice I swore would be perfect for the radio asked, "Champ, good to see you again. How are you?"

FIGURE 19.1 Texas Governor Potrait's in the Main Rotunda

I immediately replied, "Yes, sir. Good morning! Quite well, actually!"

We shook hands and started walking toward the senate chamber floor. On the way, he asked what I had learned from Governor Abbott about the executive branch of Texas. I responded briefly, "The executive branch is plural, in that the power of the executive is spread across several individually elected offices that may act independently of the governor's wishes to be as aligned as possible with the view of citizens or some other calling. And how this impacts his job, of course."

Patrick responded, "Very good. The questions are, though: What are those other officials in charge of overseeing? Who are they? And, my favorite, what are they representative of in provision of services? That is what we will be exploring today, but for now, it's time to introduce a key term, *bureaucracy*, the system of nonelected officials administering government policies and programs,[1] or as I like to joke in all seriousness, based on the roots of the term,

---

1   https://www.vocabulary.com/dictionary/bureaucracy

a governing system that is 'the form of rule by offices and desks!' You see, the word *bureau* is French for "desk" or "office," which when you combine it with the Greek word *kratos* (or κράτος in Cyrillic), meaning "rule" or "political power," you get bureaucracy."

I almost fell on the floor when I heard that, but then I asked, "What do you mean by non-elected officials?"

Patrick furthered, "I am an elected official since I had to win election to obtain my position in the government. In reality, the overwhelming majority of people working for the government simply had to pass an interview with their supervisor. The hired guns, so to speak, range from the high school teachers you spent the last four years with, to people building the roads you drove on to get here (or at least those who were supervising what the contractor was actually building in some cases), inspectors making sure that restaurants have clean kitchens, if filling stations are actually giving you the amount of fuel you are paying for, police officers writing you a speeding ticket, the driver of the buses you took to school, and the people you want to keep an eye out for in November and December: game wardens. The list goes on and on."

I remarked, "So what do they all have in common?"

After thinking for a second, Patrick stated, "They are all colloquially referred to as bureaucrats or persons with a position in the government that implement a policy or program created by the other legislators and myself, or some other lawmaking assembly such as a district school board. Remember, the state has a unitary government structure, and the unit with all the power in the state is the legislature. What we tell those agencies to do is practically sacred, and the agencies are expected to act within the bounds of the power that we grant them or face the Sunset Commission and be shut down."

By the time we were done with that short conversation, and after a brief pause in our discussions, we had walked up the stairs to the second floor and down the hall, and we arrived on the floor of the senate—of which Patrick was the presiding officer, remembering from my experience a few days prior. Once inside the chamber and figuring we would just be talking at some of the desks, I grabbed the one closest to the front of the room after going over the railing. Looking at me quizzically from his chair at the podium, after walking on, he murmured, "Are you coming?"

I replied, "Yes, sir, but where are we going?"

He spoke coolly in that radio voice again. "My chambers, of course! We must go through this small passageway to the office space behind my desk. Governor Abbott's office here is much more available to the public, while mine is a bit more off the beaten track."

I sprang to my feet and followed along quickly. What I saw when I entered the hallway was outstanding. At one end of the hall, a section of the modern plaster wall has been masterfully kept open for any of the visitors to this select part of the building to see—under a

FIGURE 19.2   Viewhole of the Original Limestone Interior of the Texas State Capital Building

glass panel, of course—a piece of the original interior limestone wall that was covered during the last renovations in the 1980s and 1990s (figure 19.2). On the other end was the entrance to the lieutenant governor's reception room, known informally as the Great Room. This space, Patrick advised, "had," at least in his opinion, "some of the best art in the capitol, which includes oil paintings by Julian Onderdonk and Frank Reaugh, the so-called Texas version of famed American painter Frederic Remington."

Once seated on the Great Room's original couches—which were from the 1880s, when the room served as an apartment for the lieutenant governor—he started in on essential factoids to know about the state's bureaucracy after I asked, "Why should I care about the bureaucracy?"

He replied, "Simply put, the people in these governing agencies—in their chairs, behind their desks—are the most common form of interaction by people with the government. This circumstance is due to people needing to go to the court system no more than a few times in their life for a traffic ticket or two and maybe a divorce, while even fewer people than that will ever visit their legislator, much less the capitol building we are in now. What people do, though, constantly in their lives is obtain licenses of all kinds, such as the driver's license from the Department of Public Safety[2] in your pocket, apply to attend college at Texas A&M,[3] purchase power from the Lower Colorado River Authority,[4] and visit state parks operated by Texas Parks and Wildlife,[5] all departments that are owned and operated by the state of Texas."

I asked, "So where does the bureaucracy exist?"

---

2   https://www.dps.texas.gov
3   https://www.tamu.edu
4   https://www.lcra.org/Pages/default.aspx
5   https://tpwd.texas.gov

He remarked, "The main place of the bureaucracy is in the executive branch, but the judicial and legislative branches do have their own; they just happen to pale in comparison to that of the executive bureaucracy concerning size and scope of authority."

## A Plural Executive

I asked, "How would you compare the federal bureaucracy to that of the Texas bureaucracy?"

In response, he eventually brought up one of the best analogies I had ever heard while getting back to what Abbott had mentioned early in the morning, but first, he asked, "What is a CEO?"

I chimed in, "The chief executive officer of a business."

He went on, "Very good. Let's now assume that the federal and state bureaucracies are both large nonprofit businesses. The question is, though, who is the CEO of the federal government?"

I replied, "The president."

He continued, "Very good, and why is this?"

I responded, "Based on what Governor Abbott said, the people working for the federal government—the agency heads, at least—all get their jobs from him or her, alongside instructions on how they are supposed to enforce the regulations entrusted to them. This seemingly centralized system keeps those bureaucrats in lockstep on where to go with their agencies' policy decisions and implementations, or, I assume, they face the ax."[6]

He furthered, "You know your stuff. So now, who is the CEO of the Texas bureaucracy?"

I could only say, "Once again, after my conversation with Governor Abbott yesterday, I don't believe there is a true one. Is there one?"

He wrapped up this portion of the conversation by using a series of excellent metaphors. "I would say that the CEO of the Texas bureaucracy is like an Error 404 message on your computer; whatever it was you were looking for does not exist. Essentially, there is no central figurehead, or CEO, in the state. You must think of the state's bureaucracy like that of a Hydra from Greek mythology[7] (figure 19.3). Together, the different agency heads represent the various pieces of the state bureaucracy, but because they have their own minds and desires, and due to their elected positions, they can act however they please, so long as they keep the citizens holding them accountable happy in most situations. The issue is, the heads

6    Denise Lu and Karen Yourish, "The Turnover at the Top of the Trump Administration Is Unprecedented," *New York Times*, March 17, 2018, https://www.nytimes.com/interactive/2018/03/16/us/politics/all-the-major-firings-and-resignations-in-trump-administration.html.

7    https://www.britannica.com/topic/Hydra-Greek-mythology

FIGURE 19.3 Francisco de Zurbarán: Struggle of Hercules with the Hydra of Lerna (1634).

are still connected to the same body. Accordingly, the heads end up pulling the state in multiple directions at the same time, especially when, say, the governor is of one party, but the lieutenant governor or other elected officials are not, leading to chaos in the statehouse. The effect that this has on state governance is akin to that of the government being driven by a chicken with its head cut off, with no common goal for the direction of the state, going around in different directions, unlike what you have with the bureaucracy at the federal level, most of the time."

I chimed in, "Could you cite an example of that chicken-without-a-head comparison?"

Putting back on his radio voice, Patrick went on. "Sure. In Texas, when the agency heads are all the same party, as they have been since 2002, we can get programs going very quickly without much fuss. Granted, that direction still may not be all that good either way, depending on the issue and your viewpoint. For example, look at the procurement of top-notch college football in the state. Every year from 1915 to 2011, plus 22 nonconcurrent years before that, the Aggies of Texas A&M played the Longhorns of Texas University in what is considered one of the biggest rivalries on the gridiron, if not all of sports. The rivalry took place on Thanksgiving Day weekend and often considered bigger than the main holiday itself. This was made possible due to the teams often being found in the same athletic conference, the Southwest and the Big 12 Conferences amongst others. The issue is, over the years Texas grew out of the shadows on a national level leaving the Aggies behind. The Longhorn Network through ESPN didn't really help as opposed to a conferencewide network for all school in the Big 12. In light of these events, the Aggies left the conference for the Southeastern Conference or SEC for short in most places in protest, leaving us where we are today; the only thing keeping the two from playing each other is an unwillingness to play one another[8]. Both universities are overseen by their respective board of regents that need to approve of the contracts to an extent that keep the two apart despite the whole state

---

8    Thompson, Cole. "Texas A&M vs. Texas: The Non-Existent Thanksgiving Tradition." Sports Illustrated. AllAggies, November 28, 2019. https://www.si.com/college/tamu/football/ texas-a-m-vesus-texas-the-non-existent-thanksgiving-tradition.

more likely than not wanting them to play. Whoever capitulates first could be seen as weak, so nobody takes the steps needed to be taken to endeavored. More importantly, because they are an independent state-governing agencies, their decisions stand and go against what the governor might advocate with nothing he or she could about it despite public calls by the governor to do so which happen regularly.[9] I think a state bill is regularly tried to be passed to make the game happen.[10] When they are all not the same party, the direction of the state will get stretched in different directions, big time, at least in football. Get the state agencies led by Democrats and the governorship led by a Republican the different directions will go statewide up and down the governing spectrum."

## Major State Agencies

In breaking the silence from Patrick's concluding remark on state versus federal bureaucracy, I summarized that we had compared the state and national administrations alongside the impact of both setups, defined the term *bureaucracy*, and finally looked at basic examples of what typical bureaucratic tasks are. I realized that it would be wise to learn how the agencies can be organized. Therefore, I asked, "How would you classify or organize the various state agencies and their figureheads?"

He replied, "That's easy. First is whether the agency is headed by an individual or a commission of various sizes, how the agency head obtains their job (which could be elected, appointed, or ex officio), and finally, what level of the government the group falls into—local or state."

In my head, and nodding outwardly, this seemed like a rather simple classification method to comprehend. With that in mind, the next logical step to go down was to learn about the various positions leading the state bureaucracy. In hopes of keeping everything as simple as possible, I requested that Patrick continue our conversation by telling me about the different executive branch officials of the state.

In response, he first noted, "The current set of individual elected officials each serve four-year terms, with the current terms running from January of 2015 to January of 2019, and like Governor Abbott told you earlier this week, they face no term limits, with full governing

9    Lauren McGaughy and Robert T. Garrett. "Texas Gov. Greg Abbott Pushes Revival of the Longhorns vs. Aggies Football Rivalry." Dallas News. The Dallas Morning News, August 23, 2019. https://www.dallasnews.com/news/politics/2019/02/05/texas-gov-greg-abbott-pushes-revival-of-the-longhorns-vs-aggies-football-rivalry/.

10   Cassandra Pollock,. "State Lawmaker Files Bill to Require Annual Football Game between UT and Texas A&M." The Texas Tribune, November 27, 2018. https://www.texastribune.org/2018/11/27/state-lawmaker-files-bill-require-annual-game-between-ut-and-m/.

authority in all cases under their helm. Most importantly though, most positions are easily comparable in function to many positions in general society."

That last bit helped explain a lot of the metaphors to come. For example, he showed how the Texas Attorney General[11] is essentially the state's lawyer, permanently held on retainer with responsibilities to represent the state in court when being sued in a case, alongside advising the governor and other officials on the legality of legislation or other pending actions and issues and investigating some activities of governing officials for maleficent behavior. He related the Texas General Land Office Commissioner[12] to be the state's personal full-time real estate agent, as this person has the authority to lease out public lands for drilling, ranching, or wind turbines, among many other purposes; manage the property in general; and collect rent on the leases so that the Texas Permanent School Fund[13] (which he or she also leads) gets funded. Third, the state's comptroller of public accounts[14] serves as the state's accountant, whose primary responsibility is to monitor state spending and revenues to ensure that a state budget deficit or bankruptcy filing is avoided at all costs. The final position was the agriculture commissioner,[15] leader of the Department of Agriculture, who functions like that of a property developer for the state due to his or her responsibilities of monitoring and ensuring the most bountiful harvest and livestock quality possible inside the state borders, alongside (via the consumer protection divisions) regulating items like grocery store scales and gasoline pumps to ensure accurate weights and measures so that you get what you actually pay for at the store in the same way that a property developer ensures the most profitable development of a section or parcel of land.

In moving on from elected officials to individual appointment positions, Patrick mentioned that the governor makes around 3,000 appointments during a typical four-year term; those appointees can only take office after being approved by the Senate for various terms, based on the position.[16] In showing the list of what positions the governor gets to appoint, Patrick brought out his smartphone, went to the governor's website, and came up with an impressive record.[17] The only thing, though, that stood out was that most of the positions listed seemed low on the totem pole of importance, as most were to the state board of licensing for this or that profession, or the board of regents for a university system, and so on. In hearing me mumble this, Patrick stated, "The only time Governor Abbott gets to appoint a

---

11    https://texasattorneygeneral.gov
12    http://www.glo.texas.gov/index.html
13    https://tea.texas.gov/psf
14    https://comptroller.texas.gov
15    https://www.texasagriculture.gov/About/CommissionerMiller.aspx
16    http://governor.state.tx.us/appointments
17    http://governor.state.tx.us/appointments/positions

high-level official is for any non-lawmaking office, like that of a state Supreme Court justice, which can only occur when the prior officeholder leaves the position early or dies in office; the governor accordingly gets to appoint someone to fill in for the remainder of their term."[18]

The first position he brought up here was the Texas secretary of state,[19] which he compared to being the state's human resources manager. This comparison was used due to this position being responsible for protecting the state seal and constitution, administering the Texas election code to serve as the chief election officer, and maintaining public filings in a right-hand-person kind of sense. Also, he mentioned that this is the final position that makes up the official leadership of the executive department, putting this position on par with the governor, lieutenant governor, attorney general, comptroller, and general land office commissioner, the difference being that this is the only one of the leading six of the plural executive system in Texas who is appointed.

Then he advised that all the individuals we were going to talk about going forward are agency heads in the executive branch, but not leaders of it. For example, he brought up the Texas adjutant general,[20] who leads the state and National Guard via the state's military department, serving as the leading military official, or general, in this case. Another example he mentioned here was that of the Health and Human Services commissioner,[21] who functions as the state's lead social worker due to his or her responsibility to enforce the various aid and welfare programs offered by the state.

Moving on, he talked about the various boards and commissions of the state. He noted that the terms vary by the board; they may function as an advisor to the executive leaders on prescribed items or in an official governing capacity; have anywhere from 3 to 16 members; and can be wholly elected, appointed, or both. The first agency he mentioned here seemed the most important, due to what is regulated by it. This first group was known as the Texas Railroad Commission,[22] so called because it was initially tasked with monitoring the railroads in the state back in 1891, but as the railroad regulatory functions were taken over by the federal government and the Federal Railroad Administration,[23] the commission moved to focus more specifically on its secondary role: regulating the oil, gas, surface coal production, mining, piping, and gas utility industries for safety and production compliance to provide similar services to that of a landman. He also mentioned here that you could go

---

18    Patrick Svitek, "Gov. Greg Abbott to Appoint General Counsel to Texas Supreme Court," *Texas Tribune*, November 27, 2017, https://www.texastribune.org/2017/11/27/abbott-appoint-general-counsel-replace-willett.

19    https://www.sos.state.tx.us

20    https://tmd.texas.gov/office-of-the-adjutant-general

21    https://hhs.texas.gov

22    http://www.rrc.state.tx.us

23    https://www.fra.dot.gov/Page/P0001

to the commission's website and see on a GIS app where every single well has been drilled in the state[24] (figure 19.4). This commission was noted to have three commissioners, who are all elected to staggered six-year terms of office.

Another group that he mentioned in this category was the State Board of Education,[25] which leads the Texas Education Agency to function as the state's lead educator, or teacher, due to its primary job of setting curriculum standards, reviewing and adopting instructional materials, establishing graduation requirements, and appointing board members to military reservations and special school districts. This board was shown to have 15 elected members who each represent a different district of the state, along with one who is appointed by the governor to serve as the education commissioner and chair of the board. A final entity he mentioned for this category was the Texas Commission on Environmental Quality,[26] which functions as the state's version of the federal Environmental Protection Agency,[27] or as he surmised coolly, "environmentalist," due to its responsibility for protecting the state's public health and natural resources (consistent with sustainable economic development practices) to achieve the goals of clean air, water, and proper disposal of waste. I thought of the television show *Captain Planet and the Planeteers* at this point and its work in the early 1990s to better the environment.[28] This board was shown to have three commissioners who are appointed by the governor to lead staggered six-year terms of office, with a two-term maximum limit. It then got a bit weird on two fronts.

Patrick remarked, "What comes to mind when I say the term *ex officio*?"

I replied, "Getting kicked out of office?"

He shrugged, "No, not even close. Let's put it like this: Have you ever gone and done one thing somewhere only to realize that, since you were already there, you might as well do an additional thing that needs to be done nearby?"

I winced. "No, nothing comes to mind. I try to plan out things to avoid being surprised like that. I think Governor Abbott may have mentioned the term a few days ago, though. However, the girl I'm going out with that I met a few weeks ago went to a salon for a facial, and decided that since she was already there, she should get her nails done as well. Is that the same concept?"

He went on. "I do believe that is a perfect example. She went in to accomplish one task, did the task, and proceeded to do another while there, just because. For a governmental example

---

24  http://wwwgisp.rrc.state.tx.us/GISViewer2
25  https://tea.texas.gov/About_TEA/Leadership/State_Board_of_Education/SBOE_-_State_Board_of_Education
26  https://www.tceq.texas.gov
27  https://www.epa.gov
28  https://en.wikipedia.org/wiki/Captain_Planet_and_the_Planeteers

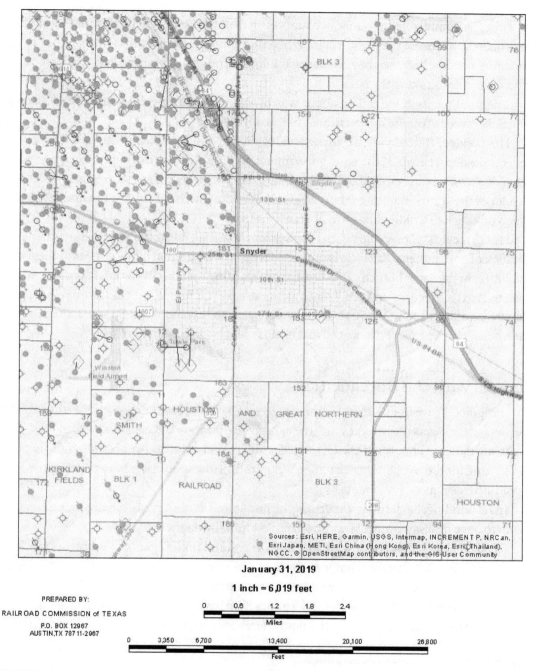

**January 31, 2019**

**1 inch = 6,019 feet**

PREPARED BY:

RAILROAD COMMISSION of TEXAS

P.O. BOX 12967
AUSTIN,TX 78711-2967

0   0.6   1.2   1.8   2.4
Miles

0   3,350   6,700   13,400   20,100   26,800
Feet

FIGURE 19.4   Overview of Oil and Gas Wells near Snyder, Texas

of this, the comptroller of public accounts is also on the Texas Racing Commission[29] just because they became the comptroller. When that commission is called to order, they function like a bookie because they regulate gambling at the greyhound and horse race tracks in the state, minus taking the bets."

The final position we talked about was probably the funniest. Lieutenant Governor Patrick[30] asked, "Where do you think I fit into all of this?"

I responded, "I would say, as you said yourself earlier, that you are an official leader of the executive department of the state government and that you are in a super-ex-officio position due to you being elected to help lead the executive branch, yet you are also the official leader of the state senate as part of the legislative branch. Also, I'll come out and say it, you keep talking like a radio talk-show host; why is that?"

He corrected, "Close. The official term is *hybrid official*, due to serving in more than one branch of government. *Ex officio* is only used when the additional office or position/responsibility is in the same branch of government. Regarding that talk-show host question, while elected to the executive branch, I, once again, in case you forgot, get paid like a regular legislator, and accordingly, I have to keep my day job as the owner of a radio station and my gig as a conservative talk-show host to make ends meet back in Houston."[31]

## Issues with the Bureaucracy

At this point, I gave a once-over to my notes to see that I had accurately classified the various leaders of the Texas bureaucracy into the appropriate positions. What stood out, though, was that we had not yet covered the characteristics[32] of and controls over bureaucratic action. In getting him to explain more on this, I inquired, "How should the bureaucrats act when making decisions or statements?"

In responding, he didn't say anything; he just stared at me. I pushed more for an answer, only to have him say, eventually, "So what did I initially do there?"

I said, in a cursed pitch, "You did nothing. You didn't take a side. You simply sat there."

He exclaimed, "Exactly! That is the role of a bureaucrat: to remain neutral as much as possible, only enforce the law as written. The comptroller does not decide what we should spend our tax revenues on, but only determines if we have the money to spend on something concocted by the legislature. The attorney general does not write policy, but only determines

29  http://www.txrc.texas.gov
30  https://www.ltgov.state.tx.us
31  http://ksevradio.com
32  Max Weber, *Theory of Social and Economic Organization* (New York: Oxford University Press, 1947).

if the actions being taken in the name of a policy and government are legal. They all remain neutral; to become partisan is the role of the governor or legislators, like me."

I then pushed for a second way they should act. In response, Patrick added, "Agencies of the state are nonhierarchical, leaving no one agency ranked higher than another, unless you are including college football and how the Aggies and Longhorns are in a tiff about who is better and why their respective universities, which are also state agencies, won't play each other.[33] Essentially, they should act as equals. While there is certainly hierarchy within agencies, the agencies are all kings of their domains, outside the influences of how their leaders obtain office (either by election or gubernatorial appointment), but even then, the governor has no further legal authority over them, and citizens aren't likely to get their guns and forcibly remove them from office as they did with Governor Davis back in 1874 when he refused to leave after being ousted in an election.[34] The problem with everyone being equal is that the agencies still have to fight for best pickings come appropriations season (January to May in odd-ending years when the legislature is in session), which leads to problems, like positioning themselves to be the most attractive, in all senses, candidate."

With those first two factors in mind, I went on. "Do the agency leaders need to be experts in their positions?"

After a minute or two of thinking, a response came: "In getting the most efficient and smoothly running operation, the leaders should be as much of an expert as physically possible—hopefully with some managerial experience. The issue is that nowhere does it state that the attorney general needs to have passed the bar exam or the comptroller be a certified public accountant.[35] However, lower-ranking officials, those practicing, but not leading, in an agency—like an engineer working for the Department of Transportation—must meet certain qualifications, like being a professional (i.e., certified) engineer, to obtain employment in the agency. Accordingly, the less professional an agency official is, the higher you get in the food chain; although, while the governor does make several political appointments, most are people who are truly certified to lead the agency they're nominated for, like a licensed nurse for the Board of Nursing Examiners. Therefore, the visionaries, the leader, and the professionals are the workers. The political appointees, or people hired due

---

33    Jake Trotter, "Aggies on Longhorns' Proposal: 'We're Booked 10 Years Out,'" ESPN, August 22, 2018, http://www.espn.com/college-football/story/_/id/24448690/texas-aggies-declined-texas-longhorn-series-renewal-proposal.

34    *Texas Landmarks and Legacies*, "Outgoing Governor Refuses to Leave. Capitol Armed," January 14, 1874, http://howdyyall.com/Texas/TodaysNews/index.cfm?GetItem=1082.

35    https://www.sos.state.tx.us/elections/candidates/guide/qualifications.shtml

to them donating during campaign season, are typically limited to areas that are advisory or not important to running the state."

I inquired, "What controls the bureaucracy?

He put out his hands to stop me and said, "Hold on there, cowboy. There are plenty of controls, and we'll get to them, but we need to cover the last characteristic, and probably the only real concern—the size of the bureaucracy. Remember, each piece of legislation passed in the legislature will impact state or local entities, as the agencies are the ones responsible in some form or fashion for implementing said policies. Therefore, whenever we act to create something, we must consider what impact it will have on the size of government. As we are Texans, we typically prefer a smaller, limited government. The problem is, every time we create a new agency, people must be hired in some form or fashion to run the entity and produce the specifics of the law, while if just a new policy is passed, someone at an existing agency must be hired or given responsibility for getting the policy enforced."

In my head, while Patrick was talking, something did not sound right. When he said *size*, the term felt a bit broad. I interrupted, "Would you please further define what you mean by *size*?"

He looked at me, flustered, and remarked, "Well, when you say *size*, two things come to mind: the actual number of employees on the staff of the government and the actual number of agencies found. For the number of employees, you need to look at the state auditor's website.[36] This group keeps track of the average number of full-time equivalent employees on the state payroll per fiscal year in the state. Per their fiscal year 2017 Summary Report on Full-Time Equivalent (FTE) Employees, we had on average during the year 327,015.7 FTE employees in state agencies and higher education institutions, which is up from 323,426.3 in the fiscal year 2016—an increase of 3,589.4, or about 1.1 percent.[37] From those totals, roughly 54 percent were in higher education in FY 2016 and FY 2017,[38] and some people say we don't put a lot of resources in education in the state—yeah, right. That is a lot of people to hire, fire, and retain. Compared to the state population—using the 28,304,000 in the calendar year 2017, and the 27,900,000 in CY 2016 from the US Census Bureau population estimates[39]—you get roughly 1.15 percent of the population being employed by the state in a given year. It gets scary when you add in employees of local government and lower education schools, but that is a topic for another day. For the number of agencies, we need to

---

36    https://www.sao.texas.gov
37    State of Texas, State Auditor's Office, "A Summary Report on Full-Time Equivalent State Employees for Fiscal Year 2017." Report No. 18-702, State Auditor's Office, Austin, December 2017, http://www.sao.texas.gov/Reports/Main/18-702.pdf.
38    Ibid.
39    https://www.census.gov/quickfacts/tx

look at the Texas State Library and Archives Commission's website[40] for the list; now this is inclusive of legislative and judicial entities, but minus agencies that have been decommissioned. There are 179 state agencies (assuming all University of Texas campuses and the like are the same) employing 328,000 state workers to serve the 28,304,000 citizens, alongside anybody passing through when applicable."

In furthering this last characteristic and the primary concern, I proposed that he discuss what the state does to reduce the size. He responded dutifully, "Remember, we are just talking today about the state bureaucracy, not federal or local. In reducing the size of the government, three primary paths are available, each with their downsides. First, we can privatize services. This option occurs when we hire a private company to provide the service, while we still pay for it. This option can be as simple as firing our in-house cleaners and replacing them with a professional cleaning service or as complex as hiring the Corrections Corporation of America to build, staff, and operate an entire prison on our behalf; they have ten prisons or processing facilities in the state.[41] The downside here is that the private companies can act as leeches on the system, becoming dependent on us for business, and when we no longer need the service, we cancel the contract, putting a lot of people out of work; that could make us look bad. Second, we can make local government agencies do the actions that we used to do by shifting the responsibility to them. Once again, we create them and still have a say in what they can and cannot do, much like a helicopter parent who never goes away, even after their kids turn 18. The problem is that the locals may not be able to fully support the program fiscally or socially, leaving them in a bind and the services suffering."

I interjected, "Like how county clerks keep track of property and other important records for y'all?"

Patrick concluded, "Exactly! Now, finally, my favorite as a Tea Partier, we can kill off various agencies, especially ones that have lived beyond their usefulness, like superfluous or failing school districts. The only issue here is the quality of services may go down, as users may have to travel further for the use of services, or those using it will now have to go without if no other alternative is easily found. Overall, though, as the size of government increases, people typically become more dependent on those services. The problem is, the size of government cannot increase forever and take over everything, as the source of government revenue is taxes. If there is nothing left to tax, much like a Ponzi scheme not being

---

40   https://www.tsl.texas.gov/apps/lrs/agencies/index.html

41   Texas Prison Bid'ness, "CoreCivic (formerly CCA)," accessed March 20, 2019, http://www.texasprisonbidness.org/company/corecivic-formerly-cca; CoreCivic, "Who We Are," accessed March 20, 2019, http://jobs.corecivic.com/page/show/who-we-are.

able to get new investors, the system falls apart. Therefore, you want to keep government small and the private sector looking elsewhere for business as much as possible to keep tax revenue streams flowing."

## Controls over the Bureaucracy

Patrick reached over for his office phone and made a call. Following this, with a wave of his hand, he ushered me to follow him. We walked back over to the rotunda's second-floor bal-

FIGURE 19.5    Texas State Capitol Building

cony. Waiting for us there was a server from the Capitol Grille with lunch for us. Time flew this morning, kind of funny since the bureaucracy is typically believed to move slowly. We did not speak much on the way, but I could tell that for the last part (the controls I had requested earlier), he had something special in mind. It was then that Patrick announced, like the disc jockey that he is, "Let's go on over to the top of the dome and the upper balcony just below the *Goddess of Liberty*. It's a good place to talk about the controls over the bureaucracy, as you can see all of them from there (figure 19.5). And eat lunch, of course."

I replied, "We can't. My dad and I tried to go up there earlier this week, and it was blocked off."

He responded, "Good news. Maintenance fixed the leak last night. It's open! For us at least."

We left for the upper balcony. After hiking up the two additional floors of stairs that seemed like much more, we arrived at the landing of the fourth floor. Since we came up the east side, we had to walk around the much smaller radial rotunda balcony. Then we arrived at the southwestern corner. Placed here was a narrow stairwell that took us up to the highest part (a fifth-floor balcony, you could say) of the dome's underside. Then we walked over to a spiral staircase that took us up to a hatch that led us onto the small outdoor balcony under the *Goddess of Liberty* statue's pedestal. The view was fantastic, albeit a bit breezy.

We proceeded to take the first few bites out of our burgers and made small talk about his gig as a talk-show host. I liked how he emphasized that he needed to prepare a lot beforehand, even though the show is live. Then we adjusted places as he positioned me to look due north on the horizon. I questioned, "How does standing out on this balcony in the heat help the process of learning about what controls the bureaucracy?"

He smiled. "Simple. You technically can see them all from here."

I responded, before taking another bite of my cheeseburger afterward, "Prove it!"

Going ahead full blast, he said, "I'll get there when we get there, but first, we have to put everything into perspective. Another question, what do bureaucrats primarily do?"

I replied, "I would say enforce the laws that those in the legislature craft."

He replied, "Very good. Now, some decisions we as the government make are perceived as bad by the public en masse, good by the public en masse, or good and bad at the same time, depending on your perspective. How people can react is where each of the controls lies. For example, colleges and universities can set their admission standards. Set them too high, and without enough demand for the school by people who can meet those high standards, enrollment will falter, and since schools get funding based on enrollment, there goes your support, and your school along with it, eventually. With that in mind, the first control is something called clientele groups. These are the entities that are directly affected by the policies passed in the legislature and who face regulation by the entities created or get funding from them in one form or another. If the groups like what the agency is doing, they stay in lockstep and keep on with their day-to-day lives, donating once or twice around election time to our campaigns, if applicable. If they don't like the direction of rules created by the agency, watch out for protests and money—actual forms of support, in this case— you received in the past going elsewhere. One example of this that you can see from here if you look about 5 or 6 miles dead ahead is the Texas Alliance for Life building,[42] if only Royal-Memorial Stadium[43] would move, of course. This group is antiabortion and will stick everything into the game to stop any support for abortion by the government from going forward like they were playing a massive game of hokey pokey. You try to give more funding to Planned Parenthood[44] from state funds, and they will throw a fit at the agency—Health and Human Services,[45] most likely—and will work to get the agency killed off or at least their lead administrators fired. Remember the abortion bill debate that was filibustered by Senator Wendy Davis a while back; protests from pro- and antiabortion groups caused a riot in the rotunda below our feet."[46]

I replied, "So clientele groups are essentially special interests who want to see policy get passed in their favor, or else."

42   https://www.texasallianceforlife.org
43   University of Texas Athletics, "Darrell K Royal—Texas Memorial Stadium at Joe Jamail Field," accessed March 20, 2019, https://texassports.com/sports/2013/7/24/facilities_0724133148.aspx.
44   https://www.plannedparenthood.org
45   http://www.hhsc.state.tx.us
46   Helen Davidson, "Texas Abortion Bill Defeated by Wendy Davis Filibuster and Public Protest," *Guardian*, June 26, 2013,. https://www.theguardian.com/world/2013/jun/26/texas-abortion-vote-defeated-deadline-wendy-davis.

He responded, "You got it. For the next control, we must turn clockwise to the east. Let's turn."

After shifting positions again, we were looking down on the roof of the senate chamber. Patrick spoke up: "What happens down there in the senate, and on the opposite side in the house, that may impact the bureaucracy?"

I blubbered, "You pass laws that fund the agencies or give money to private entities to provide services for you?"

He went on, "Very good. Those laws are called appropriations bills. Though, more important to remember, the more the agencies keep us happy in the chamber, the more likely we are to support them monetarily when it comes budget season. Legislative support is key to the agencies' future. For this control, you need to consider that the laws passed by the legislature are not the final version of a policy. The agencies tasked with enforcement create many of the rules that go along with the legislation. Now let's go look to the south."

Once repositioned, Patrick continued, "Who lives in that little white house across the street?"

I responded, "Governor Abbott?"

He replied, "What control does he have regarding financing?"

I noted, "He gets to approve of the appropriations, but more importantly, he can veto entire bills, or just portions of them, that could kill funding for the whole of an agency. This result is what happened to the financing for the Travis County district attorney (DA) and the Public Accountability Office after their district attorney was arrested on a drunk driving charge a while back. The DA did not quit her position, so the funding for her agency was cut by Governor Perry in a line-item veto.[47] A very straightforward control. So, if the governor is not made happy, there goes your support."

Moving on, Patrick remarked, after turning to the west-facing portion of the balcony, "So now that we have looked out in all four directions, what is the most common thing that you see in any direction?"

I remarked, "Housing?"

He furthered, "Once again, excellent. Citizens live in those houses. Those citizens are the fourth control. If the bureaucracy makes a ruling that people are not in favor of, especially here in Texas due to our abundance of elected positions, the citizens can rally and vote them out of office in the next election, just like that. With this being Austin, no matter

---

47   Sarah Rumpf, "Political Payback: Rick Perry Indicted in Power Struggle with Democrat-Controlled DA Office," *Breitbart*, August 16, 2014, http://www.breitbart.com/texas/2014/08/15/political-payback-rick-perry-indictment.

what way agencies decide, there will always be someone to protest. Let's go back to facing the north for the remainder."

Once we were positioned again, Patrick continued, "Look out here. Most of the buildings that you see physically house the offices of the bureaucracy, everything from the UT campus, state office buildings—hell, even the courthouse. That is all the actual government. We might make the law, but those other groups then go through and enforce it for us. The question is, though, who else has agencies among us here in Austin?"

I furthered, slightly confused, "Uncle Sam?"

Patrick moved on. "Very good. Our last control deals with the federal government. You may be unaware, but a large portion of our state revenues comes from the federal government. For example, in fiscal year 2017, the state of Texas received $38,365,630,033 from the feds, which was about 34.5 percent of state revenues in that year.[48] The only other revenue to come close was our sales tax, at $28,900,035,304, which was 26 percent of revenues in the fiscal year 2017.[49] We in Texas might not always like what the feds do, but we might not want to bite the hands that feed us as the state would go belly up or at minimum make a large number of changes in our spending patterns. As an example of this, look at the sanctuary city and state debate. Some cities and states have refused to work with federal immigration officials to arrest immigrants who came here illegally, so President Trump on multiple occasions has threatened to pull funding from law enforcement grants to these areas unless they begin to work with immigration officials.[50] What are your thoughts on all of this?"

In summing it all up, I surmised, "So for an agency to survive, it must maintain support, either from the groups that fund it or the public that supports it and ensure that the proper people are operating it. With everyone on board giving more support, the agency gets more funding, more funding gets them more power, and with more power, they can take on additional responsibilities to stay in the game and institutionalize themselves in the upper echelons of state politics to avoid getting shut down, unlike those that don't get the support. Why do I see Tim Taylor of the TV show *Home Improvement* or Captain Kirk from *Star Trek* making a good point here, as it is all about your group needing 'more power!'?"

In ending our conversation out here, Patrick concluded, "Because that is what you need to get to stick around longer than a session or two. More power!"

---

48 Comptroller.Texas.gov, "Transparency: Revenue by Source for Fiscal Year 2018 (All Funds, Excluding Trust)," accessed March 20, 2019, https://comptroller.texas.gov/transparency/reports/revenue-by-source.

49 Ibid.

50 Julia Manchester, "16 States Argue DOJ Lacks Authority to Impose Trump's Threatened Cuts to Sanctuary Cities' Funding," *The Hill*, February 1, 2018, http://thehill.com/homenews/state-watch/371841-16-states-argue-doj-lacks-authority-to-impose-trumps-threatened-cuts-to.

Once back down the stairs on the second-floor rotunda with our trash in hand, I asked, "What else is there to know about the state bureaucracy?"

He replied, "Plenty, but one thing, though: Most of those decisions made by the agencies are designed to slow society and steer things in a different direction, but do you really want a random guy going out there and shooting haphazardly, a king ruling with an iron sword (or pen, today), or people in society not taking into account how their plans affect others? Some decisions made by the bureaucracy are stupid, yes, but for the most part, the agencies are acting to hopefully better society. The trick is to get fewer, but more important, commonsense decisions made. Have a good day, Champ!"

I shook his hand, thanked him for his time, and wished him a good rest of the day in his office. After that, I walked down the stairs and out the north doors of the building to enjoy the free afternoon, thinking about all I learned about the actual officials who run the government. These are the people who are responsible for making decisions that people go on to complain about later. The issue is, many of those decisions are made in hopes of getting the best system of governance in place to help as many people as possible without getting people overly reliant on government service.

---

**QUESTIONS TO CONSIDER** REGARDING THE EXECUTIVE BRANCH BEYOND THE GOVERNOR:

1. The first main topic of the chapter discusses what bureaucracy and bureaucrats are. Please define each term, give an example from your life of both, and explain why they are a good match, in detail.
2. The second main topic of the chapter discusses plural executive. Please recap the comparison made between the state and federal executive, state the system you prefer the most, and explain why, in detail.
3. The third main topic of the chapter discusses different major state agencies. Please select the agency that stood out to you the most, state how you relate to that agency in your day-to-day life, and explain why, in detail.
4. The fourth main topic of the chapter discusses issues with the bureaucracy. Please identify the main problem, state how that issue relates to your life, and explain why, in detail.
5. The final main topic of the chapter discusses controls over the bureaucracy. Please identify what each of the controls is, select the one that relates to how you deal with other people the most, and explain why, in detail.

## FIGURE CREDITS

# Chapter 20

# Laws and Their Enforcement

# Police Jurisdiction

One of the worst fears I have is policophobia, better known as fearing the police.[1] It all started when I was 16 and got my driver's license. I had just taken and passed my test at the Texas Department of Public Safety office.[2] With my paper license in my wallet and my dad in the passenger seat, I left the parking lot and ran a red light by accident, thanks to a lead-foot disease that had not yet been cured. Unfortunately, there was a cop coming up from behind at the intersection who immediately flashed his lightbar to pull me over and give me a moving violation: speeding. I felt horrible and realized that the police or law enforcement of some kind are everywhere. Ever since, every time I see one on the road, I get tense and pray, "Please don't pull me over, pretty please!" even though I am going the speed limit and not doing anything else wrong to the best of my knowledge, like not wearing my seat belt.

Therefore, to overcome my fears and advance my trek, my goal for today was to learn about the law enforcement agencies and judicial system that handle the accused once the arrest report is finished. The problem was, since my dad and I, outside of that one traffic ticket, had never really been in trouble with the law, this was the one area where I had no credible contact to schedule a tour or something with for my trek, so today I was going to have to get over my fears in a jiff and get creative. Thankfully, I took a leap and learned the best way to approach a cop is just go up and speak with them. From what I learned, today was my last day learning about state-level government agencies and my first learning about federal-level government agencies.

I arrived at Shipley's Donuts on West Anderson Lane in north central Austin just after 7:00 a.m.[3] I figured this would be an excellent time to catch some peace officers of all kinds just before or after a shift change. About ten minutes after I arrived, I had a dozen fresh glazed doughnuts and some coupons for free coffee at the store in my arms. Just then, my prayers were answered when a wearisome group of law enforcement officers walked through the front door. I could tell that they were from all different agencies, as the six different officers had on six different uniforms. It turns out that the six officers were all lieutenants with the University of Texas at Austin Police Department,[4] the Austin Police Department,[5] the Federal Bureau of Investigation,[6] the Travis County Sheriff's Office,[7] the Texas Rangers,[8] and the

---

1   https://www.howtopronounce.com/policophobia
2   https://www.dps.texas.gov
3   http://www.shipleydonutsnorthaustin.com
4   https://police.utexas.edu
5   http://www.austintexas.gov/department/police
6   https://www.fbi.gov
7   https://www.tcsheriff.org
8   http://www.dps.texas.gov/TexasRangers

Texas Highway Patrol,[9] who all get together after shifts occasionally to discuss significant cases and keep the back channels open when the mains were clogged over this complexity called jurisdiction over cases. Lucky me, I do believe!

Before the officers could reach the counter, I went up to the lieutenant from the Austin Police Department with my box of doughnuts wide open and asked if, in exchange for buying them breakfast, would they speak to me about their various agencies' roles in law enforcement?

Lieutenant John Samson turned to his colleagues to discuss the proposition. He then turned and said, "You are under arrest for attempted bribery of a peace officer."

My mouth and hands dropped when he said this. Luckily, the University of Texas lieutenant grabbed the doughnuts and coffee coupons from my hands before the food fell too far. I could only think that the doughnuts would now make a good peace offering to the boys down at lockup. At that point, it got a bit weird when, while I was handcuffed, the officers walked me over to the large table in the corner instead of the back of one of their squad cars, and the university police lieutenant cashed in the coupons for six steaming-hot cups of coffee. After sitting down, with all six of the lieutenants sitting around the table looking at me with steaming cups of coffee in front of them, I felt very flustered. Lieutenant Billy Heisenberg of the Travis County Sheriff's Department, with one of my doughnuts in hand, then asked, "So what exactly is it that you want to know?"

Out loud, I said, "Ummm . . . what exactly is it that I am under arrest for?"

He replied, "Well . . . we aren't arresting you, but we figured the best way to inform you of the legal process in the state, and the country for that matter, would be to give you the full arrest experience. However, attempted bribery of a peace officer means that you tried getting a favor from a police officer, like being let off the hook in exchange for something."

I said, with the handcuffs still on, "Okay, that makes sense, and since we are on talking terms now and y'all are getting a hot breakfast on me, let's find out why Samson arrested me, and not one of you other guys."

Heisenberg said, "Kid, the answer to that is a term better known as *jurisdiction*, or the right, power, or authority to administer justice by hearing and determining controversies.[10] Regarding making arrests, a big portion of our jobs as police officers of various types, jurisdiction depends on where the offense occurs and the circumstances of the offense. For example, think of a doughnut. Everything from the outermost part of the doughnut on is the entirety of Travis County. Everything where the hole in the doughnut is, is the city of Austin. Also, let's assume, for sanity's sake, that other cities like Pflugerville don't exist, to make this metaphor work more easily. Where the actual doughnut is, is the jurisdiction of

---

9   https://www.dps.texas.gov/tle/index.htm
10  http://www.dictionary.com/browse/jurisdiction

the county and the sheriff's department. Where the hole in the doughnut is, is the jurisdiction of the city and the Austin Police Department. We don't typically mix coverage and leave handling crimes to our jurisdictions unless necessary."

I spoke up here, stating, "That makes sense."

Heisenberg continued, "It gets even more complicated. Do you see where the extra-large pieces of glaze have built up on the inside of the hole in the doughnut? That piece of glaze is the University of Texas at Austin campus, which is within the city limits of Austin but is the responsibility of the campus police over that of the city and county, as Lieutenant Aggie Bevo represents the state agency that owns that property—although, after an arrest, those accused are typically turned over to the county sheriff for prosecution and processing, as they have the facilities to do so, such as the actual courts. Also, see this crack over here in the glaze on the actual doughnut? That crack is Interstate 35. This area is where Lieutenant John Jimenez of the Texas Highway Patrol has primary jurisdiction, as it's the highway and state property. The jurisdiction of the campus police and highway patrol blends with that of mine and the city, but we still avoid each other's turf as much as possible, with agreements determining who has primary jurisdiction here and there."

I asked, "What about you, in the fancy cowboy hat?"

Ranger Martin Mayberry of the Texas Rangers (not the baseball team in Arlington) said, "I'm a Texas Ranger. I can go anywhere in the state, but I only investigate serious statewide crimes like, and I quote from the Texas Rangers' website, 'major incident crime investigations, unsolved crime/serial crime investigations, public corruption investigations, officer-involved shooting investigations, and border security operations.'[11] Think of serial murders, etc. Those are my bread and butter. I'm like a jack-of-all-trades: I can do a little bit of investigating everywhere when the proper time comes."

Following this, I said, "Okay, so that is all of your jurisdictions explained. So what are your duties when in your zones of jurisdiction?"

Then, Agent Clifton Gow from the Federal Bureau of Investigation interjected, "Hold up there stranger; the federal government will not be overlooked in these proceedings. We do not handle speeding tickets, like the sheriff's office or city police, nor do we have very narrow physical jurisdiction like the university police or highway patrol. We are like the Texas Rangers; we can go anywhere and investigate anything, but we focus on terrorism, counterintelligence, cybercrime, public corruption, civil rights, organized crime, white-collar

---

11    http://www.txdps.state.tx.us/TexasRangers

crime, violent crime, and, most interestingly, weapons of mass destruction.[12] The difference is, we can go nationwide. If you need to go abroad, speak with the CIA."[13]

Bevo spoke up. "Let's get a bit more specific gentleman, shall we? In short, the university police and I oversee enforcing campus laws, like campus smoking bans or parking regulations, deterring campus crime, and responding to a crisis. The Austin Police Department, more easily spoken as APD, and Samson oversee enforcing city laws, like code enforcement and deterring urban crime. Heisenberg over there and the county sheriff's department oversee enforcing state laws and deterring rural crime. Jimenez and the highway patrol oversee regulating traffic laws on the interstate and other major thoroughfares. Ranger Mayberry and Agent Gow, as previously stated, are like free agents: They can go anywhere when called on, as their jurisdictions are prescribed by the state and federal government, respectively."

With that stated, I asked, "So who is the most important out of the lot of you?"

Samson responded, "That depends on where you are. In the city, it's the APD and me. In the county, Heisenberg, and the sheriff's office, and so on and so forth. Wherever you are, the law enforcement agency with that jurisdictional coverage will always be most important. Overall, every law enforcement agency serves a similar purpose, 'to protect and serve,' which is the official motto-slash-slogan of the Los Angeles Police Department,[14] but the APD does win the race by a mile when you get down to it, as Austin is where most of the county population lives today."

## Types of Crime

With the different law enforcement agencies' duties explained and when and where they could act, I went on to inquire what the different types of crime were. "What are the different types of crimes in society?"

Jimenez of the highway patrol replied, "There are two basic classifications of crimes.[15] The first are felonies. These are the more serious types of crimes. Then you have misdemeanors, the less serious types of crimes.[16] From there, though, the crimes can be further divided by more specialties, for a variety of reasons, in certain cases."

---

12    https://www.fbi.gov/investigate
13    https://www.cia.gov/index.html
14    Los Angeles Police Department, "The Origin of the LAPD Motto," accessed March 22, 2019, http://www.lapdonline.org/history_of_the_lapd/content_basic_view/1128.
15    Attorney General of Texas, "Penal Code Offenses by Punishment Range," last modified March 2018, https://www.texasattorneygeneral.gov/files/cj/penalcode.pdf; an explanation of the Texas Penal Code; all other crime classification examples were pulled from this source.
16    https://www.britannica.com/topic/felony

Concurring, Bevo of the University of Texas at Austin Police Department stated, "John, would you mind if I explained misdemeanors?"

Jimenez nodded, and Bevo continued, "As John has said, a misdemeanor is the less serious classification of crime. These are things you will get arrested for but won't be damaging to your ability to fully function later on in life, such as the removal of your ability to vote or easily get a job, and are punishable by the county or a city. Such examples of these crimes are underage drinking or smoking, moving violations like running a stop sign, possession of a minor amount of narcotics, and, of all things, catching and keeping flounder shorter than a foot in length, among many more examples. Also, some crimes, like theft, are typically a felony unless under a small dollar value—$1,500, last I checked."

Samson spoke up. "I'll take felonies. Kid, these are, as previously stated, much more serious crimes that are punishable by the state and that will certainly damage your ability to function later in life, as it will be dramatically more difficult to get a job and it cedes your right to vote in every state but Maine and Vermont for an extended period of time—two years past the end of your sentence in Texas, only during imprisonment in 14 states and Washington DC, 22 states during imprisonment and for a short period of time afterward, and indefinitely in the remaining states.[17] Remember, these are when someone attempts to or kills somebody else, robs someone, breaks into another's property, has some indecent type of behavior with a child, stalks someone, marries more than one person at a time, and so on. The real Texas example of this, though, is cattle rustling, better known as stealing a bull or cow.[18] No matter what, that is a felony. Back in the day, you could be hung on sight if caught red-handed in the act by the owner."

It was at that point Gow added in, "I will take a gander at the specialty classifications. Son, the three main specialty classifications are federal, victimless, and white-collar crimes. Remember, these crimes all still fall into the classifications of being a felony or misdemeanor, but due to other special circumstances, they are further subdivided unofficially, mostly for reporting services I'd say. Let's take federal crimes as an example—my jurisdiction to investigate. This brings up that whole pesky matter of jurisdiction again. Let's say that you are out at sea and someone gets pushed overboard on purpose and is lost; that is a federal crime due to there being no state control over said waters in our territorial sea. It gets even worse when in international waters, as the jurisdiction to investigate by me at the FBI depends on several factors. 'The location of the vessel, the nationality of the perpetrator or victim,

---

17   National Conference of State Legislatures, "Felon Voting Rights," December 21, 2018, http://www. ncsl.org/research/elections-and-campaigns/felon-voting-rights.aspx.

18   Julián Aguilar and Miles Hutson, "Cattle Theft Still a Modern-Day Problem in Texas," *Texas Tribune*, October 28, 2015, https://www.texastribune.org/2015/10/28/cattle-theft-still-modern-day-problem-texas.

the ownership of the vessel, the points of embarkation and debarkation, and the country in which the vessel is flagged all play a role in determining whether there is federal authority to enforce the laws of the United States."[19] In another case, stalking is stalking, but if you do it on federal property, that is a federal crime, as the federal government has jurisdictional control over that area. In another case, if you commit a crime and cross a state or international border, that becomes a federal crime, as no one state has full jurisdiction. Lastly, who employs the president and postal workers?"

I responded, "The federal government?"

Agent Gow continued, "Very good. So, if you harmed one of the postal workers while they are on duty, who would want to prosecute you?"

I answered, "The federal government . . . specifically you at the Federal Bureau of Investigation, their police-slash-investigatory force?[20] This would be like the state, via the Texas Rangers, prosecuting me for harassing the governor."

Agent Gow went on, "You got it, as we have jurisdiction over the matter, as the person is in their employ. Granted, the US Postal Inspection Service might want to have a crack at you first and protect their own if it's a postal employee who's been attacked.[21] Now, let's talk victimless crimes."

Ranger Mayberry then spoke, leaving Agent Gow looking perturbed as his jurisdiction had been violated. "Very good. Prostitution, along with other crimes, like using illicit drugs or gambling, are better known as victimless crimes because the persons doing the endeavor are the only ones immediately impacted by the crime, as no one else is killed, injured, or abused, although if you gamble away your life savings, you could put your family out of a home long term, but in the immediacy, you are the only one impacted. Then there is a third specialty classification called white-collar crimes. Question: Why do you think that these crimes are called white-collar crimes?"

I murmured, "The people committing the crimes are wearing white-collared shirts at the time?"

Ranger Mayberry continued, "Good, but who wears white-collar shirts?"

I responded, "Businessmen and businesswomen?"

"Excellent," Mayberry replied. "White-collar crimes are bribery, embezzlement, insider trading, or crafting a Ponzi scheme, for example, among many others. These are crimes that

---

19    Salvador Hernandez, "Crimes Against Americans on Cruise Ships," Statement Before the House Committee on Transportation and Infrastructure, Subcommittee on Coast Guard and Maritime Transportation, March 27, 2007, https://archives.fbi.gov/archives/news/testimony/crimes-against-americans-on-cruise-ships.

20    https://www.fbi.gov

21    https://postalinspectors.uspis.gov

the average Joe on the go could not perform, as they are not in a seat of power in an entity. For example, you would need to be in a high position of power in a company to know that bad financial reports were coming out and that you should sell your stock now before it plummets. That's what happened to Martha Stewart and her company, Martha Stewart Living®, when she did some insider trading of her own.[22] On the other hand, you could make an argument for a fourth special classification, known as street or survival crimes, that people commit to survive by, for example, stealing an apple from a stand in a storefront to eat. The big difference between the two is that the storekeeper is only out a buck or two for the apple, but if someone creates a Ponzi scheme and has it all collapse around him or her, thousands of people could be out billions of dollars. This was the case of Bernie Madoff, out of New York City, back in 2008 during the financial crisis."[23]

## Criminals and Victims

I inquired, "Ranger Mayberry, you talk about different people committing different crimes, but who is the most likely to commit crimes?"

Gow replied to retake jurisdictional control, leaving Mayberry's feathers ruffled. "For that information, you need to turn to the US Department of Justice and its Bureau of Justice Statistics.[24] From there, you need only evaluate their recent report of prisoners in 2016 by statistician Danielle Kaeble.[25] From that report, if I am reading this correctly, on December 31, 2016, from table 2, there were 6,613,500 persons supervised by US adult correctional systems, of which 1,505,400 were in prison, 3,673,100 were on probation, 874,000 were on parole, and 740,700 were in local jails. Using US Census Bureau estimates for January 1, 2017,[26] the US population was 324,310,011, which means that roughly 2 percent of the population of the country at that time was someway involved in the legal system due to an arrest. Now, using appendix table 1 from that same report, here in Texas, there were 681,900 individuals making up the total correctional population, with 482,900 under community supervision and 218,500 incarcerated, the highest on all accounts compared to other states

---

22    Melvin Blackman, "Martha Stewart," CNNMoney, June 2, 2014, http://money.cnn.com/gallery/investing/2014/06/02/insider-trading-famous-cases/index.html.

23    Robert Lenzner, "Bernie Madoff's $50 Billion Ponzi Scheme," Forbes, July 13, 2012, http://www.forbes.com/2008/12/12/madoff-ponzi-hedge-pf-ii-in_rl_1212croesus_inl.html.

24    http://www.bjs.gov

25    Danielle Kaeble and Mary Cowhig, "Correctional Populations in the United States, 2016," Bureau of Justice Statistics, April 26, 2016, https://www.bjs.gov/index.cfm?ty=pbdetail&iid=6226.

26    US Census Bureau, "Census Bureau Projects U.S. and World Populations on New Year's Day," July 19, 2017, https://www.census.gov/newsroom/press-releases/2016/cb16-tps158.html.

and even the federal government. Putting these figures into more relatable terms, using appendix table 1 again, at the national level, 2,030 people per 100,000 population are in the correctional population, with 1,810 per 100,000 population under community supervision and 660 per 100,000 population being incarcerated. While in Texas, 2,430 people per 100,000 population are in the correctional population, with 1,720 per 100,000 population under community supervision and 780 per 100,000 population being incarcerated, with the states of Arizona, Alabama, Arkansas, Georgia, Alabama, Mississippi, and Oklahoma having higher rates but a lower physical number of incarcerations, and the states of Arkansas, Idaho, Indiana, Minnesota, New Jersey, Ohio, Pennsylvania, and Rhode Island having higher rates but a lower physical number under community supervision. With that info in mind, the 2016 report did not have info based on sex, race, and age, as seen in the 2014 report by E. Ann Carson, so using information from that report, at the national level there were 471 people per 100,000 population in correctional facilities, with 890 per 100,000 males and 65 per 100,000 females.[27] Here in Texas, there were 584 per 100,000 citizens in correctional facilities, with 1,081 males per 100,000 and 93 females per 100,000. Using table 10, from the 2014 report, that only displays data at the national level, additional information is available based on age and ethnicity. Based on that information, on December 31, 2014, there were 465 white males per 100,000 population in correctional facilities, 1,091 Hispanic males, 2,724 black males, and 968 other. For females, similar trends emerge, as there were 53 white females per 100,000 population in correctional facilities, 64 Hispanic females, 109 black females, and 93 other. Finally, looking at age, 169 18- to 19-year-olds per 100,000 population were in correctional facilities, 746 20- to 24-year-olds, 1,055 25- to 29-year-olds, 1,161 30- to 34-year-olds, 1,067 35- to 39-year-olds, 904 40- to 44-year-olds, 758 45- to 49-year-olds, 567 50- to 54-year-olds, 358 55- to 59-year-olds, 212 60- to 64-year-olds, and 72 people 65 years of age or older. Based on that, prisoners are more likely to be younger. Therefore, young man, if you are in Texas, male, black, and young, you are more likely to be in prison than the average citizen."

I wondered in conversation, "What about the victim, when there is an actual victim?"

Jimenez took control here. "I got that one. Using information from another report from the Bureau of Justice Statistics, this one by Lynn Langton and Jennifer Truman called "Criminal Victimization, 2014,"[28] two factors stand out, not the ones you would expect though. In this case, from table 5, evidence suggests that men are just as likely as women, and whites are

27    E. Ann Carson,. *PDF*. Washington, DC: Bureau of Justice Statistics, September 2015. https://www.bjs.gov/content/pub/pdf/p14.pdf

28    Jennifer L. Truman and Lynn Langton, "Criminal Victimization, 2014," Bureau of Justice Statistics, August 27, 2015, https://www.bjs.gov/index.cfm?ty=pbdetail&iid=5366.; http://www.bjs.gov/content/pub/pdf/cv14.pdf

just as likely as blacks, Hispanics, and other ethnic groups to be victims. Younger people and those who are not married or widowed, however, are much more likely to be victims. For example, 422,460 people 12 to 17 years of age were victims in 2014, 1.7 percent of that age group. From there, as with each older age bracket, the percentage went down. Specifically, 1.6 percent of 18- to 24-year-olds were victims, 1.5 percent of 25- to 34-year-olds, 1.2 percent of 35- to 44-year-olds, 0.9 percent of 50- to 64-year-olds, and 0.3 percent of those 65 years of age or older. I don't know if the higher victimization rate for younger people is just because they are less capable of protecting themselves or not, but either way, in the first case, being younger makes you more likely to be a victim. For marital status, those who are married or widowed saw 806,200 and 77,420 of their fellows, 0.6 percent, and 0.5 percent, respectively, in their population be victims. Whereas those who were never married saw 1,482,570 of their fellows be victims, 1.6 percent of that population, alongside 1.6 percent of those who are divorced, and 3 percent among those who are separated. In this case, being married or losing your partner to death equates to being less likely to be a victim of a crime. Overall, a person who is younger and not married or widowed is more likely to be a victim."

## Advice to Citizens

I could only sit in amazement at what I just learned, but then it hit me: What can I do to help them do their job or avoid getting arrested in my own right? But first, I said, "I know I've had you guys here for about an hour or so and I don't want to keep you from work . . ."

Jimenez said, "We are all after our shift. We've got some time this morning for you, plus, doughnuts!"

With that stated, I went on. "Okay then, if there was one thing that you could each say to a citizen, what would it be, concerning your field?"

Bevo spoke first. "Why people cannot follow the law never ceases to amaze me, as it is the best way to enforce the law. We officers cannot be everywhere at the same time. Do you not want crime in your neighborhood? Good. So, be a good person and follow the law. It is that simple."

Samson went on. "And also, why people don't report crimes amazes me. We cannot do our jobs unless people report crimes around or occurring to them. Believe it or not, most crimes are not reported because people are ashamed, do not trust the police, or a variety of other reasons. More importantly, if someone else reports the crime, or information about the crime—not to us, but to groups like Crimestoppers[29]—those individuals can get money in exchange for information, all anonymously. Their local hotline here in Travis County

---

29    http://www.crimestoppersusa.org

is 512-472-TIPS (8477) or 1-800-893-TIPS (8477). More impressively, though, you can text 'tip103 + your message' to CRIMES (274637) or do it online at Austincrimestoppers.org. I would argue, though, report info to Crimestoppers, but report the crime to us directly if you are the victim or see the crime happen when it occurs."

After that, Heisenberg made a good point: "Kid, as a last resort (I don't quite recommend this), is going beyond reporting a crime and doing something about the incident in progress. These individuals are called citizen arresters. When doing so, just be careful, as Texans can make a citizen's arrest, but only when (per section 14.1 of the Texas Code of Criminal Procedure[30]) a felony is witnessed and/or a crime against public peace is occurring. Either way, when doing so, subdue the suspect and hold them until the police arrive. More interestingly, the Ninth Amendment from the Bill of Rights states that an 'individual's natural right to self-preservation and the defense of the others is protected.'[31] Therefore, you could rely on the Constitution in case what you do in response to an incident is sketchy in and of itself, but still, report the crime, and act a hero as a last resort."

Then Mayberry said, "When making an arrest, one of three things must occur before we are entitled to act. First, we must receive a signed warrant from a judge. Second, we need to see a legitimate crime occur. Finally, someone must report a crime to have occurred. Unless one of these three situations occur, we can investigate lightly but not arrest."

Taking the cake, though, for the best response here was Jimenez, as he responded, "I cannot say it enough: When arrested, you have the right to remain silent. Use that right! I have had so many arrests take place where the perpetrator talks themselves right into a guilty plea as they openly give away all of the information in the car ride down to the station. What makes it worse is that the accused have the right to an attorney and forget to get one. Lastly, if an officer is requesting to search you or your property and you do not want them to, demand that they get a warrant. Speaking of getting permission and not getting into trouble, my wife is going to kill me if I do not get home sooner rather than later."

With everybody agreeing that they too now faced a similar fate, we all got up. Nightcrawler let me out of the handcuffs. We all shook hands and went on our merry way back to the real world. It was near 9:00 a.m. On the way out, though, I realized that I didn't even get a doughnut for myself, and I was starving. I felt good though at this point, knowing that I had an excellent start to learning about the legal process. On my way to get in line for my doughnut, Gow tapped my shoulder. When I turned around, she stated, "Law enforcement sometimes gets a bad rap with people for various understandable reasons. Therefore, I wanted to say

---

30   "Code of Criminal Procedure Title 1, Chapter 14, Arrest Without a Warrant," https://statutes.capitol.texas.gov/Docs/CR/htm/CR.14.htm

31   U.S. Constitution. Amendment 9.

in private how you should deal with the police when speaking with us, primarily when you get pulled over."

I responded, "What should I do then?"

Agent Gow iterated, "Overall, you should be cool, calm, and collected. With that in mind, when you see our emergency flashers come on, wave at us, turn on your flashers, and slow down, communicate with us that you understand that you are getting pulled over. Then, pull over to a safe location as soon as possible, preferably to the right of the road, even go to a parking lot if there is one nearby; make sure there is room for two cars to be there. Following that, once stopped, turn off the ignition and put your hands on the wheel where they can be easily seen. If the car is marked, feel free to roll down the passenger window; if not, wait until the cop is out of the car. Most importantly, stay in the car and wait for further instructions like requesting your license and insurance. Make sure that you have those in your car at all times. After that, listen to what the officer states, like your violation, and any other information they would like to inform you of. Once you get your ticket or warning, thank the officer for their service and information, and return to the road carefully and slowly.[32] Overall, be sure to communicate in everything that you do. Gotta go, see ya!"

## Types of Court Cases

All of the other information that I had learned, from jurisdiction to what was a crime, was good to know in general, but this seemed to quell my fears about the police. My day then got a bit more interesting, as while I was in line to get my doughnut—finally, as the cops ate two apiece of those that I had already acquired—a blond woman tapped me on the shoulder. She was very well dressed, so I assumed that she was a businesswoman of some kind. It turns out, though, that she was the answer to my prayers. She stated, "I was listening to you speaking with those cops for about 30 minutes. Are you in trouble?"

I replied, "Thankfully, no. I am, however, spending my summer going around to various governing agencies to learn about what they do and whether it would be the right path for me to follow in life. Unfortunately for me, the first step for learning about the legal system was the do's and do not's of arresting and getting arrested. There is a lot to learn about the process of being arrested."

She said, "I would completely agree with that. So what is the next stop on your trek?"

I went on, "I've now talked with the cops, and I think the next stop should be with an attorney so that when I get to the actual courts, I know what to do, how to act, and what is there."

---

32  "Drivers Are Freaking Out about Police Stops: This Is How to Act When Pulled Over," Driving Tests, accessed March 22, 2019, https://driving-tests.org/beginner-drivers/what-to-do-if-you-get-pulled-over-by-a-police-officer.

With that "lucky you" smirk on her face, she said, "I think I might have to be your next stop. The name is Vienna Schwartz. I am an independent defense attorney with a light case-load today. I have some time around 10:00 a.m. to speak with you if you want."

I replied, "Sssuuurrreee! I'm Champ."

After that, she gave me her business card and advised me to pack lightly for the court-house, as only the necessities are allowed into the building. With the time now being just after 9:00 a.m. and my next location in order, I had some time to spare. With a fresh dough-nut in hand, I went back to my car and took a quick nap to prepare for court. It's amazing how a good doughnut can make your day.

I awoke just after 9:30 a.m. to a home-less man rapping on my windshield and saying that I was in his spot. Confused, I turned on the ignition, plugged the Blackwell-Thurman Criminal Justice Center's (figure 20.1) address of 509 West 11th Street into my GPS, and took off. Luckily, the drive to the courthouse was only about 15 minutes (or 8 miles) away via the MOPAC expressway. Once there, just before 9:45, I parked at the central parking facility on-site garage. After getting out of the car on the fifth floor, I went down-

FIGURE 20.1   Blackwell-Thurman Criminal Justice Center

stairs and waited on the benches outside of the courthouse. At 9:55 a.m., Schwartz came up from behind and tapped on my shoulder. I shrieked, thinking it was some criminal trying to create a disturbance and get his trial delayed or something.

She asked, "Are you ready? I am due in the 390th State District Court of Texas with Judge Kocurek[33] at 11 o'clock."

I replied, "You betcha!"

After this, we went inside through security without much of a hassle. I followed Schwartz to the bank of elevators, and we proceeded up to the seventh floor. When out of the elevator, we proceeded into the courtroom directly across the hall to the right. A few court personnel were at their posts, but the judge was in her chambers, and the room was full of conversa-tion. We sat in the front row. I was looking around and turned to Schwartz and asked, "So what goes on in a courtroom?"

---

33   https://www.traviscountytx.gov/courts/criminal/district/390

She replied, "That is a rather interesting list of uses. This ranges from getting married, getting divorced, stopping discrimination,[34] settling a traffic ticket, deciding to remove life support on someone if the individual in question is terminally ill,[35] declaring someone insane, protecting copyrights and other property,[36] making a statement while on trial (Nazi Germany used the July 20 trials to embarrass public officials who tried to assassinate Adolf Hitler[37]), or using the courtroom as a classroom for law schools (such as we are doing now, in a way). Judge Judy is a real judge,[38] but let's face it, she is just entertainment. Together, she and Austin's own Matthew McConaughey as a defense attorney in the blockbuster *The Lincoln Lawyer*[39] provide examples of how courts are also used as movie and television show settings. Overall, though, unless you are being punished for a crime, each of these uses are best described as problem solving."

I sat stunned thinking with a dumbfounded look on my face, "I had no idea so much went on in court."

She shook her head in discouragement. "When you learn about court organization, you might want to double down on that look of yours right now. Until then, though, there are also two types of cases. The first is civil matters, or cases where one private citizen takes another to court to solve a problem. The other is criminal matters, where the state, really the government, brings an accused citizen to court for violating the law. This is the handling of crime and punishment. One difference between the two is the burden of proof to decide who is, for lack of a proper term, in the wrong. For civil cases, it is the preponderance of the evidence, or who is more in the wrong for what happened. In criminal cases, it is up to the prosecution to show that the accused, beyond a reasonable amount of doubt, is guilty of committing said crime."

I interrupted, "What is being broken in a civil case if you break the law in a criminal case?"

She replied, "Technically, nothing, but the law in a criminal case is called the penal code,[40] or mass listing of all punishable offenses and punishments in a jurisdiction, while in a civil case, those involved follow a civil code that deals with all or the central areas of private law and disputes in instances such as negligence in traffic accidents and illegitimate business dealings regarding how to deal with them at trial and doling out responsibility in the settlement."[41]

---

34   US Courts, "History—Brown v. Board of Education Re-enactment," accessed March 22, 2019, http://www. uscourts.gov/educational-resources/educational-activities/history-brown-v-board-education-re-enactment.

35   Terri Schiavo.org, "Timeline," accessed March 22, 2019, https://terrischiavo.org/story/timeline.

36   Reuters, "Samsung Has to Pay Apple $539 Million in Patent Infringement Case," *Business Insider*, May 24, 2018, http://www.businessinsider.com/samsung-apple-lawsuit-patent-infringement-2018-5.

37   History.com Editors, "July Plot," November 9, 2009, https://www.history.com/topics/july-plot.

38   http://www.judgejudy.com

39   IMDb, "The Lincoln Lawyer (2011)," accessed March 22, 2019, https://www.imdb.com/title/tt1189340.

40   http://codes.lp.findlaw.com/txstatutes/PE

41   https://www.britannica.com/story/what-is-the-difference-between-criminal-law-and-civil-law

## People Found in Courtrooms

I thought about what I had heard for a few minutes while Schwartz organized what she was going to discuss in court in about 20 minutes. We'd gone over specific and general court uses, types of court cases, and what codes the different court cases needed to follow. Then I wondered aloud, "Who are all of the people in the room?"

Excitedly going through the different people in the room, Schwartz replied, "The law enforcement officer is called a bailiff, and the duties are pretty self-explanatory: provide law and order in the court.[42] The woman working on paperwork is called the court clerk, and she handles the files for the cases. Let's see, the empty chair on the platform is where the judge sits, and they monitor the ebb and flow of the proceedings, making decisions on evidence, statements, and witness credibility, etc."

I interrupted, "What about where the 12 empty chairs are in the big box?"

She went on: "That is where the jury sits. In a case, there are two different juries. Before the actual case, the grand jury is presented the facts of the case by the prosecution to determine whether the state has enough information to head to trial. When the trial is actually in session, the trial (or petit) jury sits, all 12 of them, listening to the prosecutor present their case, and then the defense attorney—that's me—attacks the state's case to raise enough reasonable doubt in hopes of getting an acquittal, or innocent verdict, and then the jury decides guilt or innocence. In both juries, a unanimous decision is required. The same goes in civil cases, but the prosecution is called a plaintiff and is a private citizen. Beyond that, it's the same process. Also, all cases in Texas are guaranteed jury trials, even for simple traffic tickets that are handled by pleas of no contest a majority of the time."

Then the court bailiff called out, "Oyez, oyez, oyez! I call this court into session, the Honorable Julie Kocurek presiding."

Schwartz whispered, "Follow me when the proceedings are over. I have someone for you to meet and further inform you on important matters."

Over the next two hours, I watched Schwartz and the prosecution go through a process better known as *voir dire*, or juror selection, for their upcoming stalking trial. Along the way, certain potential jurors were called up and dismissed based on technicalities like school attendance and/or having work or family responsibilities. After that, the remaining jurors were questioned to determine their suitability on other factors, like being an expert on the case at hand, being a lawyer, or having a career field related to the case. After what seemed like mere minutes, the jury was seated, and the court was recessed for a break.

Schwartz turned around and asked, "What did you think of it?"

---

42  Judicial Learning Center, "The Players in the Courtroom," accessed March 22, 2019, https://judiciallearningcenter.org/the-players-in-the-courtroom.

I replied, "That is a lot of legal proceedings."

She said, "That is just part of the game to ensure due process for the accused, their constitutional rights not being violated, etc. Before we even got to this point in the trial, we had to deal with motions for a change of venue to get a less biased jury pool, continuance motions based on the prosecution needing more time to build up their case (luckily, the right to a speedy trial from the US Constitution helps keep those to a minimum), and plea bargaining, among so much more."

I could only agree with all of this. However, I then wondered who was it that she wanted me to speak with later today. I figured it had to be a judge, but who? Luckily, she answered that one right away with her next statement.

She continued, "Do you know where the Capitol Complex is?"

I nodded yes, as I had been there multiple times over the past few weeks.

She continued, "Good. Go to the supreme court building (figure 20.2) at the Capitol Complex and go to the courtroom of the Texas Supreme Court—not the court of criminal appeals—and the chief justice will be waiting for you. He's my uncle. Enjoy the access, and I hope you do not get too flustered when you learn how the courts are organized."

FIGURE 20.2   Texas Supreme Court Building

## Types of Court Jurisdictions

Ten minutes later, after walking east on 11th Street for three blocks, then turning north on Lavaca Street for three blocks, and finally walking one block east on 13th Street, I found myself at the back side of the Texas Supreme Court building. When walking around the south side of the structure to the main entrance, I remembered the walk my dad and I had earlier through this same area. When at the door, I went through security and found myself in the large atrium. Instead of going down the stairs to get to the tunnel, as I had done last time, I went right to the Texas Supreme Court courtroom. The court was not in session today, but Chief Justice Nathan Hecht[43] was waiting for me on the bench, doing some paperwork.

---

43   http://www.txcourts.gov/supreme/about-the-court/justices/chief-justice-nathan-l-hecht

As soon as I walked in, he looked up and ushered me to sit in a chair below the podium. He went, "Welcome to the Supreme Court of Texas!"

I could only reply, "Thanks!"

He went on, "So what exactly have you learned so far about law and order in the great state of Texas?"

I recapped, "Well, I have learned about law enforcement agencies, the laws they enforce, and where exactly it is that they operate. Following that, I got a brief introduction to how the courts operate, leaving me needing to know what exactly the courts found here are."

Hecht said, "Well, you have indeed come to the right place, as I and my fellow justices of the Texas Supreme Court, per section 31 of article 5 of the state constitution, are, and I quote, 'responsible for the efficient administration of the judicial branch and shall promulgate rules of administration not inconsistent with the laws of the state as may be necessary for the efficient and uniform administration of justice in the various courts.[44] In other words, I am the lead official on judicial matters in the state."

I said, "I do not think that I could have found a better person to speak with today for this part of the trek. Would you mind first telling me what the different courts in the state are?"

Hecht then used an interesting metaphor to explain this question. He went on: "You have to think of the various courts in the state as the different rungs of a ladder, as they are parts of a hierarchy. A common saying by people in the workforce is that they want to climb the ladder to get a better lifestyle. In any case, the various courts all have their own or shared level in the system."

I interrupted, "So, what is the lowest level?"

Hecht continued, "Before I answer that, I need to bring up the term *jurisdiction*. I'm sure you have heard this term many times thus far today, haven't you?"

I nodded in agreement while he went on. "Good, you have. Regarding court cases, a case can be heard more than once, but for different reasons. The original trial court has something called original jurisdiction, where the facts of the case are meted out to reach a verdict. If the accused is not happy with the results of the case, the individual can then petition for the case to be reviewed in a higher court with something called appellate jurisdiction, where the court reviews the procedures of a case to ensure that due process was followed and the correct verdict was reached."

I blurted, "Jurisdiction is a big topic in the legal system."

Hecht went, "That is just for cases in general. When it comes to the specific courts, it gets even more jurisdictionally specified. Look at this diagram of Texas courts here (figure 20.3)."

---

44    Texas Constitution of 1876, article 5, section 31.

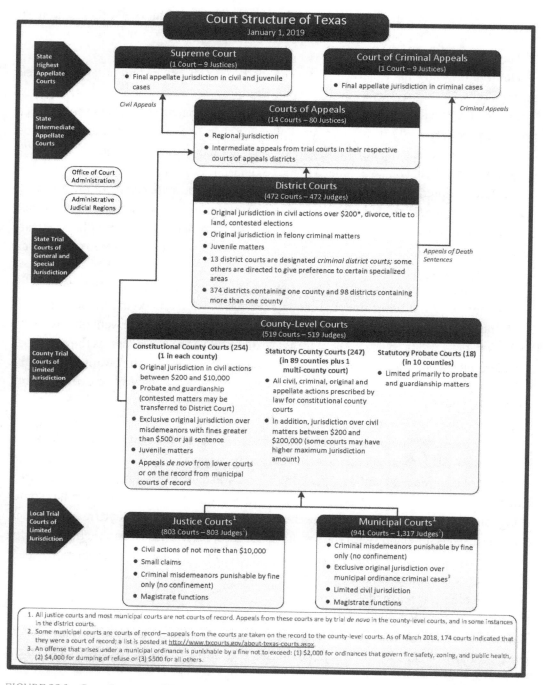

FIGURE 20.3  Court Structure of Texas

Once I took the diagram Hecht continued, "For example, at the bottom of the ladder is the municipal or city court.[45] These courts can only handle cases dealing with violations of municipal ordinances like speeding, parking tickets, or failure to maintain your property, with authority to only issue maximum fines of $2,000 and no jail time when the defendant is found guilty. For a city to get one of these courts, the city need only create it via ordinance passage, but they must pay for them on their own. Traditionally, these courts have no records of the proceedings, but in larger cities, they have been granted said authority with approval by voters to relieve the amount of appellate demand. If a court has no record, any appeal gets a new trial. Finally, for class C misdemeanors within city limits, some of these courts have shared jurisdiction with justice of the peace courts, which are run by the county."

I said, "So that is the bottom. What comes next, I assume, county courts?"

Hecht replied, "After city courts, it gets a bit complicated, as, at the county level, there is not a shortage of courts available. Using the ladder example from earlier, this next higher level would have its rung sticking out from the sides, as it is a bit wider than the rest. To be more specific, there are four different primary judicial county courts worth mentioning here with the last one being an agglomeration of different courts, all of whose (along with the city courts') main purpose in existence is to provide simple courts for simple matters."

I asked, "What differentiates the four?"

Bringing up an old topic, Hecht went, "That brings up our good old friend jurisdiction again, with each of their existences varying depending on the county, thanks to legislative manhandling. The lowest of the four is the already mentioned justice of the peace. This court handles class C misdemeanors, civil suits up to $10,000, issuing search and arrest warrants, ex officio duties such as notary publics, small claims court, and, most notably, being the coroner in counties where an official medical examiner is not found. This has judges-slash-courts here acting as the go-to guy in court matters, as the other courts are, for lack of a better term, more judicially bound in duty in court. Finally, for these courts, the number shall vary between one and eight courts, depending on the population of the county, with one being required. Oh, uh, they are also courts of no records as well."

Before moving on to discussing the three remaining county legal courts, Hecht paused to gather his thoughts for a moment. After what I just heard about the city and justice of the peace courts, I needed to collect my thoughts as well. Then Hecht asked, "Have you visited with a county government yet?"

I replied, "Yes."

---

45   For an overall explanation of courts is Texas please see the following: Jones County Courthouse—Anson, "Texas Courts: A Descriptive Summary," http://www.txcourts.gov/media/10753/court-overview.pdf.

He continued, "Well, regardless, I must bring up a county governing agency that calls itself a court but isn't, the commissioner's court. This court serves as the main legislative/governing body of county government. The county judge, beyond leading this 'so-called' court with the commissioners, also has certain judicial requirements to lead the county constitutional court, the second main county court, so called because the state constitution requires each county to have one. The problem is, many of the county judges have little to no prior judicial experience and, especially in the more populous counties, have little to no time to devote to legal concerns. In reconciling this issue, the state has created a parallel court, called the county court-at-law, the third county court, which has similar jurisdiction to hear class A and B misdemeanors and civil suits up to $100,000 in damages with a truly qualified judge."

At this point, I could hear Schwartz's comments about the organizations of the courts being complicated in my head. I agreed with her more and more. I remembered that these were only the first three with another one after that to come. Then the floodgates opened when Hecht said, "The final court at the county level is the specialty courts. One specialty version is called probate court and is specifically designed to deal with the final wishes of the deceased in regards to their assets—especially with contested wills—and custody of children under age 18. Other jurisdictions have created other specialty courts for veterans, juveniles, or family matters. The first for veterans in Texas opened in early 2014 down in Hays County."[46]

I remarked, "Sir, hearing about all of these local courts is like sitting at a stoplight with one too many lights on it where you can't tell when you are supposed to go."

Hecht responded, "That is the idea. The judicial power of the state, just like legislative and executive, was specifically designed by the constitutional writers to bifurcate power and spread it to the point that nobody can take advantage of the system fully. Speaking of spreading the power, the third rung on the ladder is the state district courts. These courts handle all felony crimes committed in the state, alongside divorces, contested elections, and issues of deed disputes, plus other not-so-readily important issues. The actual districts for these courts can cover multiple or single counties and overlap with other district courts.[47] Take a look at this map here."

After handing me the map (figure 20.4), Hecht continued, "On one end, you have Harris County with 56 district courts specifically for those residents, while on the other you have 12 district courts covering some 13 counties in central and eastern Texas. Beyond that, especially in the case of Harris County, the district court can be designated for civil or criminal

46    Laureen Chernow, "First Hays County Veterans Court Set for Spring," Hays County Government, February 25, 2014, http://www.co.hays.tx.us/first-hays-county-veterans-court-set-for-spring.aspx.
47    https://www.txcourts.gov/media/1443116/district-court-map-jan-2019.pdf

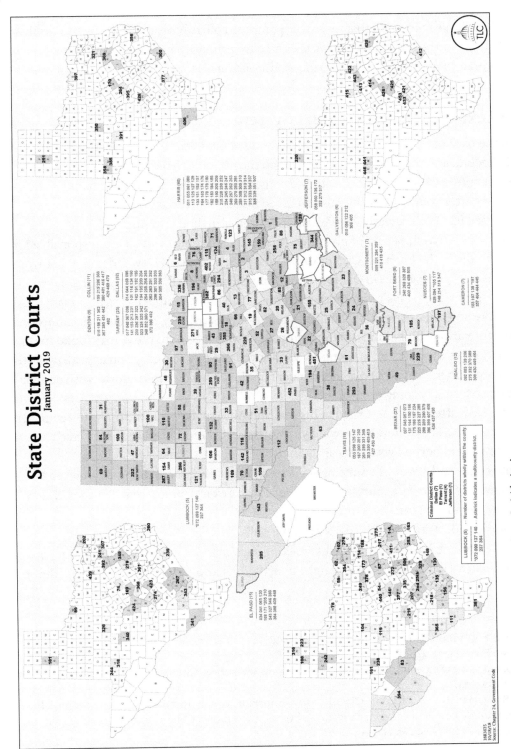

## State District Courts
### January 2019

FIGURE 20.4  Map of Texas State District Court Jurisidiction's

cases. Finally, keep in mind that up to this point the courts have all primarily had original jurisdiction; for the remaining courts, they all have primarily appellate jurisdiction."

I inquired, "So what is the fourth rung on the ladder?"

## The Texas and Federal Court System

From the back of the room, a voice rang out and stated, "Wait one moment! It is the time for the federal judiciary system to comment on the matter at hand."

Hecht spoke, "Justice Samuel Alito, welcome to my humble abode and thanks for hurrying over after your work at the Austin United States Courthouse over on Fifth Street."

I chimed in, "What exactly were you doing at the courthouse in Austin?"

Alito spoke, "Well, as part of my duties on the US Supreme Court, I am responsible for riding circuit in the Fifth US Circuit Court of Appeals based in New Orleans,[48] but from time to time, I go visit the US District Courts of Appeals as well. When there, I am responsible for 'grant[ing] stays or injunctions in both civil and criminal cases, . . . arrang[ing] bail before and after conviction, and [providing] other ancillary relief, such as extensions of time for various filings and different procedural variances[49] to the courts found in that jurisdiction. In the past, when doing so, we had to hear physical cases on appeal, up until 1869 when Congress approved of independent justices to sit on those courts, with our ability to do so formally going away in 1911."[50]

I inquired, after Hecht returned to his seat and Alito sat down at the opposing council's place from me, "So, we now know what you were doing there, but what federal court activities occur there beyond your duties?"

Alito continued, "Well, if I remember correctly, what y'all were talking about when I was coming in was the lowest courts on the ladder of the Texas court system. For the US courthouse in Austin, all I can say is ditto."

I interjected, "Ditto? Ditto? That's it? Come on!"

Alito elaborated, "My apologies, just making sure that you are paying attention. Found in the Austin US Courthouse are eight courtrooms and office space for ten different

---

48    US Supreme Court, "Order List: 582 U.S.," https://www.supremecourt.gov/orders/courtorders/062717zr1_5426.pdf.

49    Sandra Day O'Connor, "Foreword: The Changing Role of the Circuit Justice," *Toledo Law Review* 17 (1985): 523–24.

50    Sebastian Bates, "Riding Circuit: How Supreme Court Justices Can Act Alone," *Penn Undergraduate Law Journal*, March 17, 2015, https://www.pulj.org/the-roundtable/-riding-circuit-how-supreme-court-justices-can-act-alone.

justices as part of the Austin Branch of the Western District of Texas.[51] Unlike the lowest level of the Texas court system, we don't have as many different courts, just many district courts. Other branches in the Western District include Alpine, Del Rio, El Paso, Fort Hood, Midland Odessa, Pecos, San Antonio, and Waco. To top it off, there is also the Northern, Southern, and Eastern District Courts in Texas with just as many branches. Here's a map for you to keep! (figure 20.5)."

FIGURE 20.5    Map of Texas Federal District Courts

---

51    US District Court, "Office Locations," accessed March 22, 2019, https://www.txwd.uscourts.gov/court-information/office-locations/#Austin.

Hecht wanted to take his courtroom back over, so he mentioned, "As I was going to say before I was joyfully interrupted by my esteemed colleague, the fourth level of the Texas court system used to be very simple before 1891. Before that time, all appeals from the county and state district courts went directly to the court of criminal appeals or the state supreme court that you are sitting in, depending on the matter at hand, with civil and juvenile delinquency casing going here to the Texas Supreme Court, and all other cases going to the court of criminal appeals. These last two courts are also unofficially known as the courts of last resort and now make-up the fifth rung of the ladder. The state appellate process now has cases go through 14 intermediate state appellate courts to handle the ever-increasing demands for appeals. Here is another map for you to peruse. This one is of the 14 intermediate appellate courts of the Texas court system (figure 20.6)."

After handing me the map, Hecht continued. "These 14 districts are spread out across the state, but in far fewer and larger regions, to create a stopgap from keeping my court overloaded. The only vestige of the original system is that all capital-punishment cases are automatically appealed directly to the court of criminal appeals when death is sentenced. In the intermediate appellate courts, a chief justice and 3 to 15 justices sit on each bench hearing cases *en banc* (as a group) or in panels of three, while in the two courts of last resort, all nine justices serving on the courts hear each case presented."

Now wanting to take back over the ebb and flow of the courtroom, Alito argued, "The final two levels of the US court system are almost the same, except the intermediate appellate courts are called circuit courts of appeal. Texas falls under the Fifth Circuit, which hears cases on appeal from the Eastern, Western, and Middle Districts of Louisiana, the Northern and Southern of Mississippi, and the four from Texas mentioned earlier. Cases heard here on appeal are typically heard by panels of three justices and by all on the rare occasion in New Orleans, Louisiana, at the John Minor Wisdom United States Court of Appeals Building (figure 20.7). From there, cases heard on further appeals are then heard on appeal to the US Supreme Court, my court. The US Supreme Court meets at the US Supreme Courthouse (figure 20.8) on the National Mall in Washington DC, just behind the US Capitol Building. This is where nine of us hear the cases presented to the court. Oh, here is a map of the federal Circuit Court of Appeals jurisdictions (figure 20.9)."

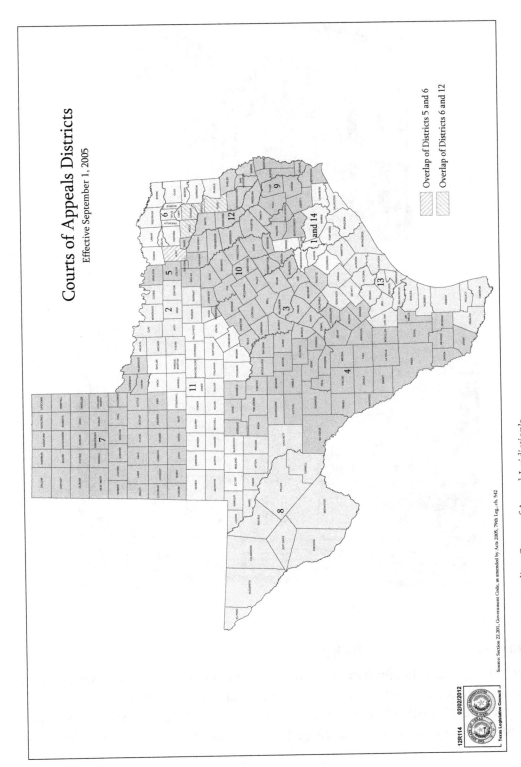

## Courts of Appeals Districts
### Effective September 1, 2005

Overlap of Districts 5 and 6

Overlap of Districts 6 and 12

Source: Section 22.201, Government Code, as amended by Acts 2005, 79th Leg., ch. 542

12R114    02/02/2012

Texas Legislative Council

FIGURE 20.6  Map of Texas Intermediate Courts of Appeal Juridiction's

FIGURE 20.7   John Minor Wisdom U.S. Courthouse, home of the United States Court of Appeals for the Fifth Circuit, New Orleans, Louisiana.

FIGURE 20.8   United States Supreme Court Building

## Qualifications to Be a Judge

After learning about the appellate courts in the state and the federal government, I asked, "What are the qualifications required to be a justice on a Texas or federal court?

Hecht said, "Now hold on a minute there. You're trying to move on when there is one more level to the Texas judicial ladder that Judge Alito has beaten me to the punch on discussing

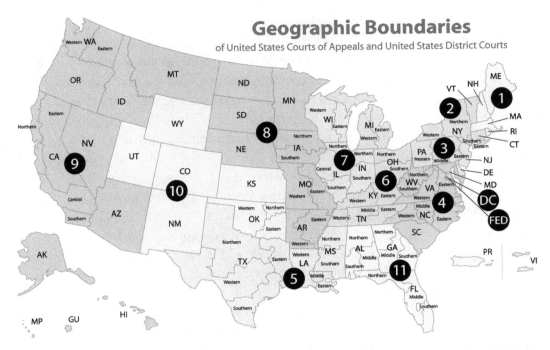

**Geographic Boundaries**
of United States Courts of Appeals and United States District Courts

FIGURE 20.9    Map of the geographic boundaries of the various United States Courts of Appeals and United States District Courts

further. That top level is the US Supreme Court. Any decision rendered by the Texas Supreme Court or the Texas Court of Criminal Appeals can be appealed to them when they issue a writ of certiorari. Beyond those cases, the US Supreme Court has original jurisdiction over cases between the United States and a state, when states have issues with other states, or when a state is suing a citizen of another state. The issue is, that court only hears about eighty cases a year,[52] meaning that for the most part, one of the appellate courts in Texas for most cases is genuinely the court of last resort. Back to your last question, though: The qualifications do depend on the court. Regardless, all judges in the state must be US citizens and registered voters. Beyond that we must turn back to the ladder. At the bottom are city courts, whose minimum qualifications vary to the point that I can't give you one.[53] Justices of the peace must merely be registered voters and US citizens. County judges on the constitution court must merely be, and I quote, 'well informed of the law.' Question: What is missing from those qualifications?"

52    Justia, "US Supreme Court Opinions by Chief Justice and Year," accessed March 22, 2019, https://supreme.justia.com/cases/federal/us.
53    Texas Secretary of State, "Qualifications for Office," accessed March 22, 2019, https://www.sos.state.tx.us/elections/candidates/guide/qualifications.shtml. A compendium on minimum qualification to run for any office in the state with their terms.

Thinking this one through, the only item that came to mind was, "There is nothing there about being a lawyer or licensed attorney."

Hecht went on: "You got it. For the most part, the people serving on these very local courts have no prior judicial or legal experience, much less a law degree. Some do, but it simply is not a requirement. What's even worse is that to start serving on the bench, those selected without prior experience are only required to take a forty-hour initial course, and a twenty-hour refresher course every year after that, on judging. Thankfully, for the remaining courts, some level of experience and a law degree are required. County courts-at-law and state district courts require you to be 25 years of age, a licensed attorney, have four years of prior experience, and be a resident of the state for two years, with the additional rider of being a resident of your district for at least six months on the county courts-at-law bench. Finally, all the appellate court judges must be at least 35 years old, have ten years of experience as a judge or lawyer, be a licensed attorney, and live in the state for at least a year, with the additional rider of living in their district for at least six months on the intermediate appellate courts bench."

I turned to Alito and asked, "What about federal courts judicial qualifications?"

Alito surmised, "Officially there are none, just be appointed by the president and get confirmed by the US Senate, and you are good to go.[54] Unofficially, it helps, though, to be on favorable terms with the US senators from your state and be of the same legal mind-set as the president. Probably, though, being a judge or having some legal experience wouldn't hurt either. I think I answered the qualifications and how they are selected, lucky me!"

## How Texas Judges Get a Seat on the Bench

I remarked, "So that is the courts themselves for both courts systems, what it takes to serve on the courts of both systems, and how federal judges are selected. So then, how do judges get selected in Texas?"

Hecht replied, "Thankfully, the state constitution writers took care of that in one fell swoop. Easily put, all judges must win a partisan election. The only exception is city judges, who are elected in nonpartisan elections, like their cities' councilmen. Wanna hear a joke about city judges?"

I nodded yes, and he went on: "Who is Jerry Jones?"

I replied, "The owner of the Dallas Cowboys."

He responded, "Nope. He's a municipal judge in Dallas."

---

54 US Courts, "FAQs: Federal Judges," accessed March 22, 2019, http://www.uscourts.gov/faqs-federal-judges.

I said, "No, he's not!"

He giddily replied, "Well, we're both right, at least theoretically for me. The one that I am referring to received his job thanks to name-brand recognition, as people think that he and the Cowboys' owner are the same person. That's the problem with nonpartisan elections: Everything depends on the recognizability of your name and not your qualifications, while for the partisan elections it all depends on what party you belong to. Finally, city judges face reelection every two or four years (depending on the city), all county and district judges face reelection every four years, and, in conclusion, all appellate court judges serve six-year terms that are staggered, with a third of the judges facing reelection every two years."[55]

Alito chimed in, "All justices on the federal court system serve until they resign their post or die. Granted, they can be impeached."

As the time was getting near 5:00 p.m., I was getting hungry and tired, and it seemed best to wrap up this discussion. I decided to ask one more question. "So what would be one thing you would want to tell people about the judiciary—a concern, maybe?"

When I brought this up, Hecht looked around with an actual air of concern about him, as apparently, I had broached a rather touchy subject about the judiciary, in Texas at least. I felt as if I had gone too far and began to pack my things and go. But then he answered, "Stay seated! I want to make sure that I have my facts in order before I get into this line of inquiry. Let's review a few things. How do all of the justices in Texas get their jobs?"

I replied, "Those positions have partisan or nonpartisan elections."

He went on, "Very good. So what must they do when the potential judges compete in an election?"

I responded, "Campaign?"

He continued, "Good. The better question is: What are some of the campaign activities people campaigning must do?"

I replied, "Answer questions about their views, make statements, and collect donations?"

He furthered, "Let's focus on the last part there, donations. For a judge, or even any politician, what could a campaign contribution for a judge be construed as in the wrong light?"

I acknowledged, "A bribe?"

He extended, "So when would it look like a bribe?"

I concluded, "When the judges are finding someone guilty or innocent or sentencing them or deciding about what to do about a case on appeal, as it may be difficult to properly punish someone if the individual made a large donation to your campaign?"

He concluded, "Exactly! Federal justices, on the other hand, have life tenure and are appointed by the president and are confirmed by the Senate, leaving them to be able to make

---

55    Ibid.

hard decisions that may be unpopular for the most part. Think *Brown v. Board of Education of Topeka.*[56] It was a complicated situation for the Warren Court to make in ending a long-standing societal norm—especially in the South—of 'separate but equal.' Imagine, what would it have looked like if X judge had made a contribution to the reelection campaign for the judge of that trial? It ultimately brings up the question: Is justice for sale in Texas? It might be. This became a much bigger issue in 2002 when, in *Republican Party of Minnesota v. White,*[57] the Supreme Court overturned the 'announce' clause in Minnesotan judicial elections that prevented judicial candidates from taking sides on issues that may come before the court that they would be deciding judges in due to the clause preventing free speech. Essentially, it turned judicial elections into real elections where those donations begin to service as bribes, theoretically of course. Well, since it's 5:00 p.m., I think we should close court for the day. It was nice meeting and discussing these endeavors with you."

Alito nodded to concur with the statement by Hecht and stated, "Champ, would you like to join me for dinner? I have some more color commentary to add to the proceedings."

I replied, "Sure, why not?"

## Opinions of the Court

Like before with the cops, I stood up and thanked Hecht for his time. Alito and I made our way to the Capitol Grill in the Capitol Extension. We made small talk along the way there and while in line for our food. Once seated, Alito stated, "On a random note, when you file for bankruptcy, you do so in US bankruptcy courts. When you have a dispute with another state's citizen, you must go to federal district court. What I wanted to talk to you about more importantly, though, is how appellate cases are decided. In the original jurisdiction court, the jury decides a verdict. At the appeals level, the justices themselves make the decision. In doing so, we write papers called opinions with the one supported by a majority of justices being called the main opinion, which becomes 'law.' Beyond that, there are dissenting opinions that are written by judges on the non-majority side of the decision, writing against the majority, followed by a concurring opinion, which is written by the justice on the majority, but who agrees for different reasons."

I interjected, "What goes into these opinions?"

Alito furthered, "Well, opinions are lengthy explanations of why the court decided a case the way it did. They also guide lower courts on how to decide or treat similar cases in the future. Beyond that, how the judge's decision is whittled down to two views, being activists

---

56    347 U.S. 483. https://www.oyez.org/cases/1940-1955/347us483
57    536 U.S. 765. https://www.oyez.org/cases/2001/01-521

or restraints. Those judges being activists make their decisions on personal feelings and the belief that everything should be viewed in a modern light, and that laws should be struck down based on changes in society, while restraints make their decisions on the belief that they should hesitate to strike down laws unless they are obviously unconstitutional and defer to the legislature for any truly drastic changes in the law."

I surmised, "It is interesting that you as justices have so much leeway in how the direction of the legal system, the law, and society itself can go."

Nodding in agreement, Alito steered the conversation to more trivial matters while taking the last bite of his burger. After about a half hour more, we said our goodbyes and headed our separate ways. On my way back to my car, I recapped what I experienced that day. First, I learned about the different law enforcement agencies found in the state, which include city police, county deputies, state troopers, Texas Rangers, and state agency forces, not to mention federal agents, alongside what their jurisdictions and responsibilities are. After that, I got a brief introduction to court uses, officials, case jurisdictions, and juries in state district court. Finally, I got acquainted with how the legal system in the state and federal governments are structured between higher and lower courts, along with problems associated with how the courts operate and form. The day was going well until I heard sirens blaring behind me and a megaphone blaring, "You there, stop. Jaywalking is illegal and stop looking at your phone while walking." Man, there are a lot of cops here with a whole lot of laws to enforce and follow alongside a massive legal system to back them up. Overall, the federal and state court systems are complex, but that complexity helps ensure that one's rights are not violated and that all matters of fact have been considered, responsibly of course.

---

**QUESTIONS TO CONSIDER** REGARDING LAWS AND THE ENFORCEMENT OF THEM:

1. The first main topic of the chapter discusses police jurisdiction. Please define what jurisdiction is, what it means for police, the police agency discussed in the chapter that would arrest you if you committed a crime at this very moment, and why, in detail.
2. The second main topic of the chapter discusses types of crime. Please identify the different crime classifications, the crime classification that most applies to you, and why, in detail.
3. The third main topic of the chapter discusses who are criminals and who are victims. Please identify who is most likely to be a criminal and a victim, the qualifications you meet, and whether you are more likely to be a criminal or a victim, in detail.

4. The fourth main topic of the chapter discusses advice that cops might want citizens to know. Please select your favorite piece of advice, what that advice entails, how that advice applies to you, and why, in detail.

5. The fifth main topic of the chapter discusses the types of court cases. Please identify what those types of court cases are, what they entail, the case that you would like to go to court for, and why, in detail.

6. The sixth main topic of the chapter discusses the people found in courtrooms. Please explain what you want to do in life, identify the person in a courtroom who most resembles what you want to do in life, and why, in detail.

7. The seventh main topic of the chapter discusses the two types of court jurisdictions. Please identify what those court jurisdictions are, what the two together are most akin to from your life, and why, in detail.

8. The eighth main topic of the chapter discusses the Texas and federal court system. Please identify the different systems and their courts, which you think is better based on the number and scope of courts, and why, in detail.

9. The ninth main topic of the chapter discusses qualifications to be a judge in the state and federal court systems. Please identify what each of the qualifications is for each of the courts, who in your opinion has the better qualifications, and why, in detail.

10. The tenth main topic of the chapter discusses how to be selected as a judge in the state and federal court systems. Please identify what each judge must do to get a seat on the bench, which in your opinion has the better system, and why, in detail.

11. The 11th main topic of the chapter discusses the main issue with how judges get their seats on the bench in Texas. Please identify what that issue is, whether you agree with the author, and why, in detail.

12. The final main topic of the chapter discusses the opinions of the court. Please identify what opinions of the court are, your favorite opinion, and why, in detail.

## FIGURE CREDITS

# Chapter 21

# Federal Enclaves

# The Concept of Federal Property

My weekend with Charity and Deacon went well. It was fun discussing my experience with the state and local agencies that I had visited over the past week and a half. Not knowing where to go next, I spent last night writing down ideas. The only logical idea that emerged was government agencies beyond the state and local level of government in Texas. I awoke this morning with my plans for the day already set out. Not by me, of course, I was awakened just after midnight by the person who had. What woke me was a black-leather-gloved hand being placed over my mouth, leaving only enough room for my nostrils to breathe. I was screaming (albeit muffled), sweating, and altogether freaked out beyond what I could comprehend at this point in the morning. Another hand was on my chest, pushing my torso into the mattress. I was pinned and quite simply unable to move. Note to self: To subdue an attacker controlling the head and chest is a great way to keep them down on the ground. After about 30 seconds, I regained my composure after I realized that I was not going to be kidnapped, molested, or have God knows what other combination of torture done to me. What also helped was the realization of who was holding me down. It was not some stranger, but someone that I knew. It was Charity's husband, Deacon. Not knowing what to say, I panted out slowly, "Deacon . . . what are you . . . doing . . . man?!"

Instead of immediately answering, he waited for what seemed like five minutes, but was probably only a few seconds, as that adrenaline got me going. Finally, he remarked, "Quiet, Champ. We don't want to wake your sister. Go put on your blackest apparel and meet me downstairs outside the garage in five minutes. No questions asked. Got it?"

I nodded my understanding. In retrospect, I probably should have asked something, but when someone has you pinned to your bed in the middle of the night, gosh darn it, you listen. I waited until he had left the room before I got out from under the sheets, to be sure, though. Without turning on the lights beyond the flashlight from my phone, I went into my closet and found an all-black tracksuit that I had no recollection of purchasing, much less putting in the closet. At this point, something told me that Charity, despite being soundly asleep, was in on this operation. Once I had changed into my black apparel and come down the stairs, Deacon was, as expected, waiting for me in his all-black attire. Once I was in front of him, he remarked, "All right, Champ, you have passed the proper attire test well. I could barely see you walking down the stairs in the dark. For our mission tonight, I rented the most unsuspicious car I could find. This vehicle will be important for us as we drive around tonight spying on one set of forward operating bases of non-Texan governing entities found in Texas. Granted, the two sets aren't enemies, but this is a lot cooler to venture through if we think that for tonight's exercise."

I replied, "Who are we spying on tonight then?"

Deacon responded, "We are surveilling the regional offices of one of the world's largest firms, the federal government of the United States of America. Hopefully, you remember your training about this secretive organization from the girl you had the date with earlier this summer. How is she by the way?

I then replied, "She's great, but why are you dressed in black?"

Deacon said, "Let's ride!"

Once in the garage, we came across one of the most, if not *the* most, decrepit-looking cars I have ever seen. I could only blurt out, "Deacon, a minivan? Why in God's name did you get this beast? How could we possibly even be inconspicuous?"

Deacon retorted, all while stripping off his outerwear, "Champ, one thing that I learned in survival school a few years back was that sometimes the best camouflage is to hide in plain sight. In the middle of the night, who is going to pull a minivan over, much less a beat-up blue clunker like this? It's the ultimate goober mobile. A cop will only think, 'There goes a dad who is about to give his kid one good hell of a telling.' That's why I am now wearing these pajamas with a robe, and you look like you just snuck out of the house to rob a 7-Eleven."

I could only look on in discouragement as to where this night would lead, but seeing as how sunrise was due in about five or so hours, I knew it would all be over soon enough. Once in the car, we backed out of the driveway. We then went to the main entrance of the Lost Creek subdivision and turned right onto State Highway 360. Once at full speed, Deacon turned to me and said, "Champ, the federal government operates out of what is known as federal buildings. Those buildings are called that because the building was built or is being used in its entirety to host the regional offices of the various federal government departments and agencies that are in the area, although that does not mean that all federal department agencies are located in them. When an agency gets to be of a certain size or gains the responsibilities that require more than just one regional hub in an area, they are often granted offices away from the central hub. When not located in one of the main federal buildings, the building is simply named after the agency that is now housed there. Also, some federal buildings carry the moniker of 'old' on them. This renaming occurs when either a new facility is built to expand offerings, or the new facility replaces the current one in its entirety but the old building remains."

I asked, "So who handles each of these buildings?"

Deacon replied, "Well, that would be the General Services Administration (GSA), I was reading their website yesterday evening (to confirm my thoughts) and there it said, I quote: 'Public Building Service (PBS) provides a variety of facilities management services to more than one million federal workers. Its facility service program's goal is to provide sustainable world-class facilities and services."[1] Of note, at each of these facilities, federal law applies while on their property as the sites function as an enclave of the federal government here in the state."[2]

I interjected, "How much property does the GSA manage?"

Deacon continued, "Well, late yesterday evening, when I was doing some background research for this particular adventure, I also came across the GSA's fiscal year 2016 State of the Portfolio Snapshot.[3] This report provides readers with the most up-to-date information about not so much what the federal government does, but what exactly its real, tangible property consists of around the country. Per that report, on page 3, the federal government portfolio consists of roughly '370.6 million rentable square feet in 8,603 active assets across the United States, in all 50 states, 6 US territories, and the District of Columbia.'[4] Overall, their rentable square feet is roughly 13.27 square miles, of which they own approximately 48 percent and lease the remainder from the private sector."[5]

I inquired, "That seems to be an awful lot of property. How do they manage all of it?"

Deacon remarked, "Well, the GSA has 11 regional managing facilities, alongside their central office that is located in our nation's capital.[6] Speaking of our nation's capital, it and the greater New York City area, Kansas City, Denver, and Chicago are the most abundant markets for federally owned or leased property.[7] The Departments of Justice and Homeland Security, the Judiciary, the Treasury, and the Social Security Administration occupy roughly 50 percent of that space as their most prominent clientele nationwide. Each of these places and more we will see tonight on our adventure."[8]

As we were about to make the turn North onto MoPac, I asked, "So what exactly does that include here in Texas?"

Thinking for a second, Deacon replied, "Well, Texas is located in the Greater Southwest Region, which is based in Fort Worth and includes 34.7 million square feet inside of 1,292

---

1   GSA.gov, "Facilities Management Overview," accessed March 22, 2019, http://www.gsa.gov/portal/content/104476.

2   US General Services Administration, "Rules and Regulations Governing Conduct on Federal Property," November 2005, http://www.gsa.gov/cdnstatic/GSA_Rules_Reg_1105.pdf.

3   US General Services Administration, "State of the Portfolio Snapshot FY 2016," 2016, https://www.gsa.gov/cdnstatic/FY_2016_State_of_the_Portfolio_Snapshot.pdf; US General Services Administration, "Rules and Regulations Governing Conduct on Federal Property."

4   Ibid., p, 5.

5   Ibid., p. 3

6   Ibid., p. 3.

7   Ibid., p. 5.

8   Ibid.

buildings.[9] Further, if I memorized that report as well as I think I did, I do believe there to be roughly 22.9 million rentable square feet here in Texas,[10] of which there are 7.42 million square feet in the DFW Metroplex, 3.3 million in the greater Houston area, 1.9 million in the San Antonio area, and, as you requested, 2.5 million square feet here in the Austin area that includes 8 owned buildings and 28 leased facilities,[11] with the remainder found elsewhere in the state."

## How Texas Monitors Federal Activity in the State

As we crossed the Colorado River, our van took the exit for West Fifth Street. At the light, we took a right and continued for 14 blocks on San Antonio Street. On the way, I asked, "Deacon, other than the research you did for this, how do you know so much about the federal government's presence here in the state?"

Deacon replied, "Well, Champ, I guess Charity hasn't told you, and you have been gone a lot since you got here, but I work for the Texas Office of State and Federal Relations under the guidance of Governor Abbott. Our mission is to, and I quote, 'increase the influence of the Governor and the Legislature over federal action that has a direct or indirect economic, fiscal, or regulatory impact on the state and its citizens, maintaining an active role for Texas in the national decision-making process.'[12] This situation is critical as the state lost its main checks and balances over the federal government with the passage of the 17th Amendment in 1913, allowing for the direct election of US instead of them being appointed by our state legislature. [13] However, the state itself still has the option to argue that they can nullify the enforcement of some, but not all, federal laws they deem unconstitutional, as was the case during the implementation of the Affordable Care Act.[14] This situation depends on the view of the Union formed by the states in 1789 to be one of a compact between states, not a true consolidation.[15] As part of this compact, the states then are believed to have retained the inherent right to judge compliance with the compact. In short, of where we are today: '(1) State officials need not enforce federal laws that the state has determined to be unconstitutional;

---

9    Ibid.
10   Ibid.
11   Ibid.
12   Office of the Texas Governor, "Mission," accessed March 22, 2019, http://gov.texas.gov/osfr/about/mission.
13   OurDocuments.gov, "17th Amendment to the U.S. Constitution: Direct Election of U.S. Senators (1913)," accessed March 22, 2019, https://www.ourdocuments.gov/doc.php?flash=false&doc=58.
14   Robert A. Levy, "Yes, States Can Nullify Some Federal Laws, Not All," Cato Institute, March 18, 2013, https://www.cato.org/publications/commentary/yes-states-can-nullify-some-federal-laws-not-all.
15   Ibid.

nor may Congress mandate that states enact specific laws. But (2), states may not block federal authorities who attempt to enforce a federal law unless a court has held that the law is unconstitutional. And (3), individuals are not exempt from prosecution by the federal government just because the state where they reside has legalized an activity or pronounced that a federal law is unconstitutional; if convicted, individuals can attempt to vindicate their constitutional rights in court."[16] Regardless, my agency and I are a watchdog over federal policy and work toward protecting my fellow state citizens and me from overburdensome policy created by the feds, in line to an extent with the compact theory."

## Branches of the Federal Government in Texas

When he finished saying that, I knew that he knew more than just how much office space they have; he also knows what goes on inside of those hallowed halls. Thankfully, to ease the tension, we then pulled up in front of a shiny looking and relatively new glass and stone building. On the side of a lower-tiered balcony, a sign read, "United States Courthouse."

FIGURE 21.1  U.S. Federal Courthouse–Austin, Texas.

I turned back to Deacon and stated, "I do believe that we have found one of those fancy federal buildings you were talking about—a courthouse, at that (figure 21.1)."

Deacon nodded his head in agreement and mentioned, "This building opened in December 2012 and is now the primary home for the Judicial Branch of the federal government and the US Department of Justice here in the Austin area.[17] They have courtrooms and office space for an agency that needs some in the area. Let's continue onward."

I interjected, "Last Friday I met Justice Samuel Alito of the US Supreme Court who was in town working in this building, I think."

After about seven more blocks on Fifth Street, we turned left and headed north on San Jacinto Street. After eight blocks, we found ourselves parked outside of a high cement

---

16    Ibid.

17    GSA.gov, "J.J. Pickle Federal Building," accessed March 22, 2019, https://www.gsa.gov/about-us/regions/welcome-to-the-greater-southwest-region-7/buildings-and-facilities/texas/jj-pickle-federal-building.

honeycombed office building. Deacon continued, "Champ, here we are. The J.J. Pickle Federal Building (figure 21.2), where agencies in need of a home can rent some of the building's 200,000 square feet of space for their work.[18] Its most famous resident was Lyndon Baines Johnson during his presidency, when he used the space as his local office, similar to the Western White House located up in Crawford that George W. Bush used during his administration at his ranch.[19] Let's drive up a block."

Once there, Deacon continued, "This building here is called the Homer Thornberry Building (figure 21.3). It is part of the federal complex in the area and was used to house the federal courts in the government complex—better known as downtown Austin—until their new building opened that we were just parked outside of. It is also connected to the Pickle Building, giving the federal government a prominent presence in the area."

Speaking up, I inquired, "Where to now?"

Deacon responded, "Time for a gumball rally[20] across the state!"

FIGURE 21.2  Front Exterior View, J.J. Pickle Federal Building located in Downtown Austin, Texas.

FIGURE 21.3  Rear Exterior View, Homer Thornberry Federal Building located in Downtown Austin, Texas.

I suddenly felt the sunrise deadline that I had dreamed of for this adventure was not about to be met. I could only say, "Hit it!"

Off we went. Once on Interstate 35, Deacon handed me a clue. It read, "Pew, pew, pew, pew, pew, pew."

Deacon asked, "So, where do you think we are going?"

18    Ibid.
19    Ibid.
20    American Gumball Rally, "Frequently Asked Questions," accessed March 22, 2019, https://www.americangumballrally.com/faq.

My only response was, "Pew, pew, pew sounds like a gun. So that would mean that we are headed toward either a police station, military base, or simply a gun range."

Deacon asked, "Which of those three do you think most likely?"

I replied, "I would say a military base, as it is their job to shoot and the Armed Forces last I checked are a nearly pure federal function outside of state guards."[21]

Deacon replied, "I'll let you know when we get there."

Over the next 45 minutes, we drove north, going through the Austin suburbs and exurbs of Round Rock and Georgetown. Then we turned west on to Texas 195 and drove through the small town of Florence along the way. Once in the city of Killeen, we turned west on to US 190, recently rechristened as Interstate 14.[22] After a mile or so, we took the spur onto T.J. Mills Boulevard that leads directly to the base. At that point, I muttered, "Deacon, if we are trying to be inconspicuous, maybe we should try not to drive onto the base looking like we are, much less attempt to drive onto the base at all!"

Deacon, cool as a cucumber, said, "Relax, we are not going to drive onto the base. That would get us thrown in the brig. We are going to pull off over here to the Marvin Leath Visitor Center[23] parking lot."

Once in the lot, we pulled into one of the spots near the building. Deacon continued, "Champ, we are now at the main entrance to Fort Hood at the Bernie Beck Gate(figure 21.4). This site was initially built during World War II to help tankers learn how to power their mechanized craft.[24] Today, that mission continues, as the base now holds the honor of being the most substantial active-duty armored post in the US military, at 214,000 acres.[25] Specifically, it houses two full divisions: the First Cavalry Division and the Fourth Infantry Division, which is mechanized, alongside 12 additional specialty units."[26]

I inquired, "So what part of the federal government does this consist of?"

Deacon continued, "It's obvious, but this is part of the US Department of Defense, which, before 1949, was called the Department of War.[27] Let's continue."

---

21    https://tmd.texas.gov/state-guard

22    Ben Wear, "Wear: You'll Never Guess How Texas Got I-14, the 14th Amendment Highway," *Statesman*, December 11, 2018, http://www.mystatesman.com/news/wear-you-never-guess-how-texas-got-the-14th-amendment-highway/Xw1IWJqoFgXaY2Ug5TQi3L.

23    Military.com, "Fort Hood Visitors Center," accessed March 22, 2019, http://www.military.com/base-guide/fort-hood/contact/visitors-center/612.

24    History of the Great Place, "Fort Hood History," accessed March 22, 2019, http://www.hood.army.mil/history.aspx.

25    Ibid.

26    Ibid.

27    *Forgotten History Blog*, "Before Rebranding, the US Dept. of Defense Was Called the "Department of War"," accessed March 22, 2019, http://forgottenhistoryblog.com/before-

We pulled out of the parking lot, being very careful to take the loop road that spits you back out onto Interstate 14, then we continued east for about 30 minutes. Along the way, as we were reaching Belton and Interstate 35 once again, Deacon handed me another clue. I read aloud, "Money for the poor! We have money for the poor!"

Deacon stated again, "So, where do you think we are going now?"

I responded, "If I remember enough of my history classes that would most likely be the Social Security Administration."

Deacon replied, "Almost there."

FIGURE 21.4  The Martin Leath Visitor Center is in the right background.

About 20 minutes later, we left the highway at Exit 301 in Temple, Texas. This action took us east onto West Central Avenue. Twelve blocks later, after crossing the railyard bridge and going through most of downtown, we turned left, going north onto North Main Street. Six or so blocks after that, we pulled into one of the parking spots immediately in front of the Social Security Office in Temple, Texas (figure 21.5). Deacon surmised, "This is one of over 1,400 agency offices that include regional offices, field offices, card centers, teleservice centers, processing centers, hearing offices, the Appeals Council, and their state and territorial partners, the Disability Determination Services,[28] all of which help distribute some of the various social insurance programs administered by the federal government. The Social Security Administration functions as an independent agency in the federal bureaucracy.[29] Here is your next clue."

FIGURE 21.5  Social Security Administration Buildng in Temple, Texas.

rebranding-the-us-dept-of-defense-was-called-the-department-of-war.

28   Social Security Administration, "About Us," accessed March 22, 2019, http://ssa.gov/agency.

29   Ibid.

As we made a U-turn on North Main Street, I opened the next envelope. The letter read, "4-H[30] and FFA[31] students, alongside their parents in the dusty pastures and trails before them, would seek this place for guidance in their quests to eventually provide sustenance."

As we turned right onto State Highway 53, I blurted out, "I assume that our next stop has something to do with farming?"

Deacon joked, "Farming, ranching, agriculture, and a whole lot of items associated with the main passengers aboard Noah's Ark."

As we were reaching the interstate feeder, I announced, "Onward to whichever branch of the US Department of Agriculture awaits us, I think."

FIGURE 21.6 USDA Service Center - Robinson, TX, just outside Waco.

For the next hour or so, we continued to make our way up the interstate. At this point, the beautiful thing I noticed about Texas is that, while in many places the state seems crowded, once you get out of the city, the countryside is still quite rural. Around Bruceville-Eddy, Texas,[32] I could see the stars in all their splendored twinkle. On the outskirts of Waco, Texas,[33] we exited off the interstate onto the Texas 340 Loop and immediately turned into the sixth driveway. Out front was merely a flagpole and facade announcing the tenant of the building: "USDA Service Center (figure 21.6)."

Deacon spoke up. "Remember, until modern times, one of the most dominant fields of work in the country, Texas not being an exception, was farming crops or raising livestock, and in many cases a mixture of the two. Every five years, Congress passes an act called the Farm Bill to create the policy for farm subsidies, the country's nutrition programs—including food stamps, known today as the Supplemental Nutrition Assistance Program—and so much more that the USDA, or Department of Agriculture, oversees, with the most recent occurring in 2014.[34] As part of that Farm Bill, the legislation,

---

30   http://www.4-h.org
31   https://www.ffa.org/home
32   http://bruceville-eddy.org
33   http://www.waco-texas.com
34   http://www.thefarmbill.com/the-bill; H.R. Res. 2624, 113th Cong. (2014) (enacted). Agricultural Act of 2014

and I quote, 'provide[s] for the reform and continuation of agricultural and other programs of the Department of Agriculture through the fiscal year 2018, and for other purposes.' This includes 'setting dollar levels for the Agriculture Department and subsidiz[ing] farmers and rural communities for a multitude of things, from protecting environmentally sensitive land to international food aid to rural Internet services.'[35] Overall, this agency, per their mission statement, goes around serving all farmers, ranchers, and agricultural partners through the delivery of effective, efficient agricultural programs for all Americans."[36]

After looking around the parking lot and saluting the flag, we then continued our way out of the parking lot through the other entrance, only to find ourselves needing to go a bit farther east to make a U-turn before we could make our way onto the ramp that would take us northbound on Interstate 35 again. Once we were through with all the meandering and back on the interstate, Deacon handed me another clue. This time it was set to music and read, "Wooly bully, wooly bully, wooly bully."

I could only reply, "Are we going where the wild things roam?"

Deacon replied, "Yeah, sort of."

After driving up Interstate 35, we took the fourth exit and turned left onto South MLK Jr. Boulevard, just after passing the new McLane football stadium on the Baylor University campus, in Waco, Texas. After driving away and crossing the bridge over the Brazos River, we turned into the parking lot of the Waco Mammoth Monument Site[37] (figure 21.7). After getting into a parking spot, Deacon mentioned, "Champ, visiting the great outdoors is one of the greatest activities a man like you or I

FIGURE 21.7 Waco Mammoth Site Sign.

can do, as it helps calm our nerves and reconnects us with our natural roots. Not only does the state have its park system, called Texas Parks and Wildlife, which operates 109 state parks, historic sites, lodges, natural areas, trailways, and tramways,[38] the National Park Service of the federal government operates 16 of its own parks, memorials, monuments, recreation

35    Ibid.
36    Farm Service Agency, "History and Mission." US Department of Agriculture, accessed March 22, 2019, http://www.fsa.usda.gov/about-fsa/history-and-mission/index.
37    https://www.nps.gov/waco/index.htm
38    http://tpwd.texas.gov/state-parks

areas, preserves, historic trails, and sites, not to mention a national seashore and wild and scenic river here in the state."[39]

I interjected, "Which one are we at now? I know it has to do with wooly mammoths."

Deacon continued, "This is the Waco Mammoth National Monument.[40] It is a paleontological site that hosts the only recorded discovery of fossils that includes the entirety of a nursery herd of Columbian mammoths from roughly 67,000 years ago. If I read the website correctly, there is even a camel with the herd. More to see, though."

Before we reached the interstate on MLK Jr. Boulevard, Deacon asked, "Big D or Cowtown?"

Not knowing the difference between the two, I stated, "I'm hungry, so let's go with the cows."

Deacon handed me another clue. I read aloud, "At the beginning of the movie *The Wolf of Wall Street*, Leonardo DiCaprio's character says the following at the end of the opening monologue, my favorite line from the film: 'But of all the drugs under God's blue heaven, there's one that's my absolute favorite.[41] My question to you is: What is that drug?"

I was not yet old enough to see that movie when it came out, much less find time to read the memoir it was based on that Deacon told me about after I read the clue aloud. Leaving me to ponder silently, I spent the next hour or so on our way up the interstate thinking, "Is he referring to an actual drug? What else is that addicting—rock and roll? Is it marijuana? No, why would we need to go to, I think Fort Worth, for that?"

Just north of Hillsboro, Texas,[42] I went to sleep. Close to 4:00 a.m., I awoke as we crossed the northern portion of Interstate 820 on Interstate 35 West. Deacon chimed in, "Morning, sunshine. Any thoughts on where we are headed? We are just about there."

I thought for a moment, as I needed a moment to adjust and had no coffee to help me do so. Deacon offered another hint: "You often carry some of their work in your wallet."

I blurted out, "Leather?"

With a disheartened look, he responded, "Not what your wallet is made of, but *in* your wallet, you. More to the point, this item is mostly made of cotton."[43]

I could only think and then repeated aloud, "Paper money?"

With a small look of excitement returning, he said, "Exactly, cotton money."

---

39    http://www.nps.gov/state/tx/index.htm

40    https://www.nps.gov/waco/index.htm

41    *The Wolf of Wall Street*. Directed by Martin Scorsese. Produced by Martin Scorsese, Leonardo DiCaprio, Riza Aziz, Joey McFarland, and Emma Tillinger Koskoff. Performed by Leonardo DiCaprio, Jonah Hill, and Margot Robbie. Hollywood: Paramount Pictures, 2013.

42    http://www.hillsborotx.org

43    Bureau of Engraving and Printing, "U.S. Currency: History of the BEP and U.S. Currency," US Department of the Treasury, accessed March 22, 2019, https://www.moneyfactory.gov/uscurrency/history.html.

Still not knowing where exactly we were going, we followed the ramp that took us off the interstate and onto US Highway 287. Just before the second exit that we eventually ended up making, a highway sign said, "Bureau of Engraving and Printing, Next Right."

After exiting the highway, we turned left and used the crossover to head south on Blue Mound Road. I thought it should be called Green Mound Road after what we were about to see, but alas, it was not. I could only think of how much security must be at this location—guards, you name it, it had to be there. Funny thing, though, the building was mostly surrounded by open fields and several small housing communities, with just the ubiquitous miles of barbed-wire fencing around the complex. About a half mile down the road, we turned left into the loop that sits in front of the complex. Deacon lectured, "Champ, the American currency that you hold in your wallet came from one of two places: the building here in front of us or the main facility located on the National Mall in downtown Washington DC. This facility opened in 1990 following a rise in demand for currency that could not be met by the lone facility in DC, which coincided with the desire for a facility to be operating away from the capital area to keep the printing process going in the face of disaster[44] (figure 21.8). Alongside printing the money here, the bureau also designs the currency with many top-notch security measures, like the hidden images and embedded stripping. Also, not only do they print money, they produce military commissions and award certificates, invitations and admission cards, and many different types of identification cards, forms, and other special security documents for a variety of government agencies."[45]

FIGURE 21.8 United State Bureau of Engraving and Printing - Fort Worth, Texas.

I surmised, "So, you are telling me that this agency is the FedEx® Office[46] of the federal government?"

Deacon concluded, "Yes, sir, I am. The Bureau of Engraving and Printing makes the paper money, and their sister agency, the US Mint,[47] produces the spare change that resides just outside of your wallet in your pocket, from mints in Philadelphia,

44 Ibid.
45 Ibid.
46 http://www.fedex.com/us/office
47 http://www.usmint.gov

Denver, San Francisco, and West Point. Both monetary production units fall under the helm of the Treasury secretary, who leads the US Department of the Treasury."[48]

At that time, a light turned on in a guard booth. I immediately spoke up, as we saw the light together. "So, where to next?"

Before he answered, we continued our way back up Blue Mound Road and found ourselves turning back onto US Highway 287 going in the opposite direction from before. After sitting quietly for a few minutes, and going south on 35 West again, Deacon offered me another envelope with a clue in it. It read, "Ze plane, ze plane!"

I stated, "This one is easy, the airport! But what are we going to see there?"

Deacon, as we were turning onto Interstate 820 going east, in an eerie voice, stated, "Government in action, of course! And get a bite to eat, maybe. The time might still be too early."

After about 10 miles, we took the off-ramp onto International Parkway, a toll road that runs right through the middle of the Dallas–Fort Worth International Airport[49]. With our tolls paid to access the airport, we found ourselves exiting for the Terminal D parking garage. Once at the gate, Deacon got the parking ticket and proceeded past many rows and levels of empty spaces. Once on the roof level of the garage, he positioned the car facing the giant spire in the middle of the massive airport. He stated, "Champ, all around you is government, or at least their control of the area all around you. The airport itself is its own special district, chartered by the state of Texas to provide international air service in North Texas.[50] Operating amid the eternal bureaucratic structure of the airport is the federal bureaucracy spreading its wings. The tower you see before us is owned and operated by the Federal Aviation Administration,[51] instructing pilots and their aircraft at the airport how to move around the terminals, the field, and the immediate airspace. All this falls under the auspices of the US Department of Transportation. Inside the terminal, before 9/11, private security contractors operated the security checkpoints. Today, the Transportation Security Administration,[52] under the auspices of the Department of Homeland Security,[53] ensures that people do not bring anything dangerous onto the airplanes. Going even deeper into the airport structure, also under the auspices of the Department of Homeland Security, is the Immigration and

48    https://home.treasury.gov
49    https://www.dfwairport.com
50    "Our Future Hangs in the Balance—Two Mile Long Terminal Planned," *Irving Daily News Special Supplement*, June 4, 1967.
51    http://www.faa.gov/about
52    https://www.tsa.gov/about/tsa-mission
53    https://www.dhs.gov

Customs Enforcement[54] group, which ensures that those entering the country are legally allowed to do so, alongside not bringing in anything that they are not supposed to, such as exotic pets or fruits. At each of the airports found here in the state—the primary commercial ones at least—each of these agencies can be found, although, in some cases, the towers are contracted out to private firms."

I interjected, "So the government is all around us. Up, down, and all around."

Deacon handed me a 20-dollar bill with the instructions, "Go get some breakfast for us in the terminal. We have one more stop to go."

I realized that since I was the only one wearing real clothes, I was going to be responsible for going out and getting dirty. Not much was offered inside the airport terminal outside of security at this hour, but the DFW Grand Hyatt[55] did have a coffee shop in the lobby that provided me the opportunity to get some coffee and danishes for breakfast. Once back in the car, we paid the small fee for going through the garage with the car and made our way back down the toll road toward Interstate 820. After a few quiet moments of chewing and sipping, we found ourselves now going south on State Highway 161. As we were going through Grand Prairie, Deacon handed me the final envelope. The slip of paper inside read, "This is where I hope no one in my family spends the rest of their life."

I could only ask, "Do you mean jail?"

Deacon responded, "Not just jail, but federal prison. We all know about the Texas Department of Criminal Justice and its 106 prisons, state jails, and other facilities, like the death house in Huntsville, here in the state,[56] which is where people convicted of crimes under state law are sent to serve their time. But no one thinks about where people go when convicted in federal court under the federal judicial system. That is what I am going to show you now."

After turning east on Interstate 20, we traveled all the way across southern Dallas and took the ramp southbound on US Highway 175. About 5 miles later, a slightly exciting sign appeared on the right: "Federal Correctional Institution. DO NOT STOP FOR HITCHHIKERS."

We proceeded to exit at the Simonds Road exit. The next intersection was a five-way stop. One of the streets to its left had a sign that read, "Federal Correction Institute."

We turned into it. Luckily, there was a significant parking lot before the main buildings. Deacon pulled into another parking spot and began speaking. He said, "Champ, this is Federal Correctional Institute Seagoville (figure 21.9). Per their website,[57] this prison houses nearly 2,000 inmates and is classified as a low-security correctional institution that also houses a

---

54   http://www.ice.gov
55   https://dfw.grand.hyatt.com/en/hotel/home.html
56   http://tdcj.state.tx.us/unit_directory/index.html
57   http://www.bop.gov/locations/institutions/sea/index.jsp

FIGURE 21.9 Main House–Federal Correctional Institute, Seagoville.

satellite camp with a detention center. This location is not where those convicted of the worst type of crimes go, but the crimes committed by the convicted inmates sent here are fairly heinous as well."

Getting a thought in my head, I asked, "Does this have anything to do with the courthouse we visited earlier?"

Deacon, after thinking for a minute, replied, "In a sense, yes. The judicial branch of the federal government tries the case in the building we saw earlier this morning, but when a person is convicted, the executive branch's Department of Justice and their Bureau of Prisons then take over care of the convict. The facility we are looking at now is just one of the 21 facilities located here in the great state of Texas that the Bureau of Prisons operates at various security levels."[58]

With that out of the way, Deacon turned on the car and drove back down the drive. Immediately before the road was a gas station. Deacon pulled in. He instructed me, "Put in 20 bucks' worth of regular and then hop in the driver's seat. I'll pay inside and use the bathroom. I'm ready to head home."

I nodded in agreement. While pumping fuel, though, I got to thinking that I might be in the great state of Texas, but the federal government indeed does have its presence. The White House and the various agencies' national headquarters might be nearly 1,400 miles away, but they have certainly found a foothold here in the state. Despite all the infighting between the two levels of government that I learned about earlier this summer, they both do seem to get along without one's facility physically attacking another. More importantly, just as I have seen so far, the federal government's presence is just as diverse as that of the state of Texas. I could work for them from home, but it might be more fun to go all the way to DC before I make that call.

When I got back in the car, I asked Deacon a question: "Deacon, you work for the Governor's Office of Federal and State Relations. How come we did not get into any of these places?"

His response: "We just raced across Texas. That was so much cooler!"

With that out of the way, I asked, "How come we didn't go to the post office? Last I checked, they are a public corporation owned by the federal government, since the Postal Reorganization Act of 1970 demoted them from a full department of the federal government."[59]

---

58   http://www.bop.gov/locations/list.jsp
59   http://about.usps.com/publications/pub100/pub100_035.htm

Deacon replied, "Well, we've all been there before, and besides it seems as if you already know something about that. But if you have to see one to make your night, go north back on US 175, take the second exit, Beltline Road. Then, go north on Beltline Road and turn right onto Seagoville Road, and one of the US Postal Service's 1,421 branches in the state will be on your immediate right[60] (figure 21.10)."

FIGURE 21.10 United States Post Office in Seagoville, Texas.

Over the drive back to Austin, I contemplated the extent of the federal government in the state and thought, "This is only what is found in Texas. How much more could be elsewhere? Area 51??"[61] Regardless, the situation here at least leaves one to believe that we are not alone here at home in the state. The "enemy" is at, or at least behind, each of their gates influencing the direction of the state whether we like it or not. It's also noteworthy that the state even has an agency set up to monitor the federal government's efforts here. The question is, to what extent should we use each of those services, and how much influence should they have?

---

60    https://tools.usps.com/go/POLocatorDetailsAction!input.action?radius=20&locationType=po&locationTypeQ=po&locationID=1381071&locationName=SEAGOVILLE&address2=&address1=15300+SEAGOVILLE+RD&city=DALLAS&state=TX&zip5=75253&zip4=9998&tollFree=800-ASK-USPS%26reg%3B%26nbsp%3B%28800-275-8777%29&latitude=32.685572&longitude=-96.5873929
61    https://www.britannica.com/place/Area-51

**QUESTIONS TO CONSIDER** REGARDING FEDERAL ENCLAVES:

1. The first main topic of the chapter discusses the concept of federal property. Please indicate what federal property is and does, something in your life that occupies a lot of space like the federal government does in Texas, and why your example is comparable to the federal government in Texas, in detail.

2. The second main topic of the chapter discusses how the state of Texas monitors the actions of the federal government in Texas. Please identify what that agency is and does, how you track the example from question 1 in your life, and whether you and/or Texas is doing enough to keep that influence in Texas in check, in detail.

3. The final main topic of the chapter discusses the actual branches of the federal government in Texas. Please identify the agency that you most relate to, what that agency does, and how you could use that agency in your life, in detail. (Feel free to visit their websites, found in the footnotes of the text.)

## FIGURE CREDITS

# Chapter 22

# Foreign Enclaves

# Leadership of a Consulate

Over the years, thanks in large part to my dad's position as a state legislator, I have traveled to Washington DC, far more times than I would care to admit. When there on a trip about two years ago, I stumbled on the section of Massachusetts Avenue NW between Scott Circle and the northern facade of the US Naval Observatory, in which embassies, diplomatic missions, and other diplomatic representations are concentrated, which I learned after today is colloquially known as embassy row. In front of each of those buildings, one finds a locked front gate, armed security guards, and flags of a foreign nature flying high in the wind over them. Also, I've seen my fair share of movies where a fellow American citizen, like Jason Bourne in *The Bourne Identity*[1] or American embassy workers in *Argo*,[2] make their way to the local embassy or consulate to evade capture by local authorities. Today served as the opportunity to learn about the other set of forward operating bases of non-Texan governing entities found in Texas, office space belonging to foreign governments.

When I began this trek across government in America and Texas, I had no idea that I would end up making a similar journey of my own, albeit under more welcome circumstances, not to mention the fact that Charity had brought up the idea of going to one such place every so often that it seemed not going would do a disservice to my trek somehow. Today's outing might not precisely be leaving the country the way one does on vacation to Mexico, but on short notice this would make do, and, as I would learn, prove essential when learning about government. Overall, I spent the day with the Mexican consular at his consulate, located in south Austin, in hopes of learning about which foreign entities are found and how they operate within the borders of the great state of Texas and the United States at large.

My dad wanted to stay out of foreign affairs due to his position in the state legislature, and Charity, whose spare time had suddenly become filled to the brim, left me to my own devices in finding a foreign governing official to shadow and interview. A few weeks back, I had come across the list of foreign states with installations in Texas on the Texas secretary of state's website.[3] In addition, I had seen the old consulate belonging to Mexico in downtown Austin a few weeks back while running around with the municipality. In looking at the list, I saw there was a total of nearly 100 different foreign states with an installation of some type in Texas. From the list, most are found in the Dallas–Fort Worth metroplex and greater Houston areas. San Antonio and the borders towns with Mexico also had sizable rosters of these entities. In Austin, though, the state capital, only eight foreign states

---

1   https://www.rottentomatoes.com/m/bourne_identity

2   https://www.warnerbros.com/argo

3   Texas Secretary of State, "Consular Offices in Texas," accessed March 22, 2019, http://www.sos.state.tx.us/border/intlprotocol/embassies.

have an installation. This list includes Ireland, Lesotho,[4] Luxembourg,[5] Mali,[6] Panama,[7] and Trinidad and Tobago,[8] which didn't make a lot of sense, but also France, which recognized Texas way back when Texas was a country of its own in 1839[9] (figure 22.1), and Mexico, for obvious geographical, industrial, and political reasons.[10] After speaking with the consular today, the geographic spread of these entities made much more sense.

FIGURE 22.1 The French Legation, built in 1840–41 and located at 802 San Marcos St., Austin, Texas, United States, is now the French Legation Museum. This building was the home of the chargé d'affaires of France to the Republic of Texas until 1846, when the Republic of Texas ceased to exist. The building was listed in the National Register of Historic Places on November 25, 1969.

When deciding which of the eight I should contact, I noticed two terms that differentiated the installations available: general and honorary consulars. I made a note to decipher the differences later, if I could get a meeting set up. With *general* sounding more official than *honorary*, this made selecting a consulate somewhat more straightforward. This situation was due to the Irish and Mexican installations being the only ones with the general status in the Austin area.[11] The one in Austin from Mexico[12] is one of 11 found in the state of Texas from that sending state. The one in Austin from Ireland[13] is one of two located in the state of Texas from that sending state (figures 22.2 and figure 22.3). Seeing as how the Mexican consulate has it own building, and the Irish one is in an office building, I hedged my bets on the Mexican consulate being the better of the two to speak with for information.

4   http://www.sos.state.tx.us/border/intlprotocol/embassies/lesotho.shtml

5   http://www.sos.state.tx.us/border/intlprotocol/embassies/luxembourg.shtml

6   http://www.sos.state.tx.us/border/intlprotocol/embassies/mali.shtml

7   http://www.sos.state.tx.us/border/intlprotocol/embassies/panama.shtml

8   http://www.sos.state.tx.us/border/intlprotocol/embassies/trinidad.shtml

9   Joseph W. Schmitz, "Diplomatic Relations of the Republic of Texas," Texas State Historical Association, June 12, 2010, https://tshaonline.org/handbook/online/articles/mgd01.

10   Sylvester Turner and Laura Murillo, "Texas and Mexico: Ties That Bind," *Houston Chronicle*, October 23, 2016, http://www.houstonchronicle.com/opinion/outlook/article/Texas-and-Mexico-ties-that-bind-10147611.php.

11   http://www.sos.state.tx.us/border/intlprotocol/embassies/ireland.shtml; http://www.sos.state.tx.us/border/intlprotocol/embassies/mexico.shtml.

12   http://consulmex.sre.gob.mx/austin

13   https://www.dfa.ie/irish-consulate/austin

FIGURE 22.2 Official version of the Flag of the United Mexican States or Mexico, adopted September 16, 1968, by Decree (Published August 17th 1968), Ratio 4:7. The previous version of the flag displayed a slightly different Coat of Arms. It was redesigned to be even more resplendent due to the upcoming Mexico City 1968 Olympic Games.

FIGURE 22.3 Map of United State Consular Regions in Mexico.

FIGURE 22.4 Austin Consulate of Estados Unidos Mexicanos.

In setting up an interview, the phone numbers were right there on the website, so I called during the last week of June to set up an appointment. Thankfully, I didn't need to contact the Irish consulate as, after introducing myself in Spanish over the phone to the Mexican version, I had an appointment all set up. After about ten minutes of conversation, I had an appointment set up for today, to begin right at 9:00 a.m. In wanting to be as prepared as possible, I had my passport in my shirt pocket in case I needed it, a Spanish app on my cell phone for any emergency translations, and a globe-trekker spirit in my mind to get me through it all. Not wanting to be late, I left Charity's house just before 8:00 a.m. to ensure that I would arrive at the consulate just after 8:30 a.m. It was easy to find the consulate, at 5202 East Ben White Boulevard, Suite 150, just after Montopolis Boulevard when going westbound (figure 22.4).

Once parked just after 8:35 a.m., I made the short walk to the front of the building from the immense freshly resealed parking lot. Once in the cavernous brick lobby, I found myself face to face with the security guards for the consulate, who said, "Hola, señor, ¿Cómo podemos ayudarle hoy?"

I replied, "Hola, soy Champ Cove. Tengo una cita con Consular Gutierrez."

The guard responded, while picking up his phone, "Uno momento, señor."

After a brief pause and some back and forth the guard said, "Señor, please go into the conference room to my right."

Once through the sparsely filled lobby and adjoining waiting area and into the conference room, I found a seat with my back to the lobby. About five minutes later a woman saw me through the window opening next to a door opposite to the one that I had entered, came into the room, and spoke: "Hola Campeón, ¿Cómo estás?"

I replied, "Muy bien, ¿Y tú?"

She replied while I thought, this is the woman from the phone a few weeks ago, "Muy bien. Consular Gutierrez will be with you momentarily."

Not really knowing where to begin, I spent a few minutes jotting down some questions beyond the one about the difference between general and honorary consular that I had jotted down earlier.

## Status of Foreign Enclaves

Consular General Gutierrez came in after a few moments and said elatedly, in English, thankfully, "Hola, young man. I hear you are doing wonderful today. I am Consular General Carlos Gutierrez. Welcome to our little enclave in the world. How was your drive here today?"

I replied, "Austin traffic was mixed, but I arrived just when I wanted to. How are you?"

Gutierrez replied, "I'm good but busy. Changing laws here and back home always keep me on my toes. What would you like to know as we begin our discussion here today?"

I replied, "Well, I spent the short time waiting for your arrival preparing questions for you. For example, when I was looking for an official to interview, I saw the terms *general* and *honorary* used a lot to title different officials. What is the difference?"[14]

Thinking for a second or two, Gutierrez remarked, "You are getting ahead of yourself. Let me tell you of the duties held by someone in my position. I am the consular general of the United States of México to Austin. A consular is an official appointed by the government of one country to look after its commercial interests and the welfare of its citizens in another country.[15] In doing so, I primarily lead the efforts taken to help the foreign nationals of my country go about their daily lives while located here. Also, I help local Texans perform trade with those of my homeland, alongside a multitude of other items, like speaking with professors for research, people seeking knowledge on Mexico like yourself, or those seeking to get a visa to come to visit Mexico. Of note, a visa is an endorsement issued by

---

14   Unless otherwise noted, all material discussed from this point forward was retrieved from an actual interview with Consular General Rosalba Ojeda y Cárdenas in the room described above in June 2014. Thank you for your valuable time and helping with this project. Of note: A June 24, 2015, interview with the new consular general with the *Texas Tribune* is used to provide updated content and direction: Julián Aguilar, "New Consul Takes On Mexico's Texas Diaspora," *Texas Tribune*, June 24, 2015, https://www.texastribune.org/2015/06/24/carlos-gonzalez-gutierrez-tt-interview.

15   http://www.dictionary.com/browse/consular

an authorized representative of a country in a passport, permitting the passport holder to enter, travel through, or reside in that country for a specified amount of time, for tourism, education, employment, etc."[16]

I replied, "So you would call yourself the agent of Mexico akin to a sports agent dealing with a team on behalf of their client, the athlete?"

Gutierrez continued, "That's the idea. Therefore, as a general consul, or agent in your wording, and getting at your first question finally, I work my position in a full-time capacity, with the same pay and benefits granted to other bureaucrats back home in México. An honorary consul performs much of the same tasks. The difference is that honorary consuls are not employees of the sending nations, nor are they always actual nationals of the sending nation in many cases. More interestingly, some honorary consulars pay for the opportunity of providing these services out of their own pockets while keeping their full-time private positions in various other endeavors."

Thinking I could get a relaxed, fun side job out of this, I inquired, "What would I need to purchase?"

He replied, "All of the equipment required to piece together travel documents like passports, an official document issued by the government of a country to one of its citizens

FIGURE 22.5 Mexican Embassy in Washington DC.

authorizing travel to foreign countries and authenticating the bearer's identity, citizenship, right to protection while abroad, and right to reenter his or her native country[17] and attendance in classes to learn about the country to which the consular is now representing."

With that in mind, I asked, "So, how does your position and installation vary from the consular and consulate in Washington DC?"

Looking ready to educate me fully with a certain Latin flair, Gutierrez remarked, "My counterpart and their structure in Washington are not a consular operating out of a consulate (figure 22.5). They are ambassadors operating out of an embassy,

---

16   http://www.dictionary.com/browse/visa
17   http://www.dictionary.com/browse/passport?s=t

or a body of persons entrusted with a mission to a sovereign or government.[18] The ambassador has much of the same responsibilities as I do, except they have one more—much more important, in reality—job to perform. This individual is charged with being a diplomatic official of the highest rank, sent by one sovereign or state to another as its resident representative in negotiating with the foreign state.[19] To put it shortly, our current ambassador, Gerónimo Gutiérrez, works on behalf of our home nation's leader, President Enrique Peña Nieto, and with US Secretary of State Mike Pompeo, who works on behalf of your President Trump over issues impacting both countries, like immigration policy and structures.[20] Gerónimo and I work directly for the Ministry of Foreign Affairs,[21] the Mexican version of the US Department of State,[22] headed by the Secretaria de Relaciones Exteriores[23] (figure 22.6). Consulates and consulars can be anywhere, unlimited in number, and of any rank, for that matter, but the embassy and its ambassador can only be found in the receiving nation's capital city, all of which operate under the instruction of the 1961 Vienna Convention on Diplomatic Affairs[24] between nations on how these entities must be set up."

FIGURE 22.6 Secretariat of Foreign Affairs of Mexico (logo of 2012).

Thinking aloud, I said, "Those diplomatic relations are a bit more complicated than I thought. Here's an easy one, so are we really on foreign soil here in this building?"

Confidently, Gutierrez remarked, "Yes, we are, to an extent. Local authorities have no jurisdiction within this building. I have the option to call them in if there is a disturbance, but without my request for their assistance, I can block them from entering if they attempt to enter outside of extraordinary circumstances like that of an explosion or attack, which happened just a few years ago, back in 2014 at our old location near downtown[25]. To bring

18    http://www.dictionary.com/browse/embassy

19    http://www.dictionary.com/browse/ambassador

20    American Immigration Council, "Immigrants in Texas," October 4, 2017, https://www.american-immigrationcouncil.org/research/immigrants-in-texas.

21    https://www.gob.mx/sre/en

22    https://www.state.gov

23    https://www.gob.mx/sre

24    United Nations, "Vienna Convention on Diplomatic Relations," *Treaty Series* 500 (1961): 95. http://legal.un.org/ilc/texts/instruments/english/conventions/9_1_1961.pdf.

25    Jim Forsyth and Jon Herskovitz, "Man Dies after Shooting at Mexican Consulate, Other Sites in Texas," Reuters, November 28, 2014, https://www.reuters.com/article/us-usa-texas-shooting-austin/man-dies-after-shooting-at-mexican-consulate-other-sites-in-texas-capital-idUSKCN0JC1BW20141128.

the situation close to home, on my command, I could have you removed from the complex if I wanted to with no questions on your behalf allowed. Also, I am responsible for hiring and firing those working beneath me, who are all typically Mexican nationals, and we operate together as a group separate from local authorities, who have no control over what goes on on our property for regulations like zoning. It's like I am the ruler of my own little fiefdom. Although, looking at the time nearing 10:30 a.m., if we went out the door in which you entered, we would come across a very packed room, which means that the parking situation is very tight outside the building despite the generous amount of parking we now have, which is US territory. In those situations, we do work together with the local governments to resolve issues as much as possible, as it is a bit beyond our borders. We ran into those problems a lot at our old location in downtown Austin."[26]

## Perks and Issues of Working for a Foreign Enclave

I interjected, "I hate parking problems as well, especially here in Austin, but I can't help but notice, your position seems to be quite prominent. What are some of the perks? And are there any downsides?"

After gathering his thoughts for a second, he continued, "I do have some very nice perks as part of my position here. I have full diplomatic immunity from prosecution, a card for tax-exempt shopping wherever I go, payment of no income taxes here (as we are paid in Mexico, not the United States, via pesos), and I receive many invitations to important social events like family weddings of host-nation presiding officials. For my post, there are very few downsides, as a position here in Austin, and the United States in general, is in a very stable political and economic climate with low crime rates, lots of Spanish speakers, and a generally high standard of living. On the other hand, postings in places like our embassy in Addis Ababa, and Ethiopia[27] would be quite a challenge and very different, due to the less-than-stable political environment, high crime rates, and the lack of Spanish speakers, nothing like what happened during the Iran hostage crisis[28] (figure 22.7) in 1979—when 52 US embassy officials were held captive for 444 days by Iranian students in response to the US handling of the former shah of Iran's future—would be expected to happen here. The only real incidents that we deal with here that truly throw hurdles in the way of my staff are when people

26    Nancy Flores, "Mexican Consulate Moves to Larger Austin Office to Meet Growing Need," *Statesman*, December 11, 2018, http://www.mystatesman.com/news/local/mexican-consulate-moves-larger-austin-office-meet-growing-need/JPSZqX7JkuCX8loE8oH6zN.

27    http://embamex.sre.gob.mx/etiopia

28    History.com Editors, "Iran Hostage Crisis," June 1, 2010, http://www.history.com/topics/iran-hostage-crisis.

are attempting to make use of consulate services become angry and local law enforcement needs to get involved in quelling the situation."

It was at this point that one of Consular Gutierrez's assistants walked in to say, "Señor Gutierrez. Usted tiene una llamada importante del Ministerio. ¿Le gustaría que yo muestro su huésped alrededor para usted?"

Gutierrez, as he was getting up, then replied "Sí, de inmediato. Muéstrele los tres departamentos principales que tenemos aquí."

FIGURE 22.7 Iranian students climb the fence of the United States Embassey in Tehran, Iran, at the start of the Iranian Hostage Crisis.

The man came over to me and introduced himself, "Hello, Champ, if I heard your name correctly earlier when you walked into the building. Follow me. Consular Gutierrez has an important phone call from our ministry back home that requires his immediate attention, and he has instructed me to show you around for a little while before you depart. I'm Raul."

I remarked, "Howdy, Raul. You got it right. Where to first?"

Raul continued, "In looking at what exactly it is we do here, I think it is wise that we go back to where you first entered the building. We will then work our way back here."

After making small talk exiting the room and going back into the atrium from before, I stopped in the doorway. All I could think was, "Dear God, there are so many people in need of help, where to begin? It was empty an hour or so ago when I walked in here."

Out loud though, I asked, "Where did the people here in the lobby come from today? How many people are seen here daily?"

Raul's response was merely, "Most people here are living in Austin, but we also serve the larger hill country as part of a 23 county area. Number-wise, the only number I can give is many. The line can go out the door on many occasions back into the United States. People can be waiting all day for help. Most are Mexican nationals looking for aid and abetting, though."

## Divisions of a Mexican Consulate

After standing for a few more moments taking it all in, Raul motioned that we go to the back of the lobby. Here, Raul continued, "The first of our main divisions found at the consulate is called Documentation. Here, Mexican nationals living in Texas can come and get a copy of their birth certificate, a new passport, or something called a 'matricula,' which is a Mexican identity card, alongside a variety of other documents issued by our government. Overall, the concerns handled here are for minor day-to-day issues where nobody is found in a life-or-death struggle."

I interjected, "So this particular place is a cross between the Texas Department of Public Safety,[29] where I got my driver's license a few years ago, and the county clerk back in Harris County, where I can go get a copy of my birth certificate?"

Raul responded, "From what I know about Texas government, you are on the right track. Let's go to the other side of the lobby."

After walking through the crowd of people, Raul advised, "Over here in Protections, the issues handled by this group are of a much more serious nature. Some come here for obtaining legal advice for how to deal with local employers who refuse to pay them due to their various statuses. That is a big issue for our nationals here in the States. Other legal issues handled here are people granting wills of power, known here in the States as a power of attorney document, to family members back home. Others are seeking help getting work visas to get employment in or to move full-time to the States. Most notably, this group helps facilitate the return of people back to Mexico when necessary. This occurs when children need to be sent back home after the parents are placed under arrest, fall ill, or one of several other unimaginably horrible circumstances. We step in after being notified of a situation by Texas Child Protective Services[30] or another family member who is unable to handle the children long term. We work a lot with the airlines, Greyhound®, and Mexican bus companies that operate here to facilitate the repatriations. We typically send a staffer who needs to go home for family business along with them to keep track of any minors. We help adults get back home as well, but children are our priority. Of note, since the election of President Trump, the last two issues have taken up much of our time here and more.[31] Let's go back to my office."

Processing all this new information in the context of the mass of people helped put the job duties of Gutierrez into reality. Once seated in Raul's office down a side corridor, Raul really came into his own. He stated, "Here at the consulate, I am the head of the department called Community Affairs. The other departments we stopped by today have much more specified duties: get IDs or get people home, respectively. Here, our services depend on the season. It's best to think of our work here as something called 'weeks.' Typically, most

---

29   http://www.txdps.state.tx.us/DriverLicense/index.htm
30   http://www.dfps.state.tx.us/child_protection
31   Jennifer Medina, "Mexican Consulates Flooded with Fearful Immigrants," *New York Times*, February 17, 2017, https://www.nytimes.com/2017/02/17/us/mexican-consulates-flooded-with-fearful-immigrants.html.

weeks, my staff and I promote the education of some issue to people in our community and improve their lives in that area. This week, for example, we are putting on financial literacy."

I posited, "Is that why all of the bank booths are set up in the lobby?"

Raul continued, "You guessed it. Most of the time, beyond the booths, events are hosted at local churches, parks, and a variety of other places to get the word out. At these events, the consulate provides information about how the staff can help people in need in that area and allow outside groups to reach people here more easily. Beyond basic banking, we are focusing this week on avoiding fraudulent activities like scams and how to avoid check-cashing fees. During the health weeks, nationals are given free health screenings for conditions like diabetes and sports equipment to support a healthy lifestyle. *Balones de fútbol* are very popular. For the education weeks, people are given info about how to earn a GED, and community centers and schools are given official Mexican textbooks to encourage more efficient learning of Spanish-speaking-only or English-as-second-language students."

I remarked, "So these event weeks are like job or health fairs?"

Raul replied, "Exactly. My favorite part of this job, though, is our sponsorship of local events beyond the 'weeks.' Our biggest sponsored event is the Festival de la Cinema Austin.[32] That event shows films that document issues facing México to bring awareness to them here and raise money to fix the issue. Also, we sponsor several soccer clubs in the area as doing so is another great way to make people aware of our services."

Then, close to 11:00 a.m., Gutierrez stormed into the room and stated, "Campeon, go get your things. We need to run to the airport. Raul, give him your tie."

No more than a minute later, I found myself in the backseat of a GMC Yukon with the consular. When going to get in the car, I noticed a fancy set of diplomatic plates adorning the vehicle. Then, when settled and to pass the time, I asked, "What exactly is your set day-to-day schedule?"

Gutierrez articulated, "That does not exist. Essentially, it varies. Some days I am speaking with the Texas secretary of state.[33] Then, I go to a major incident involving many nationals in the area. After that, I attend meetings and do paperwork. I might not be the actual one helping people get IDs or sending them back home, but it is my job to ensure that those functions here get done. If anything, I am a manager of a business. My favorite thing, though, is appearing on local TV and radio shows to speak about upcoming events being put on by the consulate."[34]

---

32    https://www.austintexas.org/film-commission/festivals
33    https://www.sos.state.tx.us/about/index.shtml
34    Aguilar, "New Consul Takes On Mexico's Texas Diaspora."

## Qualifications to be a Consular General

At this point, I could only think that the perks just got cooler. I mean, 15 minutes of fame—very cool. To keep the conversation going, I asked, "How did you get into your field of work?"

In his response, I learned that he was well prepared for his duties. Gutierrez iterated, "Getting here has been the culmination of a lifetime of work with no set qualifications.[35] I received a bachelor's degree in international relations from El Colegio de México, followed by earning a master's degree in international relations from the University of Southern California. After that, I joined the Foreign Service of Mexico in 1987, which is what consular and embassy authorities are unofficially known to be serving in around the world.[36] During that time, I have served as a career diplomat as the consul for Community Affairs at the Consulate General of Mexico in Los Angeles, California, from 1989 to 1995, the director of Community Affairs of the Program for Mexican Communities Abroad of the Ministry of Foreign Affairs from 1995 to 1999, counselor for Latino Affairs of the Embassy of Mexico in the United States of America from 1999 to 2003, executive director of the Institute of Mexicans Abroad from 2003 to 2009, consul general of Mexico in Sacramento from 2009 to 2015, and as the consul general of Mexico in Austin ever since. I've done a lot in service of and in the name of government and people of Mexico."

I remarked, when we passed the airport terminal's main building, "I would say that you are prepared for the position here in Austin based on your education and experience. Question, though: Where are we going? The main terminal is on the other side of the airport."

Gutierrez remarked, "Our ambassador to your country is about to touch down here in Austin. It was an unscheduled stop due to a mechanical issue with the plane. We are here to do one of the last duties of my position, meet-and-greets. We do them to welcome important visitors to the area, give them a tour, or help them accomplish some goal. This time we are going to drive the ambassador and his travel companions over to the main terminal for a commercial flight back home. When they fly non-commercial, we get to drive onto the tarmac to meet the plane. This should be fun."

Once on the tarmac and standing around waiting for the plane to taxi over, I remarked, "You have a hectic job, and all sorts of crazy things happen."

Gutierrez nodded in agreement. He advised, "You are welcome in Mexico anytime, and, as an American, you do not need a visa, unless you are planning on staying over 180 days or working while there."[37]

---

35    Ibid.

36    Kate McKay, "So You Want My Job: Foreign Service Officer/Diplomat," *Art of Manliness* (blog), November 26, 2017, https://www.artofmanliness.com/2013/04/25/so-you-want-my-job-foreign-service-officerdiplomat.

37    Secretaría de Relaciones Exteriores, "Consulado General de México en San Francisco," accessed March 22, 2019, https://consulmex.sre.gob.mx/sanfrancisco/index.php/visas-traveling-to-mexico.

Seeing as how I knew he was going to be busy for a lengthy period, I just stated, "Thank you so much for the large piece of your and your staff's time I received today. I learned a lot about how foreign governments operate here in the state and the country at large."

At that point, he nodded to say "you are welcome" and proceeded up to the plane that had just pulled in front of us to make his presence known. Overall, I felt that this agency is there to help the people who are in a true grey area of society, no matter their legal status here in the United States.

---

**QUESTIONS TO CONSIDER** REGARDING FOREIGN ENCLAVES:

1. The first main topic of the chapter discusses the leadership of a consulate. Please identify who those persons are, how they differ, the one you find least important, and why, in detail.

2. The second main topic of the chapter discusses the status of foreign enclaves. Please identify what that status is, a situation that is like that in your life, and why, in detail.

3. The third main topic of the chapter discusses perks and issues of working for a foreign enclave. Please identify what the perks and issues are, a country that you would like to visit, whether being consular there would have more perks or issues, and why, in detail.

4. The fourth main topic of the chapter discusses the central divisions found at a Mexican consulate in the United States. Please identify what those divisions are, similarities from your life, and why, in detail.

5. The final main topic of the chapter discusses the ideal qualifications to have to be a consular general. Please identify what those ideal qualifications are, whether you qualify to be one today, and why, in detail.

---

# Chapter 23

# Congress

# Uses of the US Capitol Building

Over the preceding four weeks, I had learned an extensive amount of detailed information on what governing entails in Texas. Amid that process, I was exposed to various aspects of the federal government as they related to the Texas governing process. Similarities and differences between the constitutions, political history, and judicial proceedings are some of my favorites. However, to give learning about the federal government a fair shake, I needed to go to Washington DC for a portion of my trek. Therefore, today, after flying in late last night from Houston, I began the process of paying that debt. En route, the Fourth of July fireworks going off everywhere were a real sight to behold at 40,000 feet.

FIGURE 23.1 Aerial view from above the U.S. Capitol, looking west along the National Mall, Washington, D.C. The main character on tour walks from the trees on the right to the lowest building on the left.

I spent the day learning about the legislative branch of the federal government. Specifically, the branch that, once again, "ha[s] . . . the power to make laws."[1] In doing so, I spent today at the US Capitol Building on the eastern end of the National Mall (figure 23.1) in downtown Washington DC.[2] I had been looking forward to visiting here since my Uncle Tommy and father took me to the Texas version back in Austin a few weeks ago, to inform me on the ins and outs of lobbying government and lawmaking in Texas, respectively. Overall, today I saw many of the same procedures as in lawmaking back home in Texas, the structure in the morning and process in the afternoon, but at a much different pace.

On Monday of last week, I sent my representative, John Culberson of Texas's seventh congressional district,[3] an email to request a meeting. Getting a meeting with your representative is a bit difficult due to their busy schedules ranging from committee hearings, going back and forth to the district in Texas, and spending time on the floor dealing with legislation, alongside other things Culberson's staff were not at liberty to discuss.[4] I was,

1   http://www.dictionary.com/browse/legislative-branch
2   https://www.nps.gov/nama/index.htm
3   https://culberson.house.gov
4   Congressional Management Foundation and Society for Human Resources Management, "Life in Congress: The Member Perspective" (report, 2013), http://www.congressfoundation.org/storage/documents/CMF_Pubs/life-in-congress-the-member-perspective.pdf.

however, offered a free tour of the US Capitol by one of Culberson's interns who are available to anyone who requests one. After today's experience, I discovered that those interns are the real workhorses of Congress due to all the running around they do, delivering messages and helping whip up support for various initiatives when not giving tours.[5] With that in mind, I had responded to their offer by requesting a very in-depth tour due to wanting to ensure my understanding was without gaps. In doing so, I was told to meet an intern by the name of Becky at 8:00 a.m. at a place called the Summer House on the northwest corner of the Capitol grounds.[6]

After discovering where that location was following getting dressed, I left my hotel and went to the nearby Du Pont Circle Metro Station on the Metropolitan Washington Area Transit Authority's Metro System and rode five stops to Union Station Metro Station on the Red Line.[7] After leaving the physical Union Station building,[8] I walked south through Columbus Circle and Lower Senate Park.[9]

Once across Constitution Avenue, I progressed along the trails that surround the Capitol Building and found myself face to face with the ornate brick structure of the Summer House (figure 23.2). It was then that I saw a middle-aged woman with a sign having my name emblazoned on it. I announced, "Hi Becky, I'm Champ."

She turned to see me and stated, "Welcome to Washington DC! Are you ready for your trek here in the nation's Capital to begin?"

FIGURE 23.2  Summerhouse - U.S. Capitol Grounds.

I replied, "You bet! Question, though: Why are we meeting here and not at the office?"

Becky responded, "Before you get some one-on-one time with the rep, I hope, there are some sites to see here in the great outdoors that provide some context on the primary proceeding that occurs here, lawmaking. First up, where we are now, of course, is the

5    https://www.house.gov/educators-and-students/college-internships; https://www.house.gov/employment/positions-with-members-and-committees

6    Architect of the Capitol, "Summerhouse," accessed March 22, 2019, https://www.aoc.gov/capitol-grounds/summerhouse.

7    https://www.wmata.com

8    https://www.unionstationdc.com

9    Architect of the Capitol, "Senate Fountain," accessed March 22, 2019, https://www.aoc.gov/capitol-grounds/senate-fountain.

Summerhouse that has been in use by travelers since 1880 to rest after their travels here from around the world. This open hexagonal structure with a fountain in the middle was built in response to the additions of the new House and Senate Chambers and the need to spruce up the grounds after the preceding years of construction. Since DC is built on a swamp, it can be scorching and humid, so this structure is designed to help alleviate that scourge and provide cooling. Let's trek on!"

Becky and I proceeded to walk south along Northwest Drive, making small talk on the paths past one monument, and stopped in front of another that was across First Street. I asked, "What are these three large structures around us here?"

Becky replied, "The large white marble monument that we just passed is known as the Peace Monument.[10] It was erected to commemorate naval deaths at sea during the Civil War and was completed in 1878. The monument features statues representing grief, history, and victory, all emotions of war. Due west of here, just in front of the Capitol Reflecting Pool,[11] is the Ulysses S. Grant Memorial,[12] with the old general himself sitting atop his horse surrounded by four lions. Beyond that, if you look in the distance to the south ahead of us, you see the James A. Garfield Memorial,[13] with him standing atop a pedestal surrounded by four seated goddesses. Along with the Summerhouse, to an extent, each of the monuments here helps provide space for commemorating those who have had a large impact on our country's past. That is the first context for today's learning. Let's make sure that we stop at the crypt to get the full effect of that context later. Lastly, if you look due east, you find yourself looking up at the rear of the Capitol Building, which brings us to context number two, a place for the people of our fair land to make their visions for the future of our country heard. For example, since 1981 the rear, west-facing, portion of the Capitol Building looking out onto the National Mall is where presidents have been making their inaugural addresses from the platform just above the fountain, outlining the goals of their administration[14] (figure 23.3). Also, where we are now is where people have protested what goes on in the hallowed halls of Congress, such as

10    Architect of the Capitol, "Peace Monument," accessed March 22, 2019, https://www.aoc.gov/map/peace-monument.

11    Architect of the Capitol, "Capitol Reflecting Pool," accessed March 22, 2019, https://www.aoc.gov/capitol-grounds/capitol-reflecting-pool.

12    Architect of the Capitol, "Ulysses S. Grant Memorial," accessed March 22, 2019, https://www.aoc.gov/capitol-grounds/ulysses-s-grant-memorial.

13    Architect of the Capitol, "Garfield Monument," accessed March 22, 2019, https://www.aoc.gov/capitol-grounds/garfield-monument.

14    White House Historical Association, "Presidential Inaugurations," accessed March 22, 2019, https://www.whitehousehistory.org/presidential-inaugurations.

the Stephen Colbert and Jon Stewart Rally to Restore Sanity and/or Fear.[15] Just north of here on Pennsylvania Avenue was the Women's March that occurred the day after President Trump's inauguration in January 2017,[16] among many more examples."[17]

I remarked as we continued walking south on the trail, "When I was at the Texas state capitol a few weeks ago they too had many memorials and places for people to cast out their visions for what government should be."

Just as we were reaching the corner of Southwest Drive and Independence Avenue, Becky furthered, "Champ, spot on of you to notice that similarity. Keep in mind, though, when the state of Texas as we know it today was crafted in 1876, the state used our national version of government as an example of how to craft their government. Granted, if you remember how long the state's constitution is, they went into much more detail than the federal version, but you've already spent a day on that, yes?"

FIGURE 23.3 President Barack Obama gives his inaugural address to a worldwide audience from the West Steps of the U.S. Capitol after taking the oath of office in Washington, D.C., Jan. 20, 2009.

I nodded in concurrence, and Becky continued, "As we look southwest from our location, three important structures come into view. First, due west of here is the US Botanic Garden, in operation since 1850 here and in its current facility there since 1933, with the premise to foster agriculture that may be used to improve on the overall prosperity of the nation.[18]

---

15    Jason Horowitz, Monica Hesse, and Dan Zak, "Jon Stewart, Stephen Colbert Host Rally to Restore Sanity and/or Fear on Mall," *Washington Post*, October 31, 2010, http://www.washingtonpost.com/wp-dyn/content/article/2010/10/30/AR2010103001573.html.

16    https://www.womensmarch.com/march

17    Michelle Goldchain, "D.C.'s Most Famous Protests, Rallies, and Riots, Mapped," Curbed DC, January 12, 2018, https://dc.curbed.com/maps/dc-washington-march-protest-rally-riot.

18    US Botanic Garden, "Brief History of the U.S. Botanic Garden," accessed March 22, 2019, https://www.usbg.gov/brief-history-us-botanic-garden.

Catty-corner to us is Bartholdi Park, which opened in 1932 as an inside place of outdoors fanfare to go and sit in.[19] The park's most promising use is for citizens to be able to go and hone their horticulture skills to make their gardens at home even more promising, not to mention the impressive fountain at its center. The gardens, the US Capitol Visitor Center, and the Library of Congress, and well the main building itself really, due east of here, provide the third context of Congress, a place to learn."

During a pause in Becky's train of thought, I inquired, "What are the three buildings that you glossed over in your spiel there?"

Becky commented, "Ahh yes, those three buildings. Due south and southwest of our current location is where we are headed next, the actual offices of our US representatives housed in the Rayburn, Longworth, and Cannon House Office Buildings. Of note, senators have their offices on the north side of the Capitol Complex in the Dirksen, Russel, and Hart Senate Office Buildings. Also, to the southwest of here two or three blocks away is the Ford House Office Building that houses the office of the architect of the Capitol, who oversees the complex, along with various committee offices."[20]

I interjected, "Let me guess, these office buildings and a majority of the other buildings in town represent the fourth context of Congress, office space?"

Becky concluded, "Right you are, young man. Those government agencies must be placed somewhere, why not all around town? Let's cross the street and enter the Rayburn Building to head to Representative Culberson's office."

Becky and I then walked across Independence Avenue to the sole entrance to the Rayburn House Office Building (figure 23.4), located on the north facade. Once through the doorway

FIGURE 23.4 View of the Rayburn House Office Building from United States Capitol dome, taken on July 12th, 2007, by Rebel At.

and security, we turned right, then left, and then a final right to find ourselves at the southwest corner of the building in front of office 2161. Once we were through the doorway, a woman behind the desk said, "Becky! Good morning! How was your walking tour?"

Becky replied, "Florence, this is Champ. Champ, this is Florence. We're having a good time, right Champ?"

19   US Botanic Garden, "Bartholdi Park," accessed March 22, 2019, https://www.usbg.gov/bartholdi-park.
20   Architect of the Capitol, "Congressional Office Buildings," accessed March 22, 2019, https://www.capitol.gov/html/LAY_2010062882107.html.

I remarked, "Very nice tour thus far. I'm hoping it can only get better by being able to speak with the rep!"

Florence, with her calendar machine in tow, said, "I think he just came in and has a few moments to spare. Becky, feel free to go next door and see if he is willing to do a bit of speaking with a new potential voter."

I interjected, "What do you mean go next door? Isn't this his office?"

Becky and Florence looked at each other with that look of knowing that only two long-term friends can give each other when they know they can show off. Becky ushered me out the door while saying, "Follow me, Champ—we might have to work on the name, though, now."

Once outside the office, we made a 180-degree turn, and Becky spoke, "What do you see surrounding the doorway we just came from?"

I replied, "A Texas flag; the US flag; a plaque with Culberson's full name, position, state, and office number; another plaque representing the state welcoming us in; and a ledger for us to sign saying that we visited."

Becky replied, "Good, but what about the other doors?"

I replied, "Every other door or so has roughly these same items, but those in between have none. Why is that?"

Becky comically stated, while pushing me toward the blank door to the right of the door we just came out of, "Let's see what's behind door number two!"

After going through the door, my jaw dropped as we came across a small cubicle farm. I could see the walled-off space of the office we just came from digging into this larger room. In the distance was another walled-off office space. I remarked, "You mean to tell me that every representative and senator has a faux office?"

Becky remarked, "Well, maybe not all, but how else would you keep people from just storming into a place of business like ours? I mean, in a house, you don't just walk through the front door into the bedroom or kitchen; you go through a grand entry and the like."

I shook my head in the stupidity of my incompetence and the genius of the office staff. Becky motioned that we head to the walled space in the rear of the room, past all the cubicles of people working and taking phone calls. Once at the doorway, Becky knocked. This action was followed by a shout calling for us to enter the room. The man spoke. "Becky, come in, and who do you have there with you?"

Becky iterated, "Well, sir, this is a new voter from our district, and he is here in the Capitol wanting to know more about what all it is we do we here in the legislative branch of the federal government."

The man spoke, "Well young man, I'm your representative here in Washington DC, John Culberson of the seventh district of Texas, just one important office of 36 important ones we have in the state. California has the most representation, with 53. I guess that

that is the only thing not bigger in Texas. Now, sit down if you please so that we may get more acquainted."

## Minimum Qualifications to Serve in Congress

Now sitting in Culberson's office, not knowing what to ask, I blurted out, "What are the minimum qualifications to serve in Congress?"

Double-checking his notes—he kept them under a desk protector—Culberson surmised, "Officially, for the House, a person need only be a US citizen for seven years, be 25 years of age, and maintain residency in their district during their time in office. Meanwhile, for those serving in the Senate, the qualifications go up, as you need to be a US citizen for nine years, be 30 years of age, and still maintain a residency in your district during your time in office, anywhere in the state in their case."[21]

I interjected, "Compared to what I learned a few weeks ago about the Texas legislature, those qualifications seem to be on par with the more noteworthy assembly, the Senate, having more stringent qualifications than the less noteworthy assembly, the House. It's almost like the state legislature is the minor league for the more qualified professionals found here in Congress, due to the age minimum being higher, as its 21 and 26 in Texas and 25 and 30 here for the two houses, the House and Senate, respectively."

## Traits of Members of Congress

Then and there, the conversation moved on in hushed tones as Culberson advised, "Unofficially, boy, it helps to meet three additional qualifications. First, it helps to be of the dominant race in your district, as that is how citizens in the districts in many states are typically drawn/grouped together. The state governments that get to draw all the districts in their respective states are good at doing that, by the way.[22] Second, it also helps to be an attorney, as attorneys are typically political science undergrads, and a large amount of their time in law school goes far in depth on the various aspects of lawmaking, such as constitutional law classes, giving them special training.[23] Third,

21    Jack Maskell, *Qualifications of Members of Congress* (Washington, DC: Congressional Research Service, 2015). https://fas.org/sgp/crs/misc/R41946.pdf. This document is a lengthy insight into the minimum qualifications to serve in Congress.

22    Justin Levitt, "Who Draws the Lines?," All about Redistricting, accessed March 22, 2019, http://redistricting.lls.edu/who.php.

23    Jennifer E. Manning, *Membership of the 114th Congress: A Profile* (Washington, DC: Congressional Research Service, 2016). http://fas.org/sgp/crs/misc/R43869.pdf.

having access to large amounts of capital is also very beneficial, as it costs a lot to run for office."[24]

I interjected, not wanting to waste the representative's time, "How many members are in each chamber, and what other similar information in that vein should I know?"

Culberson furthered, "There are 100 members in the Senate and 435 voting members in the House, with six nonvoting members—one for each of the six largest US territories (Puerto Rico, Washington DC, Guam, Mariana Islands, American Samoa, and the US Virgin Islands). These have limited voting rights in committee, with none on the main floor on the final passage of legislation.[25] Those serving in the House, like myself, serve two-year terms, while those serving in the Senate serve for six-year staggered terms, with a third of the body up for reelection every two years. Before 1913, though, senators were appointed by state legislatures, not directly elected by state citizens, as has always been the case in the House. On top of that, there are no term limits in either house. More importantly, each member solely represents their own equally populated districts, the House at least, and earns an annual salary of $174,000."[26]

I commented, "That's quite a lot more money than the representatives back home make isn't it?"

Culberson remarked, "I've come a long way salary-wise since my time in the Texas House a decade and a half or so ago; $174,000 annually is a lot more than the $7,200 annually I got back there. To keep things rolling, let's cover some key terms now, all right partner?"

## Key Terms for Congress

I said, "Sure, what terms do you have in mind?"

Thinking for a moment and nodding, Culberson spoke, "Well as you know our primary purpose here is to make laws."

I interjected, "Duly noted, so continue."

Culberson continued, "Good. The problem is that there are 541 members here in some capacity. We are a diverse group of individuals with individual and group-held interests.

---

24    David Knowles, "U.S. Senate Seat Now Costs $10.5 Million to Win, on Average, While US House Seat Costs, $1.7 Million, New Analysis of FEC Data Shows," *New York Daily News*, March 11, 2013, http://www.nydailynews.com/news/politics/cost-u-s-senate-seat-10-5-million-article-1.1285491#.

25    Aaron Secklenberg and Chiqui Esteban, "Over 4 Million Americans Don't Have Anyone to Vote for Them in Congress," *Washington Post*, September 28, 2017, https://www.washingtonpost.com/graphics/2017/national/fair-representation/?noredirect=on&utm_term=.7249ae1afa43.

26    Carol Luther, "The Average Salary of a Newly Elected Congressman," Chron, last modified March 26, 2018, https://work.chron.com/average-salary-newly-elected-congressman-7774.html.

FIGURE 23.5 United States President Barack Obama meets with members of the Congressional Hispanic Caucus in the State Dining Room of the White House, March 18, 2009.

The two main groups we fall into is Republicans and Democrats, our political parties. Under those groupings, to get work done while here, we have formed caucuses (figure 23.5), formally known as Congressional Member Organizations, along those lines,[27] which are 'a closed meeting of a group of persons belonging to the same political party or faction usually to select candidates or to decide on policy.'[28] Keep in mind the caucuses I'm referring to here focus on the policy-making functions, not the candidate selection ones, outside of selecting leadership roles while here. Membership in these organizations can be found from both houses or just in one and represents a wide variety of interests. Some of the more notable groups outside of the political parties are the Congressional Black Caucus, where members of color get together to discuss policy that affects that portion of society[29] (figure 23.6); the House Liberty Caucus, which is made up of those in the house fighting for personal freedoms;[30] and the Congressional Caucus for Women's Issues, which focuses on commenting on policy that directly impacts women.[31] Beyond those, there are groups for everything[32] from riding bikes[33] to Sri Lanka."[34]

I commented, "These caucuses are ways to discuss policies beyond traditional party lines further then, right?"

Culberson remarked, "Exactly, as they are simply ways for representatives to promote the interests of themselves or their district or anything. The main item they must do is that at the start of each session of Congress they must register with the Committee on House

27    https://www.gop.gov; https://www.republican.senate.gov; https://www.democrats.senate.gov; https://www.dems.gov

28    https://www.merriam-webster.com/dictionary/caucus

29    https://cbc.house.gov

30    https://www.facebook.com/libertycaucus

31    http://www.wcpinst.org

32    Committee on House Administration, "Congressional Member and Staff Organizations," accessed March 22, 2019, https://cha.house.gov/member-services/congressional-memberstaff-organizations.

33    https://blumenauer.house.gov/congressional-bike-caucus

34    *Daily News* (Sri Lanka), "Congressional Caucus on Sri Lanka Renewed for 115th Congress," July 27, 2017, http://www.dailynews.lk/2017/07/27/local/123373/congressional-caucus-sri-lanka-renewed-115th-congress.

Administration[35] and provide them with the name of the caucus, a statement of purpose, the group's officers, and any staffer's employee designated to work on issues related to the group. These organizations can be very effective at times at promoting policy."[36]

I commented, "It sounds as if you have been here for a while. Does that give you an advantage?"

Culberson surmised, "Overall, yes, on the one hand, regarding elections, this makes me an incumbent, key term number two for you, or 'a person who has a particular office or position.'[37] In the electoral process, I can use my record in Congress of pushing through legislation, data only available to governing officials, and anything else akin to having a head start in a foot race to get an advantage on my electoral opposition."[38]

FIGURE 23.6 Congressional Black Caucus Foundation Entrance.

I interjected, "What about while in office?"

Culberson iterated, "I would argue that that gives me seniority. Since I've been here a while, I know how everything works behind the scenes in the lawmaking process. Therefore, I can get initiatives pushed through better than somebody who is new here and knows nothing about the process outside of what they read in school textbooks. Beyond passing regulatory bills, additional work we do here in Congress can be classified as district service,[39] any project like highway dollars and hurricane relief from Harvey a year or two ago that benefits everyone in our district equally, for lack of a better term. On the other hand, there is casework, or something that I have pushed through that benefits an individual directly—your

35  Ibid 32.
36  https://www.everycrsreport.com/files/20170126_R40683_d1a42fb55c704a89651698237bd-d57650ac85b52.pdf
37  https://dictionary.cambridge.org/us/dictionary/english/incumbent
38  https://culberson.house.gov/issues; https://culberson.house.gov/biography/myrecord.htm
39  Representative Lizzie Fletcher, "Help with a Federal Agency," accessed March 22, 2019, https://fletcher.house.gov/forms/casework.

tour here, for example—in addition to cutting through the red tape of a federal agency when a citizen is facing a problem they can't resolve on their own, obtaining an American flag that has flown over the Capitol Building, or for someone about your age, a recommendation for admittance to one of the nation's service academies. Do you want to be an airman?"

I replied, shell-shocked, "No, I'm not a running at 4:30 in the morning man, and I get seasick at 30,000 feet, but thanks though! Also, does the term *pork barrel spending* need to be brought up here?"

Culberson remarked, "It certainly may. That term you are referring to is defined as 'the act of using government funds on local projects that are primarily used to bring more money to a specific representative's district.[40] It's a politician like me working to benefit my constituents solely to maintain their support and vote rather than improving the country at large."

I interjected, "Isn't that what you just told me half your job is?"

Culberson concluded, "You bring up a good point young man, but what exactly differentiates that from other things government does, like providing water and roads at the local level, regulation of services at the state level, and national defense at the national level, which are all readily available for you to take advantage of daily? At what point does legislation become something that benefits a certain community or an individual versus the country at large? Also, would you condemn getting somebody a flag or helping bring work/relief to our community to be as bad as making deals to get a pointless project or agency set up in our community?"

I blurted out, "The point at which the concept of the project sounds beyond belief?"

Culberson replied, "Let's say I don't know, so we can turn to the experts on this matter, the interest group known as Citizens Against Public Waste[41] and their 2018 annual publication, *Congressional Pig Book*.[42] From that publication, if any item meets one of seven qualifications, '[r]equested by only one chamber of Congress; [n]ot specifically authorized; [n]ot competitively awarded; [n]ot requested by the President; [g]reatly exceeds the President's budget request or the previous year's funding; [n]ot the subject of congressional hearings; or [s]erves only a local or special interest,' it is deemed pork barrel spending."

I replied, "That statement does clarify things in some ways and does the opposite in others. I see how hurricane relief does specifically benefit one community, but if you don't help Texas and do help Florida, it seems a bit unfair; but, I guess, projects must be set up somewhere. What other terms do you have for me?"

---

40   http://www.businessdictionary.com/definition/pork-barrel-spending.html

41   https://www.cagw.org

42   Citizens Against Government Waste, "2018 Congressional Pig Book," accessed March 22, 2019, https://www.cagw.org/reporting/pig-book.

Culberson pondered to himself for a moment before speaking. "This is the last term for you today, and quite possibly the main function of Congress. That term is *congressional oversight* (figure 23.7), more commonly referred to as *bureaucratic oversight*. This function occurs when we 'review, monitor, and supervis[e] federal agencies, programs, activities, and policy implementation.'[43] In other words, after we create a new federal agency or program, let's use the creation of the US Department of Homeland Security in 2002,[44] we must ensure that those new—and current ones, for that matter—agencies are doing what they are supposed to be doing. In creating the Department of Homeland Security, we created a new cabinet-level agency to place 22 different agencies then found under several different departments under one roof

FIGURE 23.7 US Congress' House of Representatives, Committee on Foreign Affairs, Hearing on the North Korean Nuclear Program. The hearing took place on March 5, 2013. It was chaired by Representative Ed Royce (R-California), with the ranking member being Representative Eliot Engel (D-New York). Testimony was given by a panel of experts composed by Dr. David Asher (Senior Fellow at the Center for a New American Security), Dr. Sung-Yoon Lee (Professor at The Fletcher School of Law and Diplomacy) and Ambassador Joseph De Trani (President of Intelligence and National Security Alliance).

to coordinate their similarly minded purposes better, protecting our citizens here at home from threats foreign and domestic, natural or human-made. For example, the Office for Domestic Preparedness came over from the Department of Justice, and the Federal Emergency Management Agency (FEMA) transitioned from being an independent agency, like how the postal service is today, and had their services consolidated under the FEMA brand due to their offerings being so similar. We reduced redundancies in this case as part of our oversight duties. Now, regarding the actual oversight when they begin work, one of the most recent prominent examples of this occurred in the fall of 2015 when then-Democratic presidential candidate Hillary Clinton was brought in to answer for her and her department's conduct during the invasion of our consulate in Benghazi, Libya, in 2012 when she was secretary of state.[45] Overall, Secretary Clinton failed to protect our ambas-

---

43    Definitions.net, s.v. "congressional oversight," accessed March 22, 2019, https://www.definitions. net/definition/congressional+oversight.

44    https://www.dhs.gov/history

45    Leigh Ann Caldwell, "Five Takeaways from Clinton's Benghazi Testimony," NBC News, October 23, 2015, https://www.nbcnews.com/politics/2016-election/five-takeaways-clintons-benghazi-testimony-n449506.

sador and three consulate staffers, and we brought her to task over it in a congressional hearing, to mixed results. Now, do you have any other questions, young man?"

I replied, taking mental note of the less-becoming parts of my father's job, as they do the same thing back home, "No sir, but where should I go next?"

Culberson spoke to Becky, who was seated silently in the back of the room, "Becky, give this young man a tour of the rest of the complex from the inside and make sure that he sees what we have going on in the House this afternoon."

Becky replied, "Yes, sir!"

## The US Capitol Building

Becky and I walked back out the door to the hallway. Once out the door, Becky stopped to get her bearings. I must admit the small windowless corridors in many cases do get a bit confusing. We headed back the way we came, turning left at the first corner and then right at the next. The difference is, instead of turning left to exit the building at the entryway we came in earlier, we passed it, only to turn right down an escalator to the basement levels of the building. Now wanting to get my bearings I asked, "Where are we going? Isn't the Capitol right across the street?"

Becky replied, "Well, if you are keeping count like I am, this is going to be context number five, underground connections. You see, each of the office buildings here at the Capitol has a tunnel leading to the main Capitol Building, and the other ones for that matter.[46] Hell, with proper ID, we could walk all the way to the Supreme Court building and the Library of Congress if we wanted to."

I thought out loud, "This day is déjà vu. Are all government buildings in the world connected underground to their various respective auxiliary buildings, or is it just me?"

Once at the bottom of the escalator, Becky replied, "Here in DC and Austin, yes. In other places, I don't know and don't care for the time being. Either way, follow me. Also, guess what?"

As we passed through a doorway, I replied, "What?"

Becky yelled elatedly, "It gets even better. We get to take a train over to the big house!"[47]

Once we were aboard the waiting train, Becky furthered, "All buildings on the Senate side are connected by trains to the main building, but we are the only building on the House side to have one. Everyone else must walk. Ours opened in 1965, but the system that first

---

46    Carmonamedina, "US Capitol Tunnel System [1035x800px], [OC]," r/MapPorn, Reddit, October 10, 2016, https://www.reddit.com/r/MapPorn/comments/56vhfv/us_capitol_tunnel_system_1035x800px_oc.
47    Tom, "United States Capitol Subway System: A Brief History," Urban Ghosts Media, September 29, 2017, https://www.urbanghostsmedia.com/2017/09/united-states-capitol-subway-history.

connected the Senate side opened in 1909 and has undergone a renovation or two since then. Before 9/11, the public could ride freely, but ever since, you must be a member, a staffer, or at least be traveling with a staffer to do so."

We spent the next minute or so traveling along the route passing the car coming from the opposing direction on the other set of rails. Once at the ride's end, we disembarked and found ourselves at the back of a short line for another line of security. Becky said, "Well Champ, now we go through airport-level screening, no liquids are allowed through here, unlike the screening we went through earlier to get into the Rayburn Building."

Once through, we found ourselves at the bottom of another escalator that took us up one level. At the top, we turned to our right, and Becky spoke. "Welcome to the lower level of the US Capitol Visitor Center located under the driveway of the Capitol Building front side. The room we are now in is formally known as Emancipation Hall (figure 23.8). Found throughout this room and the remainder of the building are two statues of famous figures from each of the 50 states that are part of the National Statuary Hall Collection.[48] Two of the more famous statues found here in Emancipation Hall are King Kamehameha from Hawaii, who unified the islands,[49] the only royalty to stand here, and Jeannette Rankin from Montana, who is famous for being the only representative to vote against our entry into both World War I and II, being the only representative at all to do so for World War II, alongside serving in these chambers for two years before women had the right to vote nationwide as the first female elected to office here in 1917.[50] What a woman!"

FIGURE 23.8 Emancipation Hall of the Capitol Visitor Center.

I asked, "What about Texas?"

Becky concluded, "Forgive me for not paying my respects. Sam Houston stands in National Statuary Hall[51] in the old House Chamber, while Stephen F. Austin resides in the Hall of

48    Architect of the Capitol, "National Statuary Hall Collection by Location," accessed March 22, 2019, https://www.aoc.gov/capitol-hill/national-statuary-hall-collection/nsh-location.

49    National Park Service, "Kamehameha the Great," last modified February 28, 2015, https://www.nps.gov/puhe/learn/historyculture/kamehameha.htm.

50    US House of Representatives, "Rankin, Jeannette," History, Art & Archives, accessed March 22, 2019, http://history.house.gov/People/Listing/R/RANKIN,-Jeannette-(R000055).

51    Architect of the Capitol, "Sam Houston," accessed March 22, 2019, https://www.aoc.gov/art/national-statuary-hall-collection/sam-houston.

Columns.[52] Both marble statues reside on pedestals made from rock quarried in Texas. Let's look at the showpiece. Follow me!"

While Becky was speaking, we advanced our way north through the hall to the middle and faced west. Becky remarked, "The main statue found here in the hall is the plaster mold that was used to cast the bronze *Statue of Freedom* that now stands atop the Capitol rotunda.[53] Freedom wears 'a helmet encircled with stars and topped with an eagle's head and feathers, the talons hanging at either side of her face. Her long, curly hair flows down her back. Her dress is secured with a brooch with the letters 'US,' and she is draped with a fur-trimmed robe. Her right hand holds a sheathed sword; the left a laurel wreath of victory and the striped shield of the United States.'[54] On either side of her plaster casting mold found here are orientation theaters showing movies to inform visitors on a wide variety of capital related topics.[55] Immediately behind *Freedom* is Exhibition Hall, which displays information on the past sessions of Congress in the exhibit entitled *E Pluribus Unum—Out of Many One.*"[56]

I interjected, "What are the sessions of Congress anyway?"

Becky remarked, "Wait till we get in the chambers for that, okay?"

Nearing 10:30 a.m., I nodded to agree, and Becky continued, "Let's go get an early lunch."

The two of us walked further north toward the northeast corner of the room. Once past the elevator, we found ourselves at the Capitol Cafe and its various dining options. After going through a set of serpentine lines, we entered the central area to select our food. Becky went for a salad, and I had the pizza slice combo. After paying and sitting around eating for a while, I joked, "I assume you eat here a lot?"

Becky replied, "I wouldn't say here, here, but in the Capitol Complex each of the buildings has its eatery or two to enjoy. Now that we are stuffed let's go get some better seats."

Following that remark, Becky and I stood and put our trays on the moving racks that took them to the dishwashers. The washers had a lot of business today, from what I could tell. Then we went back to the entrance that we came through earlier. Once through the exit, we went back into Emancipation Hall. There, we entered another set of serpentine lines. I asked, "What better seats were you referring to back there? We seem to be standing now."

---

52    Architect of the Capitol, "Stephen Austin," accessed March 22, 2019, https://www.aoc.gov/art/national-statuary-hall-collection/stephen-austin.

53    US Capitol Visitor Center, "Restoring the Original Statue," accessed March 22, 2019, https://www.visitthecapitol.gov/exhibitions/capitol-story/statue-freedom/restoring-original-statue.

54    Ibid.

55    US Capitol Visitor Center, "Orientation Theater," accessed March 22, 2019, https://www.capitol.gov/html/SPAN_2010083067765.html.

56    https://www.visitthecapitol.gov/exhibitions

Becky replied, "The next context of Congress is viewing government in action. To do so, we need to get you a timed entry ticket from the clerks here. Following that, we'll head upstairs and hit the House viewing gallery."

About 30 seconds later, we had our passes and proceeded up the escalator on the north side of the hall. Once off the escalator, we walked past the north gift shop and went to use the facilities in the northwest corner. Once through, we walked due south past a set of stairs and two additional escalators. We then headed into a room at the southwest corner of the upper level where we turned in all our belongings. Once through with that, we stood in a holding pen to wait for our turn to begin the process of entering the gallery. About five minutes later, we proceeded through the door opposite where we entered, made a U-turn, and went up the escalator we just passed. On the way up, Becky spoke. "The room at the top of the stairs is formally known as the Crypt (figure 23.9). It was planned that after the passing of George Washington his body would be placed on display here at the Capitol, like what is being done with the body of Vladimir Lenin in Moscow.[57] There is a small enclave at the back of the room that his body was supposed to be stored in at night and brought out during the day. The idea was that making all representatives walk past the body would make them consider the views of the founding fathers when lawmaking.[58] Now found in the enclave is the storage room for the iconic Lincoln catafalque that those lying in state at the Capitol rest on,[59] all part of the memorial process that we discussed earlier today. Ohh, this room also contains the Magna Carta Case, a gold case that held the Magna Carta when the document was on loan to the United States for the Bicentennial celebration in 1976, and statues of the 13 original colonies as part of the National Statuary Collection we discussed earlier."

FIGURE 23.9  Crypt of the U.S. Capitol.

57    Dasha Fomina, "A Guide to Visiting Lenin's Mausoleum," Culture Trip, February 26, 2017, https://theculturetrip.com/europe/russia/articles/a-guide-to-visiting-lenins-mausoleum.

58    Architect of the Capitol, "How the Crypt Got Its Name," accessed March 22, 2019, https://www.aoc.gov/blog/how-crypt-got-its-name.

59    Architect of the Capitol, "The Lincoln Catafalque," accessed March 22, 2019, https://www.aoc.gov/nations-stage/lincoln-catafalque.

At the top of the stairs, I decided to walk in silence. The 40 Doric columns of brownstone surmounted by groined sandstone arches were very becoming of a crypt and per the guide taking us to the viewing gallery also support the floor of the rotunda two stories above. During a brief pause here to allow the rest of our group to catch up, our tour guide mentioned, "Once done viewing our government in action in the gallery, beyond the columns in the crypt lies the old chamber of the US Supreme Court, where they met until the 1930s, when they received their current building. And my personal favorite, set in stone at the center of the room, lies a white marble compass that shows where the four quadrants of the district meet. Also, there is a placard on the wall to memorialize the first official telegraph being sent by Samuel Morse to his friend Alfred Vail in Baltimore, Maryland, on May 24, 1844."[60]

## Sessions of Congress

Wanting to get my bearings straight, I made a note to come back here later. Either way, once done hiking up what seemed like endless stairs and what I counted as three different security checks traversed since entering the main building, Becky and I finally found ourselves in the viewing gallery of the house. I asked, "So when is the special session going to get started today?"

Becky replied, "Ohh, that. We don't have those here. You see, back in Texas, there is a 140-day regular session followed by any 30-day max special sessions called for by the governor. In Congress, per article 1, section 4, 'The Congress shall assemble at least once in every Year, and such Meeting shall be on the first Monday in December unless they shall by Law appoint a different Day.' This occurred with the ratification of Amendment 20, sections 1 and 2, that sees the previous Congress end at noon on the third day of January with the new Congress to begin their terms at noon on the same day following an election of new representatives. In between those third days in January, we are off and on as much as quarreling lovers in a spat."

I interjected, "So what are they when on and what are they when off?"

Becky continued, "When Congress is 'on' again, they are in meetings of Congress. Here in the summer of 2018, we are in the 115th Congress. Due to this being an even-numbered year, as part of being required to meet every year, we are in the second session with the odd-numbered years being the first session of the respected Congress. When in physical session meeting with one another, the meetings of Congress can be classified as *daily*, which consists of routine business; *special*, which includes congressional meetings between

---

60    US House of Representatives, "The Capitol's First Official Telegraph," History, Art & Archives, accessed March 22, 2019, https://history.house.gov/HistoricalHighlight/Detail/35992.

the end of sessions and full Congresses; *extraordinary*, which occurs when the president calls us into session when we are off to consider items of utmost importance; *joint*, which is where the House and Senate meet together to hear the president's State of the Union address (figure 23.10) or to count ballots in the Electoral College; *pro forma*, which a short meeting of only a few minutes to officially welcome us back to business after a break but no real business is tended to; *lame duck*, which is when we meet in November and December fol-

FIGURE 23.10  2018 State of the Union Speech by President Trump on U.S. House Floor during a Joint Session of Congress.

lowing an election to further consider legislation, but before the official end of our terms; *closed*, which allows us to review confidential information; and finally, *executive*, to consider treaties and nominations.[61] We do have a lot of sessions here; it all just depends on what we are doing and when we are doing the legislation for one or the other to come in to order."

I inquired, "If that's what they are when on again, what the hell are they when off again?"

Becky replied, "When Congress is not in session they are in recess, the most notable of which is the August recess that allows representatives and senators to go back to their districts long term to spend time with family, work and meet with constituents, and do anything else that needs tending to back home.[62] These periods can be contentious due to something called recess appointments, or 'a presidential appointment made under the executive's power to fill vacancies when the Senate is not in session subject to later confirmation by the Senate'[63] to ensure the continuation of government services provided by agencies. Of note, per the Supreme Court, the recess need be more protracted than ten days for this power to be used.[64] The problem comes when the people nominated are unpopular and unable to pass confirmation hearings that occur once the Senate is back in session. Either way, without further confirmation, the recess appointment ends at the end of the current session of Congress."[65]

I could only reply, "I'm glad none of my relationships have been that exciting!"

---

61    US Senate, "Sessions of the Senate," accessed March 22, 2019, https://www.senate.gov/general/Features/Sessions.htm.

62    Henry B. Hogue, Recess Appointments Frequently Asked Questions (Washington, DC: Congressional Research Service, 2015). http://www.senate.gov/CRSpubs/3d313cc2-9515-4533-b1f0-3f762cd09007.pdf.

63    https://www.merriam-webster.com/legal/recess%20appointment

64    Ibid., 66.

65    Ibid.

## Different Houses of Congress

After a momentary pause, Becky remarked, "What are your thoughts on role-play?"

I remarked, "What do you have for me?"

Becky spoke, "Think about the old traditional roles of a husband and wife. The man was expected to go out and provide for the family while the wife was expected to tend to the home and children. For the roles of the House and Senate, I would say that the House is like the husband and the Senate is like the wife."

I interjected, "What do mean by that?"

Becky continued, "Well, those role assignments have to do with what each house is responsible for in fulfilling their duties. For example, the House before us, going along with the provider theme, per article 1, section 7, subsection 1 of the US Constitution,[66] 'All revenue bills shall originate in the house,' in other words, bring home the proverbial bacon to the family, tax bills in our case here. In addition to that, serving as the family disciplinarian, per article 1, section 2, subsection 5,[67] the House 'shall have the sole Power of Impeachment,' in other words, begin the process of administering justice when an official governing acts inappropriately."

I remarked, "That analogy of the House being the provider makes sense, but what about the Senate?"

Becky furthered, "The Senate, on the north side of the complex from our current positions, going along with the tending to the home and children, per article 2, section 2, subsection 2,[68] shall have final say over all treaties with other countries and appointments made to applicable federal government positions like judges and department heads. In other words, it is like, in keeping with our traditional gender roles theme, a wife giving her blessing to a major decision made by her husband before he goes and does it. Now, going along with the impeachment power of the House, 'the Senate,' per article 1, section 3, subsection 6,[69] 'shall have the sole Power to try all Impeachments,' in other words, be the final say over punishing any suspected governing official misbehaving by removing them from office. When I was growing up, my mom was always the enforcer."

I interjected, "So why did you choose the traditional gender roles analogy to discuss the roles of the federal legislative assemblies?"

Becky asserted, "Well, overall, the two houses are tied at the hip, always needing to work together to keep the family as strong as possible. Now while they each have separate their

---

66    U.S. Constitution, article 1, section 7, subsection 1.
67    U.S. Constitution, article 1, section 2, subsection 5.
68    U.S. Constitution, article 2, section 2, subsection 2.
69    U.S. Constitution, article 1, section 3, subsection 6.

duties and responsibilities, like the ones I just told you about, per article 1, section 7, subsection 2,[70] '[b]oth houses shall approve of legislation before being sent to the President for approval.' In other words, unless both people agree on what to do in the relationship nothing gets done, lawmaking in this case. Now where it gets interesting in this metaphor is later on in article 1, section 7, subsection 2,[71] where '[i]f after such Reconsideration two thirds of that House shall agree to pass the Bill, it shall be sent, together with the Objections, to the other House, by which it shall likewise be reconsidered, and if approved by two thirds of that House, it shall become a Law.' In other words, like any good couple going against their parents' wishes to marry, they can decide that they are in it for the long haul and go elope without their blessing, like a quickie wedding in Vegas, for example."

I responded, "Based on what you said there, the US House and Senate do sound like a married couple in their relationship to each other. A question, though: How does the lawmaking process vary between what occurs here and back in Texas?"

It was then that Becky handed me a copy of a lawmaking explanation sheet[72] that was eerily like one that I had received earlier on in the summer from my dad (figure 23.11). Both were vividly colorful documents explaining the lawmaking procedures in their respective assemblies. I could only see minor differences; here the presiding officer of the Senate is the vice president and there is no requirement for a three-fifths vote before discussing a piece of legislation. I commented, "This seems so like the lawmaking process back home. What differences am I missing?"

Becky quipped, "Simple: Other than having much more time to consider legislation, nearly 700 days here versus 140 back home every two years, there is no reading requirement of legislation here, only that a copy of the legislation discussed must be available to those on the floor. They tried to work on that with consideration of Senate Bill 1571 as submitted by Rand Paul of Tennessee, but the bill failed to be considered by the Committee on Rules and Administration.[73] That bill would have required Congress to show where the authority to regulate whatever was being regulated came from, citation of what was going to be changed, and the bill to be read in its entirety on the floor before consideration, among other items."

I commented, "It seems as if then the main difference between Congress and the Texas legislature is, beyond physical location, the amount of time for consideration and changes in membership due to reapportionment."

---

70    U.S. Constitution, article 1, section 7, subsection 2.
71    U.S. Constitution, article 1, section 7, subsection 2.
72    David Dreier, "Floor Procedure in the U.S. House of Representatives," Committee on Rules, Majority Office, accessed March 22, 2019, http://archives-democrats-rules.house.gov/archives/floor_man.htm.
73    Rand Paul, "S.1571—114th Congress (2015–2016): Read the Bills Act," Congress.gov, June 15, 2015, https://www.congress.gov/bill/114th-congress/senate-bill/1571.

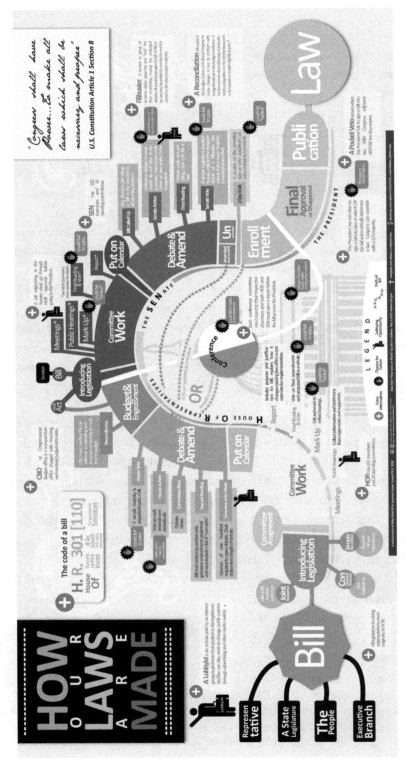

FIGURE 23.11 This "How Our Laws Are Made" infographic by Mike Wirth and Dr. Suzanne Cooper-Guasco won first prize in the Sunlight Foundation "Design for America Competition" 2010.

Becky concluded all that she had to say on Congress to me by stating, "I think that's really about it regarding Congress. You've been on the grand tour and all. I wish we could have pushed through a piece of legislation like I assume you saw back in Texas a few weeks ago, but the lawmaking process isn't set up for such an endeavor here. You may stay here until 4:30, when the House adjourns for the day, but I need to get back to the office. I have a 2:30 tour to give. Thanks for listening!"

I stood, said thanks, hugged Becky, and returned to my seat. Over the next two hours, I sat and watched. Not much occurred here outside of legislators speaking for an allotted five minutes on legislation; the filibuster last I checked was still available to those in the US Senate.[74] I could only ponder that even though I traveled so far to be here, the differences were few and far between. Either way, I have tomorrow's White House tour to look forward to experiencing. Maybe the president is different from the governor, though the lawmaking process here is not all that different from the process back home in Texas, outside of time allotted and pay. I'll see.

---

74    Dreier, "Floor Procedure in the U.S. House of Representatives."

**QUESTIONS TO CONSIDER** REGARDING CONGRESS:

1. The first main discussion topic of the chapter, and parts later, discusses the various uses of the US Capitol Building beyond lawmaking. Please identify your favorite use, how that use relates to your life, and why, in detail.

2. The second main discussion topic of the chapter discusses the minimum qualifications needed to serve in Congress. Please identify what those qualifications are, the qualifications you meet, and whether you qualify to serve at present.

3. The third main discussion topic of the chapter discusses traits of members of Congress. Please identify your most interesting trait, how you relate to that trait, and why, in detail.

4. The fourth main discussion topic of the chapter discusses key terms for Congress. Please define what those terms are, identify the one that relates most to your life, and explain how, in detail.

5. The fifth main discussion topic of the chapter discusses the various sessions of Congress. Please identify your favorite session and indicate what goes on during that session, how that session relates to your life, and why that session relates most, in detail.

6. The final main discussion topic of the chapter discusses the duties of the different houses of Congress. Please identify the different roles, your duties in your household, the house of Congress your duties at home relate most to, and why, in detail.

## FIGURE CREDITS

# Chapter 24

# The Presidency

# President's Park

Earlier this summer, I spent a full day and early morning with the governor of Texas learning about his duties. I then proceeded to spend the rest of the day with the lieutenant governor of Texas. Throughout my time with those two men, I learned about the executive branch of Texas, of which, due to the power traditionally held by the governor in many other states being distributed to a smattering of six individually elected individuals, such as the lieutenant governor, the executive branch of Texas is classified as plural. One item explicitly made clear during my time there is that that is not the case in Washington DC, as the president is a genuinely singular executive due to the office being entrusted with a wide variety of leadership duties like appointing judges and other officials. Therefore, I spent today learning about the leader, or dare I say, chief executive officer, of the executive branch of the federal government.

In arranging for my official tour of the White House, I had to go through the same process of getting the US Capitol tour, contact my representative in Congress. Thankfully, I sent the email requesting the tour three weeks early, so I was able to meet the deadline for the self-guided White House tour.[1] Since my tour time was not until 10:00 a.m., Becky from yesterday was gracious enough to give me an additional walking tour of a place called President's Park, a site belonging to the National Park Service,[2] and the surrounding areas. Therefore, I was instructed to meet her at 8:00 a.m. just outside the McPherson Square Station on the Blue, Orange, and Silver Lines of the WMATA Metro System. Unlike yesterday, I had to make a transfer at Metro Center Station after going three stops on the Red Line from Dupont Circle Station. One stop later, after taking a Blue Line train toward the Franconia-Springfield Station, I emerged from the escalator to a muggy morning breeze hitting my face. After going out the station exit covering on the Vermont Avenue side, I could see Becky purchasing what looked to be a morning coffee from a street cart. I called out, "Becky, good morning!"

Becky replied, while hugging me, "Good morning. Are you excited for your big tour today?"

I replied, "You bet, but what's the story behind all the street carts?"

Becky noted, "These street carts and, more so in modern times, food trucks are an institution in DC (figure 24.1), as they are on nearly every street corner and near every major attraction, like down on the National Mall.[3] They can be found serving food to those passing through on a walk or those wanting to escape the office doldrums to get some fresh air. Respite is here for them, be it lunch, or an afternoon pick-me-up. A cap on the number of

---

1   White House, "White House Tours," accessed March 22, 2019, https://www.whitehouse.gov/about-the-white-house/tours-events; this and all other information discussed in this chapter regarding the tour was obtained through this website.

2   https://www.nps.gov/whho/index.htm

3   https://www.nps.gov/nama/index.htm

vendors was put in place about twenty years ago, along with a moratorium on new licenses being granted by the district and tighter regulations, resulting in there being seven hundred fewer today than there were back then.[4] I would get a hot dog, the traditional fare from these carts, but it's not lunchtime, so coffee it is."

I interjected, "Good to know! For the tour though, where shall we begin, after I get my morning caffeine as well, of course?"

Becky pondered to herself for a moment while I got my coffee. She said, as we walked south on Vermont Avenue, "Depending on how you see it, we technically have already begun. Unlike the Capitol Complex in Austin for the state, the offices and parks in DC don't truly have a beginning and an end. For example, if you look up behind you, the building where you exited from the Metro is also the headquarters for the US Department of Veterans Affairs, who are here, as part of a cabinet-level agency in the executive branch of the federal government, straight from their website, 'to fulfill President Lincoln's promise 't care for him who shall have borne the battle, and for his widow, and his orphan' by serving and honoring the men and women who are America's veterans.'[5] This agency runs a massive health care provision infrastructure, veterans' cemeteries, and a whole host of other duties to take care of veterans once they return from duty. Also, across Vermont Avenue from us is the home of the Export-Import Bank of the United States, an independent federal agency, meaning they don't fall under a department, that helps provide financing for the export of American goods abroad when the private sector is not willing to do so to ensure vitality in the economy by supporting American jobs."[6]

I propositioned, "So, unlike in Austin where a majority of the state agencies are concentrated around the main Capitol Building, here, nearly everything in the district is owned or operated by the federal government."

FIGURE 24.1 Cash 4 Books at a hot dog stand close to George Washington University.

4    Nick Sibilla, "'Dog Days' Documentary Profiles D.C.'s Dogged Street Vendors," *Forbes*, September 1, 2014, https://www.forbes.com/sites/instituteforjustice/2014/07/31/dog-days-documentary-profiles-d-c-s-dogged-street-vendors/#24bec53825cf.

5    US Department of Veterans Affairs, "About VA," last modified April 11, 2018, https://www.va.gov/landing2_about.htm.

6    Export-Import Bank of the United States, "About Us," accessed March 22, 2019, https://www.exim.gov/about.

Becky furthered, "Unless it is a restaurant, hotel, or private residence, it's either a federal office or closely related to one in some fashion. Just keep in mind that everything we will see today relates to the business of the executive branch of the federal government, or 'the branch of government charged with the execution and enforcement of laws and policies and the administration of public affairs.'[7] Now, with that in mind, we have progressed to H Street at the northwest corner of Lafayette Square[8]" (figure 24.2).

FIGURE 24.2 Aerial view of President's Park in Washington, D.C. encompassing Lafayette Square (foreground), the White House, and the Ellipse (background).

I commented, "Okay, lead on, but what is the statue due south of us across the street?"

Once we were across the street, Becky replied, "This is one of several monuments found in the President's Park Lafayette Square section. Specifically, this one, at the northwest corner, is General Kosciuszko's statue, remembering the contributions of a Polish general who came to the colonies in 1776 to, from what I can tell, solely help the colonies defeat the British, as he returned home at war's end to help with an uprising against Russian occupiers controlling his homeland.[9] This and the three other statues at each corner of the square are in place to commemorate the help of influential Europeans during the Revolutionary War."

We continued heading south along what is now Madison Place. Along the way, Becky noted, "To our right at the center of the park is the General Andrew Jackson statue, with him atop his horse riding into battle. At Jackson's foot is the Bernard Baruch Bench of Inspiration, where Bernard "Barney" Baruch met Presidents Wilson and Roosevelt and other important people to offer his advice away from where he could be taped.[10] Now, let's stop here and turn our attention to the buildings across the street to our left, as, like the White House before us, they too serve a role in the governing process today and in yesteryears."

7    https://www.dictionary.com/browse/executive-branch

8    GSA.gov, "Lafayette Square, Washington, DC," accessed March 22, 2019, https://www.gsa.gov/real-estate/historic-preservation/explore-historic-buildings/heritage-tourism/our-capital/lafayette-square-washington-dc.

9    History.com Editors, "Tadeusz Kosciuszko," November 9, 2009, https://www.history.com/topics/american-revolution/tadeusz-kosciuszko.

10    http://allenbrowne.blogspot.com/2012/08/the-bernard-baruch-bench-of-inspiration.html

Once our motion was entirely arrested about halfway down the street, Becky continued, "Champ, most of the buildings before you house a portion of the Executive Office of the President, which aids and abets the president with the backing needed to properly govern and was created in 1939 by President Franklin D. Roosevelt. Accordingly, the Executive Office is home to some of the president's most important advisors.[11] The group helps the president communicate his message and mission to the world at large and is overseen by the White House chief of staff.[12] Overall, it is one of the many worker groups assisting the president in doing his job. Bringing these buildings into the governing fold was an effort in the 1960s led by local leaders and First Lady Jaqueline Kennedy to preserve them after plans emerged to raze them, to be replaced by modern federal-styled buildings.[13] As part of that process, all the buildings seen here along with the multistoried one behind them were connected by a courtyard at their rear as part of the President's Park founding."[14]

I interjected, "Other than being right across the park from the White House, why were they not razed?"

Becky continued, "Simply put, their former occupants, the most important of which, at least in my opinion, is the Cutts-Madison House at the north end of the block, where the wife of President James Madison, Dolley, lived from 1837 to 1849[15] following the death of her husband. A bit further down is the structure known as the Benjamin Ogle Tayloe House, informally known as the Little White House of President McKinley due to the president and other politically powerful people often dining and visiting here at the time when Senator Mark Hanna regularly hosted scheduled Sunday breakfasts to discuss actions and important decisions of the federal government of the day.[16] Now, the lesser-known building of this block south of us is the National Courts Building, which houses the US Court of Appeals for the Federal Circuit[17] that is on par with the other US Circuit Courts of Appeals and the US Court of Federal Claims, which was established in 1855 to provide an avenue by which citizens could file money claims against the federal government as

---

11    White House, "The Administration," accessed March 22, 2019, https://www.whitehouse.gov/the-trump-administration.

12    Ibid.

13    Ibid.

14    Ibid.

15    Joel D. Treese, "The Dolley Madison House on Lafayette Square," White House Historical Association, May 25, 2016, https://www.whitehousehistory.org/dolley-madison-house-on-lafayette-square.

16    James Morgan, *Theodore Roosevelt, the Boy, and the Man* (New York: Macmillan, 1919).

17    US Court of Appeals for the Federal Circuit, "Court Jurisdiction," accessed March 22, 2019, http://www.cafc.uscourts.gov/the-court/court-jurisdiction.

established by the Tucker Act.[18] This is the one building here that belongs in the judicial branch, not the executive branch."

Becky then ushered us south toward Pennsylvania Avenue and remarked as we approached the street, "Champ, the statue you see to our right is the namesake for the square, French general Marquis de Lafayette, who led the French troops that aided and abetted our efforts to become an independent nation. It is the second of the four statues honoring contributions of Europeans during our Revolutionary War. As we turn right to go east, the one in the distance is for Rochambeau, another French general who led the French Expeditionary Forces at the time, and in the distance catty-cornered from our location in the park is General Friedrich Wilhelm von Steuben, of Germanic descent, who served as major general of the Continental army during the American Revolutionary War and taught troops the essentials of military drills, tactics, and discipline. His most notable offering toward the cause is his text *Regulations for the Order and Discipline of the Troops of the United States* that served as the standard US drill manual until the War of 1812."[19]

I remarked, "Washington certainly has a lot of memorials.[20] Where to next?"

It was then that I focused back on where I was. The square itself was very quiet, but emerging from the tree-lined lawns onto Pennsylvania Avenue Northwest, the shouting of various protesters using microphones suddenly came into focus, along with tour groups and a wide variety of other noisemakers. I remarked, "Is it loud here or is it just me?"

Becky remarked as we walked west on Pennsylvania Avenue, "Welcome to ground zero for that group of activities. Just as people protest outside the Capitol, so do they here, the most famous of which went on from August 1, 1981, to January 15, 2016; activist Concepción Picciotto was the primary guardian of an around-the-clock sit-in post protesting nuclear armament around the world.[21] Her post was on the northern sidewalk of Pennsylvania Avenue Northwest between the White House and the Andrew Jackson statue I mentioned earlier."

Once at the Rochambeau statue on the southwest corner of the square, I asked, "What are the houses ahead of us across the street from the White House?"

---

18    US Court of Federal Claims, "Frequently Asked Questions," accessed March 22, 2019, https://www.uscfc.uscourts.gov/faqs.

19    National Park Service, "Von Steuben Monument," accessed March 22, 2019, https://www.nps.gov/vafo/learn/historyculture/steubenmonument.htm.

20    Office of Congressman Scott Peters, "Tours Booked through Congressman Peters' Office," http://scottpeters.house.gov/sites/scottpeters.house.gov/files/DC-Visitor-Guide-Rep-Scott-Peters.pdf.

21    Caitlin Gibson, "Concepcion Picciotto, Who Held Vigil outside the White House for Decades, Dies," *Washington Post*. January 25, 2016, https://www.washingtonpost.com/local/concepcion-picciotto-who-held-vigil-outside-the-white-house-for-decades-dies/2016/01/25/e0f829e2-c3b0-11e5-a4aa-f25866ba0dc6_story.html?noredirect=on&utm_term=.d6e1c656f949.

Becky explained, "Those buildings also play a role in the governing process. For example, as we are approaching the east end of Pennsylvania Avenue, the white building now to our right with the extended canopy is known as Blair House (figure 24.3), which is where foreign dignitaries visiting Washington stay, or president elects spend their last night before their inauguration, as a matter of convenience and importance.[22] The large gray structure to our left is the Eisenhower Executive Office Building[23] (figure 24.4) that originally housed the State, War and Navy Departments once completed in 1888 and now houses most offices for White House staff like the Council of Economic Advisors, who offer the president objective economic advice on the formulation of economic policy;[24] the National Security Council, which serves as 'the President's principal forum for considering national

FIGURE 24.3 The President's Guest House in Washington, D.C.

FIGURE 24.4 Eisenhower Executive Office Building, Washington D. C.

security and foreign policy matters with his senior national security advisors and cabinet officials';[25] and the Office of Management and Budget, which helps the president 'in meeting his policy, budget, management and regulatory objectives and to fulfill the agency's statutory responsibilities.'[26] Of note, this is the principal office of the Executive Office of the President I mentioned earlier and rounds out information on a vital tool of the president, the workers."

I offered, "So, this and the other buildings we've seen and will see are like the floors in an office tower below the one where the executive sits, which would be the West Wing for our situation?"

Becky remarked, "More or less, yeah. Let's go south now on 17th Street for a bit."

---

22    http://www.blairhouse.org

23    White House, "Eisenhower Executive Office Building," accessed March 22, 2019, https://www.whitehouse.gov/about-the-white-house/eisenhower-executive-office-building.

24    https://www.whitehouse.gov/cea

25    https://www.whitehouse.gov/nsc

26    https://www.whitehouse.gov/omb

Along the way, we talked a bit more about a variety of topics not noteworthy to my trek and counted seven different food carts and trucks. It was just after we crossed E Street Northwest that I had to stop and do a double-take. I remarked, "The president doesn't have a shadow office like Representative Culberson did yesterday or the opposition in the British Parliament,[27] right?"

Becky replied, "No, but you are not alone in thinking that to be true, as this building looks an awful lot like a carbon copy of the White House. This building is home to the headquarters of the American Red Cross, which has the aim of preventing and alleviating human suffering in emergencies by mobilizing the power of volunteers and the generosity of donors.[28] They offer tours of their historic building on Wednesdays and Fridays to see the historical artifacts and artwork inside.[29] Oh, and just before we crossed the last street there, to our left, south of the Eisenhower Building, is the First Division Memorial commemorating all those who have died and served in the army's First Division since World War I.[30] Also, just south of the First Division Memorial is the Butt-Millet Memorial Fountain that serves to memorialize Archibald Butt, military aide to President William Howard Taft, and Francis Davis Millet, the vice chair of the US Commission of Fine Arts, who were friends that died in the sinking of the *Titanic*."[31]

FIGURE 24.5 Headquarters building of the Daughters of the American Revolution, Washington DC.

I noted to myself that I should donate to the Red Cross when I get the chance, as you never know when another Harvey will appear and wipe out everything. After we crossed D Street, Becky noted, "The building we are now standing before is the Daughters of the American Revolution Genealogical Society DC Headquarters (figure 24.5). The library

---

27    https://www.parliament.uk/site-information/glossary/shadow-cabinet; Ex: https://labour.org.uk/people/shadow-cabinet

28    https://www.redcross.org

29    Museums USA, "Museum Info: American Red Cross," last modified May 25, 2011, http://www.museumsusa.org/museums/info/14476.

30    National Park Service, "First Division Monument History," accessed March 22, 2019, https://www.nps.gov/whho/learn/historyculture/first-division-monument.htm.

31    National Park Service, "Butt-Millet Memorial Fountain History," accessed March 22, 2019, https://www.nps.gov/whho/learn/historyculture/butt-millet-memorial-fountain.htm.

at the front and their Constitution Hall for live events at the rear together promote this nonprofit, nonpolitical volunteer women's service organization dedicated to promoting patriotism, preserving American history, and securing America's future through better education for children.[32] Further south of us before the National Mall is the Organization of American States, which is a member states organization designed for the 35 nations of the Americas, to have a place to resolve issues and promote the common welfare in the Americas,[33] aka diplomacy headquarters."

I remarked, "These groups must have had outstanding real estate agents, as they havet great, if not the greatest, real estate in the whole city. I mean, talk about access. Where to next?"

Becky had us cross 17th Street Northwest at C Street Northwest toward an ample green space. Once we were across, Becky remarked, "Welcome to the southern section of President's Park. The large open space you see before us and to our left here shortly is known as the Ellipse, which has a 1-kilometer circumference walking path. In the distance, at the northernmost point of the ellipse is the location of the seasonal National Christmas Tree[34] and Menorah."[35]

I interjected, "No National Crescent for the Islamic faithful?"

Becky stated, "I think there probably won't be one for a while, but if you really want to make a note of where you are, just north of the tree and menorah is the Zero Milestone that is used by distance measures signs for the distance to Washington DC on all American highways.[36] Let's keep walking for a bit and stop at the southernmost point of the ellipse."

About two minutes later, we stopped, and Becky said, "Champ, this is by far my favorite place in DC. Here, we are roughly halfway between the White House and the Washington Monument. Other than in New York City and Central Park or Flushing Meadows, to the best of my knowledge, there is no other place that you can go in the middle of a metropolis and be so far away from buildings. Just take in the peace. From our position, to the southwest and east are the Bullfinch Gatehouses at the corners of 15th and 17th Streets at Constitution Avenue. They were originally constructed at the base of Capitol Hill in 1828 by Capitol architect Charles Bulfinch, where we were yesterday, but were moved here in the 1880s when the Capitol Building and surrounding grounds were being reconstructed."[37]

I interjected, "Wasn't that when the Summerhouse was constructed in the 1880s?"

---

32   https://www.dar.org
33   http://www.oas.org/en
34   https://thenationaltree.org
35   https://nationalmenorah.org
36   Federal Highway Administration, "Zero Milestone—Washington, DC," US Department of Transportation, accessed March 22, 2019, https://www.fhwa.dot.gov/infrastructure/zero.cfm.
37   National Park Service, "U.S. Capitol Gatehouses And Gateposts" (report, National Park Service, 1973), http://npgallery.nps.gov/AssetDetail/NRIS/73002120.

Becky remarked, "Out with the old and in with the new. Can you guess what replaced what?"

I smirked, "Yep, the Summerhouse replaced the Gatehouses!"

Becky continued, "Speaking of places to relax due south of here between the Washington Monument and us are Enid Haupt Fountains that serve, as intended by former first Lady Bird Johnson, to frame the White House in water coming out of 3.5-billion-year-old rock at the main entrance from the National Mall to President's Park as part of her grounds improvement project.[38] Lastly, between us here and the gatehouse to our southwest is the Second Division Memorial that's used to remember 'our dead' from the division's service in World War I; the memorial is most remembered for the flaming sword at its middle that commemorates the defense of Paris.[39] Let's walk over to the west side of the ellipse."

Once there, about five minutes later, Becky continued, "Champ, the time has come for our honor to be upheld. Raise your right hand with your three middle fingers to the sky. Repeat after me, 'On my honor I . . .'"

FIGURE 24.6 Boy Scout Memorial in President's Park, Washington, D.C.

I responded, "On my honor, I . . . wait a minute. Why are we saying the Boy Scout Oath?"

Becky remarked, "You see Champ, the young lad on this statue, the Boy Scout Commemorative Tribute Memorial (figure 24.6), in uniform, is leading the two allegorical figures of a man and woman. They represent 'American Manhood and Womanhood and the ideals they will pass onto the youth.' This monument was erected in 1964 to commemorate 50 years of Scouting that occurred in 1959 and is located where the first Scouting Jamboree took place in 1937.[40] Let's walk toward 15th Street Northwest."

Once we had walked around the pool of the Boy Scout memorial, we found ourselves staring at a tall rectangular block of granite. Becky mentioned, "This is the Original Patentees Memorial. These patentees did not invent something, but they were the original settlers to the area that would eventually become Washington

---

38    City Walking Guide, "Enid Haupt Fountains," accessed March 22, 2019, https://www.citywalking-guide.com/presidentspark/enidhauptfountains.

39    National Park Service, "Second Division Memorial (U.S. National Park Service)," accessed March 22, 2019, https://www.nps.gov/places/second-division-memorial.htm.

40    National Park Service, "Boy Scout Commemorative Tribute Memorial History," accessed March 22, 2019, https://www.nps.gov/whho/learn/historyculture/boy-scout-memorial.htm.

DC. Their names are engraved at the bottom with a tobacco plant on the east, a wild turkey on the south, a stalk of corn on the west, and a fish on the north sides representing the different industry of the area at its founding.[41] Let's walk to the north."

When we were at the northwest corner of E Street Northwest and 15th Street Northwest, Becky had us stop. I asked, "Seems we've found another monument?"

Becky replied, "Right you are Champ. The one to our northwest is the General William Tecumseh Sherman Monument dedicated to the famed American Civil War general that shows him sitting atop a horse, designed so that he is depicted as he was when he rode up Pennsylvania Avenue Northwest as leader of the Army of the Tennessee on May 24, 1865, to celebrate the end of the Civil War. Murals on each side represent the general at various battles throughout the war, with one of him beside a campfire.[42] To our southwest is the Ellipse Visitor Pavilion that is a great place to use the bathroom and learn more about the statues we've seen here. The large building to our southeast is the US Department of Commerce, which operates 'to create the conditions for economic growth and opportunity'[43] via ensuring fair trade, providing data, conducting the census, and, of all things, running the National Weather Service,[44] and more. This building also hosts the White House Visitor Center that allows those who don't get on the tour a place to explore the iconic structure.[45] Lastly, to the east is Pershing Park, which was built to honor General of the Armies John J. Pershing's leadership during World War I. A statue of him stands at the middle, in an area called the American Expeditionary Forces Memorial, with him preparing to look through binoculars as he plans his next move in battle."[46]

At this point, I had to jump in. "Is it me, or do the monuments never end here in the district?"

Becky confidently stated, "They never end. Let's walk north for a while on 15th Street."

Our journey north took us past some hotels and regular-looking office buildings to our right. The one building on our left was ornate, with its long stretches of Ionic columns. Once we returned to the stretch of Pennsylvania Avenue Northwest that runs in front of

41   National Park Service, "Explore the Southern Trail (Ellipse)," accessed March 22, 2019, https://www.nps.gov/whho/planyourvisit/explore-the-southern-trail.htm.

42   National Park Service, "Explore the Northern Trail (Lafayette Park)," accessed March 22, 2019, https://www.nps.gov/whho/planyourvisit/explore-the-northern-trail.htm#CP_JUMP_2801803.

43   US Department of Commerce, "About Commerce," accessed March 22, 2019, https://www.commerce.gov/page/about-commerce.

44   https://www.weather.gov

45   National Park Service, "White House Visitor Center," accessed March 22, 2019, https://www.nps.gov/whho/planyourvisit/white-house-visitor-center.htm.

46   National Park Service, "Pershing Park (U.S. National Park Service)," accessed March 22, 2019, https://www.nps.gov/articles/pershing-park.htm.

the White House, we turned west, to our left. At the second line of bollards, we stopped so that we could lean on them and relax. Becky remarked, "Do you smell that?"

I replied, "No? What do you smell, our stinking feet?"

Becky continued, "No, I smell something much more desirable: money."

I interjected, "Wait, where? Is this where the factory is? I know of the one in Fort Worth."

Becky furthered, "No, no. Even better, this is where we spend it. The long Ionic-columned building we just passed is home to the US Department of the Treasury, which according to its website, is tendered 'to maintain a strong economy and create economic and job opportunities by promoting the conditions that enable economic growth and stability at home and abroad, strengthen national security by combating threats and protecting the integrity of the financial system, and manage the U.S. Government's finances and resources effectively.'"[47]

I conjectured, "Isn't that kind of similar to what the Commerce Department does?"

Becky opined, "In principle, yes, but the Treasury deals with distributing, making, and protecting the value of money that's important to Main Street, while Commerce deals more with items relating to Wall Street. Also, the Bureau of Engraving and Printing here in DC is on the south side of the mall, with free tours available each day, show up at the ticket booth on Raoul Wallenburg Place Southwest, and you are good to go.[48] Now, to our north is where the banks sit, even closer to the White House than that of some of the Executive Office buildings. Bank of America and PNC Bank each have a branch right there for your convenience, and I'm sure their lobbying efforts. The last building that we see here regarding finance is the Freedman's Bank Building, which is an annex of the Treasury. That building was erected on the original site of the Freedman's Bank, which was established to help finance the aspirations of African Americans following the end of slavery.[49] Sadly, though, this is where our tour this morning ends. Just up there on our left are the serpentine lines where your tour continues inside the White House. Have fun!"

Becky and I exchanged hugs and went our separate ways. After getting in line and showing my ticket to the uniformed Secret Service agents, I had some time to think. I could only ponder what I would see from here on out. About 15 minutes later, right on time for my entry ticket, I found myself going through security and entering the White House grounds at the northern end of E Executive Avenue Northwest.[50]

---

47    US Department of the Treasury, "Role of the Treasury," accessed March 22, 2019, https://home.treasury.gov/about/general-information/role-of-the-treasury.

48    Bureau of Engraving and Printing, "Take a Tour," US Department of the Treasury, accessed March 22, 2019, https://www.moneyfactory.gov/washingtondctours.html.

49    US Department of the Treasury, "Freedman's Bank Building," accessed March 22, 2019, https://home.treasury.gov/about/history/freedmans-bank-building.

50    WH Info, "White House Tour 2019," accessed March 22, 2019, https://whitehouse.gov1.info/visit/tour.html; White House tours are self-guided.

As we walked along the path south toward the East Wing of the White House, many signs were in place reminding us to stay on the beaten path or face the consequences. Intermingled were signs indicating historical events. My favorite was the one reporting that a plane crash occurred here on September 12, 1994, when Frank Eugene Corder stole a Cessna 150 and crashed it into the South Lawn,[51] and that a military helicopter mechanic named Robert Preston wanting to alert the president to his rejection from flight training stole a Bell UH-1B Huey helicopter from Fort Tipton and landed it at the White House to try and meet with the president over an issue he had with the government.[52] Who knew?

About a third of the way down the drive, a series of gates had us turn right, right across the street from the Treasury Building. Once past another checkpoint and up a flight of stairs, I finally entered the East Wing. There was a desk with a National Park ranger giving info and answering questions. The walls were lined with paintings of past presidents and first ladies. My favorite was of Nancy Reagan in a long, red, formal gown. After going up a small ramp, we turned right into an area called the East Colonnade (figure 24.7) that separated the Kennedy Garden from the Family Theater.[53]

FIGURE 24.7 President Barack Obama runs down the East Colonnade with family dog, Bo, on the dog's initial visit to the White House on March 15, 2009. Bo came back to live at the White House in April. (Official White House Photo by Pete Souza).

## Minimum Qualifications to Be President

In the East Colonnade,[54] there were several historical photos on the northern side, ranging from FDR's first-ever presidential radio address to, my favorite, presidents and their dogs. On

---

51   Maureen Dowd, "Crash at the White House: The Overview; Unimpeded, Intruder Crashes Plane into White House," *New York Times*, September 13, 1994, https://www.nytimes.com/1994/09/13/us/crash-white-house-overview-unimpeded-intruder-crashes-plane-into-white-house.html.

52   Christopher Freeze, "The Time a Stolen Helicopter Landed on the White House Lawn," *Air & Space Magazine*, March 21, 2017, https://www.airspacemag.com/history-of-flight/prestons-wild-white-house-ride-180962400.

53   White House Museum, "Family Theater," accessed March 22, 2019, http://www.whitehousemuseum.org/east-wing/theater.htm.

54   White House Museum, "East Colonnade," accessed March 22, 2019, http://www.whitehousemuseum.org/east-wing/east-colonnade.htm.

the one small open wall space on the southern side of the hall that is mostly windows, the National Park Service had a large informational board. The top part read, "Want to live here? See below!" Listed below were the three minimum formal qualifications to be president of the United States: Be a natural born citizen of the United States,[55] be 35 years of age, and live in the United States for at least the last 14 years.[56] The asterisk next to the first requirement below stated, "a citizen from birth that has no need to go through naturalization proceedings."

I thought aloud to myself, "Only 16 years to go before I can run; better put this option to join the government in some way on the back burner."

## Presidents and Prime Ministers

Looking back at the sign, the bottom part read, "PMs and presidents: What gives?" Listed below were differences between presidents and prime ministers: Both lead their respective governments, but the prime minister must first get the party that they lead in control of Parliament before they can ascend to power, while the president is elected individually; due to always having their parties in control of the legislative branch, prime ministers have an easier time governing to a point, and due to being elected by the public, presidents need not have extensive history with their respective political parties.[57]

A further sign on the middle column read, "The cost of the key to your new home, Mr. President, is a mere 270 votes in the electoral college."

Further research on my iPhone® informed me that each state gets one Electoral College vote for the number of US Senators and Representatives in Congress, with DC getting as many as are held by the lowest-apportioned state—three, under current conditions—with each state holding their mini election and the winner of the state's election getting the totality of votes, outside of a few circumstances.

An additional sign on the seventh column read, "Mr. President, your lease, er, the term is for four years, renewable for one additional four-year term maximum."[58]

A small sign on the last column read, "Enjoy your time here, sir; keep in mind your approval rating only goes down from here while in residence."[59]

---

55    Neal Katyal and Paul Clement, "On the Meaning of 'Natural Born Citizen'," *Harvard Law Review*, March 22, 2018, https://harvardlawreview.org/2015/03/on-the-meaning-of-natural-born-citizen.

56    U.S. Constitution, article 2, section 1, clause 5.

57    Michael Ray, "What's the Difference Between a President and a Prime Minister?," *Britannica*, accessed March 22, 2019, https://www.britannica.com/story/whats-the-difference-between-a-president-and-a-prime-minister.

58    U.S. Constitution, Amendment 22, section 1.

59    Gallup, "Presidential Approval Ratings—Gallup Historical Statistics and Trends," accessed March 22, 2019, https://news.gallup.com/poll/116677/Presidential-Approval-Ratings-Gallup-Historical-Statistics-Trends.aspx.

## The Interior of the White House

Physically entering the White House and being exposed to what a person must do to earn the position, how long they can stay, and what happens afterward to their popularity while in office was an exciting experience. I pondered this as I sat in the front chair of the Family Theater. Once through in the colonnade, I entered the visitors' foyer to a massive bust of Lincoln looking at me, and several more portraits and paintings of presidents on the wall.[60] Catty-cornered to the entrance of the foyer is the exit that leads to the Center Hall of the ground floor of the White House. To your left is the Vermeil Room, so called due to everything, and I mean nearly everything, being vermeil green.[61] Next door is the China Room, so named because the room has a set of fine china from every administration's time in office.[62] This would not be a great place to release a bull. Before I headed upstairs to the State Floor, I looked in the Library Room.[63] These rooms were great to see, but nothing noteworthy stood out.

Once up the stairs to the State Floor, I exited the stairs to the right and found myself in the East Room, which serves as the main event and reception room in the Executive Mansion.[64] From what I recall, this is the only room that goes from the front to the back of the mansion. At this point, I seemed to remember a series of concerts hosted by the Obamas while Mr. Obama was in office.[65] Upon exiting at the far end of the room, I ended up walking through three more rooms of color, the Green,[66] Blue,[67] and Red,[68] rooms that were all equal in decor to that of the Vermeil Room on the ground floor. The exit at the far end of the Red Room leads into the State Dining Room, which is used for state dinners hosted by the first family.[69] On my way out to the Cross Hall, I peeked into the Old Family Dining Room, where smaller state dinners or staging for events in the bigger room occurs.[70] Once in the Cross Hall (figure 24.8), I surmised that the rooms found on this floor are designed to conduct relations with entities foreign and domestic, while viewing the presidential portraits that lined the

---

60   http://www.whitehousemuseum.org/east-wing/visitors-foyer.htm
61   http://www.whitehousemuseum.org/floor0/vermeil-room.htm
62   http://www.whitehousemuseum.org/floor0/china-room.htm
63   http://www.whitehousemuseum.org/floor0/library.htm
64   http://www.whitehousemuseum.org/floor1/east-room.htm
65   "U.S. President Barack Obama Speaks during an 'In Performance at the … News Photo." Getty Images, accessed March 22, 2019. https://www.gettyimages.com/event/president-obama-hosts-the-pbs-in-performance-at-the-white-house-concert-585572145#president-barack-obama-speaks-during-an-in-performance-at-the-white-picture-id492687592.
66   http://www.whitehousemuseum.org/floor1/green-room.htm
67   http://www.whitehousemuseum.org/floor1/blue-room.htm
68   http://www.whitehousemuseum.org/floor1/red-room.htm
69   http://www.whitehousemuseum.org/floor1/state-dining-room.htm
70   http://www.whitehousemuseum.org/floor1/family-dining-room.htm

FIGURE 24.8 President Barack Obama walks down the Cross Hall towards the East Room prior to a prime time press conference, Wednesday April 29, 2009.

walls.[71] After a few minutes, I decided to make my way out of the Executive Mansion through the Entrance Hall, informally known as the President's Front Door.[72] I figured at this point the bedrooms are off limits, oh well. Guarding the exit door in the Entrance Hall were two marines. Once I was at the door, the marine to my right then asked, "Champ?"

I replied, "Yes, but how did you know?"

A mystery voice to my rear shouted, "Take him down, take him down, take him down!"

## Powers of the President

All I knew next was that I had a bag over my head, I was woozy from hitting the floor hard, and that I was being carried away by a group of people who I assume were guards. The stress of the situation caused me to pass out. I still don't know how much later it was, but I found myself slowly waking up a bit groggy. From what seemed nearby, a voice articulated in a thick Queens accent,[73] "Who are you? What are you doing here? We have you on camera exploring highly sensitive government buildings all over our great country. Explain yourself, now!"

I slowly remarked while stammering, "I'm Champ, . . . Champ C-Cove. I've only been in town for two days . . . I'm just here to learn about the government so that I could join it one day, I swear. I only got in here due to requesting a tour from my congressman, Congressman Culberson. Call him, I met him yesterday, and he'll fill you in on everything. . . I swear on my mother's life. I solemnly swear that I am not up to no good."

The voice that I first heard when waking then spoke. "I don't believe you. Agent, take off his hood. I need to see his eyes to get to the heart of the matter here."

Once the hood was off and my eyes adjusted to the light, my jaw could only drop. It was none other than President Donald Trump himself. I was seated in a chair right across the world-renowned Resolute Desk—which is made from timbers of the HMS Resolute, an

71   http://www.whitehousemuseum.org/floor1/cross-hall.htm

72   http://www.whitehousemuseum.org/floor1/entrance-hall.htm

73   Jeff Guo, "Donald Trump's Accent, Explained," *Washington Post*, February 9, 2016, https://www.washingtonpost.com/news/wonk/wp/2016/02/09/whats-up-with-donald-trumps-voice/?noredirect=on&utm_term=.d2fcaad6c750.

FIGURE 24.9 Panorama of President Donald Trump's Oval Office on January 26, 2017. Trump is sitting at the desk.

abandoned British ship discovered by an American vessel and returned to the Queen of England as a token of friendship and goodwill. When the ship was retired, Queen Victoria commissioned the desk from William Evenden, Royal Naval Dockyard at Chatham, England, and presented to President Rutherford Hayes in 1880"[74]—from the man himself in the Oval Office (figure 24.9). He sat there with the look of joy in someone's eyes when they've pulled off a great prank. Trump said, "Hello Champ, welcome to my current humble abode. Sorry about you passing out. Agent Chuckson with the hood didn't get it on cleanly and quickly and proceeded to hit you in the head."

Agent Chuckson shouted in from the next room, "Sorry Champ!"

I shouted, "Apology accepted, for now, and as for you, sir, I need some info. Who put you up to this and what are your powers to deal with this situation as president?"

Trump spoke, "That would be your father. Remember, when he was a Marine, he was stationed here in the White House on a tour of duty. Over the weekend, he called his old sergeant who works with us here now as a lead, which led us to craft our little soiree here for you."

I remarked, "I need to talk to people in my family about surprise ambushes such as this. So, does this affair go on my record at the FBI or what?"

Trump spoke, "Champ, as I read in the Constitution which, as you know I read very well, states per article 2, section 2, clause 1, I 'have Power to Grant Reprieves and Pardons for Offences against the United States, except in Cases of Impeachment.'[75] Therefore, I charge you, theoretically of course, with trespassing on White House grounds and that's not impeachment, so I now absolve you. I was able to do this for my first turkey last year on Thanksgiving, fascinating stuff going on there."[76]

---

74   http://www.whitehousemuseum.org/furnishings/resolute-desk.htm
75   U.S. Constitution, article 2, section 2, clause 1.
76   Ali Vitali, "Trump Pardons Thanksgiving Turkeys, Jokes about Killing Obama's Birds," NBC News, November 21, 2017, https://www.nbcnews.com/politics/white-house/trump-pardons-two-thanksgiving-turkeys-jokes-about-killing-obama-s-n822951.

I chimed in, "Oh thank God, but what about help with my parking tickets back home?"

Trump responded, "Not a federal crime, so no dice in aid there. Sorry, buddy. Now, speaking of dealing with paperwork, the most common form of paperwork to cross my desk back at Trump Tower was probably documents requiring my signature to approve of deals made by one of my many illustrious ventures. Here, though, the most common form I see is legislation needing my approval. My ability to act here derives from article 1, section 7, clause 2 of the US Constitution.[77] This is a very lengthy section, but if I may shorthand this . . ."

I interjected, "Please!"

Trump continued, "Overall, I have ten days in which to act.[78] During that time, if I like what I read, I may sign the legislation, and it shall become law post haste. Now, if I disagree with said legislation, I may issue a regular veto and return it with my objections to the bill's original house for reconsideration, where that and the other house must both have two-thirds of members reapprove the bill, at which point in time it would become law in what is known as a veto override. On the other hand, if I take no action on the legislation, after the ten-day period of course, if Congress is still in session the bill shall become law, but if they are no longer in session, the bill dies due to Congress not being able to reconsider the legislation and I have, therefore, used my pocket veto."

I inquired, "What about the line-item veto?"

Trump concluded, "Like with the parking tickets back home kid, no dice. Unlike your Texan governor, I am unable to cross out sections, especially spending sections, of legislation that I dislike and keep the rest. For me here, it's an all-or-nothing scenario regarding the passage of or vetoing legislation. Keep in mind that the veto power of governors varies from state to state."[79]

I remarked, "So you and the Texas governor can both approve or reject legislation, but your rejecting . . . er . . . vetoing powers differ. What's another power that you have in office?"

Trump rose and waved his hand for me to follow him. We left the Oval Office through the western door, walked past a small study, and went through a dining room and out into a hall all while making some small talk. After turning left, we walked past two doors labeled "Senior Advisor"—and at this point I swear I could see his daughter Ivanka—went past an elevator, went into another small doorway, and turned right to find ourselves knocking at a door with the big letters "VP" written on the door's window. A muffled "Come in" was

---

77    U.S. Constitution, article 2, section 7, clause 2.

78    Mitchell A. Sollenberger, The Presidential Veto and Congressional Procedure (report, Congressional Research Service, 2004), http://www.archives.gov/files/legislative/resources/education/veto/veto-procedure.pdf; Detailed info on veto and veto override procedure.

79    John Haughey, "State-By-State Guide to Gubernatorial Veto Types," CQ, November 14, 2016, https://info.cq.com/resources/state-by-state-guide-to-gubernatorial-veto-types.

heard through the closed door after Trump rattled the doorknob. Once inside, Trump said, "Mike, hey there, this is Champ Cove from Texas. He is here on a little field trip learning about government and how to get involved with government, the presidency in this case."

Vice President Mike Pence rose and came over to speak with me at the door. "Young man, welcome to my humble abode here. Sir, how may I be of assistance?"

Just then, a judge, an ambassador, and a secretary walked by reminiscing. Trump called them into the room.

Once they were in, Trump spoke. "Champ, this is retiring Supreme Court justice Anthony Kennedy, UN Ambassador Nikki Haley, and Energy Secretary, and your former governor, Rick Perry."

In unison, the three replied, "Hi Champ and, sir, how can we be of assistance?"

Trump remarked, "Play along of course. Champ, what did each of the other four people in the room say to me at one point in time?"

I replied, "What'd they say to you at one point in time, sir?"

Trump joked, "Thanks for the job, sir!"

I could hear the bu-dum-stah of a drum set in my head at that one, but Justice Kennedy remarked, "Not me directly sir, but I get what you are going after by stating that joke. Champ, what I believe Mr. President over there is going after is his ability in article 2, section 2, clause 2 of the US Constitution, along with Amendment 25, clause 2,[80] for Mr. Vice President over there, that with the advice and consent of the US Senate the president may appoint 'Ambassadors, other public Ministers and Consuls, Judges of the Supreme Court, and all other Officers of the United States, whose Appointments are not herein otherwise provided for, and which shall be established by Law.'"

Trump chimed in by saying, "Don't forget about article 2, section 2, clause 3,[81] which allows me to make appointments without Senate approval to any vacancy that occurs during a recess of the Senate that shall expire at the end of the Senate's next term unless the Senate goes on to approve of that appointment in that next term."

I spoke, "Wait a minute, does this have anything to do with your position as a singular executive rather than a plural executive, like back home in Texas?"

Secretary Perry maintained, "Bullseye. All those position equivalents back home are elected individually by you and me in an election, most of them anyhow. The only major position I could appoint was my secretary of state."

I could hear the wah-wah of a horn going off in my head at that one, but Secretary Haley remarked, "Remember, each of these appointments are important due to them being selected

---

80    U.S Constitution, article II, section 2, clause 2 and amendment XXV, clause 2.
81    U.S Constitution article II, section 2, clause 3.

to lead the federal agencies that provide you and I with goods and services, like regulating nuclear energy production in the Department of Energy by the Nuclear Regulatory Commission[82] or provision of air traffic control in the Department of Transportation led by the Federal Aviation Administration."[83]

I remarked, "Thank you all for the valuable insight on presidential appointments. What power would you like to discuss next sir?"

Everybody but Pence followed us out of the office and went on their way. Once in the quiet peacefulness of the hall, but before Trump could respond to my question, several Secret Service officers ran up to us and hurried us down several corridors, a set of stairs, down more halls, and into what was, from what I could tell, a highly secretive room. Either way, I couldn't keep track of where I was and had been; I was just glad not to have another bag put over my head at this point. Now seated at a long table, Trump spoke. "Champ, you know that I know a lot, a huge amount so to speak, regarding my job here. You see that guy in with the briefcase in here with us. He's my best friend, as he always has a football with him. You see, I use to own a USFL team, the New Jersey Generals.[84] It always great to have a football to play around with you see."

I shouted, "I'll go long!"

The mysterious man said, "I would throw, but I'm handcuffed to this particular football and not to mention it's a lot heavier than a normal football."

Trump said, "Champ, welcome to the Situation Room.[85] A room most notably pictorialized when my predecessor Obama sat here with Hillary Clinton, Joe Biden, and other West Wing officials on May 2, 2011, the night Osama bin Laden was killed by Navy Seals during a raid on his compound in Pakistan, watching the events on the big screen to your left[86] (figure 24.10). Also, thanks again Chuckson for your help on getting us down here."

Agent Chuckson from out in the hall stated, "You are welcome again, sir!"

I interjected, "The power, sir?"[87]

---

82  https://www.nrc.gov

83  https://www.faa.gov/jobs/career_fields/aviation_careers

84  Arash Markazi, "5 Things to Know about Donald Trump's Foray into Doomed USFL," ESPN, July 14, 2015, http://www.espn.com/espn/story/_/id/13255737/five-things-know-donald-trump-usfl-experience.

85  http://www.whitehousemuseum.org/west-wing/situation-room.htm

86  Alex Lockie, "Here's the Story behind One of the Most Iconic Photos from the Bin Laden Raid," *Business Insider*, May 2, 2017, https://www.businessinsider.com/situation-room-bin-laden-raid-2017-5.

87  Information on the ability of the president to act militarily was gathered from the following source: James C. Ho, "The Sword and the Purse (Part 2); The President as Commander in Chief," Heritage Foundation, accessed March 22, 2019, https://www.heritage.org/the-constitution/report/the-sword-and-the-purse-part-2-the-president-commander-chief.

Trump remarked, "Ahhh, yes. The man with the briefcase holds the tool that I may use to launch a nuclear weapon against our enemies at will. All I must do is open the briefcase, read off a set of numbers and letters that authenticates that I am giving an official command to launch a nuclear weapon to the Pentagon, and 15 minutes later it's in Pyongyang or Moscow or Timbuktu or wherever I deem fit to attack under those circumstances.[88] This is the literal form of my duties as outlined in article 2, section 2, clause 1 of the US Constitution that reads, 'The President shall be Commander in Chief of the Army and Navy of the United States, and of the

FIGURE 24.10 U.S. President Barack Obama and Vice President Joe Biden, along with members of the national security team, receive an update on Operation Neptune's Spear, a mission against Osama bin Laden, in one of the conference rooms of the Situation Room of the White House, May 1, 2011. They are watching live feed from drones operating over the bin Laden complex.

Militia of the several States, when called into the actual Service of the United States.'[89] In other words, I'm the lead military official of the United States. Other than when Truman launched the nuclear strikes on Hiroshima and Nagasaki, the last, and only, real time a sitting president led troops into battle was when George Washington put an end to the Whiskey Rebellion himself in 1794.[90] Advocates of unchecked presidential power on wartime affairs argue that I have substantive constitutional power to engage our military forces in hostilities. This is bolstered by article 2, section 1, clause 1,[91] that vests the entirety of the 'executive Power' in a single individual, me in my current position as president. My most significant action under this power came on April 13, 2017, when I dropped a bomb on a terrorist encampment of tunnels and caves in Afghanistan."[92]

I interjected, "Sir, if there is one item I've learned over the last few weeks, it's that the government has checks and balances. What are the checks on this balance?"

88    Alana Abramson, "What Donald Trump Would Have to Do to Launch Nuclear Weapons," *Time*, January 3, 2018, http://time.com/5085723/nuke-button-donald-trump-nuclear-weapons-north-korea.

89    U.S. Constitution, article 2, section 2, clause 1.

90    History.com Editors, "Whiskey Rebellion," October 30, 2017 https://www.history.com/topics/early-us/whiskey-rebellion.

91    U.S. Constitution, article 2, section 1, clause 1.

92    Robin Wright, "Trump Drops the Mother of All Bombs on Afghanistan," *New Yorker*, July 10, 2017, https://www.newyorker.com/news/news-desk/trump-drops-the-mother-of-all-bombs-on-afghanistan.

Trump articulated, "The debate over checks and balances on this power, accordingly, is the extent to which Congress's constitutional authority allows them to restrict my actions. You see under article 1, section 1, Congress only enjoys only those legislative powers 'herein granted.' In other words, while I have broad authority to act in war and other related affairs, Congress does not. For examples of what Congress can do, you must refer back to article 1, section 8, clauses 8 to 16, which, among other things, limits them only to declare war, grant letters of marque and reprisal (letting a private citizen wage war/act on behalf of the United States), raise and support armies, provide and maintain a navy, make rules for the government and regulation of the land and naval forces, provide for calling forth the militia to execute the laws of the union, suppress insurrections and repel invasions, provide for organizing, arming, and disciplining the militia, and governing such part of them."

I interjected, "What about the role of the states in hostilities?"

Trump conferred, "They have little to no authority on this matter, as article 1, section 10, clause 3 of the Constitution expressly prevents states from doing so unless with 'consent of Congress,' unless they are 'actually invaded, or in such imminent danger as will not admit of delay.'[93] By contrast, no such limitation on executing my war powers can be found in article 2 of the Constitution. Interestingly, the only real checks on my duties as commander in chief by Congress are that they may drastically limit the military resources that I may use to wage war. Thus, I may be commander in chief, but unless Congress provides the resource, I can't command the resource in a conflict. Therefore, due to their mastery of the purse strings of the federal government, I am unable to engage in hostilities without Congress, like another world war."

Chuckson, listening in, shouted, "Tell him about Congress's biggest attempt to control your position as president, sir!"

Trump obliged: "In 1973, Congress passed the War Powers Resolution to limit the commander-in-chief power of the president following actions taken by Johnson and Nixon in Vietnam, who were only armed with the Gulf of Tonkin Resolution that allowed them to 'take all necessary measures to repel any armed attack against the forces of the United States and to prevent further aggression' by North Vietnam in a conflict that would last several years.[94] The issue with the Gulf of Tonkin Resolution was that it was very broad in scope/focus, which allowed a lot of leeway for everyone involved to get what they wanted: a long-protracted war without real congressional approval. Regardless, Nixon vetoed

---

93   U.S. Constitution, article 1, section 10, clause 3.

94   History.com Editors, "Vietnam War," October 29, 2009, https://www.history.com/topics/vietnam-war/vietnam-war-history.

the legislation, and Congress went on to override the veto enacting the resolution. The resolution, in short, limits my ability as president to engage US forces in hostilities for more than 60 days, absent a declaration of war or specific congressional authorization, and requires I consult with Congress regarding military deployments.[95] Presidents since have largely ignored the resolution since such as when in Operation Desert Shield in late 1990 to early 1991 as President H.W. Bush held that he as president needed no 'authority' from Congress to execute the United Nations resolutions authorizing member states to use 'all necessary means' to remove Iraq from Kuwait.[96] Congress has not done an excellent job at checking this power."

I chimed in, "Well, if it makes your position more powerful, why fight it?"

Trump noted, "Remember, there is a certain etiquette to conflict. Speaking of which, we need to go to a different room to further discuss my powers. Chuckson!"

Chuckson stated, "Yes sir!"

Trump declared, while signaling for me to rise, "Clear a path; Champ and I are headed to the Diplomatic Reception Room."

Chuckson and the other agents led us through the two doors at the front of the Situation Room, up a small flight of stairs, to the end of the hall, to the right, and then a left up a full flight of stairs, and past what I think is the Cabinet Room, where the president meets with department officials to discuss policies and agendas as part of his official advisory board.[97] After continuing and turning right, we went through a doorway onto the West Colonnade of the White House and headed back into the Executive Mansion. Letting curiosity get to me, I asked, "Sir, what is the room to our left here?"

Trump held, "That room, I assume you watch the news from time to time, is where the great press secretary briefs the media and press on events occurring in the administration and is formally called, of all things, the Press Briefing Room.[98] Funny enough, that room used to be an indoor pool and spa. When reporting and not covering a briefing, the press can be found on the northwest lawn of the White House reporting the news from their annex. Let's walk toward South Lawn Road for a moment and take in the view of the South Lawn."

I followed, and we stopped after walking to where the sidewalk here met the road. Trump remarked, "Champ, what you see before us now is the recreational section of the grounds. In the distance are the basketball and tennis courts. Beyond that is the vegetable garden

---

95    Library of Congress, "War Powers," last modified November 27, 2017, https://www.loc.gov/law/help/war-powers.php.

96    Ibid.

97    http://www.whitehousemuseum.org/west-wing/cabinet-room.htm

98    http://www.whitehousemuseum.org/west-wing/press-briefing-room.htm

put in place by the Obamas. There are also several outdoor sitting areas over there. A bit closer and to our right is the White House pool and playground. Lastly, immediately to our right is the Rose Garden, where many formal ceremonies are performed, like the wedding of Tricia Nixon to Edward Cox in 1971."[99]

I commented, "Isn't this where the helicopter picks you up?"

Trump responded, "This is the best place for choppers to land and take off. I assume you know about the one helicopter that landed here illegally?"

I replied, "You betcha, sir."

Trump concluded, "Good. Also, other big presidential perks are the private jet known as Air Force One, which is a specially modified Boeing 747-200,[100] Camp David, the private presidential resort in Catoctin Mountain Park in Frederick County, Maryland,[101] and the Presidential State Car, informally known as the Beast, which is essentially a Cadillac version,[102] among others. Now, as we turn and walk back inside if you look up to the top two floors of the residence, those floors are home to the areas where presidents, like me, live while in office. A few of the more famous rooms are the Queen[103] and Lincoln[104] Bedrooms, so named due to most visiting heads of state staying there and being where the former president Lincoln's furniture is kept from his time here, respectively. Back inside, let's go."

Once back at the residence, we turned right and entered the Palm Room, so called due to all the palm trees in the room.[105] The two most visually stunning pieces though were the murals of Liberty and Justice opposing each other on the west and east walls, respectively. We exited through the door in the northeast corner of the room. This took us into the Center Hall that I came through when I first entered the building. About halfway down, Trump and I turned right into a room not seen on the self-guided tour earlier. Once inside, Trump directed me to sit at the door closest to the outside entrance while he sat at the one closest to the interior entrance. He said, "Champ, no other location in this spectacular building plays as important a role as this room. I can wine and dine in this room or that room, but here is where I make my first impression. This room

99    http://www.whitehousemuseum.org/grounds/rose-garden.htm
100    https://www.whitehouse.gov/about-the-white-house/air-force-one
101    https://www.whitehouse.gov/about-the-white-house/camp-david
102    Bruce Brown, "U.S. Secret Service Introduces Cadillac Beast Presidential Limo," Digital Trends, September 28, 2018, https://www.digitaltrends.com/cars/secret-service-cadillac-beast-presidential-limo.
103    http://www.whitehousemuseum.org/floor2/queens-bedroom.htm
104    http://www.whitehousemuseum.org/floor2/lincoln-bedroom.htm
105    http://www.whitehousemuseum.org/west-wing/palm-room.htm

is known as the Diplomatic Reception Room (figure 24.11).[106] The massive mural you see on all the walls was put in place by Jacqueline Kennedy in 1961 and is entitled *Views of North America*, featuring 32 beautiful scenes of North America in the 1820s when the piece was crafted."

I interjected, "What power were you wanting to discuss here though, sir?"

Trump furthered, "All right. Champ, it is fair to say that you are the unofficial dignitary from Texas visiting today. This is where visiting dignitaries and heads of state and I first meet when they visit Washington. Due to article 2, section 2, clause 2[107] granting me the power to 'make Treaties' and 'appoint Ambassadors,' my final official power is to serve as chief diplomat with 'Advice and Consent of the Senate,' of course, by them approving my actions with two-thirds approval on treaties and now one-half approval, respectively, on ambassadors. Due to these approval minimums, Congress has more influence over my decisions in this realm. Accordingly, I am known as the chief diplomat of the US government. Just an FYI, a chief diplomat is 'a person appointed by a national government to conduct official negotiations and maintain political, economic, and social relations with another country or countries.'"[108]

I asked, "Other than meeting them here or there and wining and dining them over there, what formally does this power entail?"

Trump declared, "Young man, that would include three specific duties. I already mentioned the first, treaties, or 'any legally binding agreement between nations'[109] that per the Vienna Convention of 1986 on the Law of Treaties between States and International Organizations or between International Organizations must be in writing, must be governable by international law, must always make the name of the agreement irrelevant, and can simply be an exchange of notes.[110] Examples here include the North American Free

FIGURE 24.11  President Donald Trump greets Elder Archbishop Demetrios and Father Alex Karloutsos of the Greek Orthodox Archdiocese of America in the Diplomatic Receiving Room, Friday, March 24, 2017, prior to the Greek Independence Day Celebration at the White House. (Official White House Photo by Benjamin Applebaum).

---

106   http://www.whitehousemuseum.org/floor0/diplomatic-room.htm
107   U.S. Constitution, article II, section 2, clause 2.
108   https://www.dictionary.com/browse/diplomat
109   Main Reading Room, "What Is a Treaty?," Library of Congress, accessed March 22, 2019, https://loc.gov/rr/main/govdocsguide/TreatyDefinition.html.
110   Karl Zemanek, "Vienna Convention on the Law of Treaties between States and International Organizations or between International Organizations," Audiovisual Library of International Law,

Trade Agreement that my staff and I are currently reworking between us, Mexico, and Canada. A light form of treaties is known as executive agreements that typically cover the implementation of treaties.[111] My favorite though, granted I have yet to use it, is the diplomatic recognition where I can formally and unilaterally recognize the existence of other countries thanks to my powers outlined in article 2, section 3[112] that reads 'he shall receive Ambassadors and other public Ministers.' The most famous of these incidents occurred on May 14, 1948, when the Provisional Government of Israel proclaimed the new State of Israel. On that same date, the United States via President Truman recognized the provisional Jewish government as the de facto authority of the Jewish state.[113] The document recognizing the state and the recognition via telegraph are on reserve at the National Archives, our nation's record keeper."[114]

I remarked, "How might this power relate to the day-to-day running of the federal government, sir?"

Trump continued, "One last bit of power as the chief diplomat is my power granted by article 2, section 3, that mandates me to 'take Care that the Laws be faithfully executed.' The question is, how do I do that job?"

I replied, "Hold a news conference and answer questions?"

Trump continued, "The answer to that question is what my predecessors and I have issued. Specifically, we have issued a series of executive orders, proclamations, and administrative orders. The prior is 'a signed, written, and published directive from the President, like myself, that manages operations of the federal government.'[115] One of the more impactful orders I have given was number 13835 that strengthens prior order efforts to restrict trade and commerce with Venezuela due to their continual societal deterioration thanks to the adoption of socialistic policies.[116] Proclamations 'communicate information on holidays, commemorations, federal observances, and trade'[117] to the

accessed March 22, 2019, http://legal.un.org/avl/ha/vcltsio/vcltsio.html.

111    US Department of State, "Treaty vs. Executive Agreement," accessed March 22, 2019, https://www.state.gov/s/l/treaty/faqs/70133.htm.

112    U.S. Constitution, article II, section 3.

113    National Archives, "U.S. Recognition of the State of Israel," accessed March 22, 2019, https://www.archives.gov/education/lessons/us-israel.

114    https://www.archives.gov/about

115    American Bar Association, "What Is an Executive Order?," November 27, 2018, https://www.americanbar.org/groups/public_education/publications/teaching-legal-docs/what-is-an-executive-order-.

116    Executive Office of the President, "Prohibiting Certain Additional Transactions with Respect to Venezuela," *Federal Register*, May 24, 2018, https://www.federalregister.gov/documents/2018/05/24/2018-11335/prohibiting-certain-additional-transactions-with-respect-to-venezuela.

117    Ibid 117.

various affected agencies, while the latter 'are used to manage administrative matters of the federal government.'[118] These are all akin to the CEO of a company excusing workers early for a holiday or making the final decision on whether to launch a new initiative. The difference is the orders are for more severe measures while the latter two directives are for more trivial matters. Either way, I did plenty of these back at Trump Tower. "

I inquired, "As president, what are other important powers that you hold?"

Trump commented, "To answer that, we turn back to article 2, section 3. From that section of the Constitution, I must 'report on the State of the Union,' and I do so annually when I stand in Congress and deliver a speech by the same name. In my speech, when I make calls for new laws to be enacted, I fulfill my mandate to Congress to 'recommend to their Consideration such Measures as he shall judge necessary and expedient." Also, as a check on the power of Congress, I may, 'on extraordinary Occasions, convene both Houses, or either of them and in Case of Disagreement between them, concerning the Time of Adjournment.' This means that if Congress refused to end their term and begin anew, after an election cycle, for example, I could do it for them and allow the new term/session to begin. The amount of time and energy it takes to be a president or CEO is immense."

I remarked, "Sir, thank you so much for your time. Before I go, is there anything else you could tell me?"

Trump stated, "Oh yes, but now is the time for a late lunch. Follow me. Chuckson, get some sandwiches brought up to the South Portico."[119]

Chuckson stated, "Yes, sir," and then whispered into his earpiece mic, "Send his favorite sandwiches, meatloaf I believe,[120] up to the South Portico" (figure 24.12).

FIGURE 24.12 Inauguration of Franklin Delano Roosevelt at the White House on 01/20/1945 on the South Portico.

118    Ibid 117.

119    http://www.whitehousemuseum.org/floor1/south-portico.htm

120    Holly Van Hare, "A Complete Guide to Donald Trump's Favorite Foods Slideshow," Daily Meal, October 20, 2017, https://www.thedailymeal.com/healthy-eating/complete-guide-donald-trump-s-favorite-foods-slideshow/slide-14.

# History of the Presidency

Following that, Trump and I walked out the door behind me out onto the patio between the residence and South Lawn Road. We then turned right and went up the outdoor staircases to find ourselves on a balcony with a fantastic view of the Washington Monument. The spartan area had a lone set of chairs with a table between them that we sat in. Once seated, Trump began by asking, "Champ, have you ever considered how my current position got to the point that it has? Why we have a monument to Washington[121] standing before us?"

I spoke, "Not entirely, but I do know that President Washington established many norms for the position like the name 'Mr. President,' giving the State of the Union report as a speech, retiring after twoterms, visiting his home while in office to vacation, and, of all things, when to do government business and when to meet with guests in the morning and the evening, respectively."[122]

Trump responded, "Very good, but how did we get to have a position for him to set a precedent? That is in our history. Remember, before our start, we were a series of British colonies. We had a king or queen. The most relevant king to our history as an independent nation, King George III, used a series of colonial governors to implement his policies here. The governor ruled along with a series of assemblies in each of the colonies that were elected by colonial citizens who often resisted the governor by withholding funds, of which, along with a council serving as cabinet and judiciary, set up the system of divided government and checks and balances that we have today. Regardless of exact set-up from colony to colony, these governors served as the face of the king here in the colonies who were prone to abuse their power by calling irregular sessions of the assemblies and threatening punishment to those who disagreed with them."[123]

I interjected, "But what does that have to do with your position?"

Trump countered, "Everything. What would you do in a position where for all relevant time you dealt with a person, individual, a lackey, a tyrant in truth, for the king?"

I replied, "Easy, get rid of them as soon as humanly possible."

Trump furthered, "That's exactly what we did. Under the Articles of Confederation, per article 3, that governed us through the Revolutionary War and the immediate years afterward, 'The . . . states hereby severally enter into a firm league of friendship with each

---

121  https://www.nps.gov/wamo/index.htm

122  Mary Stockwell, "Presidential Precedents," George Washington's Mount Vernon, accessed March 22, 2019, https://www.mountvernon.org/library/digitalhistory/digital-encyclopedia/article/presidential-precedents.

123  Digital History, "Chapter 3: Government in England and the Colonies," http://www.digitalhistory.uh.edu/teachers/lesson_plans/pdfs/unit1_3.pdf.

other,"[124] that per article 2, '[e]ach state retains its sovereignty, freedom, and independence, and every Power, Jurisdiction and right, which is not by this confederation expressly delegated to the United States, in Congress assembled.' Now regarding actual management of the confederation, article 5, '[f]or the more convenient management of the general interests of the United States, delegates shall be annually appointed in such manner as the legislature of each state shall direct, to meet in Congress' to provide management of the new nation. What really gets interesting is under article 9 that reads, 'The United States in Congress assembled, shall have the sole and exclusive right and power of determining on peace and war,' in clause 1, or clause 2 that reads, 'The United States in Congress assembled shall also be the last resort on appeal in all disputes and differences now subsisting or that hereafter may arise between two or more states concerning boundary, jurisdiction or any other cause whatever,' among others. The only real mention of a true executive comes in clause 5 that reads, 'The United States in Congress assembled shall have authority to appoint a committee, to sit in the recess of Congress, to be denominated "A Committee of the States," and to consist of one delegate from each state; and to appoint such other committees and civil officers as may be necessary for managing the general affairs of the united states under their direction.' Accordingly, at no point in the Articles of Confederation did our founding fathers go about and create a permanent executive, only one sit and serve at the direction of Congress when they, Congress, were not in session."

I replied, "Sir, I don't know about you, but that reading of the Articles of Confederation is the epitome of responding to the abuse of power by denying power to an individual. The problem is, if I remember enough, it did not turn out well for us as a country under the Articles."

Trump noted, "No, no it did not. Realizing the shortcomings of our Articles and the need for a true executive to be in place, among other problems, the constitutional convention was called to occur in Philadelphia in 1787. From that convention and subsequent ratification of the Constitution in 1788, the presidency came into being thanks to the presence of article 2 on April 4, 1789, when George Washington took the oath of office that is found in the final clause of section 2. Up until the 1930s, a few presidents here or there took strides to expand the influence of the presidency. For example, Andrew Jackson helped emerge the party system by giving appointments to faithful followers. Also, Lincoln, thanks to the Civil War, suspended habeas corpus and increased the size of the Army beyond congressional mandate, alongside blockading southern ports without approval. However, no one more than FDR upended the system so much. Overall, the position of the presidency was a weak one, with severe subservience to Congress being exercised by prior inhabitants to my position that changed with the presidency of Franklin Delano Roosevelt in the 1930s and

---

124    Articles of Confederation; various cited clauses in the text.

1940s. This situation came into being due to FDR and Congress pushing through the New Deal programs that further regulated the economy, alongside World War II pushing him to the forefront of foreign affairs, not to mention the rise of technology like the radio making it easier for the president to reach out to the people in a way that Congress cannot, singularly, nor anyone else before. For an example of this, think of the movie *The King's Speech* that dramatized the importance of nationwide speech making against the backdrop of the UK's entry into World War II.[125] This is somewhat akin to my press conferences and TV show hosting gigs, among others."[126]

I interjected, "How do we see this today?"

Trump stated, "That, young man, is the rise of the imperial presidency."

I contended, "The imperial presidency, what now?"

Trump collected his thoughts for a moment and continued, "Yes, Champ, the imperial presidency. This is a term first coined in historian Arthur M. Schlesinger Jr.'s 1973 book by the same name.[127] In that work, Schlesinger argues that since World War II, presidents have used times of crisis to expand their power, primarily due to war-making in this case, beyond what is mandated/allowed/acceptable under the Constitution."

I connected everything I had heard earlier in the day by interrupting, "Wait, this concept is all that was started by FDR, put into greater effect by Johnson and Nixon during Vietnam, and George H.W. Bush in Iraq put together, that you mentioned earlier in the Situation Room, not to mention, based on what you said earlier regarding the ability of your position to make war provided Congress has provided resources for you to use, this is certainly the truth."

Trump remarked, "That work, fortunately, has not been the final say on the matter. A 2002 work by Donald Wolfensberger, a former congressional staffer for 28 years, argues that that position of the presidency may be over, with some conditions.[128] He notes that George W. Bush was elected in 2000 as the first president not to be elected under the guise of a national crisis since before World War II, thanks to the ever-present Cold War. Granted, that precondition changed on September 11, 2001, following the attacks on the World Trade Center and the Pentagon that brought about the War on Terror.[129] The question Wolfensberger brings to the forefront is what may come going forward regarding President George W. Bush's

125   http://www.kingsspeech.com

126   Cristen Tilley, Nathan Hoad, and Ben Spraggon, "See If You Can Guess Which US TV Network Mentions Trump the Least," ABC News, December 13, 2017, http://www.abc.net.au/news/2017-12-13/donald-trump-news-media-coverage/9125810.n.

127   A.M. Schlesinger Jr., *The Imperial Presidency* (New York: Houghton Mifflin, 1973).

128   D.R. Wolfensberger, "The Return of the Imperial Presidency?," *Wilson Quarterly* 26, no. 2 (2002): 36–41.

129   Richard Jackson, "War on Terrorism," *Britannica*, November 19, 2018, https://www.britannica.com/topic/war-on-terrorism.

reaction to the conflict. Is it a long-term sustained new front in expanding the presidency's influence, or is it something that goes by the wayside after a few years?"

I inquired, "So what happened?"

Trump replied, "It's obvious, the imperial presidency is back and bigger than ever. We immediately invaded Afghanistan following the attack as that was where we thought at the time Osama bin Laden was hiding, and in 2003 invaded Iraq, again, under the guises that he was harboring weapons of mass destruction that turned up empty on further inspection, amid the various covert operations that are still ongoing 17 years later.[130] Remember how we got Osama? We also increased funding for intelligence services, capturing and interring terrorists in Cuba at Guantanamo Bay, and greatly stepped up our cooperation with other national intelligence services.[131] Here at home we have implemented the USA PATRIOT Act that allows for greater surveillance activities, the reorganization of intelligence services under the US Department of Homeland Security, and more established security screening and protocols at airports, borders, and public events.[132] I mean, look at what I have done beyond the MOAB we discussed earlier. Using the Politifact.com Trump-O-Meter,[133] out of 102 tracked promises from my time on the campaign trail, I have kept 13 promises and com-promised on 7, giving me a whopping 19.6 percent, for lack of a better term, success rate for my plans on everything from growing the economy at 4 percent[134] to cutting off immigra-tion from terror-prone nations[135] to improving access to services for veterans by initiating a hotline to the White House[136] to fair trade.[137] Of note, I have work on 41 other promises in the works with some not being able to be tallied into the kept category, due to me needing to be out of office. Compared to my predecessor over his eight years in office, he kept or compromised on 404 of 533, roughly 75.7 percent of promises that he made. With six years to go, I look forward to keeping more and more of my promises and, either way, you don't

130    Ibid.

131    Ibid.

132    Ibid.

133    https://www.politifact.com/truth-o-meter/promises/trumpometer

134    Miriam Valverde, "Grow the Economy by 4 Percent a Year," *PolitiFact*, August 7, 2018, https://www.politifact.com/truth-o-meter/promises/trumpometer/promise/1414/grow-economy-4-percent-year.

135    Miriam Valverde, "Suspend Immigration from Terror-Prone Places," PolitiFact, June 26, 2018, https://www.politifact.com/truth-o-meter/promises/trumpometer/promise/1402/suspend-immigration-terror-prone-places.

136    Miriam Valverde, "Create Private White House Veterans Hotline," PolitiFact, August 9, 2018, https://www.politifact.com/truth-o-meter/promises/trumpometer/promise/1342/create-private-white-house-veterans-hotline.

137    Bill McCarthy, "Raise Tariffs on Goods Imported into the U.S.," PolitiFact, July 11, 2018, https://www.politifact.com/truth-o-meter/promises/trumpometer/promise/1411/raise-tariffs-goods-imported-us.

see Congress working to advance any causes of note. Granted, the Democrats, the party not in power in Congress, did try to promote their Better Deal plan back in the spring of 2017, to little fanfare,[138] with candidates like Alexandria Ocasio-Cortez in the House proposing a so-called Green New Deal.[139] Beyond that, the Republicans, who are in charge, have deferred to me for guidance on what to accomplish, primarily."[140]

I inquired, "In what other ways can I see the impact of the imperial presidency in play?"

Trump replied, "Well, that last part I mentioned about promoting the agenda for the party in Congress puts me in the position of being the unofficial party leader, as so much of what we call for on the campaign trail leads to legislation considered and passed in Congress. Beyond that, as president, I am the head of state and government. Therefore, I'm not just the CEO, remember the executive orders we discussed earlier, I'm also the public affairs director responsible for guiding the country through tough relations with other countries.[141] The amount of work my predecessors and I have done here has made the presidency the leader of the free world due to our dominant economy and militarism since the end of World War II, as well as us being the only major country on the planet to have used nuclear weapons against another country following such a large conflict. Along similar lines here at home, following Hurricane Harvey, I visited your fair state to help with and inspect recovery efforts being led by the Federal Emergency Management Agency alongside local agencies to serve here as the manager of crisis.[142] Presidents also push for ideal policies, with the most notable one in recent memory being President Obama's Patient Protection and Affordable Care Act that took nearly two years from identifying the policy desired to him signing the legislation into law.[143] Lastly, presidents like myself have done a lot of work to grow the economy, as Obama sought to boost spending on infrastructure via the American Recovery and Reinvestment

138    https://abetterdeal.democraticleader.gov

139    Danielle Kurtzleben, "Rep. Alexandria Ocasio-Cortez Releases Green New Deal Outline," NPR, February 7, 2019, https://www.npr.org/2019/02/07/691997301/rep-alexandria-ocasio-cortez-releases-green-new-deal-outline.

140    Dan Balz, "Trump Dominates the GOP Base. Party Leaders Live with the Consequences," *Washington Post*, November 11, 2017, https://www.washingtonpost.com/politics/trump-dominates-the-gop-base-party-leaders-live-with-the-consequences/2017/11/11/3f2a14de-c6f3-11e7-84bc-5e285c7f4512_story.html?utm_term=.4ed608e62dd8.

141    Madeleine Sheehan Perkins, "The World Leaders President Trump Has Met So Far—and What Happened," *Business Insider*, August 1, 2017, https://www.businessinsider.com/world-leaders-trump-has-met-so-far-2017-7.

142    Hailey Branson-Potts and Noah Bierman, "Trump Visits Texas, Hailing Officials' Harvey Response and Promising 'Costly' Federal Aid," *Los Angeles Times*, August 29, 2017, http://www.latimes.com/politics/la-na-pol-trump-harvey-texas-20170829-story.html.

143    Affordable Health California, "Timeline: Affordable Care Act," accessed March 22, 2019, http://affordablehealthca.com/timeline-obamacare.

Act[144] to my Tax Cuts and Jobs Act of 2017 that drastically reduced taxes and supercharged the private section up and down the economic ladder."[145]

## Tools Available to the President

At a loss for words, I could only sit and think about the ability of the presidency to lead. Thankfully, the meatloaf sandwiches arrived. Trump shouted, "Chuckson, get in here. You are bound to be hungry as well."

As Chuckson sat down, he stated, 'I do love your meatloaf sandwiches, sir."

Trump said, "You are welcome."

About 10 minutes later and after juicy behind-the-scenes gossip from Trump's days as host of *The Apprentice*, Trump told Chuckson, "Chuckson, can you please have my clubs brought down to us here?"

Chuckson radioed in the request, and not three minutes later an intern ran up the stairs with the clubs. Upon seeing this, Trump motioned for us to rise and head back down the stairs which we had just come up. Once at the bottom, we walked across South Lawn Road and stopped. Trump put his bag down and asked, "Champ, what do you think is my favorite sport?"

I replied, "Well, based on the fact that you or the Trump International Corporation owns a multitude of golf courses and the fact that you just had your clubs brought down, I'm gonna say golf."

Trump said, "Yes, very good of you to remember. As I already mentioned we have a putting green here on-site, I feel at this point it is wise to use it to end our time together today. Another question, do you use a driver to put your ball into the hole?"

I replied, "No, not unless you are in a limited club situation."

Trump furthered, "Right you are; so I should, therefore, use the right club for the shot that I am about to partake in?"

I responded, "Yes, sir!"

Trump made a tremendous 25-yard shot that landed just off the green (figure 24.13) to the right of the hole and commented, "Therefore, when I govern, I need to use the right club as well. Beyond the executive office staff, I'm sure Becky told you about them earlier, which are like my drivers due to them doing so many long-term projects for me like budgeting via the

---

144    https://www.gpo.gov/fdsys/pkg/BILLS-111hr1enr/pdf/BILLS-111hr1enr.pdf
145    https://www.whitehouse.gov/wp-content/uploads/2018/02/WH_CuttingTaxesForAmericanWorkers_Feb2018.pdf

FIGURE 24.13 President Barack Obama and Vice President Joe Biden practice their putting on the White House putting green April 24, 2009. Official White House Photo by Pete Souza.

OCB, there are additional clubs for me to use.[146] For example, on the long shot I just took, at least for our circumstance here on the White House grounds, I used my hybrid 8-9 iron. The hybrid I just used here represents what Mike Pence, our vice president, offers. You see, he is a hybrid official as he is officially elected to the executive branch, but he has many powers in the legislative. For example, he is the presiding officer of the US Senate with the ability to cast tiebreaking ballots when tied, while here in the executive branch he plays the role of substitute president when I'm incapacitated for whatever reason, like in surgery, as I sign my powers over to him as required by the 25th Amendment of the US Constitution for a time until I'm capable of resuming my duties and formally notify Congress.[147] Beyond that, he plays the role of balancing the electoral ticket. While he has lots of experience in government as the former governor of Indiana, I've only been the CEO of Trump International. I have the big ideas, he helps me sell and enforce the;[148] Originally, that was the whole idea when first enacted, along with him checking in on my health and doing tasks that I ask him to do. In more recent times, they have taken on the role of advising me on important issues.[149] Remember how he jumped to his feet earlier to help me out? Of note, him taking the position does not typically lead to taking my position in his own right unless I die in office. The last two people to do so with a president dying was George H.W. Bush in 1988 and Martin Van Buren in 1836."[150]

I interjected, "Who else might be a good tool, sir?"

Before he answered, we walked our way to the green, Trump took a few practice shots with his club and went on to chip his ball within two feet of the hole. He stated while we walked

146    Brent Kelley, "Hybrid Golf Clubs: The Future of Recreational Golf," ThoughtCo, September 25, 2017, https://www.thoughtco.com/meet-the-utility-hybrid-clubs-1560505.

147    U.S. Constitution, Amendment 25.

148    Andrew Downs, "Mike Pence Is Everything Donald Trump Is Not," *Washington Post*, July 14, 2016, https://www.washingtonpost.com/opinions/mike-pence-balances-the-gop-ticket-in-every-way/2016/07/14/83cf3f08-49de-11e6-90a8-fb84201e0645_story.html?utm_term=.dcf4ad0768a6.

149    Beth Py-Lieberman, "How the Office of the Vice Presidency Evolved from Nothing to Something," Smithsonian.com, November 18, 2014. https://www.smithsonianmag.com/smithsonian-institution/how-office-vice-presidency-evolved-nothing-something-180953302.

150    Ibid.

onto the green, "Champ, on a short chip shot, as I took a few moments ago, it is wise for me to use my sand wedge. In governing, on those short shots, my predecessors and I have and love to bring into play our wives, officially known as the First Lady, aka FLOTUS.[151] My wife Melania does such a wonderful job here, doesn't she? Either way, first ladies while in office have traditionally taken on humanitarian issues. These are issues like women's health by Laura Bush during her time that led to the establishment of the Laura W. Bush Institute for Women's Health at the Texas Tech University Health Science Center in 2007,[152] women's equality by Rosalynn Carter,[153] childhood obesity thanks to Michelle Obama's Let's Move! campaign,[154] raising children as my lovely wife has primarily set her focus on raising our son, Barron[155] (recently she has worked to expand her influence) and national beautification thanks in large part to Lady Bird Johnson.[156] The one exception was by and large my former opponent Hillary Clinton, as she was a true activist on health care and met with dignitaries to play a large role in foreign policy, all without a security clearance I might add, to be just as or more so influential than her husband on many fronts.[157] Either way, they are issues that need attention while in office but are not quite on the front burner of importance. We're busy you know?"

I replied, "What else do you have for me, sir?"

Trump took out his putter, lined up with the hole, and proceeded to make the 2-foot putt. It was then that everyone watching began to clap like what happens when Tiger Woods makes a tournament-clinching birdie. Trump remarked, "Okay Champ. Now as head of the executive branch of the federal government I have two final executive titled powers. First is something called executive immunity, or the 'immunity granted to officers of the executive branch of government from personal liability for tortious acts or omissions done in the

151    White House, "Melania Trump," accessed March 22, 2019, https://www.whitehouse.gov/people/melania-trump.

152    https://www.laurabushinstitute.org

153    National Women's Hall of Fame, "Rosalynn Carter," accessed March 22, 2019, https://www.womenofthehall.org/women-of-the-hall/voices-great-women/rosalynn-carter.

154    "Let's Move," accessed March 22, 2019, https://letsmove.obamawhitehouse.archives.gov.

155    Mary Jordan, Emily Heil, and Josh Dawsey, "Inside Melania Trump's Complicated White House Life: Separate Schedule, Different Priorities," *Washington Post*, May 6, 2018, https://www.washingtonpost.com/lifestyle/inside-melania-trumps-complicated-white-house-life-separate-schedules-different-priorities/2018/05/06/60f6f07e-4703-11e8-9072-f6d4bc32f223_story.html?utm_term=.805c428fcc61.

156    Texas Architecture, "Lady Bird Johnson and the Beautification Movement," University of Texas at Austin School of Architecture, May 2015, https://soa.utexas.edu/work/lady-bird-johnson-and-beautification-movement.

157    Patrick Healy, "The Résumé Factor: Those 2 Terms as First Lady," New York Times, December 26, 2007, https://www.nytimes.com/2007/12/26/us/politics/26clinton.html.

course of carrying out their duties.[158] Which of the leading powers that I discussed to you earlier might need to use this power and why so?"

I responded, "I guess that would be your duties as commander in chief as your decisions to send troops into battle to kill or be killed might be a liability for you. Obama's decision to send a clandestine raid into Pakistan to kill Osama bin Laden would seem to be a perfect fit for this."

Trump furthered, "Perfect, young man. Now before we move on from this subject a May 28, 1998, editorial by the *New York Times* that discusses a nine-to-zero US Supreme Court ruling making note that while I have immunity from items relating the fulfillment of my official duties, civil matters are not immune from such blockages.[159] See my dealing with Trump University where I offered courses in real estate investing that many believed to be worthless and who sued to get their money that was settled in March 2017 for $25,000,000, two full months after I took office.[160] Now, who might I need to consult in these dealings?"

I replied, "I would say an attorney and at that level of dealing, a darn good lawyer at that."

Trump remarked, "That is correct, and I certainly did, followed by hiring outside attorneys at his guidance. Now regarding my position here as president, I have something called executive privilege, 'a privilege . . . not to disclose confidential communications that would impair governmental functions.'"

I interjected, "Such as one has between you and an attorney[161] or you and your preacher[162] or you and your doctor?"[163]

Trump continued, "Exactly. Per the National Public Radio website in an article by Eric Weiner, nowhere does this right officially exist in the Constitution, but presidents from both sides of the aisle have used this tool.[164] The most notable case regarding this tool was the *United States v. Nixon* ruling that found a need for such a tool to exist, but denied President

158    https://definitions.uslegal.com/e/executive-immunity

159    *New York Times*, "The Limits of Presidential Immunity," May 28, 1997, https://www.nytimes.com/1997/05/28/opinion/the-limits-of-presidential-immunity.html.

160    Camila Domonoske, "Judge Approves $25 Million Settlement of Trump University Lawsuit," NPR, March 31, 2017, https://www.npr.org/sections/thetwo-way/2017/03/31/522199535/judge-approves-25-million-settlement-of-trump-university-lawsuit.

161    John C. Busby, "Attorney-Client Privilege," Legal Information Institute, October 15, 2018, https://www.law.cornell.edu/wex/attorney-client_privilege.

162    Enrichment Journal, "Pastoral Confidentiality: An Ethical and Legal Responsibility," accessed March 22, 2019, http://enrichmentjournal.ag.org/201002/ejonline_201002_pastor_confid_.cfm.

163    S. Petronio, M.J. Do Corcia, and A. Duggan, "Navigating Ethics of Physician-Patient Confidentiality: A Communication Privacy Management Analysis," *Permanente Journal* 16, no. 4 (2012): 41–45. https://www.ncbi.nlm.nih.gov/pmc/articles/PMC3523934

164    Eric Weiner, "What Is Executive Privilege, Anyway?," NPR, June 28, 2007, https://www.npr.org/templates/story/story.php?storyId=11527747.

Nixon the right to use it as part of the Watergate break-in investigation case as the matter at hand was criminal in nature (he gave the go for the operation to cover up the break-in) and not related to his official duties.[165] Of note, while it seems to be a rather useful power, doing so is not a truly common occurrence as that while seemingly useful President Obama first used this tool in June of 2012, three and a half years into his first term, while his predecessor used it six times, Clinton used it 14 times, H.W. Bush did it once, and Reagan used it three times.[166] I have yet to do so as of October 5, 2018. Beyond that, Champ, I don't believe I have anything else to speak to you about today. Let's walk."

Trump put his putter back into his bag and had us start walking back to the Executive Mansion. We made small talk along the way. We went back through the Diplomatic Reception Room, turned right in the Center Hall, turned left up to the stairs, turned right in the Cross Hall, and made our way into the Entrance Hall. Before I exited, Trump stopped and spoke, "Champ, the weight of the world is on the backs of the presidency. My predecessors and I have made decisions good and bad, right and wrong, and those walking back and forth along the line of legality. If you'll excuse me, I need to go and tend to business and Make America Great Again. Thanks for visiting and have a great day."

I shook Trump's hand and walked through the doors I had hoped to step out of hours earlier. Once outside I went down the stairs to the right and made the walk down the driveway toward Pennsylvania Avenue Northwest. Along the way, I realized that the president is much like the governor back home. Both oversee their respective branches of government. The significant difference is that the president is a singular position, while the governor of Texas is not, due to the president having the additional widespread ability to nominate all judges and significant cabinet officials, among others. Either way, they both are in charge, just of vastly different affairs.

---

165    Ibid.
166    Boston.com, "History of Presidential Use of Executive Privilege," June 20, 2012, http://archive.boston.com/news/nation/washington/articles/2012/06/20/history_of_presidential_use_of_executive_privilege.

**QUESTIONS TO CONSIDER** REGARDING THE PRESIDENCY:

1. The first main discussion topic of the chapter discusses the sights to see when touring President's Park. Please identify the item seen on that tour that stood out most to you, what that item promotes, and why the item stood out to you, in detail.

2. The second main discussion topic of the chapter discusses the minimum qualifications needed to become president. Please identify the minimum qualifications, the qualifications you meet, and whether you qualify to serve as president.

3. The third main discussion topic of the chapter discusses presidents and prime ministers. Please indicate what the two positions are, their differences, the one you feel to be more powerful, and why, in detail.

4. The fourth main discussion topic of the chapter discusses the rules of the position of president. Please identify the rule that seems the most ridiculous, what that rule entails, and why you feel the rule to be ridiculous, in detail.

5. The fifth main discussion topic of the chapter discusses the interior of the White House. Please identify the room that seems the most useful, what that room entails, and why you feel the room is most useful, in detail.

6. The sixth main discussion topic of the chapter discusses the powers held by the president while in office. Please identify the power that you feel is most relatable to how you run your life, what that power entails, and why the power relates to your life the most, in detail.

7. The seventh main discussion topic of the chapter discusses the history of the presidency. Please rehash that series of events and how they relate to where you are today in your life, in detail.

8. The final main discussion topic of the chapter discusses the tools available to the president to execute his duties. Please identify the tool that you relate to the most in how you deal with schoolwork, what that tool entails, and why, in detail.

## FIGURE CREDITS

# Section IV

## Office Politics

# Chapter 25

# American Domestic Policy

## Concept of Public Policy

On Thursday and Friday of last week, I had been on some quite lengthy tours. I walked around buildings, upstairs, through corridors, along balconies, and, at times, with armed security. While with Congress, I was able to sit in the viewing gallery and view the painfully slow process Congress goes through to pass legislation. While with the president, I saw first-hand the struggles a CEO might deal with when trying to implement policy put forth by the board of directors, Congress in this case. Add that to what I had learned about running government back home in Texas, and I feel about topped off when it comes to dealing with who is in government and what they go through, the quote-unquote government office spaces. What I hadn't really learned about at this point is wha exactly it is that the government produces to run the country, and parts of the state for that matter. The question is, what's in a bill, and why is this bill over that bill being considered for law, much less becoming law? For example, why were my father and the rest of the Texas legislature having a special session over liquid water, and not water vapor, or frozen water for that matter? I could let it go, but this slight oversight on my behalf could not be shaken.

One of the short conversations that I left out of my write up from last Friday around President's Park and my walk with Becky was how to gather more information about what goes into the laws that are passed and implemented. When Becky and I passed the Organization of American States (OAS) last Friday, she pointed out that the building behind the OAS building was the headquarters of the US Department of the Interior, and that it had a small museum offering some useful insight on my dilemma.

Friday, on my walk home from the White House, I realized how close the museum was to the hotel I was staying in. All I had to do was ride one stop to Farragut North Metro Station on the Red Line and then take a short walk. Therefore, for my adventure today, at about five minutes after 9:00 am, I found myself walking south on 17th Street Northwest, past many of the sites that I had seen a few days before with Becky after exiting the station. After six blocks, I turned right on New York Avenue Northwest, went a block, and turned left on 18th Street Northwest. Three blocks later, I turned right onto C Street Northwest, walked half a block, and found myself standing at the foot of my desired location, the Stewart Lee Udall Department of the Interior Building (figure 25.1). At this point, little did I know

FIGURE 25.1 Main Entrance to the United States Department of the Interior Building.

that my trek this morning would be so akin to my conversations to come. I correctly used my resources.

After going up a short flight of stairs, I entered the building through the center set of doors and into a massive atrium (figure 25.2). Upon entering the lobby, I was asked by a security guard about where I was heading. I replied, "The Department of the Interior Museum.[1] It's this way, correct?"

The guard replied by pointing me to his and his assistant's right to head through security. Once through with security, the guard from before was waiting for me and stated, "Follow me."

I nodded in agreement with his guidance, and we progressed through a short walk down a corridor with a white-and-gray tiled floor. The corridor seemed to come right out of a scene from an Indiana Jones film thanks to the impressive set of white marble engravings set into the wall by, as I would read later, Gifford Beal, Maynard Dixon, John Steuart Curry, and Allan Houser. My favorite mural was one of a herd of bison congregating around a newborn (figure 25.3). After seeing that mural, I remarked, "Hey that mural is based on the national mammal, the bison."

FIGURE 25.2 Entrance Atrium to the United States Department of the Interior Building.

FIGURE 25.3 Stone Buffalo Mural.

The security guard stated, "The bison is the animal found on the seal of the Department of the Interior since 1912 and was selected as the national mammal, based on the wording of the National Bison Legacy Act,[2] due to their historical importance to native tribes of North America and prominent role in the cattle industry of today. There is a very safe phrase to

---

1   https://www.doi.gov/interiormuseum
2   House Resolution 2908, 114th session of the US Congress, second session.

say around here, 'Go Bison!' Also, we're here at the museum (figure 25.4). The tour is self-guided, feel free to start wherever you like, but I find it's best to start from the left with the video and then go right along the wall."[3]

I replied, while shaking the guard's hand, "Thank you!"

At the entrance of the museum is a small informational panel that covers museum hours, the museums founding, and additional information on upcoming major events. The room at the far back of the museum was empty and closed off by shut glass doors and retractable belt barricades. Doing as instructed, once in the main room of the museum (figure 25.5), I turned to the left and found myself in front of a small wooden bench on which to sit and watch a video discussing what the Interior Department handles. I sat for

FIGURE 25.4 Main Entrance to the Department of the Interior Museum.

a while, but the movie showing didn't quite pique my curiosity, so after about five minutes I rose and went to the exhibition nearest my right. This static display on the wall was entitled *The Department of Everything Else* (figure 25.6). The far-left portion of the display had a large golden Department of the Interior Seal with a short background on the

FIGURE 25.5 Main Room of the Department of the Interior Museum.

3    Unless otherwise noted, all information presented here was gathered from a visit by the author to the museum in Washington, DC, in July 2018.

origin, need, and eventual founding of the department alongside what the department focuses on maintaining today, "[p]eople, land, and water—honoring cultures and heritage, stewarding resources, and supplying energy."

Beyond that, the rest of this exhibit covered a whole corner of the room and showcased how the history of the department paralleled that of the nation. Overall, if the nation needed something done and nobody else was able to do something about it, then the Department of the Interior was

FIGURE 25.6 Department of Everything Else Information Timeline.

put up to the task. The physical items on display here included an original set of surveying benchmarks put in the ground when what would become the Department of the Interior was under the helm of the US Department of the Treasury's General Land Office. Beyond that, there was a land deed for 120 acres of land, a first-edition *National Geographic* magazine, a judge's gavel, a radio studio on-the-air sign, and, of all things, a case filled with a crushed stone of some kind. Each of these items helped offer insight on the broad range of responsibilities of the department, hence the "Department of Everything Else" nickname from before.

It was then that a man stormed into the room flustered. I remarked, "You all right, sir?"

The man replied, "Physically, I'm fine, but emotionally, I'm torn. I've been tasked by my boss to complete the remainder of the room to build up some good press for his reelection campaign, and I've now got the museum curator's version of writer's block, exhibitor's block You're young, what would you want to see back here?"

I replied, "You mean behind the glass doors? If so, and well, if you want my honest opinion..."

The man interjected, "That would be helpful. Of course!"

I continued "Well, I've seen enough government buildings and agencies inside them over the last month or so to know what government does, but I've yet to see anything on why what is being selected to accomplish was chosen. For example, why does seemingly every city in the United States have a great subway system, but my hometown of Houston has a token one, at best?"

The man replied, "Easy: Poor soil/environmental conditions, cost, a history of flooding, and, well, different strokes for different folks.[4] But back to your point about what is lacking—an exhibition that focuses on public policy."

4    Dug Begley, "If You Were Wondering Why Houston Doesn't Have Subways," *Highwayman* (blog), Chron, November 15, 2012, https://blog.chron.com/thehighwayman/2012/11/if-you-were-wondering-

I interjected, "Public policy what now?

The man replied, "Okay, public policy is any goal-directed course of action, taken by a government, to deal with an issue faced by the public.[5] For example, if you look at the exhibit behind you, in hopes of keeping the newfound country we all know and love today as simple as possible, Congress only created the Departments of War, State, and Treasury to manage the country. After a period, following the Louisiana Purchase in 1803 from France and the 1840s mantra of Manifest Destiny, our nation's call to expand westward,[6] the country had grown from 867,746 square miles primarily found on the east coast, in 1790, to 2,940,042 square miles in 1850, based on census tracking, from the Atlantic all the way to the Pacific Ocean.[7] This great expansion included your home state of Texas in 1845, resolution of the Oregon boundary dispute with Great Britain in 1846, and the acquisition of land from Mexico thanks to the Treaty of Guadalupe Hidalgo in 1848. We were, really still are, four times as big as we once were. The eminent need for a single department of government to control, distribute, and monitor said land was then therefore ever present. This led Congress, on March 3, 1849, to create the US Department of the Interior, to fulfill our eventual mission of 'conserv[ing] and manag[ing] the Nation's natural resources and cultural heritage for the benefit and enjoyment of the American people, provide scientific and other information about natural resources and natural hazards to address societal challenges and create opportunities for the American people, and honor the Nation's trust responsibilities or special commitments to American Indians, Alaska Natives, and affiliated island communities to help them prosper.'"[8]

I inquired, "Who are you, man, and why do know so much about the history of this department?"

The man replied, "Simple, my name is Secretary Ryan Zinke. I'm the guy in charge of this entire department. Who are you?"

I replied, "Good response, and I'm Champ, Champ Cove. I'm on a mission to learn about the government this summer and a friend last week told me about the museum here to help me learn about government policy. And, regarding your blank walls in the back, I do believe my life would be greatly improved with information on what public policy entails,

why-houston-doesnt-have-subways.

5    Public Administration, "Public Administrators and Public Policy," accessed March 21, 2019, https:// www.angelo.edu/faculty/ljones/gov3301/block6/objective5.htm.

6    History.com Editors, "Manifest Destiny," April 5, 2010, https://www.history.com/topics/ westward-expansion/manifest-destiny.

7    United States History, "U.S. Population, Land Area and Density, 1790–2000" accessed March 21, 2019, https://www.u-s-history.com/pages/h986.html.

8    https://www.doi.gov/whoweare

the different types, the process of constructing policy, and what exactly various major policies of the government entail today."

Zinke just said, while opening the closed glass doors from before and undoing the retractable belt barricade, "Follow me."

## Distinction between Domestic and Foreign Policy

A few moments later, the lights for the back room were on, and Zinke was thinking critically, or at least his ponderous facial expressions were indicative of that. He remarked after a minute or so once we were in the back room, "Okay, let's look at the small wall here to our left before we go into the main part of the back room. Now, I've given you the basic definition of public policy; it should also be noted that public policy can deal with almost anything, but if you had to separate everything into two separate piles, I would first make the distinction between domestic and foreign policy."

I inquired, "What's the difference?"

Zinke started while moving his hand on the wall, "At the top here is going to be the general definition, but I'm thinking domestic policy definition right here below it, reading 'the set of decisions that a government makes relating to things that directly affect the people in its own country,'[9] and then below that, the definition of foreign policy reading 'a country's ways of dealing with other countries.'"

I chimed in, "I see what you are going for here sir, but let's make the text large so that everyone can easily read it, and from what I just heard you say there, it would appear that domestic policy deals with issues that you and our country's government have full control over while foreign policy deals with items that our government does not have full control over."

Zinke remarked, "That's correct, and we can put in something that alludes to that right here around the corner, but next to that, how about something that expresses how the two sets of policies impact one another. Now, tell me, do you think a stick of melting butter transitioning into a tommie gun, or vice versa, would be better at the top, middle, or bottom of the display?"

I asked, confused, "Uhh, guns and butter, sir?"

## The Guns and Butter Debate

Zinke replied, "Yes, guns and butter. For the entirety of our existence, our resources have predominately been finite. At times we have been able to squeeze more out of the proverbial

---

9   https://dictionary.cambridge.org/us/dictionary/english/domestic-policy

tube, but eventually, we'll run out. Take peak oil for example.[10] For years people have been stating that we'll run out of fossil fuels, but we haven't yet, and we keep finding more. Granted, the stuff is certainly more expensive today. Regardless, butter here represents domestic spending on infrastructure such as roads or where we spend our health care dollars.[11] The tommie gun represents defense spending; the nukes maintained by the federal government don't come cheap,[12] ya know? We only have so much money to spend, so we must decide how best to spend it. The debt is already at $21 trillion on its way to $22 trillion, and who knows how much more after that; and all things considered, we got to start cutting spending somewhere, but where?[13] Where do you stand, Champ, on the issue here?"

I replied, "Butter does make toast taste good, but I do like my guns back home, and I don't think I could live without both."

Zinke stated, "That's okay, you can have both, but you can only have so much of both (figure 25.7). Get rid of or manufacture one less gun, and you can get more butter, and vice versa. Overall, when we are producing, we must decide what we are going to venture into. For an example of this, we have the National Forest Service, based in the US Department of Agriculture.[14] That agency has responsibility for 154 national forests and 20 grasslands in 43 states and Puerto Rico, with the mission to sustain the health, diversity, and productivity of the nation's forests and

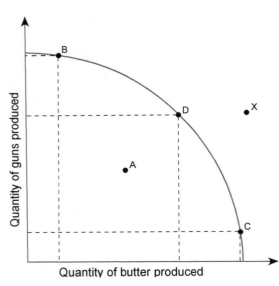

FIGURE 25.7 A diagram showing the production possibilities frontier (PPF) curve for producing "Gun" and "butter." Point "A" lies below the curve, denoting underutilized production capacity. Points "B", "C", and "D" lie on the curve, denoting efficient utilization of production. Point "X" lies outside the curve, representing an impossible output for existing capital and/or technology. Shift of PPF to point "X", will change if their improvement of factors of production (i.e., Capital and/or technology).

10   Peak Oil Barrel, "What Is Peak Oil?," accessed March 21, 2019, http://peakoilbarrel.com/what-is-peak-oil.

11   Todd Harrison, "The New Guns versus Butter Debate" (Perspective paper, CSBA, May 2010). http://csbaonline.org/uploads/documents/2010.05.24-The-New-Guns-Versus-Butter-Debate.pdf.

12   Reuters, "U.S. Nuclear Arsenal to Cost $1.2 Trillion over next 30 Years: CBO," October 31, 2017, https://www.reuters.com/article/us-usa-nuclear-arsenal/u-s-nuclear-arsenal-to-cost-1-2-trillion-over-next-30-years-cbo-idUSKBN1D030E.

13   http://www.usdebtclock.org

14   https://www.fs.fed.us

grasslands to meet the needs of present and future generations covering 193,000,000 acres of land.[15] Now, from that land, in fiscal quarters one through three of the fiscal year 2018, 1,579,135 board feet of lumber (MBF) has been harvested from those millions of acres.[16] The question is, should the government work to preserve those lands or should logging companies be allowed to come in and harvest the timber? What we have to decide here is, do we want to have more forests to visit and that produce oxygen via photosynthesis, which we need to breathe, or do we want more boards of lumber to use and build houses with (so long, of course, as houses continue to be made of wood primarily)? Either way, this whole decision-making process is an example of a simple production-possibility frontier. Of note, this is a simplification of much larger factors to consider. In your case, I assume you have limited time here in the nation's capital. So, how have you chosen which places to visit?"

I replied, "Yes, I have a limited amount of time to be here, and I need to visit places that will help me on my quest. Spending time elsewhere only makes me another tourist, not a learner."

Zinke stated, "Excellent, finite resources and how best to use them for your needs and interests. I think butter on top melting into a gun at the middle of the wall here will be best and then have text and graphs discussing what we are talking about here surrounding it to get the point across. Another question for you, what do you think of the timeline exhibition in the front room?"

I stated, "I think the timeline is excellent as it moves from the agency's founding to how the department became what it is today in an easily consumable form. Why do you ask?"

## Stages of Policy Development as They Relate to Slavery

Zinke contended, "I think the left wall here in the room needs a timeline. I'm thinking stages of policy development on the bottom (figure 25.8), like the one up front, and then stages of slavery occurring in the United States on the top."

I interjected, "Slavery sir?"

Zinke furthered, "It's a powerful example of the different stages of policy development and how they relate to one of the darkest eras of our country's storied past."

I replied, "Explain sir, in detail; this could be ugly if not done well."

Zinke offered, "No problem. Now, depending on who you ask, the major steps in policy development can vary in the number of steps and what those steps are, like how we all have

---

15   https://www.fs.fed.us/about-agency

16   US Forest Service, "Cut and Sold (New)—CUTS203S" (report, US Department of Agriculture, July 20, 2018), https://www.fs.fed.us/forestmanagement/documents/sold-harvest/reports/2018/2018_Q1-Q3_CandS_SW.pdf.

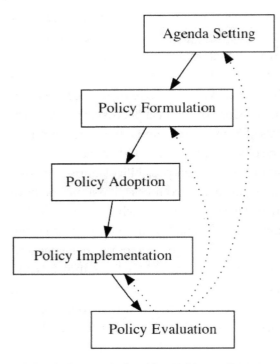

FIGURE 25.8 Stages in the Policy Making Process.

an American accent here in the United States, but there is a certain French twist in Louisiana or Kennedyesque turn of phrase in Boston. For me, I'm a five-step policy development man.[17] Of note, the process can be viewed somewhat as a never-ending process as looking back at what has been done often leads into starting the process all over again in some different light. In general, though, you must first build your agenda, which is defined as defining and prioritizing the issues facing government. For an example of this concept today in this debate over slavery, look for the work currently being undertaken by Black Lives Matter, 'a chapter-based, member-led organization whose mission is to build local power and to intervene in violence inflicted on Black communities by the state and vigilantes.' [18] They want the agenda to be focused as much as possible on ensuring that the black community is not marginalized by society at large, in short, no slavery, no discrimination, only pure equality for all. For our conversation here, we are setting the agenda by establishing the goal of ending slavery. Now let's assume that the Black Lives Matter group existed way back in the in the day when slaves were first brought on a permanent basis into what is now the United States to fit into our timeline. The members of Black Lives Matter today would be the modern equivalent of early abolitionists like Benjamin Lay, Olaudah Equiano, Anthony Benezet, and Moses Brown.[19] As a side note, this info will go in a square on the wall on the bottom of the line with the info on the top of the line discussing how this relates to slavery."

After a pause, Secretary Zinke continued, "I do believe that we have arrived at stage two, that is policy formulation, or the discussion of potential measures on an issue and deciding which is the best measure to take to resolve that issue. At this point, it's fair to say that there

17    "Policy," http://amgov.cnlawrence.com/pdf/Policy.pdf; All info on the policy steps were gathered from this pdf.

18    https://blacklivesmatter.com/

19    Andrews, Evan. "6 Early Abolitionists." History.com. A&E Television Networks, May 3, 2016. https://www.history.com/news/6-early-abolitionists.

were certainly people who were against slavery, but they had not made much headway in getting the government to adopt a policy in their favor. The question is, what happened to reach that point of deciding on a one-way path for all to take long-term, the government at least?"

I interjected, "Well, what'd it take to get on that one-way street sir?"

Secretary Zinke then went on, "Using my friends at USHistory.org and their timeline of slave history[20] to help us out here, the first permanent slaves were brought by the Dutch to Jamestown, Virginia, in 1619. Regarding individual states, Massachusetts first recognized slavery as legal in 1641 via the Body of Liberties, and by 1750 each of the British North American colonies had legalized the practice in some form or another. For the nation as a whole, the federal government sat out the debate at this point and punted the proverbial ball to the next generation by including in our Constitution, article 1, section 9, clauses 1 and 4 that banned Congress from prohibiting the importation of persons for 20 years so long as they were deemed 'proper to admit' under a state's laws, with article 5 banning amendment of clauses 1 and 4 until 1808 to enshrine the institution of slavery. Accordingly, the states until that time had free reign to do as they pleased on the issue. The question is, at this point, what did the states do?"

I interjected, "Well, what'd they do sir?"

Zinke replied, "Overall, two clear paths emerged. First, the North began on the road to freedom when Pennsylvania's legislature passed a legislative action entitled An Act for the Gradual Abolition of Slavery on March 1, 1780. This law was the first democratic means of abolishing slavery in the world and stands out from the rest by setting a precedent for how northern states would end the practice of slavery, gradually, as there was fear that just releasing thousands from bondage overnight might lead to more problems, like where would they all go and what would they do once free? The year 1777 then saw the Vermont Republic partially ban slavery and fully do so when they joined the Union in 1791. In 1783 the Massachusetts Supreme Court declared slavery unconstitutional, and New Hampshire passed their gradual abolition act. Connecticut and Rhode Island did so as well in 1784. The 1787 Northwest Ordinances banned slavery in those territories ceded by Virginia. The year 1799 saw New York begin their gradual abolition that would see all slaves freed by 1829. The year 1802 saw Ohio ban slavery. The year 1804 saw New Jersey abolish slavery, with the Michigan Territory banning slavery in 1807. The year 1820 saw Indiana ban slavery along with the Compromise of 1820 banning slavery above 36 degrees and 30 minutes north latitudinally nationwide in any new territories remaining from the Louisiana Purchase while

---

20    V. Chapman Smith, "American Anti-Slavery and Civil Rights Timeline," UShistory.org, accessed March 21, 2019, http://www.ushistory.org/more/timeline.htm; All info on slavery in the United States was gathered from this website unless otherwise noted.

admitting Missouri as a slave state.[21] Illinois territory began gradual abolition in 1828, and rounding out northern abolition was Kansas via the Wyandotte Constitution in 1859 establishing the future state as a free state, with years of armed conflict there preventing final statehood from occurring until 1861."

I then surmised, "Well, sir, it seems that by the Civil War the north had fully eradicated the blight on society, but what about the other path you mentioned earlier?"

Zinke then continued, "Well, that would be the South maintaining the status quo on their slaveholding, keeping them. Other than the beforementioned admittance of Missouri in 1820 as a slave state the only other change was Texas, which, when gaining independence from Mexico in 1836, restarted the practice of slavery after being forced to make all slaves indentured servants to keep them in bondage when Mexico abolished slavery in 1824 while they were a part of their Union."

I then forged the thought, "Sir, using what I learned before back in Texas at the Institute of Texan Cultures this feels to me like a social cleavage, or a sharp division, a split so to speak in society with the division being over the future of slavery in the country with norther favoring the view that that slavery is bad while the south takes the opposite side on the matter. This eventually led to the Union dividing temporarily? Also, how might this scenario lead into stage 3, whatever that is?"

Zinke then elaborated in his best Yoda, from Star Wars, impression, "A social cleavage situation this situation is, but what the final decision for our country as a whole is next of most concern."

I then grumbled, "Scary this will be I see."

Zinke expanded, "Ahh, making a final decision about how to handle the problem. You can ponder all day, not that the situation we are discussing would take all day to reach a final decision, but making that final decision regarding what to do is always the most difficult step as it makes everything permanent; think cold feet but on the national stage. Step number three, therefore, Champ, is policy adoption, or getting the government to approve of the final legislation. This step required federal intervention with their approach being a bit back and forth at the beginning until finally agreeing with the northern states at the end. Specifically, during the Revolutionary War, from 1775 to 1783, the Atlantic slave trade was banned in the United States in its totality by the Continental Congress. Under the US Congress we have today, the first Slave Trade Act in 1794 banned US ships from participating in the slave trade, along with the second rendition of the act in 1801 banning US citizens from doing so leaving the work to be done by foreign powers. Following the ban on amending

---

21    History.com Editors. "Missouri Compromise." History.com. A&E Television Networks, October 29, 2009. https://www.history.com/topics/abolitionist-movement/missouri-compromise.

article 1, section 9, clauses 1 and 4 of the US Constitution, expiring on January 1, 1808, the Act Prohibiting Importation of Slaves was passed in 1807 to take effect on January 1 of the following year, making the importation and exportation of slaves a crime nationwide. The year 1823 saw the nation of Liberia on the African continent, founded by the American Colonization Society, to house freed slaves. Overall, initially, national policy aligned more with the work by done by northern states."

I then spoke, "How did national policy swing back toward the policy of southern states?"

Zinke iterated, "Turning the tide of national policy back toward the South was the 1821 Adams–Onis Treaty bringing Florida into the Union as a territory to help southern states get back slaves who had escaped there, as Spain had not been willing to help with repatriation. Until 1850, no other major action occurred regarding slavery at the national level until the Fugitive Slave Act of that year required the return of all fugitive slaves to their owners regardless of where they were now. Making things worse was the *Dredd Scott v. Sanford* decision in 1857 holding that former black slaves and their descendants were unable to gain American citizenship and that slaves aren't entitled to freedom even if they had lived in a free state for years. Now then, despite policies being passed in their favor toward the end was the election of Abraham Lincoln in 1860 that led to all but five—Missouri, Kentucky, West Virginia, Maryland, and Delaware—slaveholding states to leave the Union and begin the Civil War. This point in time is when the social cleavage over views on slavery reached a climax."

I then spoke, "What was the climax sir?

Zinke continued, "That climax came about via the inception of the Republican Party in 1854 who held their first convention in Philadelphia in 1856 comprising Conscious Whigs, Anti-Slavery Democrats, and the Free-Soil Party. The overall purpose of the party was to set about ending the practice of slavery in the United States nationwide. This position came to fruition in 1863 with the passage of the Emancipation Proclamation that abolished slavery in territory controlled by the Confederate States of America, and the passage of the 13th Amendment in 1865 banning the practice of slavery nationwide. The 14th Amendment, ratified in 1868, granted citizenship to all blacks, and the 15th amendment, ratified in 1870, granted black male suffrage. "

I interrupted, again. "Sir, to me that sounds like problem solved, mission accomplished, end of slavery, woo-hoo! However, we are only on step number three. What am I missing?"

Zinke spoke in a dull tone, "Champ, that would be step four, policy implementation or the actual government agencies, courts, policemen, and individual citizens working to implement the newly enshrined into law policy. For what happened with slavery and its abolition, one must look at what happened in our country following the Civil War."

I lamented, "This can't be good."

Zinke furthered, "Nope, everyone has their own epiphanies here. Immediately after the Civil War, the Freedman's Bureau was established by the federal government in 1865 to help former slaves settle in their newfound freedom, with many going north and west. The year 1866 saw the beginning of Reconstruction, the planned redevelopment of the South following the Civil War by so-called Radical Republicans in hopes of punishing the South for leading the country into armed conflict and bring them more in line by being anti-slavery. This movement first saw success via the Civil Rights Act of 1866, covering citizenship and inherent rights, and another in 1875 that focused on equal protection in public accommodations. The 14th Amendment strengthened the prior while the latter was ruled unconstitutional in 1883. Then came along 1896 and the *Plessey v. Ferguson* decision that established the doctrine of 'separate but equal' that by 1910 saw every former Confederate state establish some form of Jim Crow system of laws that enforced racial segregation."

I inquired, "Sir, there is a term here I know of that relates to this, but I can't think of it. Thoughts?"

Zinke remarked, "I know what you are going after here. That term is *institutionalized racism*, or the situation in which 'racial oppression is imposed on subordinate racial groups by dominant racial groups through institutional channels,'[22] the Jim Crow laws in a nutshell.[23] The main street example of this from recent times is a real estate practice known as redlining or the 'discriminatory practice by which banks, insurance companies, etc., refuse or limit loans, mortgages, insurance, etc., within specific geographic areas, especially inner-city neighborhoods.'[24] Real estate agents would refuse to show houses in white areas to blacks and vice versa."

I asked, "What brought about an end to this, sir?"

Zinke commented, "That would be stage five of the policy development process, policy evaluation and revision, where government agencies go back and decide if any additional measures are needed to enforce the original policies measures better, or if the original plan in and of itself needs to be revoked. This decision, for lack of a better term, was made following World War II; it began with Executive Order 9808 by President Truman establishing the Presidential Commission on Civil Rights, which eventually led to the desegregation of the military, among other places. Bringing the issue to a head, the US Supreme Court in the landmark case *Brown v. Board of Education of Topeka, Kansas* that ended segregation in public schools led to the not-quite-so-great system of forced busing to integrate public

22    Encyclopedia.com, s.v. "institutional racism," accessed March 21, 2019, https://www.encyclopedia.com/social-sciences/encyclopedias-almanacs-transcripts-and-maps/institutional-racism.

23    History.com Editors, "Jim Crow Laws," last modified March 13, 2019, https://www.history.com/topics/early-20th-century-us/jim-crow-laws.

24    https://www.dictionary.com/browse/redlining

schools that flamed fires of its own regarding racial tensions.[25] However, what truly ended the official tyranny of whites over blacks in the US was the Voting Rights Act of 1965 that banned poll taxes and literacy tests, among other things, along with the Civil Rights Act of 1968 that covered discriminatory practices in other areas of life, like housing, ending among other things the practice of redlining from before."

I then asked, "What are the takeaways from this, sir?"

Zinke surmised, "Regarding the five stages, policy awareness is those early pioneers raising concerns over the use of slavery in the United States. Policy formulation is the decision by northern states to abolish slavery gradually while the southern states made the decision to hold the status quo and maintain their slaveholding. Final policy adoption was, after some back and forth, made by the national government when they took steps to first ban the slave trade early on in our countries history and the practice of slavery as a whole following the Civil War. However, due to our federal system of government the implementation of said policy was not so straightforward as the practice of slavery was banned at the national not enough action was taken to prevent discrimination from occurring. This led to the policy evaluation and revision stage when the federal government took further action and banned those practices as well. In the adoption of any policy at any level in any kind of a government the same general steps take place. Rounding it all off though is the work done by Black Lives Matter and the like, raising awareness that more may need to be done and starting the whole process over again on some other aspect of the issue."

I then interjected, "Good summary sir, but where will this information go in the exhibit?"

Zinke murmured, "I think this will go in a full floor-to-ceiling panel entitled 'Takeaways' at the far right of the wall. Anyway, specifically, the practice of slavery was in existence for 246 years, from 1619 to 1865, in at least some part of the country. It only became a significant issue in need of attention during the last 85 years, the time it took from us to go from the first state to take action in Pennsylvania ending slavery gradually to the practice being banned via the 13th Amendment. For 103 years after, 1865 to 1968, the presence of Jim Crow laws and their kin were segregating the races and were finally ended by acts of Congress via the Voting and Civil Rights Acts of the era. Overall, it took us 349 years to go from everyone having slaves to having no formal discriminatory policies in our country that were institutionalized at a grand scale. This is upward of 17 generations of a family, assuming a new generation got their start every 20 years or so. Overall, workable policy for society takes time to evolve into something that works for everyone."

---

25  Douglas DeWitt, "busing," in *Britannica*, accessed March 21, 2019, https://www.britannica.com/topic/busing; Brian Duignan, "Brown v. Board of Education of Topeka," in *Britannica*, accessed March 21, 2019, https://www.britannica.com/event/Brown-v-Board-of-Education-of-Topeka.

I then inquired, "Sir, if I was wanting to do something the influence the policy process along the way, maybe get something started, what advice might you give me?

Zinke thought for a minute and concluded, "By and large, anyone in the United States today can go about their business and largely not face opposition by a government to what they seek to accomplish. Granted, there is the issue of keeping the public health and safety in good order, but that's an issue for another day. What I'm saying is that while we have put an end to the torrid role of government in discrimination, much more work needs to be done to get pockets of civilization in line. That's why academics always say they have '95 percent certainty' confidence level that they have proved something when publishing,[26] ruddy outliers. In our case, there will always be some stupid racists in existence no matter what you do. The challenge is weeding out their influence in society."

I replied, "So you are saying that after a point you've got to move onto some other problem our you'll be stuck forever focusing on a problem that's no longer a problem or not worth the effort to further eradicate the issue."

Zinke stated, "But, if you are wanting to focus on a problem, you might find more success when focusing on a specific item as opposed to a generality as it helps those in power know what needs to be fixed, i.e., segregationist policies obviously created a separate, but non-equal solution that could be fixed by putting everyone in the same schools, etc. Also, when protesting policy, make sure that what you are doing is targeted at fixing the problem. For example, Black Lives Matter protesters left protesting a city council meeting in Sacramento to go shut down a portion of Interstate 5 during rush hour, which did not go well with drivers back west in California.[27] Blocking the freeway certainly gets the word out about an issue, but blocking traffic doesn't get us to a solution, and that's what people really want. If anything, doing so would lead to less support for their cause by the average Joe on the go. Either way, we've arrived back at stage number one. I wonder where we'll end up with their effort to set the agenda. Now, speaking of a problem in need of repair, let's turn to the back wall of the room here."

I asked, "What's your idea, sir?"

---

26    "Confidence Intervals," accessed March 21, 2019, http://www.stat.yale.edu/Courses/1997-98/101/confint.htm.

27    Laurel Wamsley, "In Sacramento, Protesters Shut Down Freeway and Block Entrance to Kings Game," NPR, March 23, 2018, https://www.npr.org/sections/thetwo-way/2018/03/23/596383836/in-sacramento-protesters-shut-down-freeway-and-block-entrance-to-kings-game; Tylt, "Is Blocking Freeway Traffic a Good Protest Tactic?," accessed March 21, 2019, https://thetylt.com/culture/is-blocking-freeway-traffic-a-good-protest-tactic.

Zinke replied, "Champ, my boy, I think we've covered what policy is, the debate in general, and the process that is undergone to get the policies passed. The question now is, what other policy areas should be displayed in our new exhibit?"

I interjected, "Various issues that can teach us about other items to face when setting the agenda and eventually solving the problem?"

Zinke held, "Good point. For this wall, at the center-middle let's put the text 'Major Domestic Policy Areas of Today!' Now, to tie this new area into the timeline we just created, I'm thinking of same-sex marriage; thoughts?"

I replied, "Good with me, but how?"

## Same-Sex Marriage

Zinke declared, "Time is of the essence, my boy! What we learned from slavery is that making proper policy can take time. Action on slavery took nearly 400 years, officially at least, to change, but what about what happens when public opinion does an immediate about-face on a controversial issue? That, Champ, is the debate over same-sex marriage, granted there are always going to be some people who view the subject as taboo, but opinion on same-sex marriage has dramatically shifted in a relatively short period compared to slavery. Using a fact sheet of research from the Pew Research Institute, in 2001, 57 percent of Americans had an unfavorable view of same-sex marriage, against 35 percent that viewed the subject favorably.[28] Fast-forward to 2017, 62 percent of Americans viewed the practice as favorable, against 32 percent who didn't.[29] More importantly, the results on the fact sheet from earlier indicate that this dramatic shift is across all generational, religious affiliation, political ideology, race, and gender divides."[30]

I interrupted, "That's a big turnaround, sir, but how did this shift play out legally?"

Zinke spoke, "Thanks to our friends at *USA Today*, there is a readily available timeline to consider that I read last night, seeking ideas for this space funnily enough![31] It's a long timeline, but in short, 1973 saw Maryland become the first state to prohibit same-sex marriage. The year 1998 saw Hawaii, of all places, do the same. The year 2003 saw Massachusetts bar the practice, followed by an additional 11 states in 2004 and another seven in 2006. Then, the tide turned. The year 2008 saw legal same-sex marriages allowed in California and

28   Pew Research Center, "Changing Attitudes on Gay Marriage," June 26, 2017, http://www.pewforum.org/fact-sheet/changing-attitudes-on-gay-marriage.

29   Ibid.

30   Ibid.

31   Richard Wolf, "Timeline: Same-Sex Marriage through the Years," *USA Today*, June 26, 2015, https://www.usatoday.com/story/news/politics/2015/06/24/same-sex-marriage-timeline/29173703.

Connecticut. Iowa, Vermont, New Hampshire, and DC followed in 2009. New York allowed the practice in 2011. Washington, Maine, and Maryland joined the ranks in 2012. The year 2013 saw Rhode Island, Delaware, Minnesota, New Jersey, Hawaii, Illinois, and New Mexico do so as well. The year 2014 saw bans disappear in Oregon, Pennsylvania, Indiana, Colorado, Kansas, North Carolina, South Carolina, West Virginia, and Wyoming. In other states along the way, bans were overturned, but marriages were halted until appeals could be heard. Everything ended when, on June 26, 2015, in *Obergefell v. Hodges*, the US Supreme Court legalized same-sex marriage nationwide. Overall, from the first ban in 1973 to the practice of banishment being outlawed in 2015, the process took a paltry 42 years to venture through. Using the Pew data from earlier, the last time opposition outnumbered support was in 2010, only two years after the first approval for same-sex marriages occurred in 2008, only to sky-rocket from there, all right around when the push for legalization occurred. Overall, with a great amount of universal support, change in policy can occur quite quickly. Support for the abolition of slavery was certainly prevalent, but it was not universal, i.e., the North-South divide on the matter, so the process of ending the practice took a lot longer to occur in its various forms (slavery and segregation)."

I inquired, "So what's the problem, then?"

Zinke spoke, "The problem isn't marriage in and of itself, but whether the government should be regulating marriage in the first place. Should what goes on between two people in their home be their business? Why does the state have to get involved? Accordingly, bans on same-sex marriage bans have technically opened a can of worms."

I interjected, "What worms, sir? You mean like unintended consequences?"

Zinke replied, "Exactly. A week after the approval for same-sex marriages occurred, a Montana polygamist went on to sue the state for the right to legally marry his spiritual second wife; the practice is banned under state and federal law.[32] This can of worms was opened thanks to the dissenting opinion of Chief Justice Roberts in the *Obergefell v. Hodges* case that reads, 'If not having the opportunity to marry "serves to disrespect and subordinate" gay and lesbian couples, why wouldn't the same 'imposition of this disability' . . . serve to disrespect and subordinate people who find fulfillment in polyamorous relationships?'[33] The question still is, why is the government in the regulating morality business?"

I imposed on the conversation, "It shouldn't really."

32   Laura Zuckerman, "'I Want Two Wives or I'll Sue': Polygamist's Demand after US Gay Marriage Ruling," Mirror, July 3, 2015, https://www.mirror.co.uk/news/world-news/i-want-two-wives-ill-5992752.
33   576 U. S. ____ (2015); https://medium.com/@e/dissenting-opinion-of-justice-john-c-roberts-f5e2ab4f1349

## Black Markets and Marijuana

Zinke asked, "Here's a good question to keep the exhibit planning going. Where do you buy your weed from?"

I stood there for a minute taken aback. I then said coyly, "Weed, sir? Me, sir? No, not me sir. What's marijuana? I've never heard of such a thing."

Zinke said, "Oh come on, you know about pot. Grass. Ganja. Cannabis. Reefer. Mary Jane. Chronic. You know all the nicknames, don't you? Come on! Be honest!"

I relented, "Okay, fine, I do. My family owns a convenience store, and I know for certain that we don't have it, and we would be the place to have the merchandise to sell if the product was legal. We're very convenient after all, and I assume everyone does it. You know, come to think it, there's always this El Camino in the parking lot that my dad has always told me to avoid. Is that where you get it?"

Zinke explained, "Very good. That guy, in the El Camino represents a part of society known as the black market (figure 25.9), or 'the illicit buying and selling of goods in violation of legal price controls, rationing, etc.'[34] I mean, weed has been illegal under federal law since the passage of the Controlled Substances Act of 1970, medicinal uses included. However, despite the illegality, the 2015 National Survey on Drug Use and Health found that marijuana is the most commonly used illicit drug, with 22.2 million people admitting to using the drug in the month prior to the survey.[35] Using US Census Bureau estimates for July 1, 2015, the population was 321,418,820,[36] meaning that at least roughly 6.9 percent of the population used marijuana at that point in the year. Overall, you have a decent-sized portion of society going 'To hell with the government. I'll get it and smoke the stuff wherever I can get it. I can do bad all by myself.' Either way, states are mad due to a lot of money being spent on items that aren't being taxed to fill their coffers, to provide you and me with

FIGURE 25.9  Black market speculant on graffiti. Kharkiv, 2008.

---

34   https://www.dictionary.com/browse/black-market; For a good read on black markets go here: https://www.investopedia.com/articles/economics/12/mechanics-black-market.asp

35   SAMHSA, "Results from the 2015 National Survey on Drug Use and Health: Detailed Tables," accessed October 18, 2018, http://www.samhsa.gov/data/sites/default/files/NSDUH-DetTabs-2015/NSDUH-DetTabs-2015/NSDUH-DetTabs-2015.htm.

36   https://factfinder.census.gov/faces/tableservices/jsf/pages/productview.xhtml?src=bkmk

services, but people are happier due to the potentially lower costs, less regulation, and more straightforward access to needed goods and services by going to the black market."

I interjected, "What about the individual states? Are they towing the line set by the feds or what?"

Zinke replied, "Overall, most states now allow for the use of marijuana, but not all usage is the same. There is recreational usage, and there is medicinal, using for pleasure versus helping with health-related matters, respectively. As this issue is still changing, I'll discuss both, not just the prior. According to the website Fool.com, a site offering oddball stock investing advice, and their immaculate timeline on the subject,[37] California passed *medical* marijuana usage in 1996. Alaska, Oregon, Washington, and Washington DC followed soon after, in 1998. Maine did so as well in 1999 with Colorado, Hawaii, and Nevada doing so in 2000. The year 2004 saw Montana and Vermont legalize medical marijuana, with New Mexico and Rhode Island following along in 2007, followed by Michigan in 2008. New Jersey followed suit in 2009, Arizona in 2010, and Delaware in 2011. Then, the states went a bit further. Colorado and Washington State approved *recreational* marijuana use in 2012, with Massachusetts allowing for medical usage in the same year. Illinois and New Hampshire legalized medical marijuana in 2013, followed by Minnesota and New York allowing for medical marijuana and Alaska and Oregon allowing recreational use in 2014. California, Nevada, and Massachusetts legalized recreational marijuana in 2016, with West Virginia doing so as well in 2017. Arkansas, Florida, North Dakota, Ohio, and Pennsylvania legalized medical marijuana in 2016. In 2018, Oklahoma has opened the doors to medical marijuana, and Vermont is now allowing for recreational use. Meanwhile at the federal level, not much has happened as using it is still illegal, but the Obama administration in 2009 issued the Cole Memo, limiting enforcement of federal marijuana laws in states that have legalized marijuana, which was overturned by the Trump administration in 2018.[38] Either way, recreational marijuana usage is more legally acceptable than ever in recent memory."

I concluded, "It appears that on this front people, the states rather, have options to suit their desire to get involved with marijuana."

---

37    Keith Speights, "Timeline for Marijuana Legalization in the United States: How the Dominoes Are Falling," Motley Fool, September 24, 2018, https://www.fool.com/investing/2018/09/23/timeline-for-marijuana-legalization-in-the-united.aspx.

38    US Department of Justice, "Memorandum for Selected United State Attorneys on Investigations and Prosecutions in States Authorizing the Medical Use of Marijuana," April 7, 2017, https://www.justice.gov/archives/opa/blog/memorandum-selected-united-state-attorneys-investigations-and-prosecutions-states; US Department of Justice, "Justice Department Issues Memo on Marijuana Enforcement," January 4, 2018, https://www.justice.gov/opa/pr/justice-department-issues-memo-marijuana-enforcement.

Zinke remarked, "That's the truth. What are your thoughts on lighting for the exhibit?"

I replied, "I guess a literal spotlight for each of the issues you put on the wall here would be cool, but why bring that topic up now sir?"

## Trade-Offs and Energy

Zinke noted, "It's another important issue to discuss, of course. Have you ever wondered who or what keeps the lights on? Is the power fairy waving her magic wand while running on a treadmill, or is there an army of prisoners biking with generators to keep the bulbs shining brightly at night?"

I interjected, "Obviously not, but what's the big issue to discuss here, sir?"

Zinke remarked, "This issue takes us back to the guns and butter debate from before. You see, when it comes to energy supplies in the United States, some markets are regulated while others are not. The major trend in energy supplies, at least when it comes to powering your home, is deregulation or the opening of competition for choosing your electricity provider, but not the entities transmitting and distributing the electricity to your home.[39] In short, you may choose where you buy your electricity and gas. More importantly, thanks to our friends at Electricchoice.com,[40] we have an up-to-date list of deregulation efforts in the gas and electricity markets of the various states. For our conversation, let's only look at the deregulation of electricity markets. At this time, only 17 states have deregulated theirs, and Texas is the most deregulated, with 85 percent of residents being able to select where they buy their electricity from. This is due to certain municipalities choosing in their charters to continue to supply electricity to their residents. Rhode Island, Ohio, and Pennsylvania kicked off the trend in 1996. New York, Illinois, and Oregon deregulated in 1997. Connecticut, Massachusetts, New Hampshire, and Michigan did so in 1998. Delaware, Maryland, and New Jersey went along in 1999. Maine fell in line in 2000. Washington went with the plan in 2001, followed by Texas in 2002, leaving Virginia to lead up the rear in 2007."

I interjected, "So, what's the benefit here then, sir?"

Zinke noted, "Remember how from before we had to decide whether to have more guns or butter?"

I remarked, "Yeah, what about it?"

---

39   Daniel Ciolkosz, "Electricity Deregulation," Penn State Extension, March 4, 2019, https://extension.psu.edu/electricity-deregulation#section-6.

40   Electric Choice, "Map of Deregulated Energy States & Markets (Updated 2018)," accessed March 21, 2019, https://www.electricchoice.com/map-deregulated-energy-markets.

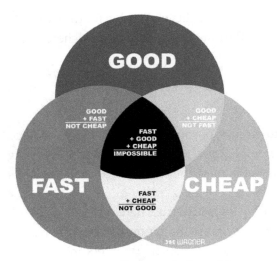

FIGURE 25.10 A Venn-diagram style chart of the "project triangle" showing visually the potential overlaps between speed, quality and low cost, along with the "inability" to accomplish all three.

Zinke continued, "What that choice is referring to is the concept of trade-offs (figure 25.10) or 'a situation in which you accept something bad to have something good.'[41] In general, the goods you buy and the services you pay for can only be two of the following: good, cheap, and fast. Therefore, if the service is good and cheap don't expect to get the item all that fast. If it's cheap and fast, don't expect it to be all that good, while if it is fast and good it'll probably cost a lot. That's just how the market works. Regarding guns and butter from before, we have to tradeoff a certain number of guns to certain more amount of butter when considering our finite societal resources."

I inquired, "What are the trade-offs with dealing with deregulated energy?"

Zinke uttered, "For this, let's imagine that you are a newly minted adult. You get a new deluxe apartment. You see, focusing in on Texas, again, back on January 1, 2002, Senate Bill 7 went into effect, deregulating the purchase of electricity in the state outside of those municipalities that were engaged in the production and sale of the product. My question for you is, under those circumstances, what do you value the most in selecting your energy? Do you want clean energy, green energy, inexpensive energy, or energy that always works?"

I responded after thinking for a bit, "Under those circumstances, I guess I would say because I'd be more likely than not broke, I would go with inexpensive energy."

Zinke remarked, "Okay, but what might the trade-off be, then?"

I replied, "I would assume that the lowest cost energy supplies might come from fossil fuels. Therefore, due to their generators being long paid off and obtainment methods being welldeveloped, I get a lower price but run the risk of the resource being pollutive, while if I go with the provider who solely focuses on bringing biomass electricity to market, due to that being a newer, greener fuel, it's going to be more expensive due to well, being new."

---

41   https://dictionary.cambridge.org/us/dictionary/english/trade-off

Zinke replied, "In general that would be correct, but it's more complicated than that. When it comes to pricing the electricity, per the US Energy Information Administration,[42] the fuel itself plays a significant role. It helps to be selective in choosing what you use to heat and cool your home along with what you use to cook your food, as the cost will vary depending on your fuel source."

I interjected, "Could you comment on green energy a bit, sir? The topic of your trade-off scenario interests me!"

Zinke furthered, "It's all about the type you select to use, renewable or nonrenewable. Nonrenewable resources are those 'resources of economic value that cannot be readily replaced by natural means on a level equal to its consumption.'[43] Fossil fuels are great examples of nonrenewable resources in that their formation takes billions of years while wind, water, and solar energy do not, seeing as how the wind is always blowing, the rivers running, and the sun shining day in and day out. Beyond that, powerplants themselves have construction, maintenance, and operating costs to keep them running. Also, the transmission lines bringing you the power must be built, maintained, and monitored. At the same time, if you buy pure wind or solar energy and the wind stops blowing or the sun doesn't shine, you might need a backup source. Lastly, as we talked about earlier, the way the market is regulated will impact the price. Overall, it's great that many can choose who they buy their power from based on what they want their power to be, but you will pay the price for the source. The wind is always blowing and turning the turbines, but don't forget about the birds that get hit by the big spinning blades.[44] Now, on another note, how come you are not at work right now?"

## Subsidies and Welfare

I replied, "Well, you see, I'm on this big trek learning about government, so I'm just not currently working. I'm on what you might call a vacation."

Zinke furthered, "Okay, but where do you live back home?"

I replied, "At home with my parents as I recently graduated and have yet to start school this fall at Texas State in San Marcos."[45]

Zinke the furthered, "What's your rent?"

---

42    Energy Information Administration, "Factors Affecting Electricity Prices," accessed March 21, 2019, https://www.eia.gov/energyexplained/index.php?page=electricity_factors_affecting_prices.

43    James Chen, "nonrenewable resource," In *Investopedia*, last modified January 4, 2018, https://www.investopedia.com/terms/n/nonrenewableresource.asp.

44    Michael Hutchins, "Understanding the Threat Wind Energy Poses to Birds," American Bird Conservancy, May 9, 2017, https://abcbirds.org/wind-energy-threatens-birds.

45    https://www.txstate.edu

I replied, "None, my parents aren't making me pay rent. Either way, hell, they only pay me minimum wage at the family corner store, so I couldn't afford to move out if I did."

Zinke stated, "So what are your parents doing in your life, then?"

I remarked, "Subsidizing my existence?"

Zinke said, "Very good. Subsidies, at least regarding government, are 'a direct pecuniary aid furnished by a government to a private industrial undertaking, a charity organization, or the like.[46] Without that support, certain activities that currently exist might not be able to thrive much longer."

I interjected, "How does that relate to me, then?"

FIGURE 25.11 Visual of a Moral Hazard.

Zinke stated, "The term to use here is a *moral hazard* (figure 25.11), or 'the risk that an individual or organization will act irresponsibly or recklessly if protected or exempt from the consequences of an action.[47] In simple English, because you don't pay your parents for rent—or utilities, for that matter, more likely than not—you don't feel the need to cut your water consumption, turn off the lights when you leave the room, or limit the movies you order on your cable box, as you don't bear the burden of paying for them. Your parents pay the bills, and you're used to it, so you don't think about these expenses.

I inquired, "Are you bringing up welfare now?"

Zinke remarked, "Why not? Humans are our greatest resource. Every company has its Human Resources department since humans are so important! Now to discuss subsidies, yes, I do need to bring up welfare or 'the financial or other assistance to an individual or family from a city, state, or national government.'[48]

I interjected, "So, what's the problem here, then?"

Zinke noted, "We'll on one hand that would be the cost of doing so. For example, using data from our friends at USGovernmentSpending.com and their amazing data tables on total government spending in the fiscal year 2019,[49] the federal government is planning on spend-

46    https://www.dictionary.com/browse/subsidies

47    https://www.dictionary.com/browse/moral-hazard?s=t

48    https://www.dictionary.com/browse/welfare

49    USGovernmentSpending.com, "Government Spending Details in $ Billion: Federal State Local for 2019—Charts," accessed March 21, 2019, https://www.usgovernmentspending.com/ year_spending_2019USbn_20bs6n#usgs302.

ing $1,052,100,000,000 on Social Security and $631,000,000,000 on Medicare programs. Meanwhile, federal, state, and local governments are planning on spending $731,800,000,000 on Medicaid and $458,400,000,000 on other welfare programs, including money for family and children, unemployment, workers compensation, and housing. Together, that is $2,873,300,000,000 in a single year being given away in some form or another."

I inquired after a brief lull, "Where exactly is that money coming from?"

Zinke noted, "Well the first two are financed by direct taxes taken from each of your paychecks—remember the taglines FICA and Medicare the next time you look at your earnings statement—while any other number of other measures finances the rest. For example, a recent Curbed.com article discussed how Proposition C in San Francisco, if approved this fall by voters, would have companies based there that make more than $50,000,000 in revenue pay an extra 0.5 percent gross receipts tax, increasing the section of the city's budget paying for homeless programs by 70 percent.[50] Beyond that example, paying for these programs could come from any number of resources, general funds or some other specified tax."

I inquired, "What other problems are associated with welfare?"

Zinke furthered, "Well beyond the cost of doing so, that article I just mentioned says it all. Most people are not against helping those in need, but nobody wants to see someone taking a handout who doesn't need one. Overall, we must debate the extent to which we should help our fellow man and how best to do so. Should we encourage people to go out and get a job to advocate more personal responsibility, or is investing money into a solution the better way, like what is going on currently in Stockton, California, where the city will be giving 100 residents $500 a month for 18 months to test the impact of providing a universal basic income beginning in February 2019, based on an idea promoted by Martin Luther King Jr. before his death in 1968 and championed by others today like potential democratic presidential nominee Andrew Yang who made the policy the central tenant of his campaign?[51,52] Now, speaking of people problems, my kids are growing up and need to move out. May they move in with you?"

---

50    Adam Brinklow, "Twitter CEO Tweeted Off over Prop. C Homeless Tax," Curbed SF, October 22, 2018, https://sf.curbed.com/2018/10/22/18009508/twitter-ceo-dorsey-prop-c-homeless-tax-election.

51    Kate McFarland, "Stockton, CA, US: New Details Revealed in Planned Basic Income Demonstration," Basic Income Earth Network, August 23, 2018, https://basicincome.org/news/2018/08/stockton-ca-us-new-details-revealed-in-planned-basic-income-demonstration; Jordan Weissmann, "Martin Luther King's Economic Dream: A Guaranteed Income for All Americans," *Atlantic*, January 20, 2014, https://www.theatlantic.com/business/archive/2013/08/martin-luther-kings-economic-dream-a-guaranteed-income-for-all-americans/279147.

52    Stevens, Matt, and Isabella Grullón Paz. "Andrew Yang's $1,000-a-Month Idea May Have Seemed Absurd Before. Not Now." The New York Times. The New York Times, March 18, 2020. https://www.nytimes.com/2020/03/18/us/politics/universal-basic-income-andrew-yang.html.

I had to jump back a little at the proposition and ponder. I said, "I'm going to say no, but why do you ask?"

## Immigration

Zinke said, "Well, the last issue for me to discuss here with you before we move on to other items for our exhibit is immigration, or 'the movement of non-native people into a country to settle there.'[53] The question is how to sort those individuals. You could distinguish them by immigration status; legal immigrants have permission to be in the country they are now in, while illegal immigrants do not. Each year we set the number of immigrants our country will take in, which immigrants we will take, where to resettle them when here, and update the policies; in general, we choose to enforce said specific policies."

I interjected, "Like the wall that President Trump wants to build?"[54]

Zinke furthered, "Exactly! Now, for what our country has chosen to legislate on this issue, I'd like to turn to my friends at the Migration Policy Institute and their 2013 timeline of major US immigration laws from 1790 to the present.[55] Let me bring it up here on my phone!" (figure 25.12).

I posited, "You like timelines, don't you sir?"

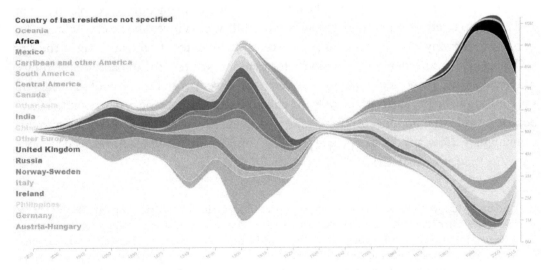

FIGURE 25.12 Figure displays the effect of United States immigration law on sources of immigration.

53 https://www.thefreedictionary.com/immigration
54 https://www.whitehouse.gov/issues/immigration
55 Migration Policy Institute, "Major U.S. Immigration Laws, 1790–Present," March 2013, https://www.migrationpolicy.org/research/timeline-1790.

Zinke continued, "Yep! Okay, back on point, from their timeline, they consider 33 US policies on immigration to be major. Some of the more interesting ones were related to world events, like the 1945 War Brides Act that allowed currently serving or honorably discharged members of the Armed Forces to bring their foreign-born wives and children back home with them, but regarding what we see going on today in America, two major policies stand out. The first was the 1924 National Origins Quota Act, also known as the Johnson–Reed Act. That act placed a limit on the number of persons who could immigrate into the United States each year going forward at no more than 2 percent of each nationality's proportion of the foreign-born US population in 1890, based on the census done in that year. Of note, exemptions were made for certain professions, students attending school in the United States, and the spouses and minor children of US citizens. This act was deemed discriminatory due to it leaving little immigration from places other than western Europe, your French, German, and British, for example, as those groups were the primary senders of immigrants before 1890. Now superseding that law was, or dare I say is, the 1965 Immigration and Naturalization Act, also known as the Hart–Cellar Act, which abolished the National Origins Act's quota system and replaced it with a system focused on admitting immigrants based on family members already here and the needs of employers, with no cap on the number of immediate family members (spouse, parents, and children). This has led to a massive shift in the demographic makeup of the country ever since, with millions of immigrants from outside of western Europe.[56] For example, the 1950 US Census had a racial breakdown of 89.5 percent white, 10 percent black, and .5 percent other. The 1960 US Census had a racial breakdown of 88.6 percent white, 10.5 percent black, and 0.5 percent other. Consistently, but ten years later, five years after the 1965 Immigration and Nationality Act, the makeup transitioned into 87.5 percent white, 11.1 percent black, and 1.4 percent other, slow change but change none the less. Forty years later, in 2010, the breakdown was of 72.4 percent white, 12.6 percent black, 5 percent Asian, 6.2 percent some other race, 2.9 percent two or more races, and 0.9 percent American Indian or Native Alaskan, or other. A dramatic shift that can and is attributed to the 1965 law being implemented.[57] Overall, based on the implementation of that act, the United States is expected to become a minority-majority state by 2042. Granted, changes in family procreation habits certainly helped speed up the process of demographic changes."

I interjected, "Sir, what do you mean by a minority-majority state?"

---

56    History.com Editors, "U.S. Immigration Since 1965." March 5, 2010, https://www.history.com/topics/immigration/us-immigration-since-1965.

57    US Census Bureau, "A Look at the 1940 Census," http://www.census.gov/newsroom/cspan/1940census/CSPAN_1940slides.pdf; all demographic data discussed here came from here.

Zinke noted, "Oh, it means 'a population in which more than half represent social, ethnic, or racial minorities, and in which fewer members of the more socially, politically, or financially dominant group are represented.'[58] In other words, whites will still make up the most significant percentage of the population but will not be the majority of it eventually."

## Truths about Public Policy

After a few minutes of pondering, I suggested, "Sir, I do believe the back wall is filled to the brim with each issue under its spotlight. Let's move on to the wall to the right of the main entrance when entering the room."

Zinke commented, "What do you have in mind?"

I articulated, "Well, a while back I spoke with the chairs of the Democratic, Libertarian, and Republican Parties of Texas. The major item we discussed was the party platform that they figuratively stand on to win over the masses. From that, the parties wish to give you various amounts of access to government services, but I want to have something more interactive."

Zinke inquired, "Like what?"

I continued, "Sir, I'll admit, I already knew a thing or two about the marijuana legalization, specifically that of recreational legalization in Colorado. Sir, I want to have a place where people can paste on the wall their opinions, a live Facebook or Twitter feed where people can post their reactions to government policy changes."

Zinke interrupted, "What are you thinking of as an example of this concept?"

I concluded, "Well, I remember this photo of a woman in Colorado who on the first day of the legalization of recreational marijuana ran outside to greet the friendly local beat cop to take a photo with him and her giant marijuana stalk. She went on to become known as the 'Meanwhile in Colorado' meme. Also, there were these Girl Scouts who started selling Girl Scout cookies in front of a marijuana dispensary in California.[59] Either way, I call it the 'People Do Weird Stuff When Things Change Wall!'"

Zinke stated, "I think that's a great idea, but we now need to focus on some additional formal takeaways. We can put this info on the last remaining wall fully in this room that we have not yet already put info onto. Now, we already have that workable policy can take time, but what else is important? For that, my friends Clarke Cochran, Lawrence Mayer, T.R. Carr, Joseph Meyer, Mark McKenzie, and Laura Peck in their esteemed publication known as *American*

---

58    https://www.dictionary.com/browse/majority-minority
59    Josh Hafner, "Girl Scout Reportedly Sells 300 Boxes of Cookies outside of California Pot Shop," *USA Today*, February 7, 2018, https://www.usatoday.com/story/money/nation-now/2018/02/07/mysterious-girl-scout-sells-300-cookies-outside-california-pot-shop/316042002.

*Public Policy: An Introduction*,[60] offer four main options to choose from when formulating and eventually adopting and implementing policy. Frist, they argue that there will be disagreement about what constitutes a problem that needs to be solved by the government. Remember the issue of whether the government should regulate marriage? Second, the two sides of an issue may never agree on what should and should not be done to resolve the issue. Remember how we still debate how it is best to off welfare services to the citizenry? Third, there may exist no socially acceptable solution to a problem. Remember how it can be seen as harsh to just throw people here illegally back to where they came from but at the same time it still be seen as improper to just allow everyone in no matter what? Lastly, most policies can be written to offer some leeway as to how to interpret the policy in question. Remember how the states are adopting various forms of an at-large policy en route to an overall universal adoption?"

I interjected, "Let's finish out the room with a wall that sums up everything. This could be a cool chant! 'What do we want?'"

Zinke noted, "Government regulation, I assume?"

I furthered, "When do we want it?"

Zinke remarked, "When they have an excellent reason to get involved!"

Nearing noon, I remarked, "Thanks for letting me help you here, sir, but I'm getting hungry. Do you have any suggestions?"

Zinke stated, "Sure. Follow me!"

We made our way into the main hall and turned left. We passed an original building water fountain and then took the first left down an escalator to the basement. Once at the bottom, we found ourselves in a large atrium. Dead ahead was a place called the Bison Bistro. Zinke stated, "There you go, the best, and the only, food in the whole building. Thanks for the help. The man in orange will be ever so delighted."

We shook hands and went our separate ways. I then paid tribute to the bison industry and bought a bison burger. Following that, I grabbed a table and had my fill. In the distance, I noticed a small store and declared, "Time to spend some money on souvenirs!"

The woman sitting behind me asked, "Question is, which souvenirs and how much of your finite pocket change can you spare to spend?"

I dropped my head and sulked, contemplating the vast knowledge of all around me when it comes to finite resources, only to realize that that is what life is all about—making decisions about what to do and the requirement to face the good and bad consequences of doing so. Life's just one long string of decisions. The question is, what should I do to learn about what to do in situations when I can't make the decisions unilaterally?

---

60   https://www.cengage.com/c/american-public-policy-an-introduction-11e-cochran; Clarke E. Cochran, Lawrence C. Mayer, T. R. Carr, N. Joseph Meyer, Mark McKenzie, and Laura Peck, *American Public Policy: An Introduction*, 11th ed. (Boston: Cengage Learning).

**QUESTIONS TO CONSIDER** REGARDING AMERICAN DOMESTIC POLICY:

1. The first main discussion topic of the chapter defines the concept of public policy. Please define the term *public policy* and explain what the word means to you, and why, in detail.

2. The second main discussion topic of the chapter discusses the difference between domestic and foreign policy. Please define what each is, provide an example of both from your life, and explain why they are good examples, in detail.

3. The third main discussion topic of the chapter discusses the guns and butter debate. Please spell out what that debate is, describe a time in your life when you had a similar decision to debate, and explain why, in detail.

4. The fourth main discussion topic of the chapter discusses the stages of policy development as they relate to slavery. Please identify the five stages of policy development and what went on regarding slavery during each of the stages. Then identify a situation from your life where you went through similar stages to accomplish something and relate them to the stages of policy development, in detail.

5. The fifth main discussion topic of the chapter discusses the unintended consequences of same-sex marriage adoption. Please explain what unintended consequences are, what was an unintended consequence of same-sex marriage adoption, a situation from your life that saw an unintended consequence emerge, and why it is an unintended consequence, in detail.

6. The sixth main discussion topic of the chapter discusses the concept of black markets and how they relate to marijuana. Please explain what a black market is, a good from your life that is on the black market, the consequences of you buying that good from the black market, and why, in detail.

7. The seventh main discussion topic of the chapter discusses the concept of trade-offs and how they relate to energy. Please explain what a trade-off is, a trade-off from your life that you made recently, and why it's a good example, in detail.

8. The eighth main discussion topic of the chapter discusses the concept of subsidies and moral hazards and how they relate to welfare. Please explain what subsidies and moral hazards are, a time from your life when you propped something up, and why that situation relates to those terms, in detail.

9. The ninth main discussion topic of the chapter discusses the concept of immigration. Please explain what immigration is, the types of immigration, how the concept of immigration presented here relates to your life, and why, in detail.

10. The final main discussion topic of the chapter presents different truths regarding public policy. Please identify the truth that relates to your life and explain why, in detail.

## FIGURE CREDITS

# Chapter 26

# American Foreign Policy

## Texas Higher Education Coordinating Board ACGMSLOs

*For Federal Government 2305: Upon successful completion of reading the book and taking the associated course, students will be able to do the following:*

1. Explain the origin and development of constitutional democracy in the United States
2. **Demonstrate knowledge of the federal system**
3. Describe separation of powers and checks and balances in both theory and practice
4. **Demonstrate knowledge of the legislative, executive, and judicial branches of the federal government**
5. **Evaluate the role of public opinion, interest groups, and political parties in the political system**
6. Analyze the election process
7. **Describe the rights and responsibilities of citizens**
8. **Analyze issues and policies in US politics**

*For Texas Government 2306: Upon successful completion of reading the book and taking the associated course, students will be able to do the following:*

1. Explain the origin and development of the Texas Constitution
2. Describe state and local political systems and their relationship with the federal government
3. Describe separation of powers and checks and balances in both theory and practice in Texas
4. Demonstrate knowledge of the legislative, executive, and judicial branches of Texas government
5. Evaluate the role of public opinion, interest groups, and political parties in Texas
6. Analyze the state and local election process
7. Identify the rights and responsibilities of citizens
8. **Analyze issues, policies, and the political culture of Texas**

# Advice from George Washington

I remember my debate teacher back at Langham Creek High School telling us in class that there will always be two sides of the same coin. The coin that I started evaluating yesterday dealt with aspects of policy making regarding domestic issues, items that an individual, our country, in this case, has full control over. I did so by helping design a new exhibit at the US Department of the Interior with Secretary Zinke for their free public museum.[1] On the way down to the basement deli and gift shops, Zinke made a recommendation for another site that I should go visit to help me fulfill my lofty quest that would help with the opposite side of the coin.

FIGURE 26.1 The Harry S. Truman Building located at 2201 C Street, NW in the Foggy Bottom neighborhood of Washington, D.C. It is the headquarters of the United States Department of State.

Specifically, Zinke suggested that I go over to the US Department of State Harry S. Truman Building (figure 26.1) and tour the Diplomatic Reception Rooms located in the appropriately named Foggy Bottom section of the district. The other side of the coin is foreign policy, or "general objectives that guide the activities and relationships of one state in its interactions with other states."[2] This side of the coin is the one that we as a country do not have full control over. The issue is, the tour is not a show up whenever you like; it's more of a call ahead and make a reservation kind of thing and hope the stars are on your side.[3] Luckily, I called the number on their website that Zinke helped me look up before he went back to work and got the process rolling on the way back to my hotel. After about 15 minutes of ensuring there was room for the 9:30 a.m. tour this morning and providing my identification information for what I assume is a lengthy background check, my visit was booked. I was instructed to arrive at the entrance to the US Department of State Building on 23rd Street Northwest no later than 9:15 a.m. this morning.

With that information in mind and putting into practice my knowledge from yesterday of using my resources most efficiently, I decided that it was best to take the Metro as I had done on my first trip days earlier but go two additional stops past the McPherson Square

---

1   https://www.doi.gov/interiormuseum
2   https://www.britannica.com/topic/foreign-policy
3   https://diplomaticrooms.state.gov/tours

Metro Station to the Foggy Bottom-GWU Metro Station (figure 26.2) and walk from there. At the top of the escalators taking passengers to street level from the station, I entered the hustle and bustle of the busy downtown Washington DC melee. To my left was the impressive facade of the George Washington University Hospital.[4] Beyond the usual souvenir and hot dog vendors there was an out-of-sorts pie seller-protester group, but, most noticeably, there

FIGURE 26.2  Foggy Bottom-GWU Metro Station Entrance.

was a 46-inch high bronze bust, sitting atop a 68-inch-high brown granite base, of George Washington himself[5] helping provide ambiance to the entrance of the George Washington University campus.[6]

A few minutes later, with my bearings set and a pie for later, I turned south, right if you were immediately leaving the escalator from before, and proceeded to walk four and a half blocks south to the State Department Building. Along the way, one building stood out from the rest. Between E Street Northwest and Virginia Avenue Northwest on 23rd Street Northwest is the modernist-style headquarters of the Pan American Health Organization (figure 26.3), a subdivision of the World Health Organization, focusing on health-related issues in the Americas.[7] The front part of the building is a large honeycombed circular theater complex with a curved, glass-fronted main building at

FIGURE 26.3  Headquarters building of the Pan American Health Organization, the World Health Organization's arm for the Americas, in Washington DC in the USA.

the rear that is adorned by 29 round bronze seals representing the founding nations of the Pan American Health Organization back in 1902, set in black stone. Seeing the health organization building here made for a nice contrast with the dominant federal styling of most buildings in the district. I knew the district was the main epicenter of activity in the country,

---

4  https://www.gwhospital.com
5  Wally Gobetz, "Washington DC—Foggy Bottom: GWU—George Washington Bust," Flickr, June 7, 2009, https://www.flickr.com/photos/wallyg/3628745370/in/photostream.
6  https://www.gwu.edu
7  https://www.paho.org/hq/index.php?lang=en

FIGURE 26.4 Champ Cove Photograph with Diplomatic Reception Rooms Tour Badage.

but I had no idea about the international flare going on at the same time, other than state embassies.

Just before 9:15 a.m., I found myself waiting with a small group of other obvious tourists in front of the 23rd Street Northwest entrance of the State Department Building.[8] At 9:15 a.m. on the dot, the security agents called us into the tan security tent to process us for entry. I showed my driver's license to the guard; he found me on the day's approved entry list, and I was processed through the screening process. A French family behind me in line was denied entry due to not bringing the required documents, as they didn't bring their passports as requested. This requirement is part of the security protocol for non-US citizens, due to the sensitive nature of the activities going on in the building, international relations, or "relations across the boundaries of nation-states."[9] Once inside, we passed another ID check and were issued guest badges to the building (figure 26.4). Afterward, we were ushered to an isolated area of the lobby to await our tour guide, who had not yet reported for duty, and ordered to hang any large items and coats on the provided hangars and racks. Once seated in one of the insufficient number of provided chairs, I picked up my phone to take a selfie with my badge and the large seal located on the wall. Not a second after I had posed with my phone for a selfie, the guard at the gate yelled, "No photos! Put all your phones and cameras away immediately, or you will be removed from the building!"

I immediately dropped my phone to my side, turned it off, and put it away in my pocket, hopefully never to be seen again, at least for the time being. It was at this moment I realized that I wasn't in Kansas anymore and that the severe nature of the building's business was

8    The author gathered any pertinent information not directly cited on a tour of the Diplomatic Reception Rooms in July of 2018.

9    Department of International Relations, "What Is IR?," accessed March 21, 2019, https://internationalrelations.sfsu.edu/what-ir.

beyond what I had expected. Just after 9:30 a.m., our tour guide, Patricia, came into view. She began by stating, "Good morning everyone. Welcome to the United States Department of State, where we negotiate away our problems. If you want to fight, feel free to go across the Potomac River and have fun with the boys in uniform at the Pentagon (figure 26.5). Just let us have a chance at dealing with the issue beforehand."

The lot of us had a good chuckle at that one-liner. After a pause, Patricia continued in a very joking parlance, "Now, everyone, I do have a few rules to advise you of regarding the tour. Photos are not allowed at any time unless I or one of our lovely guest tour guides, the armed guards in white shirts, tells you that you may do so. Also, do stay with the group; this is not a self-guided tour, and you going on a self-guided tour of your own is a felony, so stick together, or we'll be glad to get you a private suite at the nearby FBI J. Edgar Hoover Building (figure 26.6) for the night while we investigate you. If nobody has any questions, follow me!"

Everybody remained silent. After about ten seconds, Patricia waved us forward to follow her. She provided some information on the building itself. "All right everyone

FIGURE 26.5  The Pentagon, headquarters of the US Department of Defense.

FIGURE 26.6  Standing on Pennsylvania Avenue NW and look up F Street NW at the J. Edgar Hoover Building, the headquarters of the Federal Bureau of Investigation in Washington, D.C., in the United States.

the building we're now progressing through was completed as it looks today in January 1961 to bring the seven thousand, at the time, State Department employees under one roof allowing for the use of 1.3 million square feet of office space. The secretary and his staff are up on the seventh floor with the rest of the department divisions vertically aligned over multiple floors to allow staff to be closer to one another, and those of similar rank in the various departments to be on the level with the others. Like in the rooms we are about to visit, everything must be equal, or calamity strikes, and seeing as how our job is to avoid that with other nations, why not do so as well with ourselves? Also in the building is a library for use by our staff, an international conference area, exhibition hall, smaller conference rooms, offices for delegates, a delegates' lounge, an auditorium capable of seating eight hundred people that was used by President Kennedy for press conferences most famously, but for you all, those are all off limits.[10] As we turn left, here follow me."

It was at this point that I tuned out for a bit. The walls of the building are bright white, and the low ceilings provide the ambiance of entering a secret underground lair, which now that I think about it is precisely what I have seen in every spy movie that I've ever witnessed. I'm thinking of Jason Bourne for some reason at this point.[11] The highlights of what I remember seeing here were to my right, a television studio where, I guess, important state department broadcasts are delivered. I stopped and put my head up against the window only to be left with the guard glaring at me while waiting patiently for me to continue my trek. After a minute, he stated sternly, "Keep moving please."

I remembered at this point watching an episode of my favorite television show, *The Americans*, and how in an episode entitled "Tchaikovsky" the main character, Elizabeth, goes on the same tour that I was on now, makes a mad dash to a secret meeting in the department cafeteria, and once it is noticed she is missing, pandemonium breaks out while everyone is looking for her.[12] I at this point decided it best to keep up with the group.

About 200 feet later our group turned right and stopped about 500 feet later for a bathroom break. Our guards never broke ranks, and we were counted meticulously and repeatedly and told to stand squarely against the wall. We were held up by a mother and daughter in the bathroom taking their time. After about ten minutes, we were then allowed to move into the adjacent elevators once all were accounted for. We were divided into two different lifts for the ride up to the eighth floor to view the reception rooms there; the reception rooms on the seventh floor were not open to tours that day. I had a feeling that the rooms here are of a similar function to that of the Diplomatic Reception Rooms at the White House, international relations, but I had the impression that the rooms here are where a lot of the dirty behind-the-scenes work goes on before all the pomp and circumstance at the White House. Of note, a guard went with each elevator group, and each elevator had an operator to ensure that we only went to the right place. We were not allowed to leave until the guard

---

10    US Department of State, "Extended, Remodeled New State Building," accessed March 21, 2019, https://history.state.gov/departmenthistory/buildings/section29.

11    Rotten Tomatoes, "The Bourne Collection," accessed March 21, 2019, https://www.rottentomatoes.com/franchise/the_bourne_collection.

12    Scott Tobias, "The Americans Recap: Slippery People," *Vulture*, April 5, 2018, http://www.vulture.com/2018/04/the-americans-recap-season-6-episode-2-tchaikovsky.html.

had secured the elevator. Also, of note, when you have an elevator key, the alarm doesn't go off when you hold the door open. Either way, about 45 seconds later, we found ourselves entering a room of spectacular grandeur.

Then, at that moment, a booming voice came from just out of view of our elevator. The voice said, "Hello everyone! Welcome to the Diplomatic Reception Rooms tour! I am United States secretary of state Mike Pompeo. Follow my voice over here."

When we were face-to-face with the secretary, our tour guide, Patricia, stated, "Wow, sir, your presence is so unexpected! Are you going to give the full tour for me?"

Pompeo stated, "Yes ma'am! It will be a nice change of pace to speak with citizens who aren't politicians. May I go ahead and get started?"

Patricia nodded for him to do so. Pompeo stated, "Once again everyone, welcome! The room that you are now standing in is called the Edward Vason Jones Memorial Hall (figure 26.7), one of 42 rooms available to my staff and I to conduct our business with the other nations of the world.[13] We'll see only a small minority of those rooms today, but we'll make the most of the opportunity. This room is named for the architect who spent years of his life revamping each of the rooms that we are to visit today. This room is modeled after the drawing room at Marmion, an eighteenth-century house in King George County, Virginia. The faux marble pilasters and cornices help create an aura of opulence for visiting dignitaries like

FIGURE 26.7 Edward Vason Jones Memorial Hall at the United State Department of State.

yourself. The furniture consists of Boston- and Philadelphia-styled furniture from the late eighteenth century that primarily sits in the extension of the room to my right. My favorite pieces, though, are the busts of George Washington, John Jay, and Marquis de Lafayette.[14] Who wants to tell me why George Washington might be a part of that trio of busts?"

I uttered, "He's a founding father, if I'm not mistaken."

A woman next to me asked, "Didn't he provide some essential pieces of advice for our foreign policy going into the future?"

13   *Wikiwand*, s.v. "Diplomatic Reception Rooms, U.S. Department of State," accessed March 21, 2019, http://www.wikiwand.com/en/Diplomatic_Reception_Rooms,_U.S._Department_of_State.

14   US Department of State, "Diplomatic Reception Rooms," accessed March 21, 2019, https://diplomaticrooms.state.gov/Room/?id=386012d3-ff51-e711-8107-1458d04e2fb8.

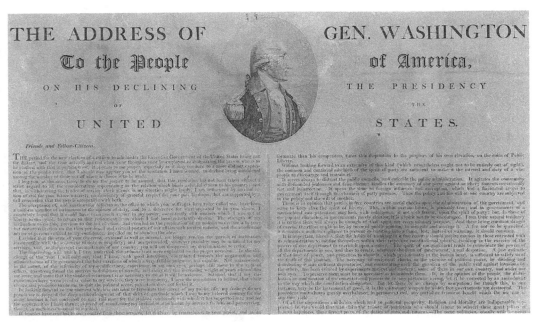

FIGURE 26.8  Broadside, Washington's Farewell Address, Page One.

Pompeo stated, "Why, yes he did. What you are referring to is Washington's Farewell Address[15] (figure 26.8). That address that was written to offer parting words to the country he had lived in, loved, and worked tirelessly for most of his life, and covered topics related to foreign policy as part of an overall campaign, stated as such in paragraph 43, that 'they may be productive of some partial benefit, some occasional good; that they may now and then recur to moderate the fury of party spirit, to warn against the mischiefs of foreign intrigue, to guard against the impostures of pretended patriotism; this [I] hope will be a full recompense for the solicitude for your welfare, by which they have been dictated.'"

I interrupted, "So, what's the advice?"

Pompeo continued, "Everyone, relevant information from his farewell address regarding dealing with other nations boils down to five useful pieces of advice. The first includes Washington's advice to 'cultivate peace and harmony with all' from paragraph 31 and to create 'just and amicable feelings towards all' from paragraph 32 that together calls for us to reach peaceful relations with anyone willing. Second, paragraph 33 implies while paragraph 40 explicitly calls for us to 'steer clear of permanent alliances with any portion of the foreign world'; i.e., be independent of the affairs of other nations as much as possible. This situation

15    OurDocuments.gov, "Transcript of President George Washington's Farewell Address (1796)," accessed March 21, 2019, https://www.ourdocuments.gov/doc.php?flash=false&doc=15&page=transcript.

is pertinent, he writes in paragraph 33, as 'attachment of one Nation for another produces a variety of evils. Sympathy for the favorite Nation, facilitating the illusion of imaginary common interest, in cases where no real common interest exists, and infusing into one the enmities of the other, betrays the former into a participation in the quarrels and wars of the latter, without adequate inducement or justification.' Adding on to this is a call, his third piece of advice is for us to avoid foreign entanglements, when in paragraph 37 Washington states that 'it must be unwise in us to implicate ourselves, by artificial ties, in the ordinary vicissitudes of her politics, or the ordinary combinations and collisions of her friendships or enmities.' This call is made to us in the context of the constantly quarrelsome nature of European affairs that we are physically foreign to, thanks to our position of being an ocean away. Regarding trade, in his fourth piece of advice, Washington tells us 'in extending our commercial relations, to have with them as little political connexion as possible' in paragraph 36 due to trade being a place for us to connect and develop good future relations healthily. Lastly, paragraph 42 concludes by stating, 'There can be no greater error than to expect or calculate on real favors from nation to nation' summarized as, we shall expect the need to exist as independently as possible in our affairs with others and not depend on anyone to, in military speak, to cover our six."

Another man in the group said, "I get the advice, but where do we stand with this information today?"

Pompeo furthered, "Well, we aren't what we used to be at our country's founding, as we've gone in a variety of slightly different directions. Regarding the first piece of advice, creating harmony with all, from the Pew Research Center's Spring 2017 Global Attitudes Survey that polled people in 38 countries from around the world, including our citizens, only 19 countries had a 50 percent or more very favorable or somewhat favorable view of the United States. This list includes the United States, Vietnam, Israel, the Philippines, South Korea, Poland, Nigeria, Hungary, Italy, Ghana, Japan, Tanzania, Senegal, Kenya, South Africa, Columbia, Brazil, and the United Kingdom.[16] Also, we do host the United Nations, an intergovernmental organization to promote 'the maintenance of international peace and security.'[17] Regarding alliances, our membership in the North Atlantic Treaty Organization (NATO), a mutual self-defense pact with 28 other countries in Europe and North America, means that we've been allied with at least eleven countries, Belgium, Canada, Denmark, France, Iceland, Italy, Luxembourg, the Netherlands, Norway, Portugal, and the United

---

16    http://www.pewglobal.org/database/indicator/1/survey/19
17    United Nations, "What We Do," accessed March 21, 2019, http://www.un.org/en/sections/what-we-do.

Kingdom, to hold back communism since August 24, 1949, the day of the group's founding.[18] That's borderline permanent. Hell, even further if you include our alliances with the United Kingdom and France in World War I and II. Regarding foreign entanglements, using the 2017 listing of US military bases overseas kept by David Vine at American University, our military has roughly 800 different types of bases in nearly 80 countries around the world.[19] When it comes to trade, I would argue that we follow this advice most closely, as based on trade statistics from the Department of Commerce's International Trade Administrations Office of Trade Policy and Analysis, our top 30 trade partners are all, excluding China, for the most part with countries that we are on good terms with, like Canada, Mexico, Japan, and the United Kingdom.[20] Finally, regarding expecting favors, I think my comments on our mutual defense pact in NATO covers that topic quite well. Now, everyone, please follow me into our next room."

## Major Players in Foreign Policy

About a minute later, the group was settled after multiple advisories to not touch the numerous valuable, mesmerizing artifacts. Pompeo stated, "Alright everyone, welcome to the Entrance Hall (figure 26.9) that is modeled on the interior of two 1700s Georgian plantations on the

FIGURE 26.9 The Entrance Hall at the United States Department of State.

James River in Virginia, Carter's Grove and Westover.[21] My favorite piece in here is the Tabriz rug overlaying the mahogany floor. Now, a question, who does everyone think the most important people on the scene are when issues of foreign policy arise here in the United States?"

The mother of the girl who slowed us down earlier said, "President Trump."

I chimed in quietly, "Congress."

18    North Atlantic Trade Organization, "What Is NATO?," accessed March 21, 2019, https://www.nato.int/nato-welcome/index.html.

19    David Vine, "List of U.S. Military Bases Abroad, 2017 (version of 2017-05-14)," AU Digital Research Archive, 2017, https://dra.american.edu/islandora/object/auislandora:55685.

20    US Department of Commerce, "Top U.S. Trade Partners," https://www.trade.gov/mas/ian/build/groups/public/@tg_ian/documents/webcontent/tg_ian_003364.pdf.

21    US Department of State, "The Entrance Hall," accessed March 21, 2019, https://diplomaticrooms.state.gov/Room/?id=326012d3-ff51-e711-8107-1458d04e2fb8.

The girl from earlier said, "Peppa Pig!" making no comment on what she meant by that, which brought a small chuckle to the group.

Pompeo stated, "Okay, the first two of you are spot on. Keeping in order, President Trump and his predecessors play the role of being our chief diplomat by negotiating deals, treaties, and other agreements, not to mention serving as commander in chief of the Armed Forces. Most importantly, for me at least, he's responsible for hiring me, my lieutenants, and my primary on-site staff around the world, ambassadors and consular generals. Now as part of checks on the powers of the president, Congress approves of treaties and agreements made by the president, confirms my and my colleagues' appointments, and, most importantly, controls spending."

Another woman stated, "Don't forget the power to declare war thanks to article 1, section 9, clause 1 of the US Constitution."

Pompeo stated, "Very good and thanks to you all for paying such good attention. Beyond those two players, we also have—no, not Peppa the Pig—special interest groups that lobby our government's decisions, or at least those making the decisions, to help them achieve a goal of some kind in dealing with other nations. An example of these groups is homeland changers, who, using the mission statement of the Cuban American National Foundation as an example, seek to achieve, 'as its mission, the unwavering commitment to bring freedom, democracy, and respect for human rights to Cuba.'[22, 23] Beyond that, there are human rights groups like Amnesty International whose mission 'is to undertake research and action focused on preventing and ending grave abuses of these [human] rights'[24] around the world. A final group consists of economic groups, like the National Foreign Trade Council, whose mission is to '[advance] global commerce by advocating for public policies that foster an open, rules-based international trade and investment regime.'[25] Lastly, for our final major player, we have the federal government itself, specifically that of the bureaucracy; this includes my department, the US Department of State that focuses on negotiating with other states, the Defense Department that physically fights with other states, and the Treasury that cuts the checks to pay for everything when dealing with other states. I'll offer more insight on those agencies later, though."

---

22    Cuban American National Foundation, "Purpose," accessed March 21, 2019, http://www.canf.org/about-us/purpose.

23    https://votesmart.org/interest-groups/NA/32#.W-MS9JNKiUn; this is a great reference for information on interest groups of all kinds like those discussed in the Special Governmental Interests chapter.

24    Amnesty International, "Amnesty International's Statute," accessed March 21, 2019, https://www.amnesty.org/en/about-us/how-were-run/amnesty-internationals-statute.

25    National Foreign Trade Council, "National Foreign Trade Council 2017 Goals and Priorities" (report, NFTC, March 7, 2017), http://www.nftc.org/default/general information/2017goalsandpriorities.pdf.

## Goals for Foreign Policy

I chimed in, "That's a lot of people to work with when conducting business. What does it take to get people on track for everything?"

Pompeo announced, "Goals, wonderful goals."

I asked, "Like what goals?"

FIGURE 26.10 The Gallery at the United States Department of State.

Pompeo ushered us into the next room. Once in what seemed to be a really elaborate hallway, he stated, "Now everyone, welcome to the Gallery (figure 26.10), the hallway that takes us to the main areas of our operation here, at least what you may see on the tour. This was the first room renovated to their current look back in 1965. At either end of the hall are Palladian windows paying tribute to our first Secretary of State Thomas Jefferson. Beyond the furniture and keeping with the rug theme are the Bakhtiari and Persian rugs covering the floors from the early 1900s.[26] Like with foreign affairs, it is good to have solid flooring to stand on. With that information in mind, that takes us to foreign policy goal numero uno, advocating human rights. The United States has a high standard of living, 17th out of 80 ranked countries, according to a recent *U.S. News & World Report* article on the subject.[27] Therefore, we advocate the same high standards in our foreign policy by working for that for others. Action here is taken by signing on to agreements like what was produced on May 25, 2000, at the United Nations Convention on the Rights of the Child: Optional Protocol on the Sale of Children, Child Prostitution and Child Pornography that we were a signatory on.[28] Beyond that, we offer troops and aid in kind to the United Nations Peacekeepers, an international group that 'helps countries navigate the difficult path from conflict to peace'[29] that currently consists of 14 missions around

26    US Department of State, "The Gallery," accessed March 21, 2019, https://diplomaticrooms.state.gov/Room/?id=346012d3-ff51-e711-8107-1458d04e2fb8.

27    *U.S. News & World Report*, "The 80 Countries with the Highest Quality of Life," accessed March 21, 2019, https://www.usnews.com/news/best-countries/quality-of-life-full-list.

28    OHCHR, "Optional Protocol to the Convention on the Rights of the Child," General Assembly Resolution A/RES/54/263, May 24, 2000, https://www.ohchr.org/en/professionalinterest/pages/opsccrc.aspx.

29    https://peacekeeping.un.org/en

Africa, Asia, and Cyprus in the Mediterranean Sea.[30] Lastly, we encourage citizens like you all to go out and embark on goodwill missions around the world by supporting you via our missions here in the State Department that consists of various embassies, consulates, and other diplomatic posts.[31] One of my favorite examples of this is the group called People to People International that started under the Eisenhower presidency to encourage greater understanding of various nations around the world as part of the United States Information Agency at the time of that group's founding."[32]

At this point, the idea of traveling about on some far-flung mission had a certain appeal. Once my focus returned to hallway after a bit of daydreaming, I heard Pompeo say, "Let's see, to my left and right, respectively, are the Martha Washington Ladies' Lounge (figure 26.11) and the Walter Thurston Gentlemen's Lounge (figure 26.12). Feel free to gaze on the northwest Persian rug, the finest in our collection, in the gentlemen's lounge and the Ming-type Chinese rug from the 1880s in the ladies' lounge, but don't go in, as sacrifices must be made, keeping us to only stand here on the rugs here in the gallery."

The tour took a pause while we each went from room to room to look at the artifacts at a distance from behind the barricades. After about ten minutes I asked aloud, "Why can't we go in? Does that relate to foreign policy goals in some way?"

FIGURE 26.11 The Martha Washington Ladies' Lounge at The United States Department of State.

FIGURE 26.12 The Walter Thurston Gentlemen's Lounge at The United States Department of State.

---

30    United Nations, "Where We Operate," accessed March 21, 2019, https://peacekeeping.un.org/en/where-we-operate.

31    US Department of State, "What Is a U.S. Mission?," accessed March 21, 2019, https://www.state.gov/discoverdiplomacy/docs/208084.htm.

32    https://ptpi.org/about

FIGURE 26.13 The Ratification of the Treaty of Münster, 15 May 1648.

Pompeo stated, "Actually, yeah. You see, while we talked about human rights first and foremost, that goal is often least important due to that goal being a conflict of interest at times with the other two. Therefore, that goal is used as a bargaining chip; we ignore this to obtain that. Not to mention, we have the Peace of Westphalia as proclaimed by the Treaty of Münster[33] (figure 26.13), entered in 1648, that helped establish the sovereignty of states over their own lands, leaving us in a bind to tell other states how to run theirs. The rugs out here in the hallway are just as important as the ones in the two lounges, but we sacrifice these two out here to keep the other two in there in their best condition, plus we don't want any of you to try and put a spy device into one of the couches and cause all sorts of calamity, like that woman spy did in *The Americans*[34] when she went on the exact same tour as you are on now!"

## Eras in Foreign Policy

I asked, "So what are the two other goals that are more important than human rights?"

Pompeo articulated, "Okay. Let's go over here to the gentlemen's lounge. Notice how in here there are multiple surfaces to write on. In here we work to come to an agreement and secure our standing in the world. In here it is all about peace of mind through ensuring national security. Similar to how the rooms overtime have been upgraded, so too has our foreign policy. Originally, under the guise of advice given by Washington himself that we discussed earlier, in the eighteenth and nineteenth centuries our policy primarily consisted of following the mantra of isolationism, or 'the policy or doctrine of isolating one's country from the affairs of other nations by declining to enter into alliances, foreign economic commitments, international agreements, etcetera.'[35] Granted, we did invade Canada and fight against the British in the War of 1812 that eventually saw this very White House

33    *Britannica*, s.v. "Peace of Westphalia," accessed March 21, 2019, https://www.britannica.com/event/Peace-of-Westphalia.

34    Scott Tobias, "The Americans Recap: Friendly Fire," *Vulture*, May 17, 2018, https://www.vulture.com/2018/05/the-americans-recap-season-6-episode-8.html.

35    https://www.dictionary.com/browse/isolationism

of ours here in DC be burned to the ground in 1814, but we were provoked by their restrictions over trade with France imposed on us by them.[36] In short, the fight came to us, not the other way around. Following that, in the first half of the twentieth century, we went back and forth between isolationism and interventionism, or 'the policy or doctrine of intervening, especially government interference in the affairs of another state or in domestic economic affairs.'[37] Intervention came during World War I, on behalf of our allies, France and the UK, followed by settling back into isolationism during the interwar years of the 1920s and 1930s."

## Schools of Thought in Foreign Policy

I inquired, "What's the big picture on these two eras, sir?"

Pompeo stated, "Okay, good idea to summarize everything up to here. These first two eras bring to light something known as the realist school of foreign policy. This school of thought focuses on states serving as central actors in a conflict, the absence of supranational authority guiding states, states acting rationally to seek the best deal possible while maximizing their interests at the behest of others, and, finally, states seeking more power and self-preservation.[38] Remember, we fought the Brits in the War of 1812 to keep our trade routes intact, we fought Mexico in the Mexican-American War following their threats against us regarding the annexation of Texas, we fought the South in the Civil War to preserve the Union, and we fought the Spanish in the Spanish-American War in response to being attacked via the USS *Maine* exploding, all done to preserve our self-centered standing in the global society away from others."

I posited, "Where does World War II figure into this train of thought?"

Pompeo furthered, "That would be a turning point as we have yet to turn back toward our isolationist ways of yesteryear since that conflict. Accordingly, the driving force of our foreign policy from the end of World War II to the 1980s can be surmised as containment, or 'an act or policy of restricting the territorial growth or ideological influence of another, especially a hostile nation,'[39] and deterrence, 'the maintenance of military power for the purpose of discouraging attack,'[40] regarding the spread of communism. The term *MAD*, short for "mutually assured destruction," should ring a bell here, as we participated

---

36    History.com Editors, "War of 1812," October 27, 2009, https://www.history.com/topics/war-of-1812/war-of-1812.

37    https://www.dictionary.com/browse/interventionism?s=t

38    http://www.unc.edu/depts/diplomat/item/2011/0104/oped/op_smith_idealism.html

39    https://www.dictionary.com/browse/containment

40    https://www.merriam-webster.com/dictionary/deterrence

in the Korean[41] and Vietnamese[42] Wars to keep communism from spreading any further than its primary operating bases in China and the Soviet Union. Not to mention, we also participated in more isolated events such as the Cuban missile crisis[43] and backing of the Mujahidin in Afghanistan to keep the Soviet Union from taking over their country.[44] Now, to tie this third era to the first two, our enemies up to this point in time primarily consisted of other states, the British, the Japanese, Mexico, Spain, the Soviet Union, etc."

I interrupted, "But where does that leave us today, sir?"

## Enemies of the United States

Pompeo furthered, "Good question; now, I should say that our modern enemies do still consist of other states. Those states are just now a smaller portion of the opposition pie. Today we take a more case-by-case approach to the tactics that we use to deal with our enemies. For example, in the 1980s President Reagan started the process of détente, or 'the relaxation of strained relations or tensions (as between nations)'[45] toward the Soviet Union. In addition, toward North Korea today each time they go on the news and make some big show of force about how they will launch their nuclear missiles to obtain total world domination, we retaliate likewise but to a far greater extent by also posturing, or 'behavior or speech that is intended to attract attention and interest,' by flying our B-2 Spirit Stealth Bombers and requisite support craft over them to say 'That's fine; launch your one nuke, but we're going to retaliate with much more force' to encourage them to stop their bellicose rhetoric in the matter.[46] Granted, since President Trump took office and they had their meeting in Singapore earlier this year, that posturing has gone by the wayside on both sides exponentially.[47] Third, continuing the trend of interventionism, we now have preemptive strikes or

---

41    History.com Editors, "Korean War," November 9, 2009, https://www.history.com/topics/korea/korean-war.

42    History.com Editors, "Vietnam War," October 29, 2009, https://www.history.com/topics/vietnam-war/vietnam-war-history.

43    History.com Editors, "Cuban Missile Crisis," January 4, 2010, https://www.history.com/topics/cold-war/cuban-missile-crisis.

44    Alan Taylor, "The Soviet War in Afghanistan, 1979–1989," *Atlantic*, August 4, 2014, https://www.the-atlantic.com/photo/2014/08/the-soviet-war-in-afghanistan-1979-1989/100786.

45    https://www.merriam-webster.com/dictionary/detente

46    James Griffiths and Brad Lendon, "US Warns of N Korean 'provocations' as It Sends Bombers, Carriers to Region," CNN, October 30, 2017, https://www.cnn.com/2017/10/30/asia/north-korea-bombers-cosmetics/index.html.

47    Jonathan Marcus, "Trump Kim Summit: What Did It Actually Achieve?," BBC News, June 14, 2018, https://www.bbc.com/news/world-us-canada-44484322.

something 'said or done before someone else has a chance to act or attack so that their plans or actions are prevented from happening,[48] as was the case with Iraq when we invaded on March 19, 2003, to prevent them from using their supposed weapons of mass destruction that were never found.[49] Granted, we could probably invade North Korean quite easily; the difference is the data on the presence of nukes and the like are much more solid than those in Iraq."[50]

I posited, "Sir, I thought you said that we have shifted away from state-centered entities?"

Pompeo furthered, "Okay good point, and yes. That brings us to the last focus of today in foreign policy, intelligence gathering or the gathering of intelligence 'to reach a conclusion often intuitively from hints or through inferences.'[51] Here you have non-state actors like the Islamic State, the multitude of Somali Pirates, Al Qaeda, or the regular nut on the street here at home all seeking to achieve some private aim like terrorism, hijackings, or to simply shoot up the place. We as a country have placed so much into this, like that of the military, we have a whole office set up to perform this task led by the director of national intelligence 'to coordinate the other 16 Intelligence Community Components (FBI, CIA, etc.) based on intelligence consumers' needs that began under reforms as initiated by the passage of the Intelligence Reform and Terrorism Prevention Act of 2004.[52] I mean, you just never know when someone like the underwear bomber on the Delta flight,[53] shoe bomber on the American flight,[54] or Vegas strip shooter[55] is going to hit. Intel here is priceless."

Another woman inquired, "So what do the last two eras you discussed there represent?"

Pompeo concluded, "Ma'am, that question takes us to the idealist Wilson's school of foreign policy that focuses our attention on spreading our so-called values like democracy, capitalism, and its varied entities. In doing so, we intervene as much as possible and have imperialistic tendencies, be it physically expanding our territory or greatly exhausting foreign resources

---

48    https://www.macmillandictionary.com/us/dictionary/american/preemptive

49    History.com Editors, "War in Iraq Begins," November 24, 2009, https://www.history.com/this-day-in-history/war-in-iraq-begins.

50    Uri Friedman, "The Return of the Iraq War Argument," *Atlantic*, March 21, 2018, https://www.the-atlantic.com/international/archive/2018/03/iraq-north-korea-war/555929/.

51    https://www.merriam-webster.com/dictionary/gather

52    Office of the Director of National Intelligence, "U.S. National Intelligence Overview 2013," https://www.dni.gov/files/documents/USNI 2013 Overview_web.pdf.

53    *New York Times*, "Umar Farouk Abdulmutallab," https://www.nytimes.com/topic/person/umar-farouk-abdulmutallab.

54    CNN Library, "Richard Reid Fast Facts," last modified January 2, 2019, https://www.cnn.com/2013/03/25/us/richard-reid-fast-facts/index.html.

55    *Independent*, "Stephen Paddock," accessed March 21, 2019, https://www.independent.co.uk/topic/stephen-paddock.

and then leaving the territory to shrivel up and rot.[56] Remember, we fought the Vietcong in Vietnam, the North Koreans on the Korean Peninsula, engaged in the blockade of Cuba, and so much more to prevent the spread of communism. I won't even talk about the acts of Senator Joseph McCarthy and his efforts here at home to prevent the spread in his series of congressional hearings.[57] More recently, we invaded Iraq under the guise of preventing them from using their weapons of mass destruction as a possible 'cover story' to allow our oil companies access to their oil fields,[58] all of which was/is done to expand our standing in the global society. Adding together the fact that we were the only major player in World War II to not receive much damage and our entrance proving a turning point in the conflict, we have now become a hegemon, or 'something (such as a political state) having dominant influence or authority over others.'[59] Either way, it's a lot harder to see what's coming than it was before when dealing with just states, as standing army unit movements are easier to track than purchases at Walmart. Let's head over to the ladies' lounge doorway to talk about ensuring economic prosperity."

Once at the other end of the hallway in front of the entryway to the ladies' lounge, Pompeo then continued, "For ensuring economic prosperity, the final foreign policy goal of these here United States, or 'the capacity of having the money necessary to fill your needs and many of your desires,'[60] we emphasize this most when dealing with friendly nations to our cause who will work with us and show us no ill will. In getting people money, we take measures to keep solid job growth and high employment, retain access to affordable energy, promote foreign direct investment, and keep inflation low. We achieve these aims by joining organizations like the World Trade Organization, whose purpose is to 'open trade for the benefit of all' by operating a global system of trade rules, acting as a forum for negotiating trade agreements, settling trade disputes between its members, and supporting the needs of developing countries.[61] More recently, we have signed, threatened to leave more than anything, under President Trump, 14 free trade agreements with a total of 20 countries, like Australia, the Central American region, Canada,

---

56    http://www.unc.edu/depts/diplomat/item/2011/0104/oped/op_smith_idealism.html

57    History.com Editors, "Joseph McCarthy," October 29, 2009, https://www.history.com/topics/cold-war/joseph-mccarthy.

58    Antonia Juhasz, "Why the War in Iraq Was Fought for Big Oil," CNN, April 15, 2013, https://www.cnn.com/2013/03/19/opinion/iraq-war-oil-juhasz/index.html.

59    https://www.merriam-webster.com/dictionary/hegemon

60    Taylor Hall, answer to "What Is the Definition and Some Examples of the Term "Economic Prosperity"?," Quora, August 29, 2015, https://www.quora.com/What-is-the-definition-and-some-examples-of-the-term-economic-prosperity.

61    World Trade Organization, "The WTO," accessed March 21, 2019, https://www.wto.org/english/thewto_e/thewto_e.htm.

Mexico, and South Korea among others,[62] that 'reduce the barriers to trade between two or more countries, which are in place to help protect local markets and industries,' like tariffs and trade quotas with varied results.[63] The last action used here is open-skies agreements, which remove quotas on the maximum number of flights between states to allow as much trade and movement as possible.[64] We now have these agreements with a little over 120 different countries around the world and on every continent and at every level of economic development."[65]

I interrupted, "So why go the extra mile to sign all these agreements?"

Pompeo concluded, "The hope is, by breaking down barriers, the government acting as a middleman in this case, to trade, that then allows costs of providing goods and services to go down, which leads to lower prices for the consumer and hopefully a better standard of living for all involved. Now everyone, let's go through the doorway to our left at the opposite end of the hall from where we entered."

This part of the conversation seemed akin to the required trade-offs discussed yesterday when dealing with domestic policy. I and the others followed orders and were faithfully escorted by our armed guards. The room we were now in was a tasteful color of blue that felt as if we were now walking in the sky itself. The statue of Thomas Jefferson in the alcove at the far end of the room stood out prominently. After a few minutes of wandering around the room, Pompeo stated, "All right everyone, welcome to the Thomas Jefferson State Reception Room (figure 26.14).[66] The big room behind us is the Benjamin Franklin State Dining Room (figure 26.15).[67] Together, these two rooms form the core areas of the reception rooms

FIGURE 26.14  The Thomas Jefferson State Reception Room at The United States Department of State.

62    US Department of State, "Outcomes of Current U.S. Trade Agreements," accessed March 21, 2019, https://www.state.gov/e/eb/tpn/bta/fta/c76143.htm.

63    Matthew Grimson, "What Is a Free Trade Agreement?," ABC News, April 7, 2014, https://www.abc.net.au/news/2014-04-07/free-trade-agreement-explained-bilateral-fta-tpp/5371314.

64    US Department of State, "Open Skies Partnerships: Expanding the Benefits of Freer Commercial Aviation," July 5, 2017, https://www.state.gov/e/eb/rls/fs/2017/267131.htm.

65    Ibid.

66    US Department of State, "The Thomas Jefferson State Reception Room," accessed March 21, 2019, https://diplomaticrooms.state.gov/Room/?id=366012d3-ff51-e711-8107-1458d04e2fb8.

67    US Department of State, "The Benjamin Franklin State Dining Room," accessed March 21, 2019, https://diplomaticrooms.state.gov/Room/?id=3a6012d3-ff51-e711-8107-1458d04e2fb8.

FIGURE 26.15 The Benjamin Franklin State Dining Room at The United States Department of State.

for hosting large functions. The key to remember here is that we should best use our resources by placing events into the room of appropriate size. Here in the smaller reception room, in its neoclassic design, would be best for a smaller, more intimate event like entertaining an up-and-coming country that we want on our side. Jokingly, of course, as they don't exist, I'm thinking Wakanda would be a good start here for you Marvel fans, due to their recent outing into the public world thanks to their abundant stores of vibranium.[68] However, when we need to pull out all the big guns and stops, the dining room is the place to be, and that brings us to the last item for us to discuss on our tour of the rooms today, the various options available to engage other states with."

## Tools of Foreign Policy

I interrupted, "What tools fit best in here sir?"

Pompeo stated, "You are really interested in the subject matter here, aren't you young man?"

I replied, "You don't know the least of it sir. I traveled all the way here to DC to find the right place for me to get into government. The amount of travel offered by your department really stands out to me, sir."

Pompeo stated, "See me at the end of the tour, young man. I have an idea! Now, here in the small room, to get the ball rolling with another country, I, or the president, might find the opportunity on occasion to make a public statement of some kind. A great example of 'a written or spoken announcement on an important subject that someone makes in public' dates to our dealings with the Soviet Union. Afraid of leading our great nations into war, President Kennedy, making a statement of solidarity with Berliners and challenging oppression wrought by the Soviet Union against their people, made the infamous statement 'Ich bin ein Berliner'[69] in June 1963 following the completion of the Berlin Wall (figure 26.16). A more modern example of this is President Trump's tweeting, with one of the more infamous examples being his tweet of 'Covfefe' that united the nation over trying to decipher the

68    *Marvel Database*, s.v. "Wakanda," accessed March 21, 2019, http://marvel.wikia.com/wiki/Wakanda.
69    Jesse Greenspan, "JFK Tells West Berliners That He Is One of Them, 50 Years Ago," History.com. June 26, 2013, https://www.history.com/news/jfk-tells-west-berliners-that-he-is-one-of-them-50-years-ago.

message.[70] The president's tweets actually have their own museum in New York City, Chicago, and Los Angeles hosted by *The Daily Show with Trevor Noah* and Comedy Central."[71]

I interrupted, "How can we bring up the relations a notch, sir?"

Pompeo furthered, "Well, young man, that would be diplomacy or 'the art and practice of conducting negotiations between nations.'[72] As an example of this concept, nearly 24 years after president Kennedy's speech at the Berlin Wall, in 1987 President Reagan went on to make his famous 'Mr. Gorbachev, tear down this wall' speech in hopes of getting the Soviet premier back to the meeting room to discuss reducing their respective nuclear stockpiles after prior negotiations had fizzled out. Five months later, in December 1987, the two superpowers met, negotiated, and signed the Intermediate-Range Nuclear Forces Treaty that drastically reduced the number of nuclear missiles on European soil[73] (figure 26.17). Leading the way in this process is the department that we are in now, the State Department, where we have the mission 'to advance the interests of the American people, their safety and economic prosperity, by leading America's foreign policy through diplomacy, advocacy,

FIGURE 26.16  KN-C29248 26 June 1963 President Kennedy's address to the people of Berlin. Rudolph Wilde Platz, West Berlin, Federal Republic of Germany.

FIGURE 26.17  C47450-20, President Reagan and Soviet General Secretary Gorbachev shake hands after signing the INF Treaty ratification in the Grand Kremlin Palace during the Moscow Summit. June 1, 1988.

70    Matt Flegenheimer, "What's a 'Covfefe'? Trump Tweet Unites a Bewildered Nation," *New York Times*, May 31, 2017, https://www.nytimes.com/2017/05/31/us/politics/covfefe-trump-twitter.html.
71    Comedy Central, "The Donald J. Trump Presidential Twitter Library Book," accessed March 21, 2019, http://www.cc.com/shows/the-daily-show-with-trevor-noah/trump-twitter-library.
72    https://www.merriam-webster.com/dictionary/diplomacy
73    History.com Editors, "Reagan Challenges Gorbachev to Tear Down the Berlin Wall," November 13, 2009, https://www.history.com/this-day-in-history/reagan-challenges-gorbachev-to-tear-down-the-berlin-wall.

and assistance.'[74] Overall, we negotiate on behalf of the American people in hopes of avoiding something much worse, like nuclear war, by acting essentially as a mediator, of which I'm the chief of that aim. With that in mind, young man, what is your name?"

I stated "Champ, sir. Champ Cove of Texas."

Pompeo furthered, "Champ, would it be wise for me to give each of you your own personal tour?"

I replied, "It would be nice, but probably not the best use of our resources as time is a valuable thing to waste."

Pompeo iterated, "Very good young man. Today, we all have a common interest, learn about the amazing rooms that we are exploring today. Accordingly, we all got together and began this amazing tour. This brings us to tool three, foreign alliances, or 'a formal agreement or treaty between two or more nations to cooperate for specific purposes.'[75] In keeping with the trend of relating these items back to the Soviet Union, think about our relations with them during the twentieth century. During World War I, the Treaty of London of September 5, 1914, linked the British Empire, France, and the Russian Empire, along with ourselves when we entered the war in 1917, with the aim of defeating the Central Powers. Keeping with tradition, with the aim of defeating the fascist Mussolini of Italy, the Japanese Empire, and Hitler of Nazi Germany, the same powers allied themselves again during World War II under the guise of the Declaration of the United Nations on January 1, 1942. In both wars, multiple other countries signed on to the various alliances (figure 26.18).[76] Sadly, as we all know, ten-

FIGURE 26.18 British Prime Minister Winston Churchill, U.S. President Franklin Roosevelt, and Soviet leader Joseph Stalin met at Yalta in February 1945 to discuss their joint occupation of Germany and plans for postwar Europe. Behind them stand, from the left, Field Marshal Sir Alan Brooke, Fleet Admiral Ernest King, Fleet Admiral William D. Leahy, General of the Army George Marshall, Major General Laurence S. Kuter, General Aleksei Antonov, Vice Admiral Stepan Kucherov, and Admiral of the Fleet Nikolay Kuznetsov. February 1945.

---

74   US Department of State, "What Is the Mission of the U.S. Department of State?," accessed March 21, 2019, https://www.state.gov/discoverdiplomacy/diplomacy101/issues/170606.htm.

75   https://www.dictionary.com/browse/alliance

76   https://www.britannica.com/topic/Allied-Powers-international-alliance; Avalon Project, "A Decade of American Foreign Policy 1941–1949: Declaration by the United Nations, January 1, 1942," Lillian Goldman Law Library, Yale Law School, accessed March 21, 2019, http://avalon.law.yale.edu/20th_century/decade03.asp.

sions arose, and the Soviet Union drifted away, taking many satellite states along with them like Poland and East Germany. In response, on April 4, 1949, via the Washington Treaty, the United States and ten other countries grouped together, like I said before, and created the North Atlantic Treaty Organization, a mutual self-defense pact with 28 other countries in Europe and North America to hedge against aggression by the Soviet Union and their communistic tendencies. Finally, to finish off the room, it's wise now to discuss international organizations, or 'organization[s] established by a treaty or other instrument governed by international law and possessing its own international legal personality.'[77] One type of group here is known as nongovernmental organizations, commonly referred to as NGOs, which are private groups focused on resolving an issue. A good example of an NGO is the Sea Shephard Conservation Society (figure 26.19), with their mission 'to end the destruction of habitat and slaughter of wildlife in the world's oceans in order to conserve and protect ecosystems and species.'[78] They are most famous for their show on Animal Planet, *Whale Wars*, that catalogued their *privately* funded and guided efforts to prevent Japanese whaling vessels from killing animals for use in research and food.[79] On the other hand, most relatable to our aims here, government tools are international governmental organizations, or 'an entity created by treaty, involving two or more nations, to work in good faith, on issues of common interest.'[80] It's akin to an alliance, but is more open in membership and mission. They have the aim of being 'a mechanism for the world's inhabitants to work more successfully together in the areas of peace and security, and to deal with economic and social questions,'[81] which means, in short, to set

FIGURE 26.19 MY Steve Irwin of the Sea Shephard Conservation Society Approaching Melbourne.

---

77    Peace Palace Library, "International Organizations," accessed March 21, 2019. https://www.peace-palacelibrary.nl/research-guides/international-organisations-and-relations/international-organizations.
78    Sea Shepherd, "Mission Statement," accessed March 21, 2019, https://seashepherd.org/mission-statement.
79    https://www.animalplanet.com/tv-shows/whale-wars
80    Harvard Law School, "Intergovernmental Organizations (IGOs)," accessed March 21, 2019, https://hls.harvard.edu/dept/opia/what-is-public-interest-law/public-service-practice-settings/public-international-law/intergovernmental-organizations-igos.
81    Ibid.

FIGURE 26.20 United Nations Headquarters in New York City, view from Roosevelt Island.

the international agenda, mediate bargaining in affairs, and provide a place for innovativeness in facing pending issues. The most notable of this type of group is the United Nations (figure 26.20) that we discussed earlier today, an intergovernmental organization to promote 'the maintenance of international peace and security.'[82] A local branch of their work is located right up 23rd Street in the home base of operations for the Pan American Health Organization, a subdivision of the World Health Organization, which is a system organization of the United Nations. This group acts along the guidelines set forth by the United Nations' main deliberative assembly, policy-making, and representative organ, the General Assembly, membered by any and all willing nations of the world, and the Security Council that responds to major global incidents in need of further discussion that is membered by five permanent nations, ourselves, Russia, China, the United Kingdom, and France, along with ten other nations that rotate for two-year stints. The difference is that the former policies are optional while the latter decisions are required to be followed."[83]

I interrupted, "Sir, those methods seem to deal with dealing with another country before something has occurred, or at least in the immediate aftermath, but what about after the fact?"

Pompeo stated, "For that young man, let's all go in the Benjamin Franklin State Dining Room behind us."

Once in the immense room, Pompeo stated, "Young man, in referring to your questions from before, you and I and the president himself have been known on more than one occasion to stick our foot in our mouths when making a public statement. Once that happens, the work of a diplomat then gets started at working to keep a conflict from going nuclear and greatly impacting everyone and everything. If things in one-on-one negotiations can't smooth issues over, we then join alliances, and intergovernmental organizations help provide us with a great team to continue discussing the conflict with. Unfortunately, from time to time none of that works to resolve the issue. When that happens, we must seek other more formidable options to get our opposition in a conflict over to our side. Take, for example, our current dealings

---

82   United Nations, "What We Do."

83   https://www.britannica.com/topic/United-Nations; http://www.un.org/en/sections/about-un/main-organs; http://www.un.org/en/sections/about-un/funds-programmes-specialized-agencies-and-others/index.html

with North Korea. This provides a good example of the foreign economic policy tool, or the actions that governments take in the economic field toward their relationship with other states. However, despite having a healthier dialogue with that nation now than we have had in quite some time, we still impose sanctions on them, preventing, among other items, '[a]ll transactions or dealings involving the North Korean government or the Workers' Party of Korea; [t]he importation into the United States, direct or indirect, of any goods, services, or technology from North Korea; [v]essels and aircrafts that have visited North Korea within the last six months, or engaged in a ship-to ship transfer with such a vessel, from visiting the United States; and [t]he importation into the United States of any goods, wares, articles, and merchandise mined, produced, and manufactured wholly or in part by North Korean citizens or nationals' which are enforced by the Treasury Department.'[84] If they fully shut down their nuclear capabilities, we go a different route

here, as we could begin to open trade with them by signing a free trade agreement like the ones we have with other countries around the world that we discussed earlier. Until then, in the meantime, thanks to our friends at the US Agency for International Development (figure 26.21), we could offer aid and add them to the list of 142 countries around the world receiving money from the United States to develop their countries.[85] We still offer aid through the World Food Programme,[86] but we could be doing so much more beyond basic humanitarian aid if they would just work with us more than they currently do now on resolving our differences.[87] I'm looking forward

FIGURE 26.21 A U.S. Marine Corps UH-1Y Venom with Joint Task Force 505 prepares to depart from Tribhuvan International Airport, Kathmandu, Nepal, May 19 during Operation Sahayogi Haat. JTF 505 along with other multinational forces and humanitarian relief organizations are currently in Nepal providing aid after a 7.8 magnitude earthquake struck the country, April 25 and a 7.3 earthquake on May 12. At Nepal's request the U.S. government ordered JTF 505 to provide unique capabilities to assist Nepal.

84    US Department of State, US Department of the Treasury, and US Department of Homeland Security, "Risks for Businesses with Supply Chain Links to North Korea," July 23, 2018, https://www.treasury.gov/resource-center/sanctions/Programs/Documents/dprk_supplychain_advisory_07232018.pdf.

85    USAID, "Why Our Work Matters: Worldwide," accessed March 21, 2019, https://results.usaid.gov/results.

86    World Food Programme, "Democratic People's Republic of Korea," accessed March 21, 2019, http://www1.wfp.org/countries/democratic-peoples-republic-korea.

87    Jacob Wang, "An Overview of Humanitarian Aid to North Korea," *Claremont Journal of Law and Public Policy*, February 2, 2018, https://5clpp.com/2018/02/02/an-overview-of-humanitarian-aid-to-north-korea.

to our next peace conference to continue our talks with them.[88] Lastly, if we act in a team effort on this front, we can also offer financing for various initiatives. For example, the World Bank 'provides financing, policy advice, and technical assistance to governments of developing countries,'[89] or we can work with our friends at the International Monetary Fund 'to ensure the stability of the international monetary system—the system of exchange rates and international payments that enables countries (and their citizens) to transact with each other.' The prior is like a traditional bank loan while the latter is a payday loan type financier."

A guy to my rear announced, "Sir, I recently finished a Dave Ramsey Financial Peace University Course, and he advised us all to go debt free.[90] What if one of those countries taking out a loan becomes destitute? What would you recommend I do if in your position as secretary of state?"

Pompeo articulated, "You could always get a lawyer and file a lawsuit, the next tool, or 'a legal action by one person or entity against another person or entity, to be decided in a court of law'[91] against another country so long as they harmed you in some way."

FIGURE 26.22 International Court of Justice hearing in the case of "Application of the Interim Accord of 13 September 1995 (the former Yugoslav Republic of Macedonia v. Greece)"

I interjected, "Like if they invade you or something?"

Pompeo furthered, "Well, yeah! As part of our membership in the United Nations, we are entitled to have cases heard at the International Court of Justice (figure 26.22), their judicial arm.[92] Specifically, from their website they hear cases that are 'legal disputes between States submitted to it by them (contentious cases) and requests for advisory opinions on legal questions referred to it by United Nations organs and specialized agencies (advisory proceedings).'[93] As an

---

88    Russell Goldman, "A Guide to Trump and Kim Jong-un's Meeting in Vietnam," *New York Times*, February 8, 2019, https://www.nytimes.com/2019/02/08/world/asia/trump-kim-summit-north-korea-vietnam.html.

89    World Bank, "Who We Are," accessed March 21, 2019, https://www.worldbank.org/en/who-we-are.

90    https://www.daveramsey.com/fpu#in-progress=0&center=32.912768,-100.935494

91    https://www.law.cornell.edu/wex/lawsuit

92    International Court of Justice, "How the Court Works,", accessed March 21, 2019, https://www.icj-cij.org/en/how-the-court-works.

93    Ibid.

example of the prior, on June 7, 2016, the Philippines successfully won a case here arguing that China violated their sovereign territory when they built a wide variety of military installation on islands in their domain.[94] For us, when one of our naval vessels, the USS Vincennes, shot down an Iran Air A300B aircraft flying from Tehran to Dubai on July 3, 1988, they initiated court proceedings against us on May 17, 1989, seeking damages and other restitution for lives lost that we settled out of court in the following years."[95]

I inquired, "What if that doesn't work?"

Pompeo stated, "Well, there is always the last resort tool, warfare or 'a state of usually open and declared armed hostile conflict between states or nations.' Just as you have the right to defend yourself if you are attacked, so do we. This idea is known as the castle doctrine, more commonly referred to as stand your ground laws today in modern nomenclature.[96] Remember, we might have been helping to deliver supplies to our eventual allies in the United Kingdom prior to entering World War II as part of the Lend-Lease Program,[97] but once we were attacked at Pearl Harbor on December 7, 1941 (figure 26.23), we went on to declare war the following day by a vote of 470 to 1 in

FIGURE 26.23 Photograph taken from a Japanese plane during the torpedo attack on ships moored on both sides of Ford Island shortly after the beginning of the Pearl Harbor attack. View looks about east, with the supply depot, submarine base and fuel tank farm in the right center distance. A torpedo has just hit USS West Virginia on the far side of Ford Island (center). Other battleships moored nearby are (from left): Nevada, Arizona, Tennessee (inboard of West Virginia), Oklahoma (torpedoed and listing) alongside Maryland, and California.

On the near side of Ford Island, to the left, are light cruisers Detroit and Raleigh, target and training ship Utah and seaplane tender Tangier. Raleigh and Utah have been torpedoed, and Utah is listing sharply to port.

Japanese planes are visible in the right center (over Ford Island) and over the Navy Yard at right. U.S. Navy planes on the seaplane ramp are on fire. Japanese writing in the lower right states that the photograph was reproduced by authorization of the Navy Ministry.

---

94    Larisa Epatko, "International Court Rejects China's Claims in South China Sea," PBS, July 12, 2016, https://www.pbs.org/newshour/world/international-court-rejects-chinas-claims-south-china-sea.

95    International Court of Justice, "Aerial Incident of 3 July 1988 (Islamic Republic of Iran v. United States of America)," accessed March 21, 2019, https://www.icj-cij.org/en/case/79.

96    National Conference of State Legislatures, "Self Defense and 'Stand Your Ground'," July 27, 2018, http://www.ncsl.org/research/civil-and-criminal-justice/self-defense-and-stand-your-ground.aspx.

97    US Department of State, "Lend-Lease and Military Aid to the Allies in the Early Years of World War II," accessed March 21, 2019, https://history.state.gov/milestones/1937-1945/lend-lease.

Congress.[98] Fast-forward three and a half years, and we and our allies had won the conflict. Today, looking back at a lot of our discussion, nearly everything from our lawsuits at the International Court of Justice to holding back aid from North Korea to President Trump, Kennedy, and Reagan making public statements all lead back to working to prevent, or at least contain, acts of war."

I inquired, "Who do our combatants consist of, sir?"

Pompeo offered, "That would be one of three different groups. First is our Armed Forces, or the government-sponsored defense, fighting forces, and associated organizations of a state. For us, this consists of our Navy,[99] Army,[100] Marine Corps,[101] and Air Force.[102] These are the uniformed groups we send overseas to fight our battles, of which, we have been at war for 225 of our 242 years of existence.[103] Beyond that, we have our homeland defenders, or the groups designated with protecting our physical borders. For us, that consists of our Coast Guard at sea,[104] the US Customs and Border Protection on land,[105] and the Transportation Security Administration at major transit hubs."[106]

A man with a thick Russian accent stated, "My friend, so why does your military not patrol your borders like back in my homeland?"

Pompeo stated, "Good sir, that would be the Posse Comitatus Act of 1878[107] that along with the Insurrection Act of 1807[108] limits the ability of the federal government to use our Armed Forces for domestic law enforcement duties. Therefore, you have our Armed Forces primarily overseas with the homeland defenders working here at home. However, troops can be sent to the border, but they must only do so in support of the homeland defenders' work, such as the case I suspect will emerge when the president escalates tensions with our neighbors to help protect the border from migrants by 'providing helicopter support for border missions, installing concrete barriers and repairing and

98    History.com Editors, "The United States Declares War on Japan," November 16, 2009, https://www.history.com/this-day-in-history/the-united-states-declares-war-on-japan.

99    https://www.navy.mil

100   https://www.army.mil

101   https://www.marines.mil

102   https://www.af.mil

103   *Washington's Blog*, "America Has Been at War 93% of the Time—222 out of 239 Years—since 1776," Centre for Research on Globalization, January 20, 2015, https://www.globalresearch.ca/america-has-been-at-war-93-of-the-time-222-out-of-239-years-since-1776/5565946.

104   https://www.uscg.mil

105   https://www.cbp.gov/careers

106   https://www.tsa.gov

107   "Overview of the Posse Comitatus Act," http://www.rand.org/content/dam/rand/pubs/monograph_reports/MR1251/MR1251.AppD.pdf.

108   Insurrection Act of 1807, ch. 39, 2 Stat. 443, 443.

maintaining vehicles."[109] They will help find people, but the actual Border Patrol will be making arrests. Lastly, backing up the other two groups is our intelligence agencies, or 'a governmental agency that is devoted to the information gathering (known in the context as "intelligence") for purposes of national security and defense."[110] For us, we have the Federal Bureau of Investigation, the Central Intelligence Agency, and the Defense Military Agency, whose missions are to 'to protect the American people and uphold the Constitution of the United States,'[111] 'preempt threats and further US national security objectives by collecting intelligence that matters, producing objective all-source analysis, conducting effective covert action as directed by the President, and safeguarding the secrets that help keep our Nation safe,'[112] and 'provide military intelligence to warfighters, defense policymakers and force planners in the Department of Defense and the Intelligence Community, in support of U.S. military planning and operations and weapon systems acquisition,'[113] respectively. I would argue that the FBI focuses their work more domestically, while the CIA does so abroad, with the DMA doing so universally so long as it pertains to military endeavors."

The Russian-accented man from before asked, "To what extent does America fund its military?"

Pompeo argued, "That, sir, is quite a lot. From our friends at USGovernmentSpending.com, in fiscal year 2017 we spent $598.7 billion on the military, $175 billion on veterans affairs, and $46.3 billion on foreign aid, for a grand total of $823 billion, accounting for 20.65 percent of total government spending in that year. Further estimates suggest that these numbers will go up to $732.4, $212.4, $44, and $988.8 billion respectively, accounting for 21.48 percent of total federal spending in 2018.[114] When it comes to war, we are like the rug in this room, immense, as we here are standing on a Savonnerie-style carpet that measures 120 x 80 feet and weighs over 8,000 pounds, with design elements including the Great Seal of the United States, symbols of the four important crops of the early Republic, the four seasons, and, in the field, 50 stars representing the States of the Union."[115]

---

109    Astrid Galvan, "This Federal Law Limits What US Troops Deployed at the Border Can Do," *Military Times*, October 31, 2018, https://www.militarytimes.com/news/your-military/2018/10/31/federal-law-limits-what-us-troops-deployed-at-the-border-can-do.

110    http://www.yourdictionary.com/intelligence-agency

111    https://www.fbi.gov/about/mission

112    https://www.cia.gov/about-cia/cia-vision-mission-values

113    http://www.dia.mil/About

114    https://www.usgovernmentspending.com/defense_spending; USGovernmentSpending.com, "Defense Share of Federal Spending," accessed March 21, 2019, https://www.usgovernmentspending.com/spending_chart_1935_2020USf_20s2li011mcn_30f_Defense_Share_Of_Federal_Spending#view.

115    US Department of State, "The Benjamin Franklin State Dining Room."

FIGURE 26.24 "The Spirit of 76" is a painting that was made to honor the bravery and patriotism in the United States as it declared independence from Great Britain.

I inquired, "How does this compare to other countries?"

Pompeo stated, "$610 billion for what China, Russia, Saudi Arabia, India, France, the UK, and Japan spent combined versus $578 billion for us, when only looking at military-military spending, based on 2017 spending."[116]

Just then, Pompeo's watch buzzed. He stated, "Sorry folks, the Cambodian government is waiting for me downstairs and I need to run. Before I go, let's wrap things up appropriately. Let's walk back into the corner to the left of the way we entered this room. Here lies my favorite painting in the collection, by Archibald Willard, circa 1875, *The Spirit of 76*[117] (figure 26.24). This painting has what looks to be a worn-out Uncle Sam playing a drum standing between a short drummer boy and slightly taller fifer leading troops into an unknown battle. This painting says a lot about our foreign policy. Overall, we operate with the goal in mind to create an ideal world of peace, open trade, and understanding of our differences. See our humanitarian work with the UN and USAID, demolishing trade barriers thanks to our many free trade and open skies amendments, and embassies around the world working with one country after another. Unfortunately, our economic interests guide us, leading us into situations that might not be tenable, publicly at least. See our dealings with Saudi Arabia; they kill a journalist at their embassy in Turkey on what is their soil and we bat no more than an eye at them to keep our access to their oil and in support of their opposition to Iran in the proxy war waged in Syria.[118] As a result, we decide what to do based on what exactly it is we get from a deal being made at that time.

---

116    Peter G. Peterson Foundation, "U.S. Defense Spending Compared to Other Countries," accessed March 21, 2019, https://www.pgpf.org/chart-archive/0053_defense-comparison.

117    US Department of State, "Spirit of 76," accessed March 21, 2019, https://diplomaticrooms.state.gov/Item/?id=ea917e86-0152-e711-8106-1458d04eb810.

118    Al Jazeera, "Jamal Khashoggi Case: All the Latest Updates," February 12, 2019, https://www.aljazeera.com/news/2018/10/jamal-khashoggi-case-latest-updates-181010133542286.html.

Sometimes, we build some good bridges for long-term engagements. At other times, we send in planes that can get in and out real fast to get whatever we need. Overall, we go forth regardless of the stretch of soil that lies before us. Have a great day, all."

Pompeo left the room quite quickly. Patricia from earlier stated, "All right folks. We have another tour here shortly, so I need to get you guys out and them in. Thanks for visiting, but remember, your dealings with others is no different than our work internationally with other nations. We have been allies with some countries for over a century and been at odds with others. Your foreign policy is how you best interact with others. Are you always at odds and quarreling? Are you making catty remarks that come back to bite you? Your tools are our tools; they just have a different name attached to them."

Of note, I don't know how or why, but when I returned to my hotel room that night, there was an informational pamphlet on becoming a courier for the State Department waiting for me at the hotel.[119] It felt nice to be recruited.

---

119    https://www.state.gov/m/ds/about/c77947.htm

**QUESTIONS TO CONSIDER** REGARDING AMERICAN FOREIGN POLICY:

1. The first main discussion topic of the chapter discusses the advice given by George Washington regarding our country's future foreign policy. Please explain what that advice consisted of, the advice you deem most prudent to follow, and why, in detail.

2. The second main discussion topic of the chapter discusses the major players in foreign policy. Please identify who the players are, rank them in order from most to least important in your opinion, and identify why you put them in that order, in detail.

3. The third main discussion topic of the chapter discusses our goals for foreign policy. Please identify what those goals are, rank them in order from most to least important in your opinion, and identify why you put them in that order, in detail.

4. The fourth main discussion topic of the chapter discusses the different eras in foreign policy. Please explain what the four main eras are, the one you feel is best for us as a country to head back to or remain in, and why, in detail.

5. The fifth main discussion topic of the chapter discusses the two schools of thought in foreign policy. Please identify the two schools and explain what the schools consist of, the one you feel matches the way you like to deal with people overall, and why, in detail.

6. The sixth main discussion topic of the chapter discusses the enemies of the United States over time. Please identify what those enemies are and what they consist of, the enemy that relates most to your life, and why, in detail.

7. The final main discussion topic of the chapter discusses the tools of foreign policy. Please identify each of the tools and explain what each tool consists of, the tool that you like to use the most when dealing with other people, and why, in detail.

# Chapter 27

# Civil Liberties

# Difference between Civil Rights and Civil Liberties

When I woke up this morning, my head had an excruciating amount of pain. I've never had a migraine before, but I assume that this amount of pain was what one would feel if they had one. I wasn't back in my hotel room in a nice warm and cozy bed as I had hoped. Instead, I found myself on top of a hard metal bench surrounded by a sort of people that I would not say that I have ever had relations with of any kind, much less being locked in a small eight-by-ten-foot jail cell together. No matter how I sliced it, today was not getting off to a great start. Being stuck where I was, and the time being 6:00 a.m. per the clock on the wall outside the cell, I spent the next half hour muttering to myself the possible ways that I could have found myself in this predicament. About 20 minutes in, though, it hit me: I had eaten the pie I had bought early yesterday on my way home from the Diplomatic Reception Rooms tour, and apparently that pie had gone bad, or worse, there was something less than desirable in the pie that I reacted to. The latter seemed more likely, based on the freshness and good visual appeal of the pie itself.

With that realization in mind, I rose into a sitting position, took better note of my surroundings, stood, walked to the front of the cell, and yelled, "Hello, anybody out there? What do I gotta do to get out of here? Hello?"

For around ten minutes, I got no response other than those of my fellow cell mates telling me to hush my mouth for waking them. My favorite was, "You're in jail moron, and they will tell you where you can go and when you can go there. Have you not read the 13th Amendment to the US Constitution?"

I replied, "No, but why do you bring it up, smelly?"

The man rose and yelled, "Man, that smell's you, but since you ask, I'm a constitutional lawyer here in DC, and that tells you all you need to know about me. For the 13th Amendment though, specifically section 1, which reads, 'Neither slavery nor involuntary servitude, except as a punishment for crime of which the party shall have been duly convicted, shall exist within the United States, or any place subject to their jurisdiction,'[1] you and I are now slaves to the man, the government, the 5-0, whatever you want to call them until we have served time for our crime (figure 27.1)."

I replied, "I thought we had gotten rid of slavery with that amendment?"

The man replied, "Private slavery, yes, but with a strict interpretation of the document the government still retains that right as a punishment for you and me when we break the law. "

I could only think in my head now of the terrible mistakes that I have made and the untenable consequences to come. I asked the guy, "What else can you tell me about the Constitution regarding our current predicament?

The man asked, "Your civil rights or your civil liberties?"

I replied, "How about both?"

---

1    U.S. Constitution, Amendment 13, section 1.

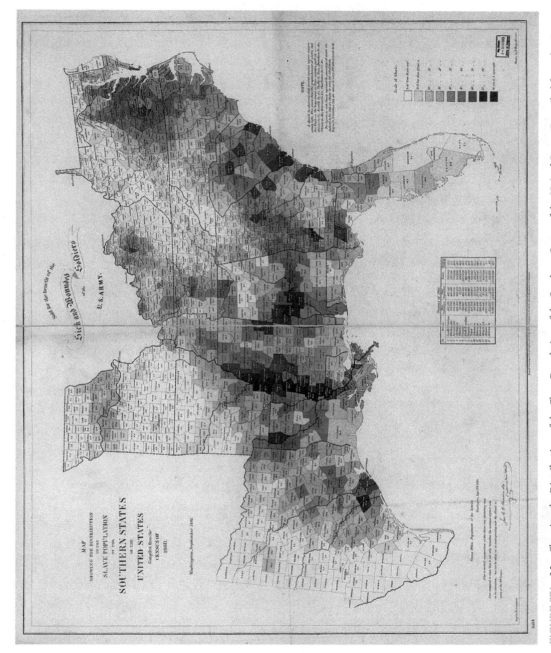

FIGURE 27.1 Map Showing the Distribution of the Slave Population of the Southern States of the United States Compiled from the Census of 1860.

The man replied, "Well then, where to begin? How about definitions. Civil rights 'concern the basic right to be free from unequal treatment based on certain protected characteristics (race, gender, disability, etc.) in settings such as employment, education, housing, and access to public facilities.'[2] You have a civil rights issue when you face discrimination in a setting due to a protected characteristic preventing you from accessing something, like when a potential landlord refuses to rent an apartment to you based on the color of your skin. On the other hand, civil liberties 'concern basic rights and freedoms that are guaranteed—either explicitly identified in the Bill of Rights and the Constitution or interpreted or inferred through the years by legislatures or the courts by the government.'[3] The former concerns ensuring fairness in life when dealing with other people while the latter provides fairness in life when dealing with the government. Now given the fact that we are stuck here behind bars, liberties are our game for today, but talking about one always leads to the other."

I nodded in concurrence to the information gathered and followed up by asking, between grunts made by our other cell mates to hush up, "So what are some other examples of my rights that I should be knowledgeable of under our current predicament?"

Before the man could answer, he rose and waddled his way over to the toilet in the room that had no privacy barriers and relieved himself. He flushed the toilet, buttoned his pants back up, and returned to his metal bunk. He stated, "That depends on where you are, as the federal government and state governments are all separate legal entities."

I interjected, "I spoke with the US secretary of the interior a few days ago. We talked about marijuana use and how each state had different standards for it, like how some states ban the sale, use, and possession altogether while other states allow for medical usage and still others allow for full recreational usage. It's quite a patchwork of laws come to think of it now that I mention the circumstances."

The man continued, "Exactly, and for some more extreme rights and liberties think about your right to exist. Back in Argentina during the Dirty War of 1976 to 1983 (figure 27.2), an estimated thirty thousand people disappeared as part of

FIGURE 27.2   Memorial to the Disappeared

2     Findlaw, "Civil Rights vs. Civil Liberties," accessed March 21, 2019, https://civilrights.findlaw.com/civil-rights-overview/civil-rights-vs-civil-liberties.html.

3     Ibid.

a political war led by the army against left-wing political parties who were protesting the right-wing government. No trials ever occurred, and many people were taken away, blindfolded, and never seen again. Most went to a detention center of some kind where they were tortured for information until made mad to the world. Following that, they were taken on death flights and dumped into the Atlantic Ocean after having blocks of cement tied to their ankles to help hasten their drownings and disappearances."[4]

I tuned out of the conversation for a moment, swallowed the vomit that had come into my throat at hearing those words, and then prayed to God that I would not face a similar fate today. Once the man realized that I had tuned out, he yelled, "Dammit boy, pay attention. We don't have anything else to do for now, so we are going to talk about this stuff that you are unaware of that could save your life. You could have killed somebody while you were out there last night and face hardtime if you don't get your things in order post haste. Speaking of getting things in order, we're damn lucky to have a lot of the liberties and rights that we have at all."

I interjected, "What do you mean, lucky to have them at all?"

The man yelled in his best Medea impression, "Oh good Lord dear child, pay attention. We have a lot of work to do with you. For this topic, we need to go back to the founding of our country."

I interjected, "You mean the Constitutional Convention of 1787?"

The man replied, "The one and only. Remember, the original purpose of that meeting was to hash out differences between the states regarding the Articles of Confederation. After weeks of arguing, the founding fathers decided that in that situation the best resolution for all would be, to begin with, a whole new document . . . er . . . Constitution for the country, a fresh start to the country so to speak. In the document that was produced, certain protections from government were enshrined, most notably article 1, section 9, clauses 2 and 3, that provide for '[t]he Privilege of the Writ of Habeas Corpus [to] not be suspended, unless when in Cases of Rebellion or Invasion the public Safety may require it . . . [and] No Bill of Attainder or ex post facto Law shall be passed.'[5] In short, unless anarchy envelops the country, you and I as part of the criminal process must be presented to a judge in a court of law before punitive proceedings may begin, while section 3 ensures that '[a] legislative act that singles out an individual or group for punishment without a trial'[6] cannot be enacted or

---

4    Fern Coll, "Who Were the Disappeared?," *Chimu Blog*, December 10, 2016, https://www.chimuadventures.com/blog/2016/12/dirty-war-argentina.

5    U.S. Constitution, article 1, section 9, clauses 2 and 3.

6    "Bill of Attainder," accessed March 21, 2019, http://www.techlawjournal.com/glossary/legal/attainder.htm.

enforced alongside no punishable act committed when said act was legal that is now illegal can be punished in a court of law."

I asked aloud, "Hey, isn't there something about knighthood in there?"

The man furthered, "That's article 1, section 9, clause 8, that reads, '[n]o Title of Nobility shall be granted by the United States: And no Person holding any Office of Profit or Trust under them, shall, without the Consent of the Congress, accept of any present, Emolument, Office, or Title, of any kind whatever, from any King, Prince, or foreign State.'[7] In short, there can be no formally created class of citizenry higher than others, alongside those in power being restricted from accepting gifts or ranking of any kind from another state or head of one. Depending on who you ask, President Trump is currently in hot water over this clause. This point is the argument made in *Blumenthal et al. v. Trump*. That case argues that President Trump is violating the emoluments clause of the Constitution due to the potential conflict of interests that arise from his shares in ownership of the Trump Organization that is still operating while he is in office via the Trump Organization's numerous business dealings with and in other states, via those states approving of trademarks, paying for rooms and events at Trump properties, renting space, and other unknown items with other countries that have certainly been expedited due to Trump's position as president of the country.[8] Granted, Congress can always say, 'Go for it with those business deals due to your company being so large and it being complicated for you to separate yourself from the company to have the whole issue go away,' but seeing as how *Blumenthal et al.* refers to a group of congressional people, that won't likely happen anytime soon. Either way, the case is in the hands of the federal court system now.[9] Taking this case a bit further, if the charges rendered against President Trump become criminal in nature, the *Blumenthal et al.* case is currently a civil court matter for reference; the president would have the right to a jury trial in the matter, as article 3, section 2, clause 3, indicates, 'The Trial of all Crimes, except in Cases of Impeachment, shall be by Jury.'[10] Of note, the Seventh Amendment guarantees a right to a civil trial by jury as well."[11]

I replied, "I bet if there is negligence found in the civil trial by President Trump impeachment charges will be filed instead, but I guess that they would also need to show that any payments directly impacted his decision-making, which is a lot harder to do for a conviction. What else came directly from the original articles of the Constitution?"

---

7    U.S. Constitution, article 1, section 9, clauses 10.
8    Constitutional Accountability Center, "Blumenthal, et al. v. Trump," accessed March 21, 2019, https://www.theusconstitution.org/litigation/trump-and-foreign-emoluments-clause.
9    Ibid.
10   U.S. Constitution, article 3, section 3, clauses 3.
11   U.S. Constitution, Amendment 7.

The man the replied, "That's it."

I sat dumbfounded. "What do you mean, that's it?"

The man furthered, "As originally written, those are the only civil liberties granted to or banned for the regular citizenry."

I muttered, "Seems a bit lacking, seeing as how we had had that whole Revolutionary War to get away from King George III who had committed so many grievances against us, not to mention that entire Declaration of Independence thing that spelled out said objections in detail, 23 if I'm not mistaken, such as my personal favorite, 'For cutting off our Trade with all parts of the world'[12] that I enshrined in my head due to my record mark selling popcorn back in the day with the Scouts[13] being threatened by a den mom who argued that I should only trade in my neighborhood lest I make her son feel bad."

The man concluded, "Okay, but you are right. The issue is you are also looking at the issue out of context. Our founding fathers did want to include more liberties, just as the citizenry at the time led most notably by George Mason of Virginia did. The problem is, they were more focused on seeking the establishment of the updated version of the country's government following our disastrous time under the Articles of Confederation and had to let a few things go by the wayside to advance their cause as a group.[14] For example, no ruling on voting rights were rendered until Amendment 15 became ratified in February 1870, when New York and Nebraska did so to ensure that no restrictions could be made on account of race, with the next major item, protection of voting rights for women, not coming until August 1920, when Tennessee ratified the 19th Amendment[15] (figure 27.3). Hell, we didn't even establish a minimum voting age until July 1, 1971, when we ratified the 26th Amendment establishing 18 as that minimum (figure 27.4), and the banishment of poll taxes and being prevented from voting for not paying taxes of any kind didn't come around until January 23, 1964, when we passed the 24th Amendment.[16] Even funnier regarding voting rights, those living in our nation's capital couldn't even vote for president until March 29, 1961, when we passed the 23rd Amendment giving them electors in the Electoral College equal to that of the least-populated state in the Union.[17] Residents in

---

12    U.S. Declaration of Independence, indictment 16.

13    https://www.trails-end.com

14    History.com Editors, "Bill of Rights Passes Congress," March 3, 2010, https://www.history.com/this-day-in-history/bill-of-rights-passes-congress.

15    U.S. Constitution, Amendments 15 and 19.

16    U.S. Constitution, Amendments 24 and 26.

17    U.S. Constitution, Amendment 23.

FIGURE 27.3   Women's Suffrage Protest

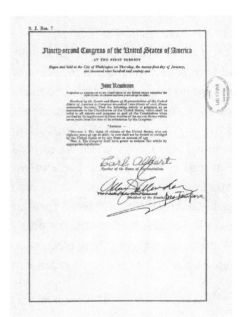

FIGURE 27.4   Joint Resolution Proposing the Twenty-sixth Amendment to the United States Constitution.

DC only have a delegate to Congress in the House and no senators like other US territories.[18] Lastly, we didn't obtain the right to directly elect our US senators until the passage of the 17th Amendment on April 8, 1913, that took this right from our state legislators, weakening their checks and balances over the federal government.[19] Together, this gave the founding fathers at the convention the look of 'Meh?' on the matter to the populace."

## How We Got the Bill of Rights

I replied, "So what happened?"

The man argued, "That would be the first order of business in the new Congress. Led by James Madison, on September 25, 1789, the House of Representatives first approved of 17 different amendments, of which 12 went on to receive the necessary Senate approval to go before the states.

---

18   Christopher Davis, "Delegates to the U.S. Congress: History and Current Status" (report, Congressional Research Service, 2015), https://fas.org/sgp/crs/misc/R40555.pdf.

19   U.S. Constitution, Amendment 17.

Of those 12, by December of 1791, the states had ratified 10 of the 12 potential amendments that went on to be known as the Bill of Rights[20] (figure 27.5). Of note, the two other amendments not to receive ratification dealt with representation of Congress based on the 1789 population and the ability of Congress to raise their pay, the latter of which went on to receive ratification by the states in 1992, 203 years after its first proposal, thanks to ratification of the 27th Amendment.[21] The lawmaking process can be slow under our current system of government, though one time that our government acted fast on something was on January 16, 1919, when they prohibited the production and sale, but not the consumption, of alcohol via ratification of the 18th Amendment, only to go back 14 years later when it became obvious that nobody was following the law when on December 5, 1933, we ratified the 21st Amendment repealing the 18th. This chaos gives a lot of insight on regulating morality as many people will keep on doing something no matter what the circumstances are."

FIGURE 27.5    The US Bill of Rights

20    NCC Staff, "On This Day, Congress Proposes the Bill of Rights to the States," *Constitution Daily* (blog), National Constitution Center, September 25, 2018, https://constitutioncenter.org/blog/on-this-day-congress-proposes-the-bill-of-rights-to-the-states.
21    U.S. Constitution, Amendment 27.

I celebrated to the chagrin of my neighbors, "Isn't that the idea, and who cares? We are now protected from the government! Woohoo! Wait a minute. Why aren't you not happy as I am right now at this information?"

The man questioned, "What do you mean by *government*?"

I replied, "You know, the government. States, the feds, and the locals. What am I missing here?"

The man furthered, "Boy, I said it earlier. I'll repeat it; you need to keep on reading. Look at this."

## How the Bill of Rights Was Applied to the States

The man handed me a pocket version of the Constitution that he was still able to hold on to for some reason. I was told to open to page 5 and then read aloud a highlighted paragraph. The paragraph read, "*Congress* shall make no law respecting . . ."

After a minute of silence, I rambled aloud, "These amendments then only restrict the federal government from violating these rights. Accordingly, the states can do as they please on these matters due to their unitary status over local governments and strict separation of power from the feds based on the Tenth Amendment, which reads, 'The powers not delegated to the United States by the Constitution, nor prohibited by it to the States, are reserved to the States respectively, or to the people.'[22] That ain't good, is it?"

The man noted, "No, no it's not."

The man that I'd been speaking with continued, "Like what you learned with Secretary Zinke, the process of getting these protections from the federal government to also be applied to the state government's powers is also a slow-moving process that didn't exist until the 1930s."

I interjected, "Explain."

The man furthered, "Simple: Late great 1833 and the Supreme Court decision in *Barron v. the Mayor and City Council of Baltimore, Maryland*.[23] In this case, Barron, the owner of a profitable deep-water wharf within the limits of the city of Baltimore, faced damages from actions taken by the city when they, as part of their municipal functions, repaved and regraded streets that brought in sediment from the surrounding hills that ruined the ability of Barron to profitably operate his business.[24] As the actions of the city caused damages, Barron

---

22    U.S. Constitution, Amendment 10.

23    Legal Information Institute, "Barron v. Mayor & City Council of Baltimore," accessed March 21, 2019, https://www.law.cornell.edu/supremecourt/text/32/243.

24    Ibid.

argued before the court that under the eminent domain clause of the Fifth Amendment of the Constitution the city owed him damages.[25] The Supreme Court in their decision, written by Chief Justice John Marshall, ruled that the clause only serves as a limitation on the exercise of power by the government of the United States, not the individual governments of the states, and that, accordingly, the court has no jurisdiction over the matter at hand in the suit.[26] Of note, going back to my statement earlier about how your liberties vary by location, this is another perfect example as no stipulation exists preventing the states from taking such actions on their own to protect you from their governments. The situation is just that nothing existed at the time stating that they had to provide said provisions. Pure dual era of federalism here."

I replied, "That sucks. So where did we go from there?"

## Civil Rights Prescribed by the Constitution

The man went on, "Well, we fought the Civil War from 1861 to 1865. In the aftermath of that conflict, we passed the Reconstruction, aka the Civil War, Amendments.[27] We already discussed the 13th Amendment banning slavery and the 15th preventing discrimination regarding voting and race, but the real kicker for change came with the 14th Amendment, section 1, that reads, "All persons born or naturalized in the United States, and subject to the jurisdiction thereof, are citizens of the United States and the state wherein they reside. No state shall make or enforce any law which shall abridge the privileges or immunities of citizens of the United States; nor shall any state deprive any person of life, liberty, or property, without due process of law; nor deny to any person within its jurisdiction the equal protection of the laws.'"[28]

I noted, "There is a lot to that amendment. Don't be afraid to flesh that one out a bit more, please."

The man stated, "I would if you'd stop interrupting me, boy. Either way, the first sentence established the doctrine of birthright citizenship where if you are born in the United States and not the product of a representative of a foreign state here on official business, you are a full-fledged citizen, no questions asked. The arcane term *anchor baby* comes up in discussions here, as many examples exist of women coming to United States territory to give birth,

---

25    Ibid.
26    Ibid.
27    Documents of Freedom, "The End of Slavery and the Reconstruction Amendments," accessed March 21, 2019, https://www.docsoffreedom.org/student/readings/the-end-of-slavery-and-the-reconstruction-amendments.
28    U.S. Constitution, Amendment 14, section 1.

either legally, as part of birth tourism, most notably in Saipan by Chinese mothers,[29] and illegally, as part of a long-term scheme to obtain welfare benefits and eventual sponsorship of themselves later in their lives by the child by sneaking across the border. The sponsorship for citizenship happens when the child born here comes of age so that the child may move to the US to put the process into motion due to them having US citizenship—thanks to our country's immigration laws being set up for such actions to occur.[30] In the world, only 35 countries offer universal birthright, *jus soli* if you are a Latin language lover, with an additional four offering it under certain circumstances.[31] Of developed countries, only ourselves, Canada, and Luxembourg fall on either list with a sheer majority of the other countries coming from North and South America."[32]

I noted, "Understood, get born here, and you are one of us; please continue."

The man went on, "The first third of the second sentence there, formally known as the privileges and immunities clause, prevents the states from taking actions that would strip citizenship of citizens and other like matter, but for our discussion here, the final two-thirds is what matters most; the due process and equal protection clauses. Specifically, the middle-third, that reads once again, 'nor shall any state deprive any person of life, liberty, or property, without due process of law,' is the crux of the matter. This one sentence single-handedly applies the protection of rights found in the Bill of Rights that the federal government may not abridge to the states."

I interjected, "So what's the problem? Let's celebrate!!"

The man, now shaking his head in utter disappointment at me, asked, "Did I specifically say that it's time to celebrate?"

I replied, "No, but you said the Bill of Rights is now applied to the states, and it does make sense to think that an appropriate reaction."

The man continued, "Well, it does, but remember for that to be the law of the land, the Constitution must be interpreted to mean as such, and with the dual federalism of the era that wasn't the case. Remember Jim Crow laws of the late 1800s and the first half of the 1900s, the concept of separate but equal, and the like? I wouldn't say that the concept of

---

29    Jon Emont and Nancy Borowick, "Saipan: The Island Where Chinese Mothers Deliver American Babies," *Wall Street Journal*, December 22, 2017, https://www.wsj.com/articles/the-island-where-chinese-mothers-deliver-american-babies-1513852203.

30    Federation for American Immigration Reform, "Birthright Citizenship," last modified August 2010, http://www.fairus.org/issue/societal-impact/birthright-citizenship.

31    Ashley Collman, "More than 30 Other Countries Recognize Birthright Citizenship—Here's the Full List," *Business Insider*, October 30, 2018, https://www.businessinsider.com/countries-that-recognize-birthright-citizenship-jus-soli-2018-10.

32    Ibid.

applying the Bill of Rights to the states was off to the races from the start. That would take still more time. Another 65 years to be precise, until 1937."

I asked, "What happened in 1937?"

The man stated, "The Supreme Court strikes back of course, against itself this time. In 1937 the court decided that the due process clause of the 14th Amendment protected rights that are 'of the very essence of a scheme of ordered liberty' and that they should begin the process of applying those rights over time as justiciable violations arose so that they could determine if the infringed right met the test they had established.[33] In the case in question that brought about the ruling to slowly apply the Bill of Rights to state governments, *Palko v. Connecticut*, the problem for Palko, officially Palka as court documents misspelled his name, was that the violation of the double jeopardy clause of the Fifth Amendment that he filed his appeal on was felt to not meet that 'ordered liberty' test as he was charged with first-degree murder for killing two police officers, but convicted of second-degree murder giving him a life sentence rather than the death penalty for the killing two police officers, and that the actions by the state of Connecticut, in the second trial, only corrected an error made in the first and didn't count as a whole new trial and that allowed him to go on and get executed by the State of Connecticut via electrocution."[34]

I could only reply, "Poor Palka. Either way though, to me at least, that sounds exactly like double jeopardy as they held a whole new trial for a crime that he was already convicted of committing. If the state erred in its action, why punish the guy already getting the short end of the stick even more? Regardless, what do we call this process today?"

The man offered, "That process is what we in the industry refer to as selective incorporation or, 'a constitutional doctrine through which the first ten amendments of the United States Constitution (known as the Bill of Rights) are made applicable to the states through the due process clause of the Fourteenth Amendment'[35] as established by the ruling in *Palko v. Connecticut*. Since that ruling, the entirety of the First, Second, and Fourth Amendments have been applied to states, while the Fifth Amendment is lacking that status due to the right to indictment by a grand jury not being incorporated. The Sixth Amendment is lacking due to the right to a jury selected from residents of crime location not being incorporated, and the Eighth Amendment is lacking due to the prohibition against excessive fines not being incorporated.[36] The entirety of the Third, Seventh, Ninth, and Tenth Amendments have not

---

33    Legal Information Institute, "Palko v. Connecticut," accessed March 21, 2019, https://www.law.cornell.edu/supremecourt/text/302/319.

34    Ibid.

35    Legal Information Institute, "Incorporation Doctrine," accessed March 21, 2019, https://www.law.cornell.edu/wex/incorporation_doctrine.

36    Ibid.

been applied in any right.[37] The Tenth Amendment is irrelevant to this discussion because it already applies to the states, thanks to the wording of the amendment: 'The powers not delegated to the United States by the Constitution, nor prohibited by it to the states, are reserved to the states respectively, or to the people.'[38] The eighth and sixth will more likely than not be fully applied by the end of the year due to the case of *Tyson Timbs v. Indiana* over the issue of excessive fines being brought before the court of the state of Indiana's decision to confiscate his $42,000 Land Rover over the events of drug deal where he used the car to drive to a sale of drugs to undercover police officers. Overall, applying the Bill of Rights to state government proceedings is still an ongoing affair requiring the opinion of the court to settle disputes on the issue."

I remarked, "Your comment earlier about the slow-moving process of lawmaking in the United States sounds all too much the norm now."

It was at that moment, a bit before 8:00 a.m., that a guard walked down to the gangway between cells banging a gong to wake everyone up and stating, "Chow in five boys. Chow in five."

I asked, "So what do we talk about now?"

The man stated, "I'm going to ponder whether we get syrup with our pancakes."

I stated, "So what happens next to us in the legal process? What does the Constitution offer protection-wise for us in our upcoming series of events?"

The man stated, "You are like a lamb thrown to the wolves here, aren't you boy?"

I could only reply, "Well I'm just here in DC to learn about how to join the governing ranks best, and quite frankly I'm endeavoring through a side I wish not to be a part of any more."

The man continued, "Good. I think it's best that we first then discuss the Fourth Amendment, which reads, 'The right of the people to be secure in their persons, houses, papers, and effects, against unreasonable searches and seizures, shall not be violated, and no Warrants shall issue, but upon probable cause, supported by Oath or affirmation, and particularly describing the place to be searched, and the persons or things to be seized.'[39] In short, the police when investigating a crime or going about their business can't search you and confiscate something without probable cause or obtaining a warrant to do such a thing."

I asked, "What is probable cause?"

The man furthered, "Probable cause is 'the legal standard by which a police officer has the right to make an arrest, conduct a personal or property search, or obtain a warrant

---

37    Ibid.

38    Tim Zubizaretta, "Supreme Court Hears Arguments on Whether Eighth Amendment Excessive Fines Clause Applies to States," Jurist, November 29, 2018, https://www.jurist.org/news/2018/11/supreme-court-hears-arguments-on-whether-eighth-amendment-excessive-fines-clause-applies-to-states.

39    U.S. Constitution, Amendment 4.

for arrest. While many factors contribute to a police officer's level of authority in a given situation, probable cause requires facts or evidence that would lead a reasonable person to believe that a suspect has committed a crime.[40] This could be when an officer of the law smells an illegal substance on you, he or she sees you in the process of buying or selling a banned substance, etc.[41] Also, don't forget about the time and place of something occurring like being in a back alley at 2:00 a.m. and then making a run for it when a police officer asks to speak with you.[42] Most importantly, don't try to figure out if a cop has probable cause—say, 'No, I do not consent to a search,' and the officer should pull back from what they are doing and then either let you go or wait for a warrant to proceed.[43] Either way, don't confess to anything as that gives them permission.'[44]

I replied as granola bars were handed to us through the bars of the cell door, "Unless they already have a warrant, don't give them permission, but what if they do have a warrant?"

The man replied, "Get the hell out of their way! But, if you are so inclined, based on the amendment's end wording, 'particularly describing the place to be searched, and the persons or things to be seized,'[45] ensure that those standards are met in the warrant with your attorney later, as you can then employ the exclusionary rule, or constitutional precedent derived from *Mapp v. Ohio*[46] that 'prevents the government from using most evidence [and confessions[47]] gathered in violation of the United States Constitution'[48] if you are trying to get off the hook for something due to malfeasance by the government in question to the search. Of note, the one time that the federal, but not state, government is banned from seizing your home is if the home is to be used for quartering soldiers during peace and war without your consent based on the Third Amendment preventing the government from doing so.[49] Also, now that I think about it, the one thing that you can be compelled to do by the constitution is to pay a tax on all of your income per the 16th Amendment, which reads, 'The Congress shall have power to lay and collect taxes on incomes, from whatever source

---

40    https://www.flexyourrights.org/faqs/probable-cause
41    Ibid.
42    Ibid.
43    Ibid.
44    Ibid.
45    Ibid. 37.
46    Legal Information Institute, "Mapp v. Ohio," accessed March 21, 2019, https://www.law.cornell.edu/supremecourt/text/367/643.
47    384 U.S. 436 Miranda v. Arizona.
48    Legal Information Institute, "Exclusionary Rule," last modified June 2017, https://www.law.cornell.edu/wex/exclusionary_rule.
49    U.S. Constitution, Amendment 3.

derived, without apportionment among the several States, and without regard to any census or enumeration.'"[50]

I interjected, "That sounds all good as to what happens before you get into court, but what about when you get into court?"

The man stated, "Information on that subject comes from the Fifth Amendment, which reads, "No person shall be held to answer for a capital, or otherwise infamous crime, unless on a presentment or indictment of a Grand Jury, except in cases arising in the land or naval forces, or in the Militia, when in actual service in time of War or public danger; nor shall any person be subject for the same offence to be twice put in jeopardy of life or limb; nor shall be compelled in any criminal case to be a witness against himself, nor be deprived of life, liberty, or property, without due process of law; nor shall private property be taken for public use, without just compensation.'"

I had to state for sanity reasons, "Break that down for me, please."

Sounding eloquent, the man furthered, "Of course, good sir. The second and fourth sections, as separated by semicolons, no double jeopardy and eminent domain requirements, we discussed earlier in the day, but the first and third are new for us here. The first section presents the requirement for a grand jury session to be held to have a formal indictment be handed down before that of the petit-slash-trial jury in all criminal cases excluding times of war, in military service, or if the country is under duress. On the other hand, the third covers your right to not self-incriminate, i.e., state anything that will cause you harm. Therefore, people may plead the fifth in a trial to not have charges be brought against them and refuse to speak with the cops when they investigate a crime."

I interjected, "Is that it for what goes on before trial; should we move on to what goes on during the trial in court?"

The man stated, "I think it is about time to advance on, but one thing to keep in mind..."

A guard came to our door and shouted, "Cove, Champ, and Smith, John, step forward." This event was followed by the bars sliding open and us being ushered forward and handcuffed before transfer. Over the next ten minutes, we were walked through corridors, searched, sequestered, and finally marched into a room with a camera and a TV. The guard then instructed, "Wait here, when the TV turns on answer the questions posed by the judge."

Over the next ten minutes, Smith and I waited. After a minute, though, Smith stated, "Welcome to arraignment court where we enter our pleas and the path that our fates takes us begins."

I whispered, "What advice you got now?"

---

50    U.S. Constitution, Amendment 16.

Doe answered, "What I tried getting at earlier before we were interrupted is from the Eighth Amendment and your right that '[e]xcessive bail shall not be required,'[51] which means in short that the government can require you to pay a bail, or 'a sum of money given to a law court by a person accused of a crime so that the person can be released until the trial, at which time the money will be returned,'[52] but that amount must be in line with the crime."

I stated, "So if I'm in here for public intoxication, I can't be forced to pay a million bucks to get out of here today?"

Smith stated, "That's correct, and the remainder of the Eighth Amendment comes into play after the trial, assuming you go to one, and you get convicted and punished as the latter two sections of the Amendment prevent 'excessive fines imposed, nor cruel and unusual punishments inflicted,' which means in short that you can't be fined a billion dollars for public intoxication as that is an amount that maybe 100 people in the whole country can pay, nor can you be put through a physical punishment that is deemed cruel and unusual."

I interjected, "What do you mean by *cruel and unusual*?"

Smith stated, "There is quite a debate on what exactly is 'cruel and unusual,'[53] but there are some general guidelines."

I remarked, "Like what?"

Smith argued, "When it comes to assigning the punishment, said punishment cannot be duly unnecessary, cruel, inhuman, or degrading, arbitrary in nature, nor can the punishment be against public will and be something that is clearly rejected throughout society.[54] The main case cited on this matter is *Gregg v. Georgia* that found that capital punishment, death sentences, are legal and not cruel and unusual in all cases so long as a defined, process and procedure is entered into when handing down such as sentence via a separation of guilt and punishment phases, jury findings that severity of the crime and attributes of the convicted merit such a punishment, and the punishment can be shown to be inline with other similar cases and sentencing."[55]

I inquired, "Where does that leave us today?"

Smith stated, "Looking at capital cases, firing squads, hanging, gassing, lethal injection, electrocution, and life imprisonment are allowed while burning at the stake, being drawn and quartered, dismemberment, and anything for minors, under 16 in most cases, is not

---

51    U.S. Constitution, Amendment 8.

52    https://dictionary.cambridge.org/us/dictionary/english/bail

53    Bryan A. Stevenson and John F. Stinneford, "The Eighth Amendment," National Constitution Center, accessed March 21, 2019, https://constitutioncenter.org/interactive-constitution/amendments/amendment-viii.

54    Stevenson and Stinneford, "The Eighth Amendment."

55    Oyez, "Gregg v. Georgia," accessed March 21, 2019, https://www.oyez.org/cases/1975/74-6257.

allowed.[56] Of note, like what we said before with your rights and liberties varying from state to state, that principle applies here too as some states have no death penalty and each state may choose their punishments.[57] Regarding lesser crimes, life imprisonment for public intoxication isn't allowed as the punishment doesn't match the crime."

A voice echoed from afar, "Mr. Smith, wonderful to see you again. Are we sober yet?"

Doe stated, "Yes, ma'am, I do believe so."

The voice coming from a judge on the TV screen stated, "Good, let's begin."

Smith stated, "I'd like to make a statement. The lad here in the room is amid an adventure to learn about his civil rights."

The judge stated, "You two are the only ones on my docket for today, so go ahead. I know that you are an attorney and will provide good information on the subject, but seeing as where we are, let's focus on the Sixth Amendment, please."

Smith said, "Mr. Cove, the Sixth Amendment reads in the first part that, '[i]n all criminal prosecutions, the accused shall enjoy the right to a speedy and public trial.'[58] For us today, that means that we can compel the state, represented by the prosecution attorney, to move ahead with the trial if they continually attempt to delay proceedings and hamper our lives. Also, our trial must be done in public, as our proceedings cannot be held in private to ensure that the prosecution doesn't pull anything funny. In the second part, Amendment 6 reads that the verdict in said trial should be given 'by an impartial jury of the State and district wherein the crime shall have been committed, which district shall have been previously ascertained by law.'[59] Therefore, if your case goes to trial, your trial may be moved to ensure that the jury is not biased, as occurred in the O.J. Simpson murder trial where the court granted a change of venue that saw the trial setting be moved from Santa Monica to Downtown Los Angeles."[60]

The judge on the TV screen chimed in and said, "To ensure a speedy arraignment as part of your trial proceedings I'll take over here and discuss the next and the last part of Amendment 6 that requires the accused 'to be informed of the nature and cause of the accusation; . . . [and] to have the Assistance of Counsel for his defence.'[61] Accordingly, Mr. Cove, you are formally charged with public intoxication. How do you plead?"

---

56  Death Penalty Information Center, "Methods of Execution," accessed March 21, 2019, https://death-penaltyinfo.org/methods-execution.

57  Ibid.

58  U.S. Constitution, Amendment 6.

59  Ibid.

60  Michael Abrams, "Venue Change in Simpson Case," *Los Angeles Times*, October 12, 1995, http://articles.latimes.com/1995-10-12/local/me-55971_1_prosecution-gil-garcetti-peremptory-challenges.

61  U.S. Constitution, Amendment 6.

I responded, "After speaking with my attorney, Mr. Smith here next to me, as per my constitutional rights, I plead guilty and toss myself on the mercy of the court."

The judge replied, "The court accepts your plea and releases you on 30 days of probation and no fine or court costs.[62] Please don't let me see you again in here, young man, and safe travels back to Texas. Of note, before you go, the final portion of the Sixth Amendment that we have not covered reads that a person may 'be confronted with the witnesses against him; to have compulsory process for obtaining witnesses in his favor.'[63] Accordingly, had the case here gone to trial, you have the right to have all witnesses brought before you to testify and call those in your defense with help from the courts, a character witness so to speak in regular parlance. Now, in getting those witnesses to court, don't forget to send out your subpoenas, 'a writ commanding a person designated in it to appear in court under a penalty for failure,'[64] or face the possibility of those people not having any incentive to show up for your defense other than out of the good of their heart, which I, as an attorney and judge, would not count on. Teeth in the matter always help in defense and prosecution. As for you, Mr. Smith, the district is dismissing all charges due to your provision of community service here in the court and for the rest of the day in informing Mr. Cove of his rights. Lastly, you are both free to go, and I'm glad to see that either of you didn't have to take your right to defend yourself in court as per your implied right under the Sixth Amendment.[65] Good day!"

Following that, Smith and I were released from the DC Central Detention Facility (figure 27.6) at 19th Street Southeast and D Street Southeast. While making some small talk, we went north on 19th Street Southeast for six blocks to the north entrance of the Stadium-Armory Metro Station. Before going down the stairs to get onto the platform and catch a train, Smith had us sit on a bench for the nearby busses. Once seated, he contemplated, "Look west now. The building complex before you is one of the most

FIGURE 27.6   The Washington, DC, Central Detention Facility

62    Code of the District of Columbia, –"§ 24–604. Public Intoxication; Confidential Records," accessed March 21, 2019. https://code.dccouncil.us/dc/council/code/sections/24-604.html.
63    U.S. Constitution, Amendment 6.
64    https://www.merriam-webster.com/dictionary/subpoena
65    Justia US Law, "Self-Representation," accessed March 21, 2019, https://law.justia.com/constitution/us/amendment-06/16-self-representation.html.

FIGURE 27.7 D.C. Armory located at 2001 East Capitol Street, NE in Washington

diversified complexes in the district. This building is the DC Armory (figure 27.7). Not only does the complex host a 10,000-seat multi-purpose arena, it is also home to the District of Columbia National Guard.[66] The facilities are managed by the Washington Convention and Sports Authority and were constructed and opened 78 years ago, in 1941.[67] Now, what right comes to mind when you consider our setting and 'pew . . . pew . . . pew . . . pew' ringing out?"

I replied, "I'm going to bet my Second Amendment rights, which reads, 'A well regulated militia being necessary to the security of a free state, the right of the people to keep and bear arms shall not be infringed.'[68] In short, as every good Texan knows we have the right to bear arms, not own bear arms or show bare arms, but to bear armaments."

Smith mentioned, "Very good, young man, you know that you have a right here, don't you?"

I replied, "Yes sir!"

Smith furthered, "Okay then, you take the 'individual rights' model that interprets the amendment to read that an individual has the right to bear arms, which is in line with the Supreme Court's interpretation in *District of Columbia v. Heller*[69] that found that the term 'militia' and the rest of the first half of the amendment is an introductory or prefatory clause and doesn't instill or distill any right, unlike the latter half that does your right to bear arms. Had the court taken the opposing view they would be arguing for the 'collective rights' model that holds that one must first be part of a 'well organized militia' before having a right to bear arms.[70] The decision in *Heller* argued that at the time of writing a 'well organized militia' was everyone and that not taking this view would have solidified the 'type of state-sponsored force against which the Amendment was meant to protect people'[71] from."

66   https://dc.ng.mil

67   http://eventsdc.com/Venues/DCArmory.aspx

68   U.S. Constitution, Amendment 10.

69   Oyez, "District of Columbia v. Heller," accessed March 21, 2019, https://www.oyez.org/cases/2007/07-290.

70   T.J. Martinell, "The 2nd Amendment: Individual, Not Collective Rights," Tenth Amendment Center, August 29, 2015, https://tenthamendmentcenter.com/2015/08/29/the-2nd-amendment-individual-not-collective-rights.

71   Ibid 69.

I replied, "Obviously, I have the right to bear arms, but what exactly does that right involve in practice? I have a general understanding of this in Texas, but I feel that there is more to the story."

Smith noted, "Ahh, yes. The formalities of the subject go across many lines. State versus federal rights to regulate and all the key terms that are out there. The question is where to begin to discuss this matter. First, one must consider the gun being purchased. For that, one must consider the legislation put forth by the National Firearms Act of 1934.[72] From that act, the portion that still stands prominently in place today is the different defined classes of guns that range from machine guns that fire automatically and continuously once the trigger is pulled and held down to short barreled rifles and shotguns, suppressors to silence the noise made by guns, and destructive devices like bombs and grenades. Any other weapon that can be fired falls into the "Any Other Weapon" category, like handguns that can be concealed, and are not regulated by this act. The National Firearms Act was enacted following years of gangland crime that was rampant during the Prohibition era that included such notable events as the St. Valentine's Day Massacre of 1929 and the attempted assassination of President Franklin D. Roosevelt in 1933, among others. In seeking to curtail these crimes, to prevent their sale and transfer, the act required all these weapons to be registered and taxed at $200 when registering with the US Secretary of State as an owner or purchase, an amount that was quite burdensome at the time. Therefore, the average public is heavily restricted from owning automatic rifles and anything other than a handgun, or at least the purchase of said gun. Years later, the US Supreme Court decision in *Haynes v. United States* held that the federal government does have the right to regulate firearms but cannot compel someone to register a weapon that they already have, as doing so violates their Fifth Amendment rights to privacy.[73] Congress later went on to rewrite the law making it impossible for anyone except a government to register one of these weapons effectively barring their eventual ownership and purchase by private citizens."[74]

I interjected, "If I'm taking this in correctly, the federal government has a right to determine what guns I can and cannot purchase."

Smith furthered, "That's the idea, but now one must consider the actual purchase of a gun. Federal law, specifically as passed under the Gun Control Act of 1968, holds that no gun seller may sell a gun 'to any person knowing or having reasonable cause to believe that such

---

72    Bureau of Alcohol, Tobacco, Firearms and Explosives, "National Firearms Act," accessed March 21, 2019, https://www.atf.gov/rules-and-regulations/national-firearms-act.

73    Justia, "Haynes v. United States, 390 U.S. 85 (1968)," accessed March 21, 2019, https://supreme.justia.com/cases/federal/us/390/85.

74    Ibid.

person"[75] is under indictment for a felony, is a fugitive from justice, is an unlawful user of or addicted to any controlled substance, has been adjudicated as mentally defective or has been committed to any mental institution, being in the country illegally, been discharged from the armed forces under dishonorable conditions, has renounced his citizenship, is subject to a court order that restrains contact with someone, or been convicted of a misdemeanor for domestic violence."[76] To enforce this, Congress passed the Brady Handgun Violence Prevention Act[77] in 1993 that required backgrounds checks and a minimum five-day waiting period before a purchase can be made via licensed seller and created the National Instant Criminal Background Check System (NICS)[78] in 1998 to help expedite the background checks as required in the 1993 law. Of note, when you see and hear people talking about increasing gun sales regulation, closing the private seller no background check requirement loophole is what they are seeking to enact into law."

I replied, "I do believe that these acts heavily restrict the ability of large swaths of the population from owning or at least buying a gun. Where should we go from here to discuss this matter?"

Smith surmised, "It's time to bring the states back into the discussion. This is prudent, as no two states have the same restrictions and requirements for gun purchasing. For example, using data from the State Firearms Law Project at Boston University and the Gifford's Law Center that was tabulated in a summary article entitled "Understanding Key Terms in The Gun Control Debate" by Shayna Orens and Gabriele Carotti-Sha in Newslea,[79] 11 factors are identified as restricting the sale and eventual use. For now, let us focus on the seven factors that focus the state vantage on a purchase. Overall, from that report on page 6, 38 states allow you to purchase handguns at age 18, with the rest allowing you to do so at 21. For long guns, 23 states have no minimum age, 23 states allow you to buy at age 18, two at age 21, and two at lower ages (16 in Vermont and 14 in Minnesota if outside a city, within cities at 18). Also, seven states, inclusive of California, Connecticut, Hawaii, Illinois, Massachusetts, New Jersey, and Rhode Island, all require you to get a license before purchase. On top of that, five states, inclusive of California, Connecticut, Hawaii, Massachusetts, and Oregon,

75    Bureau of Alcohol, Tobacco, Firearms and Explosives, "Gun Control Act," accessed March 21, 2019, https://www.atf.gov/rules-and-regulations/gun-control-act.

76    Ibid.

77    Bureau of Alcohol, Tobacco, Firearms and Explosives, "Brady Law," accessed March 21, 2019, https://www.atf.gov/rules-and-regulations/brady-law.

78    Federal Bureau of Investigation, "National Instant Criminal Background Check System (NICS)," accessed March 21, 2019, https://www.fbi.gov/services/cjis/nics.

79    Shayna Orens and Gabriele Carotti-Sha, "Understanding Key Terms in the Gun Control Debate," Newslea, March 2, 2018, https://1.cdn.edl.io/vtJmMmYWMqtjBtRAl8XEHkP5Ltxq9X8J9NBLBMnPHy-wMnYbC.pdf.

all require sellers to report all sales without mentioning if only licensed or all sellers must do so. Beyond licenses, six states, inclusive of California, Connecticut, Hawaii, Maryland, Massachusetts, and Rhode Island, all require buyers to undergo safety training before purchase. Now with those conditions met, nine states, inclusive of California, Colorado, Connecticut, Delaware, Nevada, New York, Oregon, Rhode Island, and Washington State, all require a background check for buyers without making a note of whether it applies only for purchases through licensed sellers or for all sellers. On top of that, five states, inclusive of California, Connecticut, Hawaii, Illinois, and Rhode Island, require waiting periods before a gun sale beyond those of federal law we discussed earlier. Lastly, five states, inclusive of California, Connecticut, Hawaii, Maryland, and New York, ban ownership, or at least use, by those convicted of a misdemeanor."

I interjected, "For some states, most notably California, Connecticut, Massachusetts, and Rhode Island, citizens face a lot more restrictions on buying a gun than elsewhere. If I'm keeping track correctly, citizens in the 38 states not mentioned by you face no restrictions other than federal ones when buying a gun."

Smith held, "That is correct. Beyond that, only in Hawaii, the state with the most restrictions, must you register the ownership of a gun with the state. Therefore, most states have decided to focus on regulating the use of said guns as opposed to the purchase aspect, leaving federal law as the minimum standard, the third thing to consider when discussing guns. This transition for us brings up the debate over concealed and open carry weapons where the prior allows one to be able to carry a hidden gun outside of the house whereas the latter requires the gun to not be concealed. You can conceal carry in all 50 US states as well as the District of Columbia, but 38 states do require you to have a permit to do so, with 8 states, inclusive of California, Connecticut, Delaware, Hawaii, Maryland, Massachusetts, New Jersey, and New York, as well as DC, giving authorities wide latitude to reject applications, 15 with limited discretion to do so, and the final 15 authorities must issue the permit without restriction.[80] On the other hand, you can open carry without a license in 31 states, 15 states require a license, with five states, inclusive of California, Florida, Illinois, New York, and South Carolina, as well as the District of Columbia, banning open carry entirely."[81]

I noted, "It seems as if the states that most heavily restrict gun purchases also heavily restrict gun use."

---

80   Giffords Law Center to Prevent Gun Violence, "Concealed Carry," accessed March 21, 2019, https://lawcenter.giffords.org/gun-laws/policy-areas/guns-in-public/concealed-carry/#state.
81   Giffords Law Center to Prevent Gun Violence, "Open Carry," accessed March 21, 2019, https://lawcenter.giffords.org/gun-laws/policy-areas/guns-in-public/open-carry/#state.

Smith further commented, "We'll make causation with that correlation here in a moment, but for now, one additional restriction needs to be considered: stand your ground laws, or laws that allow people to use deadly force in self-defense in a public space. This means you can shoot your attacker, even if they have not fired, and not go to jail or prison if it is deemed that your life was in danger.[82] Otherwise, it's murder. Thirty states have such provisions on the books.[83] Of note, the four heavy hitters we identified from before, California, Connecticut, Massachusetts, and Rhode Island, and the District of Columbia, from what we've learned about, now fall into the category of not having this law on the books."[84]

At this point, I became curious and asked, "Why did you mention these heavy hitters again?"

Smith remarked, "Let's try and make that correlation I was telling you about from before. Now depending on who you ask, to keep the crime rate down, most notably violent crime, including murder and nonnegligent manslaughter, rape, robbery, aggravated assault, property crime, burglary, larceny-theft, and motor vehicle theft, that one would often consider to go along with high gun prevalence, you should have more guns in the community, under the logic that if everyone knows that everyone has a gun, then people will be less likely to go up and rob someone and vice versa, your standard pro-gun lobby view like that of the National Rifle Association.[85] Opposing that are anti-gun rights activists who feel that more guns lead to more violence, like that of the Coalition Against Gun Violence.[86] Now to get the tale of the tape, using data from the 2017 Federal Bureau of Investigation report on crime in the United States,[87] there is no correlation with either set of beliefs, as California, ranked 16th, Connecticut, ranked 44th, Massachusetts, ranked 27th, Rhode Island, ranked 43rd, and the District of Columbia, ranked 1st, are intermingled equally throughout the other states that have no real restriction on purchase or use, based on their violent crime rate per 100,000 population. Two states that seem to banter the headlines about whose side to take are Texas and California, which have nearly the same rate at 439 and 449, respectively. The district's rate is highest at 1,005 per 100,00, and the lowest is in Maine at 121 per 100,000 population. Overall, other factors are at play when determining what the crime rate in an area will be. Let's catch a train. I'm done with this subject for now."

---

82   Giffords Law Center to Prevent Gun Violence, "'Stand Your Ground' Laws," accessed March 21, 2019, https://lawcenter.giffords.org/gun-laws/policy-areas/guns-in-public/stand-your-ground-laws/#state.
83   Ibid.
84   Ibid.
85   https://home.nra.org
86   https://www.csgv.org
87   Federal Bureau of Investigation, "Crime in the United States," accessed March 21, 2019, https://ucr. fbi.gov/crime-in-the-u.s/2017/crime-in-the-u.s.-2017/topic-pages/tables/table-4.

TABLE 27.1  Violent Crime Per Capita by State in 2017

| State | Number of violent crimes in 2017 | Violent crime rate per 100k population in 2017 |
|---|---|---|
| District of Columbia | 8,236 | 1,005 |
| Alaska | 5,966 | 829 |
| New Mexico | 14,585 | 783 |
| Tennessee | 42,459 | 652 |
| Louisiana | 26,477 | 558 |
| Nevada | 19,924 | 556 |
| Arkansas | 16,563 | 555 |
| Missouri | 31,720 | 531 |
| Alabama | 25,878 | 524 |
| Arizona | 32,542 | 508 |
| South Carolina | 25,137 | 506 |
| Maryland | 29,019 | 500 |
| Oklahoma | 17,855 | 465 |
| Delaware | 4,859 | 453 |
| Michigan | 45,782 | 450 |
| California | 174,796 | 449 |
| Illinois | 56,054 | 439 |
| Texas | 121,064 | 439 |
| South Dakota | 3,636 | 422 |
| Kansas | 11,665 | 413 |
| Florida | 88,700 | 408 |
| Indiana | 26,516 | 399 |
| Montana | 3,886 | 377 |
| Colorado | 19030 | 368 |
| North Carolina | 37,767 | 363 |
| Georgia | 40,268 | 358 |
| Massachusetts | 25,975 | 358 |
| West Virginia | 6,633 | 350 |
| Wisconsin | 17,716 | 320 |
| Pennsylvania | 40,389 | 313 |
| Nebraska | 5,661 | 306 |
| Washington | 22,101 | 305 |
| Ohio | 35,759 | 298 |

| State | Number of violent crimes in 2017 | Violent crime rate per 100k population in 2017 |
|---|---|---|
| Iowa | 9,170 | 293 |
| Mississippi | 8,411 | 286 |
| Oregon | 10,983 | 282 |
| North Dakota | 1,905 | 281 |
| New York | 74,315 | 257 |
| Hawaii | 3,452 | 251 |
| Utah | 7,406 | 239 |
| Minnesota | 13,365 | 238 |
| Wyoming | 1,431 | 238 |
| Rhode Island | 2,529 | 232 |
| Connecticut | 8,180 | 228 |
| New Jersey | 21,861 | 228 |
| Idaho | 3,876 | 226 |
| Kentucky | 10,452 | 226 |
| Virginia | 18,495 | 208 |
| New Hampshire | 2,668 | 199 |
| Vermont | 851 | 165 |
| Maine | 1,649 | 121 |

We went into the adjacent Metro station. On the way down to the underground platform at the Stadium-Armory Metro Station, Smith asked, "Champ, what did we just pass through?"

I replied, "Turnstiles sir?"

Do asked, "So what do they represent?"

I responded, "The dividing line between those who have paid to ride the trains and those that haven't, a go-no-go separation, so to speak."

Smith concluded, "Very good young man. For us though, it's one item that you may come across in your time carrying, or using, a gun in spaces where guns are banned. Using your state of Texas as an example, guns are banned from polling places on election day, courts, racetracks, beyond security at the airport, within 100 feet of the Huntsville Unit in Huntsville on an execution day, in prison, liquor stores, and certain state-owned lands.[88] However, you may carry at an assisted living facility, amusement park, place of worship, and any meeting of a government entity freely unless the operator has given effective notice via oral communication,

88    Giffords Law Center to Prevent Gun Violence, "Other Location Restrictions in Texas," last modified September 14, 2018, https://lawcenter.giffords.org/other-location-restrictions-in-texas.

a card or other document on which is written the following language: 'Pursuant to Section 30.06, Penal Code (trespass by holder of license to carry a handgun), a person licensed under Subchapter H, Chapter 411, Government Code (handgun license law), may not enter this property with a handgun'; or a sign posted on the property that includes the prior quoted text in both English and Spanish, appearing in contrasting colors with block letters at least one inch in height; and displayed conspicuously clearly visible to the public.[89] Granted, due to the rise in school shootings, some schools are going in the opposite direction of banning guns in schools by arming and training their teachers to use guns to defend students."

I could only reply while waiting on the westbound train platform, "There is a lot of restrictions on the sale and use of guns sir. It seems most wise to stay at home and only shoot there, but where are we going now?"

Smith remarked, "Champ, I've saved the best for last; church!"

I stated, "First Amendment, sir?"

"Nothing's better than that, young man!"

Following that back and forth, we rode a Silver Line train eight stops to the Metro Center Metro Station that I had traversed multiple times over the past several days. We then transferred to a Red Line train going toward Shady Grove Metro Station and got off four stops later at Cleveland Park Metro Station. Along the way, Smith mentioned, "We are not going to see a lot from the inside, but we will see some impressive sights, okay?"

I replied, "Okay."

Once out of the station, we walked 3 miles west on Ordway Street Northwest and south five blocks on 34th Street Northwest. Once we made the turn south, our destination came into view. About a block out, Doe posited, "Here before us is one of the most spectacular sights in the district, Washington National Cathedral[90] (figure 27.8). The other spectacular religious sight is the Latter-Day Saints DC temple.[91] Beyond the glorious traditional stylings of the cathedral that is run by the Episcopal church, this cathedral is

FIGURE 27.8   The Washington National Cathedral, also known as the Cathedral Church of Saint Peter and Saint Paul, located at 3101 Wisconsin Avenue, NW, in the Massachusetts Heightsneighborhood of Washington, D.C.

89    Ibid.
90    https://cathedral.org
91    https://www.lds.org/locations/washington-dc-temple-visitors-center?lang=eng#d

known for its gargoyle collection that adorns the outside of the building; my favorite is Darth Vader."[92]

I replied, "So what is there to discuss about the first fifth of the First Amendment to the US Constitution that reads 'Congress shall make no law respecting an establishment of religion, or prohibiting the free exercise thereof?'"

Smith held, "Well then, the nuts and bolts of the matter it is. The first half provides for the separation of church and state in that the business of the church shall not mix with the state; the state shall not proclaim a church such as Baptist or Catholicism or Taoism as the only religion of the land, like what Peter Griffin did on an episode of *Family Guy* when he created the Church of the Fonz after having a falling out with his primary church.[93] As was the decision laid down in the decision of *Zorach v. Clauson*, which upheld accommodationism, proclaiming that the nation's 'institutions presuppose a Supreme Being' and that government recognition of God does not constitute the establishment of a state church, which the Constitution's authors intended to prohibit, which is why 'In God We Trust' appears on our money, prayer is allowed at meetings, and you get to 'tell the truth, the whole truth, and nothing but the truth (so help you God/under pains and penalties of perjury),' when being a witness in court."[94]

I asked, "What determines if something has overstepped the bounds?"

Smith replied, "That would be the Lemon test as established by the US Supreme Court in *Lemon v. Kurtzman*[95] that concluded that government action does not violate the establishment clause if it '[h]as a significant secular (i.e., non-religious) purpose, . . . [d]oes not have the primary effect of advancing or inhibiting religion, and . . . [d]oes not foster excessive entanglement between government and religion.'[96] In short, a government may provide resources to help a daycare run by a church so long as the money is only used toward that purpose."

I replied, "What about the other half?"

Smith concluded our time here by stating, "Okay the latter half of the first fifth of the First Amendment is better known as the free exercise clause, which allows you to go to church on Sundays (for Christians), pray in the streets on Fridays, sacrifice animals, go door to door spreading your faith, and wear specific religious clothing, like Jewish men and the kippah, more commonly known as a yarmulke. For the government to get in the way, the government would need to show that their action is based on them having a compelling interest, or when a

---

92    Washington National Cathedral, "Take a Gargoyle Tour at Washington National Cathedral," accessed March 21, 2019, https://cathedral.org/events/category/tours/gargoyle.

93    *Family Guy Wiki*, s.v. "Church of the Fonz," accessed March 21, 2019, https://familyguy.fandom.com/wiki/Church_of_the_Fonz.

94    Oyez, "Zorach v. Clauson," accessed March 21, 2019, https://www.oyez.org/cases/1940-1955/343us306.

95    Oyez, "Lemon v. Kurtzman," accessed March 21, 2019, https://www.oyez.org/cases/1970/89.

96    Ibid.

governmental interest (as in protecting the public) is so important that it outweighs individual rights.[97] In other words, do whatever it is you want, but if you want to sacrifice a goat you need to do it sanitarily and not steal your neighbor's to do so, or the more common requirement that all those seeking to attend a public school to be immunized to prevent a spread of measles, as the religious exemption in some circumstances allowed in 17 states has been shown lead to outbreaks, as was the case of a recent one in the Pacific Northwest.[98] Also, there can no human sacrifices or flying planes into buildings in the name of some god, as was decided in *Schenck v. United States* by the US Supreme Court.[99] That pretty much about covers freedom of religion."

I replied, "Where to next sir?"

Smith started walking back the way we came and held, "The station from which we came of course!"

About 20 minutes later, we found ourselves walking back underground to the platform at the Cleveland Park Metro Station. From there, we rode a Red Line train back into the city for four stops and transferred at Metro Center Metro Station to a Blue Line train toward Franconia-Springfield Metro Station.

Four stops later we found ourselves exiting the above-ground platform at Arlington Cemetery Metro Station. We proceeded to walk along Memorial Avenue toward what at first glance appeared to be a large park. About halfway up the road, Doe stopped and said, "Champ, before us lies the final resting place of many of our nation's greatest citizens: war heroes to presidents to astronauts to judges and congressmen and women. This assembly is formally known as Arlington National Cemetery[100] (figure 27.9). The hallowed grounds were established in

FIGURE 27.9    Arlington House also known as the Robert E. Lee Memorial in Arlington National Cemetery. Section 32 of the cemetery is in the foreground.

---

97    Ronald Steiner, "Compelling State Interest," Free Speech Center and the John Seigenthaler Chair of Excellence in First Amendment Studies, accessed March 21, 2019, https://www.mtsu.edu/first-amendment/article/31/compelling-state-interest.

98    WFTS Digital, "Religious Exemptions for Vaccinations in Question Following Measles Outbreak," ABC Action News, February 2, 2019, https://www.abcactionnews.com/news/state/religious-exemptions-for-vaccinations-in-question-following-measles-outbreak.

99    Oyez, "Schenck v. United States," accessed March 21, 2019, https://www.oyez.org/cases/1900-1940/249us47.

100    https://www.arlingtoncemetery.mil

their current use during the Civil War to bury the mass of war dead on the grounds of Arlington House, the former estate of Confederate general Robert E. Lee's wife, Mary Anna Custis Lee (a great-granddaughter of Martha Washington). Now while as morbid as you or I may feel this to be, no other place can help us discuss another fifth of the First Amendment, 'the right of the people peaceably to assemble.' No other place in or near our nation's capital can indeed display what a mass of people truly amounts to on a day-to-day basis. In total, over 400,000 gravesites are strewn across 623 acres of land chosen for is views of Washington DC, being high above the river to prevent graves from being unearthed, and the overall pleasantness of the land on the hills. With that in mind, you have the right to assemble with any of your peers to partake in any action in which you please. What action would you like to gather as a group to partake in, Champ?"

I replied, "I'd love to throw a parade for dogs and go on the biggest mutt-struts ever and get into the *Guinness Book of World Records*! What about you, Mr. Smith?"

"That's none of your business, but what might get in the way of in partaking in your right to assemble?"

"Traffic?"

"Yes! Traffic! As much as traffic might be the plague for us all and as nice as a nice group dog walk would be, the cars need to take people where they need to be, ambulances for people to the hospital, and cyclists to get in the way in their special ways. Therefore, costs may be incurred by municipalities and the like in ensuring that safety and public health are maintained during the assembly. Accordingly, the US Supreme Court in *Cox v. New Hampshire*[101] considered the constitutionality of a Manchester, New Hampshire, ordinance that set a fee from a nominal amount up to $300 for marches and parades to be held in their jurisdiction. The ordinance in question was challenged by a band of Jehovah's Witnesses who, without seeking the required permit, conducted a march and handed out leaflets to passers by during their assembly. In their decision, the Supreme Court upheld both the permit requirement and the fee with Chief Justice Hughes, writing for the court, 'We perceive no constitutional ground for denying to local governments that flexibility of adjustment of fees which, in the light of varying conditions, would tend to conserve, rather than impair, the liberty sought.'[102] Covering what you can say when assembling requires bringing up the case of *National Socialist Party of America v. Village of Skokie*.[103] While no one can argue that the original Nazis and any of their modern followers are of the right sort, they still have a

---

101    Oyez, "Cox v. New Hampshire," accessed March 21, 2019, https://www.oyez.org/cases/1940-1955/312us569.
102    Ibid.
103    Oyez, "National Socialist Party of America v. Village of Skokie," accessed March 21, 2019, https://www.oyez.org/cases/1976/76-1786.

right to assemble. A group of Nazis in 1978 requested a permit to march as a group in front of the Skokie, Illinois, city hall to protest the Skokie Park District's ordinance requiring a bond of $350,000 to be posted before the issuance of a park permit. It's important to note that the village was primarily inhabited by Jews at the time and the mayor testified that the demonstration could lead to uncontrollable violence because of the circumstances that ultimately saw the permit be denied. The Nazi group appealed to no avail through the state of Illinois court system only to find haven in the Supreme Court who decided that the group had unjustly been denied a permit to march. Let's go for a walk."

Once done talking, Smith led us down Memorial Avenue away from the cemetery. This led us across the Arlington Memorial Bridge back into the district from Virginia. About twenty minutes later, we found ourselves at the footsteps of the Lincoln Memorial.[104] Once standing squarely at the base of the steps, Smith stated, "Alight Champ, one of the more famous assemblies seen here in Washington DC occurred on August 28, 1963, when Dr. Martin Luther King Jr. gave his famous 'I Have a Dream' speech at the top of these very steps to a crowd of hundreds of thousands of people.[105] Dr. King and his followers came here to protest many of the still rampant at the time Jim Crow laws and failures to prevent discrimination based on race as part of the larger civil rights movement. Overall, while Dr. King's speech and the multitudes that were gathered certainly qualify as assembly, with the goal in mind to seek an end to unfair government practices put forth by bureaucrats on certain parts of the population, like African Americans, the goal of the speech constitutes, another fifth of the First Amendment . . ."

I chimed in "'. . .and to petition the Government for a redress of grievances.' I got you on this one sir. When I was back in Texas learning about interest groups, I learned about this section as it enshrines our right to speak to or at least toward governing officials to influence them either poorly or positively, all depending on your view, but thanks for putting this right in a new perspective!"

Smith remarked, "All right kid, you knew your stuff there, but let's march onward!"

We spent the next forty minutes walking the length of the National Mall along the Lincoln Memorial Reflecting Pool, past the World War II Memorial, the Washington Monument, and in front of the many Smithsonian Museums. At Seventh Street Northwest, we turned north for one block, then went east on Constitution Drive Northwest for one block before turning north on Sixth Street Northwest. Once across Pennsylvania Avenue Northwest, we

104    https://www.nps.gov/linc/index.htm
105    History.com Editors, "'I Have a Dream' Speech," November 30, 2017, https://www.history.com/topics/civil-rights-movement/i-have-a-dream-speech.

FIGURE 27.10   Front pages of newspapers, displayed at the Newseum, an interactive museum of news and journalism, located in Washington, D.C.

walked half a block and stopped in front of the Newseum[106] museum facade and the front-page copies of various newspapers from around the world that gave away the point behind our latest stop (figure 27.10). Smith began by stating, "Champ, it's time to discuss the second to last fifth of the First Amendment, no 'abridging the freedom . . . or of the press;' When I say *press*, what comes to mind for you?"

I replied, looking up at the facade of the museum, "Newspapers, pamphlets, magazines, and books from when our country was founded, but for today I'd say websites, films, radio, television shows, social media, and god knows what else."

Smith furthered, "Very thorough the list there; like newspapers though, that list might be out of date by tomorrow. Regardless, like your right to assembly, the media may publish as they see fit, but various items exist to keep them in check in what they print. First, from the government, they may invoke something called prior restraint, which occurs when they prevent something from being published.[107] This may be done in the form of a judge issuing a gag order, which blocks a press agent from publishing information about a trial. The major case on this right came in *Nebraska Press Association v. Stuart* where the Supreme Court held that a judge in Nebraska's gag order about a trial was unconstitutional when broadcasting the confession of the accused.[108] The only time when gag orders issued under these circumstances are held up is when the perceived violator of First Amendment rights sufficiently shows that doing so is necessary to prevent harm to a defendant's right to a fair trial. From the public, the press may be restrained after the fact when a person discussed is shown to be harmed by a publication. The key term to understand here is *defamation*, or 'the act of communicating false statements about a person that injure the reputation of that person.'[109] When done in print, this is known as libel, where if done orally is known as slander. In this case, the person who has been damaged by the defamation must show that actual malice

---

106   http://www.newseum.org

107   Joe Hashmall, "Prior Restraint," Legal Information Institute, accessed March 21, 2019, https://www.law.cornell.edu/wex/prior_restraint.

108   Oyez, "Nebraska Press Association v. Stuart," accessed March 21, 2019. https://www.oyez.org/cases/1975/75-817.

109   https://www.merriam-webster.com/dictionary/defamation

has occurred, which is when the one who has published the statement has done so knowing that the report is blatantly false or is knowingly done in a way to have reckless regard for the truth of the matter at hand.[110] Setting the standard for how judges may rule in this case is *New York Times v. Sullivan*, which held that the plaintiff in a civil case must prove that actual malice has occurred by showing the court with "clear and convincing" evidence that actual malice has occurred.[111] In other words, unless you can prove that you were targeted by the publisher, it is very difficult to receive damages."

I interjected, "What about in court? A neighbor of mine is a reporter, and she often gets called into court."

Smith concluded our discussion by stating, "Odds are unless your neighbor is really up to something she should'nt be, she is being requested to give up the sources she used to write an article. There exists something known as a shield law. A shield law allows the reporter to not testify in a case and not be thrown in jail.[112] The charge levied when this occurs is called contempt as the witness, the reporter, in this case, is refusing to comply with an order given by the court, giving up their source. Under federal law, no shield exists where, depending on which state you are in, reporters have a full or partial shield in place, forty states, and the district, or no shield from being held in contempt as is the case in ten states.[113] Being thrown in jail is not supposed to be a punishment, but rather a ruse for compliance. Let's walk some more."

Without going inside the Newseum, we turned and went back how we came onto the National Mall. Along the way, we stopped and got a hot dog from a cart and made some small talk. Once back on the mall in the center grass area between the museums on the north and south side, Smith stated, "Champ, we are at an end. Once our conversations end here, I shall have completed my punishment as described by the court this morning. One final fifth of the First Amendment remains, 'Congress shall make no law . . . abridging the freedom of speech.' I'm happy to report that you have the right to say whatever it is you may wish. On a personal note, I still retain my right to call you a nincompoop based on what is that you say. On a professional note, I encourage you to watch your mouth still. Specifically, the government, when the situation comes to you expressing yourself, may act to block your speech when you pose

---

110    https://www.law.cornell.edu/wex/defamation

111    Oyez, "New York Times Company v. Sullivan," accessed March 21, 2019, https://www.oyez.org/cases/1963/39.

112    Johnathan Peters, "Shield Laws and Journalist's Privilege: The Basics Every Reporter Should Know," *Columbia Journalism Review*, August 22, 2016. https://www.cjr.org/united_states_project/journalists_privilege_shield_law_primer.php.

113    AM, "Number of States with Shield Law Climbs to 40," Reporters Committee for Freedom of the Press, accessed March 21, 2019, https://www.rcfp.org/journals/number-states-shield-law-climbs.

a 'clear and present danger,' as was decided in *Schenck v. United States*[114] regarding the distribution of a leaflet opposing the draft in World War I. Therefore, you cannot shout "fire" in a movie theater if there is no actual fire, as this might cause an unnecessary stampede, causing death and the like. The ruling of the Supreme Court in *Gitlow v. New York* expanded the clear and present danger test to include actions that lead to 'evil[s].'[115] This standard in use today is known as the imminent lawless action test and was established in 1969 by the decision in *Brandenberg v. Ohio*, where now the state must show that the speech it is seeking to stop is 'directed to inciting or producing imminent lawless actions and is likely to incite or produce such actions.'[116] In other words, the bar set by the court for states to meet to block speech has been raised restricting their ability to block speech."

At this point, I saw a plaque in the ground that read, "On October 11, 1987, The NAMES Project AIDS Memorial Quilt[117] first laid here." I asked, "Sir, what was this 'quilt' about mentioned on this sign here on the ground?"

Smith remarked, "For us here, it is another point to discuss when advocating your freedom of speech. Specifically, in response to the murders of gay San Francisco supervisor Harvey Milk and mayor George Moscone in 1978, a man by the name Cleve Jones and his friends organized a march to remember those men. In 1985 Jones was made aware of thousands of men and women who had been lost to AIDS and in response propositioned his fellow marchers that year to write on placards the names of friends and loved ones who had died of the disease. At the end of the march, Jones and others taped the placards to the walls of the San Francisco Federal Building. As a result, the placards came out akin to a patchwork quilt. From there, the idea came to start the Names Project. Two years later, thanks to donated time, effort, and sewing machines, the final quilt was produced and put on display here and has appeared multiple times since at this spot, with the most recent occurrence in 2012. The question is, do all people find such a topic fit for public display?"

I replied, "Probably not."

Smith furthered, "Now, nobody did protest, but that brings us to the discussion of obscenity and what could be considered obscene. In 1973 the Supreme Court decision in *Miller v. California* determined that material is obscene by holding that '[t]he basic guidelines for the trier of fact must be: (a) whether 'the average person, applying contemporary community standards' would find that the work, taken as a whole, appeals to the prurient interest . . . (b)

---

114    Oyez, "Schenck v. United States," accessed March 21, 2019, https://www.oyez.org/cases/1900-1940/249us47.

115    Oyez, "Gitlow v. New York," accessed March 21, 2019, https://www.oyez.org/cases/1900-1940/268us652.

116    Oyez, "Brandenburg v. Ohio," accessed March 21, 2019, https://www.oyez.org/cases/1968/492.

117    Yasif Lateef, "The AIDS Memorial Quilt," NAMES Project Foundation, accessed March 21, 2019, https://www.aidsquilt.org/about/the-aids-memorial-quilt.

whether the work depicts or describes, in a patently offensive way, sexual conduct specifically defined by the applicable state law; and (c) whether the work, taken as a whole, lacks serious literary, artistic, political, or scientific value."[118] In short, the court avoided establishing a national standard for what is or isn't obscene, leaving it up to a local standard while offering a framework to do so. In the one case that places an actual limit on obscene material, child pornography is banned thanks to the decision in *Osborne v. Ohio*.[119] In the major congressional statement on this matter, looking at porn in general, the Children's Internet Protection Act requires libraries to put porn filters on computers or face a loss of federal funding, which was upheld as constitutional in *United States v. American Library Association*, as if a patron asks for the filters to be removed, the library may easily do so and therefore is not overly restricting your freedom of speech.[120] For the NAMES Project in San Francisco there is undoubtedly no issue, but putting the quilt in a socially conservative part of the country might raise an eyebrow. Overall, you have a freedom of speech to express yourself, but the further you move away from objectivity to subjectivity, the more you risk your rights being stripped away."

I stated, "That's a lot to take in sir, but it seems that if I keep on the straight and narrow to back up my opinions clearly, I can express myself. Anything else?"

Smith concluded our time together by stating, "There is the Ninth Amendment to the US Constitution that reads, 'The enumeration in the Constitution, of certain rights, shall not be construed to deny or disparage others retained by the people.' In other words, you have additional rights not explicitly stated in the document, but since there is no way to enumerate them we have this amendment serving as a catchall allowing you th ability to get them interpreted in your interests later on. Bye, Champ!"

And like that, Smith was no longer with me. I was left in an open field to ponder my rights. Is it legal for me to stand here? What could be considered legal for me to do so? All I knew at this point was that I wanted to exercise my Ninth Amendment rights to a shower and headed back to my hotel for a nap in a proper bed.

---

118   Oyez, "Miller v. California," accessed March 21, 2019, https://www.oyez.org/cases/1971/70-73.
119   Ibid.
120   Oyez, "United States v. American Library Assn., Inc," accessed March 21, 2019, https://www.oyez.org/cases/2002/02-361.

**QUESTIONS TO CONSIDER** REGARDING YOUR CIVIL LIBERTIES:

1. The first main discussion topic of the chapter discusses the difference between civil rights and civil liberties. Please explain what civil rights and civil liberties are, the most important in your opinion to discuss, and why, in detail.

2. The second main discussion topic of the chapter discusses how we got the Bill of Rights. Please explain the events that transpired that allowed us to get the Bill of Rights, what that process relates to from your life, and why, in detail.

3. The third main discussion topic of the chapter discusses how the Bill of Rights was applied to the states. Please identify what process is called and explain what that process relates to from your life, and why, in detail.

4. The remainder of the chapter discusses your civil liberties as prescribed by the Constitution. Please select one of those liberties, identify what it consists of, and explain where you get that liberty from, how you use it today, and why that liberty stood out to you, in detail.

## FIGURE CREDITS

# Chapter 28

# Making and Spending of the People's Money

## Texas Higher Education Coordinating Board ACGMSLOs

*For Federal Government 2305: Upon successful completion of reading the book and taking the associated course, students will be able to do the following:*

1. Explain the origin and development of constitutional democracy in the United States
2. Demonstrate knowledge of the federal system
3. Describe separation of powers and checks and balances in both theory and practice
4. Demonstrate knowledge of the legislative, executive, and judicial branches of the federal government
5. Evaluate the role of public opinion, interest groups, and political parties in the political system
6. Analyze the election process
7. Describe the rights and responsibilities of citizens
8. **Analyze issues and policies in US politics**

*For Texas Government 2306: Upon successful completion of reading the book and taking the associated course, students will be able to do the following:*

1. Explain the origin and development of the Texas Constitution
2. Describe state and local political systems and their relationship with the federal government
3. Describe separation of powers and checks and balances in both theory and practice in Texas
4. Demonstrate knowledge of the legislative, executive, and judicial branches of Texas government
5. Evaluate the role of public opinion, interest groups, and political parties in Texas
6. Analyze the state and local election process
7. Identify the rights and responsibilities of citizens
8. **Analyze issues, policies, and the political culture of Texas**

# Role of the Comptroller in Texas

I arrived into Austin-Bergstrom International Airport on United Flight 6008 from Washington Dulles International Airport at 11:26 a.m. After spending a bit less than a week in the nation's capital, my wallet was on empty; I barely had enough cash on me to pay for parking. To get some money, it was time that I went to the bank to cash a check Charity had given to me before I had left for my trip. The check had a note on the memo line reading, "Happy Birthday. Spend WISELY!!!" The issue is, I was unable to deposit the check into my bank account and get the money immediately, as I had spent my last few dollars buying souvenirs and what not on my last day in Washington DC. I hate how you must have the funds in your bank account to cash a check, even if it is not written off your bank account. So naturally, I needed to take the check to Charity's bank to cash it. Charity and Deacon keep their funds at Piggy Bank, which is primarily located in the Houston-Galveston area but has a branch in Austin to service the large group of customers who go between the two cities daily. Unfortunately, that one location is found at the corner of 15th and Guadalupe Streets in downtown Austin—right around the same places downtown that I'd been traveling to before I had been to DC.

FIGURE 28.1    Texas Medical Association Building.

After making the drive from the airport, I arrived in front of the Texas Medical Association Building (figure 28.1), which held the bank's branch on the first floor. Following the signs, I found myself pulling into the parking garage entrance on the west side of the building. Once parked on the roof, I took the elevator down to the first floor and went in through the handy in-garage entrance to the building to avoid the already scorching Austin sun. After going down a long hallway with a few offices on either side, I found myself in the lobby atrium, which had the entrance to the bank. When walking through the door, I heard from the manager on duty who was standing nearby: "Good morning, sir. Welcome to Piggy Bank! How may we help you?"

I replied, "I need to cash a check, ma'am."

The manager spoke. "Well, you'll need two forms of identification and must be willing to let us scan your fingerprint into our system for record-keeping services. If that's all right with you, follow me."

I stated, "Will my driver's and open-carry licenses be enough? And sure, why not?"

After that short conversation, we walked through the waiting area and found ourselves at the teller line. The manager stated, "Larry, this young gentleman needs to cash a check."

As I approached the counter, I replied, "Thank you, ma'am, and hi, Larry, I'm Champ. How are you?"

Larry remarked, "I'm doing well. We have been open about four hours, and no difficult transactions to process just yet, although, looking at the size of this check, I might have to get my manager to approve of this big transaction. Also, it almost lunchtime for yours truly!"

Puzzled, I replied, "It's a $200 check, and no, you don't. You're kidding, right?"

Larry continued, "I don't know. You are not a client of the bank, it's not a terribly local account, and you probably want small bills. That's a classic conception of potentially fraudulent activity. Fraudulent activity while small now may be a first attempt on your part to come back and make a bigger play later. It looks like, though, that this is probably from a relative perhaps, so I think I can take a risk on you. Stick your right thumb on the scanner, please."

Sticking my arm out, I placed my right thumb onto the scanner. My face and the room glowed as the scanning device moved up and down on the small scanner. Larry, looking mesmerized by the glow, then asked me, "While that is going on, may I have your two forms of ID, please?"

A few moments later, the scanner stopped, and I moved my arm back to my side. Larry was finishing copying the information from my driver's license and was about to start writing the information from my open-carry permit onto the check when he spoke: "Open carry? Are you concealed or open now?"

I replied, "No, no, no. Never to a bank or a government building. I carry the card in my wallet so that when I do carry, I won't be without it, a far graver offense."

Larry replied, while writing down the info, "Good to know. How would you like your bills doled out?"

I said, "Let me have a hundred, a fifty, two twenties, and a ten."

Larry swiped the check through his microreader machine, typed the dollar amount into the computer, and waited to determine if the check would clear. After an affirmation from the system to proceed, he reached down to his drawer and retrieved the bills. Following this, he counted the money on the counter. While I was waiting, I saw a fire engine–red Camaro with large white pinstripes tear by the window behind the counter. Then, with the money in hand, I waved and said, "Thanks, Larry. I hope the rest of your day goes smoothly!"

Then, as I began to move back toward the entrance doorway, a wave of glass flew in my direction. Luckily, I was shielded by a fake fig tree and was able to duck to avoid the shrapnel. Following that, the same Camaro from before came into view. A man with a pair of silk stockings over his head yelled out the passenger door, "Frank, you idiot! This establishment is not the convenience store! That's on the other side of the lobby!"

The man behind the wheel said, "Hey, Bob, way to use our real names, you nincompoop! On my way through the main building doors, I decided to go left instead and see if we could hit the big time!"

Then the man who was waiting behind me in the teller line finally crawled up to my hiding place behind the desk customers could use to write their transaction slips on and went, "What the hell is happening? I got a big piece of glass across my face, and I can't see a thing with all this blood."

I could only reply, "I think this is a robbery in progress. An unplanned one at that, so hang on!"

I could only think, "I wish that I had open-carried my pistol today!"

A few moments later, Bob yelled out, "All right everyone, this is now officially a holdup. We don't want to hurt anyone, so stay where you are! We are going to walk around and take your valuables from you, one person after another. You tellers will go first, and don't even think about hitting one of the magical buttons or typing a fancy code into your computers!"

Immediately after that, the two robbers ran past the blinded man and me, right up to where Larry had been shocked frozen. The robbers jumped the counter, pushed Larry to the floor, and raided his till. Bob kept a watch on the lobby while Frank did the swiping. Then, after what seemed like minutes but was probably only seconds, Bob jumped back over the counter and came up to my location. Bob said, "Wallets and watches, please. No funny business, you two."

After giving away our items, Bob marched the blinded man, Larry (who had just been dragged from behind the counter), and me over to the vault on the other side of the lobby. Over the next few minutes, the other bank employees and patrons in the lobby were also herded with us into the vault. I counted a total of nine people, including myself, in the vault that we were now locked in. A woman who appeared to work for the bank asked, "Where's Paula? What did they do with Paula?"

I shouted, over a room full of panicked murmuring, "Who's Paula?"

The same woman from before replied, "She's the woman who greeted you at the door and walked you over to Larry to get your check cashed. She has a heart condition!"

Since I was the only calm one in the room, I yelled, "Okay everyone, calm down. We are locked in here. Let's not use up all the oxygen, assuming that is that there is no outside source providing some to the room. I don't hear any fans, so let's assume we have a fixed amount of air."

The blinded man pushed his phone into my hand and went, "Boy, come here. I need to let my office know what happened to me. I need you to call them for me quickly. Since I'm an elected official, letting them know could help expedite the removal process, assuming the hostage crisis we are now in doesn't take all night, that is. The number is . . ."

After turning his phone right-way-up, I dialed as the blinded man continued: ". . . five-one-two-four-six-three-four-eight-six-five."

After a few rings, a woman spoke. "Yes, Mr. Hegar, did you need us to bring a document to you at the bank?"

I declared, "No, this isn't Mr. Hegar. My name is Champ Cove. I was cashing a check a little after noon at Piggy Bank in their downtown Austin branch when it was held up. We were all herded into the vault and locked in. A man who was blinded by some shrapnel, I guess that to be Mr. Hegar, told me to call his office to let y'all know what happened to him."

Shocked, the woman shrieked, "Comptroller Hegar is hurt, we will send for . . ."

Suddenly, the line went silent. I looked down. The phone was dead. A funny thought then ran through my head: "I could learn a lot from this blinded man about the government and work to keep the calm about the room at the same time. Yes, a twofer."

## Role of the Comptroller

I asked the blinded man, I mean Mr. Hegar, "What is a comptroller? I've heard the term earlier over the last few weeks, but I'd like to know more."

Mr. Hegar said, "I am one of the leaders of the state's executive branch. I'm on an even par with that of the governor, just not as well known, as everyone knows who the cheerleaders and jocks are, not the athletic trainers. Officially, I'm the state's accountant, as I oversee balancing the state's checkbooks, distributing funds, estimating revenues, and ensuring that we stay on budget, among other things.[1] If you were trying to find a similar position in the federal government, I'm akin to Treasury Secretary Steven Mnuchin of the federal government, who does much of what I do in addition to 'maintain[ing] a strong economy, foster[ing] economic growth, and creat[ing] job opportunities by promoting the conditions that enable prosperity and stability at home and abroad.'[2] In other words, I keep track of the checkbook; he tinkers with the economy by adjusting various interest rates to ensure the booming economy today stays that way by intervening."

I interjected, "What do you do, specifically, though?"

Mr. Hegar continued, "Specifically, per article 3, section 49(a-b) of the state constitution,[3] I am required to submit to the Texas Legislature a certified amount of available cash on hand and anticipated revenues for the next biennium budgetary cycle. This is important, as the legislature is not permitted to spend any funds more than those amounts unless

---

1    https://comptroller.texas.gov/about/mission
2    https://www.treasury.gov/about/Pages/Secretary.aspx
3    Texas Constitution of 1876, article 3, section 49(a).

there is a codified emergency, which requires a four-fifths approval vote in both chambers to go forward, with the excess spending via the borrowing of monies—something that does not happen all that often, if ever in Texas.[4] If the legislature does spend more without the said vote, I am required to reject and return to the legislature any appropriation in violation of this requirement.[5] Plus, I oversee the various trust funds for education—one for higher and one for lower education.[6] Wait a minute, why do you want to know? Are you one of the robbers trying to pump me for information to go for a massive heist or something later?"

I replied, "No, no, no, no . . . it's just that I am on the tail end of a trek this summer to learn about the government found here in the state and our country at large. And quite frankly, one of the items not yet crossed off my list was how the state, or any government, earned and then spent the public's money it collected. If I'm not mistaken, after what I just learned, you are probably the best one to speak to about all that in the entire state."

Mr. Hegar spoke: "Normally, I would be busy overseeing the financial affairs of the state but seeing as how we are all locked up in here, and you did help me get in here safe and sound, not to mention make the phone call for me, everyone gather 'round. This tall Texan tale should help keep us from going crazy while waiting around in here. Here is my tabulating tale."

## Levels of Government and Their Primary Tax

After a pause allowing everyone else in the vault to get closer, Mr. Hegar continued. "Well, beyond the whole keeping track of current and expected revenues gig, one of the most important of my duties is to collect all tax revenue owed to the state of Texas by the marketplace. This collection is just one part of the tax-collecting infrastructures of the country at large, as in the big picture, the federal, state, and local governments all collect their own various, sometimes overlapping depending on your jurisdiction, levied taxes. The difference is who is collecting and which tax they are collecting on. Up top, the federal government typically focuses on taxes derived from your income. The next time you look at your paycheck,[7] look for the lines typically labeled as Federal Income, FICA, shorthand for Federal Insurance Contributions Act,[8] and Medicare, with the prior collected to fund general government spending and the latter two to fund the main government entitlement programs of Social Security and Medicare. The federal government can collect this tax based on the

---

4    Ibid.

5    Ibid.

6    https://comptroller.texas.gov/about/mission

7    Aliciamadamczyk, "Learn How to Read Your Pay Stub," Money.com, April 07, 2016, http://time.com/money/collection-post/4273993/money30-day-4-learn-your-pay-stub.

8    https://www.investopedia.com/terms/f/fica.asp

16th Amendment to the US Constitution[9] that allowed of the income tax to be collected, which was approved of by the states in 1913."

A tall man in the back asked, "I made $72,000 last year. Do you know how much I am going to need to pay after I file my extension?"

Mr. Hegar, who, even through the blood on his face, I could tell, had one of those perplexed looks on his face due to the specificity of the question, said, "You will need to speak with an accountant, or the IRS for that matter,[10] on any specifics based on your tax situation due to possible deductions and the like causing you to owe or be owed a refund, but here's how it goes, in a nutshell. The income tax is known as a progressive tax, due to the greater amount of money you earn, the greater the percentage of your income you are required to pay from your paycheck.[11] For example, if you are single, keep in mind there are different tax brackets for various situations like being married or filing as the head of household, for income earned in calendar year 2018, you will pay 10 percent of everything up to $9,525, which is $952.50. Beyond that amount, the next bracket is $9,526 up to $38,700.00, where you pay the 10 percent from the lower bracket plus 12 percent of the new bracket, which is an additional $3,500.80. Above that, there are five additional brackets, where you pay far higher percentages. The highest bracket is 37 percent of everything over $500,000, plus $150,689.50 from the entirety of what was owed from the lower brackets.[12] After that, you then get to make any deductions and potentially get a refund or find that you owe more than you have already had deducted from your paychecks. This slightly confusing method is why some people call for a flat tax, where everyone pays an equal percentage of everything.[13] For the FICA, this can be broken up into individual lines or condensed, but expect to pay 6.2 percent, or 12.4 if you are self-employed, for the Social Security Old Age Survivor and Disability Insurance Fund.[14] For Medicare, expect to pay 1.45 or 2.9 percent if you are self-employed, to cover medical care of the old, both of which, like the federal income tax, are further deducted from your paychecks."[15]

Another one of the loan officers, a man, spoke up. "So, what is the second level of tax collection?"

---

9    U.S. Constitution of 1776, Amendment 16.

10    https://www.irs.gov

11    https://www.investopedia.com/terms/p/progressivetax.asp

12    Kelly Phillips Erb, "New: IRS Announces 2018 Tax Rates, Standard Deductions, Exemption Amounts and More," *Forbes*, January 30, 2019, https://www.forbes.com/sites/kellyphillipserb/2018/03/07/new-irs-announces-2018-tax-rates-standard-deductions-exemption-amounts-and-more/#2d5f07683133.

13    Tonya Moreno, "Tax Terms: Understanding the Flat Tax System," Balance, February 6, 2019, https://www.thebalance.com/what-is-a-flat-tax-system-3193253.

14    http://www.ssa.gov/OACT/ProgData/taxRates.html

15    Ibid.

Mr. Hegar continued. "Here in Texas, listed on my agency's website at https://comptroller. texas.gov/taxes/a-to-z.php, there are 31 possible taxes and fees that a citizen of the state or passer-through could expect to pay, based on their situation, to either us or one of the local governments.[16] From that list, nearly everything under the sun can be seen there, but what goes to the states, at least here in Texas, are primarily the various sales and use taxes. Beyond the sales taxes, one of the oddballs that stands out from that action-packed field of competitors is the four nine-one-one emergency service fees that are obtained when you pay your monthly landline or mobile phone bills, totaling 56 cents a month, which are then forwarded along to us by your telecommunication provider or the person who sold you your prepaid phone, which is 2 percent of the gross sale price of the phone.[17] One of the more risqué fees is the sexually oriented business fee paid by owners of live nude entertainment establishments that also serve alcohol, who must pay five dollars for every client who enters their establishment.[18] That fee's why you pay a cover charge when walking into the door of one of those establishments. One other more common tax here is the franchise tax, which any chartered or organized business in Texas must pay for the privilege of operating in the state based on their revenue and sales.[19] One tax that is by default a Texas specialty, due to the significant presence of oil and gas in the state, is the severance taxes, where producers must pay 4.6 percent of the market value of the crude oil and 7.5 percent of the natural gas when extracted, with various exceptions for both.[20] Finally, one that I always find odd, seeing as how it taxes something that is quite the necessity in the state, is the Cement Production Tax, where, and I quote, '[a] tax is calculated based on the amount of cement distributed, sold or used by the person for the first time in intrastate commerce at 55 cents per ton.'"[21]

Larry, finally coming out of his state of shock, inquired, "What of the actual sales tax that you originally spoke of?"

Mr. Hegar supplanted, "Ah, yes. Those prior-discussed taxes are all on top of the more common—and profitable, for that matter—local and state sales taxes on goods purchased, which can add up to 8.25 percent of the goods sold, 6.25 for the state, no matter what, and up to 2 for the local entities, which includes cities, counties, transit authorities, and various special-purpose districts that have elected to collect on them.[22] We use a unified collection system for the sales taxes, so we (the state) are also responsible for returning the portion

---

16    https://comptroller.texas.gov/taxes/a-to-z.php
17    https://comptroller.texas.gov/taxes/911
18    https://comptroller.texas.gov/taxes/sobf
19    http://comptroller.texas.gov/taxinfo/franchise
20    https://comptroller.texas.gov/taxes/crude-oil; https://comptroller.texas.gov/taxes/natural-gas
21    https://comptroller.texas.gov/taxes/cement
22    https://comptroller.texas.gov/taxes/sales

of the collection due to the respected local governments. For example, in May of calendar year 2018, we collected $2,758,373,000 from the state portion of the sales and use tax alone and another $3,228,303,000 from the franchise tax.[23] A sales tax is also known as a regressive tax, where the less money you have, the more you pay, as poorer people pay a greater percentage of their income for this than higher-income earners. Of note: We do not collect a state income tax, as article 8, section 24 bans the practice specifically."[24]

A woman seated to my right inquired, "I went to the corner store last week for a pack of cigarettes for my weekend fishing trip I was going on, but I paid a lot more than just a regular sales tax on the purchase. What's up with that?"

Mr. Hegar replied, "Well, when it comes to sales taxes, not all items sold are taxed equally. There are narrow-based taxes, also referred to as sin taxes, which are designed to be paid by only a small percentage of the population—smokers like yourself, ma'am, in this case—in hopes of deterring their use as much as possible. For cigarettes, you pay $1.41 per pack for a conventional package of 20 cigarettes, or a $1.76 per pack of 25 cigarettes, roughly $71.50 to $88.00 for every 1,000 cigarettes you buy.[25] This tax is typically included, but, like the sin taxes on alcohol, mixed beverages, or gasoline, these items can also be shown as an additional tax line on the receipt, if so desired by the establishment selling the merchandise.[26] The general sales and use tax are also known as a broad-based tax, as they are designed to be paid by everyone on everything."

A female customer who had been listening quietly spoke up. "Are there any exceptions to the rules in this matter?"

Looking intrigued, Mr. Hegar declared, "My dear, next time you are at the grocery store, be sure to only buy unprocessed foods like fruits, vegetables, and deli items, as year-round you do not have to pay a dime in sales taxes on the purchase of those items.[27] You know what, I will do you one better. On August 10–12 of this year, keep in mind the dates do vary from year to year, but it's typically the second full weekend in August, the state has a sales tax holiday on the purchase of most clothing, footwear, and school supplies priced under a hundred bucks, even if you put the item on layaway. If you buy your nonperishable needs for the year and groceries that weekend, you walk out the door with

---

23    https://comptroller.texas.gov/transparency/revenue/watch
24    Texas Constitution of 1876, article 8, section 24.
25    https://comptroller.texas.gov/taxes/tobacco/cigarette.php
26    http://comptroller.texas.gov/taxinfo/mixbev/mb_sales.html
27    http://texreg.sos.state.tx.us/public/readtac$ext.TacPage?sl=R&app=9&p_dir=&p_rloc=&p_tloc=&p_ploc=&pg=1&p_tac=&ti=34&pt=1&ch=3&rl=293; Title 34, part 1, section 3, subchapter O, rule §3.293.

a wallet full of savings—roughly eight dollars per every hundred you spend depending on where you are spending."[28]

After listening back and forth for a few more minutes about the minutia of the state and our glorious sales and use tax, I inquired, "So what goes on with the local governments and taxation?"

After another pause, Mr. Hegar continued, "Beyond their portion of the sales and use tax, local governments primarily tax property. When it comes to property, there is real, like land and buildings, and personal, such as clothes and televisions, intellectual ideas, and the like, among many other types depending on who you ask. When it comes to taxing property, local governments tax real property. The state did so as well until 1968, when it was dropped in favor of the previously mentioned sales and use tax, as article 1, section 1-E now bans the practice."[29]

The same woman from before interjected, "How come the property tax on my home keeps changing every year?"

Mr. Hegar posited, "Well, ma'am, that could be for one of two reasons. In one case, the county, city, school, or various other special districts in the area could raise their tax rate (the amount per unit of an activity being taxed), which they can do at will through their pre-determined budgeting practices. Or, more commonly, the County Appraisal District, which is responsible for setting the value of property in the area, could assess your property value, which is part of the tax base, to be higher than it was before, causing the rate to have more value to tax and accordingly raise your tax bill.[30] Formally, this is called an ad valorem tax, where something is taxed based on the value of it."

## Why Do We Tax?

I interjected, as the conversation was becoming heated, "So why tax?"

Mr. Hegar, with a look of bewilderment on his face, replied, "Well, son, that is the politics of the matter. When it comes to why tax, the real answer, in one aspect, is controlling. When governments tax, the entity may desire to regulate behavior. Higher taxes on something may make the item less desirable for people to purchase, thus restricting the use of the item—like the cigarette tax or the sexually oriented business fee. This tax is levied to reinforce behavior, as a lower tax would make the product more desirable. The exception for fruits and vegetables, once again, is a great example. On the other hand, the government's tax

---

28    http://www.comptroller.texas.gov/taxinfo/taxpubs/taxholiday/d
29    Texas Constitution of 1876, article 1, section 1(e).
30    http://scurrytex.com/index.php/Property_Tax_Process

is based on the benefits received—what the taxed get when taxed. An excellent example of this is the tax levied on gasoline purchases, which here in Texas is 20 cents per gallon.[31] The federal amount is 18.4 cents per gallon, for a total of roughly 38.4 cents per gallon on every gallon of gasoline sold in Texas.[32] The benefits received come in the form of the money being earmarked for highway construction and rehabilitation, mass transit projects, or related ecological disaster-site cleanup.[33] The final reason to tax someone is based on their ability to pay, as the tax is apportioned based on their higher or lower income, or some other factor. This reason is pertinent, as someone with a substantial income can afford to pay more of their income and still live comfortably, whereas someone on minimum wage could spare only small amounts to help benefit society."

I posited, after noticing a trend, "Mr. Hegar, it seems as if many of those taxes are initially levied onto business, live-nude entertainment, and severance fees on oil and gas companies, et cetera, correct?"

Mr. Hegar responded, "Well, yes."

I furthered, "The whole point of a business is to make money, but with paying all of those fees, how do the businesses ensure their profits are still being made?"

Mr. Hegar argued, "Let's focus on that sexually oriented business fee, again. When you enter the establishment, you must pay something called a cover charge. The fee, as I stated before, is only $5, but many places will have you pay $20. This covers their fee and puts a bit of extra kip into their pockets on top of what the business gets from food and beverage sales. Toilets use a lot of water, and a bunch of drunk people in a room need to use the toilet a lot, and water isn't free. How else are they going to pay that bill? Either way, this procedure is something called a tax shift. Overall, the business is passing along the cost of whatever it is they must pay in fees to the state directly on to you. It would be the same as a fast-food restaurant being forced to pay higher wages due to a mandated minimum-wage increase and passing along the cost to you by raising menu prices."

I commented, "So I guess the buck always stops with me or whoever else is participating in the economy. What other revenues are there?"

Mr. Hegar gathered his thoughts for a moment. "Those other revenue sources can include monies earned from federal funds, license and permits being issued, interest and investment monies, direct sales of various services, claim settlements, land sales, and various streams like lottery ticket sales,[34] all of which bring in roughly $12 billion a month for the state to go

---

31    https://comptroller.texas.gov/taxes/fuels/gasoline.php
32    http://www.fhwa.dot.gov/ohim/hwytaxes/fe21b-97.pdf
33    https://comptroller.texas.gov/taxes/fuels/gasoline.php
34    http://www.texastransparency.org/State_Finance/Revenue/Revenue_Watch; Revenue by source table.

back and spend. In May of 2018, this was $12,339,318,000 in total revenues. Going back to the bonds item that I brought up earlier, if the legislature did choose to borrow money, they would issue something called bonds (an instrument of indebtedness of the bond issuer to the holders[35]), which can be classified as revenue where revenues, based on whatever is being built, pay off the bond, or general issuance bonds, where an entity's general fund is used to pay off the bonds. It's the government's version of taking out a loan."

## Appropriations

While feeling that the topic of revenues had been dragged out to death, I expressed, "So how does the government spend the tax revenues it brings in?"

Mr. Hegar commented, "Champ, technically, the state, or any government for that matter, does not spend money. The state appropriates, or sets aside, money for its application to use and to the exclusion of all other uses.[36] It's still spending, but due to a lengthy budgeting process, it's a whole different animal."

I continued, "So how do y'all appropriate, then?"

Mr. Hegar commented, "Well, Champ, you may have heard me say the term *biennium budget cycle* earlier. That means that the state, via the legislature and under the guidance of the legislative budget board and the governor, appropriates funds for two years at a time, due to the legislature only meeting, regularly, once every two years. Our next budget for 2020 and 2021 goes into effect in September 1 after being passed in the legislative session. That budget in the appropriations process follows that same procedure as a regular law seeking approval. When budgeting, though, governments typically follow one of two methods. In the first case, called line-item budgeting, each year an entity takes what they spent in the prior year on an item or program and then decides to go back and adjust the amount spent on that item accordingly. The only issue is, without controls for performance or necessity of the thing, agencies tend to keep spending endlessly on topics that are now out of date, like schools buying typewriters instead of investing in computers. On the other hand, governments may take a zero-based approach where, each year or budget cycle, agencies all function as if they are starting an entirely new agency without regard to what they have performed in the past. All program activities and services must be justified again to continue to receive funds, all based on a cost-versus-benefit weighing against other ranked items of importance. The difference is that the first takes a historical approach, while the latter assumes a clean slate to need. The federal government follows the same process, but on an annual

---

35 https://www.investor.gov/introduction-investing/basics/investment-products/bonds
36 http://www.dictionary.com/browse/appropriation

basis when they get around to making a budget instead of passing a continuing resolution.[37] The feds main issue now is deficit spending due to an increase in mandatory spending on things like entitlements."[38]

The woman who had asked about why she paid a lot more in taxes on her cigarettes inquired, "So, what exactly did the state spend during the last session?"

Mr. Hegar turned to his briefcase and took out a file of papers. He passed the documents around and stated, "Lucky for you guys, I was on my way to a local Rotary Club today for lunch as the speaker, and I have a budget summary, entitled 'Why It Matters: Certifying The 2018–2019 Texas State Budget'[39] right here with me. Overall, the state, via the legislature, has appropriated $216.8 billion of spending, an increase of $7.4 billion over the 2016–2017 budget, which is about $7,871 per state resident, an increase of 94 dollars per resident over the 2016–2017 budget.[40] In determining the values a state holds dear, it is best to look closely at what is explicitly appropriated. In the 2016–2017 cycle, lower education (K–12), received $58.4 billion, this time they received $59.9 billion, an increase of $1.5 billion from the last budget.[41] Higher education (undergraduate on up) received $20.5 billion, a $0.6 billion increase from last time.[42] Medicaid received $62.4 billion, an increase of $1.2 billion.[43] Transportation spending is now $26.6 billion, an increase of $3.5 billion.[44] All totaled, that's $169.4 billion, roughly 78.28 percent of total appropriations. The rest is spent on a multitude of services, from prisons to pet projects of individual legislators.[45] Altogether, the appropriations represent the societal issues the state feels it most appropriate for the government to handle today."

As a group, the rest of the audience and I spoke in unison: "That's a lot of spending!"

I asked, "What about federal spending?

Mr. Hegar offered, "Ahh yes, the money pit. Thanks to our friends at usgovernmentspending.com and their user-friendly spending visualization tools, we know that the federal government is appropriating a whopping $4,406,700,000,000 in fiscal year 2019, with $984,400,000,000 of the $4.6 trillion in deficit spending. Of the $4.6 trillion, $1.1 trillion

---

37  https://www.gao.gov/key_issues/federal_budgeting/issue_summary
38  Ibid.
39  Comptroller.Texas.gov, "Certifying the 2018–2019 Texas State Budget," accessed March 21, 2019, https://comptroller.texas.gov/about/media-center/infographics/2017/budget-certification.
40  Ibid.
41  Ibid.
42  Ibid
43  Ibid.
44  Ibid.
45  Edgar Walters and Chris Essig, "A Closer Look at the Final Texas 2018–19 Budget," *Texas Tribune*, June 6, 2017, https://apps.texastribune.org/final-budget-2017.

is being spent on pensions, that's your old age and survivors from before, $1.23 trillion on health care, inclusive of Medicare, Medicaid, medical research, and the like, $112.5 billion on education, $949.9 billion on defense, $347.9 billion on welfare, your food stamps and unemployment benefits, $42.3 billion on protection, your federal law enforcement agencies and prison system, $94 billion on transportation, $53.8 billion on general government, $110.1 billion on other spending, and my personal favorite, $363.4 billion on interest payments on the trillions we are already in debt for."[46]

After a long, drawn-out silence due to the staggering figures presented, from memory I might add, I asked, "How do people feel about all of that spending?"

Mr. Hegar submitted, "As a state, Texas tends to be fairly conservative. Accordingly, fewer taxes and less future spending is ideal. But take schools, for example; a hundred or so years ago, we were using one-room schoolhouses; we were far more rural and for the most part self-sufficient, all while not seeing much need for much, if any, additional government intervention in the future. Now ask yourself: 'Are we like that today?' If you can't say yes, then things have changed, and a greater role of the government is, for lack of a better term, needed. The better question is: What do we want that role to be? Taking on only the bare minimum, or ever-present, making decisions on what farmers will grow and who will marry whom? People or groups individuals take part in, such as interest or pressure, all take a stand on something. Whoever is loudest will typically get the most buck for their banging."

I asked, "Where do we go from here?"

Instead of getting an answer, the vault door began to open behind our group slowly. After a few moments, fresh air swirled throughout the room. It felt as if a beautiful sense of enlightenment entered the room. The funny thing is, though, four of the officers who were there helping us to freedom looked very familiar. I could only remark, "Lieutenant Samson, Lieutenant Heisenberg, Lieutenant Bevo, and Ranger Norris? What are all of you doing here? How could you have . . .? What's happening?"

Bevo answered, "The guys who attempted to burglarize this place were idiots. Behind this building, on 14th Street, is the headquarters of the Combined Law Enforcement Associations of Texas[47] and the Travis County Sheriff's Officers Association.[48] Depending on the day, there are more officers there than in the actual various law enforcement headquarters here in the county. When the call went out, the lot of us ran over and intervened. The two guys

46   Christopher Chantrill, "Federal Budget," USGovernmentSpending.com, accessed March 21, 2019, https://www.usgovernmentspending.com/federal_budget_detail_fy20bs22019n_0010404150517072#usgs302.
47   http://www.cleat.org
48   http://tcsoa.org

gave up after ten minutes, but it took us an hour and 15 minutes for Paula, the manager, to recover enough to help us access the vault holding you all. For now, though, let's get y'all out and treated."

About five minutes later, Mr. Hegar was on a gurney, being carried to an ambulance. While walking alongside, I asked him to answer the question that I had raised earlier. In response, he replied, "I do not know, but you must get involved to make change occur. If you want more for education, you must demand it. If nothing occurs, you must join the legislature and get it appropriated yourself. Just like making a budget at home, if you want more money, you need to get another job, or, if you retire, expect less spending power and adjust accordingly."

With that in mind, I spent the next few minutes speaking with an officer. As my car was in the garage and blocked in with police tape, I decided to give Charity a call for a ride. The funny thing is, when I called, her phone's ring, the classic phone's "brrrnngg . . . brrrnngg," was playing right behind me. I turned and found myself being hugged by Charity straight away. Charity stated, "I'm so happy you are all right. Mom, Dad, and I were so worried. Let's get you something to eat. Also, you are with me tomorrow!"

On the way to the car, I pondered what I had learned during the hour or so that I was stuck in the vault. Governments levy taxes to earn revenues. What taxes are levied is all decided based on a variety of circumstances and goals of the government in question. More importantly, when the governments spend, better stated as appropriate, what they earned in revenues, it says a lot about what they stand for. When I make my first adult budget, I should put my money where my mouth is and keep an eye out for appropriate sources of revenue and expenditures.

**QUESTIONS TO CONSIDER** REGARDING MAKING AND SPENDING OF THE PEOPLE'S MONEY:

1. The first main discussion topic of the chapter discusses the role of the comptroller in Texas. Please define what a comptroller is and explain the job duties/functions, who from your life could be a comptroller, and why, in detail.

2. The second main discussion topic of the chapter discusses the different levels of government and their primary tax. Please identify each level of government and explain what they primarily tax, the tax and associated level that applies most to your current situation, how that tax applies to you, and why/how, in detail.

3. The third main discussion topic of the chapter discusses the reasons why we tax. Please identify what those reasons to tax are, rank them, in your opinion, from most to least annoying, and indicate why you put them in that order, in detail.

4. The final main discussion topic of the chapter discusses appropriations. Please explain what appropriations are, the appropriations mentioned in the book that you found most annoying/shocking/etc., and why you found that spending to be that way, in detail.

# Chapter 29

# Political Symbols

# What Symbols Are

On the way home last night from the bank robbery, Charity and I discussed each of the different places that I'd been and concluded that I'd seen every relevant government entity in the country and nearly every set of policy areas that I could. The one thing we agreed I should still see is something that helps each state and the country at large put their best forward. Adding to the fact that Charity didn't want to let me out of her sight due to all I'd been through, there was only one thing left for me to see.

With that backstory in mind, one common thread from the last weeks was that various symbolic items were prevalent at the multiple sites I'd been. This list includes the flags outside of the Mexican consulate here in Austin; the six flags that have flown over Texas etched into the front, reverse, and floors of the state capital; and a multitude of other things that I have seen along the way. Here and there I had picked up some meaning of each, but I lacked information on the totality of the symbols together as a whole, if there was one. Therefore, to better make sense of the symbols that I had seen, I ended up spending today with my sister Charity. This set of circumstances also proved convenient, as she earned her stripes to inform me on this topic due to her graduating from the University of Texas at Austin a few years ago with a bachelor of arts in advertising[1] with a focus on symbology. Therefore, the goal of today was to experience many of the different items that the state of Texas and our national government have chosen to use to represent themselves to others around the world. This turned out to range from A to T—armadillos to toads, that is, in Texas, and bison to roses for America.

Accordingly, close to 7:30 a.m., when I was sitting at the kitchen table eating some cereal, I knew my day was about to begin as from the corner of my eye I saw Charity enter the kitchen in a somewhat coordinated outfit. Standing in the doorway, she stated, "Good morning, little brother. Are you ready to get started?"

I could only nod in agreement, as I could not put into words the totality of what she was wearing. In a nutshell, from head to toe, she was wearing what I assumed were every single state clothing symbol known to man, along with a few other garments that were probably symbols of some kind as well. Eventually, after a minute of silence and her gesturing me to get more involved in the conversation, I replied, "Do you want me to discuss your clothing, or do you just want me to go get in the car?"

Charity replied, "Yes, but for now let's focus on the clothes. You see, everything that I am wearing comprises the totality of officially unofficial symbolic Texas clothing. You see, my dress fabric has an essential pattern to it. This pattern is called the bluebonnet tartan[2]

---

1    https://advertising.utexas.edu/undergraduate/major-advertising
2    Texas House Concurring Resolution (TX HCR) 242, 71R, 1989.

(figure 29.1). Tartans are fabric schemes that were originally used to identify members of different clans in Scotland. Our tartan, as the name suggests, is supposed to resemble the state flower, the bluebonnet[3] (figure 29.2). The tartan, in some ways, looks like a field on the side of the highway, in bloom with them during the spring. The state flower designation is due to the bluebonnet being as prosperous in the state as the shamrock is in Ireland, not to mention the fact that it looks like the lone star found on the state flag at the right angle."[4]

I interrupted, "Stick to the clothes, Charity, or I am going to need some additional coffee to keep up with your infinite wisdom this morning, and the pot is just about out, and I don't want to make any more."

She replied, "Oh, you hush. Now, look at my gorgeous shoes. My cowboy boots are the state's official footwear. This symbol got its start in post–Civil War cattle drives, with famous boot makers such as Justin[5] and Lucchese[6] promoting their user-friendliness for the cowboys back in the 1800s, and the expansion of western-movie-driven entertainment via the 1950s and the emphasis that they can be worn with almost everything has made them a part of popular culture ever since[7] (figure 29.3). To go with my boots, this small silver clasp on the leather strand wrapped around my neck is called a bolo tie, which is the state tie (figure 29.4). This was selected due to its representation of the determination, independence, and individualism that are in the makeup of so many great Texans, alongside conjuring feelings that harken people back to the 'pioneer' era and western culture of the state."[8]

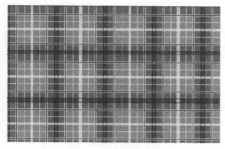

FIGURE 29.1  Blue Bonnet Tartan.

FIGURE 29.2  Blue Bonnets.

---

3   § 3101.008. STATE FLOWER. TX HCR 144, Texas Senate Concurring Resolution (TX SCR) 12, 27R, 1901.
4   Ibid.
5   https://www.justinboots.com
6   https://www.lucchese.com/ourheritage
7   TX HCR 151, 80R, 2007.
8   TX HCR 12, 80R, 2007.

FIGURE 29.3   Cowboy Boots and Hat.

FIGURE 29.4   H. Bud Chadwickson, author and Factuarian. A fictional character used in promotional material for Republic Wireless wearing his infamous bolo tie.

I remarked, "I always wondered what that thing around your neck was. A lot of people still wear them, but what about your earrings? They look nice and special."

Charity continued, "Well if you have to know, they are two state symbols in one. The stones are made of Texas blue topaz, the state gem.[9] The large 'Lone Star' you see beveled into them is the state gemstone cut[10]".

I remarked, "Just like the bluebonnet tartan, it plays right into the state flag again. I see a trend here. What about the hat?"

With a big smile on her face, Charity concluded, "Thankfully, all of my letter writing a few years back when I was still in school paid off. Back in the 2015 state legislature, the state house and senate, via House Concurrent Resolution Number 35, based on the logic of, 'the wide brim provid[ing] the face, neck, and shoulders of the wearer shade from the sun and cover from the rain while enduring the elements on a ranch or cattle drive,'[11] all of which harken back to our days of living off the land successfully, finally made the cowboy hat a state symbol. I look so good today, don't I? I want to go and show myself off. Let's get me some breakfast. However, if I were to add some additional ones of my own to the list of clothing items, I would add spurs due to their use in working cattle,[12] and really, western wear in general due to it all being so synonymous with the lifestyle of the cowboy that much of what I am wearing relates to."[13]

---

9    TX HCR 12, 61R, 1969.

10   TX HCR 97, 65 R, 1977.

11   TX HCR 35, 84R, 2015.

12   Tracy Schumer, "Ode to the Spur," High Minded Horseman, May 11, 2010, http://www.highminded-horseman.com/2010/05/11/ode-to-the-spur.

13   Alexia Wulff, "A Brief History of American Western Wear," Culture Trip, September 26, 2016, https://theculturetrip.com/north-america/usa/articles/a-brief-history-of-american-western-wear.

While I was gathering my things, I shouted down the stairs, "Charity, are there any clothing symbols for the federal government?"

Shouting louder than I ever could up the stairs, Charity replied, "Unfortunately, no, even though there are several noteworthy contenders like blue jeans, since they became popular en masse following James Dean wearing them in *Rebel Without a Cause* in 1955 and service members introducing them to the world during World War II."[14]

After a few minutes, and me showering and getting dressed, we were in Charity's car, ready to keep the day going. Along the way to the as yet unknown destination I inquired, "What exactly are symbols? I think before we go any further, we should discuss that matter for clarity."

After a minute, Charity responded, "Well, in short, symbols are 'something that stands for or suggests something else because of a relationship, association, convention, or accidental resemblance.'[15] It can be a word, sound, gesture, an idea, or, in my case, a proper visual image of something. Think about how the Deathly Hallows represent the life, really death, choices of the Peveril brothers from *Harry Potter and the Deathly Hallows*.[16] The cloak represents the one who greeted death as an old friend. The stone represents the one who died for love. The Elder Wand represents the one who died for power. Put together, and you have the tools to defeat death by hiding from him, bringing back a loved one who has passed, and sending others to their demise, scary stuff, but very representative of how life choices can impact you. And don't forget about the three-finger salute from *The Hunger Games* trilogy being representative of saying thanks, giving admiration, speaking goodbye to someone you love and eventually becoming a symbol of rebellion against the capital."[17]

I stayed silent to take in a lot of the symbolism that just made me rethink entertainment from my early childhood. My mind was blown. Luckily, after driving a stretch on SH 360, from Charity's home in the Lost Pines subdivision, we took the flyover to US Highway 290 and went to the Whataburger located where SH 71 exits to the north. I asked as we pulled in to the drive-through, "Let me guess: This is a symbol too?"

Charity remarked, "Sadly, no, but luckily, Whataburger[18] is an official state treasure due to its amazing hamburgers. Look at the big sign on the window claiming as such (figure 29.5).

---

14   AMC Filmsite, review of *Rebel without a Cause*, by Stewart Stern, accessed March 21, 2019, http://www.filmsite.org/rebel.html.

15   https://www.merriam-webster.com/dictionary/symbol

16   Pottermore, "The Deathly Hallows," accessed March 21, 2019, https://www.pottermore.com/explore-the-story/the-deathly-hallows.

17   *Hunger Games Wiki*, s.v. "Three Finger Salute," accessed March 21, 2019, http://thehungergames.wikia.com/wiki/Three_Finger_Salute.

18   Texas House Resolution (TX HR) 723, 77R, 2001.

FIGURE 29.5    Whataburger. A Texas Treasure.

FIGURE 29.6    Austin Zoo Entrance.

Even though you already ate, I'll order something small for you out of commitment to today's mission."

A few minutes later, with food in hand, we continued west on SH 71. I asked, "So where are we off to now?"

Charity, in between bites, responded, "A place where you could have a good use for the rest of the bread from your biscuit there: the Austin Zoo and Animal Sanctuary,[19] where I am now at the final stage of updating my senior collegiate project from around three years ago, that is still on exhibition there" (figure 29.6).

I asked, "Is that the one you were working on for the Texas State Preservation Board as an intern?"[20]

She replied, "You remembered! Thank you so much! They oversee the Bullock Museum,[21] where I now work full time and we went to earlier in the summer, and since the museum is about history and the zoo is about animals, they felt that placing this project there, or here I guess now that we are almost there, would be a bit better of a place for it. Accordingly, we worked out an agreement where the zoo tends to the animals, and we tend to the displays themselves. It's nice going to the zoo occasionally to check on things now that I'm out in the real world."

We turned onto Circle Drive for the final travel segment of traveling to the zoo. Near 9:00 a.m., we were in the parking lot. At the gate, Charity flashed her badge to get us in for free, and we were off to the traveling, now permanent, I guess, exhibition building just to the right of the entrance.

At the door, Charity remarked, "Remember, my project here was to assemble the different state animal symbols into one big exhibition for a new segment of the zoo to help expand

19    http://austinzoo.org
20    http://www.tspb.state.tx.us; http://www.thestoryoftexas.com/about/board-of-directors
21    https://www.thestoryoftexas.com

the overall complex. The first room houses the ones that fly in the air, so when this door opens, do not open the next one until this door closes."

I nodded my understanding. Then, once inside the entry stockade, I felt a look of awe on my face due to the pretty creatures floating around in flight. After going through the second door, Charity remarked, "If you look off into the dark corner to our right, you should see an animal that looks like a pair of black fuzzy dice dangling from the ceiling. Those two animals are a breeding pair of Mexican free-tailed bats, the state flying mammal (figure 29.7). They were selected due to their innate ability to help regulate the local ecosystem—they eat mosquitoes—just as any good Texan works hard to keep the environment clean.[22] The Congress Avenue bridge downtown has millions of these animals dwelling there during the summer that leave to hunt in the evening. Now let's look over to the left."

FIGURE 29.7    Mexican free-tailed bats exiting Bracken Bat Cave.

I clarified, "I remember seeing those bats there about two weeks ago. They look even better up close and personal. And the red and black fluttering butterflies?"

Charity continued, "Those are monarch butterflies, to be exact, the state insect. This insect was selected due to Texas being the birthplace of the species each year, leaving state citizens across the land to witness this species 'literally' bloom with massive quantities of them each year as they return to breed the next generation.[23] Unfortunately, what you see swooping down from the rafters eating the butterflies on occasion is the mockingbird, our state bird (figure 29.8). That bird was selected to represent the state due to it being known to fiercely protect its home and dying to do so, as any 'true' Texan would.[24] I believe this selection also pays homage to the Alamo defenders who died there.

FIGURE 29.8    Northern Mockingbird.

22    TX SCR 95,74R, 1995.
23    TX HCR 94, 74R, 1995.
24    TX SCR 8, 40R, 1927.

FIGURE 29.9    Bald Eagle landing on Douglas Fir tree at Long Lake Waterfront B&B Nanaimo BC, Vancouver Island BC.

Also, next month in the area behind the curtain over here will be a bald eagle (figure 29.9) exhibition, where injured specimens will be placed while rehabbing from wounds. They were selected on June 20, 1782, as the emblem of the United States of America, 'because of its long life, great strength, and majestic looks, and because it was then believed to exist only on this continent.' The turkey was also considered at that time to be our national symbol.[25] I'm happy with the way it turned out, as turkeys are delicious to eat."

I interjected, "Charity, what is that growing buzz I hear from way up in the rafters?"

Charity concluded here, "I don't know, I did not put any bees or hornets into this exhibit. However, if the buzz is coming from a hive of western honey bees,[26] I'll take credit, as those bees are the state pollinator due to their 'essential role in the pollination of crops [as this]

FIGURE 29.10    Western Honey bee on a Flower.

this industrious insect enables the production of at least 90 commercially grown crops in North America' (figure 29.10). Regardless, let's go into the next room and get back down to earth before we get stung. Follow the same door rules as before, please, and hurry!"

From there, we entered a long-elevated platform that had viewing portholes on either side that looked to the outdoors directly or into an air-conditioned room. After walking a few feet, Charity said, "Look at the floor. Embedded into the ground here are the back-bones of the state dinosaur, Paluxysaurus jonesi, a Brachiosaurus in layman's terms, more or less. It was selected due to the creature being seemingly as big as the state is today, not to mention being native to the area many, many, many, many years ago."[27]

---

25    Elizabeth Nix, "How Did the Bald Eagle Become America's National Bird?," History.com, February 25, 2015, https://www.history.com/news/how-did-the-bald-eagle-become-americas-national-bird.
26    TX HCR 65, 84R, 2015.
27    TX HCR 16, 8R, 2009.

That comment made the phrase "walking with dinosaurs" a little too realistic, not as scary as *Jurassic Park* or *Jurassic World*,[28] though, or live action as *Walking with Dinosaurs: The Arena Spectacular*.[29] There was an additional door to the right after we left the aviary, but Charity advised that we go through that door after walking to the other end and back, where the dinosaur skull is. Looking to the left at an outdoor pen, I saw a ubiquitous sight in the Austin area. Charity announced, "You noticed the Texas longhorn, didn't you? Those longhorns are the large state mammal, due to their being a 'cornerstone' of the state's cattle industry, alongside the long horns on their head[30]. The question is, where is the American Bison that should be in the pen with it, that was selected by Congress via the National Bison Legacy Act in 2016 to be our national mammal due to its importance to Native Americans livelihoods over time, presence on our currency, and their placement on the Department of the Interior's seal among other reasons.[31] I hope the animal's not sick or something, as they are borderline threatened. Of note, the state bison herd is found at Caprock State Park,[32] and the state longhorn herd is the Foundation Herd of the Texas Parks and Wildlife Department.[33] Although, if you look a bit closer to the ground, you might see some shiny armored balls rolling across the terrain. Those are nine-banded armadillos that serve as the small state mammal due to their real ability, like many Texans, to 'change and adapt' to their surroundings to protect themselves and others[34] (figure 29.11). This one is funny because their ability to defend themselves is to curl up into a ball and roll away, which kind of goes against the idea of Texans being known to stand up and fight—a profound contradiction. The longhorn and the armadillo are always put together due to legislation that was passed to make the designation official, after a statewide contest showed that

FIGURE 29.11   Nine Banded Armadillo Playing in the Grass.

---

28   http://www.jurassicworld.com

29   https://www.dinosaurlive.com

30   TX HCR 178, 74R, 1995.

31   U.S. House Resolution (US HR) 2908, 114th, 2016.

32   TX HCR 116, 75R, 1997.

33   Texas Senate Concurrent Resolution (TX SCR) 79, 61R, 1969.

34   TX HCR 178, 74R, 1995.

Texans felt that both deserved to be honored as Texas symbols, instead of just one as the state mammal."

As we were walking, I asked, "What is the horse doing here over in the next pen? Shouldn't that be in an exhibit for Kentucky and their derby?"[35]

Ready to pounce, Charity pointed out, "The horse is too an important part of our state's heritage. What do you think the cowboys rode to round up the herd on the ranch, the state dinosaur? That is the state horse, the American quarter horse, due to the breed playing a pivotal role 'in horse shows, racing, ranching, recreational riding, and other endeavors' of the state industries.[36] Now, let's go down to the dinosaur's head at the far end of the platform."

After admiring the head for a few minutes, we moved on to the small walled display that used a bit of natural sunlight to brighten it up. I stated, "I like the Texas horned frog you got over here. What's it doing here, beyond the obvious?"

FIGURE 29.12   A Small Texas Horned Lizard.

Charity answered, "Good question. The Texas horned lizard (figure 29.12), if I remember from the accompanying house resolution on the wall over there, has no specific reason given to call it the state reptile.[37] I bet, though, that the state legislature was thinking it would be good due to its resourcefulness in the heat and the ability to inflate itself, like any good Texan, to scare away its enemies, and the ability to shoot blood out of its eyes also garnered it some credibility.[38] Let's head back to the door you noticed earlier. On the way, though, I would like to show you my favorite display."

About halfway back, we walked through a lacy blue curtain to our now current left that led to a glass display case. Charity spoke through tears: "At zoos, you traditionally can't touch the animals, much less take one home with you. This exhibit is the one exception. The dogs you can see here through the display case are puppies up for adoption. They are all blue lacy dogs (figure 29.13), the state dog breed. Like

FIGURE 29.13   Blue Lacy Dog.

35   https://www.kentuckyderby.com
36   TX HCR 53, 81R, 2009.
37   TX HCR 141, 73R, 1993.
38   https://www.youtube.com/watch?v=xodVcgJ8bco

the rest of the animals and their abilities to defend themselves, this breed of dog was selected due to their essential role in ranching operations by fending off predators and vermin like javelinas.[39] The Lacy Game Dog Association volunteers their time on weekends to make sure that puppies are available.[40] It's getting hot, even in the shade, so let's go for a swim—figuratively, of course."

After remembering that I don't have a place to live, I decided against making an adoption, but I did get a few wet licks on my chin before we left. We walked back down the walkway and into that door I saw earlier that Charity had steered me away from. The door led into a large, inverted-U-shaped, Plexiglas-covered path. On both sides, at the beginning all you could see was dirt. As you walked further, the soil, which became sand at a point, began to slope down into a beachhead on both sides. For the remaining, I swear, hundred feet or so, on both sides of the hallway, were large bodies of water. The left was labeled "Salt water." The right was labeled "Freshwater." Charity motioned to look to the left and mentioned, "In here are the state crustacean, sea turtle, and saltwater fish. Do you see the two flying discs toward the back?"

Still looking, I said, "Yes."

Charity continued, "Those two animals are Kemp's ridley sea turtles (figure 29.14). This animal was selected due to their species' use of the Padre Island National Seashore, near Corpus Christi, as one of their two primary nesting sites.[41] The school of fish you see here in the foreground is inhabited with red drum (figure 29.15). They're our state saltwater fish due to their 'demonstrating the hardiness and adaptability so often found in the Lone Star State,'[42] their importance to the local fishing industry, and being a prize catch for any

FIGURE 29.14    Kemp's Ridley sea turtle nesting.

FIGURE 29.15    Caught off the Gulf Coast of Louisiana. This is a mature red drum but not a "bull red," the nickname given to red drum longer than 26 inches.

---

39    TX HCR 108, 79R, 2005.
40    http://lacydog.org/rescue
41    TX HCR 31, 83R, 2013.
42    TX HCR 133, 82R, 2011.

fisherman casting away from the many gulf coast piers. Finally, if you look at the bottom, you can see a school of Texas gulf shrimp, the state crustacean. They were selected due to the shrimp being, 'Like barbecue and Tex-Mex, one of the signature foods of Lone Star cuisine and an essential part of the economy and the cultural heritage of our state.[43] The rest of the fish you see are other species common to the coastal areas of Texas, like flounder."

After staring in awe for a few minutes, we turned to look at the freshwater river bank that had a slow-moving current flowing toward us. Toward the right side, the scenery was set up for marshland now that I had a better view of it. Coming from the otherwise silent tank was a constant "ribbit . . . ribbit . . . ribbit."

I asked, "Charity, how many of those infernal things do you have croaking in there? Those things keep me up at night back home in Houston. What are they doing here?"

Charity replied, "The Texas toad (figure 29.16) is the state amphibian due to its ability to display a 'hardy determination that Texans are known for' and being capable of surviving in the many diverse habitats that make up the state landscape and terrain.[44] The noise is the only real downside, but they do deserve a place here. Think, we could have them or mosquitos; you decide. Let's walk down a bit."

A few moments later, after seeing what was swimming in the water, I was reaching for my imaginary fishing pole. I stated, "Let me guess: the Guadalupe bass is the state fish because They are only found in Texas, and their massive plentitude serves as 'a living testament to the sparkling purity of the state's freshwater purity'?"[45]

Charity nodded her head in agreement. "Now, let me guess: You read the bill that made this one a designation on our way in, right over there on the wall, didn't you? I don't care. You are trying to do my job now, hmm. Also, if you look at the surface of the water, you can see our state waterlily, the Nymphaea Texas Dawn (figure 29.17) that was

FIGURE 29.16   Texas Toad.

FIGURE 29.17   Nymphaea Texas Dawn.

---

43   TX HCR 122, 84R, 2015
44   TX HCR 18, 81R, 2009.
45   TX HCR 61, 71R, 1989.

chosen without any real connection to our heritage other than being crafted in Texas and its 'its unique beauty and resilient character.[46] I'm hungry, again. Let's go."

After finishing the walk to look at the other various fish common to Texas that were in the tank, like gar, we left Charity's exhibition to head back to the parking lot. A few minutes later when back on the road, just after we turned off Circle Road, Charity plugged in her iPhone® and pressed her iTunes® app. I was still a bit tired, so I didn't say much, but the tunes that played must have been related to our trip. There were a few just short sayings, like "friendship." There was also some lyrics, like "Bluebonnets, blue lovely Bluebonnets, More beautiful than all the rest. Texas chose you for her flower, And we love you best, Bluebonnets." My favorite, though, was "Texas, O Texas! Your freeborn single star, Sends out its radiance to nations near and far. Emblem of freedom! It sets our hearts aglow, With thoughts of San Jacinto and glorious Alamo." There was also a poem read with my favorite verse being "Rocks and hills hold fast the secret." The last tune was a simple phrase "in God we trust."

Forty minutes later, we arrived at the capitol after going on US 290 and MOPAC to downtown Austin. We used the underground parking garage and proceeded to enter the restaurant in the extension's basement. Before we got out of the car, I asked, "Aren't you going to tell me what all that music we just listened to has to do with today?"

Charity replied, "We'll now that you ask, the word *friendship* that you heard off and on is our state motto that was selected due to the name Texas being derived from the Indian word *Tejas*, meaning friendship, and the word being emblematic of the universal spirit existing in Texas and reflecting the spirit that has always influenced our people.[47] More importantly, our state flower song is "Bluebonnets," which explains the bluebonnet ode that you heard. Also, our state song is "Texas, Our Texas," which was selected due to, well, why not.[48] A majority of the tunes, our state music is western swing, which was selected due to it being 'a lively sound that has enjoyed enduring popularity over the course of nearly a century, . . . [that] . . . reflects the ethnic diversity of Texas by encompassing many of the musical traditions that were introduced to the state by the groups that settled here,'[49] not to mention the fact that it gets you moving and grooving.'"

I spoke aloud, "Glad to see that music has not been left out in the cold regarding our state symbols, but what about our national music symbols?"

---

46    TX HCR 24, 82R, 2011.
47    TX HCR 22, 41st, 4CS, 1930.
48    TX HCR 24, 43R, 1933.
49    TX SCR 35, 82R, 2011.

## Categories of Federal and State Symbols

Charity didn't say anything, but she motioned to follow her inside. Once in the grand gallery, we walked south and stopped immediately in front of an American flag. She put her hand over her heart and said aloud, "I pledge allegiance to the flag of the United States of America" and ended with " I, therefore, believe it is my duty to my country to love it, to support its Constitution, to obey its laws, to respect its flag, and to defend it against all enemies."

After a round of applause from the bystanders, Charity pulled me in close and said, "The first line I spoke is from our national pledge of allegiance, and the last was from our national creed that was adopted by Congress in 1918.[50] The last phrase you heard back when we were in the car was our nation's motto that was made official via a 1956 Joint Resolution of Congress to replace 'E Pluribus Unum' and was selected from the fourth verse of Frances Scot Keys' Star Spangled Banner poem due to it saying, 'And this be our motto.' A bit obvious, but it works."

As we walked past various committee rooms and the gift shop I told Charity what she said was very beautiful, but I made a special point to say, "Where is this food you referred to when you said you were hungry a while back at the zoo?"

Then, as we arrived at our lunchtime destination, the Capitol Grill,[51] Charity gave her best Vanna White pose, and I could only hang my head in shame due to my poor whiny behavior.

I mumbled, "I forgot about this place from a week ago, oh boy."

When walking in the door, Charity, ignoring my grumbling, stated, "Just like the exhibit at the zoo, I had a hand in preparing our lunch. Not cooking it of course, but the actual selecting of the dishes to be served. This was something that I worked on this last spring as an assignment with the museum. Specifically, we will be dining on dishes that have been selected to represent our state. Bon appétit."

When we walked into the restaurant, the short-order cooks and the head chef all yelled, "Hey there, girl, we moved your spread to the far side of the room. Check it out!"

In response, Charity yelled, "Thanks for the tip!"

Then, she turned to me and said, "The first item I want you to look at is what many of the dishes are being cooked in. Believe it or not, the cast iron Dutch ovens (figure 29.18) you see here are the state cooking implement. This common kitchen item was selected due to their use by Texans ever since the original Spanish explorers came here centuries ago.[52] What you see inside the first Dutch oven today is the state dish, chili.[53] Chi(), as you know, is a

---

50    State Symbols USA, "Pledge & Creed," accessed March 21, 2019, https://statesymbolsusa.org/symbol-official-item/national-us/state-cultural-heritage/pledge-allegiance.

51    http://austincapitolgrill.com

52    TX SCR 9, 79R, 2005.

53    TX HCR 18, 65R, 1977.

spicy stew that contains a mixture of peppers, meats, tomatoes, and, most notably, beans, and deserves the rank of state symbol because the state is the dish's birthplace as well as the home of the international chili cook-off, and a Texan is the champion cooker in most years. Next to it, in the second Dutch oven, is our state bread, Pan de Campo. This delicacy takes the role of state bread due to 'its elegant simplicity' and 'its role as a redolent reminder of the state's storied past and the vaqueros of South Texas.'[54] In the last one is the salsa half of the state snack, chips and salsa."

The head chef came over and advised, "This dish is good as an appetizer. More importantly, chips and salsa (figure 29.19) deserve the rank of state symbol due to being found in virtually every home in the state, its use of traditional state crops, folk medicine lore, and its importance to a variety of industry."[55]

Charity replied, "You remembered what I told you about the dish from the legislation mandating it—good for you, Taco!"

Taco, the head chef, continued, "I'll show you even more of what I know. Look over here, kid. We got three side dishes that also fall into the rank of state symbols. In the first bowl, in front of the Dutch ovens, you are looking at the state vegetable, the sweet onion (figure 29.20), all chopped up and ready to go. This item was selected due to it originating in the state and being the first sweet onion in the world, not to mention representing a state

FIGURE 29.18    Cowboy dishing up chili and pan at noonday dinner. Cattle ranch near Marfa, Texas.

FIGURE 29.19    Chips and Salsa.

FIGURE 29.20    Fresh Picked Sweet Onion.

54    TX HCR 98, 79R, 2005.
55    TX HCR 16, 78R, 2003.

FIGURE 29.21   Jalapeños in a pile at the grocery store.

FIGURE 29.22   Chiltepin Plant.

legacy of agricultural innovation in vegetable development.[56] If you want to make your chili or salsa extra caliente, the two state peppers are available. The regular state pepper, the jalapeño (figure 29.21), is in the middle bowl and was chosen due to its representation of being 'a culinary, economic, and medical blessing to the citizens of the Lone Star State . . . and serves [as] . . . a distinctive reminder of our state's unique heritage and diverse culture.'[57] In the last bowl is the state native pepper, the chiltepin (figure 29.22). This duplicate pepper was selected because it is the only native pepper to Texas and played a role in the creation of red-hot Texas chili.[58] If you want, feel free to eat the chiltepin and test your manhood."

I replied, "Thankfully, when I was 13 at summer camp in Burnet, Texas, at Camp Longhorn,[59] I had already passed that pivotal test with flying colors. Only a big glass of milk saved my taste buds from extinction. Good times. What are the meats over there on the platters?"

Charity and Taco exchanged looks. Charity said, with a concerned tone, "Champ, that is red drum fish and longhorn beef. Despite being a state symbol, they are both quite tasty. Therefore, they made the spread. Let's look over here at the desserts, though, to pick up our spirits."

After moving down the counter, Charity continued, "On the first platter are the state pastries, the sopapilla and strudel (figures 29.23 and 24). These delicacies were selected due to their representation of the tremendous cultural differences found in the state,

56   TX HCR 148, 75R, 1997.
57   TX HCR 105, 74R, 1995.
58   TX HCR 82, 75R, 1997.
59   http://www.camplonghorn.com

FIGURE 29.23   Sopaipilla.

FIGURE 29.24   Strudel.

with the sopapilla, with honey on top, representing Hispanic south Texas and the strudel representing the German hill country.[60] Next to those is a pecan pie (figure 29.25), which remarkably covers three more state symbols: the state health nut, pie, and tree. The pecan was selected as the state tree due to its longevity and being commonplace in 152 counties, the nut because of its health benefits (with Texas responsible for 20 percent of national production), and pie due to the pecan is best enjoyed in a pie with varying quantities of syrup and nuts and ice cream."[61]

FIGURE 29.25   Pecan Pie.

At this point, I was just in awe. However, after coming to my senses (and my sister bopping me on the head for gawking at the display), I went for a serving of the state fruit, the Texas red grapefruit (figure 29.26), that was in a bowl. I was glad to make this selection for dessert, and it is a state symbol, because, as Charity put it, "It is the most profitable tree crop in Texas' and it has 'proven resolve at being a healthy food for all Texans.'"[62]

FIGURE 29.26   Texas Red Grapefruit.

After what seemed like an hour, we finally paid for the meal and sat down to eat. Little did I know, the sights were only just getting started at our table, which seemed to be a bit more decorated than the others. While our lunch here up to this point seemed random, I

60    TX HCR 92, 78R, 2003.
61    TX SB ,ch. 97, 36R, 1919 (Tree). TX SCR 2, 77R, 2001 (Health Nut). TX SCR 12, 83R, 2013 (Pie).
62    TX HCR 175, 73R, 1993.

FIGURE 29.27 Pumpkins, taken at the Hancock Shaker village.

do believe at this point it was now premeditated. Charity stated, "Champ, look here at the centerpiece. This is the state squash, pumpkin (figure 29.27). It's not carved due to Halloween being several months away, but this vegetation was selected due to Texas producing millions of them each year, it plays a pivotal role in feeding livestock during winter due to them keeping for quite a while, being a healthy food source, pumpkin pie, and, most importantly, several varieties can grow to over 1,000 pounds, making them larger than life, like many Texans are.[63] Let's eat. Your steak has to be getting cold by now."

After about 15 minutes of silence, Charity said, with a bite of steak still in her mouth, "You know, while we are here, I should give you a tour around the Capitol Building because it displays many different things important to Texas over the years."

I interrupted her by stating, "Let's keep today as much as possible for state symbols. I went on more tours of this place than I can count and I've already seen as much of it as I care to for a while."

Thinking for a few seconds, Charity said, "Fine, I get to take you over to one place before we go. No but's."

I replied, "So where are we going then?"

FIGURE 29.28 State Agriculture Museum.

Charity answered, followed by us putting our waste into the appropriate bins, "The State Agricultural Museum (figure 29.28) upstairs, of course. Lots of symbols in there, little brother. Let's go."

On the way there, I asked, "Are there any national food symbols?"

Charity responded, "Nothing official, but if I had to choose a national dish it would either be apple pie or hot dogs due their epitomization in a 1974 Chevy cars commercial that put them as such and despite both being of European heritage, they

---

63    TX HCR 87, 83R, 2013.

came into being after being brought over here by the action of immigrants."[64]

I replied, "I remember that commercial. Both are delicious in their own regard. I want a slice and a dog now. Oh, well."

Thankfully, the change in location to the museum proved prudent, as many of the state's less edible vegetation items were on display, not to mention we were staying out of the midday heat for a while longer and getting the dishes off my mind, I hoped. In getting to the first floor of the main building, we took a right out of the restaurant and found ourselves in front of the main bank of elevators. When on the first floor, we traveled to the west wing via the main rotunda. When we arrived, I could not help but stare in awe at the massive room's 1894 appearance, with what appeared to be the original furniture and, quite possibly, the original flooring. In getting started, Charity mentioned, "If you look over here in one of the bigger display cases, you will see our state fiber and fabric, cotton (figure 29.29). This symbol earned its place due to it being one of the largest crops grown in the state and how in the panhandle, from Midland to Amarillo, blooms go from dust brown to snow white each year when the crop comes in, like how the rest of the state 'blooms' with the state insect and flower each spring.[65] Let's go to the other side of the room."

After a short walk, we found ourselves looking at a group of fossils. Charity explained, "Lightning is a powerful force, as seen in the many storms that hit the state each spring, year in and year out. Anything that assumes its shape should have its power. In taking this mantra to heart, our state has selected the lightning whelk (figure 29.30) as our state shell. This shell earned the right to be a state symbol due to it being one of the most

FIGURE 29.29   Cotton harvest on the South Plains near Lubbock, Texas. Cotton stripper header pulls the cotton bolls and leaves off of the plant.

FIGURE 29.30   Sinistrofulgur perversum (Linnaeus, 1758) HMNS 1659 Galveston, TX.

64    Sally Rummel, "As American as 'Baseball, Hot Dogs, Apple Pie and Chevrolet,'" *Tri-County Times* (Fenton, MI), July 27, 2016, http://www.tctimes.com/as-american-as-baseball-hot-dogs-apple-pie-and-chevrolet/article_dd7083ea-3efe-11e6-8531-43492d385b75.html.
65    TX HCR 228, 75R, 1997.

FIGURE 29.31 Cabochon of agatized fossil palm wood from south-central United States (TX-LA).

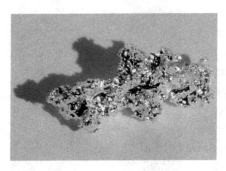

FIGURE 29.32 Natural silver nugget, 1 cm long.

common shells found along Texas coastlines and being one of the few that opens from the left side.[66] Next to it is our state stone, petrified palm wood. Petrified palm wood (figure 29.31) was selected due to Texas being a primary growth area for the palm wood tree millions of years ago and how the state produces many excellent varieties of the petrified, or stoned, remains today.[67] Beyond these symbols, every crop produced in the state can be seen in this room. As you can see, a big state such as Texas can grow a wide variety of crops. Lastly, next to the palm wood is our state precious metal, silver (figure 29.32), that was selected due to it being a 'visible part of Texas culture, reflecting the enduring influence of Spanish colonial design and the western heritage that is so much a part of the state's lore'[68] and not to mention in jewelry and tableware. This material is what the bolo tie I am wearing is made from. Now, I know it's hot, but we do need to go outside eventually. You game?"

I replied, "You bet I am!"

The time was now getting close to 3:00 p.m., and we left the museum through the doors that lead to the main hallway of the floor. We took an immediate right and found ourselves facing a brutal Texas summer heat after exiting the building that felt like we were walking into an oven. We quickly found ourselves a tall shrub to stand under for protection. Charity said, "I'm glad we picked this tree to stand under."

I interjected, "Why is that?"

Charity pointed out, "Well, this is a crape myrtle, the state shrub. This shrub plays back onto the theme we discussed earlier of state symbols looking like the bluebonnet. In the case of the crape myrtle, it kind of looks like the bluebonnet, but a lot bigger.[69] If we look a bit

---

66    TX HCR 75, 70R, 1987.
67    TX HCR 12, 61R, 1969. https://lrl.texas.gov/LASDOCS/61R/HCR12/HCR12_61R.pdf#page=4
68    TX HCR 102, 80R, 2007.
69    TX HCR 14, 75r, 1997.

closer, surrounding the crape myrtle spread out along the ground is our state native shrub, Texas purple sage (figure 29.33). This sage was chosen due to the plant being able to 'face droughts, freezes, high winds, salt spray, hungry deer, and blazing heat and keep right on performing beautifully,'[70] like any good Texan would when called to duty."

FIGURE 29.33   Texas Purple Sage (Leucophyllum frutescens).

I noticed an exciting, yet familiar vehicle passing on the street in the distance. I called out to the driver, "Sir, what kind of wagon vehicle do you have there?"

The driver slowed the drawing horses and said, "Young man, this is called a chuck wagon (figure 29.34). This is the state vehicle. It is essential to recognize it due to no other vehicle having helped so many Texans settle the west. Chuck wagons served as the storage and supply vehicles on cattle drives that ranchers drove to get cattle to market back in the day of hunger and malaise.[71] Want to go for a ride?"

FIGURE 29.34   Reenactor Dave Harkness with Chuck Wagon.

---

70   TX HCR 71, 79R, 2005.
71   TX SCR 8, 79R, 2005.

FIGURE 29.35    Prickly pear cactus in Texas.

Charity and I simultaneously said, "Yes!"

Once on the wagon, we were moseying down the road out of the capital grounds via the Grand Walk. We turned east on 15th Street. At that point, I asked the driver, "Where are you headed for your ride today?"

He responded by indicating, followed by turning his head back to the road ahead, "I am headed for UT's Frank Erwin Event Center and the Austin Rodeo.[72] It was supposed to be back in March, but it had been delayed for a few months due to scheduling conflicts with the N-C-double-A Men's Division One Basketball Tournament."[73]

In the downtime, Charity and I mostly just looked out the back of the wagon and took in the sights. But, being the expert, she is, Charity used the opportunity to show off a few more symbols just as we became cattycorner to the Erwin Center at the last remnant of Centennial Park at the corner of Red River and 15th Streets, which, as I later learned on a web search, was built in 1936 to commemorate the 100th anniversary of Texas's founding and has since been mostly razed to build the new medical school and teaching hospital for the University of Texas at Austin.[74] While waiting for the light to turn, Charity pointed out, "That cactus over there is called a prickly pear cactus (figure 29.35), the state plant. Prickly pear cacti were selected due to them being a 'denizen' of the rugged landscape, their innovative uses in cooking, and security, in addition to being able to survive in the many different landscapes of Texas, just like the state amphibian could.[75] Also, the grass surrounding the cactus is the state grass, side-oats grama. This was chosen as it can be seen on every ranch, highway median, and unmaintained plot of land to preserve the soil of the state, alongside the fact that ranchers depend on it for feeding their herds. Also, it can survive in any weather condition, as any good Texan can.[76] We Texans, as you should note by

72    http://uterwincenter.com; http://www.rodeoaustin.com

73    http://www.ncaa.com/sports/basketball-men/d1

74    Ralph K.M. Haurwitz, "UT's Centennial Park to Be Sacrificed for New Teaching Hospital," September 25, 2018, http://www.mystatesman.com/news/local/centennial-park-sacrificed-for-new-teaching-hospital/sTKi06VQdYKkeMMB1aAgHM.

75    TX HCR 44, 74R, 1995.

76    TX SCR 31, 62R, 1971.

now, like to be strong, independent types who can survive anything in the dirt before us. I think that if I were to summarize them all, it takes a lot of grit, true grit that is, to be Texan or at least represent Texans to the world. Also, before I forget, the big tree that you see in the center of what's left of the park is the mighty oak tree (figure 29.36), our national tree, that was selected in 2007 after a nationwide contest led by the National Arbor Day Foundation, not to mention its 60 some-odd species, beauty, abundant shade, and usefulness in making hardwood products."[77]

FIGURE 29.36    Mighty Oaks in San Marcos, Texas.

A few minutes later, just past 4:00 p.m., we arrived at the Erwin Center, tipped the driver, and said thanks for the ride on the traditional Texan way of getting around. Once we walked up the steps to get a closer look at the building from Red River Street, we saw some people dancing on the large open plazas surrounding the building. Charity pointed out, "Those fine Texas citizens are square dancing (figure 29.37), the state folk dance, which was selected due to it representing a combined cultural legacy of how early settlers dealt with the hardships of early domains by using the dance to build a

FIGURE 29.37    Bent Creek Ranch Square Dance Team at Asheville Mountain Music Festival.

sense of community on the plains.[78] Also, the guys with the domino set put out over there are playing the state domino game called 42, which was selected due to the game 'being a true Lone Star original and a testament to the ingenuity and fun-loving nature of Texans in times of crisis.'"[79]

A few minutes after we showed up, the woman leading the square dance invited us to join in. Charity found a nice cowboy to dance with while I danced with the leader. After about an hour of dancing to the guitar music, Charity and I stopped to get a drink of water and

77    https://www.arborday.org/programs/nationaltree
78    TX HCR 84, 82R, 2011.
79    TX HCR 153, 72R, 1991.

FIGURE 29.38    A classical guitar.

decide whether to see the rodeo events that were about to start, but before we left, Charity walloped herself on the forehead out of the blue after she was spun into the band. She said, all dazed and confused, "The guitar (figure 29.38) they are playing the music on is the state musical instrument due to many musical pioneers of the state using it to build their careers, and multiple forms of music use the guitar as a core component of their harmonies.[80] Let's go inside. My head hurts now."

Also, on the way in Charity mumbled something about how roses (figure 29.39) are our national flower due to them growing in each of the 50 states, its robustness in all seasons, bright colors, and ability to deceive the senses while being a challenge to grow.[81] I didn't quite get all of it, but at least I now knew all the national vegetation symbols as well.

Now close to 5:30 p.m., we had our tickets in hand and went through the turnstiles. We got some hot dogs and sat down to watch the events. Throughout the evening, I realized that many of the events occurring were just different activities that regularly occurred on ranches throughout the state; they were just modified for entertainment purposes to additionally help build a sense of community that links us to our past on top of the swing music and square dancing.[82] The chuck wagon races were the most interesting example of this concept. Since we were at a sports arena, I decided to ask Charity what the state sport was. Her response, back at full strength: "You are looking at it right now, the rodeo (figure 29.40), of which the current performance is by the Ghostriders, our state rodeo drill team."[83]

I asked, "Are there any other symbols that you can think of?"

FIGURE 29.39    Red rose from the rooftop at Sanmar RL Park View, South Khulshi, Chittagong.

80    TX HCR 23, 75R, 1997.
81    State Symbols USA, "The Rose." accessed March 21, 2019, https://statesymbolsusa.org/symbol-or-officially-designated-item/state-flower/rose; US HCR 1/8/1965.
82    TX HCR 21, 75R, 2013.
83    TX HCR 136, 80R, 2007; http://theghostriders.homestead.com

FIGURE 29.40   Rodeo Rider.

Charity, instead of immediately sputtering out some other long list of things, brought out her smartphone. She searched and came across a website that had a list of them that was maintained by the Texas State Library and Archives Commission.[84] In no order, she pointed out that the Commemorative Air Force is our state air force;[85] the Texas State Aquarium in Corpus Christi is our state aquarium;[86] the Lady Bird Johnson Wildflower Center is our state botanical garden;[87] the Texas Maritime Museum in Rockport is our state Maritime Museum;[88] our state bluebonnet city is Ennis;[89] our nickname is the Lone Star State;[90] our state ship is the USS *Texas* near Houston at the San Jacinto Battlegrounds (figure 29.41);[91] the state 10K is the Texas Round-up 10K in Austin;[92] the state railroad is the Texas State Railroad;[93] *The Lone Star,*

FIGURE 29.41   San Jacinto Battlegrounds Monument.

84   https://www.tsl.texas.gov/ref/abouttx/symbols.html
85   TX SCR 114,71R, 1989; https://commemorativeairforce.org
86   TX CHR 40, 69R, 1985; https://www.texasstateaquarium.org
87   TX HB 694, 73R, 2017; https://www.wildflower.org
88   TX SCR 57, 70R, 1987; http://texasmaritimemuseum.org
89   TX HCR 116, 75R, 1997; http://www.ennistx.gov
90   TX HCR 77, 84R, 2015.
91   TX SCR 101, 74R, 1995; https://tpwd.texas.gov/state-parks/battleship-texas
92   TX HCR 148, 79R, 2005.
93   TX HCR 34, 78R, 2003; http://texasstaterailroad.net

*Texas, Beyond the Sundown*, and *Fandangle* are our state plays;[94] and our tallest ship is the tall ship, *Elissa*.[95] She concluded by stating, "We might have too many symbols. We might want to make sure our legislators who decide on these things are a bit busier with other things, or we might run out of things to claim, although we have three official state hashtags, #Texas, #Texas ToDo, and #txlege, for Texas in general, tourism, and the state legislature itself, so be sure to light up their accounts.[96] I would say that we could probably use a few more at the national level, though."

I could only agree, but as stated before, the point of today was to learn about the symbols that have been used by the state and national governments to represent themselves to the outside world. This turned out to range from animals to activities, all the way down to the dinner table, with the state government doing a far better job at presenting itself to the world. For the most part, in both cases, the symbols are used to represent our heritage of surviving off the land, how we choose/chose to deal with issues that arose from living here, and standing up and fighting for our way of life. One thing, though, I felt was missing: Why is football not the state sport? I seem to remember going to games on Friday, Saturday, and Sunday each weekend in the fall, to the extent that it was a religion, not to mention baseball for the national government. I think I need to contact somebody about this. My representatives and state legislators perhaps? Either way, a diverse set of items is used to represent the state and nation to outsiders.

94    TX SB 93, 66R, 1979.
95    TX HCR 117, 79R, 2005; http://www.galvestonhistory.org/attractions/maritime-heritage/texas-seaport-museum-elissa-rentals
96    TX HCR's 105, 106, and 104, 84R, 2015.

## FIGURE CREDITS

# Chapter 30

# Reflections

O N THE WAY HOME FROM THE rodeo, Charity's inner mom came to the forefront. Explicitly, she stated, "Champ, if I've run through the list of all the places you could experience for a summer in government, I think you have checked off all the boxes. Have you given it much thought as to where you want to end up after the summer? The season's almost over, you know?"

I replied, "Yes I do know, and the stress of it all is getting to be a bit more than I'd care to admit."

She replied, "What's so stressful?"

I replied, "I guess that once I make a decision, that decision is somewhat permanent, kind of like how people make such a decision when drafting a governing document."

Charity countered, "You do realize that people switch careers all the time, right? There is no shame in picking something now and then going back later in a new direction when you realize that your first choice was not the right one. Doing so indicates that you made a thoughtful decision, eventually of course. How are you feeling now?"

I replied, "Better, knowing that insight. I guess I don't exactly know how to go about making that decision as to which road to go down."

Charity concluded while sipping her water, "Why don't you go back and summarize what you learned on each day of your trek more than you have in each of your journal entries you've made thus far and then make a decision from there?"

Accordingly, when I woke up this morning, I sat down and did just that. What follows are the lessons learned from my 29 days of travel. In general, each of those 29 days of travel is better grouped into four different sections, governing foundations based on the first 7 days, getting involved with government based on the following 5 days, office spaces based on the next 12 days, and the final 5 days consisting of office politics.

When looking back at what I had been through over the last six weeks, the trek that I had been on started on a bit of a whim when my family and I spent time at Disney World in Orlando. That whim occurred on the final full day when at the Hall of Presidents attraction. While there, during extensive conversations with the animatronic presidents led primarily by current President Trump, I first learned that government is a form or system of rules that governs a state, akin to the rules set up by parents to keep the peace in their homes. Following that, I garnered that society is like a chair being held up by laws and traditions that are enforced by institutions, without which society crumbles from within like a chair without its legs. Then, I was exposed to the terms of power, the ability to get others to act in your stead, authority, verbal permission to act, and legitimacy, power, and authority being invested to an entity by a written document of which together gives one the right to lead. Afterward, various types of government were spelled out, varying based on who has the power, authority, and legitimacy: one, many, or none. Ending Trump's time in the spotlight was his discussion on the two types of democracy, direct and indirect, which vary by the prior having to make decisions en masse and the latter having the populace elect people to make decisions for them. Former president Obama then took over and introduced five items that make democracy survive, including having regular free and fair elections, people participating, protecting rights of the people to participate, the rule of law, and notable differences between candidates in elections. President Woodrow Wilson ended the discussion by showing that political scientists have organized leadership theories in government into an elitist rule and majority rule only to conclude that the United States is a mixture of the two in something called pluralism, due to citizens selecting our leaders, but that those leaders tend to be from elitist camps of society. Overall, the exposure to these terms brought about my interest to pursue politics in the future.

On the second day, what started as a simple flight home from vacation turned into an out-of-aircraft experience. On the flight home from Orlando, Florida, to Houston, Texas, I met Dr. Derek Alderman of the University of Tennessee. He mentored me about political geography which is looking at political institutions through a geographical lens for greater understanding. In doing so, I learned the difference between nations, groups of people, and states, governed territories, and how a whole world of terms like nation-states exist when the two overlap. Following that, I learned how the state characteristics—including the size, the amount of territory had by a state, shape, how the territory of a state is distributed, location, being landlocked or not, core area, the place of major activity within a state, and boundaries of a state, the lines demarking where one state ends, and the other begins—can impact a future state's existence, as each variation makes it easier or more difficult to manage. We concluded our time together learning about state cohesion, factors focusing on the nation within a state can work to divide or build up a state's existence, like nationalism. Overall, I learned how the nation and the state work together to provide a prosperous or a disastrous state of being for the citizenry.

On day three, I explored the University of Texas at San Antonio's Institute of Texan Cultures, where I met Dr. John Davis. While there, we first viewed an exhibit on the native peoples of the area (who dated back to 10,000 BCE) and the Clovis people. This exhibit led to an interesting discussion on what drove their societies (obtaining sustenance) and how it was a metaphor for people selecting their government and what it does for them today. After watching the feature presentation in the Dome Show Theatre, I was introduced to the topic of political culture (and its original theorist, Daniel Elazar) at the national and regional level. Following that, I was enlightened by the recent work of Richard Florida, who offered additional classifications at the local level, due to the likelihood of culture pockets emerging in areas that have a drastically different view toward government than their surroundings. We also discussed the potential factors that help develop political culture before touring the exhibit hall, which housed showcases of the various sects and populations that eventually settled here in the state. While in the showcases, we discussed the impact of political cleavages (based on the different viewpoints found in the societies) and how best to deal with them by finding issues that cut across the different groups. After that, while touring the Back 40 exhibit, we discussed a Texas legislative study report that showed how our political culture could predict our spending decisions and rankings on societal dilemmas like poverty. We concluded with the thought that we develop our view toward the government that then works toward defining what our government ends up becoming that then governs accordingly producing a society that advocates the original view toward government, a vicious circle. My day ended after walking the short distance to the Alamo through HemisFair Park, where I realized that the defenders were defending their beliefs in a limited government and setting off our history of keeping that limited-government culture alive. Overall, I learned how our beliefs toward government became a reality and went on to impact our daily lives to this day.

On day four, I found myself back in San Antonio for another adventure. While there, at the Texas State Data Center on the campus of the University of Texas at San Antonio, Downtown, I met with the state's demographer, Dr. Lloyd Potter. I found it cool that he had a framed piece of legislation from 2001 that created his position. We proceeded to have an extensive discussion about the different offices that make up his agency: the legislative liaison office in Austin and the San Antonio office, where the demographic data of the state is processed. Following that, we discussed the different responsibilities he had, which ranged from required reports to the legislature on down to public speaking events for different groups that needed his information to make better business decisions. From there, we looked at the various trends found in the state's demographics. For one trend, the population is growing, but rural counties are losing population, with the growth being concentrated in the triangle formed by the cities of San Antonio, Dallas-Fort Worth, and Houston. Also, whites are facing stagnating growth, while all other ethnic groups are proliferating. The consequences of this stagnation in growth by the dominant ethnic group but massive growth had one major consequence regarding politics, which is a projected political shift from Republican-dominated politics to Democratic-dominated politics, as Hispanics, blacks, and other ethnic groups tend to vote for the Democratic Party more than the former group. After discussing trends in the demographics of the state, I was introduced to other official events that he and his organization put on to discuss their data, alongside their website, which users may make inquiries on. Lastly, the day ended with the two of us going to the legislative liaison office in Austin to make an emergency presentation to a group of legislators on the population dispersion of the state. Politics was seen during the meeting, as there was a bit of pressure by the legislators to put the numbers in a more favorable light. Overall, I learned that the demographics of the state were right at the heart of change in the state, as the trends foresaw the arrival of a new era of political control, at least at the state level.

On day five, I had the opportunity to sit in on a rather interesting presentation at the Lorenzo de Zavala State Archives and Library. The speaker that day never revealed his identity, but he came off as an expert on the important documents of not just the state, but also the country at large. After the lights in the learning center room went dark, the mystery man spoke. He first talked about why constitutions and declarations are important; they provide the governing structure and proper allegiance, respectively, followed by presenting the state's current constitution and declaration of independence from Mexico. In introducing the roles of constitutions, he brought up the main characters of the show *The Big Bang Theory* and how the roommate agreement that binds them together is nothing more than a constitution in disguise. After establishing what constitutions are and do, the darkness of the room to keep the documents safe was used as a metaphor for the differences between strict and loose government documents and how to interpret them, by the letter or spirit of, respectively. The conversation then moved on to the contents and what the goals of constitutions are when writing them. After a brief interlude as to how countries were typically formed, the mysterious man discussed the importance of the Texas and the American Declarations of Independence, which led into a long history of the Articles of Confederation and how that constitution led to the adoption of our current federal constitution. Following that, each of the states' and the federal constitutions was discussed in detail in reference to their influence on what governs us today. The experience ended with the group playing a modified version of the paperclip game, with balloons that taught us how a good constitution is one that is fair to all concerned and is designed to help regulate society but not go so far as stopping everything from occurring. Those who failed to learn the lesson ended up covered in flour. Overall, I discovered that, in a society that self-governs based on a written document, it is wise to write a document that is fair to all concerned to meet the expectations of its people, and one which, as time goes on, gets updated as necessary by their descendants.

On day six, I learned about different kinds of relationships for governments, all while being set up to start one of my own. On this day, I had a blind date with a nice young woman who works with Charity. Over lunch, the young woman I met with, Leia, informed me about the main focus of her research: federalism, the relationship between the states and the national government. We first discussed the term *sovereignty* and how the level of it represents how much independence a state has. We then moved on to discuss the three main systems of government: federalism, unitary, and confederal. Each system of government differed based on the amount of power centralization. Afterward, the discussion moved on to who had which set of powers: reserved, delegated, or concurrent by the states, the federal government, and both at the same time, respectively. We then used different types of cakes to display the difference between layer-cake and marble-cake federalism and how the different methods impact the relationship found between the states and the federal government. The cake discussion led into our following discussion on how we moved from the dual to the cooperative, and then on to the coercive eras of federalism, which was representative of how the states went from being equal to that of the federal government to Texas being subservient to the federal government, which was created by the states in the first place. The lunch date ended with a discussion of the laboratory of democracy and how letting individual states adopt a policy, seeing how it works, and then allowing other states to adopt the policy as needed to their situations, or not at all, might be a better solution for how we develop policies in the country. Overall, I learned that the relationship between the states and the federal government is much like one between two people, with their dynamics, roles, and courting procedures, which can lead to quite healthy or toxic relationships, i.e., the health of the nation at large.

Day seven found me touring the Bullock Museum in downtown Austin. I was initially going to go around with Charity, who works there, but an emergency saw her get pulled away. As an introduction to the day's activities, Charity and I listened to a mix tape of patriotic Texas and American songs on the commute to the museum. While walking around the museum by myself, I got my start standing in the middle of the first portion of the mural placed into the rotunda's floor. The museum itself functioned like that of a timeline that you walked through instead of viewing on the wall. On the first floor, not much was seen to showcase modern Texas politics, as it only offered information regarding the royal French ship named *La Belle*, along with the native populations, and those of the French and Spanish colonies, found in the state. The second floor really did a great job of presenting the state under Mexican rule and why we left; the Revolutionary War that ensued and secured our independence; our time as our own country; our first round as a fully functional US state (all the way through the process of leaving and then rejoining the country after the US Civil War), ending with the first half of the twentieth century. The events of this floor seemed to mimic the flow of relationships and stages that a high school student goes through during their time in those grades. I mean, up to this point, Texas was a part of one country, became its own, joined another, left it, and then got together all over again. The final floor did not cover anything political; instead, it just showed how Texans made their way off the land from ranching, agriculture, and oil. The funny thing was though, at each turn of the timeline, I kept channeling what I learned during my senior-year American government class. By that I mean, like Texas, the colonies got fed up with their dictatorial ruler from afar and left, had a revolutionary war that ensued to secure our independence, spent some time developing what our country was to be, and fought another war (the War of 1812) to secure that new destiny. Overall, the political history of Texas and the country at large are the same, just with different names and times.

Day eight saw my trek get out of the classroom and into the field, the field of political participation with Uncle Tommy. At the start of the day in Tommy's office, I first learned about how people's participation can be grouped into different categories based on what it is they do. I was then introduced to some of the more passive types of participation, such as voting, having a discussion, writing a letter to a public official or an editorial in the newspaper, or making a monetary contribution to a campaign. For lunch, we ate with Tommy's Rotary Club, which was a good example of service organizations and how they help you build social capitol to spend in currying favor for yourself. The afternoon saw our focus turn to more active methods of participation. During a drive in the afternoon to city hall, we almost hit a guy showing his political affiliation via a shirt, hat, and button combination outfit. We then saw political bumper stickers and billboards that along with the clothing help get your message out to the people. After the drive, we attended an Austin City Council meeting to learn about petitions, protesting, and good old-fashioned rioting. At the end of the afternoon, we went to a diner and saw how a sit-in works. Overall, I felt that there are many ways that I could participate in the political process; the issue was finding the best one for each situation that I would face.

Days nine and ten consisted of two sides to the same coin. On the ninth, the subject matter consisted of learning about elections from the perspective of the candidates involved. In the morning, I spent time again with Tommy, who introduced me to the roles of campaign director, press secretary, social media director, webmaster, and speech writer. Due to Tommy being called away, I was sent to the local office of US representative Stormy Ridge. While at her office, we discussed campaign events of party conventions, making speeches, debating, and even going door to door. I was then sent to speak with some of her employees, who doubled during election season as workers for the campaign.

The first was Ridge's financial advisor, who informed me on how candidates could raise money and what they had to do with it once collected. The second was Ridge's pollster/researcher, who informed me about the processes that she used to get the public view of the candidate and how people made decisions in the voting booth. Lastly, I spoke with Ridge's staff director, who indicated how, once other people did their jobs, it was his duty to direct people who volunteered at events on how to get the message out. At the end of it all, I realized that running for office was a very lengthy public job interview, with a staff who helped the candidate decide to run or keep running. Even the events after an election like taking the position were intense. Overall, running for office is more than just the election; it is a team effort over an extended period.

On day ten, I found myself learning about the other side of the coin, elections from the perspective of the voters helping officials get into office. First, from a commercial broadcast by the current secretary of state, Rolando Pablos, about the voter eligibility requirements in Texas, I learned that I did qualify. I was also advised of an important voter registration drive that was occurring that same day over on the West Mall on the UT campus. When I got there, I overheard Pablos's speech informing the crowd as to where citizens can go to register (other than at the event, if they did not qualify that day). While there, I was also able to listen in on a conversation had between the secretary and event-goers. The first one I overheard was on how to go vote on or before Election Day physically; the possibilities were numerous due to mail-in ballots and early voting. The next group asked about who votes and how it had changed over the years—interest in politics and a political party alongside increased wealth, education, and age, being female, and being a churchgoer get people to the polls today. Differing voting rates based on race or ethnicity have disappeared. I was then brought in to the conversation by the secretary to prove a point. It didn't work, but I was able to learn about the difference between the voting-age population and voting-eligible population and how only around half, if that, can be expected to show up to vote in Texas. The reasons behind the low turnout ranged from the socioeconomics of the state to the actual length of the ballot and how the contents of the ballot can swing turnout. The next person in line asked about keeping the sanctity of voting, showing how Texas is doing more than most to keep the process pure, thanks to voter IDs, Aussie ballots, neutral polling stations, election monitors, and the ability to have recounts. After that, a UT football player showed up in full pads to ask how exactly the voting process works here, to find that it is a three-step process thanks to primary elections being used by parties to select candidates, general elections for the totality of citizens to elect people to office, and special elections to ensure that we always have representation. I asked why Secretary Cascos knew so much about the electoral process here in the state, to find that this is what his job entails as the chief election official of the state. The next few people inquired as to how ballots were constructed, how to get on one, and who wins. Overall, I learned how I could become registered to vote and how if I did want to vote what elections are available for me to participate in.

Day 11 got off to an awkward start as two state troopers arrived at the front door to haul me to a hearing at the Texas state capitol building about the activities that I had been involved in thus far this summer. That hearing was with the Texas Ethics Commission. While being interrogated by them, I was informed on what lobbying is: direct communication to influence government. After that, I was informed on what it would take to be required to register as a lobbyist, what I would have to report if I did so, and how registering here is different than in Washington DC, under federal law. Lastly, the commission covered some additional restrictions on what I could do, regardless of whether I was required to lobby. After that, I spent the rest of the day back with Tommy and was informed on what interest groups are, professional political partitionists, formally known as pressure groups and their lackeys, lobbyists. We discussed pressure group types: economic, noneconomic, and mixed. We went on a walking tour to nearby local headquarters of various interest groups and ended up in front of the Republican Party of Texas's headquarters to discuss how political parties are different from interest groups. When back at the capitol, we discussed why these groups exist today, constitutional rights, why people join them, career advancement and the desire to influence, and the numerous controls in existence to keep interested groups' influence in check like high or low levels of professionalism in a legislature. Lastly, I had the opportunity to practice how to lobby before Tommy told me to how to do so properly. Overall, I determined that interest groups lobby government like everyone else but are more professional at doing so than the rest of us.

Day 12 took me to a far-flung place, albeit nothing official. I spent the middle part of the day having lunch with the chairmen of the Democratic, Libertarian, and Republican Parties of the state at an authentic Russian restaurant in Austin. We first discussed the idea and history of party systems in the country, as political parties were shown to operate relative to one another, feeding off the others' demises and their political gains. Regardless of circumstances, political parties differ based on their views toward accessibility to government-provided services. We discussed the Nolan chart to help determine my political affiliation. We then covered the four functions of political parties in general, along with three characteristics of American political parties. After that, we determined who the main supporters of each party were and where each party had the advantage. The discussion reached a pivotal moment when we compared each other's parties' platforms, determining that the primary difference was their views on accessibility to services. Republicans seemed to be the most restrictive, Democrats less so, and the Libertarians wanted full access for everything in their way. Our conversation ended by discussing the difference between permanent and temporary party organization and how the two each help the parties advance their causes. Overall, I learned straight from the horse's mouths about the most straightforward link between government and society and how those political parties run the government when elected to office.

Day 13 of my trek saw my experiences transition from learning about how one could participate with the government to what actual government agencies are. For the first governing agency, I didn't have to leave the subdivision I was staying in, as was the first of four days learning about the local government of the area. On tap for this day were the remnants of the former Lost Creek Municipal Utility District, now the Lost Creek Limited District. While at their main offices in the heart of the subdivision, I met with Executive Director Jim Emmons. He advised me that the limited district gets its nomenclature because they are designed to handle one solitary issue in a set geographical district—the Lost Creek subdivision, in this case—by overseeing maintenance of the community areas of Lost Creek like the trails and entrance sign along with overseeing deed restrictions. We then discussed the district's operating infrastructure; he was responsible for creating a budget and a plan for how the district would operate, followed by getting it approved by the layperson board of directors. This led to the downsides of special districts in that few people know about them which drags down functionality and usage, low participation in meetings by those affected by the districts, and poor economies of scale which then led into how the district recently was stripped of their utility service provision after the city of Austin took over those duties due to Austin being able to provide the same service at much lower costs. Lastly, a tour of the facilities showed how their facilities are right with the people who live in the community. Overall, I learned that there was not a lot to the special district responsibilities, but that was the idea, as they are designated to only provide a single service like utilities, schooling, or transit.

Moving up the ladder of local government on day 14, I spent the day dealing with the city of Austin to learn about municipal organizations. When in the office of the city manager, who runs the city under the guise of the city council, I was informed of the charter, granted by the state legislature, which created the municipal government. This document gave them considerable power but still left them exposed to further legislative mandates. Also, we discussed the difference between general law and home-rule municipal structures to note that the latter is more powerful than the prior. Later, in a city council meeting, I was tasked with asking a question about how the power can be spread out among a city's government, to learn that there can be five different options, with the power being spread evenly among a commission or held entirely by a single individual. In the afternoon, I embarked on a scavenger hunt which saw me go to the Parks Department, the Code Compliance Department, the Planning and Design Department, Public Works, and the Austin-Bergstrom International Airport to learn about what occurs in the different bureaucratic agencies of the municipality. Overall, the cities, like the states, each have their legislative assembly and chief executive but have considerably different areas which they control.

Going even further up the rungs on the ladder of local government on day 15, I found myself at the Travis County Courthouse to educate myself on the how counties are run. When I arrived, I first spoke with the county judge, who served in a similar capacity to that of the mayor of a city or president of the country. Also, I was exposed to the fact that there are 254 counties in the state, and that each county has the same basic organizational structure: the judge and four commissioners. Most importantly, unlike the city yesterday which provided numerous specialized services to the area, the county was indicated to provide general government services, like holding courts and keeping track of important records like deeds. Like yesterday, I was also charged with standing before the commission to ask questions about how they handle their precincts in the county. In the afternoon, I was able to speak with said elected county officials by going on a scavenger hunt again. The offices could be divided into three categories: record keeping, with the county and district clerks; financing, with the tax assessor-collector, the county treasurer, and county auditor; and finally, law enforcement, between the district and county attorneys, the constable, and the sheriff. My final stop came when I visited with a county commissioner who informed me on the issue of consolidating services with the city of Austin and why it won't happen due to being outlawed in the state constitution. Overall, the services here seemed to be more straightforward with more standardization practices than those of a municipality akin to that of a special district.

On day 16, I reached the final rung of the local government spectrum. I spent the day at the Capitol Area Council of Governments to learn about regional planning councils. When speaking with the director in the morning, I learned that there are 24 in the state, with 3 to 26 counties per council, some of which included districts in neighboring states and Mexico. Specifically, I was advised that COGs are formed to handle anything that is a mutual concern in a contiguous geographic area. In running the council, the director informed me of her position as the executive director to handle the day-to-day operation of the district. Legislatively, she informed me that the executive commission oversees advising the day-to-day activities of the group, the general assembly is where member entities vote on the charter amendments and the budget, and a variety of other commissions form opinions on policy to be later voted on by the general assembly. A concern was raised that a policy does not always have to be followed by member organizations. After a snack break, the Cedar Park police chief advised me how, via the CAPCOG Law Enforcement Academy, common issues among members are resolved using better economies of scale. Then a Department of Public Safety officer advised that using disaster planning by looking at the regional level is more efficient. Finally, a director from the Texas Commission on Environmental Quality advised that issues without true boundaries, like air quality, can be serviced here. We ended our discussions here by concluding that the councils seemed to function like that of the Jedi

Council from Star Wars, where those of the force from around the galaxy gather together to handle a common occurrence throughout the realm, the dark side of the force. Overall, I got the idea that entities like small counties, municipalities, and special districts facing common issues can turn to their council to reach an accord on how to tackle common problems together.

On day 17, I spent my time in what seemed like every building, corner, and room of the Capitol Complex. In the morning, my dad and I went on a tour. We saw all the memorials, monuments, adjacent structures that housed branches of Texas government other than the legislative, hidden tunnels, and, most importantly, what my dad's office looked like. I had seen it before, but it had been a while. Along with our walk, the topic of our discussion focused on the minimum requirements for obtaining his office in the house. I met most of the official, but not many of the unofficial, requirements, due to being so, well poor and unemployed. We also discussed the size of the two legislative assemblies, 31 in the senate and 150 in the house, along with how often, once every two years or whenever the governor wants, and how long their sessions were, 140 days in the biennial session and no more than 30 days in the special. The last subject seemed most important, as it had to do with how the legislative districts were drawn, as the process could be discriminatory if done wrong. After lunch, I learned about the presiding officers that lead the regular legislators through the, if I counted correctly, 21 or so steps to passing legislation in Texas. Assuming a bill had to do with spending, it must first be submitted to the house, read, approved by a committee and their subcommittee, put on the house calendar, read again, argued over on the floor, read again, and finally voted on for approval, in that order. The worst part is that wasn't even the halfway point. That whole process gets repeated over again in the senate; the difference is that two-thirds of their members must vote on whether to hear about it in the first place. Once a bill is out of the senate, a conference committee must reconcile the different versions of a bill, followed by the original house reapproving it. When done, the bill must then get approved by the governor. If he or she doesn't, then both houses, with a two-thirds vote, must reapprove it. Also, at this point, the comptroller must give their blessing on whether we can afford it before the governor gets their say. In short, there are a lot of processes to follow just to get the legislative branch up and running, much less get a piece of legislation approved of. Overall, the morning covered the structure of the state legislature while the afternoon focused on how everything worked within the legislature akin to how we learn what parts are in the digestive system in addition to what each part does.

On day 18, I had the honor of spending a full 24 hours with the governor of Texas. The day got off to a bit of an odd start, as, when I arrived at the mansion, I made my way to the wrong door and set off an alarm along the way, to find myself getting in trouble. Thankfully, things were cleared up when Governor Abbott came out to rescue me. We spend the first part of the morning touring the Governor's Mansion grounds and the inside of the building. The most notable sights were the governor's official flag, the tack marks in the banister, and the Governor's Memento Collection. Later in the morning, we took a flight to New York City via Newark Airport in New Jersey. On the flight, I was exposed to the fact that he loses his powers when not in Texas, and I learned about the minimum qualifications, the perks, the length of his terms of office, how he could get removed, and, most importantly, his legislative powers. Once in New York City after a quick helicopter ride, the rest of our discussions focused on his executive powers. While in the New York City, we focused on the governor's duties as head of state, equivalent to that of a club doorman. This situation was evident, as he was a guest on *The Daily Show with Trevor Noah*, where he was promoting the state, and we attended the National Governor's Association annual meeting, where we did some glad-handing. After flying back to Austin on a late-night flight and getting some shuteye in the mansion, we went over to the governor's office, where we went over his remaining executive powers, which focus on his role as head of government, equivalent to that of a club manager. The fact that he was part of a plural executive seemed to diminish his demeanor, but he did still seem to have a fair bit to do. Overall, it seemed as if the governor was the true leader of the state albeit somewhat in a diminished capacity. The issue is that his hands were tied, due to so much of his authority being spread out among other leaders of the state when compared to that of the president. This was one of those days that left me wanting to know more.

From Day 19, I learned that the governor is only the tip of the iceberg regarding what makes up the executive branch of Texas government. What makes up the rest is something better known as the bureaucracy, the actual agencies on the ground enacting state laws, and was the focus of today. The day began when I met up with Lieutenant Governor Dan Patrick in the rotunda of the capitol building after walking downstairs from the governor's capitol office. While walking over to his office, we discussed what I had learned the day before about our state's bureaucratic setup, due to the plural executive being in effect and how it may impact the running of the state. Once in his office, which used to be an apartment for the holder of his office, we compared how our bureaucratic system was different from what went on at the federal level. The most notable part from here was the basic characteristics of the bureaucracy, from how the agencies must remain neutral to its actual size. We concluded our talk here by discussing how the actual agencies can be organized by whether they are an individual or part of a commission, how they get their job, and at what level in the system they are on. After a call for some lunch to be brought up to the rotunda floor, we made our way with our bagged lunches to the top of the capitol rotunda dome, just under the *Goddess of Liberty* on the open-air platform found there. While there, I got a bird's-eye view of the different groups, agencies, and people that play a significant role in controlling the decisions made by the officials who have the final say on issues. The view was amazing, albeit a bit chilly. Overall, I learned where the actual government existed and how it's nearly everywhere, controlling nearly everything that we do.

On what I counted to be my twentieth day learning about government, I spent my time focusing on what entities are in place to enforce the laws made by the state legislature, Congress, and local governing boards and implemented by the bureaucracy. At the beginning of the day, I was exposed to six different federal, state, and local law enforcement agencies that patrolled around Travis County and where exactly it was that the individual law enforcement agencies worked—all while being handcuffed in a booth at a donut store. While with the officers, we discussed jurisdiction (where they enforce the law), their main duties, the different types of crime (felonies versus misdemeanors), who is likely to commit crimes, and who is likely to be a victim. The officers ended our discussion with the advice of why it's good to follow the law, report crimes, when to make a citizen's arrest when they can make an arrest, and why it's important to remain silent when under arrest. While there, I got lucky and started up a conversation with an attorney who agreed to fill me in on what exactly goes on in a court. When at the county courthouse, the attorney and I discussed the different people of the court and what activities, including court cases, can go on there, which proved to be a very extensive list. Most importantly, I learned about the difference between civil and criminal cases, the difference being the other private citizens or the government pressing charges, respectively. Finally, when speaking with the chief justice of the Texas Supreme Court and Justice Alito of the US Supreme Court in the Texas Supreme Court Building, I was exposed to how the court system of Texas is like that of a ladder, with higher and lower courts being in existence, alongside how it compares to that of the US court system. Also, we discussed the difference between appellate and original jurisdiction, judicial qualifications, and how we select our judges, which may be very controversial, depending on who you speak to and the system used to select judges. Overall, the bureaucracy set up by the states to enforce the law has multiple people working together to protect the rights of the accused and those at trial.

Day 21 saw myself and Deacon, Charity's husband, wake up just after midnight to visit the vestiges of the federal government in Texas. We ended up embarking on a road trip to the Dallas-Fort Worth area, and those federal offices are what we viewed along the way. We first drove around downtown Austin, where we saw the new United States Courthouse, the old Homer Thornberry Judicial Building, and the J.J. Pickle Federal Office Building. We then drove up to Killeen and learned about the Fort Hood army base. Later, in Temple, we saw the local branch of the Social Security Administration. Just south of Waco, we stopped in at the local United States Department of Agriculture service station and then went to the west side of town and saw the Waco Mammoth Site, which is part of the National Park Service. After that, we found ourselves in front of the United States Bureau of Engraving and Printing, in north Fort Worth, where the federal government prints some of the currency that we use. Then, we found ourselves at Dallas-Fort Worth International Airport, where I was introduced to the Department of Transportation's Federal Aviation Administration and its responsibility to control the skies. Also while there, we saw the Department of Homeland Security's Transportation Security Administration screening passengers before their flights. We ended our run just south of Dallas at the United States Department of Justice's Bureau of Prisons Federal Corrections Institute, Seagoville. Deacon's job at the Texas Office of Federal-State Relations, under the guidance of the governor, allowed us to have intimate knowledge of where the federal government had operations set up in the state. Overall, the federal government was found to have its fair share of office space here in the state, not to mention the General Service Administration's Public Building Service managing everything.

Keeping up with the theme of state entities with locations I ended up going abroad for day 22. In doing so, I shadowed different officials at the Mexican consulate in Austin. In the morning, I spoke with Consular General Carlos Gutierrez. We first discussed what the roles of a consular were. He is like the CEO of that station, with full authority over all matters occurring there, and he highlighted the differences between a consulate and an embassy. More importantly, he established the fact that we were on foreign soil when there. We then discussed many of the perks and downsides of working for a consulate that depended on where the consulate was located as to whether there are more pros than cons and vice versa. The day hit home when we toured the facility and saw all the people waiting to seek help from their services. While he caught up on some emails and other office functions, I was able to view officials who worked in the documentation division helping Mexican nationals obtain identification cards and copies of birth certificates. After that, I went by the protection division, which helps lost minors return home or adults get legal help for nonpayment of work done in the US by local employers. Lastly, I spent time with the community affairs division and saw how they worked to put on events in the community, which varied by the week and were aimed at improving the health and general welfare of Mexican nationals living here. We ended the day rushing to the airport in Austin to meet the Mexican ambassador to Washington DC, who had been diverted due to mechanical issues on their aircraft. On the way, though, I learned a bit more about Consular Gutierrez and how his education and lifetime career in the foreign service brought him to his current position. Overall, like that of the federal government that I had seen the day before, the consulate might not have primary jurisdiction to govern here in Texas, at least beyond their office space, but they still operate a very impressive operation, seeking to help certain parts of the population.

Day 23 consisted of me spending the first full day of my trek in the nation's capital, Washington DC. I spent the entirety of the day with a congressional intern of my representative touring the Capitol grounds and buildings. Just as was the case back home in Texas, the grounds here are full of memorials and buildings dedicated to legislator's offices and court-rooms. Once in front of my representative, John Culberson, we went over the minimum qualifications to serve in Congress, which were similar in scope, but more stringent than those in Texas, followed by the size, which is much bigger here. We then discussed some key terms like how members divide themselves into caucuses to discuss issues beyond party lines, how being an incumbent gives you an advantage due to already knowing what is going on as compared to a freshman congressman, the extent of pork barrel spending (frivolous spending by Congress), and how they are in charge of overseeing the actions of the federal bureaucracy. Becky and I walked through the tunnels connecting all the buildings on Capitol Hill to find ourselves sitting in the viewing gallery of the House. Expecting to see another rapid lawmaking process like back home, I was disappointed as the US Congress is a full-time legislative body that takes its time when making laws, due to their continuous sessions. We concluded our talks by discussing the various jobs held by the US House and Senate bodies, but from what I can tell the lawmaking process is like that of the state house back home. Overall, I learned today about the way laws are made in Washington for the country at large.

Day 24 saw my trek move from Capitol Hill to the White House. Becky was gracious enough to give me a tour of the area surrounding the White House to find more offices and memorials of the federal government. I moved onto the public White House interior tour when I learned the difference between a president and a prime minister, the minimum qual-ifications to be president, how 270 Electoral College votes makes one president, and how a president may serve no more than two four-year terms in office. However, after touring the executive mansion, I was hooded, knocked out, and taken into the inner workings of the complex. While there, I got the private tour of nonpublic spaces found in the White House by President Trump. Along the way, I learned about his official duties as a chief pardoner, approving of legislation, appointing officials to government offices, being commander in chief of the armed forces, and being chief diplomat in dealing with other nations. Over lunch on the south portico, I got an extensive history on how we created a moderately powerful presidency following our time with a too-strong executive in King George III and how not having an executive didn't work during our time under the Articles of Confederation. My time with President Trump ended while playing a hole of golf where we compared the differ-ent tools readily available for use like the vice president. Overall, as expected from my time with the governor, the president is truly like that of a CEO due to their much more exten-sive powerbase being fully in charge of an entire organization.

Day 25 saw my trek enter the final phase of subjects, office politics, which consisted of me spending my time evaluating what exactly the states and federal government have decided to do with their lawmaking authority. I got my first break here touring the US Department of the Interior's museum. While there I learned that the department got its start taking on the tasks that no other department could reasonably perform long-term and evolved overtime to handle issues that go on within our borders that we are fully in control over. Following that, the US secretary of the interior came in and informed me of what public policy is. We proceeded to turn the barren back room of the museum into a new world-class exhibition by including specs on the guns and butter debate as a euphemism for whether we should invest more of our resources in domestic goods or weapons of war. I learned about the five steps endeavored through to craft new policy: build your agenda, formulate the best possible policy, get the policy approved of, implement the policy, and then go back to determine if more needs to be done to get the policy right. We looked at major domestic policy areas to show that each can teach a lesson, like how passing a policy can lead to unintended consequences, the opening of black markets, or how selecting a policy may require trade-offs or create a moral hazard. More importantly, a policy with widespread approval can be passed more quickly but will still take time. We ended our work together by concurring that not everyone will agree what problems are real problems, no socially acceptable solution may be available, the sides may never agree on a solution, policies can be written to have some leeway in implementation, and government should intervene here and there, but they should have good reasoning and do so at the right time. Overall, domestic policy is what our country's leaders have proposed to deal with in our society.

Day 26 saw the focus on policy switch over to foreign affairs and how we deal with other states and nations. In doing so, I received a tour of the Diplomatic Reception Rooms found at the US Department of State. Each of the rooms we visited was used by Secretary Mike Pompeo to teach some point. The first room informed the group on the foreign policy advice given by George Washington in his farewell address to have no permanent alliances, trade with friendly nations, keep out of others' business when it is not our own, expect no favors by other nations, and seek the peace whenever possible. From there, the next room identified the major players in Congress, the president, the bureaucracy, and interest groups seeking to influence the process. The next three rooms identified the three main goals of foreign policy to be human rights, which often suffers at the hand of the other two, economic prosperity and self-defense. We discussed how foreign policy had changed over time from the realist school of foreign policy to the idealist school, which saw us go from isolationism to interventionism following World War II. Lastly, each of the last rooms on tour brought up the foreign policy tools of making public statements, practicing diplomacy, joining alliances, joining international organizations, economic policies, filing a case at the international court of justice, and the one we tend to do the best at, going to war. Overall, a plethora of options is available for interacting with other countries. The question is what option to take going forward.

On day 27, my last full one in DC, I found myself waking inside of a jail cell. Once I had come to terms with my situation, my cell mate and I, Mr. John Smith, embarked on a whirlwind tour of our rights. We first hashed out the differences between civil rights and liberties with the prior protecting you from discriminatory practices by private citizens while the later does so with the government. We discussed how we got our Bill of Rights thanks to actions by the first congress only to discover the issue of those rights only protecting us from Congress and not state governments. Smith informed me on how later court cases established the concept of selective incorporation, which is where our rights do protect us from state governments, but that a separate court case must be had to apply each right to state government actions. The rest of the day was spent learning about my rights as found in the US Constitution, which range from in court, in day-to-day activities, and what I can tell the military to do when they want to use my house to house troops in war. Overall, I learned what rights I do have; the question is what those rights are, as they are still up for interpretation by the Supreme Court.

On day 28, I went back to Austin. Once on the ground, I made the transition from being accused to being a victim of a crime. While cashing a check at my sisters' bank, two men in a Camaro rammed their way into the door of the bank and robbed the bank. During the crime, bank employees, fellow customers, and I were shoved into the vault and locked in. Luckily, though, the opportunity to learn about another important part of government emerged when I found that I was being held with the state comptroller. The comptroller ended up answering our questions and telling us all about his position to pass the time. Comptroller Hegar first advised us that his two main duties revolved around reporting to the legislature how much money the state has on hand to spend and the managing of the various trust funds of the state, like the ones for education. These were in addition to handling the collections and redistributions of all taxes collected in the state for a multitude of issues. Following that, we all learned about how each level of government had its taxing specialty. We also had a good discussion on why taxes are issued and the associated issues of doing so. Beyond taxes for revenues, Hegar also showed us evidence of being able to collect revenues from visitor fees from state parks, investments, and even lottery ticket sales. Also, Hegar used copies of his report on the 2017–2018 budget cycle to inform us on how the state budgets and what exactly the state is spending money on over the next two years. Education and health care were to get the biggest pieces of the proverbial spending pie. The most notable item I took away was how those who make the biggest amount of noise would typically get the biggest amounts of money. Accordingly, if I do not agree with what is being spent, I should get more involved. Overall, the government can collect revenues from a wide array of sources, but it must follow a strict method for spending, and what it spends on says a lot about its priorities.

Looking back, I spent the last day of my trek with my sister Charity. With her, I discovered what the state of Texas and the nation had chosen to represent themselves with. Those items are better known as our state and national symbols. Her degree in symbology paid off that day. Charity's clothes were representative of the clothing items that get at the heart of the state. None are found for the federal government. Breakfast and lunch featured the restaurant and foods symbols of the state. None are found for the federal government. At the zoo, many of the animal symbols were on display in the exhibit that she had worked on while in school with the federal government finally getting one. At the state capitol building, the state Agriculture Museum and surrounding grounds had all the geological and vegetation symbols on display. Lastly, a ride on the state vehicle, a chuck wagon, led us to see even more vegetation symbols and eventually took us to the Frank Erwin Center, where the state activities were on display. Along the way, the applicable federal versions were also seen, though granted, they are few and far between. Overall, the various symbols were representative of our heritage, from surviving off the land, to how we chose to deal with issues that arose from living there, to standing up to fight for our way of life. True grit was the real commonality.

In making my final choice for where to go in my career, many of the items in "Governing Foundations and Office Politics" seemed to be academic affairs requiring a lot more schooling and time spent researching. The actions in "Getting Involved and Office Space" seemed more my pace, due to the requirement to get out and about more. The one opportunity that piqued my interest was to join the foreign service, which I got my first taste of at the Mexican consulate and fully explored at the Department of State. The question is, where is my passport?

CPSIA information can be obtained
at www.ICGtesting.com
Printed in the USA
LVHW060747101122
732678LV00005B/13

9 781793 523396